*The*

*Women of England*

Barbara Kanner is on the faculty at Occidental College and is an officer of the West Coast Association of Women Historians. Her articles have appeared in several anthologies.

145712

HQ
1599
.E5
W65

# The

# Women of England

## From Anglo-Saxon Times
## to the Present

*Interpretive Bibliographical Essays*

Edited

with an Introduction by

BARBARA KANNER

ARCHON BOOKS

Hamden, Connecticut

1979

GOSHEN COLLEGE LIBRARY
GOSHEN, INDIANA

© Barbara Kanner 1979

First published 1979 as an Archon Book,

an imprint of The Shoe String Press, Inc.

Hamden, Connecticut 06514

All rights reserved

Composition in Hong Kong by Asco Trade Typesetting Limited

Lithoprinted and bound in the United States of America

*Library of Congress Cataloging in Publication Data*
Main entry under title:

The Women of England

Includes index.
1. Women—England—History—Sources.
2. Women—England—History—Bibliography.
I. Kanner, Barbara, 1925–
HQ1599.E5W65      301.41'2'0942      78-32166
ISBN 0-208-01639-2

# Contents

# Preface

The preparation of this anthology has been an enterprise in cooperative scholarship. Each of the essays is original and composed especially for this volume in a close editorial relationship. All of the contributors share my commitment to the study of women in the past, and to the integration of that study into the mainstream of English social history. Authors and editor share also the conviction that the success of such an endeavor depends upon the foundation of responsible scholarship; and that this scholarship rests heavily upon the availability and use of a very large body of reliable sources.

No doubt, the new field of women in history requires new conceptualizing of categories for historical questioning, new theoretical frameworks for interpretation, and new methodological approaches for analysis if it is to bring to light the relationship between the roles and experiences of the still comparatively obscure female population and the development of English society. But theories, methods, and interpretations must be related to the evidence that only the records, documents, and other unqualified sources can provide. These have not yet been fully explored. For this reason we have avoided prescribing a particular theoretical model, methodological approach, or philosophical guideline. Implicitly, however, the various essays do suggest how the sources can be

7

approached and how the findings may be employed in teaching and writing. Each author has selected a set of questions which he or she pursues through a critical evaluation of primary and secondary references. The selection reflects not only the particular interests and knowledge of each author, but also his or her own opinion about the kinds of questions that are appropriate and significant for the historical period and sociocultural context. Short titles or authors' names only are given in citations in the text and notes. Readers should consult the bibliographies (which are limited to these sources) at the end of each chapter for full information about the sources and references under discussion.

While preparing this book, the contributors and I sought the advice and criticism of colleagues who possess the twin qualifications of serious involvement with the subject of women in history (through teaching, guidance of theses, writing, or researching) and of proven expertise in the history of the period in question as well as the specialized topics under consideration. We feel the contributions of these advisors to be invaluable, and we want to thank them and acknowledge their assistance. Alphabetically, they include: Andrew Appleby, Joyce A. Berkman, Robert Brentano, Thomas W. Davis, Carolly Erickson, Robert T. Farrell, James Fitts, Jess Flemion, Peter Gay, Mary Jane Hamilton, Dorothy O. Helly, Richard Helmholz, C. Warren Hollister, Neil Kunze, Norma Landau, Jean L'Esperance, Gordon Mingay, Adrienne Rosen, Andrew Rosen, Daniel Scott Smith, Leo Solt, Elizabeth Vodola, and Cecile Zinberg.

At various stages in this project I have also received advice and assistance from Susan Groag Bell, Leonore Davidoff, Albert A. Hayden, Jane Jaquette, Edwin B. Kanner, Peter Stansky, and Ronald L. Stephenson. Further thanks are due to the reference and inter-library loan librarians at the University Research Library, UCLA. Finally, I must acknowledge with appreciation the technical contribution of my library assistant, Steven Halasey and my indexer, Mary Lombardi.

Barbara Kanner
Los Angeles, California
June, 1978

# INTRODUCTION

## Old and New Women's History

### BARBARA KANNER

The women of England have been represented in historical writings from Anglo-Saxon times to the present. For more than a thousand years scribes, chroniclers, legists, biographers, religionists, politicians, social reformers, and others have documented in official records and private papers the active participation of the female population in the changing patterns of English life, law, and social organization. Most of this documentation remains in manuscript form, but there are published sources also, including explicitly focused histories of women that have been available for a very long time. Modern scholarly study, however, does not yet do justice to the rich supply of sources that confirms there is a history of the women's history of England.[1]

The purpose of this anthology is to explore that history with a critical attitude, posing questions pertaining to female English experience as it has been revealed in published historical writings, as it remains still obscure in untapped archival or other sources, and as it awaits fresh and newly relevant contexts. The chronological arrangement of the chapters not only answers the question of how much investigation has been done on each historical period, but also indicates what kinds of inquiries have been made at different times, and how well these inquiries have satisfied their author's purposes. The contributors to this volume aim to illustrate the potential that probing the history of England's women holds for expanding knowledge of the English nation's history in general, and that of the still insufficiently studied half of the population in particular. The female population of England constitutes a unique grouping in society because it has always been relegated—by law, custom, and social policy—to the special category of a sex, regardless of class or ethnicity. Thus gender is a sound category of analysis, and patterns of sexual division warrant detailed study. The bibliographical essays in this volume are intended as a contribution in that direction.

The method of exploring historical questions through interpretive bibliography is only as effective as the quality of an author's ordering of priorities. Each contributor to this anthology has had to meet the challenges of limited space, and of the decision between sources and questions as his or her primary consideration. This choice is not as easy as it may seem. On the one hand, presenting a catalog of useful references under reasonable headings is a proven way to attract participants to a developing research field. On the other hand, it is the set of topics or questions—selected to address specific sources—that ultimately governs historical interpretation. In addition there is the problem of ascertaining that the bibliographical material is adequate to satisfy the questions. Not surprisingly, the number, availability, and quality of usable primary and secondary sources vary for each historical period. In some cases, subjects or questions may be in greater supply than the sources available to answer them, and it is neither responsible nor to anyone's advantage to employ guesswork, wishful thinking, or pure theory for framing doubtful conclusions to fill in voids which are actually inescapable. In the chapters that follow, each author has tried to meet these challenges of bibliomethodology.

We are aware both of our place in the tradition of historical writing about English women and of the differences between our perspectives and definitions of "women's history" and those of authors who wrote before the mid-1960s. Our approaches have been informed by recently articulated historical viewpoints, newly formed categories, and an expansion of interdisciplinary interests, techniques, and methodologies for research— many of them not traditionally historical but now incorporated into the range of social history. Besides, our interests are unavoidably (but self-consciously) influenced by the issues and writings of women's movements that have become increasingly articulate throughout the world since the mid-1960s. Thus older historical writings about women are different from ours. At the same time, we still need the information they supply, and we need to learn how they represent the climate of opinion influencing their authors.[2] A few examples from the chapters below illustrate the value of the "old" women's history to the "new," and the directions which the "new" is taking.

The earliest written sources for the history of women in England have so far yielded only fragmentary details, but they hold evidence that Anglo-Saxon women were expected to fulfill a variety of social roles, and they provide descriptions of some outstanding individuals. Sheila C. Dietrich ("An Introduction to Women in Anglo-Saxon Society"), on consulting, for example, Bede's *Ecclesiastical History of the English People*, *The Anglo-Saxon Chronicle*, various lives of women saints, and handbooks of penance,[3] designates as significant for tracing English women's social roles the casual manner in which contemporary authors commented on women as administrators, warriors, and religious figures. She concludes that "a study of Anglo-Saxon history might produce examples of women's influence and freedom of action that would make aspects of even the twentieth century appear 'dark.'" The records of these early centuries—largely descriptive, narrative, anecdotal, and biographical—set Anglo-Saxon women vividly into contemporary scenes. Of course, the Old English writers did not subject the female population to the kind of social analysis that modern historians need in order to understand how Anglo-Saxon women experienced family and community life; how they ranked in the social structure and within their social class; or how they contributed to national development. Judgment on whether or not these kinds of questions are answerable from existing evidence will be based upon new, direct consultation of the manuscript sources. To this end, Marc A. Meyer ("Land Charters and the Legal Position of Anglo-Saxon Women") has made intensive searches of archives of legal records to discover the position of Anglo-Saxon women under land law. He has been able to establish relational ties between developments in Anglo-Saxon economic politics and the functional status and power of women of wealth and property.

Kathleen Casey's perceptive treatment of women in medieval English history ("Women in Norman and Plantagenet England") convinces us that important and still unattended questions await scholarly attention. "It is hardly an exaggeration to say," she advises, "that nothing less, now, than a complete reevaluation of the entire *corpus* of medieval sources is needed to redress the balance created by neglect and misinterpretation ... [for example] the connections between production, reproduction, acculturation, and the nexus of family life in which all these meet ... are present and awaiting synthesis." The brilliant pioneering work of the early twentieth-century medievalist, Eileen Power notwithstanding, the main thrust of Casey's essay is to explain and to compensate for what she recognizes as a "real dearth of secondary writings in the field, especially in the neglected area of economic life." Evaluating books and articles of many kinds, she has relied heavily upon her own original "connective web" for analysis and interpretation. For example, in her discussion of working women's occupations, she emphasizes the close relationship that existed between the marriage bond and the production of food and services—and she designates the marriage bond as crucial to every aspect of the "conjunction of women's lives and politics in the English middle ages." Casey compares the rural domestic mode of production, in which gender differences in work assignments were not pronounced (except that women were additionally occupied with childbirth in replacement of the working population "generation by generation"), with the urban situation, especially the case of the guilds where women might enjoy certain advantages. Even here, the interconnection of guild workers through marriage ties could cancel women's independent trading status. Still to be explored is "the incongruity between women's high visibility in medieval economic life and their subordinate status in [common] law, theology, and literature." The latter is represented in the rich primary source material of contemporary medieval women's history. Casey emphasizes the importance of analyzing "the dialectical and transforming reciprocity" that existed between women's objective experiences in their roles and occupations, and their subjective experiences as symbols in a set of ideologies. Traditional medieval sources may also be consulted to this end. For example, the records of medieval law trials in the ecclesiastical, manorial and royal courts hold at least a dim contemporary reflection of the complex interplay between objective and subjective female experience. "Women in large numbers attended courts," writes Ruth Kittel ("Women Under the Law in Medieval England"), "and the extant legal documents offer ... an examination of women's activity." Litigation on marriage— and the laws of marriage themselves—reveal not only the issues that brought the parties to court, but also the definition of marriage, the nature of "consent," the rights of both partners, and the roles of their families. From a good set of manorial court rolls, says Kittel, the historian can gain "information on social structure, economy, mobility, and tenure patterns." Women's history in medieval legal manuscripts reveals the medieval mind focused on women in action, while it also provides the modern researcher with a valuable and valid starting point for pursuing the kinds of questions that Casey and Kittel suggest.

In Rosemary Masek's essay ("Women in an Age of Transition: 1485–1714"), there are at least twenty references to women authors whose diaries, autobiographies, memoirs, or treatises were written, and in some cases printed, in sixteenth- and seventeenth-century England. Especially when consulted along with women's correspondence, account books, wills, and other papers, these contemporary sources are valuable in expanding knowledge of women's history as well as social history in general. When women's documents are juxtaposed with the exclusively male-authored writings on such subjects as "the woman question," the "marriage debate," and the courtesy-conduct manuals (for ladies), modern historians should gain insight into differences between male and female perceptions of some topical issues in sixteenth- and seventeenth-century England. Such a juxtaposition may also answer the question of the extent to which the social history of the period has been written from a masculine perspective. Seventeenth-century examples of the latter include Thomas Heywood's *Gunaikeion: The Nine Books of Various History Concerning Women* (1624) and *Exemplary Lives* ... (1640). Heywood's books appear to have served subsequent writers as models for using the historical stance to reaffirm the standards of male society for "proper" female behavior. Masek describes how "woman and her nature" were attacked and defended—with the detractors of women more popular than the defenders. She says, "a debate over woman's nature—its intrinsic merits or defects—was renewed with vigor in the Tudor-Stuart era, reflecting changing values and indicating that men were recognizing women as a class while denying them higher status." Yet this was a period in which formal education for women was being advocated, and in some instances undertaken. Masek links increased activity of women in religious movements with spread of female literacy: "as women read the Scriptures and were convinced of their religious experience, they began to make their faith more public.... They organized small women's groups to which they explained the Bible, or else they preached in public places, occasionally even in the church." These linkages deserve deeper investigation and analysis than they have been given in existing secondary sources—with all respect to the recent studies to which Masek refers. Histories are wanting that evaluate the participation of women thinkers and writers in the religious controversies, and of female patrons of both the early Puritan ministers and post-Restoration nonconformists. Archives should be searched, suggests Masek, for new knowledge that will replace the laudatory descriptions of "women worthies" with more analytical writings that set women activists at the center of the movements they assisted or helped to create within their culture and society.

This suggestion undoubtedly applies to the study of the English women of the next century as well. Prescriptive literature, flat and laudatory biography, treatises intended to persuade, narrative accounts of events, observations of conditions needing remedy, and descriptions of charitable enterprise represent historically oriented eighteenth-century writing on women. Also, in the tradition of Thomas Heywood, George Ballard published *Memoirs of Several Ladies* ... (1752) and William

Alexander *The History of Women* ... (1782) to show how women might aspire to become prototypes of eighteenth-century England's standard feminine ideal. But Barbara B. Schnorrenberg, with Jean Hunter ("The Eighteenth-Century Englishwoman"), works the bibliographical guide in the direction of charting social changes that marked transitions to nineteenth-century England more than to analyzing linkages to the previous century. The Englishwoman's "life at the end of the century," write Schnorrenberg and Hunter, "was different from that at its outset. The spread of literacy, the acceptance of writing as a respectable livelihood for women, the rising birthrate and declining death rate, and the evangelical expectations of good works for the benefit of society were surely among the most important developments affecting women." Eighteenth-century periodical literature, contemporary fiction, pamphlet rhetoric, and instruction manuals by and for women await, along with official documents, the modern historian's questioning to supplement and improve upon contemporary women's history that portrayed rather than analyzed the social participation of women in transforming and modernizing England's social life. Historians of the "old" women's history have hardly noticed the advent of "literary women" who derived income from books and magazines and the advent of women philanthropists and social reformers who worked directly in charitable organizations and social movements. How women participated in organized activity in the category of "social upheaval" remains to be researched. Study of women's participation in religious movements has hardly scratched the surface. As for political activism, Schnorrenberg and Hunter, like Karl von den Steinen in the succeeding chapter ("The Discovery of Women in Eighteenth-Century Political Life") show early feminist expression in the eighteenth century as preamble to the nineteenth-century women's movement. Von den Steinen demonstrates that while we know that a number of women possessed informal political power, we must reconsider all aspects of the subject closely, and reread the manuscript sources pertaining to political action to discover just how they employed it. Neglect of investigation into the roles of women in political life—including voter activity—in eighteenth-century England may be a serious omission in political history. Von den Steinen suggests the importance of the relationship between the sociopolitical activity of female partisans and results of elections and legislation. Pursuit of this question will expand our understanding of the breadth and scope of the eighteenth-century political process at the same time as it enlarges the compass of social history to include women's roles.

   Though nineteenth-century England witnessed the development of "the great tradition of Western historical scholarship" and the advent of "scientific history," no new approach to the question of women in history was added by the historians to the models furnished by writers of the seventeenth and eighteenth centuries. For the most part, social history was a residual category, and women's participation was virtually invisible in the institutional, administrative, constitutional, and diplomatic subjects that were closely investigated and described. Yet the close analysis of State archives by the historians, and their development of techiques for gathering facts and data, constituted a legacy to contemporary commentators writing on subjects pertaining to Victorian women, just as this legacy is enjoyed by historians of women writing today. No one has analyzed the relationship between the growth of the historical profession in England and Victorian preoccupation with the gathering of social data for British population census reports and parliamentary investigative reports, although many historians were as imbued with the idea of progress and with measuring its fulfillment as were the Utilitarians. Official reports and census volumes printed after 1840, writes Sheila Johansson ("Demographic Contributions to the History of Victorian Women"), "can be used to illuminate many aspects of Victorian women's history ... [and] unpublished enumerators' schedule books ... are in many ways demographically revealing ... on the name, sex, age, marital status, occupation, birthplace, and relationship to head of each member of a household." Thus in the nineteenth century, precise information about women—often accompanied by historically oriented comment or interpretation—was written into official records that were eventually employed to guide state policy and legislation that was of direct relevance to English women of all social classes.[4] The facts and data also filtered into contemporary statistical journals, newspaper articles, and essays in the periodical press, so that factual Victorian writing on questions involving women is perhaps more often found in journalistic writing than in the books on English women of the past which were for the most part stylistically similar to the "women worthies" tradition.[5]

Thus there is a vast catalog of nineteenth-century writings focused on a very wide assortment of subjects representing interest and concern over the question of the position of women vis à vis men in society, law, and politics—an issue that was manifest in socioeconomic and even literary discussion from the 1840s.[6] The rhetoric and arguments are well known, but much less studied is the diversity of the opinions expressed in writings on "the woman question" during the century and the circumstances behind the variations in thought and reaction.[7] It is the element of diversity that Sheila Johansson underlines as the result of her close investigations of Victorian population studies that revealed to her how "complexity and diversity have always characterized the experience of

English women. ... Britain, unevenly affected by the spread of industrialization and urbanization, became regionally and socially heterogeneous to an unprecedented degree." Considering the extent to which "the Victorian woman" has been sterotyped, Johansson's vantage point is original and constructive. It is made possible, she explains, by the contributions of historical demography to recent social history and to the "new" women's history.

"Demographic research provides a natural focus for the exploration of several key dimensions of nineteenth-century experience," writes Johansson. Some examples are "the feminine role in the translation of 'progress' into improved health and greater longevity, the spread of fertility control, the role of marital status and migration in the accelerating drive for personal autonomy, and the evolution of new roles for women in and outside of family households." Regional, occupational, social class, and attitudinal (even psychological) factors explain the demographic and, consequently, the social differences among groups in the various geographical areas when fertility, mortality, marital, and migration rates are measured over time and are interpreted in the context of the dynamics of socioeconomic change. The latter is the task taken over from demographers by social historians, who have searched for the social questions that are dictated by the findings—especially those for the beginnings and the consequences of recognizable trends. To the social historian, the social factors are viewed as being not only at the very center of *causation* but also at the center of the *changing patterns*. For example, in the case of Victorian women, studying declining rates of fertility in the aggregate has not been as revealing of the roles women may have played in controlling their fertility as investigating, and then comparing, the fertility rates for trends in different local areas. Of course, the social context of the groups of women under consideration must be carefully defined and that definition should include a close questioning of the impact of industrialization, urbanization, and population expansion on the various demographic phenomena. Comparative local area studies of this kind not only assist in clarifying results of trends in the alterations in women's life-styles, occupations, and, consequently, status and goals, but also help to show formative differences in the impact on feminine as compared with masculine experience.

Another reason for considering sex-linked differentials among the consequences of demographic and modernizing transitions is to obtain a more complete and objective understanding of the social transformation of ninteenth-century England. Furthermore, consideration of these differentials contributes to an understanding of the subjective responses of Victorian women to demographic change. For example, Sheila Johansson suggests that there may be value in a reexamination of possible linkages between limitation of family size and the emergence of feminism—or at least of a feminist consciousness in the form of a feminine, individualistic "gospel" of self-realization, even among women who did not overtly claim a greater share of economic life. She proposes that Victorian novelists may have been instrumental in communicating this "gospel."

Patricia Otto Klaus ("Women in the Mirror: Using Novels to Study Victorian Women") considers this question of the role of the Victorian novel in shaping women's attitudes, opinions, and consciousness. She writes, "Much of the criticism of novel reading stemmed from the fear that girls and women would be debased by the stories they read. . . . Perhaps as damaging was the possibility that women, aspiring to unattainable fantasies, would become unhappy or undutiful daughters or wives." At least one Victorian feminist, Emmeline Pethick-Lawrence, recalled in her memoirs that the novels she and her associates read as young girls affected their lifelong interests. If novels actually fulfilled their alleged potential to sway female readers from conventional viewpoints and self-images, they appear also to have been considered by contemporaries as surrogates for teachers of morality—the work of the novelist having been described, says Otto Klaus, as "something like that of a physician or a priest." In any event, impressive evidence shows that Victorian fiction, by providing an imagined milieu to which readers responded on various levels of consciousness, was a shaping force in the process of enculturation and, thereby, a social medium deserving the attention of historians. For the study of women in the past, there is the added dimension of the successful lady novelist. "Their works enable us to read what women had to say . . . about Victorian society, the position of women, and relations between women and men. The woman novelist, though perhaps 'invisible' in a legal and political sense," says Otto Klaus, "is very visible through her writing." Yet the value of the Victorian novel for the history of women is not as dependent upon the sex of the author as upon the author's ability to create a convincing milieu for representative characters, and to develop insights into the emotions, responses, and behavior of fictional women in various circumstances and relationships. As a historical figure who makes a special type of statement about women of the time, however, the Victorian novelist is an important element to consider in historical analysis of the work of fiction. In this connection, the sex of the author is a factor not for selecting one novel over another, but for interpreting the rendition of Victorian women in fiction as compared with the realities they confronted in nineteenth-century English society.

This is not to claim for the Victorian novel the status of the historical document. As Otto Klaus cautions, it must be used with conventional evidence to ensure that its interpretation is not misleading. Some dominant themes of novels that are also of particular importance in women's history—marriage and the family, for instance—are of course more easily verifiable than others. It is undoubtedly for this reason that historically oriented writers have traditionally used scenes and dialogue from novels for illustrative purposes. There is a difference for practitioners of recent women's history, however, and this consists in the techniques they employ for weighing evidence, and in their tendency to evaluate changes over time in the portrayals of female characters in thought and action. By the end of the nineteenth century, for example, themes and characterizations in the novels exemplified the emergence and the meaning of "the new woman," and suggested female role alternatives that the early Victorian woman could not have dreamed possible.

"The new woman," representing the educated middle class, was accepted in careers and in some of the professions by the first decades of the twentieth century. Among the accomplishments of those women who held respected places in higher education and in the academic disciplines are writings of focused histories of English women and studies that incorporate discussion of England's female population. Alice Clark's *Working Life of Women in the Seventeenth Century* (1919);[8] Eileen Power's *Medieval English Nunneries* (1922) and "The Position of Women" (1926);[9] and Ivy Pinchbeck's *Women Workers and the Industrial Revolution, 1750–1850* (1930)[10] are among the best examples of historical writings about the women of England that mark a sharp contrast with previous women's history.[11] These authors employ primary sources, analytic style, and a distinct awareness of the value of including women's participation in historically oriented socioeconomic studies. Clark writes in her preface:

> The conditions under which the obscured mass of women live and fulfill their duties as human beings, have a vital influence upon the destinies of the human race ... knowledge of what these conditions have been in the past will be of more value ... than many volumes of carefully elaborated theory based on abstract ideas. [P. 5]

Clark questioned the procedure of developing theory before searching for primary evidence. Theoretical approaches, she writes, "have been abandoned and replaced by others ... still only held tentatively," and, in turn discarded "when a deeper understanding becomes possible" (p. 5). She narrowed her focus deliberately, explaining that "many records of Gilds, Companies, Quarter Sessions and Boroughs" had to be examined "*in extenso* before a just idea [could] be formed of women's position" (p. 6). Clark's book remains a starting point for studying her subject (see Masek's chapter below). Yet researchers today promise improvement over Clark's women's history by attending to questions relevant to, but left out of, Clark's discussion: demographic change, provisions of the law of marriage and unwedded status, dynamics of family-kin relationships, female deviant behavior, and sexuality.[12] Nevertheless, Clark's work on seventeenth-century English women remains a model against which historians of women today measure their own work.

This also holds true for Eileen Power's early twentieth-century studies of medieval English women at work, in nunneries, on landed estates, in contemporary literature, and in medieval theory. Of her histories, M. M. Postan wrote recently in his preface to *Medieval Women*, an anthology of Power's lectures, "From the very outset of her career as a scholar, Eileen Power was engaged on a history of women of the Middle Ages. Her ambition was to produce a study fuller and better grounded in evidence than any of the existing books on the subject" (p. 7). Convinced that women's part in the historical process belongs in the mainstream of scholarship, Power's questions about women's roles spanned social history as she defined it: the experiences in society of the inarticulate as well as the powerful. In "The Position of Women" she writes:

> The working classes, whose shoulders held the sky suspended above Church and Aristocracy.... That busy world of men and women of which we catch a glimpse in court roll and borough record, rarely raised its voice above the whistle of the scythe.... One other class, too, remained inarticulate, for we hardly ever hear what women thought about themselves. All the books, as the Wife of Bath complained, were written by men. [P. 426]

Power examined the life-styles and the roles of lower-class housewives; the "lady" who became "but amateur soldier and man-of-the-house" and farmer and participant in "manorial economy"; and the nun and prioress. On contemporary theory about women, Power observes:

> The position of women is one thing in theory, another in legal position, yet another in everyday life ... the various manifestations of women's position reacted on one another but did not exactly coincide; the true position of women was a blend of all three. [*Medieval Women*, p. 9]

Practitioners of women's history today, in quest of theoretical approaches, are having to face this same kaleidoscope of elements that determine the position of women not only at different times in the course of the female life cycle, but also within the different periods and environments of English society and through the endless, often irrational, processes of change over time.

Of the phenomena determining dynamic alterations in the English landscape, the combination of industrialization, agricultural technology, urbanization, and rapid population expansion has been undoubtedly the most transforming. Estimating its effect on women's working lives and domestic relationships, and how this estimate assists in epitomizing the period of the Industrial Revolution in the hundred years after 1750 is the focus of Ivy Pinchbeck's still unparalelled *Women Workers and the Industrial Revolution*. Like Alice Clark and Eileen Power, Ivy Pinchbeck chose as a major concern the experience of women as women, not merely as factors interacting with industrializing processes. In her preface to the 1930 edition she writes:

> This book is an attempt to give an account of the conditions governing the lives of working women during the period 1750–1850. The Industrial Revolution has been studied from many aspects, but so far, women's work during this period has not been the subject of any separate study.

Pinchbeck compares the nature and environment of handicraft industry in home-based industries of proto-industrial times with conditions ensuing from separation of home and workshop, and the advent of women's roles as wage earners. She argues that an important variable in interpreting the impact of the Industrial Revolution is the degree to which English women workers continued from the past—but in new structural and functional relationships to marketplace and family—to represent an "indispensible factor" in the productive work of the nation and thereby in the making of modern society. Pinchbeck's study also demonstrates the relationship between changes in women's occupations and the regional location of their employment. She relates occupational change also to the social transformations which accompanied revolutionary productive processes, the economy, and new demographic patterns. She analyzes variations in local conditions as relevant to changes in women's status in the community, in work roles, and in domestic arrangements. *Women Workers and the Industrial Revolution* is a multidimensional work that is not easily summarized. It is a book that has been neither revised nor equalled by another work of similar proportions for the same or a later period.[13] But ways in which the range of questions and variables could be expanded profitably for women's history and the history of the family have begun to be suggested in some valuable recent articles.[14] In more general terms, Neal A. Ferguson ("Women in Twentieth-Century England") notes the absence of the "total history" approach not only for working-class women, but also for women—working or not —of other social classes.

"The 'total' history of English women since 1900 has yet to be written from an approach that traces the interactions among economic, social, and political currents," he writes. Ferguson's survey of writings for twentieth-century women's history highlights the gap in historical studies left by Pinchbeck's terminating date of 1850, and the inexplicable absence of large-scale, closely focused studies for subsequent periods. Nevertheless, Ferguson enumerates the very long catalog of primary and secondary sources that are addressed, though less intensively, to some of the questions Pinchbeck raised—notably about women in family and employment. He emphasizes the crucial place of the history of the family among the questions indispensible for the history of the women of England—considering that the formation of industrial society resulted in changing structural and functional relationships in household and family with repercussions for women's role expectations both in society and in the home. Since, by the twentieth century, the trends of the eighteenth may be called traditional, they beg for analysis that involves questioning both the "private sphere" or domestic realm of female experience and the "public sphere" or extra-domestic activity.[15] In these two areas, Ferguson relies on the writings of earlier twentieth-century participants in the evolution of women's life-styles and also on recent feminist scholarship by sociologically oriented authors who analyze present trends with reference to historical precedents.[16]

Ferguson's connection of positive change in women's social (or "public") status to expansion of educational opportunities and institutions is an affirmation of traditional analyses. For example, throughout Doris Mary Stenton's fine survey, *The English Woman in History* (1957), women's legal, political, and social status is described as dependent upon advances in female education. Stenton's virtuoso research and analyses of primary sources from the Anglo-Saxon period to the nineteenth century were rewarded with penetrating biographical descriptions of the individual experiences, influence, and accomplishments of educated, mainly upper-class English women.[17] Relying upon discussions of educated women, as well as their own writings, Stenton reveals the impressions, reactions, and interpretations of English women to changing social, political, and economic circumstances. By showing them interacting in groups or coteries of similarly educated, articulate, and socially conscious women, she is convincing in delineating a class of female intelligensia and in some cases a corps of feminists (or proto-feminists)—all products of the educational processes of particular times and localities. This emphasis on the relationship between education and changing societal participation has not been continued in large-scale studies by historians writing after Stenton. Ferguson writes: "It is not clear why histories of education about the twentieth century have been so sex-blind." But he discusses some recent articles that appear to be pointing the way to frameworks and contexts within which late nineteenth- and twentieth-century women's education may be written in the forseeable future.

The materialization of these anticipated additions and advances in the field of English women's history will depend upon the quality and intensity of new explorations and interpretations of sources, especially of archival sources. Jeffrey Weeks ("A Survey of Primary Sources and Archives for the History of Early Twentieth-Century English Women") estimates optimistically that recent developments in social history and the revival on a large scale of the feminist movement in England have resulted in new efforts to preserve an expanding range of source materials and to increase the number of specialist archive centers in England and elsewhere. Weeks provides a detailed guide to English libraries, archives and private holdings to assist researchers in obtaining these materials and documents. His discussion is organized under eight topical headings that he evaluates as both underinvestigated by historians and vital to any study of the women of England in this century.

This brief survey, outlining the purpose of the bibliographical essays in this anthology, can only begin to suggest the historical attention that writers over a thousand years have given to the question of English women's roles and participation in socioeconomic development, at the same time that it indicates the direction that this women's history is taking at the present. The authors of these essays, in making critical judgments of the writings for each period, indicate their own opinions and approaches to the various questions they have selected for discussion. In every case, the authors are aware of the dimensions that have been added since the 1960s to the study of the social history of England, and of the development from that time of the research field designated—albeit without precision— women's history. At the time of this writing, both social history and women's history are in the process of further development and growing sophistication. Some recent articles and papers, speculating on new directions, therefore seem worthy of at least brief attention in these introductory remarks.

The term, "new social history," generally designates the study of changing social patterns that delineate social transformations over time, and historical analyses of categories of inquiry not yet considered tradi- tional in the historical discipline. Among these categories are social movements and the phenomena of social protest, demography, the devel- opment of social institutions such as the family, urban studies of the developmental kind, classes and social groups including the poor and "the inarticulate," transforming processes such as industrialization, "mental- ities" or collective consciousness, and, most recently, questions of deviance and sexuality—that is, private experience as well as public events.[18] Another connotation of "new social history" is the adaptation of method-ologies from other disciplines,[19] notably sociology and social anthropology, which has tended to convey the idea that new social history is "inter-disciplinary."[20] The tendency to consider the study of women in the past within the domain of the new social history is not a strain when the female population is considered as a gender group, as among "the inarticulate," or as a segment pertinent to interpretations in all of the categories, and when the questions and methodologies suit the purpose of evaluating women's roles and experiences in the social transformations of their societies. Yet the pair-bonding of new women's history with new social history is fragile. Specialists in women's history, after acknowledging debts in the growth of their "subspeciality" to the advent of new social history, are nevertheless critical of insufficient attention to women in studies published through the 1970s. Carroll Smith-Rosenberg writes in "The New Woman and the New History" (1975):

> But my criticism of the New Social History goes beyond the fact that it has failed to study a major segment of the population. In doing so, contemporary social historians have also ignored one of the most basic forms of human interaction—that between the sexes. The dynamics of female-male relations are central to our under-standing of the family, the church, the school, and indeed of all social institutions. This neglect of female-male interaction has contributed to another basic defect in much of the New Social History—its flirtation with functionalism and structuralism. . . . [Women's history has] begun to study groups of women never before examined and categories of human behavior and experience traditionally considered beyond the reach of historical methods. Placing women at the center of our analytic schema we have sought to construct models encompassing the complex interplay between the macrocosm of social structure and belief systems, the microcosm of family structure and the existential experience of being female.[21]

Gerda Lerner also offers a comprehensive critique in "Placing Women in History" (1976):

> While most historians are aware of the fact that their findings are not value-free and are trained to check their biases . . . they are as yet unaware of their own sexist bias, and more importantly, of the sexist bias which pervades the value-system, the culture, and the very language within which they work. . . . Conceptual models of history hitherto developed have only limited usefulness for women's history, since all are based on the assumptions of a

patriarchal ordering of values. The structural-functionalist framework leaves out class and sex factors, the traditional Marxist framework leves out sex and race factors as *essentials,* admitting them only as marginal factors. [PP. 362–64][22]

Anna Davin and Sally Alexander observe in "Feminist History" (1976):

> Most social history books nowadays boast sections on the family and the position of women, along with religion, education, popular culture and so on. But they are still tagged on, not integrated into the overall understanding of a society or even of its parts. Social history like labour history takes for granted sexual divisions at work, in the home, or in political and cultural life. The sexual division of labour disappears in discussion of men's and women's different 'roles'; domestic life is studied in a vacuum; popular culture is represented by men's clubs, self-help organizations, or football, and the absence of women is scarcely noted let alone investigated or explained.[23]

In their introduction to *The Rights and Wrongs of Women* (1976), Juliet Mitchell and Ann Oakley seek the reworking of social history and other disciplines from a feminist perspective:

> When we talk of returning to the drawing-board, we are referring to the enterprise of rewriting history; of re-interpreting the social world, both past and present, from a perspective which includes women.... Feminism is a method of analysis as well as a discovery of new material.... [It] asks new questions.... [It is] coming up with new answers.... [And it] says there is a contradiction in the social relations between men and women. This contradiction is never static as a biological opposition would be, but it shifts, moves and is moved and is therefore one force among others that effects social change and the movement of human history.[24]

In their papers for a recent international conference on women in history, Leonore Davidoff and Joan Kelly both offered critiques of recent social history and women's history with the opinion that new theoretical guidelines are essential.[25] Davidoff argued that "one of the contributions of a feminist perspective is to show that the lack of an explicit framework can narrow, even cripple, historical analysis." To the question of what kind of theory and at what level, she suggested as a guide that the "task is to bring the question of sexual divisions back into historical thinking." Her detailed discussion focused on the concept and analysis of power within sexual divisions in terms of interpersonal relationships—illustrating her points, often, from nineteenth- and early twentieth-century circumstances in

England. Prescribing new tasks for women's history, Davidoff advised that the analysis of power (especially a feminist view of power) "challenges the traditional expectation that personal, affectional, sexual and moral elements can somehow be 'factored out' of the picture."[26]

Joan Kelly's paper, "A Decade of Feminist Theory," on the other hand, focused upon a theoretical view or "vision" favoring a "unified, 'double' view of the social order" rather than an emphasis on "dualism" or sexual division. Kelly said:

> What the development of theoretical and practical consciousness over the past decade has led to, in short, is the beginning of a systemic unification in place of the dualism of a mode of production on the one hand, and a mode of reproduction on the other.... From our new position, theorists have already begun to see how earlier feminist theory ... subscribed to the simple dichotomies that [nineteenth-century bourgeois] society set up.... It is no longer adequate to ours. And once we recognize that, we also see that that split vision could never generate a fully comprehensive social theory—not even of nineteenth-century society and social movements.[27]

Kelly's and Davidoff's approaches convey difference in interpretive stance rather than differences in basic concepts about the social organization of the past—with Davidoff seeking as first priority a more penetrating historically oriented analysis of all the factors behind the tradition of dichotomizing social roles and spheres, and Kelly prescribing the development of theoretical approaches out of viewpoints more closely related to recent feminist thought and experience.

The relative value of these suggestions for inquiry into women's history awaits judgment through evaluation of the studies to which they are now and will be applied. The same must be said for judgment of whether the questions and concerns of women's history and social history will remain parallel or whether they will more firmly coincide. My prediction favors the latter. In any event, the new social history and the new women's history are, in the decade of the 1970s, weathering rapid growth and development in both cooperative and dialectical relationships. And, as the essays in this volume exemplify, the direction of historical writing on women is not only toward expanding new knowledge of social development and of women's roles in the historical process, but also toward creating new and provocative challenges for the profession of history itself.

# NOTES

1. The term "women's history" is used here and in recent publications without precise definition. The usual connotation is: any historical writing about women. I am therefore using the term broadly in reference to historically oriented comment on women in sources, as well as in secondary historical writings about women. Professional historians of women, since the 1960s, have been working toward a more accurate definition of the term to delineate a research field. My introduction does not purport to be either a detailed or a systematic historiographical discussion of English women's history. Such an endeavor would be worthwhile however, and should be undertaken.

2. As Carl N. Degler writes in his 1974 article on Mary Beard's *Woman as Force in History:* "Leopold von Ranke may have said that history ought to be written as it actually happened, but the fact is that written history is only that part of the past in which we are interested ... it is always our concerns about the present that determine which of the myriad facts of the past become known as 'history'" (p. 70).

3. Full references to these Anglo-Saxon sources will be found in Dietrich's bibliography.

4. These include nineteenth-century government inspectors' reports, commissioners' reports, census reports, as well as proto-sociological studies of the period. Some secondary works containing bibliographies that cite these documents include: Neff, *Victorian Working Women*; Roberts, *Victorian Origins of the Welfare State*; Pinchbeck, *Women Workers and the Industrial Revolution*; Pinchbeck and Hewitt, *Children in English Society*; Hewitt, *Wives and Mothers in Victorian Industry*; and McKendrick, "Home Demand and Economic Growth."

5. There are, of course, some exceptions, and these include: Eckenstein, *Women Under Monasticism* (1896); Hill, *Women in English Life from Medieval Times* (1896); Stopes, *British Freewomen* (1894); and Cleveland, *Women Under English Law* (1896).

6. Many bibliographical references are in all of the chapters of Vicinus, ed., *Suffer and Be Still* and *A Widening Sphere*; McGregor, "The Social Position of Women in England, 1850–1914: A Bibliography"; Palmegiano, *Women in British Periodicals, 1832–1867: A Bibliography*; Banks and Banks, *Feminism and Family Planning in Victorian England*; and in the notes of Holcombe, *Victorian Ladies at Work*.

7. Palmegiano found, in her intensive study of periodical literature, that "Perhaps the one absolute that emerged ... was that the [female] sex was not affected in the same way because women were not alike.... The more that writers sought to delineate true womanhood, the more confused they appeared" (p. xi). She quotes A. W. Kinglake in *Quarterly Review*, 1844: "This subject of 'Woman' is so splendid, so terrifying, so enchanting, so vast" (ibid.).

8. Contemporary reviews of Clark's book include: *Atheneum*, 2 January 1920; *Survey*, 29 May 1920; *Times Literary Supplement*, 4 December 1919.

9. See Robinton's review article on Eileen Power's writings in *Some Modern Historians of Britain*.

10. Contemporary reviews of Pinchbeck's book include: *Times Literary Supplement*, 20 March 1930; *Spectator*, 1 March 1930; *Saturday Review*, 15 March 1930; *American Economic Review*, December 1930.

11. Other writings that may be included in this category are: Abram, *English Life in the Later Middle Ages* (1913); Putnam, *The Lady* (1910); and Neff, *Victorian Working Women* (1929).

12. See Davis, "'Women's History' in Transition: The European Case," for a critical discussion of Clark's work in comparative context.

13. Titmuss makes this point in "The Position of Women: Some Vital Statistics," in *Essays in Social History*, p. 287, n. 2.

14. For example, see: Smelser, "Sociological History"; and a critique of Smelser by Anderson, "Sociological History and the Working-Class Family." Medick's "The Proto-Industrial Family Economy" is an excellent discussion. Directly focused on women's history are, for example: George, "From 'Goodwife' to 'Mistress'"; Davidoff, L'Esperance, and Newby, "Landscape with Figures." For other examples, see the

listings in Kanner, "The Women of England in a Century of Social Change, 1815–1914: A Select Bibliography, Part II," pp. 206–18.

15. For an excellent consideration of the "two spheres" see Elshtain, "Moral Woman and Immoral Man." One of the earliest proposals of this framework for analysis is that of Rosaldo, "A Theoretical Overview." A thoughtful discussion that explores the concept is Papanek, "Research on 'Sex Roles.'"

16. Among the feminist writers he discusses, Ferguson underscores the contributions of Juliet Mitchell, Ann Oakley, Sheila Allen, Diana Leonard Barker, Leonore Davidoff, and Sheila Rowbotham. There are, in addition, writings from the British Women's Liberation Movement; see, for example: Wandor, comp., *The Body Politic*; and Allen, Sanders, and Wallis, eds., *Conditions of Illusion*. A fine collection of theoretical essays on feminist scholarship is included in Carroll, ed., *Liberating Women's History*. See especially Carroll's introduction and critical review of Beard's *Woman as Force in History*, and also Smith, "Feminism and the Methodology of Women's History"; Johansson, "'Herstory' as History: A New Field or Another Fad?"; Lerner, "Placing Women in the Past"; and Mitchell, "Four Structures in a Complex Unity." See also the introduction and essays in Bridenthal and Koonz, eds., *Becoming Visible*.

17. Stenton's pioneer survey is more comprehensive than my remarks here suggest. For a thorough discussion of the contents with reference to interests explicitly germane to recent women's history see Tilly's introduction to the reprinted edition of 1977.

18. Hobsbawm's "From Social History to the History of Society" is an excellent discussion of the development of recent social history. Degler includes in his article on Beard a discussion of new social history trends. Articles in *The Journal of Social History* and *Social History* exemplify new trends also.

19. Hobsbawm discusses methodological relationships between historians and social scientists. The issue of *Daedalus* in which his article appears is devoted to methodological considerations. *Oral History; Journal of the Oral History Society* (University of Essex) is a primary source for this specialty. Psychoanalytical methodology is explored in *The Journal of Psycho-History*. Psychology of perception and the use of perception for women's history in anthropological-historical interpretation is the focus of Shirley Ardener's *Perceiving Women*. Ardener proposes to examine "the set of ideas which together represent women in the minds of those who have generated the model [of women] as well as those concepts which women themselves generate in their minds" (p. xi).

20. Hobsbawm discusses historians' methodological borrowing from social scientists, and considers how "historians with all their willingness to learn from other disciplines, are required to teach" the historicizing social scientists "who have ventured into historical source material without knowledge of the hazards" (p. 26).

21. Smith-Rosenberg capitalizes spelling of the terms "New Social History" and "New Women's History." And she writes, "There are in the mid-1970s two women's histories each reflecting orientations and trends within general historiography. One can be designated as traditional or politically oriented women's history. The second, which I will call the New Women's History is the product of a complex interaction between the political perspective of the contemporary women's movement and the methodology of the New Social History" (p. 186). She concedes, "Indeed, without the growing methodological sophistication of contemporary social history, the New Women's History could not be written.... But the path between ... is not a one-way street; the history of women has significantly expanded the concerns of contemporary social history" (p. 188). For another comprehensive discussion of the developments of women's history in relation to contemporary social history, see Lougee, "Modern European History."

22. This quotation is from Lerner's chapter in *Liberating Women's History*, a revised version of her article "Placing Women in History: Definitions and Challenges," originally published in *Feminist Studies*.

23. Davin and Alexander state among their future purposes in writing for *History Workshop*: "We want to examine the sexual division of labor in different historical contexts, under

27

capitalist and other modes of production. A reappraisal of family history will be another priority because this has so often been the only place for historical mention of women" (p. 5).

24. Introduction to *The Rights and Wrongs of Women* (p. 14). Mitchell and Oakley describe their anthology as an "anti-text; a text that could be set against the ideological message of orthodox literature on the position of women" (p. 7).

25. This conference, held at the University of Maryland, 16–18 November 1977, was entitled "Women and Power: Dimensions of Women's Historical Experience, an International Conference in Women's History." The conference was sponsored by the Conference Group in Women's History (an affiliate of the Coordinating Committee on Women in the Historical Profession) in consultation with the Women's Research and Resources Centre, London.

26. Davidoff's paper was entitled "Power as an 'Essentially Contested Concept': Can It Be of Use to Feminist Historians?" I want to thank Leonore Davidoff for a copy of the typescript and for permitting me to quote.

27. Kelly (also known as Kelly-Gadol) marks Juliet Mitchell's "The Longest Revolution" (1966) as preparing the way for conceptualizing women's history with "the four structures by which we might assess the complex position of 'woman's estate'" (production, reproduction, sexuality, and socialization). She then traces the development of "feminist theory" to 1977, concluding that "our understanding of women and society has developed accordingly." I want to thank Joan Kelly for a copy of the typescript and for permitting me to quote.

# BIBLIOGRAPHY

ABRAM, ANNIE. *English Life and Manners in the Later Middle Ages.* London and New York: 1913.

ALEXANDER, WILLIAM. *The History of Women from the Earliest Antiquity to the Present Time.* 2 vols. London: 1782. (Numerous other editions.)

ALLEN, SANDRA; SANDERS, LEE; and WALLIS, JEAN, eds. *Conditions of Illusion: Papers from the Women's Movement.* Leeds: 1974.

ANDERSON, MICHAEL. "Sociological History and the Working-Class Family: Smelser Revisted." *Social History,* no. 3 (October 1976): 317–34.

ARDENER, SHIRLEY, ed. *Perceiving Women.* London and New York: 1975.

BALLARD, GEORGE. *Memoirs of Several Ladies of Great Britain Who Have Been Celebrated for Their Writings or Skill in the Learned Languages, Arts and Sciences.* Oxford: 1752.

BANKS, J. A., and BANKS, OLIVE. *Feminism and Family Planning in Victorian England.* Liverpool: 1964. Reprint (paperback). New York: 1972.

BRIDENTHAL, RENATE, and KOONZ, CLAUDIA, eds. *Becoming Visible: Women in Modern Europe.* Boston: 1977.

CARROLL, BERENICE A., ed. *Liberating Women's History: Theoretical and Critical Essays.* Urbana, Ill.: 1976.

CLARK, ALICE. *Working Life of Women in the Seventeenth Century.* London and New York: 1919. Reprint. London and New York: 1968.

CLEVELAND, ARTHUR RACKHAM. *Woman under English Law; from the Landing of the Saxons to the Present Time.* London: 1896.

DAVIDOFF, LEONORE. "Power as an 'Essentially Contested Concept': Can It Be of Use to Feminist Historians?" Paper read at the International Conference on the History of Women, 16–18 November 1977, at the University of Maryland.

———; L'Esperance, Jean; and Newby, Howard. "Landscape with Figures: Home and Community in English Society." In *The Rights and Wrongs of Women*, edited by Juliet Mitchell and Ann Oakley. London: 1976.

DAVIN, ANNA, and ALEXANDER, SALLY. "Feminist History." *History Workshop: A Journal of Socialist Historians* 1 (Spring 1976): 4–6.

DAVIS, NATALIE ZEMON. "'Women's History' in Transition: The European Case." *Feminist Studies* 3, nos. 3–4 (1976): 83–103.

DEGLER, CARL N. "*Woman as Force in History* by Mary Beard." *Daedalus* 103 (Winter 1974): 67–73.

ECKENSTEIN, LINA. *Women Under Monasticism*. Cambridge: 1896.

ELSHTAIN, JEAN BETHKE. "Moral Woman and Immoral Man: A Consideration of the Public-Private Split and Its Potential Ramifications." *Politics and Society* 4, no. 4 (1974): 453–73.

GEORGE, MARGARET. "From 'Goodwife' to 'Mistress': The Transformation of the Female in Bourgeois Culture." *Science and Society* 37 (Summer 1973): 152–77.

HEWES, AMY. Review of *Working Life of Women in the Seventeenth Century*, by ALICE CLARK. *American Economic Review* 10 (1920): 577–81.

HEWITT, MARGARET. *Wives and Mothers in Victorian Industry*. London: 1958.

HEYWOOD, THOMAS. *The Exemplary Lives and Memorable Acts of Nine of the Most Worthy Women in the World*. London: 1640.

———. *Gunaikeion: Or Nine Books of Various History Concerninge Women*. London: 1624, 1657.

HILL, GEORGIANA. *Women in English Life from Medieval to Modern Times*. 2 vols. London: 1896.

*History Workshop: A Journal of Socialist Historians*. Vol. 1– (Spring 1976–). London.

HOBSBAWM, E. J. "From Social History to the History of Society." *Daedalus* 100 (Winter 1971): 20–45. Reprint. In *Essays in Social History*, edited by M. W. Flinn and T. C. Smout. Oxford: 1974.

JOHANSSON, SHEILA RYAN. "'Herstory' as History: A New Field or Another Fad?" In *Liberating Women's History: Theoretical and Critical Essays*, edited by Berenice A. Carroll. Urbana, Ill.: 1976.

*Journal of Psychohistory*. Vol. 4– (Summer 1976–). New York. (Continues *History of Childhood Quarterly*.)

*Journal of Social History*. Vol. 1– (1967–). Berkeley.

KANNER, BARBARA. "The Women of England in a Century of Social Change, 1815–1914: A Select Bibliography, Part II." In *A Widening Sphere: Changing Roles of Victorian Women*, edited by Martha Vicinus. Bloomington, Ind.: 1977.

KELLY, JOAN. "A Decade of Feminist Theory: 1967–1977." Paper read at International Conference on the History of Women, 16–18 November 1977, at the University of Maryland.

LERNER, GERDA. "Placing Women in History: Definitions and Challenges." *Feminist Studies* 3 (Fall 1975): 5–14. Reprint in revised edition as "Placing Women in History: A 1975 Perspective." In *Liberating Women's History: Theoretical and Critical Essays*, edited by Berenice A. Carroll. Urbana, Ill.: 1976.

LOUGEE, CAROLYN C. "[Review Essay] Modern European History." *Signs* 2, no. 3 (1977): 628–50.

McGREGOR, O. R. "The Social Position of Women in England, 1850–1914: A Bibliography." *The British Journal of Sociology* 6 (1955): 48–60.

McKENDRICK, NEIL. "Home Demand and Economic Growth: A New View of the Role of Women and Children in the Industrial Revolution." In *Historical Perspectives: Studies in English Thought and Society in Honour of J. H. Plumb*, edited by Neil McKendrick. London: 1974.

MEDICK, HANS. "The Proto-Industrial Family Economy: The Structural Function of Household and Family during the Transition from Peasant society to Industrial Capitalism." *Social History*, no. 3 (October 1976) : 291–315.

MITCHELL, JULIET. "Four Structures in a Complex Unity." In *Liberating Women's History: Theoretical and Critical Essays*, edited by Berenice A. Carroll. Urbana, Ill.: 1976.

———. "The Longest Revolution." *New Left Review* 40 (1966): 11–37.

———, and Oakley, Ann. "Introduction." In *The Rights and Wrongs of Women*, edited by J. Mitchell and Ann Oakley. London: 1976.

NEFF, WANDA FRAIKEN. *Victorian Working Women: An Historical and Literary Study of Women in British Industries and Professions 1832–1850*. New York and London: 1929. Reprint. London and New York: 1966.

*Oral History: Journal of the Oral History Society* (Essex University). Vol. 1– (1973–). Mimeographed.

PALMEGIANO, E. M. *Women and British Periodicals 1832–1867: A Bibliography*. London and New York: 1976.

PAPANEK, HANNA. "Research on Women in Society and Research on 'Sex Roles.'" *Canadian Newsletter of Research on Women* 5, no. 3 (October 1976): 18–20.

PINCHBECK, IVY. *Women Workers and the Industrial Revolution*. London: 1930. Reprint. London: 1969.

———, and Hewitt, Margaret. *Children in English Society*. 2 vols. London: 1969–73.

POWER, EILEEN. *Medieval Women*. Edited by M. M. Poston. Cambridge: 1975.

———. "The Position of Women." In *The Legacy of the Middle Ages*, edited by C. G. Crump and E. F. Jacob. Oxford: 1926.

PUTNAM, EMILY JAMES (SMITH). *The Lady; Studies of Certain Significant Phases of Her History*. New York: 1910. New York and London: 1919. Reprint. Chicago: 1970.

ROBERTS, DAVID. *Victorian Origins of the Welfare State*. New Haven: 1960.

ROBINTON, MADELINE. "Eileen Power." In *Some Modern Historians of Britain*, edited by Herman Ansubel, J. Bartlet Brebner, and Erling M. Hunt. New York: 1951.

ROSALDO, MICHELLE ZIMBALIST. "A Theoretical Overview." In *Woman, Culture and Society*, edited by Michelle Zimbalist Rosaldo and Louise Lamphere. Stanford, Calif.: 1974.

*The Saturday Review*. Review of *Women Workers and the Industrial Revolution*, by L. [sic] Pinchbeck. *The Saturday Review* 149 (1930): 333.

SMELSER, NEIL. "Sociological History: The Industrial Revolution and the British Working-Class Family." *Journal of Social History* 1 (1967): 18–35.

SMITH, HILDA. "Feminism and the Methodology of Women's History." In *Liberating Women's History: Theoretical and Critical Essays*, edited by Berenice A. Carroll. Urbana, Ill.: 1976.

SMITH-ROSENBERG, CARROLL. "The New Woman and the New History." *Feminist Studies* 3 (Fall 1975): 185–98.

*Social History*. No. 1– (1976–). London.

*The Spectator*. "Economic History [review of *Women Workers and the Industrial Revolution*, by Ivy Pinchbeck, and other works]." *The Spectator* 144 (1930): 338–41.

STENTON, DORIS MARY. *The English Woman in History*. London: 1957. Reprint, with an introduction by Louise Tilly. New York: 1977.

STOPES, CHARLOTTE CARMICHAEL. *British Freewomen: Their Historical Privilege*. London: 1894.

*Times Literary Supplement*. "Women in the Seventeenth Century [review of *The Working Life of Women in the Seventeenth Century*, by Alice Clark]." *Times Literary Supplement*, 4 December 1919, p. 707.

———. Review of *Women Workers and the Industrial Revolution, 1750–1850*, by Ivy Pinchbeck. *Times Literary Supplement*, 20 March 1930, p. 227.

TITMUSS, RICHARD. "The Position of Women." In *Essays on the 'Welfare State,'* edited by Richard Titmuss. London: 1958. Reprint. London: 1963. Reprint in revised edition as "The Position of Women: Some Vital Statistics." In *Essays in Social History*, edited by M. W. Flinn and T. C. Smout. Oxford: 1974.

VICINUS, MARTHA, ed. *Suffer and Be Still: Women in the Victorian Age*. Bloomington, Ind.: 1972.

———. *A Widening Sphere: Changing Roles of Victorian Women*. Bloomington, Ind.: 1977.

WANDOR, MICHELENE, comp. *The Body Politic: Writings from the Women's Liberation Movement in Britain, 1969–1972*. London: 1972.

WOODBURY, HELEN SUMNER. Review of *Women Workers and the Industrial Revolution, 1750–1850*, by Ivy Pinchbeck. *American Economic Review* 20 (1930): 720–21.

# An Introduction to

# Women

# in Anglo-Saxon Society

# (c. 600 – 1066)

## SHEILA C. DIETRICH

The Anglo-Saxon period seems a "dark age" only to one uninitiated in the sources for its history.[1] When those sources are examined to discover what they reveal about women in Anglo-Saxon society, the period appears almost enlightened. It is true that the documentary evidence for Anglo-Saxon history is scarce compared with that for modern England, but the returns it will provide to the student of women's roles and contributions may prove to be proportionately greater. Women (at least the upper class women usually depicted in the documents) emerge from Anglo-Saxon records possessing an impressive independence and influence. Doris M. Stenton recorded that her impulse towards writing *The English Woman in History* (1957) came from the contrast between the "masterful and independent Anglo-Saxon ladies" of whom her husband talked, and the "legally dependent, although still masterful" women of the twelfth and thirteenth centuries.[2] She was not the first to notice that contrast, nor was she the last.[3]

Before discussing the Anglo-Saxons, it is important to clarify that English history did not begin with the Anglo-Saxon settlements in the fifth and sixth centuries. Celtic and Romano-Celtic Britain preceded Anglo-Saxon England, and while there are far fewer written sources for those earlier periods, enough exists to make the reader desire more. Of relevance to women are Tacitus's references to the queens of Celtic Britain (first century A.D.), Boudicca of the Iceni and Cartimandua of the Brigantes, who had great impact on Rome's policies in Britain. There is much work to be done on women in Celtic society, particularly by historians who can draw together classical sources, archaeology, and Irish literature. Since recent scholars are moving away from the "extermination theory" (of Celts by Anglo-Saxons), to one which posits interaction and intermarriage, and since early Anglo-Saxon society felt the impact of Celtic culture through the Irish church, what is discovered of women in Celtic culture might well have a bearing on the status of women in Anglo-Saxon England.[4]

For background to Anglo-Saxon society there exist various recent general surveys. F. M. Stenton's *Anglo-Saxon England* (1943) is unsurpassed as a comprehensive study; Dorothy Whitelock's *The Beginnings of English Society* (1952) is still one of the best short introductions to Anglo-Saxon society. Both authors, as natural and integral parts of their discussions, consider individual women and also provide some general evaluations of women's status. Other works appearing between Stenton's first edition (1943) and the present have their individual strengths as general histories, but, on the whole, are less satisfactory than Stenton or Whitelock in dealing with specific women and with general questions of women's status.[5]

What picture of Anglo-Saxon women do such secondary works produce? Regarding women's involvement in political affairs (governing, giving counsel, even leading armies), there seems to be no consensus. Some works emphasize the influence and power of royal woman; others deny the significant role of women in these concerns.[6] Some works emphasize the participation of many noble women in more than household affairs; others, by discussing domestic interests at greater length, imply that Anglo-Saxon housewives fit a more recent stereotype.[7] Regarding women's participation and influence in religious life, similar disagreement exists; some works emphasize women's contribution, others remain silent.[8] Where the law is concerned a clearer picture emerges: the legal rights and legal independence of Anglo-Saxon women are favorably sketched, either implicitly or explicitly, with at least one author noting the decline in this legal independence after the Norman Conquest.[9]

The disparity of modern treatments underscores the necessity of going directly to the primary sources. In some cases this involves stripping away the accretions of another writer's bias or orientation, and asking new questions of very old records. In other cases it involves merely supplementing or complementing the partial picture already obtained. The vitality of the documents is not often reflected in secondary works, however good, and original records might repay a close look with fresh insights. The rest of this essay will focus, therefore, on introducing the primary materials relevant to women and noting special studies which offer useful commentary on them.

## Narrative and Biographical Sources[10]

A variety of sources survives which makes it possible to examine the Anglo-Saxon woman in action. One may begin such an examination with the extant narrative and biographical sources, which highlight the lives of "great women." This approach to women's history through the study of supposedly "representative" individuals might be criticized as limited or eccentric; but it is valuable since it reveals the public or political activities available to women (admittedly, a small segment of women), and thus allows a comparison of their opportunities both with those of men in their own period and with those of "great women" in later periods. Such a study also reveals the impact several women had on the course of Anglo-Saxon history, an impact that is not always adequately represented.

The *Anglo-Saxon Chronicle*,[11] although it does not mention women frequently, does contain several suggestive entries. For example, in A.D. 672, "Cenwealh died, and his queen Seaxburh reigned one year after him." Or consider the entry for 697: "the Southumbrians slew Osthryth, Ethelred's queen and Ecgfrith's sister." Was Osthryth slain because she was Northumbrian and exercising too much authority in her adopted kingdom, Mercia? It is tempting to read this entry as a quiet comment on the assertiveness of queens and the equal treatment meted out to unpopular rulers—men or women. Another terse entry which invites speculation regarding the power of the woman involved is for 722: "Queen Æthelburh demolished Taunton, which Ine [King of Wessex] had built."

The entries for 910 to 918 in the Mercian version of the *Chronicle* are more complete in documenting the political and martial activities of Æthelflæd, daughter of King Alfred of Wessex, wife of the ealdorman of Mercia, and sole ruler ("Lady of Mercia") after her husband's death in 911. Æthelflæd's political control of Mercia and her military leadership of its army were instrumental in reconquering areas taken by the Danes and in paving the way for the unification of England. At her death in 918 she left a daughter, Ælfwyn, to succeed her. The *Chronicle* indicates that in 919 Ælfwyn was deprived of authority in Mercia and taken into Wessex. This was probably done at the instigation of her uncle, Edward the Elder, ruler in Wessex, who desired the subjection of Mercia to Wessex (i.e., to his) authority.[12]

For the later Anglo-Saxon period, the late ninth to the mid-eleventh centuries, contemporary biographical works depict more fully the activities of "great women." Asser's *Life of Alfred*[13] (written c. 893), for example, while containing only incidental references to the royal women closely connected with Alfred, sketches briefly the career of a tyrannical queen who ruled several generations before Alfred's time. According to Asser, Eadburh, daughter of the Mercian king Offa (reigned c. 757–96) and his wife (queen Cynethryth), married (c. 789) the king of Wessex and gained almost complete control of his realm. All who stood in her way she deprived of life or power, and supposedly was responsible for poisoning the king himself. Asser relates this story to illustrate the origin of a "perverse" custom of the West Saxons: since Eadburh's time, they had not allowed a king's wife to sit beside him on the throne, and had denied the title "queen" to the king's wife. It was not, apparently, her exercise of power, but her abuse of power, which enraged the West Saxons against Eadburh and caused them to attempt to limit the queen's official role.[14]

For the later Anglo-Saxon period, two laudatory lives illustrate the activities of queens—*Encomium Emmae Reginae* (Praise of Queen Emma) and *Vita Ædwardi Regis* (Life of King Edward).[15] The first, commissioned by the Emma of the title, reveals how Emma, originally a member of the Norman ducal family, wished herself to be portrayed within the context of Anglo-Saxon history. She was "peaceweaver" between the defeated Anglo-Saxons, the nation of her first husband, King Æthelred (d. 1016), and the conquering Danes, ruled by the man who became, in 1017, her second husband, King Cnut. (The logic of her "claim" to represent the Anglo-Saxons is not made clear, since the *Encomium* does not mention Emma's first husband, from whom that claim derived.) The *Encomium* also reveals Emma's impact on late Anglo-Saxon history: perhaps we should seek the beginning of the Norman Conquest in 1002, when she married Æthelred, or in 1017, when her second marriage, in effect, banished her sons to Normandy.

Emma's daughter-in-law, Queen Edith (wife to the Norman-raised Edward the Confessor from 1045 until his death in 1066), commissioned a biography of her husband; *Vita Ædwardi* reveals the activities of Edith as queen and as member of the powerful Godwin family. Barlow, in his recent biography of Edward, suggests that the work originally might have represented an attempt by Edith to support her claims to rule England after her husband's death.[16] This seems a plausible theory, considering the active role that royal women played in public life during the Anglo-Saxon period. Why shouldn't Edith have seen herself as another Seaxburh or Æthelflæd?

The plausibility of this sort of question has caused at least one writer to suggest a contrast between the Anglo-Saxon period and the centuries following the Norman Conquest. In a sketchy, little-noticed, but suggestive article, B. Bandel noted the contrast between the Anglo-Saxon period—when women exercised authority in public affairs and this was taken for granted by the *Anglo-Saxon Chronicle*—and the postconquest period—when "war and government left the home," women's opportunities in governing and military leadership declined, and many chroniclers exhibited narrower attitudes toward women who did occasionally engage in such activities.[17] Bandel argues that Æthelflæd's treatment in twelfth- and thirteenth-century chronicles differs radically from that in the *Anglo-Saxon Chronicle*. Her martial exploits are neglected; her marital exploits or, more accurately, her lack of them, come to the fore. She is no longer the woman who successfully led the Mercian army against the Danes; she has become the woman who had only one child because labor pains so bothered her that she henceforth refrained from intercourse with her husband.[18]

Some vigorous women participated in government and in military campaigns in the postconquest period, but they appear to have been exceptions.[19] In the Anglo-Saxon period, men's control of government and war was certainly more usual than women's, but the evidence of women such as Seaxburh, Æthelflæd, or even, on a less heroic scale, Edith suggests that the society's view of what behavior was appropriate to a certain sex was less limiting for women than views that prevailed later. Anglo-Saxon society allowed women the mobility to step directly and without fuss into roles which involved ruling a kingdom or even, on occasion, leading an army.

RELIGIOUS SOURCES

Sources dealing with Anglo-Saxon religious life offer two kinds of information about women. Some illustrate the active position of women within the church hierarchy; others reveal the church's "official" attitude toward women in general.

Bede's *Ecclesiastical History* (completed 731), one of the most interesting and significant works for the early period, records the respected official position that many noble women held in the church hierarchy; the authority that abbesses exercised over double monasteries, i.e., institutions that included monks as well as nuns; and the various signs of sanctity that attached equally to relics of holy men and women. It was not surprising to Bede that Abbess Hilda's counsel was sought by ordinary men and kings alike, nor that the educational standards at her monastery produced five bishops; it did not bother him that an abbess of a double monastery ruled over men as well as women. She was a "shining example" to all who wished to live a good life.[20]

The letters of St. Boniface and the saints' lives that relate to his missionary work on the continent in the eighth century also illustrate the active and respected role of women in the Anglo-Saxon church.[21] Some— for example, Leoba (Leofgyth), abbess of Bishofsheim—served with Boniface in the German lands, risking their lives to help convert and educate the still pagan Germans. Others remained in England, corresponding with Boniface and producing the much needed books used in the newly established continental monasteries. The letters that passed back and forth across the Channel reveal, for example, the degree of education attained by Anglo-Saxon nuns, the desire (often fulfilled) for pilgrimage, and exceptional levels of respect and warm affection for colleagues, male and female, who were considered equals in the Christian endeavor. This was a period in which the Anglo-Saxon church excelled in intellectual and missionary fervor, and it was due as much to women such as Hilda and Leoba as to men such as Bede and Boniface. As Talbot suggests, "Never, perhaps, has there been such an age in which religious women exercised such great power."[22]

The double monasteries were not refounded after the Danish invasions; great counselor-administrator-educator figures such as Hilda do not appear in the last centuries of Anglo-Saxon England.[23] But the persistence of holy women as abbesses and at lower levels in the church is attested by numerous saints' lives; these might provide potential evidence for the role of women in religious life.[24] F. M. Stenton suggested that the "contribution made by women to the religious idealism behind the [tenth-century] English monastic revival" had, perhaps, been undervalued by historians.[25] No one has yet attempted to test that hypothesis.

The second kind of information shows that the church's "official" attitude toward women was not always consistent with the high standing women enjoyed in the Anglo-Saxon church. Some church laws of the fourth through sixth centuries reveal a bias against women based on early Church Fathers' ("patristic") attitudes toward women, which saw them as threats to men's salvation.[26] But this bias did not often surface in the actions or opinions of men who worked alongside Anglo-Saxon nuns and abbesses. For example, one church law of this period forbade the burial of a male corpse next to a female corpse until the latter had decomposed. Boniface was either ignorant of this precept and its underlying biases, or intentionally disregarded them; he requested that he and Leoba be buried in the same grave, so that they who served God "with equal sincerity and zeal" should await the Resurrection together.[27]

Church attitudes toward the female sex, marriage, and sexuality in general are also found in penitentials, medieval handbooks of penance. These were intended to establish moral guidelines for clergy and laity and to indicate the appropriate penance for a variety of sins. They illustrate the existence of, or the fear of, certain social and sexual sins and thus show the moral climate in which the Christian Anglo-Saxon woman, regardless of class, was expected to operate. For example: "If a woman practices vice with a woman, she shall do penance for three years"; "If a priest is polluted in touching or in kissing a woman he shall do penance for 40 days"; "Women shall not in the time of impurity enter a church or communicate, neither nuns nor lay women; if they presume they shall fast for three weeks"; "A husband ought not to see his wife nude."[28] (The converse is not mentioned.)

The power and influence available to women within the Anglo-Saxon church hierarchy apparently declined in the later part of the period. It is possible to posit an increasing ascendancy of the patristic view of the evil of women. This is reflected in an early twelfth-century history of the church of Durham, discussed by Gransden in *Historical Writing in England* (1974). Gransden points out that the monastic author of this work attributed to Cuthbert, seventh-century Anglo-Saxon monk, bishop of Lindisfarne, and saint, an antifeminism which he never evinced. According to Gransden, the author claims that Cuthbert excluded all women from his church, his shrine, and the cemetery of his church, inflicting terrible vengeance on female trespassers. Nothing in the sources from Cuthbert's own time supports this view, and Gransden justifiably concludes that the author was trying to provide historical precedents for contemporary attitudes.[29]

Exactly why those attitudes changed, and in what way, if any, that change in attitude was related to the decline in actual authority and position of women in the church (i.e., the relationship between the theoretical and the actual) are subjects that require further study. Women such as Hilda, Leoba, and countless other nuns and abbesses played important roles in the early church; perhaps new research would turn up equally vital, if not as obvious, contributions in the later period (as F. M. Stenton suggested might be the case for the tenth century). But if not, it is important to seek explanations for the reversal both in offical attitude toward women and in the actual place of women in the church hierarchy.[30]

LEGAL SOURCES

Just as the religious sources portray individual women's activities in the church and the church's attitudes toward women in general, the extant legal sources illustrate two aspects of women's legal status. The law codes provide a picture of the norm, a standard of conduct that was considered necessary to ensure the good order of society; we can thus perceive in the laws a normative or ideal picture of women's rights and obligations.

Business documents such as wills and charters depict the actual exercise by individual women of these rights and obligations.

The law codes present neither a completely clear nor a consistent picture of women's legal status.[31] On the one hand, certain laws can be cited which seem to suggest that Anglo-Saxon women were hedged in, not liberated, by the law. For example, a woman was under the authority of a male guardian, who was entitled to compensation if she were injured or abducted; a woman was a chattel to be bought or sold; a wife was totally subject to her husband; she was punished more severely for sexual crimes than was her husband.[32] A very selective reading of these laws would produce a grim picture of the Anglo-Saxon woman's lack of legal rights.

On the other hand, one finds laws which imply a relative equality between men and women of the same status, and which indicate a legal independence allowed to women. For example, compensation for (injury to) an unmarried woman was the same as for a free man; a wife who bore a child was entitled to one-half the couple's goods, and in the early period she could depart with her share; a wife was considered to have her own sphere of authority in the household and would not suffer her husband's punishment unless his stolen goods were found in her cupboard or chest (to which she controlled the keys); a widow's maintenance was guaranteed, and in the later Anglo-Saxon period she enjoyed the protection "of God and of the King."[33]

As the earlier mention of secondary works has indicated, the consensus of opinion is that the second set of laws is the more representative of Anglo-Saxon legal attitudes. Within a society which was, after all, patriarchal, women enjoyed relative legal independence when it was desirable and "benevolent" protection when it was necessary. As maidens they were valued and protected; as wives they appear to have been considered partners, not abject subjects, to their husbands; as widows the laws enabled them to manage their lives with virtually no interference, as long as they lived the respectable lives prescribed by "God and the King." One law, not usually cited as relevant to women, might be significant because it omits mention of them:

> Concerning the weak. 1a. Because we may know full well that the weak and the strong cannot bear an equally heavy burden, nor can the sick man bear one equal to that borne by him who is sound. 1b. And therefore we must make due allowance and carefully distinguish between age and youth, wealth and poverty, freeman and slaves, the sound and the sick. 1c. And discrimination with regard to these circumstances must be shown both in ecclesiastical amends and in secular judgment.[34]

Admittedly, arguing from an omission is not the safest method; but this law seems to imply that women were not considered weak enough or inferior enough to warrant special mention in this classification.

The portrayal of women's rights and activities in extant business documents lends weight to the perspective presented by the more favorable selection of laws, and no doubt contributed to the formation of the "consensus view." Charters and wills illustrate that women received grants of land as men did; evidently personal likes and dislikes, not rigid legal or social preference for the male line, governed bequests of "bookland."[35] Descriptions of several land disputes survive in charters, indicating that women took an active part in the legal process as oath-helpers, or as "litigants," defending their rights to land.[36] Wills made by husband and wife indicate that either spouse was considered capable of looking after the estates after the death of one partner. Wills of wealthy widows suggest the immense power many of them must have exercised, considering the number of estates, slaves, and goods they possessed.[37]

Some wills are much more than arid business documents; they convey a vivid impression of the personalities of the women who made them. For example, the possessions enumerated in the will of Wynflæd (c. 950) invite the creation of an almost epic character. She bequeathed an impressive number of estates, livestock, men and women, bracelets and brooches, gold adorned cups and buffalo horns, chests and bedclothing and tapestries, cloaks, books, tame and untamed horses—and her red tent. Another will, Ælfgifu's (c. 966–75), lacks such epic wealth, but contains an element of wry humor. She granted to her sister Ælfwaru "all that I have lent her," and to her sister-in-law Æthelflæd "the headband which I have lent her."[38] Given the oral, public, and not always deathbed nature of the wills, these seem rather pointed, facetious reminders of belongings loaned out and long since given up for lost.[39]

In these law codes and business documents we find references to women of lower classes, free peasants and slaves. The charters and wills usually were made by the secular or ecclesiastical elite, but they often mention men and women who were bound to and bequeathed with an estate, or slaves who were freed by the terms of the document. For example, Wynflæd's will bequeaths a woman weaver and a seamstress to Eadgifu. Wulfwaru is to be freed, "and she is to serve whom she pleases"; Wulfflæd is to be freed also, but "on condition that she serve Æthelflæd and Eadgifu."[40]

The law codes are of more universal relevance; the laws cited earlier apparently pertained to all classes. Other laws reveal Anglo-Saxon society as very status conscious; they clearly depict society's gradations by enumerating various classes of free and unfree. These laws define graduated compensations paid for insults to or attacks on various classes of women, from the unfree on up the social scale.[41] In theory, at least, even slave women were protected: "If a slave rapes a slave, castration shall be required as compensation."[42] There was also a sliding scale of fines for which women of different classes were liable, if they were guilty of certain crimes.[43]

Most historians assert that the last centuries of Anglo-Saxon England witnessed a drift from freedom into servitude for the lower classes.[44] Women, of course, would have been affected by that general trend. However, their status in relation to men of their own class probably remained much the same, and continued so for centuries. In this respect, the remarks made by R. H. Hilton in "Women in the Village" (fourteenth century) are relevant. He concludes that as far as their place in the economy was concerned, peasant women "enjoyed a measure of relative independence, a better situation in their own class" than was enjoyed by noble or middle-class women.[45] Given the continuity of peasant society, perhaps we can extrapolate backwards from this later evidence to the Anglo-Saxon period. In that case we can posit that at all levels of Anglo-Saxon society, women enjoyed "rough equality" with the men of the same class. For peasant women this continued after 1066; but upper class women increasingly were subject to their husbands as feudal lords.[46]

J. Scammell's interpretation of Anglo-Saxon peasant life provides a less favorable assessment of peasant women's status than that implied above.[47] Scammell argues the existence of personal limitations regarding marriage and the family on Anglo-Saxon peasants and the mitigation of these limitations in the Anglo-Norman period. Her views have roused at least one critic: E. Searle is sceptical about, among other things, using later evidence to reveal the degree of subjection of Anglo-Saxon peasants.[48] But Scammell reasserts that Anglo-Saxon society was slave based (nine percent of the male population counted by the Domesday survey was slave); that "others, perhaps the majority, inhabited a twilight of subjection and personal limitation";[49] that lords in the ninth century lent wives to some of their laborers, but maintained ownership of the women and resultant children; that women could be owned, bought, sold, or lent; and that a man might have to pay rent to his lord for his wife.[50] Further research might resolve this particular debate and clarify the general issue of peasant women's status.

LITERARY SOURCES

One of the most enjoyable adjuncts to the history of Anglo-Saxon women is a study of Old English poetry,[51] an area which seems to have received the greatest impetus from the recent interest in women. Several studies in particular offer correctives to what E. Hansen in "Women in Old English Poetry Reconsidered" has termed "intellectual benign neglect," the silence of generations of scholars on the issue of women in Old English verse. Because scholars did not see there the familiar objects of romantic love that populate later literature, they assumed that women were irrelevant to the earliest medieval poets.[52] The inaccuracy of that assumption becomes apparent when certain poems are given a close reading; the poems reveal the literary counterparts of women who appear in the *Chronicle*, in letters, and in wills.

*Beowulf*, though considered a "masculine" heroic poem, illustrates the great importance of women as "peaceweavers" (feud-healers, alliance-makers) between unrelated, often hostile, kindred or nations. A marriage alliance was often unsuccessful in keeping peace, and women were thus placed in tragic dilemmas. The poet is capable of seeing these situations from the woman's viewpoint, as the depiction of Hildeburh in the Finn episode indicates.[53]

The poems *Juliána*, *Elene*, and *Judith* all depict martial, courageous women as heroes. The first two are Christian saints: Juliana defeats the devil to emerge a victorious virgin martyr; Elene (Helen) journeys from England to the Holy Land to bring back the True Cross. The third features the Old Testament (Apocryphal) widow who saved her people by beheading Holofernes. These works suggest the acceptability of heroic female models in Anglo-Saxon culture.[54]

In addition to the heroic poems, elegies such as "The Wife's Lament" and "Wulf and Eadwacer" survive, presenting another side of the female character in Anglo-Saxon literature. Written in a woman's voice, possibly composed by women, they reveal that love, and the suffering that results from separation from the loved one, were not inventions of later medieval literature; they clearly were a part of the Anglo-Saxon emotional world as well.[55]

Similarly, "wholesome and spontaneous attitudes" towards sexuality are not the invention of recent decades.[56] Some of the Anglo-Saxon riddles (those usually labelled "obscene") describe sexual relations in enthusiastic and sophisticated "double entendres." While these might have appalled some nineteenth-century scholars, perhaps they can be appreciated today as they were in Anglo-Saxon times.

NONWRITTEN SOURCES

In addition to the various kinds of documentary evidence, there are other areas of study which contribute to an understanding of women in Anglo-Saxon society. For example, numismatics and art illuminate diverse aspects of the material culture of the Anglo-Saxons, and occasionally offer direct comment on women's activities.[57] Place-names constitute another significant area of study, one which speaks more directly to the status of women. As early as 1906 F. M. Stenton argued the existence of women landowners in Anglo-Saxon England, based on his study of place-names derived from feminine names.[58] Over three decades later his continued interest in this evidence produced a stronger statement on the place of women in Anglo-Saxon society. He illustrates how the evidence of place-names supports the view of women provided by documentary evidence, "that Old English society allowed to women, not only private influence, but also the widest liberty of intervention in public affairs," and that "women were associated with men on terms of rough equality in the common life of the countryside."[59]

Our knowledge of the material culture of the Anglo-Saxons is being increased by archaeology. This not only has supplemented our picture of royal and well-to-do Anglo-Saxons who usually appear in the documents; it also provides often our only record of lower class life, of the everyday existence of Anglo-Saxon men and women who do not usually appear in written sources.[60] In addition to providing tangible aspects of Anglo-Saxon women's existence in the form of habitations, household utensils, tools, and ornaments, several excavations have revealed a grimmer picture of life for some Anglo-Saxon women than we might glean merely from written records. For example, Page describes the "rare occurrence" of a female skeleton thrown unceremoniously in a grave on top of a carefully arranged male; he notes Scandinavian parallels and suggests a form of human sacrifice—burial of a slave or companion for the dead man. Excavation of one grave at Sewerby, Yorkshire, lends itself to a similar explanation: a female slave possibly buried alive in the same grave as her deceased mistress to serve her in death.[61] Another unusual female burial from approximately the same period (c. sixth or early seventh century) has prompted a theory of rape followed by punishment for the "dishonored" victim.[62] Future assessments of the status of Anglo-Saxon women should consider the implications of such interpretations, particularly if further archaeological research substantiates these suggestions.

If a well-born English woman of the late medieval or early modern period had looked back on her Anglo-Saxon ancestor, she would not have seen a "Golden Age" for women, as this essay might at times have implied; but she probably would have seen there much to envy. Certainly living conditions would have been a trifle more "rustic"; but she would have seen her Anglo-Saxon counterparts possessing rights, exercising alternatives, and wielding power that she could barely attain in the best of circumstances. Of course, there were hard knocks to accompany the greater independence; one could not destroy towns, lead armies, or merely "meddle" in affairs of state without taking the same risks as men. The amazing thing about the activities of Anglo-Saxon women is that those experiences, those precedents, were ignored or neglected, as women's proper roles and behavior were redefined in later medieval centuries. The role flexibility that existed for Anglo-Saxon women was reduced; the restrictiveness of sex roles was increased. As D. Stenton argues, "The feudal world was essentially a masculine world";[63] in this masculine world, "woman's place" became much more strictly defined. Aided by the tools of historical research, we can rediscover the experiences and precedents of Anglo-Saxon women; a study of Anglo-Saxon history, a familiarity with its sources, might produce examples of women's influence and freedom of action that would make aspects of even the twentieth century appear "dark."

# NOTES

I am grateful to Marc Anthony Meyer for his close reading of the first draft and his valuable suggestions, also to Robert T. Farrell for his suggestions regarding recent archaeological research.

1. For background on this period, consult the works recommended below. For comprehensive bibliographies of past work on the period, see Bonser, *Anglo-Saxon and Celtic Bibliography* and Graves, *Bibliography of English History to 1485*; for current research, consult the annual bibliographies published in *Old English Newsletter* and in *Anglo-Saxon England*, ed. Clemoes.

2. *English Woman*, p. vii. D. Stenton's chapter "The Anglo-Saxon Woman" is a good introduction to the subject. She indicates some of the primary sources, selects illuminating examples from them, and argues that these show "men and women lived on terms of rough equality with each other" (p. 28). But her rather anecdotal approach leaves the reader feeling suspended, as if the analysis of the position of women and of changes in that position has not been carried through to its logical conclusion. More questions can be asked of the sources than she asks; much of the evidence points to more forceful conclusions than she indicates. These are not failings so much as functions of the fact that the work was written almost a quarter century ago. Her work (and, one might add, the work of her husband, F. M. Stenton) is more sensitive to women in history than are many recent studies; it does not detract from her contribution to suggest that the subject deserves a fresh treatment.

3. E.g., Buckstaff, in "Married Women's Property in Anglo-Saxon and Anglo-Norman Law," in 1893 noted the more favorable legal position of Anglo-Saxon women; Bandel, in a 1955 note, "English Chroniclers' Attitude toward Women," discussed the contrast in terms of political opportunities. A more recent discussion, but one which apparently did not use D. Stenton's book, is Acworth's chapter on the Anglo-Saxon period in *The New Matriarchy*. This is less satisfactory than Stenton's; Acworth goes to the opposite extreme of inferring too much, e.g., that strong traces of matriarchy remained in Anglo-

Saxon society, indicated by the importance of queens and by the desire to marry royal widows (p. 56).

4. For Tacitus's references to Boudicca see *Annals* 14.29–37 and *Agricola* 16; for Cartimandua, see *Annals* 12.36, 40 and *History* 3.45. Tacitus also refers to the respected position of women in Germanic society in the first century: *Germania* 8, 18–20. For secondary works on the Celtic queens see Macurdy's brief chapter in *Vassal Queens*; Richmond's "Queen Cartimandua," a good example of what conclusions can be drawn from little evidence; and Dudley and Webster's *Rebellion of Boudicca*, a treatment of the subject from a Roman and military viewpoint. The most interesting chapter in *Rebellion* describes the diverse treatments of Boudicca in later historical and literary works. For the Irish background, see Binchy's "Linguistic and Historical Value of the Irish Law Tracts" and *Studies in Early Irish Law*. Meyer in his doctoral dissertation (in progress), "The Legal Status of Anglo-Saxon Women," is considering the Irish influence on the status of Anglo-Saxon women.

5. E.g., Blair, *An Introduction to Anglo-Saxon England*; Wilson, *The Anglo-Saxons*; Loyn, *Anglo-Saxon England and the Norman Conquest*; Arnold, *Social History of England*; Kirby, *Making of Early England*; Fisher, *Anglo-Saxon Age*; Finberg, *The Formation of England*. Fisher's work, although it does not offer general comments on women's status, is closest to Stenton in its comprehensive inclusion of specific women. Two recent works exemplify in different ways how not to deal with women. Page's chapter "A Woman's Place" (in *Life in Anglo-Saxon England*) is a nice blend of documentary, archaeological, and literary sources. The author provides examples of the "considerable freedom in law and practice" enjoyed by Anglo-Saxon women, making the important qualification that most of what we know pertains to the noble or well-to-do woman (p. 66). But by separating the treatment of women from other subjects (e.g., "The Working Man," "God's Thanes"), Page conveys—despite the disclaimer opening the chapter—the inaccurate impression of a "woman's place." Women were much more fully integrated into all spheres of Anglo-Saxon life, not confined, as his organization implies, to a "woman's place." Even more suspect is the approach exemplified in Rosenthal's *Angles, Angels, and Conquerors*. He includes a sprinkling of references to women throughout his work, but these tend to be simplistic, coy, or inaccurate. Perhaps the level of Rosenthal's work is best revealed in his discussion of the upper-class woman as manager of the household: "supervising packing and unpacking was a skilled task that women learned to master" (p. 112).

6. E.g., Loyn, pp. 221, 265, and F. M. Stenton's discussion of Æthelflæd (3rd ed.), pp. 324–29, emphasize women's political involvement; Kirby, p. 167, downplays the power of royal women, while Rosenthal, e.g., pp. 110–11, either ignores examples of powerful women or treats them with coyness and condescension.

7. E.g., Whitelock, pp. 94–5, emphasizes the involvement of women in concerns outside the home; Kirby, pp. 154–55, and Rosenthal convey the opposite impression.

8. Rosenthal neglects to mention the nuns and abbesses involved in Saint Boniface's eighth-century missionary work; Kirby similarly underestimates the contributions of early Anglo-Saxon religious women. The majority of other works mentioned note in varying degrees the important role of women in religious life.

9. E.g., Blair's two examples of shire court procedure implicitly illustrate women exercising considerable legal rights over land (pp. 229–31); Whitelock, pp. 94–5, 150–53, notes the high legal status and comments on the decline.

10. The categories used in this chapter are, to a certain extent, artificial; many of the sources discussed under one heading contain information relevant to other areas as well. The lives of saints, for example, could be considered biography, but are discussed as religious sources; Bede's *Ecclesiastical History*, also considered here as a religious source, contains information about the political, social, and legal structure of early Anglo-Saxon England; the *Anglo-Saxon Chronicle*, mentioned under the present heading, contains items dealing with the lives of certain abbesses.

11. The *Anglo-Saxon Chronicle* is a compilation of yearly entries (ranging from the year A.D. 1 to 1154 in one version), recorded and copied by a variety of scribes in different locations and at different times; the impetus for the compilation of the *Chronicle* is usually

GOSHEN COLLEGE LIBRARY
GOSHEN, INDIANA

attributed to Alfred, king of Wessex from 871 to 899. For the Anglo-Saxon text and discussion of two versions, see Plummer, *Two of the Saxon Chronicles Parallel*; for modern English editions which also include textual variants, see the translations by Whitelock and Garmonsway. The above quotations are taken from Whitelock's revised translation. A translation of the *Chronicle* also appears in Whitelock, ed., *English Historical Documents*, vol. 1; this comprehensive collection contains translated excerpts of many of the documents mentioned throughout this essay.

12. Wainwright's "Æthelflæd, Lady of the Mercians" is an excellent analysis of the *Chronicle* entries and of Æthelflæd's career.

13. Asser's *Life*, ed. Stevenson; the work has been translated from the Latin into modern English by Jane, by Cook, and by Giles in *Six Old English Chronicles*. Asser's discussion of the West Saxon custom and of Eadburh appears in chapters 13 to 15, under the year 855.

14. In the late tenth century a Wessex nobleman, Æthelweard, translated the *Anglo-Saxon Chronicle* into Latin for his cousin Matilda, abbess of Essen, a descendent of King Alfred; Æthelweard mentions the Wessex royal women who made continental marriage alliances, one of which produced Matilda. The participation of royal and aristocratic women in such marriage alliances constitutes a significant aspect of their political role. See Æthelweard's *Chronicle* in Giles, or in the more recent edition and translation by A. Campbell. Gransden, in *Historical Writing in England*, argues that this work (like the *Encomium Emmae Reginae* and *Vita Ædwardi* discussed below) is "symptomatic of the respected position of women in Anglo-Saxon society" (p. 45).

15. A. Campbell, ed. and trans., *Encomium*; Barlow, ed. and trans., *Vita Ædwardi*. For a modern analysis of Emma's career as queen to two kings and queen mother to two more, see M. Campbell's articles, "Queen Emma and Ælfgifu of Northampton," and "Emma, Reine d'Angleterre." For modern views of Edith, see Barlow, *Edward the Confessor*, and Cutler, "Edith, Queen of England."

16. *Edward the Confessor*, p. 299.

17. "English Chroniclers' Attitude," p. 114. For discussions of the decline in power of aristocratic and royal women in a western European context and in a French context, see, respectively, McNamara and Wemple, "Power of Women through the Family," and Facinger, "Study of Medieval Queenship: Capetian France."

18. "English Chroniclers' Attitude," pp. 115–17. Bandel's short article has limitations, but it touches on important questions and, in doing so, highlights the need for a comprehensive study of Anglo-Saxon queenship. For discussions of the influence of certain Anglo-Saxon queens, see Meyer's "Women and the Tenth Century English Monastic Reform" and Hart's "Two Queens of England."

19. E.g., Matilda Empress, claimant to the English throne after the death (in 1135) of her father Henry I; and Queen Matilda, forceful wife of the usurper Stephen, King from 1135 to 1154.

20. See Bede's *History* 4.23 for discussion of Hilda. His work exists in a variety of translations: *Bede's Ecclesiastical History of the English People*, ed. Colgrave and Mynors, features the original Latin and an English translation on facing pages; Sherley-Price's translation (*History of the English Church and People*) is an accessible paperback edition. For another early Anglo-Saxon view of religious women, see Aldhelm's *In Praise of Virginity* (in *Opera*, edited by R. Ehwald); this treatise was written c. 686 for the nuns at Barking. For background to the early English church, see Mayr-Harting, *The Coming of Christianity to England*; Blair, *The World of Bede*; Godfrey, *The Church in Anglo-Saxon England*, "Double Monastery in Early English History," and "Place of the Double Monastery"; Eckenstein, *Women under Monasticism*; Browne, *The Importance of Women in Anglo-Saxon Times*; Bateson, "Origin and History of Double Monasteries"; and Peers and Radford, "The Saxon Monastery at Whitby."

21. See Emerton, trans., *Letters of St. Boniface*, and the selection of letters and saints' lives (e.g., "Life of St. Leoba" by Rudolf, and "Hodoeporicon of St. Willibald" by the Anglo-Saxon nun Huneberc) collected in Talbot, ed. and trans., *Anglo-Saxon Missionaries in Germany*. For background studies, see W. Levison, *England and the Continent in the Eighth*

*Century*; Talbot, "St. Boniface and the German Mission"; and Bishop, "St. Boniface and his Correspondence."

22. *Anglo-Saxon Missionaries*, pp. xii–xiii.

23. F. M. Stenton speaks of the abbesses of monastic houses founded for women in the later period as "shadowy figures in comparison with the women who ruled the double monasteries in the seventh and eighth centuries. No woman in the middle ages ever held a position comparable with that of Hild of Whitby" (*Anglo-Saxon England*, 3rd. ed., p. 162). Perhaps further research (e.g., in the saints' lives) would improve the picture, making the later women less shadowy; we should also remember that late Anglo-Saxon England had no Bede to make accessible to us the lives of important religious women.

24. Lives of Anglo-Saxon women saints are conveniently collected in Capgrave, *Nova Legenda Angliae*, ed. Horstmann, and in *Lives of Women Saints*, ed. Horstmann. See also, Bethell, "The Lives of St. Osyth"; Wilmart, "La Legende de Ste. Edith"; Esposito, "La Vie de Ste. Vulfhilde"; and Braswell, "St. Edburga of Winchester." One of the most interesting Anglo-Saxon saints was born several decades after the conquest; see Talbot, ed. and trans., *Life of Christina of Markyate* for the career of an Anglo-Saxon recluse and nun in early Norman England. For an introduction to hagiography as a genre, see Delehaye, *Legends of the Saints*. Since these saints' lives are not strictly historical, and since they might contain later (i.e., postconquest) material, they should be used with caution. If used carefully, they can provide a wealth of information about Anglo-Saxon religious and social life. Anglo-Saxon history would benefit from a scholarly survey of its female saints.

25. *Anglo-Saxon England*, 1st. ed., p. 439. A similar point has been made recently by Meyer in "Women and the Tenth Century English Monastic Reform": "The role of secular and religious women in the monastic reform movement of the tenth century is a study which deserves more emphasis than it has received" (p. 36). Meyer partially rectifies this situation by analyzing, mainly through the use of charters, the role of royal widows and queens (and to a lesser extent, of other aristocratic women) as patronesses of the monastic reform movement. See his chapter in this volume.

26. Bailey, in *Sexual Relation in Christian Thought* (published in England as *Man-Woman Relation in Christian Thought*), provides excellent discussions of the development of patristic attitudes toward women and sexuality, and the complexities inherent in those attitudes. He cites (p. 73) the church law mentioned in the above discussion.

27. Talbot, *Anglo-Saxon Missionaries*, p. 222.

28. From "Penitential of Theodore" (668–690, with later additions), McNeill and Gamer, trans., *Medieval Handbooks of Penance*, pp. 185, 191, 197, and 211. There are also penances listed for adultery, making love potions, drunkenness, abortion, and infanticide. Theodore's penitential, in the original Latin, is included in West and Stubbs, ed., *Councils and Ecclesiastical Documents*, 3: 173–213. For a discussion of the penitentials as sources for history, see Oakley's article of that title; for the penitentials' relation to Anglo-Saxon law, see his *English Penitential Discipline and Anglo-Saxon Law*, and "Medieval Penance and Secular Law." The Anglo-Saxon penitentials illustrate the influence of Irish religious practices on the English church. See Bieler, *The Irish Penitentials*, as well as the selections from Ireland in McNeill and Gamer. Mayr-Harting raises an interesting question regarding women's cooperation with such codes: "Whether Anglo-Saxon women, who were accorded a high status in society and were often formidable personalities in their own right, always submitted to the male-drafted rules and codes which constitute our evidence, we cannot say" (p. 240).

29. Gransden, pp. 119–20.

30. See Southern, *Western Society and the Church in the Middle Ages* (pp. 309–12), for a brief discussion of this issue. As the following statement indicates, his explanation raises further questions: "As society became better organized and ecclesiastically more right-minded, the necessity for male dominance began to assert itself" (p. 310).

31. The law codes mentioned here range over four centuries; the earliest codes show little sign of Christian influence, while the later ones certainly were drafted under the influence of the church. This is just one indication of the way in which the society of the

later codes differed from that reflected in the earlier. But for each of the two views of women's legal status briefly sketched in the text, it is possible to select examples of laws from the early (e.g. Æthelberht and Ine) and from the later period (e.g. Æthelred and Canute); the apparent lack of consistency is not merely a matter of coming from disparate centuries. The standard edition of Anglo-Saxon laws is still Liebermann, *Die Gesetze der Angelsachsen*. For English translations (with the original on facing pages), consult Attenborough, *Laws of the Earliest English Kings*, and Robertson, *Laws of the Kings of England from Edmund to Henry I*. Citations in the text are taken from the latter two works. For general background, see *Essays in Anglo-Saxon Law*, and Pollock and Maitland, *History of English Law*; for discussions of the law and social structure, see Lancaster, "Kinship in Anglo-Saxon Society," and Loyn, "Kinship in Anglo-Saxon England." Anglo-Saxon laws should not be studied in a vacuum; it is useful to compare them with other codes, e.g. Irish and continental Germanic. For the former, see Binchy's works on Irish law; for one continental code, see Fischer, ed. and trans., *The Burgundian Code*, and Drew, "The Germanic Family of the 'Leges Burgundionum.'"

32. See, e.g., Æthelberht 75, 82; Æthelberht 31, 77, and Ine 31; Ine 57 and 2 Canute 76: lb; 2 Canute 53, 54. Æthelberht's and Ine's laws are from Attenborough; Canute's are from Robertson. One response to the interpretation that women were bought and sold is to suggest that it was only the right to a woman's *mund* (i.e., the right of guardianship over her) that was bought and sold, not the woman herself.

33. See, e.g., Æthelberht 74; Æthelberht 78, 79; 2 Canute 76: 1, 1a; Ine 38, 6 Æthelred 26, 39. Æthelred's code appears in Robertson. For an analysis of the laws that relate to widows, see Rivers, "Widows' Rights in Anglo-Saxon Law"; he argues that women's legal rights improved in the later Anglo-Saxon period, and that widows were especially fortunate in their increased independence. According to Rivers, the protection of "God and the King" meant the absence of direct male control.

34. 2 Canute 68.

35. For discussions of "bookland," see F. M. Stenton, *Anglo-Saxon England*, 3rd ed., pp. 307–12; Whitelock, *Beginnings of English Society*, pp. 153–154; and Loyn, "Kinship in Anglo-Saxon England." The distinction is usually drawn between "bookland"—land secured by royal charter, exempt from many obligations to the king, and carrying with it rights of alienation to whomever the holder prefers—and "folkland"—land governed by customary obligations to the king and obligations of descent within the kindred (with the male side probably preferred). For other discussions of land tenure, see Finberg, *Agrarian History of England*, and John, *Orbis Britanniae*. See, e.g., Robertson, ed. and trans., *Anglo-Saxon Charters*, no. 78, for a landed woman making a female relative, rather than her own son, her heir; for division of lands between daughters and sons, see, e.g., Whitelock, ed. and trans., *Anglo-Saxon Wills*, nos. 21 and 32; for grants to daughters, see *Wills*, nos. 2, 3, 17, 19. One late tenth-century Anglo-Saxon will (Æthelgifu's) is now in the United States; see Fleming, "The Old English Manuscripts in the Scheide Library," and Collins, *Anglo-Saxon Vernacular Manuscripts in America*. For an edition and translation, see Whitelock, *Will of Æthelgifu*. Sheehan's *Will in Medieval England* and Collins' "Earliest English Wills" provide general background. Legal documents also appear in Harmer, ed. and trans., *Select English Historical Documents*, and in *English Historical Documents*, vol. I. For a complete list of Anglo-Saxon charters, see Sawyer, ed., *Anglo-Saxon Charters*. See also the charter collections by Finberg and Hart.

36. See *Charters*, nos. 66 and 78.

37. See, e.g., *Wills*, no. 9, for mention of the capability of the wife; for widows, see, e.g., *Wills*, no. 3, and *Will of Æthelgifu*.

38. *Wills*, nos. 3 (Wynflæd) and 8 (Ælfgifu).

39. See the discussion of wills by M. Sheehan and by R. Collins.

40. *Wills*, no. 3. After listing others to be freed, this section concludes: "if there be any penally enslaved man besides these whom she has enslaved, she trusts to her children that they will release him for her soul's sake." For a description of the persons who labored on a late Anglo-Saxon estate, with brief mention of the yearly provisions due to

a female slave and a female cheesemaker, see "Rectitudines Singularum Personum" in Douglas and Greenaway, eds., *English Historical Documents*, 2: 813–16.

41. E.g., Æthelberht 10, 11, 16; Alfred 10, 11, 25 (in Attenborough).

42. Alfred 25: 1.

43. E.g., Alfred 18: 1–3.

44. F. M. Stenton, *Anglo-Saxon England*, 3rd. ed., p. 470; Whitelock, *Beginnings of English Society*, p. 98; Blair, *Anglo-Saxon England*, p. 261.

45. Hilton, p. 105.

46. This trend, the continuation of a status of "rough equality" for peasant women and the decline in status for aristocratic women, is suggested by D. Stenton in *English Woman*, pp. 28–29, 75–76, 348. Hilton cites this theory, but cautions that it might involve assuming too much about peasants between the Anglo-Saxon period and the second half of the fourteenth century (p. 109).

47. See Scammell's "Freedom and Marriage in Medieval England"; Searle's criticism, "Freedom and Marriage: an Alternative Hypothesis"; and Scammell's response, "Wife-Rents and Merchet."

48. Searle, p. 483. Searle argues that "wife-rent" did not exist: "In the term 'wife-rent' an implausible hypothesis is enshrined in a name; it is best forgotten."

49. "Wife-Rents and Merchet," p. 487. Scammell notes that she hopes to discuss this matter at greater length elsewhere.

50. Ibid.

51. For scholarly editions of the poems, see Krapp and Dobbie, ed., *Anglo-Saxon Poetic Records*. Among the many translations is the comprehensive collection of Gordon, *Anglo-Saxon Poetry*. For a complete bibliography on Old English literature, through 1972, see Greenfield and Robinson, ed., *Bibliography of Publications in Old English Literature*.

52. Hansen herself provides the best corrective to this attitude. In a short article she packs a wealth of insights about women in Old English poetry; she touches on gnomic poetry, *Widsith, Waldere, Juliana, Judith, Elene*, as well as discussing at greater length the women in *Beowulf*. Other, more specialized, studies include Williams, "What's So New about the Sexual Revolution? Some Comments on Anglo-Saxon Attitudes towards Sexuality in Women"; Davidson, "Erotic Women's Songs in Anglo-Saxon England"; Renoir, "Reading Context for 'The Wife's Lament.'"

53. This point is made by Hansen in her perceptive discussion of women in *Beowulf*, p. 113. For a general analysis of women as "peaceweavers," see Rosenthal, "Marriage and the Blood Feud in 'Heroic' Europe."

54. It has been suggested that *Judith* was composed to celebrate Æthelflæd's victories over the Danes. This is an attractive theory, but one which has been rejected by, among others, Chamberlain in "*Judith*: A Fragmentary and Political Poem." He places the poem in the troubled reign of Æthelred (late tenth and early eleventh century), a time when such an *exemplum* of bravery and resistance to invaders was needed (pp. 158–59).

55. Davidson, in "Erotic Women's Songs," criticizes Anglo-Saxon scholars who have been reluctant to admit that love played any part in English culture before the conquest. He argues, "despite our understanding of Anglo-Saxon society as matter-of-fact and unsentimental, there is very good reason to suppose that the cultural milieu of women, distinct from men's warrior world ... was sufficiently separate to generate popular patterns of cultural expression along other than masculine lines" (p. 455). Davidson is right to attempt to dispel the stereotype of a totally unsentimental Anglo-Saxon culture; but his method of doing so erects other stereotypes that seem equally unrepresentative of the Anglo-Saxon world. His emphasis on a separate "cultural milieu of women" which produced these poems, and his assumption that "in Anglo-Saxon times such poetry was apparently considered immoral and unmanly" (p. 460) depend on more rigid definitions of "manliness" and "womanliness" than probably existed. If Renoir's discussion of "The Wife's Lament" were the only work on Old English poetry read, it too would produce an unfortunate stereotype: he argues that the "reading context" should be a "Germanic tradition of suffering women" (p. 235).

56. This is argued by Williams, in "What's So New about the Sexual Revolution?" Her analysis of the "obscene" riddles leads her to conclude that Anglo-Saxon women actively enjoyed sexual relations, that no sanction existed against such pleasure, and that women are not portrayed in the riddles as degraded or exploited. She also provides translations of the riddles. Stewart, although not approaching the riddles from the point of view of the Anglo-Saxon woman as Williams does, also suggests that the riddles reveal the playful and joyous way in which the Anglo-Saxons viewed sexual intercourse (work in progress, "Wit and Wiht: Linguistic and Literary Analysis of the Old English Riddles").

57. D. Stenton illustrates the value of numismatics by citing the coins struck with the name and representation of Offa's queen, Cynethryth; the power of one Anglo-Saxon queen is thus made tangible (pp. 2–3, and plate 1). Of the Anglo-Saxon art works that survive, certainly much, if not all, of the embroidery and most likely some of the illuminated manuscripts were produced by women. For surveys of Anglo-Saxon art, see Kendrick, *Anglo-Saxon Art to 900* and *Late Saxon and Viking Art*; and Rice, *English Art, 871–1100*. See also Christie, *English Medieval Embroidery*.

58. "Place-Names as Evidence of Female Ownership of Land."

59. "Historical Bearing of Place-Name Studies: The Place of Women," pp. 314, 324. For comments on personal names and what they reveal of women in Anglo-Saxon society, see Woolf, "The Naming of Women in Old English Times."

60. For an introduction to this field, see Wilson, *The Anglo-Saxons*, and Wilson, ed., *Archaeology of Anglo-Saxon England*. See the reviews of current publications in archaeology by Farrell in "Year's Work in Old English Studies"; for reports on fieldwork, see the listing of sites in "Medieval Britain: Pre-Conquest" in *Medieval Archaeology*. See also Meaney, *Gazetteer of Early Anglo-Saxon Burial Sites*, and Cook, "The Evidence for the Reconstruction of Female Costume."

61. Page, *Life in Anglo-Saxon England*, pp. 75–76. See also, Rahtz, "Sewerby."

62. Hawkes and Wells, "Crime and Punishment in an Anglo-Saxon Cemetery?" For another example of archaeological-osteopathic collaboration, see their "An Anglo-Saxon Obstetric Calamity."

63. *English Woman in History*, p. 29.

# BIBLIOGRAPHY

For serious study of the Anglo-Saxon period, a knowledge of Old English and Latin is necessary; however, because most of the available records have been edited and translated, it is possible to use many of the primary sources without having this knowledge. For the benefit of people who are interested in the period but who do not have a reading knowledge of those languages, I have listed useful and accessible translations; this is by no means a comprehensive list of all editions.

ACWORTH, EVELYN. *The New Matriarchy*. London: 1965.

ÆTHELWEARD. *The Chronicle of Æthelweard*. Edited by Alistair Campbell. Medieval Texts, edited by V. H. Galbraith, R. A. B. Mynors, and C. N. L. Brooke. London: 1962.

ALDHELM. *Opera*. Edited by R. Ehwald. Monumenta Germaniae Historica. Auctorum Antiquissimorum, 15. Berlin: 1919.

ANDRE, J. L. "Widows and Vowesses." *Royal Archaeological Institute of Great Britain and Ireland* 49 (1892): 69–82.

ARNOLD, RALPH. *A Social History of England, 55 B.C. to 1215*. New York: 1967.

ASSER. *Life of King Alfred*. Edited by William H. Stevenson. Oxford: 1904.

———. *Life of King Alfred*. Translated by Albert S. Cook. London: 1906.

———. *Life of King Alfred*. Translated by L. C. Jane. London: 1908.

ATTENBOROUGH, F. L., ed. and trans. *The Laws of the Earliest English Kings*. Cambridge: 1922. Reprint. New York: 1963.

BAILEY, DERRICK SHERWIN. *The Man-Woman Relation in Christian Thought*. London: 1959. (Also published as *Sexual Relation in Christian Thought*. New York: 1959).

BANDEL, BETTY. "English Chroniclers' Attitude toward Women." *Journal of the History of Ideas* 16 (1955): 113–18.

BARLOW, FRANK. *Edward the Confessor*. Berkeley: 1970.

———, ed. and trans. *Vita Ædwardi Regis qui apud Westmonasterium Requiescit*. Medieval Texts, edited by V. H. Galbraith, R. A. B. Mynors, and C. N. L. Brooke. London: 1962.

BATESON, MARY. "The Origin and History of Double Monasteries." *Transactions of the Royal Historical Society* n.s. 13 (1899): 137–98.

BEDE. *Ecclesiastical History of the English People*. Edited by Bertram Colgrave and R. A. B. Mynors. Oxford Medieval Texts, edited by V. H. Galbraith, R. A. B. Mynors, and C. N. L. Brooke. Oxford: 1969.

———. *A History of the English Church and People*. Translated by Leo Sherley-Price and revised by R. E. Latham. Baltimore: 1968.

BELL, A. "Gaimar and the Edgar-Ælfthryth Story." *Modern Language Review* 21 (1926): 278–87.

BETHELL, D. L. T. "The Lives of St. Osyth of Essex and St. Osyth of Aylesbury." *Analecta Bollandiana* 88 (1970): 75–127.

"Bibliography." *Anglo-Saxon England* 1–(1972–).

BIELER, LUDWIG. *The Irish Penitentials*. Dublin: 1963.

BINCHY, DANIEL A. "The Linguistic and Historical Value of the Irish Law Tracts." *Proceedings of the British Academy* 29 (1943): 195–228.

———, ed. *Studies in Early Irish Law*. Dublin: 1936.

BIRCH, W. DE GRAY, ed. *An Ancient Manuscript of the Eighth or Ninth Century, Formerly Belonging to St. Mary's Abbey or Nunnaminster, Winchester*. Hampshire Record Society. London: 1889.

BISHOP, E. "St. Boniface and his Correspondence." *Reports and Transactions of the Devon Association* 8 (1876): 497–516.

BLAIR, PETER HUNTER. *An Introduction to Anglo-Saxon England*. 1956. Rev. ed. Cambridge: 1977.

———. *The World of Bede*. London: 1970.

BONIFACE. *The Letters of Saint Boniface*. Translated by Ephraim Emerton. Columbia Records of Civilization, edited by Austin P. Evans, no. 31. New York: 1940.

BONSER, WILFRID. *An Anglo-Saxon and Celtic Bibliography: 450 to 1087*. 2 vols. Oxford: 1957.

BRASWELL, LAUREL. "St. Edburga of Winchester: a Study of Her Cult, A.D. 950 to

1500, with an Edition of the Fourteenth-Century Middle English and Latin Lives." *Mediaeval Studies* 33 (1971): 292–333.

BROWNE, GEORGE FORREST. *The Importance of Women in Anglo-Saxon Times; and Other Addresses.* London: 1919.

BUCKSTAFF, FLORENCE. "Married Women's Property in Anglo-Saxon and Anglo-Norman Law and the Origin of the Common Law Dower." *Annals of the American Academy of Political and Social Science* 4 (1893): 233–64.

BYRNE, SISTER MARY. *The Tradition of the Nun in Medieval England.* Washington, D.C.: 1932.

CAMPBELL, ALISTAIR, ed. *Encomium Emmae Reginae.* Camden Society, 3rd series, vol. 72. London: 1949.

CAMPBELL, MILES W. "Emma, Reine d'Angleterre, Mère Dénaturée ou Femme Vindicative?" *Annales de Normandie* 23 (1973): 99–114.

———. "Queen Emma and Ælfgifu of Northampton: Canute the Great's Women." *Mediaeval Scandinavia* 4 (1971): 66–79.

CAPGRAVE, JOHN. *Nova Legenda Angliae.* Edited by Carl Horstmann. 2 vols. Oxford: 1901.

CHAMBERLAIN, DAVID. "*Judith*: A Fragmentary and Political Poem." In *Anglo-Saxon Poetry: Essays in Appreciation For John C. McGalliard*, edited by Lewis E. Nicholson and Dolores Warwick Frese, pp. 135–59. Notre Dame, Indiana: 1975.

CHRISTIE, A. G[RACE]. I. *English Medieval Embroidery....* Oxford: 1938.

CLUTTERBUCK, R. H. "The Story of Wherwell Abbey." *Hampshire Notes and Queries* 4 (1889): 85–96.

COLLINS, ROWLAND L. *Anglo-Saxon Vernacular Manuscripts in America.* New York: 1976.

———. "Earliest English Wills: Clues to our Society's Origins." *Trusts and Estates* 115 (1976): 816–19, 842–44.

COOK, A. M. "The Evidence for the Reconstruction of Female Costume in the Early Anglo-Saxon Period in the South of England." Master's thesis, University of Birmingham: 1974.

CUTLER, KENNETH E. "Edith, Queen of England 1045–1066." *Mediaeval Studies* 35 (1973): 222–31.

DAVIDSON, CLIFFORD. "Erotic Women's Songs in Anglo-Saxon England." *Neophilologus* 59 (1975): 451–62.

DELEHAYE, HIPPOLYTE. *The Legends of the Saints: An Introduction to Hagiography.* London: 1907.

DOUGLAS, DAVID C., and GREENAWAY, G. W., eds. *English Historical Documents, 1042–1189.* English Historical Documents, edited by David C. Douglas, vol. 2. London: 1953.

DREW, KATHERINE FISCHER. "The Germanic Family of the 'Leges Burgundionum.'" *Medievalia et Humanistica* 15 (1963): 5–14.

DUDLEY, DONALD R., and WEBSTER, GRAHAM. *The Rebellion of Boudicca.* New York: 1962.

ECKENSTEIN, LINA E. *Women under Monasticism: Chapters on Saint-lore and Convent Life between A.D. 500 and A.D. 1500.* Cambridge: 1896. Reprint. New York: 1963.

ESPOSITO, M. "La Vie de Ste. Vulfhilde par Goscelin de Cantorbery." *Analecta Bollandiana* 32 (1913): 10–26.

*Essays in Anglo-Saxon Law.* Boston: 1876.

FACINGER, MARION. "A Study of Medieval Queenship: Capetian France 987–1237." *Studies in Medieval and Renaissance History* 5 (1968): 3–48.

FELL, CHRISTINE E. *Edward King and Martyr*. Leeds Texts and Monographs, n.s. Leeds: 1971.

FINBERG, H. P. R. *The Formation of England, 550–1042*. Paladin History of England, edited by Robert Blake. New York: 1977.

———, ed. *The Agrarian History of England and Wales*, vol. 1, pt. 2, "A.D. 43–1042." Cambridge: 1972.

———. *The Early Charters of Devon and Cornwall*. 2d. ed. Leicester: 1963.

———. *The Early Charters of the West Midlands*. Leicester: 1961.

———. *The Early Charters of Wessex*. Leicester: 1964.

FISCHER, KATHERINE, ed. and trans. *The Burgundian Code*. University of Pennsylvania Translations and Reprints from the Original Sources of History. Philadelphia: 1949.

FISHER, D. J. V. *The Anglo-Saxon Age, c. 400–1042*. Longman, A History of England, edited by W. N. Medlicott, vol. 3. London: 1973.

———. "The Anti-Monastic Reaction in the Reign of Edward the Martyr." *Cambridge Historical Journal* 10 (1952): 254–70.

FLEMING, JOHN V. "The Old English Manuscripts in the Scheide Library." *Princeton University Library Chronicle* 37 (1976): 126–38.

GARMONSWAY, GEORGE N., trans. *The Anglo-Saxon Chronicle*. Rev. ed. London: 1960.

GILES, J. A., ed. *Six Old English Chronicles*. London: 1848. Reprint. New York: 1968.

GODFREY, JOHN. *The Church in Anglo-Saxon England*. Cambridge: 1962.

———. "The Double Monastery in Early English History." *Ampleforth Journal* 79 (1974): 19–32.

———. "The Place of the Double Monastery in the Anglo-Saxon Minster System." In *Famulus Christi: Essays in Commemoration of the Thirteenth Centenary of the Birth of the Venerable Bede*, edited by Gerald Bonner, pp. 344–50. London: 1976.

GORDON, ROBERT K., comp. and trans. *Anglo-Saxon Poetry*. Rev. ed. New York: 1954.

GRANSDEN, ANTONIA. *Historical Writing in England, c. 550 to c. 1370*. Ithaca: 1974.

GRAVES, EDGAR B., ed. *A Bibliography of English History to 1485: Based on the Sources and Literature of English History by Charles Gross*. Oxford: 1975.

GREENFIELD, STANLEY B., and ROBINSON, FRED C., eds. *Bibliography of Publications on Old English Literature*. Toronto: 1978.

HADDAN, ARTHUR W., and STUBBS, WILLIAM, eds. *Councils and Ecclesiastical Documents relating to Great Britain and Ireland*, vol. 3. Oxford: 1871.

HANSEN, ELAINE TUTTLE. "Women in Old English Poetry Reconsidered." *Michigan Academician* 9 (1976): 109–17.

HARMER, F. E., ed. *Anglo-Saxon Writs*. Manchester: 1952.

———, ed. *Select English Historical Documents of the Ninth and Tenth Centuries*. Cambridge: 1914.

HART, C. R. *The Early Charters of Northern England and the North Midlands*. Leicester: 1975.

———. "Two Queens of England." *Ampleforth Journal* 82 (1977): 10–15, 54.

HAWKES, SONIA C., and WELLS, CALVIN. "An Anglo-Saxon Obstetric Calamity from Kingsworthy, Hampshire." *Medical and Biological Illustration* 25 (1975): 47–51.

———. "Crime and Punishment in an Anglo-Saxon Cemetery?" *Antiquity* 49 (1975): 118–22.

HILTON, RODNEY H. "Women in the Village." In *The English Peasantry in the Later*

*Middle Ages: The Ford Lectures for 1973 and Related Studies*, pp. 95–110. Oxford: 1975.

HORSTMANN, CARL, ed. *The Lives of Women Saints of our Contrie of England*. Early English Text Society, o.s. vol. 86. London: 1886.

HUNT, NOREEN. "Appunti sulla storia della monache benedettine e cisterciensi in Gran Bretagna." *Ora et Labora* 26 (1971): 78–87, 180–86.

JOHN, ERIC. *Orbis Britanniae and Other Studies*. Leicester: 1966.

KENDRICK, THOMAS D. *Anglo-Saxon Art to 900*. London: 1938.

———. *Late Saxon and Viking Art*. London: 1949.

KIRBY, D. W. *The Making of Early England*. New York: 1968.

KRAPP, GEORGE P., and DOBBIE, ELLIOT V. K. *The Anglo-Saxon Poetic Records*. 6 vols. New York: 1931–53.

LANCASTER, LORRAINE. "Kinship in Anglo-Saxon Society." *British Journal of Sociology* 9 (1958): 230–50, 359–77. Reprinted in *Early Medieval Society*, edited by Sylvia L. Thrupp, pp. 17–41. New York: 1967.

LEVISON, WILHELM. *England and the Continent in the Eighth Century: The Ford Lectures Delivered in the University of Oxford in the Hilary Term, 1943*. Oxford: 1946.

LIEBERMANN, FELIX. *Die Gesetze der Angelsachsen*. 3 vols. Halle: 1903–16.

LOYN, H. R. *Anglo-Saxon England and the Norman Conquest*. Social and Economic History of England, edited by Asa Briggs. New York: 1962.

———. "Kinship in Anglo-Saxon England." *Anglo-Saxon England* 3 (1974): 197–209.

MACURDY, GRACE H. *Vassal Queens and Some Contemporary Women in the Roman Empire*. The Johns Hopkins University Studies in Archaeology, edited by David Robinson, vol. 22. Baltimore: 1937.

MAYR-HARTING, HENRY. *The Coming of Christianity to England*. New York: 1972.

MCNAMARA, JO ANN, and WEMPLE, SUZANNE. "The Power of Women through the Family in Medieval Europe: 500–1100." In *Clio's Consciousness Raised*, edited by Mary S. Hartman and Lois Banner, pp. 103–18. New York: 1974.

MCNEILL, JOHN T., and GAMER, HELENA M., eds. *Medieval Handbooks of Penance: A Translation of the Principal "Libri Poenitentiales" and Selections from Related Documents*. Columbia Records of Civilization, edited by Austin P. Evans, no. 29. New York: 1938.

MEANEY, A. L. *A Gazetteer of Early Anglo-Saxon Burial Sites*. London: 1964.

"Medieval Britain: Pre-Conquest." *Medieval Archaeology* 1– (1957–).

MEYER, MARC ANTHONY. "Women and the Tenth Century English Monastic Reform." *Revue Bénédictine* 87 (1977): 34–61.

———. "The Greater Royal Nunneries of Wessex: a Brief Introduction to the History of Anglo-Saxon Nunneries and Nuns, together with a Detailed Description of Their Lands and Land Holdings and an Edition of the Lansdowne Life of St. Æthelflæda and St. Merwynna." Master's thesis, University College, Dublin: 1975.

MONTALEMBERT, COUNT DE. "The Anglo-Saxon Nuns." In *Monks of the West from St. Benedict to St. Bernard*, vol. 4, book 15, pp. 357–469. London: 1896.

MURRAY-DAVEY, D. "Anglo-Saxon Nuns of the Golden Age." *Dublin Review* (1928): 282–92.

OAKLEY, THOMAS P. *English Penitential Discipline and Anglo-Saxon Law in their Joint Influence*. New York: 1923.

———. "Mediaeval Penance and Secular Law." *Speculum* 7 (1932): 515–24.

————. "The Penitentials as Sources for Mediaeval History." *Speculum* 15 (1940): 210–23.

"Old English Bibliography." *Old English Newsletter* 1– (1967–).

PAGE, R. I. *Life in Anglo-Saxon England*. English Life Series, edited by Peter Quennell. London: 1970.

PEERS, C. R., and RADFORD, C. A. R. "The Saxon Monastery at Whitby." *Archaeologia* 89.(1943): 27–88.

PLUMMER, CHARLES, ed. *Two of the Saxon Chronicles Parallel*. 2 vols. Oxford: 1892–99.

POLLOCK, FREDERICK, and MAITLAND, F. W. *The History of English Law before the Time of Edward I*. 2d ed. 2 vols. Cambridge: 1968.

RAHTZ, P. "Sewerby." In "Medieval Britain." *Medieval Archaeology* 4 (1960): 137.

RENOIR, ALAIN. "A Reading Context for 'The Wife's Lament.'" In *Anglo-Saxon Poetry: Essays in Appreciation for John C. McGalliard*, edited by Lewis E. Nicholson and Dolores Warwick Frese, pp. 224–41. Notre Dame: 1975.

REYNOLDS, J. J. "Ancient History of Shaftesbury." *The Wiltshire Archaeological and Natural History Magazine* 7 (1862): 250–71.

REYNOLDS, ROGER E. *"Virgines Subintroductae* in Celtic Christianity." *Harvard Theological Review* 61 (1968): 547–66.

RICE, DAVID TALBOT. *English Art, 871–1100*. Oxford History of English Art, edited by Thomas S. R. Boase, vol. 2. Oxford: 1952.

RICHMOND, IAN A. "Queen Cartimandua." *Journal of Roman Studies* 44 (1954): 43–52.

RIVERS, THEODORE J. "Widows' Rights in Anglo-Saxon Law." *American Journal of Legal History* 19 (1975): 208–15.

ROBERTSON, A. J., ed. and trans. *Anglo-Saxon Charters*. 2d ed. Cambridge Studies in English Legal History, edited by H. A. Holland. Cambridge: 1956.

————, ed. and trans. *The Laws of the Kings of England From Edmund to Henry I*. Cambridge: 1925.

ROSENTHAL, JOEL T. *Angles, Angels, and Conquerors: 400–1154*. The Borzoi History of England, edited by A. J. Slavin, vol. 1. New York: 1973.

————. "Marriage and the Blood Feud in 'Heroic' Europe." *British Journal of Sociology* 17 (1966): 133–44.

SAWYER, P. H., ed. *Anglo-Saxon Charters: An Annotated List and Bibliography*. London: 1968.

SCAMMELL, JEAN. "Freedom and Marriage in Medieval England." *Economic History Review* 27 (1974): 523–37.

————. "Wife-Rents and Merchet." *Economic History Review* 29 (1976): 487–90.

SEARLE, ELEANOR. "Freedom and Marriage in Medieval England: An Alternative Hypothesis." *Economic History Review* 29 (1976): 482–86.

SHEEHAN, MICHAEL M. *The Will in Medieval England: From the Conversion of the Anglo-Saxons to the End of the Thirteenth Century*. Pontifical Institute of Mediaeval Studies, Studies and Texts, no. 6. Toronto: 1963.

SIMS-WILLIAMS, PATRICK. "Cuthswith, Seventh-Century Abbess of Inkberrow, Near Worcester, and the Würzburg MS of Jerome on Ecclesiastes." *Anglo-Saxon England* 5 (1976): 1–21.

SISAM, KENNETH. "An Old English Translation of a Letter from Wynfrith to Eadburga." *Modern Language Review* 18 (1923): 253–72.

SOUTHERN, RICHARD W. *Western Society and the Church in the Middle Ages*. The Pelican History of the Church, edited by Owen Chadwick, vol. 2. Harmondsworth: 1970.

STENTON, DORIS MARY. *The English Woman in History.* New York: 1957. London: 1957. Reprint. New York: 1977.

STENTON, FRANK MERRY. *Anglo-Saxon England: c. 550–1087.* The Oxford History of England, edited by Sir George Clarke, vol. 2. Oxford: 1943; 3rd ed. 1971.

———. "The Historical Bearing of Place-Name Studies: The Place of Women in Anglo-Saxon Society." *Transactions of the Royal Historical Society* 4th series 25 (1943): 1–13. Reprinted in *Preparatory to Anglo-Saxon England: Being the Collected Papers of Frank Merry Stenton,* edited by Doris Mary Stenton, pp. 314–24. Oxford: 1970.

———. "Place-Names as Evidence of Female Ownership of Land in Anglo-Saxon England." *Academy,* 7 July 1906. Reprinted in *Preparatory to Anglo-Saxon England: Being the Collected Papers of Frank Merry Stenton,* edited by Doris Mary Stenton, p. 6. Oxford: 1970.

STEWART, ANN HARLEMAN. "Wit and Wiht: A Linguistic and Literary Analysis of the Old English Riddles." Work in progress.

TACITUS. *The Complete Works of Tacitus.* Translated by Alfred J. Church and William J. Brodribb. Edited by Moses Hadas. New York: 1942.

TALBOT, C. H. "Saint Boniface and the German Mission." *Studies in Church History* 6 (1970): 45–57.

———, ed. and trans. *The Anglo-Saxon Missionaries in Germany.* London: 1954.

———, ed. and trans. *The Life of Christina of Markyate.* Oxford: 1959.

THOMPSON, A. H. "The Monastic Settlement at Hackness and Its Relation to the Abbey of Whitby." *Yorkshire Archaeological Journal* 27 (1924): 388–405.

WAINWRIGHT, F. T. "Æthelflæd, Lady of the Mercians." In *The Anglo-Saxons: Studies in Some Aspects of their History and Culture Presented to Bruce Dickins,* edited by Peter Clemoes, pp. 53–69. London: 1959. Reprinted in *Scandinavian England: Collected Papers of F. T. Wainwright,* edited by H. P. R. Finberg, pp. 305–24. Chichester: 1975.

WHITELOCK, DOROTHY. *The Beginnings of English Society.* The Pelican History of England, vol. 2. 1952. Reprint with revisions. Baltimore: 1966.

———, ed. and trans. *Anglo-Saxon Wills.* Cambridge Studies in English Legal History, edited by H. D. Hazeltine. Cambridge: 1930.

———, ed. *English Historical Documents c. 500–1042.* English Historical Documents, edited by David C. Douglas, vol. 1. New York: 1955.

———, ed. and trans. *The Will of Æthelgifu: A Tenth-Century Anglo-Saxon Manuscript.* Oxford: 1968.

———, ed. and trans., with Douglas, David C., and Tucker, Susie I. *The Anglo-Saxon Chronicle.* London: 1961.

WILLIAMS, EDITH WHITEHURST. "What's So New about the Sexual Revolution? Some Comments on Anglo-Saxon Attitudes towards Sexuality in Women Based on Four Exeter Book Riddles." *Texas Quarterly* 18 (1975): 46–55.

WILMART, ANDRÉ. "La Legende de Ste. Edith en prose et vers par le moine Goscelin." *Analecta Bollandiana* 56 (1938): 5–101.

WILSON, DAVID M. *The Anglo-Saxons.* Ancient People and Places, edited by Glyn Daniel, vol. 16. New York: 1960.

———, ed. *The Archaeology of Anglo-Saxon England.* London: 1976.

WOOLF, HENRY B. "The Naming of Women in Old English Times." *Modern Philology* 36 (1938): 113–20.

"The Year's Work in Old English Studies." *Old English Newsletter* 1– (1967–).

# Land Charters and the Legal Position
## of Anglo-Saxon Women

MARC A. MEYER

One of the most remarkable achievements in historical scholarship in recent decades has been the judicious and creative application of charter evidence to the study of early English history.[1] The cryptic formulae of the charters often make it extremely difficult to discern precise meanings and historical implications, but through rigorous criticism and analysis they become one of the most valuable sources for the reconstruction of Anglo-Saxon history. Any discussion of Anglo-Saxon women, particularly an investigation of their legal capacity, is necessarily incomplete without reference to the land charters.[2] Until now, the application of Anglo-Saxon charter evidence has been too slight to warrant a strict bibliographic approach. In the pages that follow, possible lines of inquiry, along with some of the difficulties involved in such a study, will accompany a brief survey of women's legal capacity as it pertains to the law of property found in the land charters.

Royal charters, or landbooks as they were known in early England, created bookright—land held *in perpetuum* by the king's authority. The charters themselves are modeled on the Roman private deed, and their formulae incorporate various concepts of the late Roman vulgar law of property common in Italy and other parts of Europe.[3] The notion of perpetual tenure was originally imported into England by churchmen

57

anxious to safeguard the possessions of their cathedral and monastic communities:[4] the brief formula of *jus ecclesiasticum*, found regularly in Anglo-Latin charters, summarizes what initially meant simply the rights of the church to its property free from outside interference.[5] Because land-books gave the power of perpetual possession they were attractive to laymen; so by the mid-eighth century the laity were legitimately receiving royal charters for their estates.[6] The sentiment of the aristocracy is perhaps best exemplified by a remark made by Alfred the Great (871–99) in his translation of St. Augustine's *Soliloquies*: "Every man, when he has built himself a home on land lent to him by his lord, with his help, likes to stay in it sometimes, and to go hunting and fowling and fishing, and to support himself in every way on that loanland, both by sea and land, until the time when through his lord's favor he may acquire bookland and a perpetual inheritance."[7] Fully developed, bookright conferred on its possessor hered-itary tenure and the right of alienation, economic benefits based on demesne exploitation, and certain judicial rights and obligations. Bookright gave Anglo-Saxon men and women the power to alienate estates and hold them in their own right. That some women received bookright is itself significant, and the legal powers it conferred enhanced their legal capacity and status. Once a woman obtained bookright for an estate, she was no longer bound to the customary law governing family lands.

One must bear in mind, however, that the charters are difficult documents and must be approached with caution. The historian is presented immediately with the complicated problem of whether a charter is forged, authentic, or interpolated.[8] The Anglo-Saxons never developed a satisfactory procedure for charter authentication, and the difficulty is compounded because charters were, in fact, forged, interpolated, or badly copied. Thus, a knowledge of Latin and Old English, paleography and diplomatic is desirable (and essential to the serious researcher), although excellent editions and translations of some charters and other pertinent land documents are available.[9] Furthermore, the charters should be viewed alongside other kinds of evidence: Latin and vernacular wills, the law codes, monastic and cathedral histories and registers, a variety of other sources such as place-name evidence and saints' lives, and, of course, Domesday Book.[10]

On Christmas, 1085, when the royal court was assembled at Gloucester, King William (1066–87) ordered a survey to be made of his kingdom, affectionately known to his Anglo-Saxon subjects as the Domesday Book.[11] Although Domesday is not properly an Anglo-Saxon source, it does provide a wealth of information on both late Saxon and early Norman England.[12] From successive drafts of shire and hundred returns, culminating in the Exchequer (i) and "Little" (ii) Domesday, a picture of English society emerges. We possess a document which may have been the "terms of reference" of those who conducted the survey.[13] It records that the king ordered to be written down the name of the manor, who held it and how much it was worth in 1066 and 1086 (and occasionally for the interim period), how many people were on the estate (broken down into various social and economic categories of folk), and additional information valuable both to King William and to the modern historian. Queen Edith, the wife of. Edward the Confessor (1042–66), for example, held the estate of Kenton, Devonshire in 1066 which was assessed for the geld at three hides and one ferding. By 1086, King William held the estate with nineteen ploughs (indicating a sizable manor), thirty villeins, ten bordars, six serfs, four swineherds paying twenty shillings rent a year, eight saltworkers paying twenty shillings a year, numerous livestock, and woodland, meadow, and pasture, all of which was valued at thirty pounds a year.[14]

\* \* \*

The charters presume prior knowledge, and it should be remembered that the king was the originator of bookright and only those members of society who were valuable to him received its privileges directly. Others had to obtain booklands by inheritance, gift or purchase, and exchange. Owing to the ecclesiastical derivation of the land charters, kings initially issued diplomas only to religious individuals and communities—including abbesses, nuns, and nunneries—because they performed important functions for kings and their kingdoms.[15] When the laity legitimately obtained charters, queens and aristocratic women began to receive bookright along with male members of the ruler's mediate and extended family and other notables of the realm. Generally, actual control of real property came to a woman only after the death of her husband. The women who acquired bookright attained a degree of independence greater than those who did not. Women were unequal to each other within their sexual group, and this accounts for the fact that only relatively few women received charters in their own right.

In addition to the obvious distinction between secular and religious women, one must discriminate among seculars on the basis of social position and marital status, and among the religious between veiled nuns and those living a contemplative life within the confines of the monastery. The numerous landbooks written in behalf of women point to the fact that by far the greater number of women who received bookright from the king did so because of their familial ties with the royal house.[16] Kings issued charters to wives, stepmothers, sisters, and a variety of more distant female relatives. Not only those women born into the royal kin-group, or *mægþ*, but also women who married into the royal family were provided for by the king when he secured to them an income worthy of their royal affiliation.[17] At the same time, the king could extend the influence of the monarchy by granting large estates to secular women likely to uphold royal policy. These estates could then be converted into thegnland for the support of warriors, or loaned to them without dissipating the royal demesne. This allowed women to extend directly their activities into the social and political life of Anglo-Saxon England. Domesday occasionally records that a certain thegn was a "man" of the queen, an abbess, or laywoman,[18] or that a woman held the soke of men living on her estates. For example, Eadgifu the Fair, possessor of extensive manors in Cambridgeshire in 1066, loaned parts of her estates to her men in return for services she owed the king.[19]

A law of Æthelred (978–1016) clearly distinguishes between nuns and women who have retired from the active life to the monastery: the latter are classed with canons (i.e., priests serving collegiate minsters) and the nuns are grouped with monks.[20] Noble-born women who desired a monastic life and often served as lay-abbesses obtained fresh charters for their booklands when they entered the nunnery. The West Saxon diplomas are particularly illuminating in this regard. King Edmund (939–46) alone issued eight charters to women, variously described as "religiosa femina" or "sancta monialis."[21] King Edgar (959–75), for example, granted an estate by charter in 966 to Ælfgifu, the former wife of his brother Eadwig (955–59), the marriage having been dissolved by Archbishop Oda of Canterbury in 958 on the grounds of consanguinity.[22] The estates were sometimes given by the women to the abbey in which they resided, as in the case of Cheselbourne and Winterborne Tomson, both in Dorset, which were granted to Wynflæd, the grandmother of King Edgar and lay-abbess of Shaftesbury.[23] Ælfgyth, a nun of Wilton, donated her estate at Rollington in Bullbridge, Wiltshire to her abbey as well.[24] Other manors were alienated outside the woman's monastic home, and some were absorbed by newer foundations, like Ælfhild's manor at Culham, Oxford.[25] As the charters of Edmund and Edgar show, women who had received estates were expected to live off the proceeds of their booklands while remaining in the nunnery, and they were free to bequeath the lands to whomsoever they desired.

Identifying the grantees of the royal charters is often complicated and troublesome.[26] Many of the women are referred to as "matrona," "fidelis femina," or "nobilis femina." Only rarely do charters elaborate on these unilluminating descriptions. But toward the end of the Anglo-Saxon period it is apparent that a limited number of women belonging to the powerful provincial aristocracy began to obtain bookland directly from the king. Casual references found in some charters issued to a variety of grantees indicate that perhaps more aristocratic laywomen received bookland than the extant charters would suggest. However, the first substantial reference comes from a charter of Æthelred II issued in 985 to Wulfrun, a lady of a prominent Staffordshire family.[27] Wulfrun's family was extremely influential in the West Midlands, and for this reason she and her kindred were graced by the king's good favor. Generally, women like Wulfrun received grants of land for the purpose of endowing or founding a religious community.[28] Others sometimes obtained booklands because of their personal relationship with the king; through them he could extend royal influence on a local level by granting large and small estates with their rights of jurisdiction and obligations due the monarch.[29] All men and women holding bookland were subject to the king's justice, and so were responsible for carrying out royal policy. But the upward social mobility characteristic of the male section of society, especially in the late tenth and eleventh centuries,[30] was not effective in altering women's social status. Men of low social standing, with hopes of becoming "five-hide men," became eligible for the privilege of bookright because of the king's growing need of a professional warrior class and the increasing necessity of king's thegns to administer more adequately the expanding public law.[31] Wives and daughters of these new thegns benefited from the good fortune of their men, but did not themselves receive royal charters.[32] There can be little doubt that those women who received a royal charter came primarily from the royal household and its close associates and occasionally from the provincial aristocracy.

Distinguishing social class as a criterion for obtaining bookland is essential, and most royal and aristocratic women were legally segregated again on the basis of marital status. The notable exceptions are queens or royal consorts who acted with a high degree of independence whether widowed or married.[33] A girl still in her minority fell under the protection of a male kinsman, usually her father if he were alive, until she married, or entered a convent with her religious dowry and came under the authority of the abbess and ultimately of the bishop who consecrated her.[34] Minors might be summarily dismissed as incapable of maintaining an estate, although a writ of Edward the Confessor mentions that on the day of his birth his mother gave land to him and assigned it to his inheritance, demonstrating that minors could legally possess land in right even if they could not control and possess it in fact.[35]

Under the customary law of the vernacular law codes, a married woman was legally bound to her husband in much the same way as a minor to a father.[36] The real property she brought into the marriage remained in her possession,[37] but its maintenance was vested in her husband; he held the land and could do with it whatever he wished except permanently alienate it from his wife's possession.[38]

The wife also held additional property as the widow's portion which was given to her by her husband. This type of property, however, was not held independently of the other property of the marriage until after the death of the husband. A tract from the *Textus Roffensis*, "How a man shall betroth a maiden, and what agreement there ought to be," shows that what the man grants to his future wife in land and movable property will remain in her possession until her death.[39] This tenth-century treatise curiously fails to mention the woman's morning-gift, but does indicate that, according to custom, half the marriage property would descend to the wife or "if they have children together," all the property would go to her unless she remarries.[40] The legal and social concepts of this little treatise exemplify early English custom which sought to stress the economic prosperity of the nuclear family unit by guarding against the alienation of family land at the expense of the kin-group. The eighth-century post-obit bequest[41] of Æthelnoth, reeve of Eastry, like many other similar documents, was designed to secure land for his mediate family, and therefore he bequeathed all his property to his wife, if she lived longer than he. But, "if they have a child, it shall succeed after the death of both of them."[42] Both the treatise on the betrothal of a maiden and Æthelnoth's will assume that the wife will hold and preserve the children's share of the property until they come of age, and therefore she is forbidden to alienate the property of the marriage outside the family unless otherwise specified by her husband.[43]

The law code of Æthelberht of Kent (?552–616) also refers to property which will descend to the wife on the death of her husband, but it does not mention the woman's morning-gift.[44] This morning-gift, usually specified at the time of betrothal,[45] was intended to provide economic security for the woman after the death of her husband, as in the case of the widow's portion, regardless of whether the marriage produced children. That the property given as a morning-gift was relegated to the wife's *mægþ* is evidenced by Æthelberht 81: "If she does not bear a child, [her] father's relatives shall have her goods, and the morning-gift." However, the morning-gift was subsumed under the property holdings of both marriage partners and was thus not usually considered a separate economic holding prior to the dissolution of the marriage.[46] The traditional morning-gift, mentioned in Æthelberht's laws, did not necessarily allow an increase in the woman's legal and economic activity. The husband usually maintained the estate, though again without the right of permanent alienation.[47] The fact that many post-obit bequests of the Anglo-Saxon period repeatedly affirm the woman's possession of some morning-gifts only emphasizes further that the guardianship of the land was vested in her husband and that it was often necessary to regrant the estate to the wife after it had been in his control.[48] A law of Cnut (1016–35) dealing with the remarriage of a woman within the twelve month mourning period makes a distinction between the morning-gift and that property which descended to the wife on the death of her husband: "And if then, within the space of the year, she chooses a husband, she shall lose her morning-gift and all the property which she had from her first husband, and his nearest relatives shall take the land and the property which she had held."[49] This passage, when considered alongside other documents of the same period, discloses a more subtle characteristic of married women's property: that is, the type of morning-gift differs according to the terms of the marriage agreement made between the two interested parties. It is therefore necessary to distinguish between the traditional morning-gift and one held by book-right. In the so-called "Worcestershire Marriage Agreement," drawn up during the reign of Cnut, a dramatic departure from the customary morning-gift can be seen in that one estate given to the woman was within her right to alienate at any time.[50] Wulfric is made to state that he will give to Archbishop Wulfstan's sister, the prospective bride, two estates "for her lifetime" which will presumably descend to their children, an estate for a period of three lives which he will obtain from the religious community at Winchcombe, and an estate which she can bestow on whomsoever she pleases "during her lifetime or at her death." What has been granted in this last instance is bookright with its full powers of alienation. Evidently very anxious to enter into a marriage alliance with the archbishop,[51] Wulfric offered his sister estates of three distinct kinds: two estates to be held on precarious tenure, which accounts for "what he grants her if she should live longer than he" in the marriage treatise referred to above; an estate to be retained on conditions similar to loanland granted by episcopal and monastic landholders; and an estate to be held by bookright. That many estates granted as morning-gifts were involved in litigation[52] and donated to religious communities[53] suggest further that the kinds of tenure attached to morning-gifts depended on the contractual arrangements agreed upon by all involved parties.

A concept of community property also developed that was designed to protect married women and their children. Numerous documents attest to the importance of community property and the respect accorded women by men. A lease of land of Bishop Wærferth of Worcester, for example, typifies the Anglo-Saxon sentiment toward women's capacity to carry out the conditions stipulated in some land transactions: "And Æthelred and Æthelflæd shall hold it for all time, ... uncontested by anyone as long as they live. And if Ælfwyn [their daughter] survives them, it shall similarly remain uncontested as long she lives. ..."[54] Although the woman is merely viewed as a custodian of an estate until the coming of age of the man's heir,[55] the heir in question could be of either sex. This fact is evidenced further in a charter of King Offa of Mercia (757–96) issued in 788 in which the king is made to state that he gave an estate to his faithful minister Osbert and his wife which was to pass to their son or daughter after their deaths.[56] While both marriage partners lived, all landed property received jointly (and this was a common occurrence)[57] could be alienated by one of them only with the consent of the other. But it should be noted that in most royal and episcopal grants made to a man and woman, the man is seen as the dominant partner. Charters are issued because of the fidelity and loyalty of the king's thegn, and his wife is most often mentioned in a passive connection. It is not by her own virtue that a woman receives the estate with her husband—although she was recognized as capable of managing the estate in his absence—but only on account of her relationship to the royal minister and as a mother of his children and perserver of the basic unit of society, the family.

Similarly, joint donations of husband and wife suggest again that the woman is the passive participant. Regardless of whether the usufruct over the land was reserved, the woman usually appears as the consenting party complying with the desire of her husband. Queens are frequently mentioned as codonors of estates to both religious communities and secular persons, but it is doubtful whether their consent was actually needed. At times it would have been politic to obtain the queen's consent, but more often, particularly in relation to donations to monasteries and cathedral chapters, she was simply included as a pious benefactress for the salvation of her soul.

Many lay donations to religious communities stipulate that the donors will retain the usufruct over the estates. Reserving the usufruct was a common procedure in Anglo-Saxon England, and most of the bequests to monasteries and cathedrals can be understood in this sense.[58] Pious gifts were rewarded not only by entry into heaven but by a loan of the land for one or more lives and a means of protection for widows and children once the land was surrendered to the religious house. Thus, Æthelric made an arrangement at the Synod of Clofesho in 804 protecting his mother Ceolburh in her possession of estates at Westminster and Stoke.[59] Fearful that others with prior claims to these lands might try to seize them from his mother, Æthelric included a provision in his testament in order to safeguard the two estates in Ceolburh's possession. He did so by giving his mother a life interest in the lands with reversion to Worcester. But, "if she does not get protection in the city of Worcester, she is afterwards to seek it from the archbishop in Kent." (We are not told if the estate was then to pass to the archbishop.) By the late tenth century, it was standard to place a widow's *mundium*, or guardianship, under a bishop or the king. According to VI Æthelred 26, widows are under the protection of God (the church) and the king.[60] Clearly a woman—whether nun, vowess, or married or widowed laywoman—needed male support to ward off attacks on her possessions. For women who could obtain a royal charter or receive bookright by inheritance or gift, the perpetual tenure embodied in its formulae, backed by a strong king and the church, provided the necessary security of economic and legal stability.

After the death of her husband, and provided that she did not remarry within twelve months, the widow was free to keep or dispose of her bookland, with the king's consent, and retain her inherited family land. In the early English period a widow was still under the protection of her *mægþ*,[61] but by the tenth century, with the increasing power of the king's law, the widow was placed under royal protection. The newfound legal and economic freedom permitted to those women holding bookright accounts in part for the substantial increase in donations to monastic communities during the course of the later Saxon age.

Many royal charters granted to women were subsequently used to endow monasteries—one of the primary reasons for issuing charters to them. Queen Frithgyth made a donation to Winchester where she had been raised as a young girl.[62] The noblewoman Ælfswith made four separate donations to Glastonbury Abbey.[63] And perhaps the most generous patron of the monasteries, Queen Eadgifu, wife of Edward the Elder (899–925), supported Abingdon and Christ Church, Canterbury and assisted the leaders of the tenth century monastic reform in various parts of England.[64] Like so many other estates granted to women, lands Wulfrun received from King Æthelred in 985[65] were used to endow a new community of clerks at Wolverhampton in Staffordshire.[66] But land was not the only form of pious donation. Foodstuffs and building materials, at times equally valuable, were often given to religious communities. Ealhburg, for example, made over to St. Augustine's, Canterbury "forty ambers of malt, a fullgrown bullock, four sheep, two-hundred and forty loaves, a wey of lard and cheese, four fothers of wood and twenty hens," all of which were to be carted to the abbey every year provided that every day the community sings "on her behalf after their verse the psalm 'Exaudiat te Dominus.'"[67]

The alienation of part of the *feorm*[68] prescribed in Ealhburg's donation could conceivably have been made without holding land by charter. But the permanent alienation of land by means of charters, bequests of inheritance, and some of the morning-gifts would not have been possible unless they had been granted *in perpetuum* by the king in the first place. Real property traditionally descended to members of the *mægþ*, of which we learn much in the vernacular codes. But with the introduction of land held by royal charter, those women who received the benefits of bookright could alienate land outside the kin-group if they wished to do so.

Secular and religious women exhibit greater versatility than merely acting as grantees and donors in individual and joint land transactions. In many instances they sell, buy, and exchange property, and defend their possessory claims through litigation. Booklands can also be forfeited to the king.

Maitland remarked that "nothing for nothing is a good medieval rule."[69] Earlier charters generally record a fine, or *land-ceap*, for the privilege of bookright or for permission to transfer possession of property. Payment of a *land-ceap* is found in a charter of the 840s issued by King Berhtwulf of Mercia (c. 840–52) whereby he sold to his thegn, Forthred, nine hides of land at Wotton Underwood, Buckinghamshire for nine hundred shillings, but the charter also stipulates that an additional thirty mancuses were to be paid as a fine or tax at the time of purchase.[70] Even men and women of the early monastic communities paid for bookland.[71] King Swæfheard of Kent (c. 676–92) issued two charters in 690 which indicate that, unless otherwise stated, grants of land were paid for by the grantee. In one, Swæfheard donates to Abbess Æbba the estate "for the eternal health of my soul,"[72] a common enough formula in Anglo-Saxon charters. The other charter, also issued to Æbba, was made not only for money which she had given the king nor because they were related by blood, but for the benefit of his soul. The charter formula points to the major reasons for granting a charter to an individual.[73] Notice as well a revealing formula recorded in a West Saxon grant of 833 made to Abbess Dunn in which King Egbert (802–39) gives the estate "not for money but for the remedy of my soul and for the expiation of my sins."[74] On the other hand, King Eadred (945–55) received the specific sum of two pounds' weight of pure gold from the nun Ælfwynn for six hides at Wickhambreux, Kent.[75]

Not only kings but also queens were given "gifts" for their kindness. Bishop Ethelwold of Winchester, for example, "gave to his royal lord 200 mancuses of gold and a silver cup worth 5 pounds in return for the renewal of the freedom [of Taunton, Somerset], and to Ælfthryth, his wife, 50 mancuses of gold, in return for her help in his just suit."[76] This payment to Queen Ælfthryth demonstrates her effectiveness and influence at court,[77] but it also points to the fact that the king had little to gain materially from the transfer of property—the rights in land *in perpetuum* having been already granted. By assigning a *land-ceap*, or land tax, he could gain by giving his consent to a change of possession or renewal of liberty, and he could control better the descent of estates as well.[78]

As holders of bookright, with the right to alienate the same by sale, women were guarded by the same laws as men. Among a series of laws on testimony and witnesses, III Æthelred 3 stipulates that a person's right to alienate property must not be violated: "And there shall be no interference with purchases of land, or gifts by a lord of what he has a legal right to bestow, or purchases of legal rights...."[79] The only qualification of this right is mentioned in Alfred 41: "[he] who holds land by title-deed, which his kinsmen have left him, shall not be allowed to give it out of his kindred if there is documentary or [other] evidence that the power to do so is forbidden him by the men who first acquired it, or by those who gave it to him...."[80] And it would appear that this law was enforced throughout the Anglo-Saxon period. By mutual agreement the terms of the contract of sale were arranged in such a way as to vest rights and duties in both parties. The capacity to act in bilateral contracts of sale and purchase demonstrates the widening scope and importance of women's legal activity after the acquisition of bookright. Women are often referred to in deeds of sale, like Ælfswith, the wife of ealdorman Ælfphege, who purchased from King Edgar an estate in Wiltshire.[81]

The extant charters show that only women of high social position made independent sales or purchases of land. At the beginning of the eighth century a certain Cuthswith paid two men six hundred shillings for land in Warwickshire without mention of any man acting as her advocate.[82] Queen Æthelswith, the sister of Alfred the Great, conceded in 868 a certain part of her land to her faithful minister Cuthwulf for a specified sum of money,[83] and in the eleventh century Queen Edith purchased an estate in Lincolnshire which was subsequently granted to Peterborough Abbey by the Confessor.[84] These transactions point to the continuation of the practice of land sales by influential women.

The actions of these exceptional women cannot, of course, be taken as representative of all women. The majority of Anglo-Saxon women only took direct control of their legal and economic affairs after the death of the husband. That he kept control over communal property is evidenced by the action taken by Wiohstan when having taken in marriage Goda's anonymous daughter he took control of the four hides at Marden, Sussex.[85] Presumably with her consent, although it is not stated as such, Wiohstan sold one of the four hides to Eldfred and his wife Ealsware. The remaining three hides were alienated when Wiohstan, with his wife and daughter, made a pilgrimage to Rome and financed their journey by selling or "donating" the land to Bishop Wulfhune. This transaction illustrates the traditional legal dependence of married women on their husbands in the law of common property. Conversely, however, the extant sources amply demonstrate that a woman could sell as well as donate or bequeath part or all of her morning-gift if she retained it after the death of her husband or if it had been given *in perpetuum*.[86]

III Æthelred 3 asserts that the right of alienation of bookland by sale was embodied in the brief formula of "in perpetuum haereditatem,"[87] along with an additional right to exchange land. The early eighth-century *Testament of Mildburg* clearly shows that the formula "in propriam perpetualiter perdono potestatem" includes the right to exchange land, for "habeas facultatem donandi commutandi" follows that formula in the same part of the document.[88] Most exchanges of landed estates were probably made for administrative convenience;[89] this was perhaps King Edmund's motive for initiating an exchange of estates with the nuns of Shaftesbury. The king transferred possession of land at *Bucticanlea* for land of the old site of the defunct monastery at Tisbury[90] which he then gave to his consort Ælfgifu. She planned to bequeath the estate to Shaftesbury, but after her death Eadwig took back *Bucticanlea* and returned Tisbury to the nuns. All this was duly recorded in a reconfirmation charter of Ethelred in which he restored a wood at *Sfgcynllebar* which one of his men tried to annex as his own property.[91]

Landed estates were often lost owing to various kinds of lawful forfeiture and illegal seizure. When conditions of an agreement were disregarded, or conflicted with other claims, women were presented with the opportunity to assert themselves through litigation.[92] The list of offenses which could result in the forfeiture of property is quite extensive from the evidence of the charters alone. Larceny was accounted a serious crime and its perpetrator liable to the king's justice and the eventual loss of his estates.[93] Committing murder also resulted in the loss of property, as did harboring of a murderer by any of his kinsmen, if they had earlier declined to pay the victim's wergeld.[94] During the reign of King Æthelred a great many charters refer to confiscation of property on account of treason and desertion of the king's host.[95] And interestingly, suicide was an offense that could result in forfeiture of land.[96] But theft was perhaps the most common crime.[97] Women were certainly not exempt from the penalties resulting from misdeeds simply because of their sex. Hence, in one celebrated case, Æscwyn had given the title deed of Snodland to Rochester Cathedral, but it was stolen by some priests and sold to her son Ælfric.[98] When Ælfric died in the midst of litigation, the bishop brought charges against his widow Brihtwaru; King Edgar, finding in the bishop's favor, ordered the return of the deed and the forfeiture of the widow's estates at Bromley and Fawkham. She then pleaded with the bishop for clemency and he, moved to pity, bought back her two estates from the king and allowed her the usufruct. However, Brihtwaru's kinsman Brihtric forcefully seized the estates after Edgar's death. Although Brihtric seems to be acting in some sense as Brihtwaru's protector or custodian of her estates while she held them from Rochester, he wanted to possess them on a more permanent basis. But Brihtwaru was nevertheless involved in the suit as rightful possessor *in perpetuum* and had to account for herself in the affair.

Practicing witchcraft or magic also resulted in the loss of property. This offense was particularly associated with women during the middle ages (and for some time afterwards) and under the direction of the church, kings legislated against it.[99] That legislation and actual circumstance can coincide is shown by a late tenth-century grant whereby King Æthelred confiscated the estate of Ailsworth because a widow and her son "drove an iron pin into Ælfsige, Wulfstan's father, and it was discovered, and the deadly image was dragged out of her room."[100] The accomplices were punished for the crime: the widow's son became an outlaw after he escaped capture and she was despoiled of her property and thrown off London Bridge to drown in the Thames.

Any person holding land by book was subject directly to the king's justice. Moreover, bookright embodied the right of appeal to the king in the event of illegal seizure of land. Royal authority over holders of bookland is explicitly asserted first in I Æthelred 14: "And the king shall be entitled to all the fines which are incurred by men[101] who hold land by title deed, and on one [of these] shall pay the compensation following upon any charge, unless in the presence of the king's reeve."[102] The charters also indicate that disputes over possession of land fell under the king's providence. Queen Eadgifu, for example, sought out the king's justice in her dispute over Cooling, Kent. She is also seen in the record giving evidence and testifying in court.[103] Those women whom the king regarded as worthy of receiving a charter or those who obtained bookland by inheritance or as a morning-gift are seen to participate more actively in legal procedure in their own right[104] than those women who simply inherited a portion of the family land or were given a widow's portion on which to live after the death of a husband.

*     *     *

The noted English historian Eileen Power remarked: "The position of women has been called the test point by which the civilization of a country or of an age may be judged, and although this is in many respects true, the test remains one which it is extraordinarily difficult to apply, because of the difficulty of determining what it is that constitutes the position of women."[105] The legal capacity of women is an essential ingredient in the mixture that constitutes the position of women in any society, but legal theory and practice are often diametrically opposed. The land charters, however, offer a description of legal arrangements that are at once functional and theoretical. An equality of men and women is suggested by the legal principles found in the formulae of the landbooks and in other sundry documents related to the possession of land. Similar rights, obligations, and powers of jurisdiction were attached to all land held by charter, and all possessors were subject to royal authority whether the king himself granted the land or whether it had been obtained by bequest or inheritance. The limitation of the evidence, particularly the low survival rate of early charters, precludes an estimate of the amount of land possessed by women in any period of Anglo-Saxon history. Some impression of their involvement in bookland can be drawn from the fact that of the 1875 land documents given in Sawyer's annotated list of Anglo-Saxon charters about seven percent mention secular and religious women as grantees or donees.[106] Even though these women were few in number and limited to the upper aristocracy, it is nevertheless significant that bookright increased their status and legal capacity by expanding the sphere of their legal activities and by permitting them to manage and administer their property if they chose to do so.

The study of Anglo-Saxon women and the concept of perpetual tenure of the land charters takes on special importance for that period in history when the possession of land meant wealth, power, and influence. Particular studies perhaps will raise questions that yield only tentative conclusions, but this should not retard attempts to solve vital problems concerning women's legal and social position in early England. How did bookright affect the position and legal status of Anglo-Saxon women? What kind of political and economic power was obtained by those women who held bookland? Who actually received booklands, and what is the relationship of the patterns of its distribution to the structure of the Anglo-Saxon aristocracy? To what extent did grants and bequests of bookland affect the traditional inheritance patterns and the power and influence of the mægþ? Did bookright really allow greater legal and social freedom for women within the confines of a Germanic warrior society? Can the church be properly labeled misogynistic when it not only acquiesced in but also promoted grants and bequests of bookland to religious and secular women? Did holding bookland by women undermine the growth of feudal institutions in pre-Conquest England? Is there really a significant break in the continuity of the legal position or status of women from Anglo-Saxon to Anglo-Norman times? Has the position of women in Anglo-Saxon society been inflated beyond proper proportions? Charter evidence provides the key to these and other questions, and the outlook for future research is promising.

# NOTES

I am extremely grateful to C. Warren Hollister, professor of history, University of California at Santa Barbara, for his valuable comments and criticisms. I would also like to thank C. K. Holt and J. H. Rush for their help in the preparation of the manuscript. All errors are, of course, my own.

1. Good general surveys of previous charter research and criticism, with extensive bibliographies, can be found in Cronne, "Charter Scholarship in England"; Harmer, "Anglo-Saxon Charters and the Historian"; and Brooks, "Anglo-Saxon Charters: The Work of the Last Twenty Years."

2. F. M. Stenton in "The Historical Bearing of Place-Name Studies: The Place of Women in Anglo-Saxon Society," p. 324, relying primarily on place-name evidence, concluded that "the independence which women had enjoyed in the Migration Age was never completely lost during the centuries of Old English history." The extent of their independence had been examined earlier by Ernest Young in his study "Anglo-Saxon Family Law." Young divided Anglo-Saxon society into two classes, "the legally independent and the legally dependent; those who could act for themselves, and those who needed a guardian to act for them" (p. 142). Young was content with a much too narrow view of women's legal status and thereby made his two-pronged scheme untenable, while Stenton, on the other hand, alluded to a decline in women's legal capacity as the Anglo-Saxon period progressed. Both hypotheses concerning women's legal activities can be modified and elaborated by a detailed study of the Anglo-Saxon charters.

3. Latin formulae of the early Anglo-Saxon charters, correctly understood, illustrate that the landbooks imply grants of power and *dominium*. (See, for example, the charters listed in Sawyer, *Anglo-Saxon Charters*, nos. 7, 8, 10, 15, 1167, etc., hereafter cited as Sawyer.) The charters continually use the terms *dominium* and *possessio* to describe types of tenure. Based in part on Levy, *West Roman Vulgar Law*, John in *Land Tenure in Early England* has shown how from the seventh century onwards the Roman vulgar law, the debased Roman law of the late empire and early barbarian kingdoms, was an important factor in the development of Anglo-Saxon bookright. Viewed from the classical system, *possessio* indicates the "fact" of control while *dominium* is regarded as the "right" in principle of total mastery over movables or immovables. But as Levy has shown (pp. 61, 63–64), *dominium*, relieved of its individuality in the vulgar law, was interchangeably used with *possessio* and thus failed to preserve the distinction between ownership and the right of perpetual lease—the continual use of an object or estate. This blurring occurred mainly from the merger of *ius perpetuum* and *emphyteusis* and its subsequent appearance as *dominium* (Levy, pp. 45, 78). For a study of the transmission of Roman and Continental formulae to English charters, see Chaplais, "The Origin and Authenticity of the Royal Anglo-Saxon Diploma," and "Who Introduced Charters into England? The Case for Augustine." The question of foreign influence on the formation of the developed Anglo-Saxon law is vital to the understanding of the legal position of women. Not only Roman vulgar and Romance law, but also Irish,

Scandinavian, and ecclesiastical legislation and custom must be accounted for. This is partly the subject of my current research, "The Legal Position of Women in Anglo-Saxon England," Ph.D. dissertation in progress, University of California, Santa Barbara.

4. No charter can be said to have been accepted as authentic which dates before 669, or the arrival of Theodore of Tarsus in May of that year. But cf., Chaplais, "Who Introduced Charters" for an original and scholarly argument contrary to the majority opinion.

5. See John, *Land Tenure*, pp. 1–63.

6. For an interesting discussion on this point see John, "Folkland Reconsidered," in *Orbis Britanniae*, pp. 64–127.

7. Carnicelli, ed., *King Alfred's Version of St. Augustine's Soliloquies*, p. 48.

8. For scholarly discussion addressing the question of the authenticity of the charters, see Bruckner, "Zur Diplomatik der älteren angelsächsischen Urkunden"; Harmer, "Anglo-Saxon Charters"; and Chaplais, "Some Early Anglo-Saxon Diplomas on Single Sheets: Originals or Copies?" The forthcoming work of Simon Keynes based on his Cambridge Ph.D. thesis, "The Diplomas of King Æthelred II," will prove indispensable to the serious student of Anglo-Saxon charters. The best guides and aids to charter criticism and analysis are Sawyer, which includes an annotated list of the extant charters with manuscript references, brief summaries of the documents, where they can be found in modern editions, an extensive bibliography, and the judgements of Whitelock and Ker on the authenticity of the more difficult charters. A series of books on the early charters of England is also extremely valuable and should be used alongside Sawyer: the series includes Finberg, *The Early Charters of Devon and Cornwall, The Early Charters of the West Midlands*, and *The Early Charters of Wessex*; Hart, *The Early Charters of Eastern England, The Early Charters of Essex*, and *The Early Charters of Northern England and the North Midlands*. This series provides a detailed summary of charter contents—who was the grantor and grantee, what was the name of the estate given and what was its hide assessment, and cross-references to other charters in which the estates and persons mentioned appear. It also includes some interesting studies on particular aspects of Anglo-Saxon history with special reference to the charter evidence. Comments on the authenticity of individual charters must, however, be varified in each case.

9. The best modern editions of the charters are Kemble, ed., *Codex Diplomaticus*; Birch, ed., *Cartularium Saxonicum* (for charters up through the reign of Edgar); Earle, ed., *A Hand-Book to the Land Charters, and other Saxonic Documents*; Napier and Stevenson, eds., *The Crawford Collection of Early Charters and Documents* (a remarkable work of scholarship and a model for subsequent editions of the charters); and Campbell, ed., *The Charters of Rochester* (the first volume in a series which aims to publish all Anglo-Saxon land charters according to archive group). For the most accessible facsimile editions see Lowe, ed., *Codices Latini Antiquiores, ii, Great Britain and Ireland*; and Bruckner and Marichal, eds., *Chartae Latinae Antiquiores, part III, British Museum, London*. Good editions with translations include Harmer, ed. and trans., *Select English Historical Documents of the Ninth and Tenth Centuries* and *Anglo-Saxon Writs*; and Robertson, ed. and trans., *Anglo-Saxon Charters*. General introductions to the charters are Earle, *A Hand-Book to the Land Charters*, pp. xiii–cxi and F. M. Stenton, *Latin Charters of the Anglo-Saxon Period*.

10. See the preceding chapter in this volume for a discussion of these and other Anglo-Saxon sources.

11. The Anglo-Saxon chronicler wrote *sub anno* 1085: "So very thoroughly did he [King William] have the inquiry carried out that there was not a single hide, not one virgate of land, not even—it is shameful to record it, but it did not seem shameful to him to do—not even one ox, nor one cow, nor one pig which escaped his notice in this survey."

12. Domesday Book is used here only as a supplement to the charter evidence, but this does not diminish its great value as a source. The most accessible translations with valuable

commentary on Domesday are found in relevant volumes of the *Victoria History of the Counties of England*. The rare 1783 Farley edition of Domesday, which followed the original Domesday paleographic abbreviations, has been photographically reproduced with a translation (which must be used with caution) in single shire volumes under the general editorship of John Morris. One of the best introductions to Domesday analysis, with a good bibliography, is Finn, *An Introduction to Domesday Book*. Finn's other works that are useful are *The Norman Conquest and its Effects on the Economy: 1066–1086* and with Darby et al., *The Domesday Geography of England*—an indispensible series treating all aspects of Domesday research in groups of shire circuits which is heavily statistical in design. For a good summary see also Harvey, "Domesday Book and its Predecessors." References in Domesday Book will be cited hereafter as *DB*.

13. Finn, *Introduction to Domesday Book*, pp. 6–7.
14. *DB*, 1: 94b.
15. See Meyer, "The Greater Royal Nunneries of Wessex," and a summary of this work, "The Endowment of the Royal West Saxon Nunneries in the Late Old English Period," a paper read at the Pacific Coast Conference on British Studies held at Mills College, Oakland, Calif., 7 April 1978.
16. See Sawyer, 446, 460, 489, 562, 703, 737, 1084, 1861, etc.
17. In all fairness to the charter evidence, it should be noted that the documents are slanted in the direction of gifts to members of the royal household and their preservation by religious communities.
18. For example, see the Domesday entries for Senwell, Bedfordshire in which Walrave is mentioned as a man of Queen Edith (1: 209b); Hoggeston, Buckinghamshire in which a man of the abbess of Barking has one hide T. R. E. (1: 148b); and Buckingham with Bourton, in which Manno the Breton has four burgesses who were at one time the men of Eadgifu, wife of Syred (1: 143).
19. See *DB*, 1: 189b, 193b, 199.
20. "And it is the decree of our lord and his councillors, that men of every estate shall readily submit, in matters both religious and secular, to the duty which befits them; and most of all the servants of God, bishops and abbots, monks and nuns, priests and women under religious vows, shall submit to their duty, and live according to their rule, and zealously intercede for all Christian people" (V Æthelred 4).
21. Sawyer 460, 464, 465, 474, 482, 485, 487, 493.
22. Sawyer 737 and *ASC sub anno* 958.
23. Winterborne Tomson was given to Shaftesbury nunnery, but according to Domesday Book, it had been lost by 1066. Cheselbourne has a much more interesting history. The first mention of Shaftesbury's Domesday estate of Cheselbourne is found in a doubtful charter of 870 issued by Æthelred (866–71) to Alfstan (Sawyer 334). A charter for *Chisselburne Fifhide*, nearly identical topographically with the earlier *Cheselburnean*, was drawn up in the same year and appears to be diplomatically dependent on Sawyer 334; again, Alfstan is recorded as the grantee (Sawyer 342). Both ninth-century diplomas were copied into the Shaftesbury register along with another charter (supporting a doubtful witness list, but embodying a genuine text) granting an estate at *Cheselburne* whereby King Edmund gave the estate to "religiose sancte converscionis nomialis femine Wenflede" (Sawyer 485). This charter records a grant of seven *mansi* and thus can be viewed as a composite of the two previous grants of two hides at *Cheselburnean* and five hides at *Chisselburne Fifhide*. Edmund added another eight *mansi* to the estate and brought the assessment to fifteen hides by 942. Another charter relating to Cheselbourne bound in the Shaftesbury register records the rather insignificant grant of "tres virgas" or three-fourths of a hide made by Edgar to his minister Wulfheard in 965 (Sawyer 736). The sum total of the various Cheselbourne grants accounts for the sixteen hides at Cheselbourne in the final Anglo-Saxon charter reference to the estate whereby King Cnut allowed his minister Agemund possession of the manor in 1019 (Sawyer 955). Domesday records that Cheselbourne was held by Shaftesbury Abbey for sixteen hides in 1086 (*DB*, 1: 78b). Although the nunnery lost the estate for a time during the upheavals of the Danish invasions of the late tenth and eleventh centuries,

Shaftesbury regained possession of it by order of King William who allowed to stand a writ of the Confessor which restored the estate to the nunnery.

24. Rollington was given to Wilton nunnery some time after 944 (Sawyer 493) and by the time of the Great Survey, it was assessed with Wilton borough (*DB*, 1: 68).

25. A charter of King Edmund dated 940 grants Culham, Oxford to his kinswoman, the matron Ælfhild (Sawyer 460), and the abbey's chronicle says that Ælfhild was to hold Culham from Abingdon just as King Cenwulf of Mercia (796–821) had granted it to his sisters who gave it to that abbey. This grant by Cenwulf is not recorded elsewhere, but it will be recalled that Cenwulf's daughter was abbess of Southminster in Thanet, and of the double monastery of Winchcombe in Gloucestershire. Thus, in 940 Edmund restored Culham to the foundation, placing his kinswoman Ælfhild on the estate, for her to enjoy in the same way as the sisters of King Cenwulf had held it from Abingdon in the early ninth century. The site of St. Helen's church was traditionally the site of a nunnery, but such a foundation could not have survived more than a few years after the grant of 940 because Ethelwold, later bishop of Winchester, refounded the abbey of Abingdon with the help of Queen Eadgifu. Domesday Book ignores the ancient manor of Culham, so we do not know its fate in the late eleventh century.

26. The works of Finberg and Hart are particularly helpful in identifying the personal names found in the charters. See also Searle, *Onomasticon Anglo-Saxonicum: A List of Anglo-Saxon Proper Names from the Time of Beda to That of King John*, and Boehler, *Die Altenglischen Frauennamen*. For example, a reference in the margin of the cartulary copy of a grant of 962 issued by King Edgar refers to the grantee, Æthelflæd, as the daughter of Alfgar, the ealdorman of Essex (Sawyer 703). By this notation and an examination of Æthelflæd's will (Sawyer 1494), an identification of this woman is possible. Notice also that many charters of a more recent issue have, as in the case of some monastic charters, superseded older diplomas that possibly name another grantee: the new one being issued for various reasons, not the least being "because we no longer have the old one" (Sawyer 469). Similarly instructive, a charter of 996 issued by Æthelred reads "sicut mater ei largita est voti compos optineant," informing its reader that the estate of Abbots Bromley was once held by Wulfrun, the mother of Wulfric Spot (Sawyer 878). Domesday Book presents the same problems of identification for lesser-known persons holding estates before 1066. Much valuable information can be found in the Victoria county history introductions to the translation of shire surveys, but see also von Feilitzen, *The Pre-Conquest Personal Names of Domesday Book*.

27. Wulfrun's family was of considerable importance in the West Midlands. She herself received at least two charters (Sawyer 860, 878). Wulfric Spot, referred to in conjunction with his mother's name in Æthelred's confirmation of Æthelric's will (Sawyer 939), was the founder of Burton-on-Trent. Wulfrun's other son, Ælfhelm, was an ealdorman of southern Northumbria.

28. It is possible that Æthelred's grant to Wulfrun (Sawyer 860) was for the express purpose of founding Wolverhampton, a community of canons, but there is no direct evidence to this point. For the Domesday entries of the community see *DB*, 1: 246, 248.

29. For the obligations attached to land in Anglo-Saxon England, see Stevenson, "Trinoda Necessitas," pp. 689–703, and the interesting series of essays by John in *Orbis Britanniae*.

30. See F. M. Stenton, "The Thriving of the Anglo-Saxon Ceorl," *pp. 383–93*.

31. John, *Orbis Britanniae*, pp. 64ff.

32. Loanland, a grant of land usually for three lives, is distinct from bookland, and deserves a special study with regard to women and the law of real property. Most of our information comes from Worcester and the Oswald leases, although earlier loans survive (Sawyer 62, 1179, 1283) as well as later ones (*DB*, 1: 172b). Loans were generally the prerogative of the lesser aristocracy and relatives of the lessor. A few loans were given directly to women (Sawyer 120, 1309), while others were inherited by women whose names appear in the loan-charter rubrics (Sawyer 1261, 1324, 1330, 1349, 1350, 1356, 1420, 1425). Further loans were received jointly by husband and wife (Sawyer 1310, 1334, 1338, 1350, etc.). And unless otherwise stated (Sawyer 1280), the

descent of the loanland was not restricted to men. It is unlikely that women would have performed the many conditions attached to the Oswaldslaw loans which would have been difficult for them to fulfill. Thus, they were dependent on male assistance in order to perform the contractual obligations. Domesday records that two nuns (perhaps indicating a religious community for women at Worcester) held leases from the church at Worcester some time between 1066 and the date of the survey. One of them, a certain Eadgifu, "was to have it [Knightwick] and to perform the service so long as the brethren were willing and could dispense with it. On their number increasing under King William, she restored it [to them], and she herself, who is still living, is witness to the fact" (*DB*, 1: 172b).

33. Only women of great political influence issued charters in their own right. The most powerful English woman of the Anglo-Saxon age, Æthelflæd, the Lady of the Mercians, was the virtual ruler of the area north of the Thames valley in the West Midlands in the early tenth century. She issued charters to two of her faithful followers, an act which certainly did not require the approval of her brother King Edward the Elder (Sawyer 224, 225). The evidence does not, however, permit the suggestion that Æthelflæd created bookland rather than merely issuing a charter for a privileged area already existing but vacant. For further activities of women of the royal house, see Hart, "Two Queens of England"; Meyer, "Women and the Tenth Century English Monastic Reform"; Wainwright, "Æthelflæd, Lady of the Mercians"; Campbell, "Queen Emma and Ælfgifu of Northampton: Canute the Great's Women"; Cutler, "Edith, Queen of England, 1045–1066"; and Campbell, *Encomium Emmae Reginae*, appendix 2.

34. See Ine 23:2, Alfred 8 and VI Æthelred 2 where the abbess had the guardianship of the members of her community. That bishops' responsibilities extended to nuns, and women generally, can be seen in VI Æthelred 39 and in various hagiographical works wherein the prelate consecrates the nun (see *Vita Sanctae Ethelfledae:* B. L. MS Lansdowne 436 fol. 44r [*BHL* 2471], and Denis Bethell, "The Lives of St. Osyth of Essex and St. Osyth of Aylesbury," p. 87) and continues the close relationship with her (see Dom André Wilmart, "La Legende de Ste Edith en prose et vers par le moine Goscelin," pp. 87–88).

35. Sawyer 1148.

36. See Wihtred 12; Ine 7, 57; and II Cnut 72, 72: 1.

37. Such is certainly in evidence in the will of Ælfflæd, the wife of Earl Bryhtnoth (Sawyer 1487). For a valuable discussion of the descent of the estates of Ælfgar (Sawyer 1483) and his daughters Ælfflæd and Æthelflæd (Sawyer 1494), see L. Lancaster, "Kinship in Anglo-Saxon Society—II."

38. An incident in the chronicle of Ramsey (*Chronicon Abbatiae Rameseiensis*, pp. 135–40) relates how control of the estate at *Athelintone* remained with the married woman. The manor belonged to Dacus's wife by a former marriage. When Bishop Ætheric visited the couple, Dacus became drunk and the bishop proposed a low price for the property. Dacus received his wife's consent to sell the estate, but in the morning with the clearing of the mist in his swollen head he attempted to obtain a release from the hasty agreement he had made. Ætheric pleaded his case to King Cnut emphasizing the wife's consent: the king upheld the agreement.

39. See Sawyer 1459.

40. See Æthelberht 78, 81; Ine 57; and VI Athelstan 1 for the division of family property.

41. For a discussion of the nature of Anglo-Saxon wills, see Hazeltine's introduction to *Anglo-Saxon Wills*, Whitelock ed., pp. vii–xl. But cf., John, *Land Tenure*, pp. 168–77. See also, the preceding chapter in this volume.

42. Sawyer 1500.

43. See Sawyer 1514 whereby Dunn gave his title deed to his wife but stipulated that it was to be turned over to St. Andrew at Rochester after her death.

44. Æthelberht 78: "If she bears a living child, she shall have half the goods left by her husband, if he dies first."

45. For example, Sawyer 1461 states: "Here is declared in this document the agreement which Godwin made with Brihtric when he wooed his daughter. In the first place he gave her a pound's weight of gold, to induce her to accept his suit, and he granted her the estate at Street with all that belongs to it, and 150 acres at Burmarsh and in addition 30 oxen and 20 cows and 10 horses and 10 slaves."

46. Sawyer 1500.

47. Anglo-Saxons queens were certainly an exception to the rule. It is recorded in the E-version of the *ASC sub anno* 1003 that "Hugh, the French fellow, whom the Lady [Emma] had appointed as her reeve" was responsible for the Danish host laying waste to the area round Exeter. Exeter was probably part of Emma's lands which she received on marrying Æthelred. If we can trust Gaimar, a notably late source (Gaimar, *L'estoire des Engleis*, p. 131), Emma was given Rockingham and Rutland with Winchester upon her marriage in 1002. (We also know that Winchester was part of the dower of Queen Edith [*Carmen de Hastingae Proelio*, pp. 40–41] and this might be the reason which lies behind the Confessor's survey of royal burgal property in that city in the 1050s.) It is perhaps equally crucial in determining the extent of landed estates held by the queen in the early eleventh century that Queen Edith held extensive manors in Rutland T.R.E. (*DB*, 1: 219, 292b). These great women undoubtedly held and controlled their own lands. It cannot be said that the history of Anglo-Saxon queenship has been written. Such a work would be extremely valuable for Anglo-Saxon studies.

48. For example, see Sawyer 1485, 1487.

49. II Cnut 73a. The continuation of Old English custom into the Anglo-Norman period is evident from a passage in Domesday Book in which we read: "And after King William came into this land Bishop Ailmer seized it [Plumstead] for a forfeiture, because a woman who held it married within a year of her husband's death" (*DB*, 1: 199). An unmarried or widowed woman who possessed large estates by bookright had much to offer a prospective husband. Perhaps Cnut's law can be viewed as positive legislation designed to protect women from ambitious guardians and suitors trafficking in rich heiresses. However, the evidence is too slim to substantiate the claim. But there were wealthy heiresses, like Æthelgifu, whose considerable holdings must have attracted ambitious men. For Æthelgifu's will, see Sawyer 1497, which is thoroughly discussed in Whitelock et al. *The Will of Æthelgifu.*

50. Sawyer 1459.

51. A study of marriage alliances for both the royal house and the aristocracy has never been made for the Anglo-Saxon period. Is marriage to be seen as useful in providing heirs, or useful in that it can be employed in dynastic associations?

52. See Sawyer 1458.

53. See Sawyer 1236, 1486.

54. Sawyer 1280. Ælfwyn was the daughter of Ealdorman Æthelred and Æthelflæd, Lady of the Mercians, who was "deprived of all authority in Mercia: she was taken to Wessex three weeks before Christmas." (*ASC sub anno* 919).

55. Sawyer 1485: "Then to my wife Ælswith, if she live longer than I and maintains the property in accordance with the confidence I have in her, ... she is to possess the estate at Batcombe for her time and after her death it is to pass into the possession of our son Ælfweard if he is still alive."

56. Sawyer 128.

57. Sawyer 100, 128, 458, 462, 561, etc.

58. Sawyer 1187, 1221, 1503, 1525, 1529, 1536, etc.

59. Sawyer 1187.

60. "And all widows who lead a respectable life shall enjoy the special protection of God and of the king."

61. See also Æthelberht 75, 76; and Ine 38. For a discussion of the legal position of widows see Rivers, "Widow's Rights in Anglo-Saxon Law."

62. Sawyer 310. This charter is spurious, but perhaps embodies a genuine tradition of Frithgyth's donation.

63. Complete charters do not exist for Ælfswith's donations, but they are recorded in *Index Chartarum, I*, a list of the contents of a lost Glastonbury cartulary which was printed by Hearne, *Johannis ... Glastoniensis Chronica sive Historia de rebus Glastoniensibus*, and appear as Sawyer 1720, 1748, 1761, 1762.

64. See Meyer, "Women and the Tenth Century English Monastic Reform," pp. 38–45.

65. Sawyer 860.

66. Sawyer 1380.

67. Sawyer 1198. A variety of other reasons for donating land to a monastery are given in the charters. The widow Wihburh conceded one hide of land to Worcester in the mid-eleventh century as soul-scot (Sawyer 1227). Ramsey Abbey was given three estates by Ælfhild who had been granted the usufruct over the lands during her lifetime for the support of her children and herself. She made a further provision that if the community would accept her daughter's son Adnoth as a monk, they would receive an additional estate (Sawyer 1808).

68. When an estate was booked, the royal *feorm*—in Latin *pastus* or *vectigal* (Sawyer 52)—or food rents, constituted an important part of those rights inherent in the charter. What had once directly supported men of the warrior class or the king himself, now supported the cathedral or monastery and select notables of the kingdom.

69. Maitland, *Domesday Book and Beyond*, p. 379.

70. Sawyer 204: "Ego, Berchtwulf, cyning, sile Forthrede minum thegne, nigen higida lond, in Wudotune in ece erfe ... ond he salde to land ceape .XXX. mancessan, on nigen hund scil'l', with þaem londe, him in ece erfe."

71. See Sawyer 210, 448, etc.

72. Sawyer 11.

73. Sawyer 10.

74. Sawyer 270.

75. Sawyer 535. Some of the charters simply record that the estate was granted "pro ejus placabili pecunia" (Sawyer 448). Others, like Sawyer 535, do list a specified sum to be paid (Sawyer 534, 563, etc.).

76. Sawyer 806, but the charter cannot be accepted as totally authentic.

77. For gifts to queens involving land transactions see D. Whitelock, et. al., *The Will of Æthelgifu*, pp. 20–21.

78. In the Anglo-Saxon wills, the heriot took the place of the *land-ceap*. The widow was required by law (II Cnut 70) to pay her deceased husband's heriot to his lord. This perhaps accounts in part for the twelve-month delay before a widow could legally remarry (V Æthelred 21 : 1; and II Cnut 73).

79. Æthelred's law is reiterated in II Cnut 81.

80. The written word was mysterious to the Anglo-Saxons, and the holy anathemas and testimony of bishops and other great men, secular and ecclesiastic, further substantiated the claim that a written contract was far better than simple oral testimony. Not many accounts of sale and purchase survive, probably because a royal charter was issued in subsequent years to the buyer or to his heir, but the few that do remain indicate that a written instrument was often desirable and necessary. As recorded in an interpolated charter written shortly before 883, a minister of King Burgred bought an estate at Marlcliff in Cleve Prior, Worcestershire, for "mille siclis." After his death it was arranged that his wife was to receive the land for her support. Cuthulf, a kinsman of Burgred's minster, purchased the estate from the woman (also demonstrating that it was in her power to sell it) because she wanted to make a pilgrimage to Rome. Æthelred, ealdorman of Mercia, ordered the transaction reduced to writing so that Cuthulf could enjoy the land and bequeath it to his heirs without the interference of any one (Sawyer 222). In this way, any claims arising from the woman's kin-group could be defeated easily.

81. Sawyer 866. The estate was subsequently granted to Glastonbury by King Æthelred in 987, as related in the charter. How Æthelred could grant an estate that Ælfswith had earlier purchased is not clear, but perhaps he simply confirmed her own gift to the abbey.

82. Sawyer 1177.
83. "mile quingentis solidis argenti et auri vel quindecies centum siclis" (Sawyer 1201).
84. Although this writ of the Confessor (Sawyer 1029) is of doubtful authenticity, it probably embodies a genuine tradition of Edith's purchase.
85. Sawyer 1206.
86. In a ninth-century record of a land dispute, Ætheldryth had told a certain Oswald that an estate in Wiltshire was fully in her power to sell "forþ hit waes hire morgengifu" (Sawyer 1445).
87. For example, see Æthelred's charter, Sawyer 886.
88. Sawyer 1800. The complete Testament of Mildburg is printed and analyzed in Finberg, *The Early Charters of the West Midlands*, pp. 197–216.
89. Leobwin made over an estate at Alton valued at fifteen hides to the community of monks at Winchester, but stipulated that unless the community gives it "in return for another estate which is nearer and more convenient for them," they were never to alienate the property (Sawyer 1513). On the secular side, Wulfric Spot made an exchange of land for an estate which was more convenient to him, with the king's permission and with the witness of his advisors (Sawyer 886).
90. In the mid-eighth century there was an abbey at Tisbury (Sawyer 1256) that became part of the endowment of Shaftesbury nunnery in the tenth century. This is just one example of a West Saxon royal monastery superseding an older, extinct private monastery.
91. Sawyer 850.
92. It was often stipulated that a tenant could not forfeit his lord's property if it was held by a precarious tenure by the man. Thus, we learn in an interpolated charter that King Cnut granted an estate at Folkstone with the provision that the grantee, his priest Eadsige who had become a monk at Christ Church, Canterbury, would hand over the estate to his community after his death: "... and he cannot alienate it from the holy monastery by gift or sale or loss in a lawsuit of forfeiture" (Sawyer 981). Eadsige's tenure was not *in perpetuum*—he obtained from the king a life interest in the land to help in his support during his years as a monk. Christ Church itself held the estate as bookland; Eadsige, having only the usufruct, could not lose it because of some conflict of interest or public crime. See also Sawyer 1224, 1536.
93. "per puplicum latroncinium" (Sawyer 753).
94. See II Edmund 2 and Sawyer 926.
95. Although treason occurred constantly throughout the Anglo-Saxon period (see Sawyer 1211, 1212), many sources for the reign of Æthelred, like Wulfstan's *Sermo Lupi ad Anglos*, suggest that it had a particularly crippling effect at just that time. See Sawyer 926, 927 (a text which should be used with caution), 934, 939.
96. For *agenslaga*, see Bosworth and Toller, *An Anglo-Saxon Dictionary*, Suppl., p. 29, and Robertson, *Anglo-Saxon Charters*, p. 338.
97. See Sawyer 254, 443, 753, 886.
98. Sawyer 1457. Rochester held Bromleah, Kent in 1066 for six solins, but with land for thirteen ploughs (*DB*, 1: 5b). Snodland, Kent was also held by the cathedral for six solins (*DB*, 1: 5b). This dispute is discussed at some length by Whitelock, *Anglo-Saxon Wills*, pp. 128–29.
99. See Ine 57 and II Athelstan 6.
100. Sawyer 1377.
101. The OE "men," translated by Robertson as Mod. (E) "men" in her edition and translation of the later Anglo-Saxon laws (*The Laws of the King of England from Edmund to Henry I*, p. 55), should be rendered "those" to eliminate the false impression of sexual bias on behalf of Æthelred's law makers.
102. This law of Æthelred, ultimately based on the seventh-century Ine 6, provided the foundation for II Cnut 13:1 which states "if he has land held by title-deed, it shall be forfeited into the hands of the king without regard to the question of whose man he is."
103. The dispute over Cooling is discussed by Harmer, *Select English Historical Documents*, no. 23.

104. The evidence for the activity of women in litigation is not always consistent: Queen Eadgifu defended her claim in court, Queen Edith requested a shire court to pronounce a judgment concerning a certain Wudumann to whom she had entrusted her horses and who had witheld her rent (Sawyer 1241), and Abbess Eadgifu gave sureties along with Abbot Leofric to preserve the concord between their two communities (Sawyer 1452). But at the same time, a certain woman sent her brother-in-law, Thurkill the White, as her advocate into court when she reaffirmed that her son Edwin had been disinherited (Sawyer 1462). Thurkill's wife's name was Leofflæd. They had many estates in Hereford at the time of the conquest in 1066 along with her brother Leofwine. Wellington was in Thurkill's possession in 1066 and was held by Hugh the Ass in 1086 (*DB*, 1: 187). Cradley, the other estate mentioned in the dispute, belonged to the canons of Hereford in 1086 (*DB*, 1: 182). Women appear in the hundred and shire court records as sureties, witnesses and oath-helpers, and initiators of judicial procedure. And well over two hundred signatures of women (although most of them were queens' attestations) appear in the witness lists of the charters. But the fact remains that by and large women were dependent on male guardians to fight a suit or defend a claim to family land. See Sawyer 1442, 1452, 1454, 1457, 1458, 1462.

105. Power, "The Position of Women," p. 401. (Power's article has recently been made into a very readable survey of women in the middle ages, Power, *Medieval Women*, ed. by Postan [Cambridge: 1975].)

106. This figure does not include those charters issued to religious communities for women or double monasteries, but only reflects the charter activity related to individual women.

# BIBLIOGRAPHY

BETHELL, DENIS. "The Lives of St. Osyth of Essex and St. Osyth of Aylesbury." *Analacta Bollandiana* 88 (1970): 75–127.

BIRCH, WALTER DE GRAY, ed. *Cartularium Saxonicum*. 1885–99. Reprint (3 vols. and index). New York: 1964.

BOEHLER, M. *Die Altenglischen Frauennamen*. Germanische Studien 98. Berlin: 1931.

BROOKS, NICHOLAS. "Anglo-Saxon Charters: The Work of the Last Twenty Years," in *Anglo-Saxon England 3*, edited by Peter Clemoes, pp. 211–31. Cambridge: 1974.

BRUCKNER, A., and MARICHAL, R., eds. *Chartae Latinae Antiquiores, Part III*, British Museum, London. Olten: 1954.

———. "Zur Diplomatik der älteren angelsächsischen Urkunden." *Archivalische Zeitschrift* 61 (1965): 11–45.

CAMPBELL, ALISTAIR, ed. *The Charters of Rochester*. London: 1973.

———, ed. *Encomium Emmae Reginae*. Camden Society, 3rd series, vol. 72. London: 1949.

CAMPBELL, MILES W. "Queen Emma and Ælfgifu of Northampton: Canute the Great's Women." *Mediaeval Scandinavia* 4 (1971): 66–79.

*The Carmen de Hastingae Proelio of Guy Bishop of Amiens*. Edited by Catherine Morton and Hope Muntz. Oxford: 1972.

CARNICELLI, T. A., ed. *King Alfred's Version of St. Augustine's Soliloquies.* Cambridge, Mass.: 1969.

CHAPLAIS, PIERRE. "The Origin and Authenticity of the Royal Anglo-Saxon Diploma." *Journal of the Society of Archivists* 3 (1965–69): 48–61.

———. "Some Early Anglo-Saxon Diplomas on Single Sheets: Originals or Copies?" *Journal of the Society of Archivists* 3 (1965–69): 315–36.

———. "Who Introduced Charters into England? The Case for Augustine." *Journal of the Society of Archivists* 3 (1965–69): 526–42.

*Chronicon Abbatiae Rameseiensis.* Edited by William D. Macray. Rolls Series. London: 1886.

CRONNE, H. A. "Charter Scholarship in England." *Brimingham University Historical Journal* 8 (1961): 26–61.

CUTLER, KENNETH E. "Edith, Queen of England, 1045–1066." *Mediaeval Studies* 35 (1973): 222–31.

EARLE, JOHN, ed. *A Hand-Book to the Land Charters, and Other Saxonic Documents.* Oxford: 1888.

FEILITZEN, O. von. *The Pre-Conquest Personal Names of Domesday Book.* Uppsala: 1937.

FINBERG, H. P. R. *The Early Charters of Devon and Cornwall.* Dept. of English Local History, occasional paper no. 2. Leicester: 1953.

———. *The Early Charters of the West Midlands.* Leicester: 1961.

———. *The Early Charters of Wessex.* Leicester: 1964.

FINN, R. WELLDON. *An Introduction to Domesday Book.* London: 1963.

———. *The Norman Conquest and Its Effects on the Economy: 1066–1086.* London: 1971.

———, Darby, H. C., et al. *The Domesday Geography of England.* Cambridge: 1977.

GAIMAR, GEOFFROY. *L'estoire des Engleis.* Edited by Alexander Bell. Anglo-Norman Text Society, 1960. Reprint. New York: 1971.

HARMER, F. E. "Anglo-Saxon Charters and the Historian." *Bulletin of the John Rylands Library* 22 (1938): 339–67.

———, ed. and trans. *Anglo-Saxon Writs.* Manchester: 1952.

———, ed. and trans. *Select English Historical Documents of the Ninth and Tenth Centuries.* Cambridge: 1914.

HART, CYRIL R. *The Early Charters of Eastern England.* Leicester: 1966.

———. *The Early Charters of Essex.* Dept. of English Local History, occasional paper no. 10 (rev. ed.). Leicester: 1971.

———. *The Early Charters of Northern England and the North Midlands.* Leicester: 1975.

———. "Two Queens of England." *The Ampleforth Journal* 82, pt. 2 (1977): 10–15, 54.

HARVEY, SALLY. "Domesday Book and Its Predecessors." *English Historical Review* 86 (1971): 753–73.

HEARNE, T., ed. *Johannis ... Glastoniensis Chronica sive Historia de rebus Glastoniensibus.* 2 vols. Oxford: 1726.

JOHN, ERIC. *Land Tenure in Early England.* Leicester: 1960.

———. *Orbis Britanniae and Other Studies.* Leicester: 1966.

KEMBLE, J. M., ed. *Codex Diplomaticus Aevi Saxonici.* 1839–48. Reprint (6 vols.). Vaduz: 1964.

KEYNES, SIMON. "The Diplomas of King Æthelred II." Ph.D. dissertation, Trinity College, Cambridge, 1977.

LANCASTER, LORRAINE. "Kinship in Anglo-Saxon Society." *British Journal of Sociology* 9 (1958): 230–50, 359–77. Reprinted in part in *Early Medieval Society,* edited by Sylvia L. Thrupp, pp. 17–41. New York: 1967.

LEVY, ERNST. *West Roman Vulgar Law: The Law of Property.* Memoirs of the American Philosophical Society, vol. 29. Philadelphia: 1951.

London. British Library, MS Lansdowne 436 "Vita Sanctae Ethelfledae" (*BHL* 2471).

LOWE, E. A., ed. *Codices Latini Antiquiores, ii, Great Britain and Ireland.* Oxford: 1935.

MAITLAND, F. W. *Domesday Book and Beyond.* 1897. Reprint, The Fontana Library, 1961.

MEYER, MARC ANTHONY. "The Greater Royal Nunneries of Wessex: A Brief Introduction to the History of Anglo-Saxon Nunneries and Nuns together with a Detailed Description of Their Lands and Landholding and an Edition of the (Lansdowne) Life of St. Ethelfleda and St. Merwynna." M. Phil. dissertation, University College Dublin, 1975.

————. "Women and the Tenth Century English Monastic Reform." *Revue Bénédictine* 87, nos. 1–2 (1977): 34–61.

MORRIS, JOHN, gen. ed. *Domesday Book.* In progress, Chichester: 1976.

NAPIER, A. S., and STEVENSON, W. H., eds. *The Crawford Collection of Early Charters and Documents now in the Bodleian Library.* Oxford: 1895.

POWER, EILEEN. *Medieval Women.* Edited by M.M. Postan. Cambridge: 1975.

————, "The Position of Women." In *The Legacy of the Middle Ages,* edited by C. G. Crump and E. F. Jacob, pp. 401–33. Oxford: 1926.

PUGH, RALPH B. *The Victoria History of the Counties of England, General Introduction.* London: 1970.

RIVERS, THEODORE J. "Widows' Rights in Anglo-Saxon Law." *American Journal of Legal History* 19 (1975): 208–15.

ROBERTSON, A. J., ed. and trans. *Anglo-Saxon Charters.* 2nd ed. Cambridge Studies in English Legal History, edited by H. A. Holland. Cambridge: 1956.

————, ed. and trans. *The Laws of the King of England from Edmund to Henry I.* Cambridge: 1925.

SAWYER, P. H., ed. *Anglo-Saxon Charters: An Annotated List and Bibliography.* London: 1968.

SEARLE, W. G., ed. *Onomasticon Anglo-Saxonicum: A List of Anglo-Saxon Proper Names from the Time of Beda to That of King John.* Cambridge: 1897.

STENTON, F. M. "The Historical Bearing of Place-Name Studies: The Place of Women in Anglo-Saxon Society." *Transactions of the Royal Historical Society* 4th series, 25 (1943): 1–13. Reprinted in *Preparatory to Anglo-Saxon England: Being the Collected Papers of Frank Merry Stenton,* edited by Doris Mary Stenton, pp. 314–24. Oxford: 1970.

————. *The Latin Charters of the Anglo-Saxon Period.* Oxford: 1955.

————. "The Thriving of the Anglo-Saxon Ceorl." In *Preparatory to Anglo-Saxon England: Being the Collected Papers of Frank Merry Stenton,* edited by Doris Mary Stenton, pp. 383–93. Oxford: 1970.

STEVENSON, W. H. "Trinoda Necessitas." *English Historical Review* 29 (1914): 689–703.

WAINWRIGHT, F. T. "Æthelflæd, Lady of the Mercians." In *The Anglo-Saxons: Studies in Some Aspects of Their History and Culture Presented to Bruce Dickins,* edited by Peter Clemoes, pp. 53–69. London: 1959. Reprinted in *Scandinavian England: Collected Papers of F. T. Wainwright,* edited by H. P. R. Finberg, pp. 305–24. Chichester: 1975.

WHITELOCK, DOROTHY, ed. and trans. *Anglo-Saxon Wills.* Cambridge Studies in English Legal History, edited by H. D. Hazeltine. Cambridge: 1930.

————, et al., ed. and trans. *The Will of Æthelgifu: A Tenth-Century Anglo-Saxon Manuscript*. Printed for the Roxburghe Club. Oxford: 1968.

WILMART, DOM ANDRE. "La Legende de Ste Edith en prose et vers par le moine Goscelin," *Analecta Bolandiana* 56 (1938): 5–101, 267–303.

YOUNG, ARTHUR. "Anglo-Saxon Family Law." In *Essays in Anglo-Saxon Law*, edited by Henry Adams, pp. 121–82. Boston: 1876.

# Women

# in Norman and Plantagenet England

## KATHLEEN CASEY

The lives of all women in England between the Norman conquest in 1066 and the death in 1399 of Richard II represent conflicts common to all of Europe at this time. Yet in England, the grinding edges of descending feudal and ascending capitalistic formations cut unusual patterns. The generations on which this survey will focus lived through the passage from a Saxon to a Norman, and thence to a modern English society, fittingly equipped with a recognizably English language. Within the context of what is often regarded as a general attrition of women's rights, accompanying the transition from a feudal to a modern political economy,[1] the experience of Englishwomen may have been no better or worse than that of women in the rest of Europe, but it was peculiar, and its peculiarities are inexplicable except as part of a political experiment that proved to be both ephemeral and unique.

Between the tenth and the fifteenth centuries, the British Isles were neither an effective nor an obvious unity. A far-flung and freewheeling Scandinavian enterprise encircling the entire subcontinent drew into its orbit the islands' outer fringes and the northern and western regions. Of women in these parts we still can say very little. The rest of Britain was involved with the Continent in two different ways. Broad ties of kin, trade, and piety bound East Anglia, England's then most populous region, to

Flanders and the mouths of the Scheldt and Rhine in something resembl-
ing a colonial embrace. By the end of the twelfth century, still another
"England" was forming, which comprised much of the middle and south
of the main island, along with extensive lands across the Channel, and
looked like nothing so much as a new France.

This political experiment was constrained by a series of circumstances: by its own intrinsic features, by geography, by population, and
also by certain interactions of the female life cycle with an evolving
domestic ethic suiting special political needs. That is, changing aspirations
over the life course of certain women could clash or mesh with emerging
beliefs about the quality of domestic relations in such a way as to affect
other social solidarities. In this sense, some aspects of the role of virtually
all women constituted a political experience, although they themselves
were formally excluded from the political arena. Political activity, then,
will not be treated as a separate category in this survey. After a summary of
fundamental studies to provide background, the main dimensions of
experience touched upon will comprise: work, life and death, family and
domesticity, and the unmarried state. These facets of the female role
illuminate a concluding review of the cult of love in England, and of the
"marriage debate" in the age of Chaucer.

Of these topics, the first two deal with the medieval terms of survival:
occupations and training at all social levels and in both lay and religious
communities; the problem of an unbalanced sex ratio; vital statistics,
health, midwifery and sexuality; religious beliefs and institutions as these
concretely affected women's training and personality. As far as possible,
the emphasis will be on the largest and lowest of the status groups,
although most research, to date, has had to concern itself with the one or
two percent of the population at the apex of the social pyramid and, to
some degree, with its intermediate, usually urban segments.

The next two sections deal with the limits to female autonomy in
dealings between individuals, small groups, and a wider society. Marriage,
in the middle ages, served as a theological allegory and a form of birth
control. For lawyers and the religious it was a pious aspiration; for most
people, it was only just beginning to carry the sense of personal union that
now seems so fundamental to the arrangement. Of lesser impact than kin,
family, or religion, conjugal bonds came nevertheless to offer both
reinforcement and resistance to England's political experiments—a context in which the problems of clerical celibacy, heresy, and witchcraft also
are seen. The law of marriage and its ramifications are treated in Kittel's
chapter in this volume. My discussions of the pair-bond occur either in the
earlier sections on fertility and sexuality or later on, in terms of sexual
ideology. The account of women in families shows an emerging concept of

conjugal solidarity and domestic harmony beginning to alter the way in which families hitherto had interacted with the broader political society.

Ideologies of love and womanhood, in the final segment, turn a spotlight on the strife, both actual and literary, generated by the "conjugal debt" in all its forms at a time when at least three major languages heightened class or status differences between Englishwomen and their styles of domesticity. As vernacular cultures elsewhere solidified regional patterns, English society was slower to erase the deep divisions accented by three distinct modes of discourse.

For the sake of continuity, some digressions into the fifteenth century will at times be necessary. However, the concerns of fifteenth-century Englishwomen are not fully covered here. Already they were helping to shape the long prelude to Tudor-Stuart rule, with its distinctively English tradition and unmistakably English language. In the main, works cited will refer to the four centuries during which Anglo-Norman, Angevin, and later Plantagenet rulers did their best to straddle the Channel. Their fragile society burdened women of all classes in England with tensions above and beyond those induced throughout Europe by the complex and uneven transition to modernity.

Parenthetically, it must be stressed that many of the titles cited have been included not because they meet the highest conventional standards of medieval scholarship but because, for the time being, nothing else is available. To this extent, bibliographical comment calls for unusually heavy reliance upon the writer's own connective web of analysis and interpretation. Its task is both to explain and to compensate for the real dearth of secondary writings in the field, especially in the neglected area of economic life.

A guide to the general framework of the female experience in its medieval mutations is "Medieval Women: A Working Bibliography," by Erickson and Casey. In what follows, those of its titles will be cited whose specific focus is England, as well as certain others which seem fundamental. Many of those which for reasons of space and time did not find their way into that earlier compilation are now added.[2] For the most part, the emphasis is laid on secondary sources. It is these, rather than primary works, which are shortest in supply and least well known. While it is usually more common for historians to be overwhelmed by secondary rather than primary sources, those embarking on the study of medieval women face rather the reverse problem. It is hardly an exaggeration to say that nothing less, now, than a complete reevaluation of the entire corpus of medieval sources is needed to redress the balance created by neglect and misinterpretation. It is not the business of this survey to recapitulate the contents of that corpus. Instead, the overview provides avenues of approach to it, by recommending works whose notes and bibliographies point the way, and by suggesting the questions which should now be addressed to the old, familiar material long in print, as well as to untapped reserves of less accessible records.

Certain older works remain an indispensable starting point for any new survey: Hill's *Women in English Life*, vol. 1 (1896); Abram's *English Life in the Later Middle Ages* (1913); Wright's *History of Domestic Manners* (1862), as well as his *Homes of Other Days* (1871); and successive editions of certain texts and source collections by Coulton, notably *Medieval Panorama* (1938).[3] Their simple enumeration of detail about daily life may look uninviting, and their categories often obscure the structural links many of us now seek. Still, the connections between production, reproduction, acculturation, and the nexus of family life in which all these meet are indeed present, awaiting synthesis.

A more integrated view of the relation of institutional to economic and family life is apparent in the work of a succeeding generation of scholars. Some of Eileen Power's previously unpublished lectures have been posthumously edited by Postan and resourcefully illustrated, in *Medieval Women* (1975).[4] In *The English Woman in History* (1957), Doris Stenton dealt still more systematically with the pronounced differences between status groups while noting their common freedom to maneuver within formal cultural and legal restrictions. But all past work has encountered difficulties in making sense of the medieval material. Analytical techniques that advance beyond the citing of individual cases with contradictory features have lately found their way into specialized articles,[5] probing and disputing Stenton's hypothesis that the medieval Englishwoman's informal freedoms were eroded over time by new political and economic tendencies. Unhappily, few of these new studies relate to England, and they are in any case restricted in scope. Stenton's survey remains, to date, the strongest basic text available.


## WOMEN'S WORK

Economic relations were not dominant at this time in the same way as they are under a modern system of contractual waged labor. In feudal society a small, landed, warrior elite ruled a mass of cultivators who, unlike slaves, were the possessors in fact of the means of production, although their labor still could be coerced in a variety of ways, from force through law and custom to thought and feeling, all of which can more easily be thought of as political than as purely economic pressures. Nor were urban and rural life sharply distinct. Productivity was low and the division of work rudimentary, but from the millenium to some point around 1300 a determined assault on swamp and forest by and large favored both lord and peasant, as well as the scattered town-dwellers. Thereafter, the efficiency of feudal organization in its economic aspect is more in doubt. An agrarian crisis engulfing most of Europe between approximately 1320 and 1440 provoked or hastened the system's demise. By this time, more cultivators than ever before, of either sex, were supporting themselves mainly by a daily wage.

## Women in the Agrarian Work Force

In this predominantly agrarian economy, women provided at least half of the labor power. The female peasant has been cursorily described in the general studies, and some notion of her role in English village life may be had from works on customary law (see Kittel's chapter in this volume). As a major segment of the labor force, however, rural women have not been systematically or separately studied. Their productivity and their rewards remain virtually unknown; their part in the unending contest for advantage between lord and serf has attracted scant attention;[6] their contribution to the collapse of serfdom has not been evaluated.

Hindsight at least has revealed the permanence of the really fundamental shift, first apparent in the fourteenth century, creating some of the basic conditions for the modern "family wage." The earliest stages of this trend have not been documented, but its outlines have been sketched in Casey's "Cheshire Cat" and are confirmed in Hilton's chapter on "Women in the Village," in his *English Peasantry* (1975). The better-paying among seasonal occupations, such as reaping, fell to men, while the lowlier chores continued to be shared by both sexes, at the same equally low customary rates as before. Further evidence of this inexorable trend to differential rewards for the more marketable, and not just the higher, skills can be pulled out of Putnam's *Enforcement of the Statutes of Laborers* (1908), although no one has yet taken the time to do so. It seems significant, too, that women are conspicuously absent from the recorded scenes of the Peasants' Revolt of 1381 in eastern England, as if the conditions of waged labor that were driving up the expectations of men had no such effect on rural women.[7]

## Urban Occupations

The headstrong little towns of England could not yet muster the sophistication of their continental counterparts and it would be misleading to take as typical the experience of Englishwomen in characteristically urban occupations. What this does serve to uncover is the antagonism between women's economic potential and the legal superstructure of Anglo-Norman bureaucracy. Latent conflict was located not so much in the division of labor as in the marriage bond, a relation crucial to every aspect of the conjunction of women's lives and politics in the English middle ages. The reasons are complex, augmenting the difficulties inherent in approaching a topic about which little, so far, has been published.

First, the distinction between production and reproduction, an issue of much importance for the history of women's exploitation in the late modern period, should be recognized. But for the middle ages it must be redrawn. Most of what both sexes labored to produce was not for exchange, but for domestic use. It is valid in either case to distinguish between processing food and goods so that people may be daily restored to their functions, and the way in which those people are all replaced, generation by generation.[8] In this period, however, there appears hardly any difference between daily services and the actual production of food and goods. It is, then, to the narrow sphere most closely approaching modern employment conditions that we must look to see precisely how women's work differed from that of men: the guilds and trades.

Guild records, like manorial and other agrarian records, yield only fragmentary evidence. Almost always the sources listed deal only with the last two centuries of the middle ages. We remain in the dark about women at work before the emergence of production wherein money as capital, rather than as a simple means of exchange, took on its new and special role in the relation of land to people. Studies of women's part in organizing trade and manufacture, or of their cooperation in the workplace are rare for England: Abram's "Women Traders" (1916) and Dale's "London Silkwomen" (1933). Heaton devotes a few invaluable pages of *The Yorkshire Woolen Industry* (1920) to guildswomen.[9] But many useful details can still be gleaned from Hill's chapter on "Women in the Ancient Gilds" in *Women in English Life* (1896), and from a short section in Abram's *English Life* (1913).

Although not specifically directed to the English scene, Sister Maria Pia's account of "The Industrial Position of Women in the Middle Ages" (1925) helps put the scattered English material into perspective. If the breakup of the guilds later on threw large numbers of women into the rank and file of wage labor,[10] their earlier advantages should not be over-estimated, especially in England. The scale of medieval industry was not such that it could greatly affect the quality of life for most women. They were employed to a much lesser extent in any kind of manufacture than they were later, under the early modern "domestic" textile or "putting out" system. In retrospect, the existing studies as well as the sources reveal a need to make certain crucial distinctions that dim the nostalgic glow in which women workers of the medieval past so often appear.

The distinction between a right and a privilege can be confusing, but rightly understood, it dissolves much of the incongruity between women's high visibility in medieval economic life and their subordinate status in law, theology and literature. Smith's *English Gilds* (1870) lets the ordinances themselves show that religious and social guilds for urban workers, guilds in which women certainly functioned in almost every respect as full members, as of right,[11] must be kept distinct from occupation guilds proper, in which women's participation was often restricted in principle even while conceded as a privilege. Likewise, the exclusively female guilds (or those in which women dominated) ought not to be directly compared with those which simply allowed the widow of a master to carry on his work and membership, while in theory restricting the guild to males.[12]

Making work rules, and ultimately shaping the direction of family capital concentration, was the prerogative of those exercising a right, not simply a privilege. On the other hand, the all-woman guilds are the really interesting site of conflict. They highlight particular power situations wherein a right may, after all, be less valuable than a personal privilege: a classic example of the not uncommon primacy of sexual over economic relations.

Next, when the production of food, clothing, and household goods is judiciously separated from other kinds of manufacture, the wider range of "women's work" in the middle ages can be appreciated without losing sight of the fact that if such work then included carpentry, for example, work of that sort did not always confer an economic advantage. Higher pay for one sex rather than the other did not begin to conform to cultural patterns of sex-segregated labor until purely customary ceilings on wages and prices were removed. Some forms of production had long been more highly valued than others, but they were not consistently tied to the sexual division of labor. Baking, candlemaking or matmaking may, or may not, have been as profitable as brewing or the sale of spices—but all of these were as much "women's work" as carpentry could be. Here, economic relations were paramount, not gender patterns.[13]

Finally, the simple difference between employer and employed is compounded when the distinct consequences of production proper, on the one hand, and the trading of products, on the other, is taken into account.[14] The female entrepreneur, even in an all-woman guild, often was also the wife of a master in a related craft that subsumed and sometimes marketed her own product. Ultimate control over the market, at either end of the productive process, or over the recruitment of apprentices that decreed the future shape of the labor force, almost always lay with someone else—usually a husband, father, or brother. In the long run it would be the flexibility of the conjugal bond, and its responsiveness to personal pressure, that would adjust the relation between right and privilege in any given economic situation.[15]

## THE WOMAN TRADER

The status of the woman trader, then, is conceptually crucial. The foregoing digression is intended as a guide to using one of the most enlightening and easily available primary sources on the urban woman worker: Bateson's *Borough Customs* (1904). Most of the English statutes and ordinances collected in volume 2, like all of those in volume 1, concern only the legal relation between husband and wife. Its details, peculiar to Anglo-Norman common law and governing women's control over property, will not be explained here. Of interest, instead, are the statutory applications cited by Bateson that reflect women's situation in trading and production.[16]

The reasons for Anglo-Norman law's continued toleration of that Roman law anomaly, the *mulier mercatrix*, or woman trader, become clear. Women seem to have been at once too weak a threat to be entirely thwarted, and too great a menace, in another way, to leave entirely unregulated. Too many couples engaged in the same general line of work belonged separately to distinct craft societies, governing activities in latent conflict, and wives were potentially more than just family agents.[17] On the one hand, then, a simple trader was less able than a producer who also traded, to organize work and profitability. On the other hand, intricate marital relations that connected male and female guilds called for careful definition of the obligations of each spouse for the other's commercial debts. So Anglo-Norman lawyers allowed some scope for the woman trader, but not much.

## HOUSEHOLD MANAGEMENT IN THE FEUDAL RANKS

Working for a wage was neither the only, nor the dominant way of using labor power in this period. Much of its material as well as its intellectual production, at all social levels, was intended for use by the producer's family. In any domestic group, lay or monastic, throughout the long transition to industrial society, the key to survival remained in the hands of women, waged and unwaged, not only in urban dwellings and rural hovels, but in courts, castles and convents that were centers of political as well as economic power in feudal society. For enlightenment on the confusing role of women in its complex structures, Putnam's *The Lady* (1910) and the more recent *Baronial Household in the Thirteenth Century* (1965) by Labarge are fundamental. Power's *Medieval English Nunneries* (1922) is an exhaustive structural account of their monastic counterparts.

Ironically, the contribution of the feudal lady or abbess to her domestic group has been less appreciated from this point of view than that of the nonnoble urban or rural housewife. Historians have been dazzled by the lady's considerable exercise *de facto* of quasi-political and juridical feudal powers in theory denied her. But the power to hold court, to tax, and to wage war accrued to anyone whose tenure of land was of the honorable rather than the servile kind. These, the political aspects of feudalism, are the opposite of sex specific. The noblewoman's equally impressive, certainly sex specific and even more essentially productive domestic administration was stressed long ago by Putnam, and her insightful early work can now be profitably supplemented by two more recent studies. Labarge has imaginatively used the Montfort household accounts for *A Baronial Household*, constructing a more sophisticated social history than that of Abram despite a roughly similar organization of material. *The Household Book of Queen Isabella* (1971), edited by Blackley and Hermans, affords an opportunity to study the details of a particularly exalted lady's personal administration, and to note, among other things, its heavy dependence upon male servants.

Ambiguities in the lady's status, implicit in the evidence presented by Stenton, no less than offered by these more specialized studies, may perhaps be resolved in their terms. Labarge's discussion of "domestic space," elaborating on that of Putnam,[18] suggests why the lady enjoyed no net advantage. A household, even a comparatively well-appointed one, constantly in the process of rearrangement at someone else's pleasure, diminished her effective control over concerns wider than the household itself. If, for example, the hospitality frequently dispensed to female relatives and friends had also to serve a political purpose, we have yet to discover how often such purposes were the lady's own.

### SKILLS, TRAINING, AND DEVELOPMENT

Like the common woman, the lady herself, whether lay or religious, had to appear busy even while at leisure, employed at tasks calling for manual dexterity in a society that did not highly value them. Harris and Nochlin's *Women Artists* (1976) makes good use of Christie's *English Medieval Embroidery* (1938) in an effort to reassess the female contribution. Christie lists attributions actually preserved. In general, though, the creators of the famed *opus anglicum*, embroidered copes and wall hangings that rendered an essential service, could no more than other medieval artisans receive recognition as major artists, despite the scale of their work and its technique: lines of close stitching that followed the contours of face and drapery like the strokes of a brush.[19]

Other skills were more fatefully denied their logical fulfillment. Most education at this time was more a matter of discipline and moral example than mental development,[20] but the education of highborn women called for some degree of literacy. And in England, command of more than one language was necessary. Yet Orme's recent *English Schools in the Middle Ages* (1973) as well as Gardiner's earlier *English Girlhood at School* (1929) agree with other scholars that English education conspicuously neglected women, even those of the nobility who happened to be nuns. The vital distinction between reading and that higher level of linguistic and intellectual competence eventually flowing from manual control of a pen was formally maintained. Not surprisingly, reference to women's share in Anglo-Norman literary production is scarce indeed. The female castellan might sometimes be able to make out letters of instruction from an absent lord, or a servant's report, but like the female trader who knew how to figure, she could rarely write her name. Power's picture of *Medieval English Nunneries* shows bishops discouraging the very presence of children as pupils, and although writing, along with illumination, was still being taught to the nuns themselves, these arts seem no longer to have attained preconquest or Continental standards.[21] When innovative thought began shifting to urban centers in the twelfth century and Anglo-Norman patronage was selectively extended to the more conservative communities, English nunneries especially, among other monastic institutions, seem to have lost earlier pretensions to intellectual training.

Even those religious orders devoted to coeducation were really only interested in training people with a vocation. Sister Mary Pia Heinrich appends a near-comprehensive bibliography to her account, ending in the thirteenth century, of *The Canonesses and Education* (1924). The one indigenous English order dedicated to teaching may be pursued in Graham's *St. Gilbert of Sempringham* (1901) and Floyed's "An Extinct Religious Order" (1896).

Religious life as an alternative to marriage may very likely not have appealed as intensely or to as many women in England as seems to have been the case on the Continent. There, by the thirteenth century, women were choosing the single state in increasing numbers, creating audible concern throughout Christendom. The "woman question," as it was then perceived, debated how those prevented from following their " natural vocation" could be materially supported and morally controlled. Whether the impediments to marriage and procreation were being created by impoverishment, by resurgent piety or by an actual surplus of women is discussed, for Europe, in McDonnell's *Beguines and Beghards* (1954) and Bolton's more recent *"Mulieres Sanctae"* (1976),[22] but for England, the situation is far from clear. The nature and extent of pressures in England to expand the unmarried role or preserve the appeal of the married state can only be known or guessed insofar as the age-sex structure of English populations can be explored.[23]

## LIFE AND DEATH

The ebb and flow of life itself circumscribed options at this period even more effectively than the limits of work and resources. We are badly handicapped in all our judgments without firm figures for total populations or profiles of age and sex balance. Our estimates of life expectancy for either sex are necessarily crude and our concept of household size is ambiguous. Yet the effect of the Crusades, among other circumstances, on English society cries out to be explored along the lines followed by Herlihy in "Life Expectancies for Women in Medieval Society" (1975).

### LIFE EXPECTANCIES, THE SEX RATIO AND FAMILY SIZE

Russell's pioneering study, *British Medieval Population* (1948) suggests, among other things, that England consistently maintained a preponderance of males that would delay emergence there of the "woman question." Support for this view may be found in the exchange between Rosenthal and Hollingsworth on "Medieval Longevity: the Secular Peerage 1350–1500" (1973). McFarlane's chapters on marriage in *The Nobility* (1973) and Post's exemplary study of "The Tauke Family" (1973) illuminate the use of Cockayne's fundamental *Complete Peerage*. Raw data on family size and continuity, as these inextricably relate to the sex ratio, are encountered in unexpected places, notably Rousset's compact but valuable analysis of "La femme et la famille dans *l'Histoire ecclésiastique* d'Orderic Vital" (1969). It suggests new ways of utilizing many of the standard chronicle sources of the period.

For the peasant majority, a similar service is performed by Britton's "The Peasant Family in Fourteenth Century England" (1976), and the several studies by Raftis, Scammell and Searle dealing with peasant marriage, which are cited elsewhere. Raftis's study of the effects of the Great Plague of 1348 in "Changes in an English Village" (1967) includes useful evidence of the lesser vulnerability of women, often implied or surmised, to this particular hazard.

Reliable data may never be forthcoming. Russell's work should be supplemented by his own "Quantitative Approach to Medieval Population Change" (1964) and "Recent Advances" (1965), as well as by Wrigley's *Introduction to English Historical Demography* (1966), illuminating the inherent problems, and by special studies: Hallam's "Some 13th c. Censuses" (1958); Krause on "The Medieval Household: Large or Small?" (1957); Bean on "Plague, Population and Economic Decline in England" (1963); and Shrewsbury, *History of Bubonic Plague in the British Isles* (1970). Above all, it should be remembered that judgments as to the relation of women to property and lordship, through kindred and marriage, should bear some relation to statistical reality, however hard to come by.

## FERTILITY

Of all the vital statistics for this period, a birth rate is the most difficult to establish. Yet without some idea of it, the function of women in each status group and throughout the social apparatus as a whole cannot be fully understood. Our imperfect information does imply somewhat looser constraints on population growth up to the Black Death in 1348, and even during the weak recovery that followed, than during early modern centuries when premarital sexual activity seems to have been more firmly controlled. Crude forms of contraception were known, but the regulation of fertility was accomplished mainly by postponing marriage until the mid to late twenties, for both sexes, in the peasant majority. Although based on numerical evidence dating only from the sixteenth century, Hair's "Bridal Pregnancy" (1966) and "Bridal Pregnancy in Early Rural England Further Examined" (1970), along with Laslett and Oosterveen's "Long-Term Trends in Bastardy" (1973) provide the necessary perspective on a phenomenon still imperfectly understood.

The regime of maternity, known all too well in its personal immediacy and rigors to a medieval woman, may nowadays be construed, however roughly, in terms of its aggregate or cyclical effects upon her total environment. But these data remain incomplete without a full understanding of her sexual capacities and desires, as well as of the constraints upon them. Purely demographic data by themselves add little to our knowledge of the married pair's relations, or of women's own initiatives in releasing or suppressing a society's crucial reproductive powers.

We know that the church avoided encouraging excessive sterility even while recommending celibacy or self-control. Its teachings are surveyed by Browe in *Beiträge zur Sexualethik des Mittelalters* (1932), and in the various studies by Noonan, including *The Morality of Abortion* (1970) and *Contraception. A History of its Treatment* (1966). By and large, evidence about the dissemination of fertility lore and the practice of fertility control

94

remains to be sifted. Flandrin, examining the penitentials and other literature for evidence on "Contraception, mariage et relations amoureuses" (1969) argues that outside marriage they tended to be tolerated. Brundage argues that stable, public sexual partnerships under many guises came increasingly into favor, in "Concubinage and Marriage" (1975). Prostitution, increasingly visible during the last centuries of the middle ages, has not been reliably studied for any country. A few details on the organization of this service in England from the twelfth century are found in Bloch, *Sexual Life* (1958). The subject is important to the study of medieval fertility in that the knowledge and use of contraception and abortion are thought to have been most common among, or even exclusive to, prostitutes.[24] Nor have data yet been gathered for a study of diet and disease as crucial intervening variables in fertility, inside or outside marriage. An introduction to this topic is found in Forster and Forster, eds., *European Diet* (1975), and in Drummond and Wilbraham, *The Englishman's Food* (1939; revised by Hollingsworth, 1957).[25]

Rubin's *Medieval English Medicine* (1974) focuses on the standard views and treatments of the female reproductive system. Himes's *Medical History of Contraception* (1936) places responsibility for the prevalence of irrational methods on the church,[26] and the absence of an appropriate frame of reference even for more experimental knowledge is dealt with in O. & P. Ranum's *Popular Attitudes Toward Birth Control* (1972). The practical aspect of the ecclesiastical view of women, as well as the female culture growing up independently around birth, child care, and health can be encountered not only in Himes's work but also in Aveling's *English Midwives* (1872), and in *The Midwife and the Witch* (1966) by Forbes. Women practicing medicine in England are culled by Rubin from Power's general study of "Some Women Practitioners of Medicine in the Middle Ages" (1922).[27]

MEDIEVAL SEXUALITY: THE INDIRECT EVIDENCE

The unschooled woman of the middle ages shared with the lettered elite a far more structured view of moral and immaterial forces than do most people today. What is more, the medieval church made of sex a more public issue than it later was to become within the private family of a secularized society, and it paid as much attention to the realities of sex as to its theories on the subject. Biased and unconcerned with numbers, the abundantly documented teachings of the church actually place us in a better position to interpret our scanty demographic and economic evidence than is the case for the more recent past. We are fortunate to know as much as we do about cultural conditioning and sex-related behavior during the middle ages, despite the overwhelming tilt of the evidence toward literary sources. They let us know what people feared.

From the second century of the Christian era on, the Church Fathers who elaborated doctrine devoted a good part of their writings to the threats posed to their ideals by the facts of life. They were especially fearful of a reproductive process they could hardly ignore without causing humanity to perish. Churchmen's view of women was more defensive and ambivalent than overtly hostile, and until the thirteenth century it did not claim a "scientific" basis. But the bitterest misogynist was also the most widely read.[28] It is the responsiveness of so many people to St. Jerome and to the more malignant of the ecclesiastical views of women that really needs to be considered and explained. Erickson's chapter on "The View of Women" in her *Medieval Vision* (1976) initiates serious consideration of sexuality. Possibly the last frontier of medieval scholarship, this topic has not yet been fully related to the English context, and the following patterns of research suggest themselves from studies whose full implications for women's own sexual ethic may not at once be obvious.

PERCEPTIONS OF THE FEMALE CULTURE

Health care inevitably involved practices related to, but still distinct from others loosely and confusingly grouped under the rubric "witch-craft." Curing, but more especially intervention in fertility, came in most of Europe to be equated with diabolism and heresy, and prosecuted as such by the church and its secular arm, fearful of all thrusts for individual and illegitimate power. In England, though, the distinction between heresy and witchcraft was usually preserved, as Kelly maintains in "English Kings and the Fear of Sorcery" (1977). This and England's relative freedom from heresies of any kind meant that the female culture of remedial magic tended to develop with little interference. Even after the Continental obsession with diabolism took hold of the English, the absence of a formal inquisition meant that their accounts of witchcraft and proceedings against witches can be more reliable guides to this enigmatic area of female experience than the more dramatic Continental con-frontations. Some of the details emerge obliquely from Kelly's study, although this, like Russell's *Witchcraft in the Middle Ages* (1972), focuses on the political overtones of notable English cases, discussed below in another context. Run-of-the-mill witchcraft in England has been little explored for what it might divulge about female sexuality.[29]

Chaucer's Wife of Bath, some critics suggest, articulates what many women actually felt about sex. Others believe Dame Alys stands only for a minority clerical view of intercourse as deservedly pleasurable: Delasanta in *"Quoniam* and the Wife of Bath" (1972); Rowland in "The Wife of Bath's 'Unlawful Philtrum'" (1972); and Palomo in "The Fate of the Wife of Bath's 'Bad Husbands'" (1975). All of these uncover details of the female "subculture." In "The Wife of Bath and the Conjugal Debt" (1969), however, Cotter finds expression of a startling new version of the old Pauline doctrine: husbands only, and not wives, owe their partners sexual satisfaction.

Depictions of erotic behavior, including that of "wild" women, are collected in Randall's *Images in the Margins of Gothic Manuscripts*, and further discussed in Verdier's "Woman in the Marginalia" (1976). With possibly the least intervention of bias in a source of this kind, the English Luttrell Psalter, widely reproduced in facsimile, brings the common woman to life across the whole gamut of life and work. The clothing and fashions of the English classes, vividly expressing sexual fantasies and tension, are minutely described in the first three chapters of Baldwin's *Sumptuary Legislation* (1926).

REPRESSION AND HOSTILITY: THE LIMITS TO GROWTH

Thirteenth-century England is especially rich in the records of church administration and synodal legislation from which may be deduced the relation of theory to practice in the matter of sexual morality. For the nonspecialist, Hair's *Before the Bawdy Court* (1972) brings sexual offenders into view: unabashed, flippant, or downright defiant. In *Marriage Litigation* (1974), Helmholz lets them speak out in sizable translated excerpts from their pleas.

Circumstantial, legal, literary, and visual evidence, then, may imply that the medieval Englishwoman was not unduly inhibited. Psychic conflict and dissociation, however, are apparent, particularly in motherhood. Diatribes like *Hali Meidenhad* (Holy Maidenhood), edited by Cockayne-Furnivall may exaggerate the tribulations of maternity even in an age when it must have been a trying experience. Still, both Walker's "Widow and Ward" (1976) and Hanawalt's "Female Felon" (1976) imply for each of the major social groups a certain casualness, to say the least, toward childhood. DeMause erects this into a major theory of unhealthy personality development in "The Evolution of Childhood" (1975), although his rudimentary statistics mainly suggest that in England, child-rearing may have been modified earlier and more rapidly than elsewhere, producing an unusually wide range of practices.[30] A few of the more circumspect articles in *The History of Childhood Quarterly* probe English records of the fourteenth and fifteenth centuries for evidence of infanticide and child abuse: Kellum's "Infanticide in England" (1974) and Helmholz's "Infanticide in the Province of Canterbury" (1975).[31]

Brissaud's nightmarish study of concealed pregnancy and clandestine delivery in fourteenth- and fifteenth-century France is based on a type of record that may have no counterpart in England, so that it is hard to be sure whether or not this particularly dangerous form of sexual repression was as prevalent there as in France. "L'infanticide à la fin du moyen âge" (1972) uncovers the emotionally harmful, sometimes lethal consequences of the public shame attending those who produced irreversible proof of a private act incurring only the mildest guilt. Since infant death often resulted from concealment, concealment itself was recognized by church courts as one of the several distinct forms of infanticide. But clandestine pregnancy, unlike clandestine marriage, always flouted the interests of the propertied family. Its treatment deserves to be singled out, where possible, as an index of the control exercised over women by an authority more implacable than the church.

## FAMILY STRUCTURES AND THE CONCEPT OF DOMESTICITY

Social control over the sexual behavior of women, even those of the lowest rank, is more intricately related to the desire to maintain control over property than the more obviously political manipulations of marriage within the noble minority. This topic is most directly approached through the legal and institutional materials discussed in a subsequent chapter, along with the tensions between church and lay jurisdictions over women's property and consent. Searle's "Freedom and Marriage" (1976), on the other hand, answering Scammell's earlier "Freedom and Marriage" (1974), together with Scammell's rejoinder, "Wife-Rents and Merchet" (1976), tackle issues and structures far wider and deeper. In what may be the most technically as well as historiographically sophisticated controversy in recent medieval women's studies, these scholars dispute the general direction of, and the motivations for what may or may not have been growing control in the twelfth and thirteenth centuries over peasant marriages and dowries.[32]

The debate between Scammell and Searle illuminates the subtle distinction between material exploitation and sexual humiliation. Scammell has argued that after 1200 it seemed more desirable for even a peasant's daughter to be given formally in marriage, when land was at stake, and that this indicated higher status and increasing prospects for the twelfth-century peasant. Such reasoning nevertheless takes an instrumental view of women. Searle perceives an increasingly exploitive seigneurial reaction of which all peasants were the objects. Twelfth-century changes in the relative frequency of the marriage fine, *merchet*, and the older, customary exaction of *leyrwite*, levied for cohabitation, form the basis of the controversy as to what kind of control over female lives is involved.

Insamuch as controls involving both corporal subjection and degrees of legal freedom must at this time have tended to function increasingly as part of a total set of human relations revolving around property, the issue does not at first seem a crucial one. A rising land market could simultaneously have released some of the servile population from archaic restrictions and reduced the female serf's freedom of sexual association. But Scammell and Searle enrich a controversy fundamental to women's studies by welding it firmly to specific political and social developments—the changes wrought upon Anglo-Saxon society by Norman rule. For Searle, those setting apart the Norman generations of the eleventh century from the Angevin generations of the twelfth and early thirteenth centuries are the more fundamental. For Scammell, they differed only in degree, while Norman and Saxon societies differed in kind. In helping to resolve this issue, the study of women's place allows us to see this whole period of English history in sharper focus.

## INTRAFAMILIAL CONFLICT AND THE LIMITS OF FEMALE ASCENDANCY

Before the conquest, women's capacity to become the focus of a settlement is demonstrated by Stenton in "The Historical Bearing of Place Name Studies" (1943). He notes that more than thirty villages associated with an ancestress were still to be found in the postconquest Domesday Book. Even in the Anglo-Saxon period this phenomenon was numerically of small significance, but its total disappearance from later Norman and Angevin society reveals something of the nature of the political and institutional changes worked by experiments with state power. Painter's "The Family and the Feudal System" (1960) clarifies the limited role of women of feudal rank in a society passionately involved at all levels with land. Kelly's *Eleanor of Aquitaine and the Four Kings* (1950) and Brown's "Eleanor of Aquitaine: Parent, Queen and Duchess" (1976) describe the struggle to control children in a contest for power at the highest level.

By the fifteenth century, women of urban patriciate households, all too briefly glimpsed in Thrupp's *Merchant Class* (1948), look much more like abstractions in a marriage game than the situation in earlier centuries would allow. English kindreds, even in the pre-Norman period, no longer exclusively defined individual obligations and behavior,[33] and while kin groups still did locate the self within a descent pattern that stressed intergenerational and sibling loyalties, doubly binding women within both husband's and father's families, opportunities for self-definition, if limited, were available in the postconquest years to women inside and outside the family. Haskell's fifteenth-century "Paston Women" (1973) may look less manipulated than Thrupp's Londoners, but the generational change in sentiment epitomized by these Norfolk wives of the middling sort only brought them closer to an idealized, private domesticity barely known in the semiprivate and more flexible Anglo-Norman family.

## THE BALANCE OF HOUSEHOLD POWER IN POLITICS: SUGGESTED PATTERNS

The life cycle of women within families may have had a formative effect on politics in a sense distinct from, though hardly independent of purely demographic considerations such as the recurrent dearth of male heirs, or the size, shape, and turnover of households.[34] Much depended in this society on the quality of conjugal relations: whether or not wives and mothers were cooperative or unstable. It also hinged on the degree to which kin ties were needed to fill a power vacuum, to consolidate an experimental political order, or to compensate for the law's lack of clarity on corporations.

Implicit in such studies as that of "Marie, Abbess of Shaftesbury and her Brothers" (1965), by Bullock-Davies, or of "Henry I's Illegitimate Children" (1949), by White (as well as in the discussion of clerical concubinage, below) are the tensions between family sentiment and sexual, no less than social, aspirations. Clark carefully interprets a quantity of evidence on "Women's Names in Post-Conquest England" (1978) to mean that Norman women were a minority, and mixed marriages, promoting English speech, were common still in the twelfth century. But few wives at odds with their partner can have compensated with exceptional mobility, like Queen Eleanor, for the triple isolation of sex, class, and language. Bonds between women that could reinforce resistance to male authority were weakened in ways that call for further study: the presence in one household of several "wives," mothers, and resident nurses;[35] the frail emotional ties between mothers and children.[36] If internecine disputes and colonizing forays among men have been thought beneficial to women on Europe's mainland,[37] the net effect not just of intermarriage but also of marital relations has yet to be investigated within the English context.

Richly suggestive of individual propensities for conjugal harmony or disharmony are Rousset's "La femme et la famille" (1969) and Bezzola's chapter on "La transformation des moeurs" (1960). They see the strain of separation taking its toll of the conqueror's occupation forces, as the occupation did of family solidarities. The cumulative effect of these personal intrasexual tensions may be useful in understanding the tenurial crisis of the twelfth and thirteenth centuries, firmly set into the context of lordship divided by the Channel in the exchange between King and Holt on "Politics and Property" (1957; 1974).[38] The crucial distinction may be not simply between the greater and the lesser nobility, but between the disparate abilities of larger and smaller magnate families to withstand such tensions.

## THE DOMESTIC IDEAL: SECULAR AND CLERICAL

By the end of the thirteenth century, as ever more elaborate political networks tried to assimilate the family, Thomist theology had contributed a rigorous rationalization for subordinating women's spiritual equality to their reproductive obligations. McLaughlin's "Equality of Souls, Inequality of Sexes" (1974) explains this process. But the ideal of domestic solidarity that Rousset finds celebrated in the chronicles of Ordericus Vitalis, and enshrined in the Holy Family itself, produced a concatenation of ironies. It involved many a woman of humble rank in criminally deviant behavior, according to Hanawalt's "Female Felon" (1976) and Given's *Society and Homocide* (1977). Meanwhile, Pugh's *Imprisonment in Medieval England* (1968) finds more and more English gaols building separate quarters for female violators in the fourteenth and fifteenth centuries,[39] and even the noncriminal family was sundered by incarceration for debt. The politics of incest emerge from Kelly's account of "Canonical Implications of Richard III's Plan to Marry his Niece" (1967). This summarizes not only the unworkable incest rules, whose ambiguities were dealt with from a wholly male perspective, but also their persistent evasion by English rulers.

The ecclesiastical view of the family was thus as complex and inconclusive as its view of sex, and for the same reasons. It tried to promote both virginity and the sacramentality of marriage by consent, at one and the same time. And while favoring individual bonds of loyalty wider than those of kinship, its extended networks continued to dwarf the sense of self. But in England, its views must also be seen in the light of Anglo-Norman reluctance to share fully in the twelfth century papacy's thrust for a more moral social order all across Europe. How women stood to gain from a many-faceted struggle between pope, king, and the several levels of the church hierarchy is perceived in Brooke's "Gregorian Reform in Action" (1956) and "Married Men Among the English Higher Clergy" (1956). Partner's "Henry of Huntingdon" (1973) explains how Henry I forced concessions by assuming direct jurisdiction over priests' wives at a time when inheritance was ever more frequently tested in court. Inconsistent enforcement of canon law in England produced the inconclusive situation briefly but piquantly revealed in Moorman's *Church Life in England in the Thirteenth Century* (1954).[40]

Ironically, the preoccupation of scholars with priests' sons has obscured the fate of the equally numerous priests' daughters. The extent of their threat to the cohesion of this society is still an unknown and unconsidered quantity.

## THE UNMARRIED STATE

To sexual conflict and the marital role, religion offered the one legitimate alternative, but toward the end of the middle ages, the formal version was in decline. In England, the proportion of women living under some kind of rule may have been steady, but it was not high, never comprising more than one-fifth (or one-fourth) of all persons in religious orders, and the 140 to 150 English nunneries were in all but one or two cases small and poor.[41] Thompson's early fifteenth-century *Visitations* (1915) is one of the rarely translated episcopal records that lift the curtain on the nuns' daily life, more often undramatic than unedifying. Power's unique *Medieval English Nunneries* (1922) surveys the range of sources from the late thirteenth century forward. Brief excerpts from such material are tantalizingly dispersed among the older texts on women or on social life.[42]

The religious life of English and Anglo-Norman women looks undistinguished and essentially conservative. The post-conquest culture added barely any female saints to the Anglo-Saxon galaxy. Ecstasies, suspended consciousness and exotic expressions of religious fervor are as rare in the records as the semideviant recluse and the mystical tract. Insofar as it can be representative, Clay's *Hermits and Anchorites* (1914) shows the number of women recluses growing more rapidly than that of men only in thirteenth-century England. During the next two hundred years, male interest in this increasingly popular role seems to have quite eclipsed the female.[43]

Walling-in ceremonies that consecrated the hermit's goal of totally shutting out the senses are chillingly depicted by Cutts in *Scenes and Characters* (1925). Clerical mistrust of such practices, expressed in synodal legislation[44] as well as in the *Ancren Riwle* (or *Ancren Wysse*), a penitential for the anchoress,[45] may account for her rarity in England at a time when mysticism on the Continent was at its height.[46] The puzzling behavior in the *Life* of Christina of Markyate, by a fourteenth-century monk of St. Albans (ed. Talbot) may not genuinely reflect the personality of this twelfth-century recluse of Anglo-Saxon descent. Various modern texts, none definitive (by Walsh, Warrack, Wolters) of *The Revelations of Divine Love* of St. Julian, a holy woman of Norwich (1343–14—?), display a sensitive, detached orthodoxy. Only the richly original Margery Kempe, it seems, born in Norfolk in 1373, broke new ground as she expressed her religious enthusiasms without entirely rejecting either her marriage or the urban, middle-class framework of her life. Her memoirs, dictated like those of Julian, are the first extant self-revelatory texts by a woman in English, and they may be read in the Middle English edition by Meech and Allen or the modern version by Butler-Bowdon.[47] A fresh approach to them is the best antidote to obtuse or superficial commentary in the existing literature, although *An Apprentice Saint* (1964), by Collis, and the earlier *Margery Kempe* (1947), by Cholmeley, are useful. A comparative study of the style and syntax of Margery and Julian, Stone's *Middle English Prose* (1970) opens up one of the most promising new avenues for exploring women's consciousness in the middle ages.

Despite the close ties binding Eastern England to the Netherlands and the Rhine, the movement for a semicloistered life dedicated to piety and self-support in a lay environment, so strong in those regions, has left little trace in England. The ideals of the *beguine* (or *beghard*)[48] may have been too much at variance with the administration of vested interests in which talented Anglo-Norman women excelled. The puzzle awaits solution.

Equally sparse, at this period, or else feebly investigated, are the traces of heresy proper, or of witchcraft in England, and they are more plainly enmeshed in political developments than in a specific women's culture. In 1428, the year in which Joan of Arc's alleged witchcraft and heresy helped the French kingdom enter the final phase of its resistance to English ambitions on the Continent, a Norfolk carpenter's wife did reflect some undercurrent of articulate heresy, cast in response to female experience. Margery Backster told people that "... it were better to eat the fragments left upon Thursday night on the feasting days, than to go to market to bring themselves in debt to buy fish."[49] Like Margery of Kempe, she was referred to as a "Lollard," a tag associated with Flemish heretics, but if Lollardy did stir up rumors of sedition and incur some repressive action, it was, like *beguinage*, an enigmatic movement in England, leaving little tangible trace. Thomson's *Later Lollards* (1965) breaks new ground in listing and describing the beliefs of individuals brought to trial, but the overwhelming majority of these are men. The study is nevertheless worth searching for its profiles of women like the widow Margery Goyte, who denied the Virgin birth.[50]

Russell's *Witchcraft in the Middle Ages* (1972) probes the trial (1324–25) of Lady Alice Kyteler, a rich Anglo-Norman of Kilkenny with many enemies.[51] The case of the flamboyant and lowborn duchess of Gloucester is analyzed by Griffiths in "The Trial of Eleanor Cobham" (1969). Declared treasonable, her indiscretions called in question the legal status of peeresses just at the point when the relations of France and England were about to be finally severed, and this survey comes to a close.

Topics which have been fruitful for the study of women, particularly the unmarried, on the continent of Europe seem to bear little promise for England. Instead, sermons and literature of the thirteenth and fourteenth centuries express antagonisms shaped by a political and economic experience to which marriage is a key.

## THE CULT OF LOVE AND THE MARRIAGE DEBATE

Medieval art forms and the developed clichés of literature, even more than fables, proverbs, puns, and riddles, are virtually incapable of rendering a truthful profile of women. Maximally "defended" against obvious meaning, medieval literary sources will never yield the riches offered by the products of more recent times. The female persona moves along a continuum of artificiality, passing through personification, allegory, and symbolism to fantasy at an unconscious, perhaps infantile level.[52] Sometimes, though, and especially where such fantasies acquire an intellectual meaning, they let historians penetrate deep into the period's cultural restraints on women.

The complex themes of literary antifeminism and love symbolism in relation to feminine stereotypes may be approached through Ferrante's *Woman as Image* (1975); Kaufman's "Spare Ribs: The Conception of Woman" (1973); Morewedge's *Role of Woman in the Middle Ages* (1975); and Utley's *Crooked Rib* (1944). The contribution of women to men's mythmaking concerns Corrigan in "Chaucer's Failure with Women" (1969).

With such preparation, the entire body of chronicle records must be scrutinized for bias—a monumental task begun by Bandel in "The English Chroniclers' Attitudes" (1955) and lately resumed in McRobbie's "Woman and Love" (1972), a penetrating study of Froissart's *Chronicles.* Here, with feudal relations on the wane, an Anglo-French knight appears willing to view women of all ranks candidly, undisguised by the courtly cult of love which had suffused Europe from the twelfth century on. English society was not immune from it, despite an impression created by the linguistic diversity producing a broad or "lewd" tradition of English poetry; a scattering of spiritual and mystical productions in English, and a quantity of Anglo-Norman verse that never dealt with love at all.

Discernable refinements of the sentiments of a none-too-sophisticated Anglo-Norman and Angevin feudal nobility had already engendered new images and treatments of women by the twelfth century, partly in response to the Church's attempt to contain sex and feeling within acceptable limits. After Aliénor of Aquitaine, queen of France, became Queen Eleanor of England under rather scandalous circumstances, her cosmopolitan court encouraged England's elites to acquire a taste for the artificial relations of adulterous love. Lazar's "Cupid, the Lady and the Poet" (1976) is a compelling introduction to the critical literature, stressing three distinct modes of sentiment, all of which can be acknowledged without fragmenting perception of their common social implications. These are persuasively summarized in Gist's *Love and War in the Middle English Romances* (1947).

A less tangential or transient sequel, appealing to the broader governing class of the mid-fourteenth century and taking a different approach to sexual relations, is explained by Robbins in "The Vintner's Son" (1976). Some of those experimenting with the English alliterative revival were inspired by a new wave of the French tradition to raise the debates about women and love to a new pitch of intensity. Just as English women in the urban crafts were beginning to wield some of the economic power of women on the Continent, a literary war began to rage around marriage and that inextricably erotic and commercial transaction, the conjugal debt.

The old arguments about Chaucerian marriage have been revived by awareness of its relation to the historical study of women's roles, evident in Murtaugh's "Women and Geoffrey Chaucer" (1971); Mogan's "Chaucer and the *Bona Matrimonii*" (1969); Levy's "The Wife of Bath's *Queynte Fantasye*" (1969); Hornstein's "The Wyf of Bathe and the Merchant" (1968); and Magee's "The Wife of Bath and the Problem of Mastery" (1974), as well as articles cited earlier in connection with female sexuality. In "The Archwife and the Eunuch" (1974), Kerhan sees love and money equated, while Noll's "Romantic Conception of Marriage" (1970) puts the debate nicely in perspective. Harwood deals, as indeed do all of these essays, with the authenticity of Dame Alice in "The Wife of Bath and the Dream of Innocence" (1972). Beichner, in "Confrontation, Contempt of Court, and Chaucer's Cecilia" (1974), sees signs of a nontraditional assertiveness in yet another female stock type, while Cherniss disposes of "patient" Griselda in "*The Clerk's Tale*, the Wife of Bath's Purgatory and *The Merchant's Tale*" (1972). Women like the Wife of Bath and the elegant Prioress are seen by Henning, in "From *Eva* and *Ave*" (1977) as trapped between intellectual and sexual aspirations in a society whose prescribed female behavior induced role denial and self-hatred.[53]

Chaucer's view of marriage expresses the social as well as the literary culmination of a transitional phase in English life. The vitality of his female characters does not mean that women were gaining the upper hand in a battle of the sexes, only that they were an integral, even a crucial part of dialectical processes in English society. In a fragile reconciliation of competing values and purposes, women and the ideological meaning of woman were at once an essential and perhaps the least reliable link.

We need a way of measuring the distance of our subjects from conventional stereotypes as urgently as we need information. The biases and silence of medieval records themselves may prevent some of the enormous gaps in our knowledge from ever being filled, but approaches used by latter-day social historians illuminate such evidence as we have. At the same time, medieval perceptions themselves enhance our ability to benefit from anthropology, economic theory, demography and measurement techniques. The signs and symbols of sex and gender are indispensable keys for decoding past perceptions and realities.

Shaped by the cult of love, the mutual relations of men and women in this period could not but be strained past the level of tension engendered either in work or in family struggles over land, children and power. A conjugal bond experienced without the "mastery" of the one or the other partner seemed inconceivable.

Literary stratagems of love play outside marriage, where the persuasion as well as the service of women was the heart of the matter, differed from those inner-directed versions wherein a poet concentrated on an image he feared to destroy. But both modes reflected attitudes prevalent in the knightly class of England, as elsewhere. It demanded a style of writing and behavior appropriate to courts and also consonant with the ethic of honor that sublimated the knight's function as a fighter. Such tastes had little in common with the church's cult of spirituality. This sought a transfiguration of the questing pilgrim soul that could not occur in nature—a mysterious and elusive goal having little to do with the relations of women and men, proper or improper. For the seriously religious, on either side of the Channel, the man-woman bond linked not male and female but humanity and divinity. It celebrated the ancient myth of the androgyne, and feminine gender as well as the marriage metaphor were mined for their symbolic messages about a new type of humanity.[54]

Nevertheless, the erotic images of nuptial Christology, clustering around a garden of delights whose plants, birds, and animals insistently ornamented the oral and visual arts, only created confusion. Passionate love outside marriage sprang from the use of the marriage bond in property relations and politics, but people also believed that passionate love was wicked; that it could not become virtuous even by channeling it into marriage.

The third mode of love in the Anglo-French literary tradition excluded mutuality and extolled mastery every whit as coldly as the older themes of *fin'amors*, refined love. For all that, there is a low-key, almost genial quality about English literary antifeminism, an evenhandedness about pulpit rhetoric and a phlegmatic neutrality about devotional lyrics[55] that has sometimes been taken to mean a high degree of latitude for women, at a time when developing economic and social trends make this unlikely. Ascribing the apparent harmony in part to a complex balance of interpenetrating linguistic forces, we can perceive a high degree not of freedom but of tension.

Sex and gender roles could not disappear in this period, but they did alter and diversify, both inside and outside marriage. At the same time, new dimensions and motivations reinforced sex segregation during the late medieval expansion. The long association of femaleness with reproductive or vegetative—and, in some eyes, inferior—nature was subtly confused, from the twelfth century on, as womanhood became identified with cult and culture itself. Their legacy was only partly modified by the advent of new relations of production, and by antimonastic movements that upgraded marriage. When this situation was further complicated, as it was in England, by political conditions, the ability and willingness of women to enter into a workable partnership with men was seriously compromised.

# NOTES

1. The case for a general deterioration of women's position in the late middle ages is summarized by Stuard in her introduction to *Women in Medieval Society*. The transition from feudal to modern society may best be approached through Wallerstein, *The Modern World System*, and Dobb, *Studies in the Development of Capitalism*.

2. Useful also is Guth, ed., *Late-Medieval England 1377–1485*, a thematic annotated bibliography.

3. The most useful of Coulton's collections of translated excerpts from original material is *Social Life in Britain*.

4. See also Power's earlier essay, "The Position of Women," in Crump and Jacob, eds., *The Legacy of the Middle Ages*. Both studies survey the situation in Europe as a whole, but the author's interests and specialized knowledge center upon England. Eleanor Searle has now undertaken to compile, from Power's notes, the definitive survey that she had planned.

5. In particular, those in Stuard, ed., *Women in Medieval Society*. The introduction is valuable, and it is unfortunate that almost all the essays in this excellent volume refer to periods and places other than those dealt with here.

6. A beginning is made with the exchange between Scammell and Searle on the nature of "wife-rents" in the twelfth century. For Europe, see Coleman, "Medieval Marriage Characteristics: A Neglected Factor in the History of Medieval Serfdom."

7. Casey, "Cheshire Cat", pp. 230–31; Thrupp, "Medieval Industry," pp. 265–66; Putnam, *Enforcement of the Statutes*, esp. pp. 89–90, and passim. Also useful is the retrospective material in Clark, *The Working Life of Women in the Seventeenth Century*. The situation contrasts starkly with that of twelfth- and thirteenth-century countrywomen and men who still could hold on to land, particularly in those eastern regions that maintained the traditions of an earlier, free peasantry, described in Stenton, *The English Woman*, chap. 3. Thrupp's discussion of the way in which the saving of women's labor time by mechanical flour milling was denied the poorer peasant family because of the

artificially high cost of the new larger mills suggests yet another way in which women's productive potential was limited. The extra time for more intensive garden cultivation or textile work was not made available under an increasingly "capitalistic" style of lordship ("Medieval Industry," p. 234).

8. Reproduction involves not merely the daily regeneration of productive forces but also the way in which new ones are assured. While the former creates special conflicts for women, the female life cycle itself as it is involved with the latter, along with the cultural constraints of their society, engender still others. These have mainly to do with the distance of that female experience from male concepts of power and intellect. Both kinds of reproduction combine to restrain movements toward autonomy, but they closely converge only when the capitalistic mode of production reaches its fullest development in the late modern period, invading every aspect of life. Karl Marx did not elaborate this distinction, but I believe it is implicit in his "General Law of Capitalist Accumulation," in vol. 1 of *Capital*. See also Rubin, "The Traffic in Women," and Kelly-Gadol, "The Social Relation of the Sexes."

9. Heaton, *Yorkshire Woolen Industry*, pp. 23–24, 38, 127.

10. Thrupp, "Medieval Industry" and "The Gilds."

11. However, even in these guilds, women appear never to have been elected to the governance as "wardens": Smith, Smith, and Brentano, *English Gilds*, passim.

12. Some of the most highly remunerative crafts, such as gold thread spinning and silk weaving, were among those organized in guilds exclusive to women. Very few guilds actually prohibited the entry of women under any circumstances, while conditions of work were almost invariably the same for both male and female. Sometimes, women seem even to have enjoyed a certain advantage, as when an ordinance of Edward III in 1363 restricted male artisans to one craft while allowing women to "freely work as they have done before this time without any impeachment or being restrained by this ordinance": Hill, *Women in English Life*, 1: 55.

13. We cannot be sure about the situation of the female carpenter until more is known about the price structure of the period. On customary price ceilings, see above, note 7.

14. Thrupp notes that when merchants began to organize the entire process of production, laborers may have lost their worries over finding capital, but they also lost their independence: ("Medieval Industry," pp. 245–47). Medieval law and theology were in principle hostile to monopoly, but were much more tolerant of its practice by the employer and merchant than by consumer or day-worker. The theoretical distinction between trading and production is discussed in a quite different preindustrial context by S. Mintz, "Men, Women and Trade."

15. For example, the strength of women in the Yorkshire textile industry seems to have aroused the envy of male co-workers, resulting in their imposition of quality supervision in 1400: Heaton, *Yorkshire Woolen Industry*, p. 127. In fifteenth-century Cologne, the products of the all-female yarn spinners' guild were regularly sold by their husbands, and an all-male yarn twisters' guild was frequently in conflict with the spinners, with whom they were clearly connected (Sister Maria Pia, "The Industrial Position of Women," p. 558).

16. Legal status and practice is discussed in the ensuing chapter by Kittel. For present purposes, see Bateson, *Borough Customs*, 2: 185–86, 222–26, 227–28.

17. A London statute of 1419 decreed that although women practicing separate crafts from their husbands might hire girl apprentices, these would be bound to both husband and wife, as the spirit of the English marriage law required: Bateson, *Borough Customs*, 2: 229–30. See also note 15, above.

18. A woman's life was shaped by the house in which she lived: Putnam, *The Lady*, p. 108.

19. Heinrich, *The Canonesses*, pp. 188–89; Harris and Nochlin, *Women Artists*, pp. 15–19.

20. E.g., Wright, ed., *Book of the Knight De La Tour-Landry* (c. 1440); Furnivall, ed., *The Babees Book* (including "How the Good Wife Taught Her Daughter"). The vocational role of morality is as apparent in the thirteenth-century advice from Walter of Henley to a milkmaid, in *Husbandry*, ed. Lamond, as it is in the twelfth-century advice of John of Salisbury on the education of a prince.

21. Orme, *English Schools*, pp. 52–56; Heinrich, *The Canonesses*, p. 111. Canonesses learned practical medicine in the hospitals built outside their cloister walls, but the available knowledge was shared with most unlettered women of the period. (On that topic, see notes 26 and 27, below.) For a comparison of this with an earlier English situation and with that on the Continent, see Leibell, *Anglo-Saxon Education of Women*, and Eckenstein, *Women Under Monasticism*. By the fourteenth century, bishops no longer assumed that the nuns to whom they issued injunctions really understood any Latin: Coulton, *Social Life*, p. 451. On the other hand, Queen Mathilda, daughter of Baldwin V of Flanders and wife of William the Conqueror of England is said to have written poetry, like her two daughters who stayed on the Continent (Jourdain, "Mémoire sur l'éducation des femmes.")

22. McDonnell, *Beguines and Beghards*, pp. 82–84. See also note 48, below.

23. For a concise overview of this problem, see Russell, "Population in Europe," pp. 58–60, in Cipolla, ed., *Fontana Economic History*, a survey providing up-to-date bibliographies on most of the topics covered in this and the previous section, as well as summaries of economic and population trends between 1000 and 1500.

24. Breaking new ground is the recent article by Rossiaud, "Prostitution, jeunesse et société," which puts the topic in the context of demographic and family history rather than, as is more usual, of warfare and economic crisis. Dealing though it does with a part of Europe remote from England, the approach and methods used could form the basis for a fresh look at the English records.

25. A discussion of the limits of peasant fertility in underdeveloped economies, in Stys, "The Influence of Economic Conditions," may have a bearing upon medieval conditions. Historical demographers may soon begin to ask the new questions raised by Birdsall in "Women and Population Studies."

26. Rubin provides a good account of the treatment of miscarriages and other female disorders. Himes ascribes the prevalence of "irrational" treatments to the channeling of medical knowledge through Roman texts rather than through the more experimental Islamic sources, while Rubin concludes that such influences, seeping into England from the Continent, had created a watershed in medical knowledge by the fourteenth century.

27. The earliest record of a woman physician practicing in England dates from 1232 (Rubin, pp. 186–87). A bibliographical register is available in Talbot and Hammond, *Medical Practitioners in Medieval England*. Walker notes in "Proof of Age" that the testimony of a midwife as to date of birth was not directly accepted (p. 314).

28. The best introduction to this topic is in Erickson, *The Medieval Vision*, chap. 8, esp. pp. 192–94; see also Frazer, "The Origins of Clerical Celibacy."

29. These exceptional cases do not clearly reflect beliefs on the subject because, like most of the Continental cases from the fifteenth century forward, they confuse the normal with the bizarre and in part create what they fear. The records of witchcraft should be used with great caution. Helpful in negotiating the maze are: Thomas, "The Relevance of Social Anthropology to the Historical Study of English Witchcraft"; Monter, *Witchcraft in France and Switzerland* and "The Historiography of European Witchcraft"; as well as Kieckhefer, *Late Medieval Witch Trials*. These works represent the latest and clearest perceptions of a vexed topic. Arguments denying the existence of any kind of female subculture built around ritual and remedial magic are offered in Cohn, *Europe's Inner Demons*, chap. 8. Beyond the chronological limits of this essay, McFarlane, *Witchcraft in Tudor and Stuart England*, provides a sound model for research on community views of female sexuality. Attitudes toward the older woman as a sexual being are discussed in Ruether, "The Persecution of Witches." See also note 51, below.

30. The regularities that emerge may, of course, reflect only the greater availability of English sources. A lucid, critical summary of the value for the medieval period of Ariès' pioneering study, *Centuries of Childhood*, is included in Hunt, *Parents and Children*. Beitscher's use of eleventh- and twelfth-century French monastic charters in "'As the Twig is Bent'...: Children and Their Parents" is suggestive.

31. Using Continental sources, the well-controlled study of maternal rejection by

McLaughlin, "Survivors and Surrogates," invites emulation by English historians. Much more than the incidence of infanticide is involved, particularly the projection onto the young of adult neuroses, something which DeMause sees as typical of this period.

32. Aside from Scammell's objection to generalizing from *merchet*, it seems agreed that lords perceived more gain in exacting recognition fines than in holding serfs to unrealistic restrictions on personal decisions, especially about the disposition of their land. And this included arrangements about the marriage of daughters outside the manor.

33. That is, kin structures were neither "elementary" nor "formal" in the sense intended by Lévi-Strauss, *Elementary Structures of Kinship*. See Lancaster, "Kinship in Anglo-Saxon Society", Bullough, "Early Medieval Social Groupings", and Phillpotts, "Kindred and Clan" for the historical context of this issue. Evidence countering their denial that strongly agnatic lineage, or descent, groups existed in Anglo-Saxon society is presented by Charles-Edwards in "Kinship, Status and the Origins of the Hide," pp. 21–32.

34. Family size, even where it can be fully known, may conceal household structure, for the same statistic may result either from a combination of high fertility and a simple conjugal unit, or else from some form of multiple domestic arrangement combined with a low fertility rate. Household size, in turn, may reflect only a phase rather than a type of family structure, especially in a society subject to high mortality and considerable fluctuation, as well as to increasing class differentiation and economic pressures: see Berkner, "The Stem Family." Increasing caution among historians as to the usefulness of such measures as family and household size suggests they are of limited use in judging the quality of women's lives, and it may transpire that those measures are more important for their effect on the balance of power within a household, than in themselves.

35. Hunt, *Parents and Children*, may reflect situations not infrequent in an earlier period. Among peasants, however, they seem less likely. Land clearance owed much to the nuclear or conjugal family unit that weakened any master-servant relationship between male and female, married or not. By contrast, the peasant parcenary farming unit played an economic role similar to that of the feudal family *consortium*. Still, Homans, *English Villagers*, has not convinced all historians that an essentially patriarchal "stem" family can be identified beneath a variety of forms. The nature of the available evidence precludes knowing whether the "stem" family was indeed archaic, or a more recent outgrowth of high medieval conditions linked, according to Homans, to regions devoted to cereal cultivation. The controversy may be followed in Berkner, "Recent Research"; Britton, "The Peasant Family"; and Wheaton, "Family and Kinship." But the shape of peasant households in the eleventh and twelfth centuries is hardly at all known, while those of the thirteenth and fourteenth centuries remain shadowy despite the emergence, during the 1200s, of manorial court records permitting, here and there, a crude form of family reconstitution, as in Britton, "The Peasant Family." The techniques of family reconstitution, explained by Wrigley, have not superseded those of the genealogists, as in Cam, "Pedigrees of Villeins," in *Liberties and Communities*. The law and practice of marriage in the middle ages is discussed fully by Kittell in the ensuing essay. It should be noted here that the ease with which individuals slipped in and out of marriage in this period of lax enforcement of the laws does not necessarily imply that personal choice often intervened in the selection of mates. The claim by Shorter, in *Making of the Modern Family*, that "expressive sex" is characteristic only of the late modern period, if hard to disprove, is controversial.

36. Walker, "Widow and Ward," pp. 162, 166. Beitscher, on the other hand, has implied that the estrangement between fathers and their children was the more serious problem in feudal France ("'As the Twig is Bent,'" pp. 187–89).

37. Putnam, *The Lady*, p. 131; Herlihy, "Land, Family and Women," pp. 110–13.

38. The potential of family analysis for explaining the civil war and anarchy of 1135 to 1154 is suggested by King, "Politics and Property," pp. 114–16. Whether the struggle between Stephen and Matilda between 1135 and 1154 involved rival styles of government, each appealing to different segments of the nobility, or, as Hollister

suggests in "The Anglo-Norman Succession Debate," conflicts at a more personal level based largely on individual relationships with a strong queen, the role of women in this confused period needs to be more fully explored. For the political background, see Cronne, *The Reign of Stephen.* Erlanger, *Margaret of Anjou,* and the account of that queen of England by Dahmus in *Seven Medieval Queens* imply structural parallels in a fifteenth-century setting. An indispensable starting point for such work is the *Victoria County Histories,* of which the latest (1970) edition by Pugh provides, in his introductory volume, a bibliographical survey and a list of contents.

39. Pugh, *Imprisonment,* pp. 103, 352–53, 357–58.

40. Moorman, *The English Church,* pp. 63–67, 210–35. The equivocal stand taken by the church has been seen to reflect positions taken during its long struggle for an identity. See also Noonan, "Marriage in the Middle Ages." The techniques of content analysis used in Laeuchli, *Power and Sexuality,* might be applied to English ecclesiastical documents, particularly in the controversies over clerical celibacy.

41. This was especially true of the Cistercians, a twelfth-century innovation. Knowles and Hadcock, *Medieval Religious Houses,* pp. 250–87, contains useful statistics on nunneries. In 1066 nuns comprised one-quarter of the religious population, while in 1154 they numbered less than one-fifth (Brooke, *Europe in the Central Middle Ages,* p. 121). The number of nunneries was roughly constant from c. 1200 until the Reformation.

42. Dugdale's *Monasticon,* ed. Caley, and Cheney, *Episcopal Visitations* provide general direction for such inquiries. An appendix to the latter has interesting comparative statistics on typical infractions in male and female communities in Normandy, and *Registrum visitationem,* ed. O'Sullivan, affords a comparison between Norman and English nunneries in the thirteenth century. A guide to the superior economic position of wealthy Norman nunneries, and to the capabilities and connections of their abbesses in the final days of Angevin rule may be found in Sweeney and Hall's "An Unpublished Privilege." In addition to Power's *Medieval English Nunneries,* Hugo's *Medieval Nunneries* may be consulted.

43. Although the surviving datable records of recluses are incomplete, a tally of those in Clay, *Hermits,* Appendix C, pp. 203–63, results in a pattern too consistent to be wholly accidental:

|         | Female | Male | Unspecified | Total |
| ------- | ------ | ---- | ----------- | ----- |
| 11th c. | 2      | 9    | 0           | 11    |
| 12th c. | 14     | 65   | 36          | 115   |
| 13th c. | 52     | 88   | 44          | 184   |
| 14th c. | 37     | 147  | 38          | 222   |
| 15th c. | 41     | 122  | 34          | 197   |

44. Cutts, *Scenes and Characters,* pp. 93–151. Cheney, *English Synodalia* is a general guide to episcopal legislation.

45. Originating c. 1200, this survives in fifteen different manuscripts, of which nine are in English, two in French, and four in Latin, witnessing its broad appeal in all of the major sociolinguistic communities of England. It is hard to tell if the rule mainly reflects the tradition of literary and religious misogyny, or the actual, and apparently none too conscientious, behavior of anchoresses. See Dobson, *English Text,* among other editions of the *Ancren Riwle* in the Early English Text Society.

46. See Underhill, *Mystics of the Church*; Knowles, *English Mystical Tradition*; and, for the unorthodox tendencies largely absent from England, Lerner, *Heresy of the Free Spirit.*

47. The memoirs were dictated between 1436 and 1438, when Margery was 63 to 65 years old. More than one amanuensis was used, and the authorship of some sections is still uncertain.

48. McDonnell, *Beguines and Beghards,* chap. 8, pp. 81–100, describes the social origins of these women and the situation to which they were responding. Their version of apostolic poverty is perhaps most subtly characterized by their popularity among the patrician families of Ghent as teachers of housework (ibid., pp. 120–53, 148–49). Economic self-sufficiency, as much as piety, was their goal.

49. Coulton, *Social Life,* pp. 462–65.

50. Thomson, *Later Lollards*, p. 106. Though persistent, Lollard beliefs are described by Thomson as unorganized, unsystematic, and largely negative. See also Aston, "Lollardy and Sedition." Illuminating on the relation of heresy to the status of women in Europe is Shahar, "De quelques aspects de la femme," which contrasts hierarchical with evangelical movements in dealing with a spreading concept of the female element in divinity.

51. Wright, *A Contemporary Narrative*, may also be consulted. Cohn stresses intrafamilial tensions besetting the much-married Lady Alice, as well as social antagonisms aroused by the involvement of her and her kin in money-lending and trade with Flanders (*Europe's Inner Demons*, pp. 198–203). See also note 29, above. Goodich, "The Politics of Canonization," shows women in Europe affected by Rome's campaign against heretical tendencies of all kinds, involving a dual policy promoting sainthood and prosecuting sorcery.

52. E.g., Holland, *The Dynamics of Literary Response*, chap. 1, "Literature as Transformation," in relation to *The Wife of Bath's Tale*. Despite the dependence of such literature upon the play of underlying central fantasies, most authors cannot help but reflect change. See also Auerbach, *Mimesis*, passim.

53. The historian's right to use a fictional creation as a model for reality is sometimes plausible. So subtly drawn and psychologically believable is the Wife of Bath that, whether she be but a pantomime type cleverly endowed with life or a figure drawn from life, she can stand for the period's or her creator's involvement with the themes of sexuality and "mastery" in marriage. Precisely because she is didactic and iconographic as well as lifelike, she is the more useful. For a general account of those themes, see Kelly, *Love and Marriage in the Age of Chaucer*, with a review of the relevant literature, including Gower's *Confessio Amantis* (Confession of a Penitent Lover) and a chapter on "The Mystical Code of Married Love." See also Robbins, "The Chaucerian Apocrypha."

54. According to Bailey, *The Man-Woman Relationship*, Christianity also implied a promise about successful personal relations that had to be striven for—mutual humility and a reconciliation of the active and passive principles, of "nature" and "culture." It is not out of the question that some people, under certain circumstances, might have recognized this possibility. If some or many women did so, we stand little chance of finding out, for the marriage metaphor was more often used by men, given that women rarely were authors. Where the literary evidence can divulge anything in this respect, it is of great importance, and it seems most likely to do so where the influence of the English language predominates.

55. For the sermon literature, see Morris, ed., *Old English Homilies*; Ross, ed., *Middle English Sermons*; and Owst, *Literature and Pulpit* and *Preaching in Medieval England*. The Early English Version of the *"Gesta Romanorum,"* ed. Herrtage, affords interesting comparisons with Continental versions of this antifeminist tradition of moral tales. Brown, ed., *English Lyrics* and *Religious Lyrics*, illustrate both the similarities and the differences between English and Continental modes of piety from the thirteenth through the fifteenth centuries. About one-quarter (twenty-seven percent) of all these verses celebrate the Virgin Mary, but in a conventional vein, and only in the fifteenth century do they approach the intensity of drama and pathos common in the rest of Europe. Only two lyrics, "I Repent of Blaming Women" and "Of Women Cometh this Worldes Weal," take a position strongly sympathetic to the female sex and what it stands for. It is not impossible that the second of these could have been of female authorship, since it is one of the "Vernon" lyrics of miscellaneous provenance, but the only one of the group for which the editor fails to make an attribution. Comprehensive guides to this material are Brown and Robbins, *Index of Middle English Verse*, and Brown, *Register of Middle English Religious and Didactic Verse*. On style and syntax, especially as used by women, see Stone, *Middle English Prose Style*.

# BIBLIOGRAPHY

ABRAM, ANNIE. *English Life in the Later Middle Ages.* London and New York: 1913.
———. "Women Traders in Medieval London." *Economic Journal* 26 (1916): 276–85.
ARIÈS, PHILIPPE. *L'enfant et la vie familiale sous L'Ancien Régime.* Paris: 1960. (English editions published as *Centuries of Childhood: A Social History of Family Life.* Translated by R. Baldick. London: 1962. New York: 1965.)
ASTON M[ARGARET]. E. "Lollardy and Sedition, 1381–1431." *Past and Present* 17 (April 1960): 1–44.
AUERBACH, ERICH. *Mimesis. The Representation of Reality in Western Literature.* Translated by W. R. Trask. Princeton and London: 1953.
AVELING, JAMES H. *English Midwives: Their History and Prospects.* London: 1872.
BAILEY, DERRICK S. *The Man-Woman Relationship in Christian Thought.* London: 1959. (Published in U.S. as *Sexual Relations in Christian Thought.* New York: 1959.)
BALDWIN, FRANCES E. *Sumptuary Legislation and Personal Regulation in England.* Baltimore: 1926.
BANDEL, BETTY. "The English Chroniclers' Attitudes Toward Women." *Journal of the History of Ideas* 16, no. 1 (1955): 113–18.
BATESON, MARY, ed. *Borough Customs,* vol. 2. Publications of the Selden Society. London: 1904.
BEAN, J. M. W. "Plague, Population and Economic Decline in England in the Later Middle Ages." *Economic History Review,* 2d series, 15 (1963): 423–37.
BEICHNER, PAUL E. "Confrontation, Contempt of Court, and Chaucer's Cecilia." *The Chaucer Review. A Journal of Medieval Studies and Literary Criticism* 8, no. 3 (1974): 198–204.
BEITSCHER, JANE K. "'As the twig is bent ...': Children and their Parents in an Aristocratic Society." *Journal of Medieval History* 2, no. 3 (November 1976): 181–91.
BERKNER, LUTZ K. "Recent Research on the History of the Family in Western Europe." *Journal of Marriage and the Family* 35, no. 3 (1973): 395–405.
———. "The Stem Family and the Developmental Cycle of the Peasant Household: An Eighteenth-Century Austrian Example." *American Historical Review* 77, no. 2 (April 1972): 398–418.
BEZZOLA, R. R. *Les Origines et la formation de la littèrature courtoise en Occident (500–1200).* Bibliothèque de l'Ecole des hautes études. Sciences historiques et philologiques 313. Paris: 1960. (See particularly: part 2, vol. 1, chap. 2, "La transformation des moeurs et le rôle de la femme dans la classe féodale du XIᵉ au XIIᵉ siècle"; and part 3, vol. 1, chap. 1, "La reine Aliénor."
BIRDSALL, NANCY, "Women and Population Studies." *Signs. Journal of Women in Culture and Society* 1, no. 3, part 1 (1976): 699–712.
BLACKLEY, D., and HERMANSEN, G., eds. *The Household Book of Queen Isabella for the Fifth Regnal Year of Edward II, 8th July 1311 to 7th July 1312.* Edmonton, Alberta: 1971.
BLOCH, IWAN. *Sexual Life in England Past and Present.* Translated by W. H. Forstern. London: 1958.
BOLTON, BRENDA M. *"Mulieres Sanctae."* In *Women in Medieval Society.* Edited by S. M. Stuard, pp. 141–58. Philadelphia: 1976.

BRISSAUD, Y.-B. "L'infanticide à la fin du moyen âge, ses motivations psychologiques et sa répression." *Revue historique de droit français et étranger*, 4th series, 50 (1972): 229–56.

BRITTON, EDWARD. "The Peasant Family in Fourteenth-Century England." *Peasant Studies* 5, no. 2 (April 1976): 2–7.

BROOKE, C. R. N. *Europe in the Central Middle Ages, 962–1154.* London and New York: 1964.

———. "Gregorian Reform in Action: Clerical Marriage in England, 1050–1200." *Cambridge Historical Journal* 12 (1956): 1–21.

———."Married Men Among the English Higher Clergy, 1066–1200." *Cambridge Historical Journal* 12 (1956): 187–88.

BROWE, PETER. *Beiträge zur Sexualethik des Mittelalters.* Breslau: 1932.

BROWN, CARLETON F., ed. *English Lyrics of the 13th Century.* Oxford: 1932.

———, ed. *A Register of Middle English Religious and Didactic Verse.* Oxford: 1916–20.

———, ed. *Religious Lyrics of the 15th Century.* Oxford: 1939.

———, ed. *Religious Lyrics of the 14th Century.* Oxford: 1924. 2d ed., revised by G. V. Smithers, 1952.

———, and Robbins, Rossell Hope, eds. *The Index of Middle English Verse.* New York: 1943.

BROWN, ELIZABETH A. R. "Eleanor of Aquitaine: Parent, Queen and Duchess." In *Eleanor of Aquitaine, Patron and Politician.* Edited by William W. Kibler, pp. 9–34. Austin and London: 1976.

BRUNDAGE, JAMES A. "Concubinage and Marriage in Medieval Canon Law." *Journal of Medieval History* 1, no. 1 (April 1975): 1–17.

BULLOCK-DAVIES, CONSTANCE. "Marie, Abbess of Shaftesbury, and her Brothers." *English Historical Review* 80 (1965): 314–22.

BULLOUGH, D. A. "Early Medieval Social Groupings: The Terminology of Kinship." *Past and Present* 45 (November 1969): 3–18.

BUTLER-BOWDON, COL. W. E. I., ed. *The Book of Margery Kempe.* London: 1936. Reprint. London: 1952.

CAM, HELEN. *Liberties and Communities in Medieval England: Collected Studies in Local Administration and Topography.* Cambridge: 1944. Reprint. London and New York: 1963. (See particularly chap. 8, "Pedigrees of Villeins and Freemen in the Thirteenth Century.")

CASEY, KATHLEEN. "The Cheshire Cat: Reconstructing the Experience of Medieval Women." In *Liberating Women's History. Theoretical and Critical Essays.* Edited by Berenice Carroll, pp. 224–49. Urbana: 1976.

CHARLES-EDWARDS, T. M. "Kinship, Status and the Origins of the Hide." *Past and Present* 56 (August 1972): 3–33.

CHENEY, C. R. *English Synodalia of the Thirteenth Century.* London: 1941.

———. *Episcopal Visitations of Monasteries in the Thirteenth Century.* Manchester: 1941.

CHERNISS, MICHAEL D. "*The Clerk's Tale of Envoy*, the Wife of Bath's Purgatory and *The Merchant's Tale.*" *The Chaucer Review. A Journal of Medieval Studies and Literary Criticism* 6 (1972): 235–54.

CHOLMELEY, KATHERINE. *Margery Kempe, Genius and Mystic.* London: 1947.

CHRISTIE, A. G[race]. I. *English Medieval Embroidery. . . .* Oxford: 1938.

CIPOLLA, C., ed. *The Fontana Economic History of Europe,* vol. 1: *The Middle Ages.* London: 1972. Reprint. Hassocks: 1976; New York: 1977. (Citations in notes are to the original Fontana edition.)

CLARK, ALICE. *The Working Life of Women in the Seventeenth Century.* London: 1919. Reprint. London and New York: 1968.

CLARK, CECILY. "Women's Names in Post-Conquest England: Observations and Speculations." *Speculum. A Journal of Medieval Studies* 53 (1978): 223–51.

CLAY, ROTHA M. *The Hermits and Anchorites of England.* London: 1914.

COCKAYNE, G. E. *The Complete Peerage of England, Scotland, Ireland, Great Britain, and the United Kingdom.* New edition, revised and enlarged by V. Gibbs et al. 12 vols. London: 1910–59.

COCKAYNE, O., ed. *Hali Meidenhad.* Early English Text Society, o.s. 18. London: 1866. Revised by F. J. Furnivall, 1922. Reprint: 1973.

COHN, NORMAN. *Europe's Inner Demons. An Enquiry Inspired by the Great Witch-Hunt.* New York and London: 1975.

COLEMAN, EMILY. "Medieval Marriage Characteristics: A Neglected Factor in the History of Medieval Serfdom." *Journal of Interdisciplinary History* 2 (Autumn 1971): 205–19.

COLLIS, LOUISE. *An Apprentice Saint.* London: 1964.

CORRIGAN, MATTHEW. "Chaucer's Failure with Women. The Inadequacy of Criseyde." *Western Humanities Review* 23, no. 2 (1969): 107–20.

COTTER, JAMES FINN. "The Wife of Bath and the Conjugal Debt." *English Language Notes* 6, no.3 (1969): 169–72.

COULTON, G. G. *Medieval Panorama: The English Scene from Conquest to Reformation.* Cambridge: 1938.

———. *Social Life in Britain from the Conquest to the Reformation.* Cambridge: 1918. Reprint: 1956.

CRONNE, H. A. *The Reign of Stephen, 1135–54. Anarchy in England.* London: 1970.

CUTTS, EDWARD LEWES. *Scenes and Characters of the Middle Ages.* 5th ed. London: 1925.

DAHMUS, JOSEPH. *Seven Medieval Queens: Vignettes of Seven Outstanding Women of the Middle Ages.* Garden City, N.J.: 1972.

DALE, MARION K. "The London Silkwomen of the Fifteenth Century." *Economic History Review* 4 (1933): 324–35.

DELASANTA, RODNEY. "*Quoniam* and the Wife of Bath." *Papers on Language and Literature* 8, no. 2 (Spring 1972): 202–206.

DEMAUSE, LLOYD, ed. *The History of Childhood, Evolution of Parent-Child Relationships as a Factor in History.* New York: 1975; London: 1976.

DOBB, MAURICE H. *Studies in the Development of Capitalism.* Rev. ed. London and New York: 1963.

DOBSON, E. J., ed. *The English Text of the Ancren Riwle Edited from B. M. Cotton Ms. Cleopatra C. vi.* Early English Text Society, o.s. 267. London and New York: 1972.

DRUMMOND, J. C., and WILBRAHAM, A. *The Englishman's Food. A History of Five Centuries of English Diet.* London: 1939. Revised by D. Hollingsworth, 1957.

DUGDALE, WILLIAM. *Monasticon Anglicanum.* New ed. by John Caley, H. Ellis, and B. Bandinel. 6 vols. London: 1817–30. Reprint: 1846.

ECKENSTEIN, LINA. *Woman under Monasticism: Chapters on Saint-Lore and Convent Life between A.D. 500 and A.D. 1500.* Cambridge: 1896.

ERICKSON, C. *The Medieval Vision. Essays in History and Perception.* New York: 1976. (See particularly chap. 8, "The Vision of Women," pp. 181–212.)

————, and Casey, K. "Women in the Middle Ages: A Working Bibliography." *Mediaeval Studies* 37 (1975): 340–59.

ERLANGER, PHILIPPE. *La rose sanglante.* Paris: 1961. (English editions published as *Margaret of Anjou, Queen of England.* Translated by E. Hyams. London: 1970. Coral Gables, Florida: 1971.)

FERRANTE, JOAN M. *Woman as Image in Medieval Literature from the Twelfth Century to Dante.* New York and London: 1975.

FLANDRIN, JEAN-LOUIS. "Contraception, mariage et relations amoureuses dans l'Occident chrétien." *Annales: Economies, Sociétés, Civilisations* 24 (November-December 1969): 1370–90.

FLOYED, J. ARTHUR. "An Extinct Religious Order. Its Founder." *The Catholic World* 63 (1896): 343–53.

FORBES, THOMAS R. *The Midwife and the Witch.* New Haven, Conn. and London: 1966.

FORSTER, E., and FORSTER, R., eds. *European Diet from Pre-industrial to Modern Times.* New York: 1975.

FRAZER, CHARLES A. "The Origins of Clerical Celibacy in the Western Church." *Church History* 41, no. 2 (June 1972): 149–67.

FURNIVALL, F. J., ed. *The Babees Book: Medieval Manners for the Young: Done into Modern English.* London and New York: 1908.

GARDINER, DOROTHY KEMPE. *English Girlhood at School. A Study of Women's Education through Twelve Centuries.* London: 1929.

GIST, MARGARET A. *Love and War in the Middle English Romances.* Philadelphia: 1947. London: 1948.

GIVEN, JAMES B. *Society and Homocide in Thirteenth Century England.* Stanford: 1977.

GOODICH, MICHAEL. "The Politics of Canonization in the Thirteenth Century: Lay and Mendicant Saints." *Church History* 44, no. 3 (September 1975): 294–307.

GRAHAM, ROSE. *St. Gilbert of Sempringham and the Gilbertines. A History of the Only English Monastic Order.* London: 1901. Reprint: 1904

GRIFFITHS, RALPH A. "The Trial of Eleanor Cobham: An Episode in the Fall of Duke Humphrey of Gloucester." *Bulletin of the John Rylands Library* 51, no. 2 (1969): 381–99.

GUTH, DELLOYD J., ed. *Late-Medieval England, 1377–1485.* Cambridge and New York (For the Conference on British Studies): 1976.

HAIR, P. E. H., ed. *Before the Bawdy Court. Selections from Church, Court and other Records Relating to the Correction of Moral Offences in England, Scotland and New England, 1300–1800.* London and New York: 1972.

————. "Bridal Pregnancy in Earlier Rural England Further Examined." *Population Studies* 24 (March 1970): 59–70.

————. "Bridal Pregnancy in Rural England in Earlier Centuries." *Population Studies* 20, no. 2 (November 1966): 233–43.

HALLAM, H. E. "Some Thirteenth-Century Censuses." *Economic History Review*, 2d series, 10 (April 1958): 340–61.

HANAWALT, BARBARA A. "The Female Felon in Fourteenth-Century England." In *Women in Medieval Society*, edited by S. M. Stuard, pp. 125–40. Philadelphia: 1976.

HARRIS, ANN SUTHERLAND, and NOCHLIN, LINDA. *Women Artists: 1550–1950.* Los Angeles County Museum of Art, exhibition catalogue. New York: 1976.

HARWOOD, BRITTON J. "The Wife of Bath and the Dream of Innocence." *Modern Language Quarterly* 33, no. 3 (September 1972): 257–73.

HASKELL, ANN. "The Paston Women on Marriage in Fifteenth Century England." *Viator. Medieval and Renaissance Studies* 4 (1973): 459–71.

HEATON, HERBERT. *The Yorkshire Woolen Industry and Worsted Industries from the Earliest Times up to the Industrial Revolution.* Oxford: 1920. 2d ed., 1965.

HEINRICH, SISTER MARY PIA. *The Canonesses and Education in the Early Middle Ages.* Washington, D.C.: 1924.

HELMHOLZ, RICHARD H. "Infanticide in the Province of Canterbury during the 15th Century." *History of Childhood Quarterly* 2, no. 3 (1975): 379–90.

——. *Marriage Litigation in Medieval England.* Cambridge: 1974.

HENNING, ROBERT W. "From *Eva* and *Ave* to Eglentyne and Alisoun: Chaucer's Insight into the Roles Women Play." *Signs. Journal of Women and Society* 2, no. 3 (Spring 1977): 580–99.

HERLIHY, DAVID. "Land, Family and Women in Continental Europe, 701–1200." *Traditio* 18 (1962): 89–120.

——. "Life Expectancies for Women in Medieval Society." In *The Role of Women in the Middle Ages.* Papers of the 6th Annual Conference of the Center for Medieval and Early Renaissance Studies, SUNY, Binghamton, edited by R. Morewedge, pp. 1–22. Albany: 1975.

HERRTAGE, S. J. H., ed. *The Early English Version of the "Gesta Romanorum."* Early English Text Society, Extra Series, 33. London: 1879. Reprint: 1962.

HILL, GEORGIANA. *Women in English Life from Medieval to Modern Times*, vol. 1. London: 1896.

HILTON, R. H. *The English Peasantry in the Later Middle Ages: The Ford Lectures for 1973 and Related Studies.* Oxford: 1975.

HIMES, NORMAN E. *A Medical History of Contraception.* Baltimore: 1936. Reprint. New York: 1970

HOLLAND, NORMAN N. *The Dynamics of Literary Response.* New York: 1968.

HOLLINGSWORTH, T. H. "A Note on the Mediaeval Longevity of the Secular Peerage 1350–1500." *Population Studies* 29, no. 1 (March 1975): 155–59.

HOLLISTER, C. WARREN. "The Anglo-Norman Succession Debate of 1126: Prelude to Stephen's Anarchy." *Journal of Medieval History* 1, no.1 (April 1975): 19–41.

HOLT, J. C. "Politics and Property in Early Medieval England." *Past and Present* 57 (November 1957): 3–52.

——. "Politics and Property in Early Medieval England: A Rejoinder." *Past and Present* 65 (November 1974): 127–35.

HOMANS, GEORGE C. *English Villagers of the Thirteenth Century.* Cambridge, Mass.: 1941. Reprint. New York: 1971.

HORNSTEIN, LILLIAN HERLANDS. "The Wyf of Bathe and the Merchant: From Sex to 'Secte.'" *The Chaucer Review. A Journal of Medieval Studies and Literary Criticism* 3, no. 1 (February 1968): 65–67.

HUGO, THOMAS. *The Medieval Nunneries of the County of Somerset and the Diocese of Bath and Wells; Together with the Annals of Their Impropriated Benefices, from the Earliest Times to the Death of Queen Mary.* London: 1867.

HUNT, DAVID. *Parents and Children in History. The Psychology of Family Life in Early Modern France.* New York: 1970. Reprint. New York and London: 1972.

JOURDAIN, CHARLES. "Mémoire sur l'éducation des femmes au moyen âge."

*Mémoires de l'Académie des Inscriptions et Belles-Lettres*, 2d series, 28 (1874): 79–133.

KAUFMAN, MICHAEL., "Spare Ribs: The Conception of Woman in the Middle Ages and the Renaissance." *Soundings* 56 (Summer 1973): 139–63.

KELLUM, BARBARA A. "Infanticide in England in the Later Middle Ages." *History of Childhood Quarterly* 1, no. 3 (1974): 367–88.

KELLY, AMY R. *Eleanor of Aquitaine and the Four Kings*. Cambridge, Mass.: 1950. Reprint. London: 1952.

KELLY, HENRY ANSGAR. "Canonical Implications of Richard III's Plan to Marry His Niece." *Traditio* 23 (1967): 269–311.

———. "English Kings and the Fear of Sorcery." *Mediaeval Studies* 39 (1977): 206–38.

———. *Love and Marriage in the Age of Chaucer*. Ithaca, N.Y. and London: 1975.

KELLY-GADOL, JOAN. "The Social Relation of the Sexes: Methodological Implications of Women's History." *Signs. Journal of Women in Culture and Society* 1, no. 4 (Summer 1976): 809–23.

KERHAN, ANNE. "The Archwife and the Eunuch." *English Literary History* 41 (Spring 1974): 1–25.

KIBLER, WILLIAM W., ed. *Eleanor of Aquitaine, Patron and Politician*. Austin, Tex. and London: 1976.

KIECKHEFER, RICHARD. *Late Medieval Witch Trials: Their Foundations in Popular and Learned Culture 1300–1500*. Berkeley, Calif.: 1976.

KING, EDMUND. "The Tenurial Crisis of the Early Twelfth Century." *Past and Present* 65 (November 1974): 110–17.

KNOWLES, DAVID C. *The English Mystical Tradition*. New York and London: 1961.

———, and HADCOCK, R. N. *Medieval Religious Houses: England and Wales*. Revised and enlarged edition. London and New York: 1953. 2d rev. ed.: 1971.

KRAUSE, J. T. "The Medieval Household: Large or Small?" *Economic History Review*, 2d series, 9 (April 1957): 420–32.

LABARGE, MARGARET WADE. *A Baronial Household in the Thirteenth Century*. Toronto: 1965.

LAEUCHLI, SAMUEL. *Power and Sexuality. The Emergence of Canon Law at the Synod of Elvira*. Philadelphia: 1972.

LAMOND, ELIZABETH, ed. and trans. *Walter of Henley's Husbandry, together with an Anonymous Husbandry, Seneschaucie, and Robert Grosseteste's Rule*. London and New York: 1890.

LANCASTER, LORRAINE. "Kinship in Anglo-Saxon Society." *British Journal of Sociology* 9 (1958): 359–61.

LASLETT, P., and OOSTERVEEN, K, "Long-Term Trends in Bastardy in England." *Population Studies* 27, no. 2 (July 1973): 255–86.

LAZAR, MOSHÉ. "Cupid, the Lady and the Poet: Modes of Love at Eleanor of Aquitaine's Court." In *Eleanor of Aquitaine, Patron and Politician*, edited by William W. Kibler, pp. 35–59. Austin, Tex. and London: 1976.

LEIBELL, HELEN D. *Anglo-Saxon Education of Women from Hilda to Hildegarde*. Washington, D.C.: 1922

LERNER, ROBERT E. *The Heresy of the Free Spirit in the Later Middle Ages*. Berkeley, Calif.: 1972.

LÉVI-STRAUSS, CLAUDE. *Les Structures élémentaires de la parente*. 2d ed. Paris: 1967. (English editions published as *The Elementary Structures of Kinship*.

Translated by J. H. Bell. Edited by J. R. von Sturmer and R. Needham. Rev. ed. Boston and London: 1969.)

LEVY, BERNARD S. "The Wife of Bath's *Queynte Fantasye.*" *The Chaucer Review. A Journal of Medieval Studies and Literary Criticism* 4, no. 2 (1969): 106–22.

MCDONNELL, E. W. *Beguines and Beghards in Medieval Culture, with Special Emphasis on the Belgian Scene.* New Brunswick, N.J.: 1954.

MCFARLANE, ALAN. *Witchcraft in Tudor and Stuart England.* London: 1970.

MCFARLANE, K. B. *The Nobility of Later Medieval England.* Oxford and New York: 1973

MCLAUGHLIN, ELEANOR C. "Equality of Souls, Inequality of Sexes: Women in Medieval Theology." In *Religion and Sexism. Images of Woman in the Jewish and Christian Tradition,* edited by Rosemary R. Ruether. New York: 1974.

MCLAUGHLIN, MARY MARTIN. "Survivors and Surrogates: Children and Parents from the Ninth to the Thirteenth Centuries." In *The History of Childhood,* edited by Lloyd DeMause, pp. 101–81. New York: 1975.

MCROBBIE, KENNETH. "Woman and Love: Some Aspects of Competition in Late Medieval Society." *Mosaic* 5 (1972): 139–68.

MAGEE, PATRICIA ANNE. "The Wife of Bath and the Problem of Mastery." *Massachusetts Studies in English* (Fall 1974): 40–45.

MEECH, S. B., and ALLEN, H. E., eds. *The Book of Margery Kempe.* Early English Text Society, o.s. 212. London: 1940. Reprint: 1961.

MINTZ, SIDNEY W. "Men, Women and Trade." *Comparative Studies in Society and History* 13, no. 3 (1971): 247–69.

MOGAN, JOSEPH J., JR. "Chaucer and the *Bona Matrimonii.*" *The Chaucer Review. A Journal of Medieval Studies and Literary Criticism* 4, no. 2 (1969): 123–41.

MONTER, E. WILLIAMS. *Witchcraft in France and Switzerland. The Borderlands during the Reformation.* Ithaca N.Y. and London: 1976. (See particularly chap. 1, "The Rise and Fall of Witchcraft Theory.")

———. "The Historiography of European Witchcraft: Progress and Prospects." *Journal of Interdisciplinary History* 2, no. 4 (Spring 1972): 435–51.

MOORMAN, JOHN R. H. *Church Life in England in the Thirteenth Century.* Cambridge: 1954.

MOREWEDGE, ROSMARIE THEE, ed. *The Role of Woman in the Middle Ages.* Papers of the 6th Annual Conference of the Center for Medieval and Early Renaissance Studies, SUNY, Binghamton. Albany: 1975.

MORRIS, R., ed. *Old English Homilies of the 12th and 13th Centuries.* 3 vols. Early English Text Society, o.s. 29, 34, 53. London: 1867, 1868, 1873. Reprint in one volume: 1973.

MURTAUGH, DANIEL M. "Women and Geoffrey Chaucer." *English Literary History* 38, no. 4 (1971): 473–92.

NOLL, DOLORES L. "The Romantic Conception of Marriage: Some Remarks on C. S. Lewis' Discussion of the Kingis Quair." *Studies in Medieval Culture* 3 (1970): 159–68.

NOONAN, JOHN T., JR. *Contraception. A History of its Treatment by the Catholic Theologians and Canonists.* Cambridge, Mass.: 1966.

———. "Marriage in the Middle Ages: Power to Choose." *Viator: Medieval and Renaissance Studies* 4 (1973): 419–34.

———, ed. *The Morality of Abortion: Legal and Historical Perspectives.* Cambridge, Mass. and London: 1970.

ORME, NICHOLAS. *English Schools in the Middle Ages.* London: 1973.

O'SULLIVAN, J. F., ed. *Registrum visitationum. The Register of Eudes of Rouen.* Translated by Sydney M. Brown. New York and London: 1964.

OWST, G. R. *Literature and Pulpit in Medieval England: A Neglected Chapter in the History of English Letters and of the English People.* London: 1933. 2d rev. ed. Oxford and New York: 1961.

————. *Preaching in Medieval England: An Introduction to Sermon Manuscripts of the Period c. 1350–1450.* New York: 1965.

PAINTER, SIDNEY. "The Family and the Feudal System in Twelfth-Century England." *Speculum* 35 (1960): 1–16.

PALOMO, DOLORES, "The Fate of the Wife of Bath's 'Bad Husbands.'" *The Chaucer Review. A Journal of Medieval Studies and Literary Criticism* 9, no. 4 (Spring 1975): 303–19.

PARTNER, NANCY. "Henry of Huntingdon: Clerical Celibacy and the Writing of History." *Church History* 42, no. 4 (1973): 467–75.

PHILLPOTTS, BERTHA S. *Kindred and Clan in the Middle Ages and After. A Study in the Sociology of the Teutonic Races.* Cambridge: 1913. Reprint for the Cambridge Archeological and Ethnological Series. New York: 1972.

PIA, SISTER MARIA. "The Industrial Position of Women in the Middle Ages." *Catholic Historical Review*, n.s. 4, no. 4 (January 1925): 556–60.

POST, J. B. "The Tauke Family in the Fourteenth and Fifteenth Centuries." *Sussex Archaeological Collections* 11(1973): 93–107.

POWER, EILEEN. *Medieval English Nunneries c. 1275–1535.* Cambridge Studies in Medieval Life and Thought. Cambridge: 1922.

————. *Medieval Women.* Edited by M. M. Postan. Cambridge: 1975.

————. "The Position of Women." In *The Legacy of the Middle Ages*, edited by C. G. Crump and E. F. Jacob, pp. 401–33. Oxford: 1926.

————. "Some Women Practitioners of Medicine in the Middle Ages." *Proceedings. Royal Society of Medicine* 15 (1922): 20–23.

PUGH, RALPH BERNARD. *Imprisonment in Medieval England.* Cambridge: 1968.

————, ed. *Victoria History of the Counties of England. General Introduction.* London (Published for the Institute of Historical Research): 1970.

PUTNAM, BERTHA H. *The Enforcement of the Statutes of Laborers During the First Decade after the Black Death, 1349–1359.* New York and London: 1908.

PUTNAM, EMILY J. *The Lady: Studies of Various Significant Phases of her History.* London: 1910. Reprint. Chicago: 1970.

RAFTIS, J. AMBROSE. *Tenure and Mobility: Studies in the Social History of the Medieval English Village.* Pontifical Institute of Mediaeval Studies, Studies and Texts, 8. Toronto: 1964.

————. "Changes in an English Village after the Black Death." *Mediaeval Studies* 29 (1967): 158–77.

RANDALL, LILIAN M. *Images in the Margins of Gothic Manuscripts.* Berkeley, Calif.: 1966.

RANUM, OREST, and RANUM, PATRICIA, eds. *Popular Attitudes toward Birth Control in Pre-Industrial France and England.* New York and London: 1972.

ROBBINS, ROSSELL HOPE. "The Chaucerian Apocrypha." In *A Manual of the Writings in Middle English, 1050–1500*, vol. 4, chap. 11. New Haven, Conn.: 1973.

————. "The Vintner's Son: French Wine in English Bottles." In *Eleanor of Aquitaine, Patron and Politician*, edited by William W. Kibler. Austin, Tex. and London: 1976.

ROSENTHAL, J. T. "Medieval Longevity: The Secular Peerage, 1300–1500." *Population Studies* 27, no. 2 (June 1973): 287–93.

ROSS, W. O., ed. *Middle English Sermons*. Early English Text Society, o.s. 209. London: 1940. Reprint: 1960.

ROSSIAUD, J. "Prostitution, jeunesse et société dans les villes du sud-est au XV^e siècle." *Annales: Economies, Sociétés, Civilisations* 31, no. 2 (1976): 289–325.

ROUSSET, PAUL. "La femme et la famille dans *l'Histoire ecclésiastique* d'Orderic Vital." *Zeitschrift für schweizerische Kirchengeschichte* 63 (1969): 58–66.

ROWLAND, BERYL. "The Wife of Bath's 'Unlawful Philtrum.'" *Neophilologus* 56, no. 2 (1972): 201–206.

RUBIN, GAYLE. "The Traffic in Women." In *Toward an Anthropology of Women*, edited by Rayna Reiter. New York and London: 1975.

RUBIN, STANLEY. *Medieval English Medicine A.D. 500–1300*. New York and Newton Abbot: 1974.

RUETHER, ROSEMARY R. "The Persecution of Witches: A Case of Sexism and Ageism?" *Christianity in Crisis* (23 December 1974).

RUSSELL, JEFFREY BURTON. *Witchcraft in the Middle Ages*. Ithaca, N.Y. and London: 1972.

RUSSELL, JOSIAH COX. *British Medieval Population*. Albuquerque, N. Mex.: 1948.

———. "Population in Europe 500–1500." In *The Fontana Economic History of Europe*, vol. 1: *The Middle Ages*, edited by C. Cipolla, pp. 25–70. London: 1972. Reprint. Hassocks: 1976; New York: 1977. (Citations in notes are to the original Fontana edition.)

———. "A Quantitative Approach to Medieval Population Change." *Journal of Economic History*, 24, no. 1 (March 1964): 1–21.

———. "Recent Advances in Medieval Demography." *Speculum* 40 (1965): 84–101.

SCAMMELL, JEAN. "Freedom and Marriage in Medieval England." *Economic History Review*, 2d series, 27 (1974): 523–37.

———. "Wife-Rents and Merchet." *Economic History Review*, 2d series, 29, no. 3 (1976): 487–90.

SEARLE, ELEANOR. "Freedom and Marriage in Medieval England: An Alternative Hypothesis." *Economic History Review*, 2d series, 29, no. 3 (1976): 482–86.

SHAHAR, SHULAMITH. "De quelques aspects de la femme dans la pensée et la communauté religieuse aux 12^e et 13^e siècles." *Revue de l'histoire des religions* 185 (1974): 29–77.

SHORTER, EDWARD. *The Making of the Modern Family*. New York: 1975. Reprint: 1977.

SHREWSBURY, J. F. D. *A History of Bubonic Plague in the British Isles*. London: 1970.

SMITH, JOSHUA TOULMIN; SMITH, L. TOULMIN; and BRENTANO, L., eds. *English Gilds. The Original Ordinances of More than One Hundred Early English Gilds etc.* Early English Text Society, o.s. 40. London: 1870. Reprint: 1963.

STENTON, DORIS MARY. *The English Woman in History*. London and New York: 1957. Reprint. New York: 1977.

STENTON, FRANK M. "The Historical Bearing of Place-Name Studies: The Place of Women in Anglo-Saxon Society." *Transactions of the Royal Historical Society*, 4th series, 25 (1943): 1–13.

STONE, ROBERT KARL. *Middle English Prose Style: Margery Kempe and Julian of Norwich*. The Hague: 1970.

STUARD, SUSAN MOSHER, ed. *Women in Medieval Society*. Philadelphia: 1976.

STYS, W. "The Influence of Economic Conditions on the Fertility of Peasant Women." *Population Studies* 11, no. 2 (November 1957): 136–48.

SWEENEY, J. R., and HALL, EDWIN. "An Unpublished Privilege of Innocent III in Favor of Montivilliers: New Documentation for a Great Norman Nunnery." *Speculum* 49 (1974): 662–79.

TALBOT, C. H., ed. and trans. *The Life of Christina of Markyate.* Oxford: 1959.

———, and Hammond, E. A. *The Medical Practitioners in Medieval England. A Bibliographical Register.* London: 1965.

THOMAS, KEITH. "The Relevance of Social Anthropology to the Historical Study of English Witchcraft." In *Witchcraft Confessions and Accusations,* edited by Mary Douglas. London: 1970.

THOMPSON, A. H., ed. *Visitations of Religious Houses in the Diocese of Lincoln.* 2 vols. Lincoln Record Society and Canterbury and York Society: 1915.

THOMSON, JOHN A. *The Later Lollards, 1414–1520.* London: 1965.

THRUPP, SYLVIA L. "The Gilds." In *The Cambridge Economic History of Europe,* vol. 3: *Economic Organization and Policies in the Middle Ages,* edited by M. M. Postan, E. E. Rich, and E. Miller, pp. 230–80, 624–34. Cambridge: 1963.

———. "Medieval Industry, 1000–1500." In *The Fontana Economic History of Europe,* vol. 1: *The Middle Ages,* edited by C. Cipolla. London: 1972. Reprint. Hassocks: 1976; New York: 1977. (Citations in notes are to the original Fontana edition.)

———. *The Merchant Class of Medieval London, 1300–1500.* Chicago: 1948.

UNDERHILL, EVELYN. *The Mystics of the Church.* London: 1925.

UTLEY, FRANCIS LEE. *The Crooked Rib: An Analytical Index to the Arguments about Women in English and Scots Literature to the End of the Year 1568.* Columbus, Ohio: 1944.

VERDIER, PHILIPPE. "Woman in the Marginalia of Gothic Manuscripts and Related Works." In *Eleanor of Aquitaine, Patron and Politician,* edited by William W. Kibler. Austin, Tex. and London: 1976.

WALKER, SUE SHERIDAN. "Proof of Age of Feudal Heirs in Medieval England." *Medieval Studies* 35 (1973): 306–23.

———. "Widow and Ward: The Feudal Law of Child Custody in Medieval England." In *Women in Medieval Society,* edited by S. M. Stuard, pp. 159–82. Philadelphia: 1976.

WALLERSTEIN, IMMANUEL. *The Modern World System. Capitalist Agriculture and the Origins of the European World-Economy in the Sixteenth Century.* New York: 1974. Reprint. London: 1976.

WALSH, JAMES, S. J., ed. and trans. *The Revelations of Divine Love of Julian of Norwich.* London and New York: 1961. Reprint. St. Meinrad, Ind.: 1974.

WARRACK, GRACE, ed. *Revelations of Divine Love.* London: 1901. 14th ed. 1952.

WHEATON, R. "Family and Kinship in Western Europe: The Problem of the Joint Family Household." *Journal of Interdisciplinary History* 5, no. 4 (Spring 1975): 601–28.

WHITE, G. H. "Henry I's Illegitimate Children." In *The Complete Peerage,* edited by G. E. Cockayne et al., vol. 11, pp. 105–21, Appendix D. London: 1949.

WOLTERS, CLIFTON, ed. *Revelations of Divine Love.* Bungay, England: 1966.

WRIGHT, THOMAS, ed. and trans. *The Book of the Knight De La Tour-Landry, Compiled for the Instruction of His Daughters.* Early English Text Society, o.s. 33. London: 1868. Reprint. London: 1973.

———. *A Contemporary Narrative of the Proceedings Against Dame Alice Kyteler,*

*Prosecuted for Sorcery in 1324, by Richard Ledrede, Bishop of Ossory.* London: 1843.

———. *A History of Domestic Manners and Sentiments in England During the Middle Ages.* London: 1862.

WRIGLEY, E. A., ed. *An Introduction to English Historical Demography.* London: 1966.

# Women under the Law

## in Medieval England

## 1066–1485

RUTH KITTEL

Bracton, a thirteenth-century judge and legist, in speaking of the widow, made a statement about her role in life which might apply equally well to most medieval English women. He said that the heir was bound to defend a widow's dower[1] and to attend the local courts for her. "For she herself ought to attend to nothing except the care of her house and the rearing and education of her children."[2] A woman's proper place was in the home. Before marriage, a woman was to live under the guardianship of parents or lord. After marriage, a wife was to reside under the benevolent protection of her husband and leave the world of public life to men.

A woman who remained in the home is largely hidden from the view of the historian. Her daily life was rarely recorded. Of exceptional interest in this regard are the large collections of fifteenth-century letters: J. Gairdner, ed., *The Paston letters*; C. L. Kingsford, ed., *The Stonor Letters*; H. E. Malden, ed., *The Cely Papers*. The Paston letters, as one example, contain a wealth of information for a Norfolk squire's family concerning marriage arrangements, relations between parents and children, and a housewife's cares and concerns. The bulk of this correspondence, which numbers over one thousand letters, deals with life as it was seen from a manor house. Yet, even in this vast collection, as H. S. Bennett has pointed out, "many of the most ordinary and everyday things of life go unrecorded."[3] By and large, even among the Paston women, it was their activity beyond the home which has left evidence for the historian.

And women did venture beyond the home. Despite Bracton's advice that a widow should let the heir take care of her legal concerns, women in large numbers attended courts. We are fortunate in having records of three types of courts: ecclesiastical, manorial, and royal courts. The extant legal documents offer one of the few viewpoints for an examination of women's activity.

Ecclesiastical courts had jurisdiction in religious matters over all Christians in England, although the very rich and the very poor did not usually appear in the diocesan courts. The courts have been studied recently by Father Michael Sheehan of the Pontifical Institute of Toronto[4] and Professor Richard Helmholz of Washington University, St. Louis.[5] Both men, who have worked extensively with unpublished sources, have been interested in the conditions surrounding the contracting and annulment of marriages. Marriage was one of the major concerns of ecclesiastical law (technically known as canon law), because it was this law which defined what constituted a marriage and who could legally marry.

The historian can and should look at both the more theoretical statements of the law and the records of court litigation. On the more abstract level, the canon law has much to teach. For example, the law concluded that consent informed by marital affection made a marriage. Two individuals speaking words of present consent became husband and wife.[6] Nothing else was necessary. No ceremony. No third party. No sexual relationship. Marital consent was required of both partners. Just as the right to sexual intercourse and the strictures against adultery applied to both when married, so in the initial contract of marriage, the sexes were strikingly equal. The canon law's emphasis on consent as the cornerstone of marriage meant a basic theoretical equality between husband and wife.

Our basic sources for the canon law are the twelfth-century *Concordance of Discordant Canons* by Gratian and the thirteenth-century collection known as the *Decretals*.[7] Both are in print. These two statements of the law give us further information about consent in the contracting of marriage. To the question, "May a daughter be given in marriage against her will?" Gratian boldly concluded that no woman was to be coupled to anyone except by her free will.[8] And in the *Decretals*, it is stated that "there is no place for consent where fear and compulsion are present."[9] But this was not taken by the Church to include all degrees of fear and compulsion. The fear must be such as would sway a "steady" person. If force was judged sufficient, then the marriage was null. But how much force was sufficient? It is at this point that looking at actual marriage litigation, as recorded in manuscripts, becomes invaluable.

Judging by marriage cases in the fourteenth and fifteenth centuries, the steady woman was expected to endure considerable force. For example, the threat to take a girl by the ears and throw her into a pool of water and the threat to another girl to deny her "a certain portion of land" were not judged sufficient grounds to annul the contract.[10] When a girl was fiercely beaten with staves, however, the court did rule for annulment.[11] These cases—and others like them—reveal individual arrangements for a marriage.

If we expand our view of the position of women in society to include their families, then canon law courts again offer valuable evidence. For example, what was the extent of a woman's responsibility to her children? In one instance, a woman, Marion, brought with her into court a month-old child.

> And the woman placed the child on the ground in front of the judge, saying that she no longer wished to care for it, but that it should be taken by the father, who she asserted was the said Rowland. To which the man replied, denying it, and offered to undergo compurgation as to any carnal relations with her. Then the judge warned the woman to receive the child at her breast to nourish it with due sustenance under pain of major excommunication until the question of paternity was discussed.[12]

This is, unfortunately, all the record tells about the case. The question of how to care for the child was apparently settled out of court. But, despite the fact that we do not know the final outcome of the case, the temporary order of the judge does illustrate the woman's immediate responsibility for her child; she was to "nourish it with due sustenance."

Canon law records are still being explored. Professor John T. Noonan, Jr., of the University of California is translating the marriage sections of Gratian and the *Decretals* for publication by the Pontifical Institute of Medieval Studies. Professor Charles Donahue of the University of Michigan and Norma Adams, professor emeritus of Mount Holyoke, are editing collections of ecclesiastical cases from York and Canterbury, respectively, for Selden Society volumes. These two efforts will make available in English the basic canon law of marriage and a sample of cases.

Canon law records of marriage litigation begin in the middle of the thirteenth century and continue beyond the end of the Middle Ages. According to Richard Helmholz, there are very few changes in the law during the period from 1250 to 1500. The position of women in the contracting of marriage is one of equality with men—and that position remains basically the same throughout the medieval period.

Ecclesiastical courts theoretically applied to all Christians living in

England. These same men and women were also, however, subject to secular courts. The majority of the population were under a manorial court. Each manor or estate was subject to a lord who, as one of his rights, held his own court. And all the people who lived and worked on the manor were bound to attend that court. The law enforced in each manorial court was essentially custom, which could and did vary from manor to manor.

There are two kinds of legal manorial records available to historians. The first, custumals, record the parcels of land on the manor and the rents and services due from each plot.[13] The custumals present the "manor at rest" or a static picture of obligations, while the second source, the court rolls, show the "manor in action".[14] These records of proceedings in the court reveal the resolutions of all types of conflict on the manor, and as a result, have been called "the foremost medieval sources for what is called social history."[15] Court rolls vary in quality and comprehensiveness, but a good set will yield information on social structure, economy, mobility, and tenure patterns.

Unfortunately, these sources reveal relatively little about women. The prime concern of the documents is with the peasant's relationship to the lord. The peasant's home life and daily routine matter nothing to the lord, and as a result do not appear anywhere in the records.[16] What matters to the lord are the payment of rents, the fulfillment of services owed, and the maintenance of peace.

There were two main areas regarding women that did concern the lord and, consequently, do appear in the records. The first is marriage. Each lord had the right to the payment of a fine for the marriage of an unfree man's daughter. The court, therefore, attempted to keep account of whether women had married, and if so, whether they had paid for a license. The court kept track of marriages both on and off the manor; consequently, the records allow the historian to trace the patterns of women's mobility. For example, Ambrose Raftis has found that women moved shorter distances away from their home manor than men.[17] This is not to say that many women did not finally get far from their native village, but for most women, neighboring communities were at least their first stopping place.

Manor records provide information not only about marriage patterns, but also about land. Records from manor courts reveal how much landed property a woman received upon her husband's death. Arrangements varied from manor to manor. To give one example, in the Oxfordshire village of Cuxham, widows of half-virgate[18] tenements could claim as dower all of their husband's land.[19] There was no clear case between 1240 and 1400 of the land passing directly from father to son. The widow could farm the land on her own. There seems on this manor to have been no objection to female tenants, since one widow alone held her tenement for thirty-two years. On other manors, there are occasions of lords exerting pressure on widows to remarry.

What mattered primarily to the lord was that the obligations attached to the land be fulfilled. The competence of the holder of the land—whether male or female—was what mattered. As a result, women are not often singled out for special treatment by the court. They are treated to a large extent, with the exception of fines for marriage, on an equal basis with men. Over the centuries, the rights of women, in respect to men, did not show any noticeable changes, but the lot of the peasantry as a whole did improve.

Studies of village life have generally been of two kinds. In one category, men have attempted to describe the social order as a whole, to give a picture of manorial life over all of England. These works present valuable introductory overviews.[20] In the other category, numerous authors have studied in minute detail specific manors in an attempt to determine the range of variation within the overall pattern.[21] And finally, in the last ten years, there have appeared a few specialized studies of marriage and inheritance patterns—studies which are of especial interest to researchers concerned with the position of women.[22]

While the manor courts served small local areas coextensive with the individual manor, the royal courts had jurisdiction over almost all of England. These royal courts were comprised of the common law courts, which will be our main concern, and the courts of equity.[23] Not until 1534 did chancery, the main court of equity, begin to enroll its decisions.[24] Our knowledge of proceedings in the fourteenth and fifteenth centuries is based largely on the complainant's petition. The defendant's answer and the court's judgment are usually not recorded. Consequently, the workings of the equity courts are difficult to interpret. The sources for the common law courts, on the other hand, are more complete.

First, there are general treatises on the state of the law. Glanvill for the twelfth century, Bracton for the thirteenth, and Littleton for the fifteenth, provide brilliant summaries of their understanding of the law.[25] All are in print. Combined with a copy of *The Statutes of the Realm*, these works are invaluable places for any historian to start his study.

Second, there are the court rolls.[26] The wealth of extant material, which numbers in the thousands of rolls, is dazzling and somewhat overwhelming. It would take several researchers a lifetime to read. In comparison with the total number of rolls, very few are in print. The rolls, while they offer information about great numbers of men and women, have their limitations for the historian. The entries often follow a common form and tell little of the personal motivations and facts of the case. We may learn just the names of the parties, their employment or status, the cause of the dispute, and the relevant action of the court. It is frequently impossible to follow one specific case from beginning to end. And if a case is settled out of court or proceedings dropped, then the case may just disappear from sight. If the historian, however, is willing to read dozens or hundreds of cases, he or she will find the exceptional entry where the clerk has added to an otherwise mundane entry some colorful detail and an informal appraisal of events.

The rolls may be supplemented by yearbooks, which are anonymous notes on the proceedings of the cases.[27] Aspiring lawyers took notes on various cases as a way of learning the profession. There survives one notebook for nearly every year of the fourteenth and fifteenth centuries. Almost all of these are in print. These notebooks record "arguments about true precedents and technicalities of process"[28] from which the judicial decision emerges. What was important for the student were the legal arguments; the decision itself may never be recorded. As a consequence, the yearbooks are of more interest to the legal historian than the social historian.

The study of women and the common law seems to have captured the interest of both legal and social historians. There are those historians such as F. Joüon des Longrais who have stressed the legal aspects of the position of women.[29] And a study of the legal disabilities of free women, especially married women, throws much light on the status of women in medieval society. One example is the law regarding the control of property during marriage.[30] Glanvill, a twelfth-century legist, outlined the general results of the husband's dominance when he wrote: "since legally a woman is completely in the power of her husband, it is not surprising that . . . all her property is clearly deemed to be at his disposal."[31] The husband had the right to enjoy the land's profits and, most importantly, the right to dispose or alienate that land for the duration of the marriage. Widows and single women had the same rights as men in land law; they could buy and sell land on their own authority. But married women submitted all immediate control of their land to their spouses.

Laws regarding property arrangements for the duration of marriage tell us something about the relationship of husband and wife. The amount of land a wife acquired after marriage also reveals a woman's position in society. F. Joüon des Longrais has written a book on the changing patterns of dower[32] in the twelfth and thirteenth centuries.[33]

Land law is the most complex and intricate part of common law, but another section which is simpler in its outlines but equally interesting is criminal law. Criminal law can offer us some insights into the degree of obedience expected of wives. Bracton stated that, although as a general rule a wife should obey her husband, she "need not be obedient in heinous deeds."[34] In theory, a wife's obedience should stop short of participation in criminal activities. The law, however, allowed the possibility of a husband forcing his wife to accompany him in a crime. In a case in Wiltshire in 1249, for example, a husband was hanged for harboring a thief, while the wife was acquitted because she "was so subjected to him that she had to obey."[35]

Criminal law also includes information about injuries inflicted on women—such as assault and rape. In the twelfth and early thirteenth centuries, community attitudes towards men accused of rape are revealed in a curious combination of heavy penalties with an almost zero conviction rate. The woman, if she chose to prosecute her suit, might secure a harsh punishment, including castration and mutilation, for the offender. In practice, however, the community seemed to discourage the woman from seeking full vengeance. In the vast majority of cases, the woman abandoned her plea. If the king chose not to prosecute, the accused was free, while if the king did follow up the suit, the most the guilty criminal suffered was a fine. There seems to have been a belief that as far as royal prosecution of justice was concerned, rape was a relatively minor matter. This attitude changed in 1285; the Second Statute of Westminster decreed that a rapist convicted at the suit of either the injured woman or the king should suffer death. But the effects of that law in actual litigation have yet to be studied. Were juries willing to convict an alleged rapist when death was the prescribed penalty? Did an increase in punishment result in a lower or higher conviction rate? Such questions can be answered only by an examination of fourteenth-century court records.

A look at laws relating to rape and their enforcement can be part not only of legal history, but of social history. Social historians have recently seen the possibilities inherent in studying the criminal law for what it can reveal about women in society. As James Given, in a study of homicide in thirteenth-century England, states, "the study of the patterns of violence and murder in a given society dramatically reveals the web of inter-relationships that unite its members, and the tensions and conflicts that those relationships engender."[36] Given reports that violence in medieval England was a male preserve. Women participate less as killers or victims, and when they do commit crimes, they show different behavior patterns. Women's actions, in comparison to men's, are centered in the family. They are more likely to kill a spouse or lover than any other relative. They also choose their companions in crime from among family members. Rarely do they act alone. And Given concludes that the "chief reason why women were involved so much less frequently in homicide was that they played a much less active role in social life." A woman's world was basically her home.[3]

What Given has studied for the thirteenth century, Barbara Hanawalt has researched for the fourteenth. Her work is broader, as it concerns not just homicide, but other criminal activities. She has found that "larceny was the single most common crime among women" and that receiving of stolen goods was the only decidedly female offense.[38] In receiving, the woman is in the difficult position of deciding whether to accept members of her family with their goods into the house. Again, the woman is seen located in her home.

In both canon and manorial law, women seem to have been treated almost equally with men, and their status does not appear to have changed very much between 1066 and 1485. In the area of common law, however, women were not always treated on an equal basis with men. For example, in land law, daughters did not inherit on an equal footing with sons. Primogeniture among male children was the rule; the eldest son inherited. It may not have been until the twelfth century that daughters, in default of sons, could inherit land held by military tenure. If there was more than one daughter, the women divided the land equally among themselves. In criminal law, a woman in the twelfth and early thirteenth centuries could only bring charges against an offender for rape, miscarriage, or death of her husband. She could not bring charges for theft, burglary, or death of any other relative. But her position slowly improved. In the thirteenth century, women as plaintiffs in both criminal and land law gained greater access to the courts. The development of the jury trial during this period benefited both men and women. Finally, the courts of equity which grew in the fourteenth and fifteenth centuries may have added to the rights of women. But balanced against these increasing legal rights must be the awareness that women disappeared from the court room in one major capacity. When legal records first become plentiful in the early thirteenth century, we see women acting as attorneys, even for their husbands. By the end of the thirteenth century, lawyers have become an almost entirely male professional class. The common law courts have become increasingly the arena of men.

I have discussed the content of law and given examples from court cases at some length because I wanted to emphasize the richness of the information contained in the legal records. One last reservation must be made about these records. The people who emerge from these records are only those who were involved in litigation—whether as plaintiff, defendant, witness, juror, judge, or lawyer. But I do not think the limitation is a serious one. The courts we have been speaking of cover every social class, from the lowly peasant on the manor to the great landowning aristocrat. They cover not only the criminal, but also the one falsely accused. They cover both secular and religious matters. In many ways, they seem to cover a broad range of interests and people in medieval society. As G. R. Elton has stated: "In general, the volume of these records ... suggests vividly that not many people in England totally escaped contact with the courts."[39] If this suggestion is true, then legal records may be one of our best sources for studying medieval women.

Most of the current legal research regarding English medieval women is in the areas of common and canon laws as opposed to manorial law. In all areas, however, there is much to be done. For example, the common law records for the fifteenth century are practically untouched. They remain in manuscript.

In summary, many aspects of the lives of medieval women will always remain hidden. We will probably never have reliable statistics on when women of the different social classes married. We know very little about how they raised their children. The majority of women seemed to have stayed close to home. But when women ventured outside—for example, to participate in court trials—they often left some record of their activity. It is the historian's job to look at the laws concerning women and to examine the actions of women themselves as revealed in extant legal records.

POSTSCRIPT

Because of the nature of the available legal documents, research on the history of medieval English women based on these sources must be done by people trained in medieval studies. The reasons are commonplace to medievalists, but they may be unknown to historians in other fields. First, there is the problem of languages. The bulk of the documents are in Latin. The clerks, to whom we owe the majority of manuscripts, wrote almost uniformly in the universal language of the Middle Ages. In addition, there is the vernacular language of Anglo-Norman. In the common law courts, for example, lawyers throughout the period pleaded in Anglo-Norman, while official records were kept in Latin. Second, there is the problem of paleography. There remain vast amounts of unpublished materials, for which a knowledge of manuscript hands is necessary. For example, only two percent of the common law records for the thirteenth century are printed. In the other ninety-eight percent, there are at least 27,500 membranes in one class, the rolls of the justices itinerant. If we have a sample of records available in print for the common law, we have only a few individual cases for the ecclesiastical courts. Anyone, therefore, who wishes to study the institution of marriage, which fell under the jurisdiction of the canon law courts, must be able to read manuscript sources.

If the historian is dependent on materials that are published and in English, he or she is left with very little. And the little that does exist has already been extensively explored. Any new work on medieval English women will probably come from people trained in both languages and paleography who can work with what are often quite difficult sources.

# NOTES

1. Dower is the gift by the husband to his wife of land or chattels for her support upon his death.
2. Bracton, *De Legibus et Consuetudinibus Angliae*, f.98.
3. Bennett, *The Pastons and Their England*, p.xvi.
4. Sheehan, "The Formation and Stability of Marriage."
5. Helmholz, *Marriage Litigation*. Also see his two articles, "Infanticide in the Province of Canterbury" and "Bastardy Litigation." For a study of later courts, see Wunderli, "Ecclesiastical Courts in Pre-Reformation London."
6. Noonan, "Marital Affection in the Canonists," p. 479.
7. For England, in particular, see Powicke and Cheney, eds., *Councils and Synods*. For a study based on these documents, see Sheehan, "Marriage and Family in English Conciliar and Synodal Legislation."
8. Friedberg, ed., *Decretum Magistri Gratiani*, C.31 q.2 *dictum post* c.4.
9. Friedberg, ed., *Decretales Gregorii IX*, 4.1.14. For marriage studies based on Gratian and the Decretals, see Esmein, *Le mariage en droit canonique*, which is the standard text, and of more recent writing is Noonan, "Marriage in the Middle Ages." A good general introduction to women in the canon law is Metz, "Le statut de la femme en droit canonique mèdièval." For specific studies see Brundage's articles, "The Crusader's Wife" and "The Crusader's Wife Revisted." Finally, Sheehan's "The Influence of Canon Law on the Property Rights of Married Women in England" deserves reading.
10. York C. P. E. 85 (1362–63) and York C. P. F. 97, 98, 105 (1429–32) in Helmholz, *Marriage Litigation in Medieval England*, p. 92.
11. York C. P. F. 223 (1442) ibid., p. 93.
12. Rochester Act Book DRb Pa 2, f. 167r quoted in Helmholz "Protection of Children by Canon Law Courts," unpublished paper delivered at the AHA convention, 1973.
13. Two examples are Scargill-Bird, ed., *Custumals of Battle Abbey* and Thorpe, ed., *Custumale Roffense*.
14. Maitland, ed., *Select Pleas in Manorial Courts*, Introduction. For examples of manor rolls, see Amphlett, Hamilton, and Wilson, eds., *Court Rolls of the Manor of Hales*; Ault, ed., *Court Rolls of the Abbey of Ramsey and of the Honor of Clare*; Baildon, Lister, and Walder, eds., *Court Rolls of the Manor of Wakefield*.
15. Homans, *English Villagers*, p. 8.
16. Bennett, *Life on the English Manor*, p. 237.
17. Raftis, *Tenure and Mobility*, p. 179–80.
18. A virgate usually averages thirty acres.
19. Harvey, *A Medieval Oxfordshire Village*, p. 123.
20. For examples, see Bennett, *Life on the English Manor*; Homans, *English Villagers*; Kosminsky, *Studies in the Agrarian History of England*; Postan, *The Medieval Economy and Society*.
21. For examples, see Harvey, *A Medieval Oxfordshire Village* and Raftis, *The Estates of Ramsey Abbey* and *Tenure and Mobility*.

22. An article concerned with the marriage rate of widows on different manors is Titow, "Some Differences between Manors and their Effects on the Condition of the Peasant." There is currently a running debate between Scammell, "Freedom and Marriage in Medieval England" and "Wife-Rents and Merchet" and E. Searle, "Freedom and Marriage in Medieval England: An Alternative Hypothesis." Also see Faith, "Peasant Families and Inheritance Customs in Medieval England."

23. Courts of equity seek to administer justice beyond the strict lines of positive law, but equity soon becomes "a complex of well-settled and well-understood rules, principles, and precedents." See *Black's Law Dictionary*, revised 4th ed., 1968, pp. 634–35.

24. Elton, *England 1200–1640, The Sources of History*, p. 58.

25. Glanville, *Tractatus de Legibus et Consuetudinibus*; Bracton, *De Legibus et Consuetudinibus Angliae*; Littleton, *Littleton's Tenures*.

26. For the court rolls, see the multivolume series published by the Selden Society. They have either Latin or Anglo-Norman on one page and an English translation on the facing page. An example is D. Stenton, ed., *Rolls of the Justices in Eyre*.

27. See Selden Society publications and the Rolls Series. An example is Maitland, ed., *Year Books of Edward II*.

28. Elton, p. 175

29. Joüon des Longrais, *La conception anglaise de la saisine* and "Le statut de la femme en Angleterre dans le droit commun mèdièval." See also Kittel, "Married Women in Thirteenth-Century England." For specialized studies of wardship, see Walker, "The Marrying of Feudal Wards" and "Widow and Ward."

30. For studies regarding land, see Buckstaff, "Married Women's Property in Anglo-Saxon and Anglo-Norman Law"; this is a pioneering work, but of poor quality. For more recent work, see Bailey, "The Countess Gundred's Lands" and Painter, "The Family and the Feudal System in Twelfth-Century England."

31. Glanville, *Tractatus de Legibus et Consuetudinibus Regni Anglie*, vi, 3.

32. See note 1.

33. Joüon des Longrais, *La conception anglaise de la saisine*.

34. Bracton, f.151b.

35. Meekings, *Crown Pleas of the Wiltshire Eyre*, no. 146 (1249).

36. Given, *Society and Homicide*, "Introduction."

37. Ibid. chap. 7.

38. Hanawalt, "The Female Felon," p. 266. See her other articles: "The Peasant Family and Crime" and "Childrearing Among the Lower Classes."

39. Elton, p. 66.

# BIBLIOGRAPHY

AMPHLETT, JOHN; HAMILTON, SIDNEY GRAVES; and WILSON, ROWLAND ALWYN, eds. *Court Rolls of the Manor of Hales, 1270–1307*. 3 vols. Worcestershire Historical Society: 1910–33.

AULT, WARREN ORTMAN, ed. *Court Rolls of the Abbey of Ramsey and of the Honor of Clare*. New Haven, Conn. and London: 1928.

BAILDON, WILLIAM PALEY; LISTER, JOHN; and WALKER, J. W., eds. *Court Rolls of the*

*Manor of Wakefield.* Yorkshire Archaeological Society, Record Series, vols. 29, 36, 57, 78, 109. 1901–45.

BAILEY, S. J. "The Countess Gundred's Lands." *Cambridge Law Journal* 10, no. 1 (1948): 84–103.

BENNETT, HENRY STANLEY. *Life on the English Manor: A Study of Peasant Conditions,* 1150–1400. Cambridge: 1937.

——. *The Pastons and Their England: Studies in an Age of Transition.* Cambridge: 1922.

BRACTON, HENRY DE. *De Legibus et Consuetudinibus Angliae.* Edited by George E. Woodbine. 4 vols. New Haven, Conn.: 1915–44.

——. *On the Laws and Customs of England.* Translated by Samuel E. Thorne. 2 vols. Cambridge, Mass.: 1968.

BRUNDAGE, JAMES A. "The Crusader's Wife: A Canonistic Quandary." *Studia Gratiana* 12, Collectanea Stephan Kuttner II (1967): 427–41.

——. "The Crusader's Wife Revisited." *Studia Gratiana* 14, Collectanea Stephan Kuttner IV (1967): 243–51.

BUCKSTAFF, FLORENCE GRISWOLD. "Married Women's Property in Anglo-Saxon and Anglo-Norman Law and the Origin of the Common-Law Dower." *Annals of the American Academy of Political and Social Sciences* 4 (1893–94): 233–64.

ELTON, G. R. *England 1200–1640, The Sources of History: Studies in the Uses of Historical Evidence.* London: 1969.

ESMEIN, A. *Le mariage en droit canonique.* 2 vols. Paris: 1891.

FAITH, ROSAMOND JANE. "Peasant Families and Inheritance Customs in Medieval England." *Agricultural History Review* 14, pt. 2 (1966): 77–95.

FRIEDBERG, E., ed. *Decretum Magistri Gratiani. Corpus Iuris Canonici,* vol. 1. Leipzig: 1879–1881. Reprint. Graz, Austria: 1959.

——. *Decretales Gregorii IX. Corpus Iuris Canonici,* vol. 2. Leipzig: 1879–1881. Reprint. Graz, Austria: 1959.

GAIRDNER, JAMES, ed. *The Paston Letters.* 3 vols. London: 1872–75.

GIVEN, JAMES BUCHANAN. *Society and Homocide in Thirteenth-Century England.* Stanford, Calif.: 1977.

GLANVILLE, RANULF DE. *Tractatus de Legibus et Consuetudinibus Regni Anglie qui Glanvilla Vocatur: The Treatise on the Laws and Customs of the Realm of England Commonly Called Glanvill.* Edited and Translated by G. D. G. Hall. London: 1965.

Great Britain, Record Commission. *Statutes of the Realm,* vol. 1. London: 1810.

HANAWALT, BARBARA A. "Childrearing among the Lower Classes of Late Medieval England." *Journal of Interdisciplinary History* 7 (Summer 1977): 1–22.

——. "The Female Felon in Fourteenth-Century England." *Viator: Medieval and Renaissance Studies* 5 (1974): 253–68. Also published in *Women in Medieval Society,* edited by S. M. Stuard, pp. 125–40. Philadelphia: 1976.

——. "The Peasant Family and Crime in Fourteenth-Century England." *Journal of British Studies* 13 (May 1974): 1–18.

HARVEY, P. D. A. *A Medieval Oxfordshire Village: Cuxham, 1240 to 1400.* Oxford: 1965.

HELMHOLZ, RICHARD. *Marriage Litigation in Medieval England.* Cambridge: 1974.

——. "Infanticide in the Province of Canterbury during the Fifteenth Century." *History of Childhood Quarterly* 2, no. 3 (Winter 1975): 379–90.

——. "Bastardy Litigation in Medieval England." *American Journal of Legal History* 13 (1969): 360–83.

HOMANS, GEORGE CASPAR. *English Villagers of the Thirteenth Century.* Cambridge, Mass.: 1941.

JOÜON DES LONGRAIS, FRÉDÉRIC. *La conception anglaise de la saisine du XII<sup>e</sup> au XIV<sup>e</sup> siècle.* Paris: 1925.

―――. "Le statut de la femme en Angleterre dans le droit commun mèdièval." *La Femme* 12, pt. 2 (1962): 135–241. (Société Jean Bodin Pour L'Histoire Comparative des Institutions.)

KINGSFORD, CHARLES LETHBRIDGE, ed. *The Stonor Letters and Papers, 1290–1483.* Royal Historical Society Publications, Camden Series, 3rd series, vols. 29, 30, 34. London: 1919, 1924.

KITTEL, MARGARET RUTH. "Married women in Thirteenth-Century England: A Study in Common Law." Ph.D. dissertation, University of California, Berkeley, 1973.

KOSMINSKY, E. A. *Studies in the Agrarian History of England in the Thirteenth Century.* Translated by Ruth Kisch. Edited by R. H. Hilton. Oxford: 1956.

LITTLETON, THOMAS. *Littleton's Tenures in English.* Edited by Eugene Wambaugh. Washington, D.C.: 1903.

MAITLAND, F. W., ed. *Select Pleas in Manorial Courts.* Selden Society, vol. 2. London: 1888.

―――. *Year Books of Edward II*, vol. 1: *1 and 2 Edward II: A.D. 1307–1309.* Selden Society, vol. 17. London: 1903.

MALDEN, HENRY ELLIOT, ed. *The Cely Papers.* Royal Historical Society Publications, Camden Series, 3rd Series, vol. 1. London, New York: 1900.

MEEKINGS, C. A. F., ed. *Crown Pleas of the Wiltshire Eyre, 1249.* Wiltshire Record Society 16. 1961.

METZ, RENÉ. "Le statut de la femme en droit canonique mèdièval." *La Femme* 12, pt. 2 (1962): 59–113. (Société Jean Bodin Pour L'Histoire Comparative des Institutions.)

NOONAN, JOHN T., JR. "Marital Affection in the Canonists." *Studia Gratiana* 12, Collectanea Stephan Kuttner II (1967): 479–5.

―――. "Marriage in the Middle Ages: Power to Choose." *Viator: Medieval and Renaissance Studies* 4 (1973): 419–34.

PAINTER, SIDNEY. "The Family and the Feudal System in Twelfth-Century England." *Speculum* 35 (1960): 1–16.

POSTAN, MICHAEL MOISSEY. *The Medieval Economy and Society: An Economic History of Britain in the Middle Ages.* London: [c. 1972].

POWICKE, F. M., and Cheney, C. R., eds. *Councils and Synods, with Other Documents relating to the English Church.* vol. II, pts. 1 and 2. Oxford: 1964.

RAFTIS, J. AMBROSE. *The Estates of Ramsey Abbey: A Study in Economic Growth and Organization.* Toronto: 1957.

―――. *Tenure and Mobility: Studies in the Social History of the Mediaeval English Village.* Toronto: 1964.

SCAMMELL, JEAN. "Freedom and Marriage in Medieval England." *The Economic History Review*, 2d series, 27, no. 4 (Nov. 1974): 523–37.

―――. "Wife-Rents and Merchet." *The Economic History Review*, 2d series, 29, no. 3 (Aug. 1976): 487–90.

SCARGILL-BIRD, S. R., ed. *Custumals of Battle Abbey in the Reigns of Edward I and Edward II, 1282–1312.* Camden Society, 2d series, vol. 41. London: 1887.

SEARLE, ELEANOR. "Freedom and Marriage in Medieval England: An Alternative

Hypothesis." *The Economic History Review*, 2d series, 29, no. 3 (Aug. 1976): 482–86.

SHEEHAN, MICHAEL. "The Formation and Stability of Marriage in Fourteenth-Century England: Evidence of an Ely Register." *Medieval Studies* 33 (1971): 228–63.

———. "The Influence of Canon Law on the Property Rights of Married Women in England." *Medieval Studies* 25 (1963): 109–24.

———. "Marriage and Family in English Conciliar and Synodal Legislation." In *Essays in Honour of Anton Charles Pegis*, edited by J. Reginald O'Donnell, pp. 205–14. Toronto: 1974.

STENTON, DORIS MARY, ed. *Rolls of the Justices in Eyre: Being the Rolls of Pleas and Assizes for Lincolnshire 1218–19 and Worcestershire 1221*. Selden Society, vol. 53. London: 1934.

THORPE, JOHN, ed. *Custumale Roffense*. London: 1788.

TITOW, J. Z. "Some Differences between Manors and their Effects on the Condition of the Peasant in the Thirteenth Century." *Agricultural History Review* 10, pt. 1 (1962): 1–13.

WALKER, SUE SHERIDAN. "The Marrying of Feudal Wards in Medieval England." *Studies in Medieval Culture* 4, pt. 2 (1974): 209–24.

———. "Widow and Ward: The Feudal Law of Child Custody in Medieval England." In *Women in Medieval Society*, edited by S. M. Stuard, pp. 159–72. University of Pennsylvania Press: 1976. Also published in *Feminist Studies* 3, no. 3/4 (1976): 104–16.

WUNDERLI, RICHARD. "Ecclesiastical Courts in Pre-Reformation London." Ph.D. dissertation, University of California, Berkeley, 1975.

# Women in an Age of Transition

## 1485–1714

### ROSEMARY MASEK

Fynes Moryson, a well-known Elizabethan traveler, observed in a witticism to which even foreign visitors to England could agree: "England in generall is said to be the Hell of Horses, the Purgatory of Servants, and the Paradice of Women."[1] As this bibliographic survey will illustrate, many men and women in the sixteenth and seventeenth centuries contributed to a literature which often belies the optimism of the wits.

Modern historians of the era, 1485 to 1714, have almost wholly neglected women as a class when writing general studies of the age. The best standard surveys, for example, those in the Oxford History of England series, provide the general background but no special starting point for the student of women's history.[2] Monographs on social and economic history in general offer a challenge to the imaginative student, while such pioneering studies as Doris M. Stenton's *The English Woman in History* (1957) and Alice Clark's *Working Life of Women in the Seventeenth Century* (1919) are a real stimulus to further research. Although many scholars have found the history of women a legitimate concern, it is still difficult for academicians generally to accept this aspect of the discipline as significant.

English history of the Tudor-Stuart era, for the most part, has centered on the flow of political events and the solution of constitutional crises. In neither the political nor the religious settlements did women as a class have any influence. Nevertheless, women had contributed to the advance of Protestantism during both the sixteenth-century Reformation and the seventeenth-century civil strife. Their efforts to achieve political recognition during the latter were thwarted. Even access to education was limited in an age in which humanistic ideals triumphed. Only a few aristocratic women benefited from the enthusiasm of humanist educators. At the same time, the number of treatises on "the woman question" increased. The debate over woman's nature—its intrinsic merits or defects—was renewed with vigor in the Tudor-Stuart era, reflecting changing values and indicating that men were recognizing women as a class while denying them higher status.

Any generalizations about the economic and legal status of women must remain tentative until those studies which would make definitive statements possible have been finished. No connection between the economic, political, and religious crises of the age and women's status has been established. The extent to which the literary debate on "the woman question" reflects a continuity with traditional medieval misogyny remains unexamined. In short, a good deal more research on the subject of women in the Tudor-Stuart era is necessary in order to understand gradual changes in woman's role in all phases of social and economic life.

The most productive research will obviously occur in those areas in which women played a more noticeable part, that is, in social, intellectual, and religious life. Consequently, this essay concentrates on the literature of four subjects: the social environment, the attitude toward women expressed in the literary debate on the "woman question," education, and religion. The bibliography is, of necessity, highly selective. For example, a review of biographies of notable women and a survey of women in literature is outside the scope of this discussion.[3] The subject of the legal status of women, however, fits naturally into the realm of the social environment.

A wide variety of primary source material is available for further study: diaries, autobiographies, letters, household inventories, wills and testaments, legislation, legal documents such as Quarter Session records, borough and guild records, contemporary books on marriage, education, and religion. Family histories, biographies, and special studies written since the nineteenth century often serve as introductory guides to particular areas of interest. The essential tools are Conyers Read's *Bibliography of British History, Tudor Period, 1485–1603* (1959) and Godfrey Davies and Mary Frear Keeler's *Bibliography of British History, Stuart Period, 1603–1714* (1970). Both cite the principal manuscript and printed sources; neither was intended to be exhaustive, but rather designed to list representative materials.

Besides Stenton's book, the general histories of women for the era include Pearl Hogrefe's *Tudor Women: Commoners and Queens* (1975), her *Women of Action in Tudor England* (1977); and Carroll Camden's *The Elizabethan Woman* (1952). Hogrefe's first book is a descriptive rather than analytic study of several aspects of woman's role, including that in business and industry, but is useful as a starting point. The second describes the domestic and public lives of nine outstanding women: Mildred Cooke Cecil, Anne Cooke, Bess of Hardwick, Catherine Willoughby, Mary Sidney Herbert, Margaret Beaufort, Catherine of Aragon, Catherine Parr, and Queen Elizabeth. It is much richer in detail and has a more complete bibliography than the first book. Camden discusses the literary debate over women as well as describing the social and economic roles women played; he draws mainly on the literary sources of the era. A sound survey essay by Wallace Notestein, "The English Woman, 1580–1650," in *Studies in Social History* (1955), still has value as an overview although Sheila Rowbotham's chapter on seventeenth-century women in *Women, Resistance and Revolution* (1974) is a more provocative analysis. Roger Thompson's *Women in Stuart England and America* (1974) relies principally on secondary sources for the discussion of Stuart women and thus fails to support adequately his thesis that American women were better off than their English counterparts. On questions of demography, women's social and economic roles and marriage patterns, the student must begin elsewhere.[4]

Nothing supersedes reading the sources themselves for discovering both woman's status in society and the attitudes toward her. Extant rare books can be located by consulting *A Short-Title Catalogue of Books... 1475–1640*, ed. Alfred W. Pollard and *Short-Title Catalogue of Books... 1641–1700*, ed. Donald E. Wing, both of which are currently being revised. Most of the larger university libraries hold many of the works cited here. For the advanced student, the collections of such research libraries as the Henry E. Huntington Library, San Marino, California; the Folger Shakespeare Library, Washington, D. C.; the Newberry Library, Chicago; and the British Library, London, are most complete and should be consulted, if possible.

## THE SOCIAL ENVIRONMENT

If the status of women in the Tudor-Stuart era is to be accurately assessed, scholars must relinquish narrative and descriptive methods for a psychosocial approach to the sources.[5] It is difficult to discover precisely to what extent woman's role in the patriarchal system of the era differed from her role a hundred years earlier or later. Essentially, the social environment for both sexes was the same. Men had created the environment and women were identified with it. A woman's status depended upon that of her husband, or if she remained single, upon that of her family. Consequently, for investigations of the social relationships between the sexes, comparative family histories are a necessity.

In order to understand family history, one must also know the composition of the population. Identifying the major divisions in English society for this period is difficult primarily because of the complexity of the sources. Quantitative methods carry only so far.[6] Recently, the Cambridge Group for the History of Population and Social Structure has begun the research necessary for clarifying some of the confusion. E. A. Wrigley's *An Introduction to English Historical Demography* (1966) provides the basis for further investigation.[7] Until more population studies are completed, it will indeed be difficult to know how women's status was related to or affected by basic demographic changes. Family reconstitution studies are especially needed.

Such works as Peter Laslett's *The World We Have Lost* (1965), a valuable analysis of preindustrial society, and Lawrence Stone's *The Crisis of the Aristocracy, 1558-1641* (1965), which introduces the subject of marriage and family relationships among the upper classes, are basic starting points.[8] Several of Laslett's most useful essays on family structure, including his study of two seventeenth-century villages of Clayworth and Cogenhoe, have been collected in *Family Life and Illicit Love*. Keith Thomas notes the limitations of studies of this kind in his review essay, "The Changing Family" (1977). More useful to the beginning student is Lawrence Stone's *The Family, Sex and Marriage in England, 1500-1800* (1977). Stone identifies three patterns of family life: the open lineage family inherited from the Middle Ages and surviving until about 1630; the restricted patriarchal nuclear family, appearing around 1550 and lasting until 1700; and the closed domesticated nuclear family, emerging after 1640 and reaching fulfillment in the eighteenth century. Replete with fascinating anecdotes, graphs, illustrations, notes, and bibliography, this study makes more accessible than any other work of its kind the details of the inner lives of both commoners and patricians. His earlier study, "The Rise of the Nuclear Family," in *The Family in History* (1975), ed. Charles E. Rosenberg, may appeal more to the beginning student. Family history, even when based on personal documents, has in the past been sentimentalized, but a recent study, Alan Macfarlane's *The Family Life of Ralph Josselin* (1970), breaks new paths. Personal documents, such as the *Memoirs of the Verney Family*, provide the basis for more modern works of this kind.

Attitudes toward marriage and family life have been analyzed by James Johnson in *A Society Ordained by God: English Puritan Marriage Doctrine in the First Half of the Seventeenth Century* (1970). His views may be compared with those in Roland Frye's "The Teaching of Classical Puritanism on Conjugal Love" (1955) and John K. Yost's "The Value of Married Life for the Social Order in the Early English Renaissance" (1976). The picture of family life would not be complete without an expression of attitudes toward children. *The History of Childhood* (1974), ed. Lloyd De Mause, contains two pertinent essays for the period: M. J. Tucker's "The Child as Beginning and End: Fifteenth and Sixteenth Century English Childhood" and Joseph E. Illick's "Childrearing in Seventeenth–Century England and America." B. M. Berry discusses a medical point of view in "The First English Pediatricians and Tudor Attitudes toward Childhood" (1974), in the *Journal of the History of Ideas*. Paul Remack's "Sixteenth Century English Children: The Theory, Reality, and Importance of Socialization and Education in Tudor Society" ought to shed further light on the subject of childhood.

Societal relationships are further revealed through personal documents such as diaries, autobiographies, and letters. Unfortunately, too few Tudor women left such documents. A psychosocial analysis must depend on limited sources such as *The Diary of Margaret, Lady Hoby* (1599–1605), ed. Dorothy M. Meads; "The Journal of Lady Mildmay" (c. 1570–1617), ed. Rachel Weigall; and *The Diary of Lady Anne Clifford* (1590–1676), ed. Victoria Sackville-West.

In the seventeenth century, autobiography became a literary form in its own right. Paul Delaney's *British Autobiography in the Seventeenth Century* (1969) introduces the genre. Examples of the type are *The Autobiography of Mary, Countess of Warwick* (1625–78), ed. Thomas C. Croker; *The Autobiography of Anne, Lady Halkett* (1622–99), ed. J. G. Nichols; and *The Autobiography of Mrs. Alice Thornton* (1627–1707), ed. C. Jackson. The autobiography must be used with caution, as all too often and idealized view of life is presented, e.g., *The Memoirs of Ann Lady Fanshawe* (1625–80), ed. H. C. Fanshaw.[9] Other examples of these personal documents have been noted in William Matthews's *British Diaries: An Annotated Bibliography of British Diaries Written Between 1442 and 1942* (1950). Lucy Hutchinson's *Memoirs* of her husband's life reveals as much of her world as his.

Personal correspondence reveals patterns of social relationships and personal commitments. The frequently cited Paston correspondence, best edited by James Gairdner, is the most significant evidence of this sort remaining from the early Tudor period. *The Correspondence of Lady Katherine Paston, 1603–1627*, ed. Ruth Hughey, continues the family history into the Stuart era. Other examples of edited letters are *The Conway Letters*, ed. Marjorie Hope Nicholson, and *The Letters of Lady Brilliana Harley*, ed. Thomas T. Lewis. Dorothy Osborne's letters to William Temple had their best editor in G. C. M. Smith; a recent abridgment has been edited by

Kingsley Hart. A sequel to the Osborne-Temple love story is Julia G. Longe's *Martha, Lady Giffard, Her Life and Correspondence* (1911). Personal letters from men, like their diaries, are a fruitful source of insight into female behavior, attitudes, and status. Norman McClure's edition of the *Letters of John Chamberlain* (1554?–1628) provides such a source. A vast amount of correspondence and other family papers has been collected in the Historical Manuscripts Commission Reports, to which the chief guides are cited in Davies and Keeler, along with an annotated list of the most important collections.

Further sources for fruitful investigation of the social environment are household inventories and accounts. Family aspirations are often revealed in expenditure. As the idea of hospitality as a virtue of noble life had not disappeared, the expenses incurred in entertaining guests would surely indicate the hopes of social acceptance. To what extent did families run into debt in order to rise socially? Certainly, the hospitality extended at marriages was costly, to the regret of the families concerned. Descriptive studies which prepare the way for further study are Paul Van B. Jones's *The Household of a Tudor Nobleman* (1917); Gladys S. Thomson's *Life in a Noble Household, 1641–1700* (1937); and Lu Emily Pearson's *Elizabethans at Home* (1957). Some printed documents which introduce the type are *Estate Accounts of the Earls of Northumberland, 1562–1637*, ed. Mervyn E. James and *The Derby Household Book*, ed. Francis R. Raines.

Personal property inventories are usually supplemented by wills, which in themselves are an excellent indicator of social status. The difficulties surrounding female inheritance of estates have been noticed in Pearl Hogrefe's "Legal Rights of Tudor Women and Their Circumvention" in *Sixteenth Century Journal* (1972). T. E.'s *The Lawes Resolutions of Womens Rights* (1632) and *Baron and Feme: A Treatise of Law and Equity concerning Husbands and Wives* (1700) may have stated what was fact in law, but reality was often quite different.[10] Though women were subject to their husbands, the examples of those who managed their own affairs tempt one to think of them as more than exceptions. Women did leave property in wills more frequently than in the middle ages. Both the amount of property left to them and by them is considerable. Wives could act as executrices of wills, but to what extent they did so or how successful they were remains unknown.

Both Hogrefe's *Tudor Women* and Clark's *Working Life of Women* survey the changing role of women in industry and business, but neither measures the impact that women had on economic life. Clark drew from manuscript as well as printed sources for her pioneering work, studying government legislation, Quarter Session records, parliamentary petitions, churchwardens' accounts, borough and leet court records. She contended that capitalism lessened the relative productivity of women during the seventeenth century both by replacing family industry and by destroying domestic industry. Domestic industry, as opposed to family industry, included any activity by which goods which did not have any exchange or money value were produced for the sole use of a family. Such activities were brewing, dairy work, care of poultry and pigs, production of vegetables and fruit, spinning flax and wool, nursing, and doctoring. In the form known as family industry, all members of the family worked for their mutual benefit, sharing all income together. When the father worked away from his home on his employer's premises, family industry had given way to capitalism.

Surveying the range of women's economic activities, Clark discussed capitalists (women who invested or loaned money), agriculture, textiles, crafts and trades, and the professions. In the Elizabethan and early Stuart eras, women were active as speculators in salt, estate managers, buyers of wardships, money lenders, shipping agents, ship owners, and contractors to the army and navy. After the Restoration, fewer women seem to be involved in such capitalist enterprises. Nor were women in the professions of teaching and nursing any better off by the end of the seventeenth century. Indeed, only midwifery had reached a professional status, but as women were excluded from advanced instruction, they were gradually displaced by men practitioners. Women teachers were similarly barred from specialized training in music and dancing and did not have access to higher education at the universities.

On the opposite end of the economic scale, the women in the agricultural sector fared no better. Their families fell into three categories: those who held sufficient land for the maintenance of the entire household including servants, those who had to work for wages to supplement the income from their holdings, and those who depended completely on their wages to support themselves. Wives of well-to-do yeomen did not have to work for wages but managed the dairy, cared for poultry, garden, and orchard, and trained servants. Husbandmen's wives worked for wages, helping with the harvest, sheep shearing, raking, and other farm tasks. Wives of wage earners were the least well off, as wages were often fixed at a subsistence level. These women were employed most often only for seasonal work. Their families were small; their children died young, or if they survived, were undernourished. Clark contended that the disintegration of the village community, a consequence of the onslaught of a capitalistic system, resulted in the decline of women's economic status.

Women employed in the textile industry found themselves slowly displaced. In Kingston-upon-Hull, guild regulations drove women from worsted weaving as early as 1490 and similar restrictions can be adduced for the sixteenth century. Driven from weaving, most women found occupation as spinners. These were frequently those poor women from the rural community who bought from a local market and sold the yarn off at a profit. Women who worked with their husbands as retailers of goods were in a more protected position. They could expect to maintain their rights to the business, if their husbands died, as long as they remained widows. To what extent they were able to continue and pass the family properties on to their heirs is not known. Guild regulations made remarriage outside the guild very difficult for widows. Did women circumvent these restrictions and, if so, what is the significance of their moving beyond the guild? An analysis of the female membership of guilds would be instructive as would further study of town records. How many women actually held public office? To what extent were they able to exercise the power of that office? Typical of the printed sources for such an investigation are Mary Bateson's *Records of the Borough of Leicester* (1905) and her *Borough Customs* (1904). For guild records, the student must search the publications of the county record societies and be prepared to visit county archives.

A discussion of women's wealth and its visibility in philanthropic enterprises appears in W. K. Jordan's *Philanthropy in England, 1480–1660* (1959). He contended that women were far more secular-minded as donors than men because they gave only 18.07 percent of their wealth to religious institutions. They were far more concerned with giving relief to the poor.[11] It was notable that in some counties, according to Jordan's statistics, a large percentage of gifts of money went to unmarried women who could not maintain themselves. It may be that some of the latter turned to crime, although data on female criminals may be hard to trace. Carol Weiner contends, for example, that female criminals are under-represented in the legal records.[12]

Further research on the subject, however, would help clarify the literary view of women living on the margin. Some of these antiheroines are described in F. W. Chandler's *The Literature of Roguery* (1907). Robert Greene's *A Disputation betweene a Hee Conny-Catcher and a Shee Conny-Catcher* (1592), one of several tracts in *The Elizabethan Underworld*, ed. A. V. Judges, argued the relative merits of being a thief or a whore. His light-hearted approach to the subject was castigated in the seventeenth century, when a serious public reaction to prostitution became apparent. Thomas Dekker's *The Honest Whore* (1635) underwent not only some internal revisions but a change of title as well in order to satisfy public opinion.[13]

Prostitution continued to be a crime but seemed to be less often prosecuted in the latter half of the seventeenth century. An interesting correlation could be made between the attitudes toward the prostitute in literature and her treatment at law, as literature often reveals changing attitudes. But what can be made of *The Life and Death of Mrs. Mary Frith* (1662) or *The Memoires of Mary Carleton* (1673)? Both relate the careers of women living on the fringes of society. Do they reflect reality at all? Or do they represent literary precursors to *Moll Flanders*? Mary Carleton was allegedly the illegitimate child of an "Itinerant Fidler of Canterbury," who made good by marrying a wealthy husband, having convinced him she was a German princess. When he discovered the fraud, he threw her out and she turned to a life of crime. Transported to Jamaica, she claimed to have corrupted her associates. Eventually, she returned to England, took up her old ways, and ended her career at the end of a hangman's rope. The serious side of the subject must be explored through legal records, many of which are in print: e.g., *Kentish Sources*, ed. Elizabeth Melling, and *Middlesex County Records*, ed. John J. Jeaffreson.

## "THE WOMAN QUESTION"

Obviously, the historian must be discriminating in the use of literary sources. This holds true as much for satiric literature dealing with women of the lower classes as for the literature of "the woman question," the literature centered on the subject of woman's nature. Shakespeare's song, "Who is Silvia?" from *Two Gentlemen from Verona*, reflects the Elizabethan fascination with woman's nature, but the question had been asked long before. In fact, "the woman question" was the subject of literary debate from the late middle ages onward.

Two excellent overviews of the controversy, Louis B. Wright's chapter, "The Popular Controversies over Woman," in *Middle-Class Culture in Elizabethan England* (1935) and Carroll Camden's "Certain Controversies over Women," in *The Elizabethan Woman* (1952), discuss the wide variety of books, ballads, and broadsides available to the reading public on the question.[14] Francis Utley's *The Crooked Rib* (1944) indexes the woman question in English and Scottish literature through 1568. H. V. Routh's "The Progress of Social Literature in Tudor Times," in *The Cambridge History of English Literature* (1930) provides a general sketch. Some of the sixteenth-century arguments are summed up in Paul N. Siegel's "Milton and the Humanist Attitude Toward Women," in the *Journal of the History of Ideas* (1950). For a description of the seventeenth-century literature on the subject, Joachim Heinrich's essay, "Die Frauenfrage bei Steele und Addison" (1930) is indispensable.

Each of these surveys has its own particular purpose, leaves some bibliographical tangles, and, in the case of Heinrich, may be inaccessible to the student. Consequently, a review of the literature, while repeating to some extent the bibliography of the controversy, may shorten title searching and raise new questions about the significance of the issue. For example, Wright's chapter suggests an examination of middle-class values in light of the woman question in the seventeenth century, but the limits of his book preclude it, and no current bibliography shows the full extent of the literature. One may also consider the extent to which traditional medieval views of women were adopted by Tudor-Stuart writers. What was the impact of continental works on English writers? What, if anything, was peculiar about the English version of the nature of woman? Was there any significant difference between the sixteenth-and seventeenth-century image of woman?

Interest in woman as woman in the Renaissance was undoubtedly stimulated by humanist treatises on the nature of man and of Platonic love. It was not until the 1540s that English works on women appeared in print and, even then, many of them were translations of continental treatises. Agrippa von Nettersheim's *De Nobilitate et Praecellentia Foeminei Sexus* (1529), translated in 1542 as *A treatise Of the nobilitie of womankynde*, provided a basis for a positive view of women. Judging from the many references to it, it was an important model for later works. Translations of other foreign books, such as William Bercher's *The Nobylyte of Wymen* (1559), which derived from Ludovico Domenichi's *La Nobiltà della Donne*, still depended on Agrippa's tract.[15] The translations, as well as native English works, are ample evidence of the popularity of the subject.

English printers prospered by publishing even the slightest verse on women, their nature, and relative merits. Some printers are even credited with the composition of these rude works. Four editions of *The Schole house of women*, attributed to the printer Edward Gosynhill, set the pace for the attack, sounding the charge in 1541, 1560, 1561, and 1572. His *The prayse of all women* (c. 1542) was a weaker model for the defence than *A Dyalogue defensyve for women* (1542). Sir Thomas Elyot's *The Defence of Good Women* (1545) was the first well-argued native work. From that point until the end of the seventeenth century, the quality of attack and defense ranged from the scurrilous to the lofty. A study of the rhetoric of these works would be instructive, showing either continuity with the past or a change in attitude.[16]

The detractors of women apparently were more popular than the defenders. The abusive attack of Joseph Swetnam's *The arraignment of lewd, idle, froward, and inconstant women* (1615) proved so popular in fact that it had ten editions before 1634 and another five between 1690 and 1807. Coryl Crandall, the modern editor of *Swetnam the Woman-hater* (1620), considers that the controversy arising from the work "reflects very well a transition from a previous literary obsession with praise or dispraise of woman *qua* woman to concern with woman's mundane stature as partner of man.''[17] The validity of this assertion could be tested by analyzing the literature which preceded and that which followed. The immediate reaction to the *Arraignment*, however, was the publication of five more books related to the controversy: Daniel Tuvil's *Asylum Veneris* (1616); Rachel Speght's *A Mousell for Melastomus* (1617); Ester Sowernam's *Ester hath hang'd Haman* (1617); Constantia Munda's *The Worming of a mad Dogge* (1617); and Christopher Newstead's *An apology for women* (1620).

To what extent was a sexist bias hidden in works in praise of women? I. G.'s *An Apologie for woman-kind* (1605), William Heale's *An apologie for Women* (1609) later reissued as *The Great Advocate and Oratour for Women* (1682), Darcie's *The Honour of Ladies* (1622), and William Austin's *Haec homo* (1637, 1638, 1639) illuminate the attitude of the defenders of women. Were these books significantly different from those of the civil war era? By contrast, Samuel Torshell's *The Woman's Glorie* (1645, 1650), I. A. 's *The Good Woman's Champion* (1650), Charles Gerbier's *Elogium Heroinum* (1651), and William Hill's *A New Year's Gift for Women* (1660) represent the works of that later era.

In the post-Restoration period, writers seemed content to issue books filled with examples of worthy women. Some of these undoubtedly had their inspiration in Thomas Heywood's *Gunaikeion: or, Nine Books of Various History concerninge Women* (1624, 1657) and his *The exemplary Lives and memorable Acts of Nine of the most worthy Women of the world* (1640). Just how influential Heywood was could be discovered by an analysis of such works as *A Catalogue of Virtuous Women* (1671), John Golborne's *A friendly Apology* (1674), John Shirley's *The Illustrated History of Women* (1686), Robert Burton (i.e. Nathaniel Crouch)'s *Female Excellency* (1681), and Nahum Tate's *A Present for the Ladies* (1692). Some other works of the period were general vindications: e.g. James Norris' *Haec & Hic* (1683) and his *The Accomplished Lady* (1683). Others, like William Walsh's *A Dialogue concerning Women* (1691) and works attributed to Mary Astell, *An Essay in defense of the Female Sex* (1696, 1697) and *A farther essay relating to the female-sex* (1696), were closely argued works, depending on logic rather than on the appeal to the example of worthy women. The works toward the end of the seventeenth century appear to mark a significant change in the appeal to the reading public.

The female character, which Swetnam derided, was far more often stereotyped in sketches inspired by the Elizabethan literary interest in Theophratus's characters.[18] Sir Thomas Overbury's *Characters* (1614), Nicholas Breton's *The Good and the Badde* (1616), Arthur Newman's *Pleasures Vision* (1619), and Thomas Fuller's *The Holy and Profane State* (1642) typify seventeenth-century efforts. Writers managed to describe every type: Amazon, harlot, virgin, honest matron, shrew. Like the

Amazon, the masculine woman was satirized in *Hic-Mulier: or, The Man-Woman* (1620) and a companion piece, *Haec-Vir: or, the Womanish-Man* (1620).[19] Indeed, both male and female types were the target of satire in the sixteenth as well as seventeenth centuries. Such works as Robert Crowley's *One and thyrtye Epigrammes* (1550), George Gascoigne's *The Steele Glas* (1576), and Edward Hake's *Newes out of Powles Churchyarde* (1579) are representative.[20]

The satirists scorned current fashion for both men and women. Philip Stubbes's *The Anatomie of Abuses* (1583) and Thomas Nashe's *The Anatomie of Absurditie* (1589) specifically addressed the issue of fashion, as did William Prynne's *The Unlovelinesse of Love-Lockes* (1628), Thomas Hall's *The Loathsomeness of Long Hair* (1654), and George Fox's *The Fashions of the World Made Manifest* (1654). *Satirical Songs and Poems on Costume* complements the prose works on the subject.

Frequently, critics of women in the seventeenth century focused attention on a wife's neglect of family obligations. Incidents such as the scandal of Sir Thomas Overbury's murder aroused a vindictive spirit.[21] What was perceived as fashionable harlotry encouraged by the scandal had already found a critic in Barnaby Rich. His *The Honestie of this Age* (1614) and the expanded version of *Faultes, faults and nothing but Faultes* (1606) as *My Ladies Looking Glasse* (1616) reflected the bitterness of the issue. The invective of William Parkes's *The curtaine Drawer of the World* (1612) was overmatched by I. H.'s *This World's Folly* (1615). The aftermath of the trial saw not only the posthumous publication of Overbury's *A Wife* (1613), a tribute to his deceased wife which had sixteen printings through 1639, but also *The bloody Downfall of Adultery, Murder and Ambition* (1615), and two issues of Thomas Tuke's *A Treatise against painting and tincturing of Men and Women* (1615).

The ungenerous attitude toward married women had precedents, of course, in antimatrimonial tracts which kept alive the misogyny of the middle ages. Robert Copland's *A complaynt of them that be to soone maryed* (1506?), *The Complaynte of them that ben to late maryed* (1505?), and *The Payne and sorrow of evyll maryage* (1509). Many sixteenth-century humanist works discussed the serious side of marriage, particularly Erasmus's *A ryght frutefull Epystle . . . in prayse of matrimony* (1530?) and Agrippa von Nettersheim's *The Commendation of Matrimony* (1545). The marriage tracts of continental reformers were translated as well, for example, Henry Bullinger's *The Christen state of Matrimonye* (1541). Explicit comparisons of a virtuous wife with a faithless one appeared in nearly all contemporary works. An especially instructive book of this kind is *The vertuous scholehouse of ungracious women* (1550?), printed as *A watch-word for wilful women* (1581). One of Erasmus's colloquies, translated as *A mery Dialogue, declaringe the propertyes of shrowde shrewes and honest wyves* (1557), offered another dignified view of the married woman.

Marriage and funeral sermons are another vital source of attitudes toward married women: e.g., Phillip Stubbes's *A Christal Glasse for Christen Women* (1591), which had twenty editions by 1664; Robert Wilkinson's *The Merchant-Royall* (1607), four editions to 1615; Hannibal Gamon's *The Praise of a Godly Woman* (1627); Stephen Geree's *The Ornament of Women* (1639); William Gouge's *A Funerall Sermon preached ... At the Funeralls of Mrs. Margaret Ducke* (1646). The impression created by a majority of books was far less flattering, although occasionally, the female portrait seems real enough.

Nevertheless, a wife's offenses were standardized and had their antecedents in the middle ages. The Tudor-Stuart taste for the medieval view of women was fed by the publication of *The Boke of Mayd Emlyn* (1520), *The Proud Wyves Pater Noster* (1560), *The deceyte of women* (1560), *A mery Jeste of a shrewde and curste wife* (1590). Seven editions of Thomas Dekker's *The Bachelors Banquet* (1603), based on *Les quinze joyes de mariage*, illustrated further the English dependence on medieval literature for inspiration.

The wife as shrew or scold was also a familiar literary stereotype. Again, English writers capitalized on a rich medieval heritage as in Arthur Halliarg's *The Cruell Shrow* (1610) and *Poor Robin's True Character of a Scold* (1678).[22] Elizabethan raillery of wives ranged from mild to sharp. Thomas Delony's *The Garland of Good-will* (1593) is a pleasant contrast to Stephen Gosson's *Pleasant Quipps for Upstart Newfangled Gentlewomen* (1595). As the seventeenth century passed, complaints seem to be more vindictive, as if wives were more visible, independent, and less trustworthy. Henry Parrot derided the wasteful leisure hours wives spend together in *Gossips Greeting* (1620). John Taylor's tracts, *Divers Crabtree Lectures* (1639), *A Juniper Lecture* (1639), and Richard Brathwaite's *Ar't Asleepe Husband?* (1640) manage to make women look ridiculous. *The Womans sharpe revenge* (1640) shows that this misogynist attitude had not gone unnoticed.

Yet that attitude persisted as women's demands during the civil war period for a voice in government were heard. The anonymous *The Parlament of Women* (1640) became the source for (or was the work of) Henry Neville, who wrote *The Ladies Parliament* (1647), *An exact diurnall of the Parliament of ladyes* (1647), *Match me these two* (1647), and *Newes from the New Exchange* (1650).[23] His ridicule must have been as galling as William Blake's refusal to take anything except manners seriously. The latter's *The Yellow Book* (1656), *The Trial of the Ladies* (1656), and *A New Trial of the Ladies* (1659), as well as I. H.'s *A strange Wonder* (1642) and J. S.'s *A Brief*

*Anatomie of Women* (1653) were were convincingly misogynistic. Thomas Peck's *Balaam's Ass* (1658) was a small improvement.

After the Restoration, the attack on married women seems to have slowed, although women in general were still a peril. *A Discourse of Women* (1662, 1673) treats twenty-two vices, drawing from ancient as well as modern authors. A different version of *The Parliament of Women* was printed in 1684, and in 1697, the war between the sexes warmed up in *The Challenge ... or, The Female War*. The stereotyped image of woman, however, persisted as the most useful model for writers of both centuries. Woman's real nature or psychology was never explored by writers on the subject of "the woman question." When women did have some political power, as in the sixteenth century, the question was slightly rephrased. It was not "Who is she?" but "What does she want?"

According to John Knox, who breathed *The First Blast of the Trumpet against the Monstrous regiment of Women* (1558), she wanted far too much, especially if she were a female ruler. Those who curried the favor of contemporary monarchs had a ready solution. John Aylmer, by publishing *An Harborowe for Faithful and Trewe Subjectes* (1559), hoped to win Queen Elizabeth's approval. Others were stirred to discuss rebellion against female rulers, for example, John Fowler's translation of *An Oration against the unlawfull insurrections of Protestants of our time* (1566). Some were moved to stirring defenses of their queens, for example, John Leslie's *A defence of the ... honour of Marie Quene of Scotland* (1569) and William Leigh's *Queene Elizabeth, paraleld in her princely vertues* (1612).[24] As female political power was not an issue again until near the end of the seventeenth century, when a large literature centering on Queen Mary was published, writers could generously address court ladies, hoping for favor but without raising their efforts to a higher plane. Francis Lenton's *Great Britains beauties* (1638), a slight work devoted to Queen Henrietta Maria and her court, is a case in point.

Louis B. Wright considered that "intelligent thinking upon women's status in a new commercial society is evident in even some of the more jocular treatises."[25] How the concern for women is actually expressed in ribald and satiric pamphlets of the age certainly bears investigation. But this concern should be viewed in light of the literature which is an obvious legacy of the middle ages. The persistence of medieval misogynist attitudes, of stereotypes of all ranks of womanhood, and of English dependence on continental sources would all be subjects of fruitful examination. Even the reaction against women's extravagance in dress and behavior, when correlated with the actual fashions, could shed light on the gradual changes which custom and tradition were undergoing. As the seventeenth century drew to a close, it seems that women's intention to establish themselves as a subject of serious consideration had been frustrated, if the literature of "the woman question" can be trusted.

## THE EDUCATION OF WOMEN

"To make a woman learned and foxes tame had the same effect," quipped James I, "to make them cunning." His remark flattered women only a bit more than his mother's had. Mary, Queen of Scots, disparaged her sex as she observed, "The wisest of us is only a little less foolish than the rest." To judge by other contemporary comments, woman's intelligence, her ability to learn and to profit from that learning did not rank high. By the end of the seventeenth century, woman's intellectual capacity was viewed more positively, plans for female academies were put forward, and, in the eighteenth century, some of them were realized. In 1727, Rebecca Wellman expressed what education meant to her: "When House and Land is gone and spent, Then learning is most excelent." [26]

Women of the Tudor-Stuart era were handicapped in their efforts to develop their intellects. Their early marriages, frequent pregnancies, and only sporadic association with other adults who shared their interests and activities discouraged them from expanding their own intellectual horizons. Toward the end of the seventeenth century, when women were drawn more often into community life, they had more opportunity for discussion of ideas. But for the vast majority of women, everyday existence was simply too exhausting to allow for the development of intellectual interests. In spite of these discouragements, some women seemed to rise above their circumstances to become at least well read, if not educated. Louis B. Wright's "The Reading of Renaissance English Women," in *Studies in Philology* (1931), builds on the premise that the female literacy rate was fairly high and shows the extent to which women responded to intellectual stimuli. The increase in the book trade supports his conclusion that women were active readers.

By contrast, David Cressy shows that although the rate of female literacy rose in two areas in England between 1580 and 1700, it still was not very high. [27] The evidence adduced by Roger Schofield and by other members of the Cambridge Group for the History of Population and Social Structure must be considered as part of the background to understanding the extent of female literacy and education. For these scholars, literacy means the ability to write, not the ability to read. For this reason, both Wright's conclusions and J. W. Adamson's have to be read in light of the new demographic studies. [28]

The story of woman's education is an important part of the whole history of Tudor-Stuart education which has yet to be written. Pioneer studies have been either collections of documents, brief descriptions of particular schools, or general narratives. J. W. Adamson's *Contributions to the History of Education, 1600–1700* (1921), while fulfilling its author's purpose, did not analyze those changes in society which occur as a result of new educational goals. Joan Simon's *Education and Society in Tudor England* does illustrate the effect of the departure from medieval educational practice and the impact of humanistic ideals on English life.[29] The clerical monopoly on education gave way to lay control and patronage. Secular interest in education had been stimulated particularly by the works of the Italian humanists. As the ideas of the controlling class changed, so did the educational goals. Now the new schools were responsible for inculcating civic responsibility as well as developing fluency in the Latin language. Obviously, men were the beneficiaries of these schools, for women, after all, were not civic leaders, needed only the most rudimentary knowledge to be successful wives and mothers, and, above all, had no use for a Latin literary style.

Still, several humanists themselves suggested that the "new learning," as they termed their ideas, had value for women. Richard Hyrde's preface to Margaret Roper's *A Devout treatise upon the Pater Noster* (1525?) appears to be the first printed recommendation of such an education for women, although Juan Vives's *De Institutione foeminae Christianae* (written perhaps in 1523 and printed in Hyrde's translation in 1529) is usually viewed as the most important defense of female instruction in the "new learning."[30] The humanist attitude has been examined by Diane V. Bayne in "*The Instruction of a Christian Woman*: Richard Hyrde and the Thomas More Circle," as well as by Marie-Claire Robineau in "Richard Hyrde: A Plea for Learned Women," both in issues of *Moreana* (1975, 1967). Sir Thomas More's letter to Gonell, one of the family tutors, and Erasmus's letter to Budé provide further evidence that these humanists, at least, took the education of women seriously.[31]

Sir Thomas Elyot's translation of Plutarch's essay *The Education or bringinge up of children* (1535), dedicated to his sister Margery Puttenham, and his own *The Defence of Good Women* reveal how the humanistic ideals were adapted. Thomas Hoby's translation of Castiglione's *The Courtier* (1561) further advanced the Renaissance ideal of a gentlewoman. The aim of the training for gentility, however, was more often aesthetic than intellectual. Ruth Kelso's *The Doctrine for the Lady of the Renaissance* (1956) discusses the literature, both continental and English, which contributed to the formation of the ideal. Her bibliography is indispensable for those who wish to trace foreign influences on English humanist education.

In the sixteenth century, several notable women demonstrated the value of humanistic ideals in their lives. Of these, Margaret Roper, Thomas More's eldest daughter, and the subject of Ernest Reynolds's biography, appears a very independent intellectual. What impact her life had on her female contemporaries and successive generations remains to be judged, but her own youngest daughter, Mary, earned a small reputation for her learning. The educated woman of the Tudor era was a rare species. The linguistic and literary talents of Lady Jane Grey, Queen Elizabeth, and the five daughters of Sir Anthony Cooke, for example, could scarcely be matched by any of their contemporaries, as George Ballard's biographical sketches in *Memoirs of Several Ladies of Great Britain* (1752) attest. The lives of these women have had brief notice in such general works as Mary A. Cannon's *Education of Women During the Renaissance* (1916) and D. M. Stenton's *The English Woman in History*. The fullest account of the educated woman in the latter half of the seventeenth century is Myra Reynolds's *The Learned Lady in England, 1650–1750* (1920). Ada Wallas's *Before the Bluestockings* (1929) discusses the lives of Hannah Woolley, Damaris Masham, Mary Astell, and Elizabeth Elstob.

By contrast, the survival of medieval educational ideas for women was assured by Caxton's publication of Geoffrey de la Tour Landry's advice to his daughters (1484). This treatise proved very popular, circulating in manuscript from the late fourteenth century onward, even on the Continent. The Knight de la Tour Landry was an advocate of education for women, especially when it was religious. Almost a century later, Edward Hake, in *A Touchstone for this time present* (1574), lamented that girls were being kept from good learning and were reading instead "pernicious, unchaste and godlesse books."[32] Thomas Salter's translation of Giovanni Bruto's *La institutione di una fanciulla nata nobilimente* (1555) as *A Mirrhor mete for all Mothers, Matrones, and Maidens* (1579), served to reinforce the medieval view that women were capable of understanding only a limited number of subjects, especially those leading to a virtuous life. Richard Mulcaster's *Positions* (1581), a work on childhood education, reaffirmed the view that reading ought to lead to virtuous behavior. When Bruto's work was translated again as *The necessarie, fit, and convenient Education of a young Gentlewoman* (1598), an Italian and a French text were included with the English in order that both foreign languages might be studied. Language study, in fact, was recognized as a suitable female pursuit. Knowing French was especially helpful to the young woman who wanted to make a reputation at court.[33]

The inclusion of foreign language study, positive as it was, was negated by such comments as Richard Mulcaster's summation. For him, in "the bringing up of young maidens any kind of learning is but an accessory by the way."[34] The author of *The Court of Good Counsel* (1607) advised that a daughter be educated to that kind of life she was likely to marry into. From that point until the reign of Charles II, hardly any positive word was written about educating women. Charles Gerbier's *Elogium Heroinum* (1651) may not have been the only work to praise learned women in the era, but it had few companion pieces. Anna Maria van Schurman's argument for education was not translated until 1659, by Clement Barksdale as *The Learned Maid*; Thomas Heydon's *Advice to a daughter* (1659), though touching on subjects of importance, was of little comfort.

Consequently, in the face of much public and private discouragement, a woman learned only what her own interests, resourcefulness, and social position permitted. She could earn the reputation of a learned woman if she had the advantages of good breeding and intelligence. Yet, as Reynolds reminds us, learning might mean only "an avowed taste for reading, the faintest interest in physical phenomena, the composition of slight little poems, the writing out of prayers and meditations, even the copying of extracts into a commonplace book...."[35]

The only survey of education available to women in a formal setting is Dorothy Gardiner's *English Girlhood at School* (1929). Probably only girls of the upper classes benefited from the small amount of formal education offered. Some grammar schools admitted girls as well as boys, as study of school rosters shows. A few girls attended Rivington School, the Merchant Taylors' School at Great Crosby, Lancashire, and Wigston Grammar, Leicestershire. The first public school for girls was established in 1619 at Ladies Hall, Deptford.[36] A fuller investigation might thus modify Simon's view: "Girls probably often attended village schools. That they sometimes attended more considerable ones is suggested by orders specifically excluding them: e.g. at Harrow, 'No girls shall be received, to be taught in the same school.'"[37] Women were teaching schools early in the seventeenth century, but no one has discovered how they became qualified for their positions.[38]

Other opportunities for training existed in less formal settings. Aristocratic families still sent their children to other households for an upbringing in the life-style to which they had to become accustomed. Training for girls logically emphasized the domestic arts. Whether girls were able to learn these same arts or others in nunnery schools before the Dissolution is a moot question. In any case, any female achievement in such schools depended upon the nuns' knowledge which, Eileen Power concludes, was limited.[39]

Even though the medieval attitude seemed to prevail, some sixteenth-century writers urged that girls be given more formal schooling. Among these was Thomas Becon, who urged the founding of public schools for girls in *A new Catechisme* (1564). John Lyly's *Eupheus* (1579) so extravagantly praised Queen Elizabeth's learning that his effusiveness, along with other such praises, suggested to Foster Watson that "learning in women was thought desirable, and unconsciously may have assisted the idea of the higher education of women more than at first sight appears. . . ."[40]

Plans for schools in the seventeenth century reflect to a high degree the commitment to religious education. Nicholas Ferrar's academy established in 1624 at Little Gidding drew criticism in *The Arminian Nunnery* (1641) for being a Protestant convent. John Dury and Samuel Hartlib planned a similar academy in "Concerning an association for the Education of Children." The girls would be taught to be good and careful housewives, though those "capable of Tongues and Sciences would not be neglected but assisted toward the improvement of their intellectual abilities." In 1660, Hartlib was still interested in founding such an academy for women.[41] Indeed, the idea of a cloistered community for women specializing in religious education persisted until the end of the century in such works as Edward Chamberlayne's *An Academy or Colledge wherin young ladies may be duly instructed in the true Protestant religon* (1671), Richard Allestree's *The Ladies Calling* (1668), and Mary Astell's two parts of *A Serious Proposal to the Ladies* (1695, 1697).

At the same time, more practical views were advocated. Adolphus Speed, a member of the Hartlib-Dury circle, planned a very practical curriculum for girls in his projected plan for an academy. He would have them study such diversified subjects as shorthand, arithmetic, French, the preparation of beauty aids, home remedies, cooking, and perfume and wax-making.[42] Bathsua Makin's *An Essay to Revive the Antient Education of Gentlewomen* (1673) and Daniel Defoe's *Essay upon Projects* (1697) both envisioned a practical education for girls.[43]

Whatever her ability to learn, the woman of the Tudor-Stuart era was expected to put her knowledge to good use. A good Puritan mother particularly was " expected to read the Bible to her children and, in the absence of her husband, to conduct family worship. . . ."[44] The most frequently read books were those on piety, such as Michael Sparke's *The Crums of Comfort* (1628; 10th edition, 1629; 42nd edition, 1656); Nicholas Breton's *Auspicante Jehoua* (1597); Elizabeth Jocelyn's *The Mother's Legacie* (1624); *A Jewel for Gentlewomen* (1624). John Featley's devotional, *A Fountaine of teares emptying itself into three rivolets* (1646) was commissioned by Elizabeth Keate for other women. Featley prided himself on making his books helpful to women by writing in English and citing only Bible verses. [5]

G. E. Noyes's *Bibliography of Courtesy and Conduct Books in Seventeenth Century England* (1937) also includes books on childhood education, another subject on which women would have been avid readers. Foster Watson's *English Writers on Education, 1480–1603* (1967) lists the most significant of these for the Tudor period. Typical for the Stuart era are *The Countrymans care and the Citizens feare* (1641), J. B.'s *Heroick Education* (1657), and Francis Osborne's *Advice to a Son* (1656; six reprints to 1658).

L. B. Wright's *Middle-Class Culture in Elizabethan England* and Chilton L. Powell's English *Domestic Relations, 1487–1653* (1917) discuss many of the domestic conduct books. Though this genre was popular until the end of the century, no one has analyzed the contents of those printed in the post-Restoration era. Sir G. Wheler's *A Protestant Monastery* (1698) represents the type. Some of the conduct books contain long passages on the means of achieving the ideal marriage. At the same time, books specifically discussing marriage were popular. William Whately's *A Bride-Bush* (1617) and his *A Care-cloth* (1624) show a modern, commonsense approach to marital relations. Even a Renaissance work by Francesco Barbaro was published as *Directions for Love and Marriage* (1677).[46] How women put these directives to work may be discovered in Christine Hole's *The English Housewife in the Seventeenth Century* (1953).

Another type of ladies' book appeared toward the end of the seventeenth century as a companion piece to the conduct and courtesy books. It took a composite form, combining advice on behavior, recipes for home medical remedies, forms for personal letters, and even some "short stories." The most popular of these was Hannah Woolley's *The Acomplished Lady's Delight* (1673; 7th edition, 1696), borrowed to some extent by John Shirley for his *The Accomplished Lady's Rich Closet of Rarities* (1687; 6th edition, 1699). An earlier version of this kind of book was M. B.'s *The Ladies Cabinet Enlarged and Opened* (1654; 4 editions to 1667). The bookseller, John Dunton, appealed to female readers by publishing questions from women in *The Athenian Mercury*, a newspaper which ran from 1691 to 1697. *The Ladies Mercury*, directed to women alone, had just eight issues in February and March 1693. N. H.'s *The Ladies Dictionary*, another composite book, contained among other things definitions of women's names and short essays on such topics as love and religion.

Further insight into the problem of women's education could result from investigating the suggestion that male education in the Tudor-Stuart era was a prolongation of the puberty rite, an exercise which might be viewed as comparable to initiation into primitive societies. The *rite de passage* for girls was entirely different, according to Walter Ong, as "it opened out upon a pleasant, fanciful, romantic world."[47] What did constitute the initiation into the world for girls, if the study of Latin indeed can be viewed as a puberty rite for boys? To what extent is it true that the world girls saw was romantic? Do the domestic conduct books and "Ladies Home Journal" reading constitute the image of the romantic?

A study of school boy textbooks would bring into focus the basis of male attitudes toward women in the era. It may be extravagant to describe these books as sexist, yet it is clear that basic negative attitudes could be reinforced by their use. Foster Watson's *The English Grammar Schools to 1660* (1908) provides a starting point. Latin dialogues by Vives and Erasmus circulated widely, but whether their views of women were influential remains to be judged.

A study of what women read in the post-Restoration era might modify some of L. B. Wright's conclusions about middle-class values. Scholarly biographies of educated women are needed before the history of women's education is complete. Women whose lives have been neglected are Anne Killigrew, Lady Winchelsea, and Lady Ranelagh (Robert Boyle's sister). A study of the latter's influence on the Hartlib-Dury-Comenius circle as well as her association with members of the Royal Society would certainly expand our knowledge of the extent of female participation in intellectual adventures.

In spite of some adverse male reaction to women's efforts to educate themselves, Bathsua Makin's judgment of what it all meant hits the mark: "Had God intended Women onely as a finer sort of Cattle, he would not have made them reasonable."[48]

FAITH OF THEIR FATHERS

"Religion," claimed the author of the *Ladies Dictionary*, is "a Ladies chief ornament ... the crown of all other Excellencies." Moreover, ladies were more steadfast in their faith than men, hence it would be less necessary for them to read multitudes of books. As it was, many women left records of their piety, including discussions of their reading. Some were notorious for their open expression of faith, speaking in private and even public meetings. Others wrote religious tracts, but left their posthumous publication to loyal relatives.

The contribution of women to the outcome of the Protestant Reformation has only recently become the subject of serious investigation. Scholars have taken a biographical approach to their work, following some of the earliest descriptions of pious women. *English Churchwomen of the Seventeenth Century* (1845) and James Anderson's *Ladies of the Reformation* (1855), as well as his *Memorable Women of Puritan Times* (1862), are still useful, even though their subjects are somewhat romanticized. Scholarly biographies of women who influenced the religious life of their age have yet to be written. Emory Battis's *Saints and Sectaries: Anne Hutchinson and the Antinomian Controversy* (1962) sets a high standard for this kind of research. Another model of biographical analysis is Patrick Collinson's "The Role of Women in the English Reformation," in *Studies in Church History* (1965).

While many scholars have concentrated on explaining the process by which the Reformation occurred in England, others have turned to institutional studies.[49] Consequently, even in histories of the Catholic Reformation, the role of women has seldom been noticed. Tudor piety was exemplified in the life and works of Margaret Beaufort, countess of Richmond. As the mother of King Henry VII, she was in an admirable position to extend patronage to both the church and the universities. She founded two new colleges, established the Lady Margaret Professorship of Divinity, and even urged the king to appoint John Fisher, one of the earliest clerics to profit from that professorship, to the bishopric of Rochester. She commissioned William Atkinson to translate the French version of Thomas à Kempis's *Imitatio Christi*, supplying the fourth part herself; persuaded Fisher to publish his *Seven Penitential Psalms*; insured the publication of Walter Hilton's *Scala Perfectionis* through association with Caxton's press; and finally translated from the French another devotional book entitled *The mirroure of golde for the synful soule* (1522, 1526). Yet all her biographies must be consulted if one wants a complete picture of her religiosity.[50]

Her example was not lost on the rest of the royal household, although the faith of her grandson's wife had been well taught in Spain and reinforced with fateful consequences. Garrett Mattingly's masterly biography of Catherine of Aragon treats the strength of her religious convictions with authority. More recent studies focusing on Tudor piety are Francis G. Murray's "Feminine Spirituality in the More Household," in *Moreana* (1970); Roland Bainton's *Women of the Reformation in France and England* (1973), which sketches the lives of Catherine of Aragon, Anne Boleyn, Lady Jane Grey, Mary Tudor, Elizabeth I, and Catherine Willoughby; his "Feminine Piety in Tudor England," in *Christian Spirituality* (1975), which discusses four of Anthony Cooke's five daughters; and William P. Haugaard's "Katherine Parr: The Religious Convictions of a Renaissance Queen," in *Renaissance Quarterly* (1969).

After the Reformation, Catholic piety was fostered by many recusants, both male and female. The history of Tudor-Stuart Catholicism is only slowly being pieced together so their contribution can be identified. The *Publications* of the Catholic Record Society and *Biographical Studies, 1534–1829*, continued under the title *Recusant History*, ed. A. F. Allison, are essential sources. The latter contains a list of theses, both completed and in progress. County records often prove a valuable source for biographical information about recusants. The fate of the nuns after the Dissolution can be followed up in such documents as G. A. J. Hodgett's *The State of the Ex-Religious and Former Chantry Priests in the Diocese of Lincoln, 1547–1574.*

John Bossy has characterized Elizabethan Catholicism. A view of recusancy in southern England is presented in Alfred Southern's edition of *An Elizabethan Recusant House* (1954). Family histories are another valuable source for students of recusancy, as is made clear in Sister J. Hanlon's "These Be But Women," in *From Renaissance to the Counter Reformation* (1965), an essay showing the strength of Catholicism in the first half of the seventeenth century among the northern gentry.

The life of one of the foremost recusants, Mary Ward, has most recently been related by Mary Oliver.[51] Her role in fostering Catholic educational aims has become well known. But Catholic education abroad at St. Omer, Douai, Louvain, and Gravelines might also be studied.[52] Ward's contemporary, Sir Kenelm Digby, argued the case for Rome in *A Conference with a Lady about Choice of Religion* (1638). A. F. Allison's *A Catalogue of Catholic Books in English ... 1558–1640* (1956) reveals the extent of literature available to those who truly sought it.[53]

Conversion to Catholicism occurred throughout the seventeenth century, although the details of this process have not been fully narrated. An interesting tract recounting *The seducing of Ann ... Ketelbey ... to the Romish religion* (1700) exposes the appeal of Catholicism to a young girl who evidently wanted to defy her parents. The story ended with either desired or disastrous results, depending on one's religious point of view. The tract points up the main difficulty of reading such works with twentieth-century values in mind. Nearly all the histories of religion and tracts of the age are colored by their authors' religious preferences. Political events, such as the disclosing of a Catholic plot against the monarchy (for example, the Babington Plot, the Gunpowder Plot, or the Popish Plot) or a monarch's appointing Catholics to public office, produced an almost hysterical reaction to the possibility that papists were still lurking in dangerous places. Yet by 1689, religious intolerance waned, even though many still would not acknowledge the end of the clerical world.

Anglicanism was under attack from the moment of the Elizabethan settlement.[54] The growing strength of Puritanism yielded a fateful harvest in the civil war. After the Restoration, nonconformists of several radical sects plagued the establishment. Christopher Hill contends that the social content of Puritan doctrine in fact became part of the Anglican creed.[55] Nevertheless, the established church had its female apologists. Mary Astell, for example, in her correspondence with John Norris, explained her view of divine love, which it seemed was tinged with Platonism. Her *The Christian Religion* (1705) as well as other works, showed her loyalty.[56] The latitudinarian point of view probably had many more adherents by the end of the century. Lady Damaris Masham's correspondence with John Locke was more philosophic than religious, though she, too, was concerned with doctrine in her *Occasional thoughts in reference to vertuous Christian Life* (1705) and *A Discourse Concerning the love of God* (1696).

Godly, nonconformist women wrote devotional and theological treatises throughout the seventeenth century, though most of their works were published posthumously. Their modesty is typified in the comment made about Mrs. Theodosia Alleine's biography of her husband. Her intention, wrote the editor, was to have her work published in the style of some "worthy divine," she not imagining it should be sent forth in her own words. Praise of this kind of modesty was preached in funeral sermons for such pious women, for example, Bishop Atterbury's *A Discourse occasioned by the death of the ... Lady Cutts* (1698). Richard Baxter's *A Breviate of the Life of Margaret ... Charlton* (1681) added only a few touches of realism to an otherwise stereotyped portrait of an ideal wife. The number of these descriptions, though not large, when taken with those of pious men, constitutes a kind of Protestant hagiography.

Although education was regarded by the enlightened of both centuries as "a Hedge against Heresies," it proved otherwise. As women read the Scriptures and were convinced of the validity of their religious experience, they began to make their faith more public, going so far as to ignore Paul's injunction to remain silent in church. They organized small women's groups to which they explained the Bible, or else they preached in public places, occasionally even in the church. The sources for the history of these women are scattered, but both the standard bibliographies list relevant manuscript collections and printed documents. Additional bibliography has been incorporated in such studies as Keith Thomas's "Women and the Civil War Sects," in *Past and Present* (1958), an essay which largely supersedes E. Williams's "Women Preachers in the Civil War," in *Journal of Modern History* (1929). An essential survey of the radicals' religious ideas is Christopher Hill's *The World Turned Upside Down* (1972). The variety of opinion is fascinating, with accusations and counteraccusations filling the press in a time when censorship was relaxed.

Women frequently were abused in the press. Critics of both the Presbyterians and the Independents (Congregationalists) claimed that these sectaries allowed their women to serve in church office, to preach, even to vote. It certainly was the practice to choose widows as deaconesses to help the sick and needy, to let women vote in the separatist congregations, and to allow their preaching in New England Baptist churches.[57] But a great deal of this acitivity was considered scandalous. Women might be accepted as spiritual equals, but they could hardly be accepted as legitimate expounders of the faith, except among the Quakers. *Tub Preachers Overturned* (1647) reflected the contemporary view that only those in authority ought to interpret the faith. Women were no more qualified to do so than common workmen. Woe to the women who had special insights, such as Anne Wentworth, whose *The Revelation of Jesus Christ* (1679) was probably the result of an unhappy marriage. Her life was made miserable by those who demanded she conform.

The Quakers, by contrast, seem enlightened in all aspects of their religious practice. Quaker women were both active missionaries and writers. John Whiting's *A Catalogue of Friends books* (1708), the earliest of religious bibliographies, lists sixty-three female authors. The literature of the Quaker movement is voluminous, in fact. Joseph Smith's *A Descriptive Catalogue of Friends' Books* (1867) and the *Journal* of the Friends' Historical Society are essential guides. The Friends' Library, London, is the chief repository for manuscripts, just as the Dr. Williams Library houses a great collection of nonconformists' writings.

Biographies of leading Quakers are plentiful. An early study of the distaff side is Mabel R. Brailsford's *Quaker Women, 1650–1690* (1915). Of Margaret Fell Fox's biographers, Isabel Ross has provided the most scholarly account in *Margaret Fell* (1949). Biographies of her associates are needed, however.

The appeal of the radical religious doctrines to various social classes has been debated by Judith J. Hurwich in "The Social Origins of Early Quakers," *Past and Present* (1970), and R. T. Vann in *The Social Structure of Quakerism, 1655–1755* (1969). Whatever the social origin of the Quakers, men and women shared equally in faith. Women were not forbidden to preach, although they may have been supervised.[58] Margaret Fell Fox's *Women's Speaking Justified* (1665) loses some of its novelty when one knows that George Fox and Richard Farnworth had already written on woman's behalf. George Keith added *The Woman-preacher of Samaria* to the literature in 1674.

The female adherents contributed to the martyrology which accompanied the rise of the sect. *A Relation of the Labour, Travail and Suffering of Alice Curwen* (1680), *An Account of the Travels, Sufferings, and Persecutions of Barbara Blaugdone* (1691), and Anne Audland's *A True Declaration of the suffering of the innocent* (1655) are typical. Very moving letters and testimonies of faith from Katherine Evans and Sarah Cheevers were published during their imprisonment on the Isle of Malta (1662). Hugh Wood kept a record of female activities in *A brief Treatise of Religious Women's Meetings, Services, and Testimonies* (1684). Though Quakers held quiet meetings, they poured out their faith on paper.

The radicalism of the Quakers was mild compared to that of other religious groups, at least in the eyes of contemporaries. According to its critics, the Family of Love, for example, preached sexual freedom, if not promiscuity. If divorce was condoned under special circumstances by Puritans, it certainly became unnecessary when a group advocated free love. Thomas Edwards's *Gangraena* (1646) relates a number of tales of the seduction of young women to the sect by men who dangled expectations of salvation before them. Edwards, as a Presbyterian, rarely differentiated one religious radical from another, so he denounced Ranters and Fifth Monarchists as freely, especially as they both attracted female adherents.[59]

One of the latter, Anna Trapnel, cast herself in the martyr's role in *Report and Plea* (1654). C. Burrage's "Anna Trapnel's Prophecies," in *English Historical Review* (1911), discusses the merit of her efforts. Mary Cary's *The Little Horn's Doom and Downfall* (1651) as well as her earlier *A Word in Season* (1647) attempted to warn Cromwell of impending disaster. In a more prophetic spirit, Lady Eleanor Douglas (Davies) foretold the deaths of Buckingham and Charles I. She was such a prolific writer that C. J. Hindle assembled a bibliography of her works. Women who might be considered camp followers of leading sectaries, such as Laurence Clarkson, have found their way into *A List of some of the Grand Blasphemers* (1654). A further study of these women would shed light on the social appeal of radical opinion.[60]

The most unfortunate women in Tudor-Stuart England were those persecuted as witches. Since the witchcraft craze reached its peak during this period of religious upheaval, scholars have attempted to discover a connection between changing religious beliefs and the high incidence of accusation of witches. Alan MacFarlane has clarified the confusion in *Witchcraft in Tudor-Stuart England* (1970). The Puritans, contrary to popular belief, proved skeptical of the whole idea of witches. Nevertheless a connection between the religious ferment of the age and the pursuit of witches has been further analyzed in Keith Thomas's *Religion and the Decline of Magic* (1971). The social and anthropological background of the ideology of witchcraft, especially with respect to community expectations of its members, could be investigated further. Paul Boyer's and Stephen Nissenbaum's *Salem Possessed: The Social Origin of Witchcraft* (1974) offers an excellent research model. Mary Douglas's edition of *Witchcraft Confessions and Accusations* (1970) contains essays on comparative witchcraft which are suggestive of other research topics.

Before the quality of women's religiosity can be evaluated, bibliographies of religious works by women must be assembled. Studies of some of the religious controversies in the post-1660 period have not been discussed in terms of the contribution of women thinkers and writers. The same could be said for an investigation of women recusants in the same era, as Catholicism clearly had not lost its vitality. A study of the circle of female patrons of both the early Puritan ministers and post-Restoration nonconformists would further illuminate the strength of female piety. George L. Turner's *Original Records of English Nonconformity* (1911) provides a basis of comparison of aid given Baptists, Presbyterians, Quakers, and Congregationalists as well as more radical sects. The contribution of women to the growth of Protestantism cannot be assessed except by careful study of individuals. It is assumed that they lived the faith of their fathers, yet the nature of their faith bears further investigation. Max Weber judged women "especially receptive to nonmilitary and nonpolitical movements with orgiastic, emotional, or hysterical aspects to them." Lawrence Stone, among others, considers that women turned to religion out of a sense of uselessness and frustration.[61] Further analysis of the religious experience of women in the Tudor-Stuart era might show that women created the movements of which Weber speaks and did not necessarily feel themselves frustrated or useless.

Only some obvious possibilities for further study of women in the era have been suggested here: for example, those relating to woman's status in the social and economic life of the age, to the contemporary literary view which on the surface appears weighted by sexism but which may in fact be the means of reinforcing the value of order in society, to the nature of the limited education available to women, to the sources of women's spiritual lives. Much more bibliographic as well as biographical study must be undertaken in order that the whole realm of women's activities may be more fully understood. The possibilities for fruitful study are limited only by the sources and the ingenuity of the individual using them.

# NOTES

1. MacLehose, *Itinerary*, 3: 462.
2. These are Mackie, *The Earlier Tudors*; Black, *The Reign of Elizabeth*; Davies, *The Early Stuarts*; G. N. Clark, *The Later Stuarts*. Each has an annotated bibliography which cites significant sources of social, economic, political, intellectual, and cultural history.
3. A review of the bibliography of women in literature is an essay in itself, though the student of history will find useful such studies as K. Rogers, *The Troublesome Helpmate*; Gagen, *The New Woman*; Helton, "The Concept of Woman's Honour"; Schleiner, *Gynaikeion*. For biographies of notable women, another possible essay in its own right, the student may turn to *Lives of the Tudor Age* and *Lives of the Stuart Age*. Costello's *Memoirs of Eminent English Women* is valuable for its use of letters and portraits; Timpson, *British Female Biography* collects the lives of queens, princesses, martyrs, scholars, instructors, poetesses, philanthropists, and ministers' wives; G. Hill, *Women in English Life* includes women as doctors and philanthropists; Wilson, *Society Women*, based on personal correspondence, gives insights into arranged marriages; J. Williams, *The Literary Women of England* has been largely superseded by later works; Wilson, *Queen Elizabeth's Maids of Honour* is basically a fictionalized account with portraits; Bone, *Henrietta Maria*, among other biographies of women rulers of the age, is a scholarly study of the queen's political activities.
4. His reviewer, Beth Norton, in *Journal of Interdisciplinary History*, suggests that the realities of husband and wife relationships as well as the self-perception of American and English women might be subjects of research.
5. Gadol, "The Social Relation of the Sexes."
6. For example, see Laslett and Wall, *Household and Family in Past Time*, chapter 4 of which describes the methodology of arriving at mean household size.
7. Other studies which are demographically oriented and illustrate methodological models are Appleby, "Disease or Famine?"; Cornwall, "English Population"; Hollingsworth and Hollingsworth, "Plague Mortality Rates"; Schnucker, "Elizabethan Birth Control"; E. E. Rich, "The Population of Elizabethan England"; Wrigley, "Family Limitation"; G. S. L. Tucker, "English Pre-Industrial Population Trends."
8. Brodsky's doctoral project at Cambridge, "Marriage and Mobility in Pre-Industrial England," analyzes marriage patterns within the ranks of the middle class. The sources for this work are marriage allegations, marriage bonds, and apprenticeship records. The essential question is whether marriage patterns can be traced to demographic change. Coleman's "Medieval Marriage Characteristics" explores this possibility. D. M. Clark's "Social Considerations Underlying Marriage and Fecundity Patterns" moves from a similar premise. See also Slater, "The Weightiest Business"; Stone "Social Mobility in England"; C. S. C. Gibson, "Marriage Breakdown and Social Class"; and Maltby, "Easingwold Marriage Horizons."
9. See Allport, *The Use of Personal Documents in Psychological Science* for criteria by which to judge authentic documents. Some of the problems associated with the type are discussed in Pomerleau, "Resigning the Needle for the Pen." Masek's "Studies in the Self-Concept" will analyze such personal documents from a psychohistorical point of view. For an analysis of the medical treatment of female psychology, see MacDonald's "Mental Disorder in Seventeenth Century England."
10. A recent contribution to the subject is Glanz, "The Legal Position of English Women." McDermott's "Common Law and the Family" focuses on will making. Barbara J. Todd (University of British Columbia) is studying the extent to which widows remarried.
11. Forty-four percent went to direct poor relief; see Jordan, *Philanthropy in England*, 355, and Appendix 9: "Structure of Giving Women Donors," 382–83; Jordan's *The Charities of London* and *The Charities of Rural England* are essential background for a study of female philanthropy. Bittle and Lane have analyzed Jordan's statistics in "Inflation and Philanthropy." Contemporary attitudes toward the poor are found in Hale's *Method Concerning Relief* and *Discourse Touching Provision for the Poor*. See also Leonard, *The Early History of English Poor Relief*, and Hampson, *The Treatment of Poverty*.

12. Weiner, "Sex-Roles and Crime in Elizabethan Hertfordshire." Her research notes provide an excellent introduction to the use of county records and legal documents.

13. Peake, "The Stage Prostitute." Schleiner (University of California, Davis) finds a significant change in the attitude toward the literary prostitute. Earlier, for example, the gold-hearted whore comes from gentle lineage; later in the Renaissance, she belongs to the lower classes.

14. Although much of the research for this section of the essay was completed at the Henry E. Huntington Library, a student may find many of the works cited already in facsimile or edited form in the larger university libraries.

15. Other works dependent on Agrippa's work are *A Pleasant Discourse*, two editions of a long poem, *The Glory of Women* and *Female Pre-eminence*, and "Female pre-eminence," in *The Wonders of the Female World*. *The Praise and Dispraise of Women*, based on de Marconville's *De la bonte et mauvaistie des femmes*, represents the French influence. Although de Gournay's work, *L'Égalité des Hommes et des Femmes*, does not seem to have been translated, du Bosc's *L'Honneste femme* was translated as *The Compleat Woman* (1639), *The Accomplished Woman* (1656), and *The Excellent Woman* (1692, 1695). *The Secretary of Ladies* is another du Bosc work. Francois Poulain de la Barre's *De L'Égalité des deux Sexes* appeared as *The Woman as Good as the Man* (1677). For a commentary, see Seidel, "Poulain de la Barre's *The Woman as Good as the Man*." The example of the Dutch scholar, Anna Maria van Schurman, was added to the catalogs of worthy women.

16. Further sources for such a study are Bansley's *A Treatyse, showing ... the pryde and abuse of women*; E. More's *A ... Treatyse, called the defense of women*; Pyrrye's *The Praise and Dispraise of women*; Anger, *Jane Anger her protection of Women*; A. Gibson's *A Woman's Woorth*; Breton's *The Praise of Virtuous Ladies* and his *Pasquils Mistresse*; B. Rich's *The excellency of good women*; Ferrers's *The Worth of Woman*; and E. F.'s *The Embleme of a Virtuous woman*.

17. Crandall, *Swetnam the Woman-Hater*.

18. H. V. Routh, "London and the Development of Popular Literature."

19. The Amazon has been discussed by C. T. Wright, "The Amazons in Elizabethan Literature." A type which has had little study is the exchange-wench. See *The Ape-Gentlewoman* and *An answer to the Character of an Exchange-wench*. James I's reaction to mannish women is alluded to in such contemporary works as the letters of John Chamberlain, and Niccholes' *A Discourse, of Marriage and Wiving*. Davis points out that the "uses of sexual inversion ... are ultimately sources of order and stability in a hierarchical society." The topos "woman-on-top," might "facilitate innovation in historical theory and political behavior" (*Society and Culture in Early Modern France*, p. 130).

20. The works of other satirists are cited in *The New Cambridge Bibliography of English Literature*; see John Marston, Edward Guilpin, Joseph Hall, Samuel Rowlands, William Goddard, Ben Jonson, Henry Fitgeffrey, Henry Hutton, and Wye Waltonstall.

21. Overbury had attempted to dissuade James I's favorite, Robert Carr, from marrying Frances, Lady Essex, whose marriage to the earl had finally been annulled amidst much scandal. For his pains, Overbury was poisoned. Public opinion was shocked by the king's permissiveness and open defense of Carr; see Davies, *The Early Stuarts*, pp. 19–20.

22. The social implications of the treatment of shrews and scolds is the subject of Jackson's "The Common Scold."

23. Women's efforts to gain political recognition are the subject of MacArthur, "Women Petitioners and Parliament"; Higgins, "Women in the Civil War" and "Reactions of Women"; H. Smith, "Feminism in the Seventeenth Century." *The Parliament of Women* was printed several times in 1646 and 1647, once as *Now or Never* (1656).

24. This concern was reflected in literature: see Phillips, "The Background of Spenser's Attitude Toward Women Rulers," and "The Woman Ruler in Spenser's *Faerie Queen*"; McNeal, "Shakespeare's Cruel Queens." Weinstein, in a popular essay, "Queen's Power: The Case of Katherine Parr," concludes that the queen had little influence. Yates, "Queen Elizabeth as Astrea," treats Queen Elizabeth's political power.

25. L. B. Wright, *Middle-Class Culture*, p. 507.

26. Quoted in Kamm, *Hope Deferred*, p. 53; Wellman's inscription is written on the back page of the Henry E. Huntington Library copy of *The Whole Duty of Man*.
27. See Cressy, "Education and Literacy," and "Literacy in Pre-Industrial England"; Stone, "The Educational Revolution in England" and "Literacy and Education in England"; Schofield, "The Measurement of Literacy."
28. Adamson, "The Extent of Literacy in England."
29. Simon's book revises Leach, *The Schools of Medieval England*, which asserted that the impact of the Reformation was largely negative.
30. Vives's work had eight editions in the Tudor era; Kuschmierz's study, "*The Instruction of a Christian Woman*: A Critical Edition of the Tudor Translation" expands upon Watson's *Vives and the Renascence Education of Women*. Watson's book contains editions of Vives's "Plan of Studies for Girls"; Hyrde, "on the Education of Women"; "The School of Sir Thomas More"; Vives's "On the Learning of Women"; Elyot's *The Defence of Good Women*.
31. C. More's *The Life and Death of Sir Thomas More*; E. F. Rogers, ed., *The Correspondence of Thomas More*, nos. 63, 122; Allen, ed., *Opus Epistolarum Des. Erasmi Roterdami*, 4: 598.
32. Hake, *A Touchstone*, p. 26.
33. Lambley, *The Teaching and Cultivation of the French Language*. The goal seems contradictory.
34. *Positions*, p. 133; see Oliphant's edition of *The Educational Writings of Richard Mulcaster* for other of his views. He would allow technical training, if it were necessary for a woman to make a living, and higher education for those qualified, but they might not attend universities.
35. *Learned Ladies*, pp. 26, 425. See also Hughey, "Cultural Interests of Women"; for a collection of such writings consult Mahl and Koon, eds., *The Female Spectator*.
36. Gardiner, *English Girlhood*, p. 209; Kay, *History of Rivington and Blackrod Grammar School*; Clode, *Memorials of the Merchant Taylors*, p. 726; Carlisle, *A Concise Description of the Endowed Grammar Schools of England and Wales*, 2: 732; Meads, "An Account of the Education of Women"; P. W. Smith, "The Education of Englishwomen."
37. Simon, *Education and Society*, p. 376, n.1.
38. Coote's *The English Schoolmaster* (1596; 49 editions to 1700) was addressed to "such men and women of the Trades, as Taylors, Weavers, Shopkeepers, Seamsters, and such others as have undertaken the charge of teaching others." The free school at Norwich, taught by women, admitted both boys and girls.
39. Power, *Medieval English Nunneries*, pp. 237–84; note B, pp. 568–81. See Plumpton, *Plumpton Correspondence*, for evidence of the experience of a child "placed out."
40. Watson, *English Writers*, p. 95.
41. Webster, *Samuel Hartlib*, pp. 145, 190, 196.
42. Quoted in Turnbull, *Hartlib, Dury and Comenius*, pp. 118–19.
43. For an analysis of some of the religious, social, and personal aims of female education, see Weier, "Views on the Education of Women."
44. D. Rogers, *Matrimoniall Honour*, pp. 268–69.
45. Hull's "Chaste, Silent and Obedient," lists books specifically written for women, among which were books on cookery, domestic conduct, piety, and even those romances which Hake and Salter warned against. Woman's right to read what she chose was defended in Tyler's preface to her translation of *The first part of the Mirrour of Princely deedes and Knighthood*, one of those same romances.
46. Some of these works are analyzed in Johnson, "English Puritan Thought," in "Puritans on the Covenant and on Marriage," and in *A Society Ordained by God*.
47. Ong, "Latin Language Study as a Renaissance Puberty Rite."
48. Makin, *An Essay to Revive the Antient Education of Gentlewomen*, 23.
49. N. H., *The Ladies Dictionary*, p. 436. Several general works on women in religion provide a useful starting point for further research: e.g., Bliss, *The Service and Status of Women*; Tavard, *Women in Christian Tradition*, a significant book on the theology of women from the point of view of theological anthropology; Douglass, "Women and the Continental

Reformation"; for a less penetrating analysis than Tavard's, see Harkness, *Women in Church and Society*.

50. For example, Dickens, *The English Reformation*.
51. Halstead, *Life*; Cooper, *Memoirs*; E. Routh, *Lady Margaret*.
52. Her other biographers are Chambers, *Life*; and Salome, *Mary Ward*.
53. Gardiner, *English Girlhood*, p. 207.
54. The number of tracts arguing the Protestant cause is also large, another indication that Catholicism was not a dead issue. For example, *The Answere of a Mother unto hir seduced Sonnes Letter* was a polemic against the proselytizing of the English Catholic college at Douai. Typical of the formal replies to papism is Barecroft's *A Letter to a Lady*.
55. So much has been written about the settlement that it would be redundant to cite works on the subject. On the nature of Queen Elizabeth's religiosity, nothing has been more provocative than Graziani, "The 'Rainbow Portrait' of Queen Elizabeth and Its Religious Symbolism."
56. Astell's biographer analyzes her religious ideas: see F. Smith, *Mary Astell*.
57. C. Hill, *Society and Puritanism*, p. 560ff. A closer look by Ludlow, "Women Preachers in Mid-Seventeenth Century England," is in progress.
58. See Robinson, *A Brief Catechism*.
59. Barclay, *They Inner Life of the Religious Societies*, p. 345.
60. Morton, *The World of the Ranters* discusses many of these radicals. Capp, *Fifth Monarchy Men* describes the careers of Mary Cary and Anna Trapnel; Cohen, "The Fifth Monarchy Mind: Mary Cary and the Origins of Totalitarianism," sees her work as valuable for providing an overview of Fifth Monarch thought. The Quakers were also scorned in the pamphlet *Quakers are inchanters and dangerous seducers*. Ebel, "The Family of Love," contains a useful bibliography of the sect to 1704.
61. Quoted in Davis, *Society and Culture*, pp. 66–67.

# BIBLIOGRAPHY

A., I. *The Good Womans Champion*. [London: 1650?]

ADAMSON, J. E. *Contributions to the History of Education, 1600–1700*. Cambridge: 1921.

———. "The Extent of Literacy in England in the Fifteenth and Sixteenth Centuries." *The Library*, n.s. 10 (1929): 163–93.

AGRIPPA VON NETTERSHEIM, HEINRICH CORNELIUS. *The Commendation of Matrimony*. London: 1540.

———. *Female Pre-eminence*. Translated by Henry Case. London: 1670.

———. "Female Pre-eminence." In *The Wonders of the Female World*. [London: 1683?]

———. *The Glory of Women; or, A Treatise*. London: 1652.

———. *A Treatise of the Nobilitie and Excellencye of Womankynde*. [London: 1542.]

ALLEN, PERCY S., ed. *Opus Epistolarum Des. Erasmi Roterdami*. Oxford: 1922.

ALLESTREE, RICHARD. *The Ladies Calling*. London: 1668, 1672, 1676.

———. *The Whole Duty of Man*. London: 1659, 1677, 1680.

ALLISON, A. F. *A Catalogue of Catholic Books in English ... 1558–1640. Biographical Studies* 3, nos. 3, 4. Bognor Regis: 1956.

———, and Rogers, D. M. eds. *Biographical Studies, 1534–1829.* Bognor Regis: 1951–58. (Continued as *Recusant History.*)

ALLPORT, GORDON. *The Use of Personal Documents in Psychological Science.* New York: 1942.

ANDERSON, JAMES. *The Ladies of the Reformation.* London and New York: 1855.

———. *Memorable Women of Puritan Times.* London: 1862.

ANGER, JANE. *Jane Anger Her Protection of Women.* London: 1589.

*The Answere of a Mother unto Hir Seduced Sonnes Letter.* London: 1627. (Letter signed: I. Maad.)

*An Answer to the Character of an Exchange-Wench.* London: 1675.

*The Ape-Gentlewoman, or The Character of an Exchange-Wench.* London: 1675.

APPLEBY, ANDREW. "Disease or Famine? Mortality in Cumberland and Westmorland, 1580–1640." *Economic History Review* 26 (1973): 403–32.

*Arminian Nunnery ... at Little Gidding.* London: 1641.

ASTELL, MARY. *The Christian Religion as Profess'd by a Daughter of the Church of England.* London: 1705, 1717.

———. *An Essay in Defence of the Female Sex.* London: 1696, 1697.

———. *A Farther Essay Relating to the Female-Sex.* London: 1696.

———. *A Serious Proposal to the Ladies.* London: 1694, 1695, 1697.

ATTERBURY, FRANCIS. *A Discourse Occasioned by the Death of the ... Lady Cutts.* London: 1698.

AUDLAND, ANNE. *A True Declaration of the Suffering of the Innocent.* London: 1655.

AUSTIN, WILLIAM. *Haec Homo, Wherein the Excellence of the Creation of Women Is Described....* London: 1637, 1638, 1639.

AYLMER, JOHN. *An Harborowe for Faithfull and Trewe Subjects agaynst the Late Blowne Blast.* Strasbourg and London: 1559.

B., I. *Heroick Education.* London: 1657.

B., M. *The Ladies Cabinet Enlarged and Opened.* London: 1654.

BAINTON, ROLAND. "Feminine Piety in Tudor England." In *Christian Spirituality: Essays in Honor of Gordon Rupp,* edited by Peter Brooks. London: 1975.

———. *Women of the Reformation in France and England.* Minneapolis, Minn.: 1973.

BALLARD, GEORGE. *Memoirs of Several Ladies of Great Britain Who Have Been Celebrated for Their Writings or Skill in the Learned Languages, Arts and Sciences.* Oxford: 1752.

BANSLEY, CHARLES. *A Treatyse, Shewing and Declaring the Pryde and Abuse of Women Now A Dayes.* [London: 1550?] Reprint. London: 1841. Reprint. In *The Elizabethan Bookseller.* Waukegan, Ill.: 1942.

BARBARO, FRANCESCO. *Directions for Love and Marriage.* London: 1677.

BARCLAY, ROBERT. *The Inner Life of the Religious Societies of the Commonwealth.* London: 1876.

BARECROFT, CHARLES. *A Letter to a Lady, Furnishing Her with Scripture Testimonies.* London: 1688.

*Baron and Feme. A Treatise of Law and Equity, concerning Husbands and Wives.* London: 1700.

BATESON, MARY. *Borough Customs.* London: 1904.

———. *Records of the Borough of Leicester.* London: 1905.

BATTIS, EMORY. *Saints and Sectaries: Anne Hutchinson and the Antinomian Controversy.* Chapel Hill, N.C.: 1962.

BAXTER, RICHARD. *A Breviate of the Life of Margaret . . . Charlton.* London: 1681.

BAYNE, DIANE V. *"The Instruction of a Christian Woman:* Richard Hyrde and the Thomas More Circle." *Moreana* 45 (1975): 5–15.

BECON, THOMAS. *A Newe Catechisme.* In *The Catechism of Thomas Becon,* edited by John Ayre. Cambridge: 1844.

BERCHER, WILLIAM. *The Nobility of Women.* Edited by Warwick Bond. London: 1904.

BERRY, B. M. "The First English Pediatricians and Tudor Attitudes Towards Childhood." *Journal of the History of Ideas* 25 (1974): 561–77.

BITTLE, WILLIAM, and LANE, R. TODD. "Inflation and Philanthropy in England: A Reassessment of W. K. Jordan's Data." *Economic History Review* 29 (1976): 203–10.

BLACK, J. B. *The Reign of Elizabeth, 1558–1603.* 2d ed. Oxford: 1959.

BLAKE, WILLIAM. *A New Trial of the Ladies.* London: 1658.

———. *The Triall of the Ladies.* London: 1656.

———. *The Yellow Book.* London: 1656.

BLAUGDONE, BARBARA. *An Account of the Travels, Sufferings, and Persecutions of....* London: 1691.

BLISS, KATHERINE. *The Service and Status of Women in the Churches.* London: 1952, 1954.

*The Boke of Mayd Emlyn That Had V. Husbands and All Kuckholde.* In *The New Notborune Mayd.* London: 1842.

BONE, QUENTIN. *Henrietta Maria: Queen of the Cavaliers.* Urbana, Ill.: 1972. London: 1973.

BOSSY, JOHN. "The Character of Elizabethan Catholicism." *Past and Present,* no. 21 (1962): 39–59.

BOYER, PAUL, and NISSENBAUM, STEPHEN. *Salem Possessed: The Social Origin of Witchcraft.* Cambridge, Mass.: 1974. London: 1974.

BRAILSFORD, MABEL R. *Quaker Women, 1650–1690.* London: 1915.

BRAITHWAITE, RICHARD. *Ar't Asleepe Husband? A Bolster Lecture.* London: 1640.

BRETON, NICHOLAS, *Auspicante Jehoua.* London: 1597.

———. *The Good and the Badde.* London: 1616.

———. *Pasquils Mistresse; or The Worthie and Unworthie Woman.* London: 1600.

———. *The Praise of Virtuous Ladies.* London: 1597, 1606.

BRODSKY, VIVIEN. "Marriage and Mobility in Pre-Industrial England." Ph.D. dissertation, Cambridge University, 1976.

BRUTO, GIOVANNI M. *The Necessarie, Fit and Convenient Education of a Yong Gentlewoman.* London: 1598.

BUDÉ, GUILLAUME. *Le Correspondance d'Erasme et de Guillaume Budé.* Paris: 1967.

BULLINGER, HEINRICH. *The Christen State of Matrimonye.* London: 1541.

BURRAGE, C. "Anna Trapnel's Prophecies." *English Historical Review* 26 (1911): 526–35.

CAMDEN, CARROLL. *The Elizabethan Woman.* New York: 1952.

CANNON, MARY AGNES. *The Education of Women during the Renaissance.* Washington, D.C.: 1916.

CAPP, BERNARD. *Fifth Monarchy Men: A Study in Seventeenth Century English Millenarianism.* London: 1972.

CARLETON, MARY. *The Memoirs of . . . Commonly Styled, the German Princess.* London: 1673.

CARLISLE, N. *A Concise Description of the Endowed Grammar Schools of England and Wales.* London: 1868.

CARY, MARY. *The Little Horn's Doom and Downfall.* London: 1651.

————. *A Word in Season to the Kingdom of England....* London: 1647.

CASTIGLIONE, BALDASSARE. *The Courtier.* London: 1561, 1975.

*A Catalogue of Virtuous Women Recorded in the Old and New Testament.* London: 1671.

CATHOLIC RECORD SOCIETY. *Publications.* London: 1905–.

*The Challenge Sent by a Young Lady to Sir Thomas ... or, The Female War.* London: 1697.

CHAMBERLAIN, JOHN. *Letters.* Edited by Norman McClure. Philadelphia: 1939.

CHAMBERLAYNE, EDWARD. *An Academy or Colledge Wherein Young Ladies May ... Be Duly Instructed in the True Protestant Religion.* London: 1671.

CHAMBERS, MARY C. E. *The Life of Mary Ward.* London: 1882.

CHANDLER, F. W. *The Literature of Roguery.* Boston: 1907.

CLARK, ALICE. *Working Life of Women in the Seventeenth Century.* London: 1919. New York, London: 1968.

CLARK, DAVID M. "Social Considerations Underlying Marriage and Fecundity Patterns During the Sixteenth Century in the County of Essex," Ph.D. dissertation, Indiana University, in progress.

CLARK, GEORGE N. *The Later Stuarts.* 2d ed. Oxford: 1955.

CLODE, C. M. *Memorials of the Merchant Taylors.* London: 1875.

COHEN, ALFRED. "The Fifth Monarchy Mind: Mary Cary and the Origins of Totalitarianism." *Social Research* 31 (1964): 195–213.

COLEMAN, EMILY. "Medieval Marriage Characteristics: A Neglected Factor in the History of Medieval Serfdom." *Journal of Interdisciplinary History* 2 (1971): 205–17.

COLLINSON, PATRICK. "The Role of Women in the English Reformation Illustrated by the Life and Friendship of Anne Locke." In *Studies in Church History,* edited by G. J. Cumming. Leiden: 1965.

CONWAY, ANNE. *Conway Letters.* Edited by Marjorie Hope Nicholson. New Haven, Conn.: 1930.

COOPER, C. H. *Memoirs of Margaret, Countess of Richmond and Derby.* Cambridge: 1874.

COOTE, E. *The English Schoolmaster.* London: 1596.

COPLAND, ROBERT. *Here Begynneth the Complaynte of Them That Ben To Late Maryed.* [London: 1505?]

————. *A Complaynt of Them That Be To Soone Maryed.* [London: 1506?]

CORNWALL, JULIAN. "English Population in the Early Sixteenth Century." *Economic History Review* 23 (1970): 32–44.

COSTELLO, LOUISA. *Memoirs of Eminent English Women.* London: 1844.

*The Countrymans Care and the Citizens Feare, in Bringing up of His Children in Good Education.* London: 1641, 1873.

*The Court of Good Counsell.* London: 1607.

CRANDALL, CORYL. *Swetnam the Woman-Hater: The Controversy and the Play.* Lafayette, Ind.: 1969.

CRESSY, DAVID. "Education and Literacy in London and East Anglia, 1580–1700." Ph.D. dissertation, Cambridge University, 1972.

————. "Literacy in Pre-Industrial England." *Societas* 4 (1974): 229–40.

CROUCH, NATHANIEL. *Female Excellency, or The Ladies Glory.* London: 1681.

CROWLEY, ROBERT. *One and Thrytye Epigrammes.* London: 1550.

CURWEN, ALICE. *A Relation of the Labour, Travail and Suffering of Alice Curwen.* London: 1680.

DARCIE, ABRAHAM. *The Honour of Ladies*. London: 1622.

DAVIES, GODFREY. *The Early Stuarts*. 2d ed. Oxford: 1959.

————, and Keeler, Mary Frear. *Bibliography of British History, Stuart Period, 1603–1714*. 2d ed. Oxford: 1970.

DAVIS, NATALIE ZEMON. *Society and Culture in Early Modern France*. Stanford, Calif.: 1957.

*The Deceyte of Women, to the Instruction and Ensample of All Men*.... London: 1557.

DEFOE, DANIEL. *Essay Upon Projects*. London: 1697, 1969.

DEKKER, THOMAS. *The Bachelors' Banquet*. London: 1603. Oxford: 1929.

————. *The Honest Whore*. London: 1635. New York: 1930. Boston: 1931.

DELANY, PAUL. *British Autobiography in the Seventeenth Century*. London: 1969.

DELONEY, THOMAS. *The Garland of Good-Will*. [London: 1593.]

DEMAUSE, LLOYD, ed. *The History of Childhood*. New York: 1974. London: 1976.

*A Dyalogue Defensyve for Women*. London: 1542.

DICKENS, A. G. *The English Reformation*. London: 1964.

DIGBY, KENELM. *A Conference with a Lady about Choice of Religion*. Paris: 1638.

*A Discourse of the Married and Single State*. London: 1621.

DOUGLAS, MARY, ed. *Witchcraft Confessions and Accusations*. New York and London: 1970.

DOUGLASS, JANE DEMPSEY. "Women and the Continental Reformation." In *Religion and Sexism: Images of Women in the Jewish and Christian Traditions*, edited by Rosemary R. Ruether, pp. 292–318. New York: 1974.

DU BOSC, JACQUES. *The Accomplish'd Woman*. London: 1656.

————. *The Compleat Woman*. London: 1639.

————. *The Excellent Woman*. London:1692, 1695.

————. *L'Honneste femme*. Paris: 1632.

————. *The Secretary of Ladies*. London: 1638.

DUNTON, JOHN. *The Athenian Mercury*. London: 1691–97.

————. *The Ladies Mercury*. London: 1693.

E., T. *The Lawes Resolutions of Womens Rights*. London: 1632.

EBEL, JULIA G. "The Family of Love: Sources of Its History in England." *Huntington Library Quarterly* 30 (1966–67): 331–43.

EDWARDS, THOMAS. *Gangraena*. London: 1646.

ELYOT, THOMAS. *The Defence of Good Women*. London: 1545. Oxford, Ohio: 1940.

————. *The Education or Bringinge up of Children*. [London: 1535.]

*English Churchwomen of the Seventeenth Century*. Derby: 1845.

ERASMUS. *A Mery Dialogue Declaringe the Propertyes of Shrowde Shrewes and Honest Wyves*. London: 1557.

————. *A Ryght Frutefull Epystle* ... *in Laude and Prayse of Matrimony*. [London: 1530?]

EVANS, KATHERINE. *This is a Short Relation of Some of the Cruel Suffering* ... *of Katherine Evans and Sarah Chever*. London: 1662.

F., E. *The Embleme of a Virtuous Woman*. [London: 1650.]

FANSHAW, ANN. *The Memoirs of Ann Lady Fanshawe*. Edited by H. C. Fanshaw. London: 1907.

FARNWORTH, RICHARD. *A Woman Forbidden to Speak in the Church*. London: 1654, 1655.

FEATLEY, JOHN. *A Fountain of Teares Emptying Itselfe into Three Rivolets*. Amsterdam: 1646.

FELL, MARGARET FOX. See Fox, Margaret Fell.

FERRERS, RICHARD. *The Worth of Woman*. London: 1662.

FISHER, JOHN. *This Treatise Concernynge the Fruytfull Saynges of Davyd the Kynge . . . in the Seven Penytencyall Psalmes.* London: 1508.

FOWLER, JOHN. *An Oration against the Unlawfull Insurrections of Protestants of Our Time.* London: 1566.

FOX, GEORGE. *The Fashions of the World Made Manifest.* London: 1657. In *Gods Truth Demonstrated.* . . . London: 1706.

———. *The Woman Learning in Silence.* London: 1656.

FOX, MARGARET FELL. *Women's Speaking Justified, Proved and Allowed by Scripture.* London: 1665.

FRIENDS HISTORICAL SOCIETY. *Journal.* London: 1903–.

FRITH, MARY. *The Life and Death of Mrs. Mary Frith.* London: 1662.

FRYE, ROLAND M. "The Teaching of Classical Puritanism on Conjugal Love." *Studies in the Renaissance* 2 (1955): 148–59.

FULLER, THOMAS. *The Holy and Profane State.* London: 1642, 1884.

G., I. *An Apologie for Woman-kinde.* London: 1605.

GADOL, JOAN KELLY. "The Social Relation of the Sexes: Methodological Implications of Women's History." *Signs. Journal of Women in Culture and Society* 1 (1976): 809–23.

GAGEN, JEAN E. *The New Woman: Her Emergence in English Drama, 1600–1730.* New York: 1954.

GAIRDNER, JAMES. *The Paston Letters, 1422–1509.* London: 1904.

GAMON, HANNIBAL. *The Praise of a Godly Woman.* London: 1627.

GARDINER, DOROTHY. *English Girlhood at School.* Oxford: 1929.

GASCOIGNE, GEORGE. *The Steele Glas.* London: 1576, 1868.

GERBIER, CHARLES. *Elogium Heroinum, or The Praise of Worthy Women.* London: 1651.

GEREE, STEPHEN. *The Ornament of Women.* London: 1639.

GIBSON, ANTHONY. *A Womans Woorth.* London: 1599.

GIBSON, C. S. C. "Marriage Breakdown and Social Class in England and Wales since the Reformation." Ph.D. dissertation, London University, 1972.

GLANZ, LEONORE M. "The Legal Position of English Women under the Early Stuart Kings and the Interregnum, 1603–1660." Ph.D. dissertation, Loyola University of Chicago, 1973.

GOLBORNE, JOHN. *A Friendly Apology in the Behalf of the Woman's Excellency: Together with Some Examples of Women-Worthies.* London: 1674.

GOSSON, STEPHEN. *Pleasant Quippes for Upstart Newfangled Gentlewomen.* London: 1595. Oxford: 1942.

GOSYNHILL, EDWARD. *The Prayse of All Women.* [London: 1542?]

———. *The Schole House of Women.* London: 1541. Reprint. In *Select Pieces of Early Popular Poetry,* edited by E. V. Utherson. London: 1817.

GOUGE, WILLIAM. *A Funerall Sermon Preached . . . at the Funeralls of Mrs. Margaret Ducke.* London: 1646.

GOURNAY, MARIE DE JARS DE. *L'Égalite des Hommes et des Femmes.* Paris: 1622. Reprint. In Marie L. Schiff, *La fille d'alliance de Montaigne.* Paris: 1910.

GRAZIANI, RENE. "The 'Rainbow Portrait' of Queen Elizabeth and Its Religious Symbolism." *Journal of the Warburg and Courtauld Institute* 35 (1972): 247–59.

GREENE, ROBERT. *A Disputation between a Hee Conny-Catcher and a Shee Conny-Catcher.* London: 1592.

H., I. *A Strange Wonder, or A Wonder in a Woman*. London: 1642.
———. *This World's Folly*. London: 1615.
H., N. *The Ladies Dictionary*. London: 1694.
*Haec Vir: or, The Womanish-Man*. London: 1620.
HAKE, EDWARD. *Newes out of Powles Churchyarde*. London: 1579, 1872.
———. *A Touchstone for This Time Present*. London: 1574.
HALE, MATTHEW. *Discourse Touching Provision for the Poor*. London: 1683, 1695, 1927.
———. *Method concerning Relief and Employment of the Poor*. London: 1699.
HALKETT, ANNE MURRAY. *The Autobiography of Anne, Lady Halkett*. Edited by J. G. Nichols. London: 1875.
HALL, THOMAS. *The Loathsomeness of Long Hair*. London: 1654.
HALLIARG, ARTHUR. *The Cruell Shrow: or, The Patient Mans Woe*. [London: 1610.]
HALSTEAD, CAROLINE. *Life of Margaret Beaufort*. London: 1839.
HAMPSON, E. M. *The Treatment of Poverty in Cambridgeshire, 1597–1834*. Cambridge: 1934.
HANLON, SISTER J. "These Be But Women." In *From the Renaissance to the Counter Reformation*, edited by C. H. Carter. Toronto: 1965.
HARKNESS, GEORGIA. *Women in Church and Society*. Nashville, Tenn. and New York: 1972.
HARLEY, BRILLIANA CONWAY. *The Letters of Lady Brilliana Harley*. Edited by Thomas T. Lewis. London: 1853.
HAUGAARD, WILLIAM P. "Katherine Parr: The Religious Convictions of a Renaissance Queen." *Renaissance Quarterly* 22 (1969): 346–59.
HEALE, WILLIAM. *An Apologie for Women*. Oxford: 1609.
———. *The Great Advocate and Oratour for Women*. London: 1682.
HEINRICH, JOACHIM. "Die Frauenfrage bei Steele und Addison." *Palaestra* 168 (1930): 1–258.
HELTON, TINSLEY. "The Concept of Woman's Honour in Jacobean Drama." Ph.D. dissertation, University of Minnesota, 1952.
HEYDON, JOHN. *Advice to a Daughter*. London: 1658, 1659.
HEYWOOD, THOMAS. *The Exemplary Lives and Memorable Acts of Nine of the Most Worthy Women in the World*. London: 1640.
———. *Gunaikeion: or Nine Books of Various History Concerninge Women*. London: 1624, 1657.
*Hic Mulier: or, The Man-Woman*. London: 1620.
HIGGINS, PATRICIA. "The Reactions of Women, with speical reference to women petitioners." In *Politics, Religion, and the English Civil War*, edited by Brian Manning. New York: 1973.
———. "Women in the Civil War." M.A. thesis, Manchester University, 1965.
HILL, CHRISTOPHER. *Society and Puritanism in Pre-Revolutionary England*. London: 1964, 1969.
———. *The World Turned Upside Down*. New York and London: 1972, 1975.
HILL, GEORGIANA. *Women in English Life from Medieval to Modern Times*. London: 1896.
HILL, WILLIAM. *A New-Year's Gift for Women*. London: 1660.
HILTON, WALTER. *Scala Perfectionis*. London: 1494.
HINDLE, C. J., ed. *A Bibliography of Printed Pamphlets and Broadsides of Lady Eleanor Douglas*. Edinburgh: 1934.
HODGETT, G. A. J. *The State of the Ex-Religious and Former Chantry Priests in the Diocese of Lincoln, 1547–1574*. Hereford: 1959.

HOGREFE, PEARL. "Legal Rights of Tudor Women and Their Circumvention." *The Sixteenth Century Journal* 3 (1972): 92–105.
———. *Tudor Women: Commoners and Queens.* Ames, Iowa: 1975.
———. *Women of Action in Tudor England.* Ames, Iowa: 1977.
HOLE, CHRISTINE. *The English Housewife in the Seventeenth Century.* London: 1953.
HOLLINGSWORTH, MARY F., and HOLLINGSWORTH, T. H. "Plague Mortality Rates by Age and Sex." *Population Studies* 25 (1971): 131–46.
HUGHEY, RUTH W. "Cultural Interests of Women in England from 1524 to 1640 Indicated in the Writings of Women: A Survey." Ph.D. dissertation, Cornell University, 1932.
HULL, SUZANNE. "Chaste, Silent and Obedient: English Books for Women, 1476–1640." M.A. thesis, University of Southern California, 1967.
HURWICH, JUDITH JONES. "The Social Origins of the Early Quakers." *Past and Present*, no. 48 (1970): 156–64.
HUTCHINSON, LUCY. *Memoirs of a Life of Colonel Hutchinson.* Edited by J. Sutherland. London: 1973.
ILLICK, JOSEPH E. "Childrearing in Seventeenth-Century England and America." In *The History of Childhood*, edited by Lloyd DeMause. New York: 1974. London: 1976.
JACKSON, NOELLE. "The Common Scold: An Example of Community Control of Personal Morality." Ph.D. dissertation, University of California, Los Angeles, in progress.
JAMES, M. E., ed. *Estate Accounts of the Earls of Northumberland, 1562–1637.* Durham: 1955.
JEAFFRESON, J. C., ed. *Middlesex County Records.* London: 1886–92, 1935–37, 1973.
*A Jewel for Gentlewomen.* London: 1624.
JOCELINE, ELIZABETH. *The Mother's Legacie to Her Unborne Childe.* Oxford: 1624. London: 1894.
JOHNSON, JAMES T. "English Puritan Thought on the Ends of Marriage." *Church History* 38 (1969): 429–36.
———. "Puritans on the Covenant and on Marriage." *Journal of the History of Ideas* 32 (1971): 107–18.
———. *A Society Ordained by God: English Puritan Marriage Doctrine in the First Half of the Seventeenth Century.* Nashville, Tenn. and New York: 1970.
JONES, PAUL VAN B. *The Household of a Tudor Nobleman.* Urbana, Ill.: 1917.
JORDAN, WILBUR K. *The Charities of London, 1480–1660.* London: 1960.
———. *The Charities of Rural England, 1480–1660.* London: 1961.
———. *Philanthropy in England, 1480–1660.* London: 1959.
JUDGES, A. V. *The Elizabethan Underworld.* London: 1930, 1965.
KAMM, JOSEPHINE. *Hope Deferred: Girls' Education in History.* London: 1965.
KAY, M. *The History of Rivington and Blackrod Grammar School.* Manchester: 1931.
KEITH, GEORGE. *The Woman-Preacher of Samaria.* London: 1674.
KELSO, RUTH. *Doctrine for the Lady of the Renaissance.* Urbana, Ill.: 1956.
KNOX, JOHN. *The First Blast of the Trumpet against the Monstrous Regiment of Women.* Geneva: 1558. Edinburgh: 1733. London: 1895.
KUSCHMIERZ, RUTH LINA MARIE. "*The Instruction of a Christian Woman*: A Critical Edition of the Tudor Translation." Ph.D. dissertation, University of Pittsburgh, 1961.
LAMBLEY, K. *The Teaching and Cultivation of the French Language in England During Tudor and Stuart Times.* Manchester: 1920.

LASLETT, PETER. *Family Life and Illicit Love in Earlier Generations.* Cambridge: 1977.
———. *The World We Have Lost.* New York and London: 1965.
———, and Wall, Richard. *Household and Family in Past Time, Comparative Studies.* Cambridge: 1972.
LA TOUR LANDRY, GEOFFREY DE. *The Book of the Knight of the Tower.* London: 1484. Oxford: 1971.
LEACH, A. F. *The Schools of Medieval England.* London: 1915.
LEIGH, WILLIAM. *Queene Elizabeth, Paraleld in Her Princely Vertues.* London: 1612.
LENTON, FRANCIS. *Great Britains Beauties.* London: 1638.
LEONARD, E. M. *The Early History of English Poor Relief.* Cambridge: 1900. London: 1965.
LESLIE, JOHN. *A Defence of the Honour of Marie Quene of Scotland.* London: 1569. London: 1970.
*A List of Some of the Grand Blasphemers.* London: 1654.
*Lives of the Stuart Age, 1603–1714.* Compiled by Lawrence Urdang Associates. New York: 1976.
*Lives of the Tudor Age, 1485–1603.* Compiled by Ann Hoffman. New York: 1977.
LONGE, JULIA G. *Martha, Lady Giffard, Her Life and Correspondence.* London: 1911.
LUDLOW, DOROTHY P. "Women Preachers in Mid-Seventeenth Century England." Ph.D. dissertation, Indiana University, in progress.
LYLY, JOHN. *Euphues.* London: 1579. Reprint. In *Complete Works,* edited by R. W. Bond. Oxford: 1967.
MCARTHUR, ELLEN A. "Women Petitioners and Parliament." *English Historical Review* 24 (1909): 698–709.
MCDERMOTT, E. "Common Law and the Family in Tudor-Stuart England: Will-Making in Sixteenth and Seventeenth Century England in Its Legal Aspects." Ph.D. dissertation, London University, in progress.
MACDONALD, MICHAEL. "Mental Disorder in Seventeenth Century England." Ph.D. dissertation, Stanford University, 1978.
MACFARLANE, ALAN. *The Family Life of Ralph Josselin.* Cambridge: 1970.
———. *Witchcraft in Tudor and Stuart England.* London: 1970.
MACKIE, J. D. *The Earlier Tudors.* Oxford: 1952.
MCNEAL, THOMAS H. "Shakespeare's Cruel Queens." *Huntington Library Quarterly* 22 (1958–59): 41–50.
MAHL, MARY R., and KOON, HELENE, eds. *The Female Spectator: English Women Writers Before 1800.* Bloomington, Ind.: 1977.
MAKIN, BATHSUA. *An Essay to Revive the Antient Education of Gentlewomen.* London: 1673.
MALTBY, B. "Easingwold Marriage Horizons." *Local Population Studies* 2 (1969): 36–39.
MARCONVILLE, J. DE. *De la bonte et mauvaistie des femmes.*
MASEK, ROSEMARY. "Studies in the Self-Concept: The Case for Seventeenth-Century Women." In progress.
MASHAM, DAMARIS. *A Discourse concerning the Love of God.* London: 1696.
———. *Occasional Thoughts in Reference to a Vertuous or Christian Life.* London: 1705.
*Match Me These Two.* London: 1647.
MATTHEWS, WILLIAM. *British Diaries: An Annotated Bibliography of British Diaries Written between 1442 and 1942.* Berkeley, Calif.: 1950.
MATTINGLY, GARRETT. *Catherine of Aragon.* Boston: 1941. London: 1942, 1950.

MEADS, DOROTHY. "An Account of the Education of Women and Girls in England in the Time of the Tudors." Ph.D. dissertation, London University, 1928.

———, ed. *Diary of Margaret, Lady Hoby*. London: 1930.

MELLING, ELIZABETH, ed. *Kentish Sources*. Maidstone: 1959–.

*A Mery Jeste of a Shrewde and Curste Wife, Lapped in a Morelles Skin*. [London: 1580?]

*The Mirroure of Golde for the Synfull Soule*. London: 1522.

MORE, CRESACRE. *The Life and Death of Sir Thomas More*. London: 1626, 1971.

MORE, EDWARD. *A Lytle and Bryefe Treatyse, Called the Defence of Women*. London: 1560.

MORE, MARGARET. See Roper, Margaret More.

MORTON, A. L. *The World of the Ranters*. London: 1970.

MULCASTER, RICHARD. *Positions Wherein Those … Circumstances Be Examined … Necessarie for the Training up of Children*. London: 1581, 1887. New York: 1888.

*Muld Sacke: or The Apologie of Hic-Mulier*. London: 1617.

MUNDA, CONSTANTIA. *The Worming of a Mad Dogge*. London: 1617.

MURRAY, FRANCES G. "Feminine Spirituality in the More Household." *Moreana*, nos. 27, 28 (1970): 92–102.

NASHE, THOMAS. *The Anatomie of Absurditie*. London: 1589, 1866.

NEVILLE, HENRY. *An Exact Diurnall of the Parliament of Laydes*. London: 1647.

———. *The Ladies a Second Time Assembled in Parliament*. London: 1647.

———. *Newes from the New Exchange*. London: 1650.

———. *The Parliament of Ladies with Their Lawes*. London: 1647.

*The New Cambridge Bibliography of English Literature*. Edited by George Watson. Cambridge: 1969–74.

NEWMAN, ARTHUR. *Pleasures Vision*. London: 1619.

NEWSTEAD, CHRISTOPHER. *An Apology for Women*. London: 1620.

NICCHOLES, ALEXANDER. *A Discourse of Mariage and Wiving*. London: 1620.

NORRIS, JAMES. *The Accomplish'd Lady, or Deserving Gentlewoman*. London: 1684.

———. *Haec & Hic; or, The Feminine Gender More Worthy than the Masculine*. London: 1683.

NORTON, BETH. "[Review of] Roger Thompson, *Women in Stuart England and America*." *Journal of Interdisciplinary History* 7 (1975): 330–32.

NOTESTEIN, WALLACE. "The English Woman, 1580–1650." In *Studies in Social History*, edited by J. H. Plumb. London: 1955.

*Now or Never; or A New Parliament of Women*. London: 1656.

NOYES, G. E. *A Bibliography of Courtesy and Conduct Books in Seventeenth Century England*. New Haven, Conn.: 1937.

OLIPHANT, J. *The Educational Writings of Richard Mulcaster*. Glascow: 1903.

OLIVER, MARY. *Mary Ward, 1585–1645*. New York: 1959.

OLIVIER, JACQUES. *A Discourse of Women*. London: 1662.

ONG, WALTER J. "Latin Language Study as a Renaissance Puberty Rite." *Studies in Philology* 56 (1959): 103–24.

OSBORNE, FRANCES. *Advice to a Son*. London: 1656, 1896.

OVERBURY, THOMAS. *The Bloody Downfall of Adultery, Murder and Ambition*. London: 1615.

———. *A Book of Characters*. London: 1614. Edinburgh: 1865.

———. *A Wife*. London: 1613.

PARKES, WILLIAM. *The Curtaine-Drawer of the World*. London: 1612.

*The Parlament of Women*. London: 1640.

*The Parliament of Women*. London: 1684.

PARROT, HENRY. *Gossips Greeting*. London: 1620.

PASTON, KATHERINE. *The Correspondence of Lady Katherine Paston, 1603–1627*. Edited by Ruth Hughey. London: 1941.

*The Payne and Sorrow of Evyll Maryage*. [London: 1509.]

PEAKE, RICHARD H. "The Stage Prostitute in the English Dramatic Tradition from 1558 to 1625." Ph.D. dissertation, University of Georgia, 1966.

PEARSON, LU EMILY. *Elizabethans at Home*. Stanford, Calif. and London: 1957.

PECK, THOMAS. *Balaam's Ass*. London: 1658.

PEMBROKE, LADY ANNE CLIFFORD. *The Diary of Lady Anne Clifford*. Edited by Victoria Sackville-West. London: 1923.

PHILLIPS, JAMES E. "The Background of Spenser's Attitude toward Women Rulers." *Huntington Library Quarterly* 5 (1941–42): 5–32.

———. "The Woman Ruler in Spenser's *Faerie Queene*." *Huntington Library Quarterly* 5 (1941–42): 211–34.

*A Pleasant Discourse*. London: 1638.

PLUMPTON, EDWARD. *Plumpton Correspondence*. Edited by Thomas Stapleton. London: 1839.

POMERLEAU, CYNTHIA. "'Resigning the Needle for the Pen': A Study of Autobiographical Writings of British Women Before 1800." Ph.D. dissertation, University of Pennsylvania, 1974.

*Poor Robin's True Character of a Scold: or, The Shrewes Looking-glass*. London: 1678.

POULAIN DE LA BARRE, FRANCOIS. *De L'Égalité des deux Sexes*. Paris: 1673.

———. *The Woman as Good as the Man*. London: 1677.

POWELL, CHILTON L. *English Domestic Relations, 1487–1653*. New York: 1917.

POWER, EILEEN. *Medieval English Nunneries*. Cambridge: 1922. New York: 1964.

*The Praise and Dispraise of Women*. London: 1579.

*The Proude Wyves Paternoster*. London: 1560, 1817.

PRYNNE, WILLIAM. *The Unlovelinesse of Love-Lockes*. London: 1628.

PYRRYE, C. *The Praise and Dispraise of Women*. [London: 1569?]

*Quakers Are Inchanters and Dangerous Seducers appearing in Their Enchantment of One Mary White....* London: 1665.

RAINES, R. R., ed. *The Derby Household Book*. London: 1853.

READ, CONYERS, ed. *Bibliography of British History, Tudor Period, 1485–1603*. 2d ed. Oxford: 1959.

REMACK, PAUL. "Sixteenth Century English Children: The Theory, Reality, and Importance of Socialization and Education in Tudor Society." Ph.D. dissertation, University of Southern California, in progress.

REYNOLDS, ERNEST E. *Margaret Roper*. New York: 1966.

REYNOLDS, MYRA. *The Learned Lady in England, 1650–1750*. Boston: 1920.

RICH, BARNABY. *The Excellency of Good Women*. London: 1613.

———. *Faultes, Faults and Nothing Else but Faultes*. London: 1606.

———. *The Honestie of This Age*. London: 1614, 1864.

———. *My Ladies Looking Glasse*. London: 1616.

RICH, E. E. "The Population of Elizabethan England." *Economic History Review* 2 (1949): 247–65.

ROBINEAU, MARIE-CLAIRE. "Richard Hyrde: A Plea for Learned Women." *Moreana*, no. 13 (1967): 5–24.

ROBINSON, JOHN. *A Brief Catechism concerning Church Government*. London: 1642.

ROGERS, DANIEL. *Matrimoniall Honour*. London: 1632, 1642.

ROGERS, E. F., ed. *The Correspondence of Thomas More*. Princeton, N.J.: 1947.

ROGERS, KATHERINE. *The Troublesome Helpmate: A History of Misogyny in Literature*. Seattle, Wash.: 1966, 1968.

ROPER, MARGARET MORE. *A Devout Treatise upon the Pater Noster*. London: 1532.

ROSS, ISABEL. *Margaret Fell, Mother of Quakerism*. London: 1949.

ROUTH, ENID. *Lady Margaret*. London: 1924.

ROUTH, H. V. "London and the Development of Popular Literature." In *The Cambridge History of English Literature* 4: 487. Cambridge:1930.

———. "The Progress of Social Literature in Tudor Times." In *The Cambridge History of English Literature* 3: 93. Cambridge: 1930.

ROWBOTHAM, SHEILA. *Women, Resistance and Revolution*. New York and London: 1974.

S., J. *A Brief Anatomie of Women: Being an Invective against, and an Apologie for the Bad and Good of that Sexe*. London: 1653.

SALOME, MOTHER M. *Mary Ward: A Foundress of the Seventeenth Century*. London: 1901.

SALTER, THOMAS. *A Mirrhor Mete for All Mothers, Matrones, and Maidens*. [London: 1570.]

*Satirical Songs and Poems on Costume*. London: 1849.

SCHLEINER, WINFRIED. "Gynaikeion: Women and Society in Renaissance Literature." In progress.

SCHNUCKER, ROBERT B. "Elizabethan Birth Control and Puritan Attitudes." *Journal of Interdisciplinary History* 4 (1975): 655-67.

SCHOFIELD, ROGER. "The Measurement of Literacy in Pre-Industrial England." In *Literacy in Traditional Societies*, edited by Jack Goody. Cambridge: 1968.

SCHURMAN, ANNA MARIA VAN. *The Learned Maid or Whether a Maid May Be a Scholar?* London: 1659.

SEIDEL, MICHAEL. "Poulain de la Barre's *The Woman as Good as the Man*." *Journal of the History of Ideas* 25 (1974): 499-508.

SHIRLEY, JOHN. *The Accomplished Ladies Rich Closet of Rarities*. London: 1687.

———. *The Illustrious History of Women*. London: 1686.

*A Short-Title Catalogue of Books ... 1475-1640*. Edited by Alfred W. Pollard, et al. London: 1956.

*A Short-Title Catalogue of Books ... 1641-1700*. Edited by Donald G. Wing. New York: 1945-51.

SIEGEL, PAUL N. "Milton and the Humanist Attitude Toward Women." *Journal of the History of Ideas* 11 (1950): 42-53.

SIMON, JOAN. *Education and Society in Tudor England*. Cambridge: 1966.

SLATER, MIRIAM. "The Weightiest Business: Marriage in an Upper-Gentry Family in Seventeenth-Century England." *Past and Present*, no. 72 (1976): 25-50.

SMITH, FLORENCE. *Mary Astell*. New York: 1916.

SMITH, G. C. MOORE, *The Letters of Dorothy Osborne to William Temple*. Oxford: 1928.

SMITH, HILDA. "Feminism in the Seventeenth Century." Ph.D. dissertation, University of Chicago, 1975.

SMITH, JOSEPH. *A Descriptive Catalogue of Friends' Books or Books Written by Members of the Society*. London: 1867.

SOUTHERN, A. C. *An Elizabethan Recusant House, Comprising the Life of Lady Magdalen, Viscountess Montague*. London: 1954.

SOWERNAM, ESTER. *Ester Hath Hang'd Haman*. London: 1617.

SPARKE, MICHAEL. *The Crums of Comfort*. London: 1628.

SPEGHT, RACHEL. *A Mouzell for Melastomous*. London: 1617.

STENTON, DORIS M. *The English Woman in History*. New York and London: 1957. Reprint. New York: 1977.

STONE, LAWRENCE. *The Crisis of the Aristocracy, 1558–1641*. Oxford: 1965.

———. *The Family, Sex and Marriage in England, 1500–1800*. New York and London: 1977.

———. "Literacy and Education in England, 1640–1900." *Past and Present*, no. 42 (1969): 68–139.

———. "The Rise of the Nuclear Family in Early Modern England." In *The Family in History*, edited by Charles E. Rosenberg. Philadelphia: 1975.

———. "Social Mobility in England, 1500–1700." *Past and Present*, no. 33 (1966): 56–73.

STUBBES, PHILIP. *The Anatomie of Abuses*. London: 1583.

———. *A Christal Glasse for Christen Women*. London: 1591.

SWETNAM, JOSEPH. *The Arraignment of Lewd, Idle, Froward, and Unconstant Women*. London: 1615.

TATE, NAHUM. *A Present for the Ladies, Being an Historical Account of Several Illustrious Persons of the Female Sex*. London: 1692, 1693.

TAVARD, GEORGE. *Women in Christian Tradition*. Notre Dame, Ind., and London: 1973.

TAYLOR, JOHN. *Divers Crab-tree Lectures*. London: 1639.

———. *A Juniper Lecture*. London: 1639.

THOMAS À KEMPIS. *De Imitatio Christi*. London: 1503, 1975.

THOMAS, KEITH. "The Changing Family." *Times Literary Supplement*, 21 October 1977, pp. 1,220–21.

———. *Religion and the Decline of Magic*. London: 1971.

———. "Women and the Civil War Sects." *Past and Present*, no. 13 (1958): 42–62.

THOMPSON, ROGER. *Women in Stuart England and America*. London: 1974.

THOMSON, GLADYS. *Life in a Noble Household, 1641–1700*. London: 1937.

THORNTON, MRS. ALICE. *Autobiography*. Edited by C. Jackson. Durham: 1875.

TIMPSON, THOMAS. *British Female Biography*. London: 1854.

TORSHELL, SAMUEL. *The Womans Glorie: A Treatise Asserting the Due Honour of That Sexe*. London: 1645, 1650.

TRAPNEL, ANNA. *Report and Plea; or, A Narrative of Her Journey from London into Cornwall*. London: 1654.

*Tub Preachers Overturned, or, Independency to be Abandoned and Abhorred*. London: 1647.

TUCKER, G. S. L. "English Pre-Industrial Population Trends." *Economic History Review* 16 (1963): 205–18.

TUCKER, M. J. "The Child as Beginning and End: Fifteenth and Sixteenth Century English Childhood." In *The History of Childhood*, edited by Lloyd DeMause. New York: 1974. London: 1976.

TUKE, THOMAS. *A Treatise against Painting and Tincturing of Men and Women*. London: 1616.

TURNBULL, G. H. *Hartlib, Dury and Comenius*. Liverpool: 1947.

TURNER, GEORGE L. *Original Records of English Nonconformity*. London: 1911.

TUVIL, DANIEL. *Asylum Veneris: or A Sanctuary for the Ladies*. London: 1616.

TYLER, MARGARET. *The First Part of the Mirrour of Princely Deedes and Knighthood*. London: 1578.

UTLEY, FRANCIS. *The Crooked Rib*. Columbus, Ohio: 1944.

VANN, R. T. "Quakerism and the Social Structure of the Interregnum." *Past and Present*, no. 43 (1969): 75–88.

————. *The Social Structure of Quakerism, 1655–1755*. Cambridge, Mass.: 1969.

VERNEY, FRANCES P. *Memoirs of the Verney Family*. London: 1892. Reprint. New York and London: 1970.

*The Vertuous Scholehouse of Ungracious Women*. [London: 1550?]

VIVES, JUAN. *A Very Frutefull and Pleasant Boke Called the Instruction of a Christen Woman*. [London: 1529?]

WALLAS, ADA. *Before the Bluestockings*. London: 1929.

WALSH, WILLIAM. *A Dialogue concerning Women, Being a Defence of the Sex*. London: 1691.

WARWICK, MARY RICH. *Autobiography*. Edited by T. C. Croker. London: 1842.

*A Watch-word for Wilful Women*. London: 1581.

WATSON, FOSTER. *The English Grammar Schools to 1660*. London: 1908, 1968. New York: 1970.

————. *English Writers on Education, 1480–1603*. Gainsville, Fla.: 1967.

————. *Vives and the Renascence Education of Women*. London: 1912.

WEBSTER, CHARLES. *Samuel Hartlib and the Advancement of Learning*. Cambridge: 1970.

WEIER, KENT. "Views on the Education of Women in England, 1655–1753." M.A. thesis, University of Nevada, Las Vegas, 1974.

WEIGALL, RACHEL. "An Elizabethan Gentlewoman: The Journal of Lady Mildmay." *Quarterly Review* 215 (1911): 119–38.

WEINER, CAROL. "Sex-Roles and Crime in Elizabethan Hertfordshire." *Journal of Social History* 8 (1975): 38–60.

WEINSTEIN, MINORA. "Queen's Power: The Case of Katherine Parr." *History Today* 26 (1976): 788–95.

WENTWORTH, ANNE. *The Revelation of Jesus Christ*. London: 1679.

WHATELY, WILLIAM. *A Bride-Bush; or, A Direction for Married Persons*. London: 1619.

————. *A Care-cloth; or A Treatise of the Cumbers and Troubles of Marriage*. London: 1624.

WHELER, G. *A Protestant Monastery*. London: 1698.

WHITING, JOHN. *A Catalogue of Friends Books*. London: 1708.

WILKINSON, ROBERT. *The Merchant-Royal; or, Woman a Ship*. London: 1607.

WILLIAMS, E. "Women Preachers in the Civil War." *Journal of Modern History* 1 (1929): 561–69.

WILIAMS, JANE. *The Literary Women of England*. London: 1861.

WIILSON, VIOLET. *Queen Elizabeth's Maids of Honour*. London: 1922.

————. *Society Women of Shakespeare's Time*. London: 1924.

WOLLEY, HANNAH. *The Accomplish'd Lady's Delight*. London: 1673, 1677.

*The Womans Sharpe Revenge*. London: 1640.

WOOD, HUGH. *A Brief Treatise of Religious Women's Meetings, Services and Testimonies*. London: 1684.

WOODHAM SMITH, PHYLLIS. "The Education of Englishwomen in the Seventeenth Century." M.A. thesis, London University, 1921.

WRIGHT, CELESTE T. "The Amazons in Elizabethan Literature." *Studies in Philology* 37 (1940): 433–56.

WRIGHT, LOUIS B. *Middle-Class Culture in Elizabethan England*. Chapel Hill, N.C.: 1935.

————. "Reading of the Renaissance English Woman." *Studies in Philology* 28 (1931): 671–88.

WRIGLEY, E. A. "Family Limitation in Pre-Industrial England." *Economic History Review* 19 (1966): 82–109.

————. *An Introduction to English Historical Demography.* New York: 1966.

YATES, FRANCES A. "Queen Elizabeth as Astrea." In *Astrea: the Imperial Theme in the Sixteenth Century*, pp. 29–87. London and Boston: 1975.

YOST, JOHN K. "The Value of Married Life for the Social Order in the Early English Renaissance." *Societas* 6 (1976): 25–39.

# The Eighteenth-Century Englishwoman

## BARBARA B. SCHNORRENBERG

### with Jean E. Hunter

Many of the institutions and patterns of modern society began in the eighteenth century. In England especially, as the economic base was extended to include industrial as well as agricultural and mercantile wealth, as the population and urban centers began to grow rapidly, as English enterprise around the world prospered, social change accelerated. The old political order began to be challenged; answers had to be found for the social problems created by increasing wealth and population. Recent studies of the mob, the origins of industrialization, demographic changes, and the background of revolutionary political activity have blown away the air of Augustan calm with which the century was enveloped by earlier historians. Eighteenth-century society clearly underwent steady change; this affected living patterns, economic organization, and political assumptions. Many of these changes are being increasingly documented by scholars working in various fields, but often these studies treat lightly, if at all, the impact of change on the life of women.

This essay surveys the material available for a social history of the eighteenth-century English woman. It will also show that the changing role and increasing importance of women in eighteenth-century society was one of the vital, if often unnoticed, aspects of this society in transition. Following a brief discussion of demographic investigations and the women of the lower classes, it will concentrate on the women of the middle and upper classes, for most of the contemporary source material and later work is concerned with them. The discussion of the "woman question" in the eighteenth century will begin with a statement of the traditional view of the role and position of women. A description of the attacks on and defense of this view will show how, in nearly every aspect of her life, the English woman of the eighteenth century was challenging the old conventions of feminine behavior. Finally this study will discuss the effects on the lives of all women of the great currents of reform and change at the end of the century. Women's situation in the nineteenth century can be better understood from the perspective of these events.

A good place to start to build a picture of eighteenth-century women is to inquire who and what they were, where they lived, and how long they lived. Demographers are increasingly offering answers to these questions, despite the challenges of finding and analyzing the sources. Although there are not the easy tools of census returns for the eighteenth century, there is much data available for those who look for it. There are new studies appearing with considerable frequency, dealing with such matters as birth and death rates, average ages of menarche and marriage, number of children, life expectancy, and illegitimacy rate. These issues obviously intimately involve women; therefore, much useful information can be found here.[1] Many of these works provide primarily raw statistics and very little in the way of conclusions. A few attempts have been made to apply the statistical information to wider generalizations about society and the men and women who made it. Some of these are based on local evidence, but their conclusions are more widely applicable.[2] Others draw their conclusions from more general evidence.[3] Peter Laslett in *The World We Have Lost* (1965) and other works[4] has attempted to combine demographic and other sources for a comprehensive description of life in preindustrial England.

Demographic studies provide a large part of our information about the lower classes. There has also been some work on lower-class housing and life, especially for the rural population.[5] Much about the life of the expanding urban lower classes can be discovered in works about London and other cities, as well as those dealing with crime, the poor, and the mob.[6] A number of eighteenth-century writers were concerned with the state of the poor and their improvement;[7] these works always contain much information about women. It is far more difficult to find out about specific women of the lower classes, especially in their own words. A single exception is Hughes, *The Diary of a Farmer's Wife* (1964).

Most lower-class women worked outside the home at nearly every imaginable kind of job. There is no sequel to Clark's *The Working Life of Women in the Seventeenth Century* (1919), but some of her descriptions and conclusions apply to the early part of the eighteenth century. Other descriptions of kinds and conditions of employment for women and their wages can be found in several local and economic studies.[8] So long as society and its economic base were essentially stable, the employment conditions for lower-class women remained basically unchanged. In the country they usually worked on a male family member's holding, at both inside and outside jobs. They sometimes hired out for agricultural labor, but this work was either seasonal or highly specialized. There was also some employment in domestic service in the country. In towns most women worked in shops or manufactories or went into domestic service. Service was undoubtedly the largest single area of paid work available to women. Without wider possibilities of earning some kind of income, women could hardly be free from their dependence on men. Ultimately industrialization widened women's opportunities, but its impact in the eighteenth century was negligible. For the most part, these women continued to lead much the same kind of life as had their mothers and grandmothers.

The women of the upper and middle classes were most touched by the political, economic, and intellectual changes of the eighteenth century.[9] For these women the debate over the "woman question" had immediate relevance. The nature of women, their rights, duties, capacities, and place in society and the world were issues which involved them and their lives. The view of the holders of power was that woman's only proper role was that of dutiful adjunct to man, whether as daughter, wife, mother, or sister. She had no place outside the family and its home. Within the family, shielded from the temptations of the world, her natural virtues operated to improve the moral tone of society in general and her menfolk in particular. Women were more likely to be led astray by the temptations of the world, and so had to be protected by their men. It was the female's duty to provide a safe haven in which children could be nurtured in innocence and morality and where husbands would find refuge from the masculine wars of business, politics, philosophy, and theology. Today this view is generally called Victorian, but as several writers have pointed out, there is much evidence for it in the eighteenth century as well.[10] The ultimate statement of this view was that of Gisbourne, *An Enquiry into the Duties of the Female Sex* (1797), but it appeared in many other works throughout the century. These ranged from the unvarnished view of Alexander Pope, *Of the Characters of Women* (1735), that "Most Women have no Characters at all," to works that purported to be more serious and scholarly considerations of the question.[11] Many authors emphasized women's superior moral character and the responsibilities it imposed on them. This was a favorite thesis of clergymen, who generally supported their statements with carefully chosen scriptural authority.[12]

Many of these writers were often not taking the initative but were rather replying to events and ideas and social changes that they saw around them. What they feared most was a change in the social structure. They perceived that changes in the position of women could be extremely threatening to the status quo. Even for writers not concerned primarily with women, to write about society, whether to criticize or to portray, was to take some position about the role and nature of the female sex in that society. Yet there has been little attempt to analyze the views on women of the leading English thinkers. An exception is Williford, "Bentham on the Rights of Women" (1976). But there is much that needs to be done, especially if one starts with the assumption that concern with the "woman question" was an active issue throughout the century.

One indication that the "woman question" was alive throughout the eighteenth century was the continuing concern with women's education. This issue had several facets: the purpose of women's education, the nature and content of this education, and whether it was most satisfactorily carried out at home or at school. A great many books and pamphlets discussed these issues and the necessarily related question of the nature and duties of females. Most of these are surveyed in Schnorrenberg, "Education for Women in Eighteenth Century England: An Annotated Bibliography" (1976). There are two surveys of girls' education in England, Gardiner, *English Girlhood at School* (1929), and Kamm, *Hope Deferred* (1965). Both they and Hans, *New Trends in Education* (1951) contain useful if brief chapters relating to these questions.

The debate over education reflected the larger "woman question." The conservatives argued that women must be educated to maintain the old virtues, morals, and religion, and to accept their appointed place in the world. Thus the objects and methods of women's education were usually different from men's. But all education taught women to read, and opened to them various possibilities. The few works on literacy in England in the eighteenth century are concerned almost exclusively with men,[13] but they stress the connection between literacy and social change. As female literacy expanded, so too did schools for girls. The boarding schools noticeably increased in number in the second half of the century and were usually condemned by contemporaries for teaching only frivolity. But Miller, "Women's Education, Self-Improvement and Social Mobility" (1972), argues that the real reason for opposition was that the schools were agents of social mobility, for they taught lower-middle-class girls the behavior deemed proper for a lady. The conservatives condemned giving such girls ideas above their station in life; the more sympathetic saw it as a grave disservice to the young women. What they all feared was social change.

Improved education meant that women could engage in activities that men had traditionally reserved for themselves. An increasing number of women made their mark in the intellectual world of eighteenth-century England. The most useful descriptive catalogue of the earlier women intellectuals is Reynolds, *The Learned Lady in England* (1920). There are a number of other works on women authors and intellectuals, generally in the form of a series of short biographical sketches.[14] These often provide information unavailable elsewhere, but many repeat the same tired gossip about their subjects, often in the breathless style many authors appear to think appropriate for dealing with women. More useful in discussing the general aspects of the intellectual woman and her world are: Upham, "English Femmes Savantes" (1913); Tompkins, *The Polite Marriage* (1938); Ehrenpreis and Halsband, *The Lady of Letters* (1969); Plaisant, Denizot, and Moreux, *Aspects de féminisme en Angleterre* (1972); Halsband, "'The Female Pen'" (1974). Several contemporary or early nineteenth-century collections of biographical sketches are also important sources of information and identification: *Biographium Femineum* (1776); Ballard, *Memoirs of Several Ladies of Great Britain* (1752); Hays, *Female Biography* (1803); Elwood, *Memoirs of the Literary Ladies of England* (1843).

Women had little impact in the traditional areas of scholarship, the classics and theology, for they had no access to the universities, the seats of traditional scholarly endeavor. Two women did achieve contemporary recognition for their scholarly work. Elizabeth Elstob, a student of Anglo-Saxon, was probably the best female scholar of her day. Her career and devotion to learning are chronicled in Ashdown, "Elizabeth Elstob, the Learned Saxonist" (1925) and Beauchamp, "Pioneer Linguist: Elizabeth Elstob." Better known among her contemporaries was Elizabeth Carter, who won fame as the translator of Epictetus. The translation is today the least interesting of her works, for she traveled widely in the intellectual society of the mid-century and wrote a large number of letters. These and her other personal works were collected in several volumes by her nephew.[15] She is better served by these than by her biographer, Gaussen, *A Woman of Wit and Wisdom* (1906).

Although Meyer, *The Scientific Lady in England* (1955), argues that women were becoming increasingly aware of science early in the century, this interest was limited largely to reading and some collecting of biological specimens. The only woman who seems to have been really active as a scientist was the astronomer Caroline Herschel, who acted as her brother William's assistant and also made discoveries of her own. Her career can be studied in *Memoir and Correspondence of Caroline Herschel* (1876), as well as in several other works.[16] Caroline was content to live in William's shadow; Ogilvie, "Caroline Herschel's Contributions to Astronomy" (1975), argues that there she should remain.

Eighteenth-century English women poets have received relatively little attention. Two very early works provide some information: Dyce, *Specimens of British Poetesses* (1825), and Bethune, *The British Female Poets* (1848). Recently Fullard and Schuelle have published "A Bibliography of Eighteenth-Century Women Poets" (1974). The best-known woman poet of the century, Anna Seward, deserves better study than she has gotten in several works,[17] but other women poets have not even received this recognition.

Some women's primary contribution to the intellectual world was as friends and hostesses. Lady Mary Wortley Montagu, whose later fame rests on her letters, was friend, patroness, and foe of many literary figures in the first part of the century. As Halsband in *The Life of Lady Mary Wortley Montagu* (1956) and *The Complete Letters* (1965–67) makes clear, Lady Mary was far from satisfied with or willing to accept society's role and limitations for women. In the end she withdrew from England. Most women were less independently minded than Lady Mary, but many were disenchanted with society and the world as they found it.

In the 1770s and 1780s the group of women who came to be called the Blue Stockings attempted to create a parallel to the French Salon. In the very masculine society of London, they tried to introduce serious and informed conversation after dinner instead of cards and drink. Their failure is investigated in Tinker, *The Salon and English Letters* (1915), and Lockitt, *The Relations of French and English Society* (1920). The very name Blue Stockings became synonymous with a learned and hence unfeminine woman. This connotation was certainly unfair to most of those who were originally included under the title. This group has been the subject of several books.[18] Its heart and leader was Elizabeth Robinson Montagu— hostess, patron, and even author of a book on Shakespeare. Considerable interest has been shown in her and her important letters.[19] On the fringes of the Blue Stocking circle was Dr. Johnson's friend, Hester Thrale Piozzi, whose relationship with the great man has occasioned some interesting studies.[20]

The eighteenth century saw the emergence of two literary forms, the periodical and the novel, which gave women new means of self-expression and employment. They also provide scholars with sources of information about women. Both must be used with caution by historians. They were written primarily for sale, and while the authors might have been telling their audience what it knew and wanted to hear about its own world, they might equally have been writing for entertainment, novelty, and titillation. Novels reflected society; they did not necessarily describe it. Periodicals often expressed little more than the idiosyncratic views of their editors. However, with these caveats in mind, the historian can use both forms to expand considerably our view of the eighteenth-century English woman.

An entertaining and useful introduction to women's periodicals is Adburgham, *Women in Print* (1972).[21] White, *Women's Magazines* (1970), offers a brief survey of their history. There are a number of shorter studies describing and using these journals.[22] Perhaps the most valuable periodical is *The Lady's Magazine, or Entertaining Companion for the Fair Sex*, which began publication in 1770 and hit on such a popular combination of elevating articles, informative bits and pieces, and romantic tales that it survived for over sixty years. But more than its success makes *The Lady's Magazine* useful. During the early decades of its life, the journal opened its pages to its audience, thus offering a forum to those who would otherwise have remained unheard. In addition, it offered practical hints on housekeeping, advice to the lovelorn, and hints on rearing children. *The Lady's Magazine*, used in conjunction with other material, is a good place to begin any study of the English woman in the later eighteenth century.

Both men and women wrote novels in which women were major characters. The novel was regarded in the eighteenth century as a peculiarly female literary diversion, albeit a dangerous one. Most writers on education warned against too much, or indeed any, novel reading as likely to excite the sensibilities and frivolities which were the natural enemies of proper female character development. The historian of eighteenth-century women can use the novels in a number of ways: to discover how some women were able to support themselves by writing and what the social position of women writers was; to determine how authors depicted the life, characters, and societal demands on women in their books; and to investigate why novels were thought a threat to female propriety.[23]

Since the pioneering work of Utter and Needham, *Pamela's Daughters* (1936), which discussed the various types of heroines, there have been several studies of women and novels. Tompkins, *The Popular Novel* (1932), considers primarily lesser works. French scholars have been especially active in this area; both Séjourné, *Aspects généraux du roman féminin* (1966), and Fauchery, *La destinée feminine dans le roman européen* (1972), provide extensive and thoughtful treatment of women in novels. Another approach to the novels is Spacks, *Imagining a Self* (1976), in which the fiction and autobiographical writings of various women are compared and contrasted.

The lives of women novelists have often received more extensive treatment than their works.[24] In the early decades of the century many of them were rebels against society or at least unconventional in their life-style; this has seemed more remarkable than what they wrote. Perhaps also the difficulties of finding out much about their lives has made this quest more attractive. Sutherland, "The Progress of Error: Mrs. Centlivre and the Biographers" (1942) details the process through which gossip, legend, and invention created a story about one novelist that is nearly as complete a work of fiction as any she wrote. Of course the more famous women of the latter part of the century have been the subject of repeated books and articles. Jane Austen's bibliography is extensive.[25] For Fanny Burney d'Arblay, one can turn to the Diaries and to various biographies.[26] Maria Edgeworth, both novelist and *moraliste*, is best treated in Butler, *Maria Edgeworth* (1972), although there are a number of other works about her.

A comparison between the writing on contemporary men and women novelists will show that generally scholars have discussed women's lives and analysed the men's works. Early in the century, Daniel Defoe wrote *Moll Flanders* and *Roxanna*. His views of women have been studied in several works.[27] The work on his contemporary, Mary Manley, also a novelist and political writer, has dealt almost entirely with her life.[28] By mid-century the novel had arrived as a major literary form, and at the same time writing became an increasingly respectable career for women, as Halsband in "'The Female Pen'" has clearly demonstrated. These two developments were not unrelated, but concentration on male novelists has ignored the connection. Among the early major novelists, Samuel Richardson was clearly concerned with women's position in society.[29] Henry Fielding also had much to say about women, especially in regard to the institution of marriage.[30] Their female contemporaries, who were also a part of the London literary world, have received little attention, except for recent doctoral dissertations. Eliza Haywood and Charlotte Lennox, both of whom wrote novels and other works in the middle of the century, have at least found biographers.[31] All of these works provide historians of the eighteenth-century English woman with useful material.

The eighteenth-century writer, whether of novels, advice to young women, or tracts on education, assumed that the destiny of woman was to marry. A woman's happiness, social position, and future, depended upon the man she married. Traditionally she was supposed to have little to say in the choice of her future mate; this was a matter for more mature minds, her parents or guardians. Society, especially in its upper reaches, often placed family and financial considerations above personal ones. And if, in the best of all possible worlds, the parent never chose a husband likely to make his daughter unhappy, all too often reality saw a woman married to a man she could neither love nor respect, who had little thought for her happiness.

There can be little doubt that significant changes were occurring during the eighteenth century, both in attitudes about the nature of marriage and in the methods of mate selection. At the outset of the century most upper- and middle-class marriages were based almost exclusively on family and economic considerations and the partners, especially the women, had perhaps at most the right of rejecting a completely unsuitable pretender. Few makers of marriages worried overmuch about the emotional content of the marital relationship. By the end of the century, this pattern had changed substantially. Many individuals, especially among the middle classes, took an active role in chosing their mates. Theoretically parents now merely had the right to refuse permission to particularly unequal matches. Whereas the recalcitrant child who refused to accept the parent's decision was the object of opprobrium in the early eighteenth century, by its end the obstinate parent had become the villain. While this situation was most prevalent among the middle orders, it was even making inroads among the aristocracy. This development has never been accurately charted, nor have its implications for the lives of the women involved been investigated. Yet changing marital mores resulted in a fairly extensive literature on how to choose a spouse and on the proper relationship between husband and wife. The changing ideas about marriage are clear evidence of the increasing importance of women in a changing society.

Historians have only recently turned their attention to the history of marriage and the family and have tended to ignore the experience of eighteenth-century England, despite the crucial changes that occurred there. A useful overview is provided in an old work, Howard, *A History of Matrimonial Institutions* (1904). Hunt's popularized *The Natural History of Love* (1959) has a good section on the eighteenth century. For a demographic overview see Hajnal, "European Marriage Patterns in Perspective" (1965). Most other information is fragmentary. Useful for understanding the financial underpinnings of upper-class eighteenth-century marriage are: Habakkuk, "Marriage Settlements in the Eighteenth Century" (1950); D. Thomas, "The Social Origins of Marriage Partners in the British Peerage" (1972); Clay, "Marriage, Inheritance, and the Rise of Large Estates" (1968). Results of marriage policies pursued by noble families are discussed in Hollingsworth, "A Demographic Study of the British Ducal Families" (1957–58) and "The Demography of the British Peerage" (1964–65).

Marriage was a topic for many writers throughout the century. Among the famous, Jonathan Swift in his "Letter to a Very Young Lady on her Marriage" offered fairly conventional advice on the proper behavior of a wife. Less conventional were the numerous works of Daniel

Defoe, who discussed almost every aspect of relations between men and women both within and without the married state.[32] Defoe generally supported the more advanced view that saw marriage as a mutual relationship, imposing equal duties and rights on husband and wife. Samuel Johnson's views are summarized in Molin, "Dr. Johnson on Marriage, Chastity, and Fidelity" (1974). There are numerous other works on marriage by anonymous or lesser-known authors which are invaluable in assessing prevailing attitudes. Interestingly, generalized attacks on the married state like *The Pleasures of Single Life* (1701), while quite commonplace during the seventeenth century, were relatively rare in the eighteenth. However, there were a number of books and pamphlets directed to men with instructions on how to make the best of marriage.[33] Works for women generally stressed the need for dutiful obedience to a husband's wishes. Perhaps the most famous of these was Lord Halifax's *The Ladies' New Year Gift* (1688), which was printed again and again throughout the century. Almost equally popular during the first half of the eighteenth century was Fleetwood, *The Relative Duties of Parents and Children, Husbands and Wives, Masters and Servants* (1705).[34] In the latter half of the century the advice was somewhat more practical in tone but generally as traditional in content, in such works as Hanway, *Domestic Happiness* (1786).[35] These works all accepted, at least superficially, the view that marriage, and thus subservience to her husband, was woman's proper role. The most serious clear critique of eighteenth-century marriage was made by Mary Astell, *Some Reflections Upon Marriage* (1700). If others shared her views, they were not willing to commit themselves to such radical ideas in print.

The institutions of courtship and marriage did change in the course of the century, and in every case the importance of the woman's role increased. Two examples of eighteenth-century courtships illustrate this change in social practice. The fascinating selections from Boswell's journals, *Boswell in Search of a Wife*, portray the man of the world's approach to courting. At mid-century, two figures in the literary world, Richard and Elizabeth Griffith, when in financial straits, published their own extensive correspondence during their courtship as *Genuine Letters between Henry and Frances*. The book, which sold quite well, makes clear the dominant role of Elizabeth/Frances.[36] Not all writers who acknowledged the role of the woman in courtship necessarily approved of these changes. Mandeville, *The Virgin Unmasked* (1709), presented an unfavorable satiric picture of female strategems. A more sober view was that of Mrs. Piozzi, whose views, along with those of several other writers, were included in *A Series of Letters on Courtship and Marriage*. That there was considerable fascination with— and interest in—love and courtship is indicated by the appearance of the journal, *The Matrimonial Magazine, or Monthly Anecdotes of Love and Marriage for the Court, the City, and the Country*, which flourished briefly in 1775.

The progress toward the equality of women in courtship and the arrangement of marriages was proceeding even more rapidly than the most feminist of theorists could have imagined. In an increasingly individualistic age, personal choice in such matters seemed natural. In courtship and marriage, a woman had as much to offer as a man. She had not just purity or morality, but in the end herself, and over this women have generally maintained intellectual and spiritual, if not physical, control. This process is easily traced in the century's novels. It is a long step in the self-assertion of women from the heroines of Defoe, who are trapped in a system over which they have little or no control, to the heroines of Jane Austen, who learn to use the system. The well-known opening of *Pride and Prejudice*, "It is a truth universally acknowledged, that a single man in possession of good fortune must be in want of a wife," is a statement from the woman's point of view. She will play out her own part and, if at all possible, manipulate the system to her own satisfaction.

Marriage legalizes, authorizes, and encourages sex. Presumably eighteenth-century women were no more or less sexual beings than the women of other periods. Yet to investigate their sexuality is difficult; the sources must be largely literary and autobiographical, and almost all are veiled by the proprieties of the day. Thus far there has been no work by a psychosexual historian which focuses on this century. A few general studies offer some leads. Bloch, *Sexual Life in England* (1938), is anecdotal but does contain useful information, as does Epton, *Love and the English* (1960). Taylor's *Sex in History* (1953), like his *Angel Makers* (1973), is less useful for the eighteenth century than for other periods. Steeves, *Before Jane Austen* (1965), provides a readable and helpful survey in his chapter, "Sex in the Eighteenth Century Perspective." Dealing more specifically with women, Spacks, "Ev'ry Woman is at Heart a Rake" (1974), has attempted to indicate the prevailing eighteenth-century view of female sexuality. Sex and sexuality may not have been publicly discussed, but there was increased recognition of its usefulness as a tool and weapon for women. The wife's locked door was her ultimate barrier.

Society assumed that courtship led to marriage and marriage led to a home and children. Books of advice of all sorts for women always assumed that she would find fulfillment as daughter, wife, and mother, all positions defined in relation to men. The law also made these assumptions. The great legal work of William Blackstone seemed to give women no status at all under the common law. His maxim that "husband and wife are one, and that one is the husband," was one of the greatest stumbling blocks to the improvement of women's legal position. Yet there was more to English law than the common law, and as Greenberg has pointed out in "The Legal Status of the English Woman in Early Eighteenth Century Common Law and Equity" (1975), women who could afford it enjoyed some considerable protection in the equity courts.

It is scarcely surprising that the aspects of the law that especially concerned women were those which dealt with marriage and divorce and the resulting property settlements. Throughout the century, there appeared pamphlets dealing with these matters.[37] In 1753 the marriage law of England was refashioned by statute, 26 George II c. 33, commonly known as Lord Hardwicke's Marriage Act. Designed to regularize marriage procedures, to prevent clandestine marriages, and thus to protect the rights of parents and guardians, its impact on women's status has not been fully assessed. One eighteenth-century commentator, Madan, in *Thelyphthora* (1780–81), thought the act was harmful to women, but he was contradicted by Penn, *Remarks on Thelyphthora* (1781). It is certainly arguable that the new act in the long run improved the status of women, as it went far in eliminating a variety of abuses. That there was little protest against it by women writers and in women's periodicals at the time and later would seem to indicate that most women felt it at least did not further restrict them.

Once safely married, the wife assumed the practical responsibilities of keeping a house and bearing and rearing children. It is perhaps as difficult in the twentieth century to recreate these responsibilities as it is to really know how these women thought. The kinds of space in which the eighteenth-century housewife operated and how the houses were used can be understood somewhat from pictures and the buildings themselves.[38] But what of the life that went on inside these houses? Burton, *The Georgians at Home* (1967), provides fascinating bits about furniture, china, gardens, and amusements. A more serious glimpse of life can be found in the chapters "The Landlords at Home" and "The Farmers at Home" in Mingay, *English Landed Society in the Eighteenth Century* (1963). There are a number of works which are useful for a fuller understanding of what women did and how their homes were actually run.[39] The century saw the publication of a number of guides to housekeeping which often provide some idea of the expectations if not the realities of the housewife's life.[40] In *The Housekeeping Book of Susanna Whatman*, the wife of a paper manufacturer recorded her own experiences, providing a wealth of detailed information about an actual middle-class housewife's life.

One of the chief concerns of all women was the management of servants, without whom no house could run smoothly. Servants have attracted the interest of a number of modern scholars, but their more serious work tends to concentrate on male, not female servants, although an increasingly large number of women worked in domestic service.[41] There was an extensive contemporary literature on the management of servants, their duties, and their relations with their superiors. One of the earliest such works was *The Compleat Servant-Maid* (1683). Defoe evinced considerable interest in the servant problem, particularly that of dealing with uppity servants, a constant complaint of the eighteenth century.[42] Other useful books and pamphlets detailing the role of the eighteenth-century servant include: Haywood, *A Present for a Servant-Maid* (1743); Glasse, *The Servants' Directory* (1760); and *Laws Concerning Masters and Servants* (1767).

Like housewives in almost every age, the eighteenth-century English-woman was responsible for feeding her family, Diet remains one of the relatively unexplored subjects in history. Two general works give coverage to the eighteenth century, Drummond and Wilbraham, *The Englishman's Food* (rev. ed. 1957) and Barker, McKenzie, and Yudkin, *Our Changing Fare* (1966). There were available to the eighteenth-century housewife, perhaps for the first time, guides to cooking and meal planning. The first appeared in 1747, *The Art of Cookery Made Plain and Easy by a Lady*. This book went to at least seven editions, with the later ones bearing the name of Hannah Glasse. Glasse also wrote *The Complete Confectioner* (1742). Another guide to cooking was Verral, *A Complete System of Cookery* (1759). If none of these works could claim the completeness of Mrs. Beeton, they were at least a beginning.

A final responsibility of the eighteenth-century housewife, which undoubtedly bulked large in her life, was the need to watch over the health of her household. With doctors scarce, and not always competent when available, it behooved her to know something about medicine and health care. Numerous books were written to help her. General home medical books include: Buchan, *Domestic Medicine* (1769), which went to nineteen editions; A. Hume, *Every Woman Her Own Physician* (1776); W. Smith, *A Sure Guide in Sickness and Health* (1776); and H. Smith, *The Family Physician*. The popularity of such works indicates that they were needed by women faced with providing health care as a part of their duties as housewives.

A woman's becoming a wife was usually followed in due time by her becoming a mother. The mother's role and responsibilities were under-going important modifications. There was a greater concern with the well-being of children, whether one's own or children in general, what Caulfield calls *The Infant Welfare Movement in the Eighteenth Century* (1931). According to Plumb in "The New World of Children in Eighteenth Century England" (1975), parents, under the influence of the theories of John Locke, became increasingly interested in molding their children, in shaping both their minds and their morals. Since mothers retained the chief responsibility for child rearing, this new attitude surely had an impact on their lives. The general works on children in history, while providing useful background information, do not do much more than raise questions about mother-child relationships. The best book on eighteenth-century childhood is Pinchbeck and Hewitt, *Children in English Society* (1969, 1973), but the work raises as many questions as it answers. Other studies take their evidence primarily from the latter part of the century and have an unfortunate tendency to generalize.[43]

The relationship between mother and child began with pregnancy and childbirth, a dangerous and all too often fatal experience. Some information about what every woman who bore children faced can be gleaned from contemporary medical works like Mauriceau's *The Diseases of Women with Child, and in Childbed* (1683), translated by Hugh Chamberlen, who was a member of the famous family of man midwives which developed the obstetrical forceps. Smellie, *Theory and Practice of Midwifery* (1752–64) was the first modern obstetrical text, though by present-day standards it was written with only the slightest amount of gynecological knowledge. Another view of contemporary gynecology can be found in Gray, *Man Midwife* (1946).

Once the child was born, the parents could look to a number of sources for guidance in its upbringing. There were many works of a general nature available, offering both moral and practical advice.[44] Some of the most useful advice to mothers came from medical men. Cadogan's *An Essay upon Nursing, and the Management of Children* (1748) was an attack on the folk traditions that still played an important part in child rearing. The book was quite successful, going into several editions. There were a number of other valuable and helpful books of this kind.[45] Doctors also provided more specialized advice concerning the treatment of children's diseases. The methods prescribed have little relation to modern pediatrics, but usually represented the best knowledge available.[46] This plethora of erstwhile Drs. Spock suggests that there was a great deal of uncertainty about child rearing practices and that many mothers were seeking expert advice. It suggests also that ideas and standards of child rearing were changing. The increasing number of these publications in the latter part of the century also suggests that the rising population may well be related to a greater interest in and ability to maintain the health of young children.

The increase in books and pamphlets dealing with every aspect of women's life at home suggests several conclusions. An obvious one is the increasing literacy of women. A second is the assumption that women wanted to find better, different, or more modern ways of running their households and bringing up their families. As a very large number of these works were written by men, one can conclude that men were acknowledging more and more the importance and value of what a woman did at home. Women themselves were certainly increasingly conscious of their own worth and the responsibilities they undertook. Memoirs, diaries, letters, and the books that have been written from them, repeatedly demonstrate this self-confidence. From such sources, written by and about both men and women, the life-style and frame of reference of a cross section of middle- and upper-class women can be discovered.[47]

Not all women, even of the middle class, were able simply to stay at home and contribute to the family and household welfare and resources through housekeeping and child care. Various circumstances forced many women to earn a living; other women simply were not satisfied to be only housewives. After the middle of the century, writing was both respectable and remunerative for women. Respectability was a serious problem for the middle class; there were few careers that could qualify. Teaching, whether as a governess or in a school, was generally considered no job for a lady, even though the instructor's duty was to instil ladylike virtues and characteristics. Some writers on education regretted this prejudice, and there were certainly exceptions. For example, Hannah More's sisters ran a school and were clearly ladies of the utmost respectability.

Much less respectable than teaching was the theater, although by the end of the century such figures as Sarah Siddons[48] and Elizabeth Inchbald were beginning to improve the status of actresses. Inchbald not only acted but also wrote novels and plays and was one of the earliest drama critics. She left her *Memoirs*, as well as a large collection of manuscript letters.[49] The stage always provided an opportunity for an ambitious woman, if she had beauty or talent or both. Among accounts of some actresses who were more or less successful are: Charke, *Narrative of the Life* (1755); Pilkington, *Memoirs* (1748–54); Pearce, *Polly Peachum* (1913); and Dunbar, *Peg Woffington* (1968).

In the eighteenth century, the line between actress and prostitute was very thin, and the oldest profession offered employment to women of all classes. Perhaps one of the best descriptions of English prostitution occurs in Mayhew, *London Labour and the London Poor* (1851), which compares prostitution in nineteenth-century London with that of earlier times. Parreaux, *Daily Life in the Reign of George III* (1969), devotes three chapters to all kinds of prostitution. Stebbins, *London Ladies* (1952), describes a successful courtesan, Martha Ray, who became the mistress of the Earl of Sandwich. Also concerned with the demimonde are Bleackley, *Ladies Fair and Frail* (1909), and Boulton, *Amusements of Old London* (1901). There was an extensive contemporary literature discussing prostitution. The authors, nearly all male, were sometimes writing to encourage reform, but as often for the sake of profit and titillation. Two works purporting to be by ladies of easy virtue were Phillips, *A Letter Addressed to the Earl of Chesterfield* (1750) and *The History of Miss Katty N--- by Herself* (1757). A few writers were concerned with the redemption of the prostitutes,[50] but seldom was there much interest in why and how women became prostitutes in the first place. The fact that respectable women, who were interested in the improvement of women's status, were not supposed to know or speak of prostitution limited the serious discussion of the subject. With the general acceptance of the double standard after mid-century, women could more easily work for the reform of almost any other social ill.

Discontent with prevailing standards of female behavior was not unknown in the eighteenth century. Many women who wanted to do and did do something different, who were not content with society as they found it, were regarded merely as eccentrics. Even in the diaries, letters, novels, and other writings of seemingly conforming women, implicit or explicit criticism of the standards of English masculine society can be found. These women wanted change, and they wanted to unite the women of England in pursuit of this change. The stable society of the first half to three-quarters of the century was very difficult to shake, despite the occasional radical voices. By the end of the century, however, three great forces of change—industrialization, evangelicalism, and political radicalism—were beginning to affect English society. Women as well as men felt the impact of these forces which transformed society in the succeeding decades.

Of these three great currents of reform and change, industrialization had the least immediate effect on the position of women, though ultimately it was of great importance. Pinchbeck, *Women Workers and the Industrial Revolution* (1930), is the starting point for any investigation of industrialization and women.[51] Several recent demographic and quantitative studies have been concerned with the relationship between industrialization, female emancipation, and population growth. Tilly, Scott, Cohen, "Women's Work and European Fertility Patterns" (1976) argue convincingly that the early stages of industrialization changed women's working habits little. Women were still part of a family unit, even if working in a factory. Discovering the effects of early industrialization of women is complicated by the simultaneous rising birthrate. Did factory work for women mean more freedom, a breakdown of traditional sexual restraints, and more children? Tilly and Scott make this easy conclusion difficult to maintain. The relation, if any, between the early stages of industrialization, the rising birthrate, and the improvement of the economic or social status of women is still unclear. One of the first effects, however, of industrialization and the concurrent rise in population was the loss of jobs by women. Clark notes this beginning by the end of the seventeenth century; it is borne out by Chambers, "The Vale of Trent," and Richards, "Women in the British Economy" (1974). They suggest that the population growth and the decline of domestic industry constricted female options. By the end of the century, writers like Hays and Wollstonecraft and Maria Edgeworth openly complained that women's jobs were being taken over by men. However, McKendrick, "Home Demand and Economic Growth" (1974) argues that as consumers, women and their families benefited extensively from the new opportunities for employment.

Contemporary descriptions of the life of working women in the early days of industrialization are relatively rare. Most novelists of the period ignored economics; in the world of Jane Austen there is even less evidence of the industrial revolution than there is of the French Revolution. The Irish stories of Maria Edgeworth and the Scottish tales of Elizabeth Hamilton are about essentially agricultural societies. Not until the second quarter of the nineteenth century did novelists and other writers become really concerned with women factory workers. However, given the gradual impact of industrialization, the works of Harriet Martineau, Charlotte Elizabeth Tonna, and Mrs. Gaskell can provide useful descriptions of the lives of women during its early decades.[52]

Evangelicalism in its broadest sense also changed English society in the late eighteenth century. The evangelical movement encompassed not only specifically religious reform, such as Methodism, but also such morally inspired reforms as the abolition of slavery, the end of civil religious disabilities for dissenters, the Sunday School movement and other improvements in lower class education, and prison reform. The emancipation of women was not part of the evangelical program. In fact the movement encouraged the increasing acceptance of so-called Victorian ideas about the status of women and sex. Many of the leaders of evangelicalism firmly and clearly opposed the radical demands for equality of the sexes. Yet the movement owed a great deal to the work and support of women. Doubtless the acceptance by women of the general objectives of evangelicalism strengthened the prevalence of its traditional views of the female sex throughout the nineteenth century.

The role of individual women, such as Selina, countess of Huntingdon, in the early spread of the Methodist movement has often been noted. But it was not only the rich and well-connected women who were effected by the religious revival and its leaders. Of all the histories of Methodism, Wearmouth, *Methodism and the Common People* (1945), says the most about its impact on women. Rogal, "John Wesley's Women" (1974), talks about the leader of Methodism's perceptions of women and their role in his ministry and life. For Wesley's own works, see *Sermons on Several Occassions* and his *Journal*. Wesley's associate, George Whitfield, also stated the Methodist approach to the female sex, particularly in his two sermons, "Christ the Best Husband: or an Earnest Invitation to Young Women to Come and See Christ," and "Christ the Beliver's Husband," in his *Works*. In *Jesus Altogether Lovely* (1763) and other devotional works, and in More, *The Life of Mrs. Mary Fletcher* (1818), one meets active Methodist laywomen.

Methodism accepted a narrow Pauline view of the role of women within the church, but other Nonconformists allowed their female members much more freedom of action. Two eighteenth-century Quaker women have left accounts of their religious experiences and activities: Bevan, *Memoirs of Sarah Stephenson* (1807), and *Some Account of Sarah Grubb* (1792). Another Quaker woman, Elizabeth Fry, led the movement for prison reform.[53]

The campaign to improve the education of the poor ·cut across sectarian lines. The charity schools made their appearance early in the century; their history can be traced in the frequent *Accounts of the Charity Schools* published by the SPCK from 1704 to 1800, in Jones, *The Charity School Movement* (1938), and Mandeville, *An Essay on Charity Schools*. These schools began as Anglican, and often male, preserves, but by the end of the century the Nonconformists had joined the attempt to provide education for both boys and girls of the lower orders. The objects of this education were to instill good morals, obedience, and basic religious beliefs, and to teach a useful skill for honest employment. Such objectives were especially important for women. Two books by Catharine Cappe, *Memoirs* (1822) and *An Account of Two Charity Schools* (1800), describe the practical results of educational reform in York. Mrs. Cappe was a Nonconformist; among her associates was Faith Gray, whose family were firm but evangelical Anglicans. The importance of evangelicalism for members of the established church is detailed in Gray, *Papers and Diaries* (1927). It is often difficult to discern any sectarian differences in the writings of late eighteenth-century evangelicals on the subject of education. Anna Laetitia Barbauld was a Presbyterian, but this shows up in her essays on religious toleration, not on education.[54] Priscilla Wakefield was a Quaker, but her *Reflections on the Present Condition of the Female Sex* (1798) contains the same moral content as any of her Anglican contemporaries, although she was more concerned with economic conditions and employment than many others.

Among evangelical Anglican women, two are particularly important for their long-term effects on the education of women and society's expectation of the female sex. Sarah Trimmer began by educating her own twelve children and then spread her techniques and ideas far and wide through her stories and texts.[55] She also wrote on educational theory:

*Reflections upon the Education of Children in Charity Schools* (1792) and *The Oeconomy of Charity* (1801). The great lady of evangelicalism was Hannah More.[56] Highly educated by the standards of the day, living in the center of London's intellectual and artistic society, More first made a name and a living for herself by writing plays and poetry. She was in fact very emancipated. But even during her worldly period, More maintained the highest moral and religious standards; in the 1780s she became increasingly associated with the Clapham Sect, one of the leading evangelical groups of the Church of England. She ultimately retired from London to the country where she devoted herself to the education and well being of the lower classes. She wrote with others the *Cheap Repository Tracts*, a series of inexpensive short moral tales, which sold widely. Their basic object was to inculcate right thinking and right living through hard work, honesty, thrift, sobriety, trust in God, and acceptance of the social system. More was not really an antifeminist; her *Strictures on the Modern System of Female Education* (1799) do not admit that women are inferior to men. But she believed that society called on women to play a different role; therefore, they did not need the same education as men. Addressed to "Women of Rank and Fortune," the underlying theme of the *Strictures* was the same as the *Cheap Repository Tracts*: acceptance of one's position in life as the will of God. It is difficult to overestimate More's influence throughout much of the nineteenth century. Her life and her works were so eminently good and respectable and useful, so eminently Victorian.

In the eighteenth century, philanthropists of either sex at first worked as individuals. But as the various charitable enterprises multiplied under the impetus of the evangelical movement, the necessity to organize them became clear. Prochaska, "Women in English Philanthropy 1790–1830" (1974), asserts that while men did most of the organizing and policy making, women then, as later, did most of the work. The temperance movement of the later nineteenth century in the United States has often been cited as a primary contributor to women's organizational and leadership experience which culminated in the suffrage campaign. The abolition of slavery and the slave trade, prison reform, and the education of the lower classes provided English women with this kind of experience by the beginning of the nineteenth century.

The French Revolution and the political and social ideas associated with it was the third great current of change. In England the revolution was cheered and supported by a diverse group of radicals. The intellectuals of the radical movement clustered mainly around William Godwin; among them were several women, including his wife Mary Wollstonecraft. Many writers have taken the publication of Wollstonecraft's *Vindication of the rights of Women* (1792) as the beginning of modern feminism.[57] It is therefore easy to associate the political statement of feminism with revolutionary political ideas. But the French Revolution did not adopt a feminist policy, and many English radicals were either unsympathetic to, or unconscious of, feminism. Thus, while Wollstonecraft and her contemporaries were inspired and encouraged by the revolution and by some English radicals, their feminist ideas were not solely the result of contemporary events. They were also the culmination of the increasing feminine consciousness of the preceeding century. In fact, Wollstonecraft's book was the climax of a debate that had gone on throughout the century. Important as Wollstonecraft is in the development of modern feminism, the accidents of her time, place, and personality have often overshadowed the tradition of feminist thinking that developed in England in the course of the century.

The first avowedly feminist tract by an English author, *An Essay in Defence of the Female Sex*, was not written until the end of the seventeenth century, although a translation from the French feminist, Poulain de la Barre, *The Woman as Good as the Man*, was published in London as early as 1677. Mary Astell is now regarded by many as the first English feminist.[58] An ardent High Churchwoman, her primary interest was religion. Her most famous work, *A Serious Proposal to the Ladies* (1694), advocated a "religious retirement" where women could be educated and could separate themselves from the social pressures of the world. Feminists applaud the ideas that women could and even should exist in this retirement without men, and that the expectations of society are not necessarily the best for women. But these ideas found no public response in the early eighteenth century. More popular because more in the mainstrean of current thought were the writings on women of Defoe in *An Essay on Projects* (1697) and Steele in *The Spectator, The Guardian,* and *The Ladies' Library*. These authors defended women against their detractors by insisting that a lack of educational opportunities had stifled the natural capacities of the female sex.

But the society that developed, according to Plumb, "a sense of common identity in those who wielded economic, social, and political power"[59] was a masculine society. In the middle decades of the century only an occasional controversy about the "woman question" erupted into the public scene. When the editor of the journal *Commonsense* published an attack on women in 1738, Lady Mary Wortley Montagu, writing anonymously in *The Nonsense of Commonsense*, defended her sex. This exchange may have occasioned the appearance of the Sophia pamphlet, *Woman Not Inferior to Man* (1739). Sophia's effort was answered in *Man Superior to Woman* (1739), and she in turn replied with *Woman's Superior Excellence over Man* (1740). The identity of Sophia remains unknown, but her pamphlets aroused enough interest to be reprinted in 1751 as *Beauty's Triumph* and as late as 1780 as *Female Restoration*.

After mid-century, social and economic changes opened more doors to women. But while female figures became more prominent in intellectual and artistic circles, there were few suggestions that women should be allowed additional political rights. The first woman openly to challenge the political status quo was Catherine Macaulay Graham.[60] A radical republican who began publishing in 1763, Macaulay Graham showed little evidence of feminism until her *Letters on Education*, which appeared in 1790. It was this book, which stated firmly that there were no differences, except physical ones, between the sexes, that Wollstonecraft cited approvingly in her *Vindication*. Macaulay Graham's last work was a reply to Burke, *Observations on the Reflections*, which also won the approval of the younger English radicals who looked with favor on the events across the Channel. There were a few other works in the years before the French Revolution which celebrated women's achievements and capabilities.[61] These feminist writings culminated in Wollstonecraft's *Vindication*; she clearly acknowledged her debts to these earlier authors. The *Vindication* initiated the final and most intense debate of the century on the nature and rights of women. Wollstonecraft found both defenders and opponents. Her supporters did not always hold radical views on other issues.[62] Opponents, both male and female, were conservative in all respects. They came to the attack with great enthusiasm, if often with little wit. Gisbourne's work was an answer to Wollstonecraft, as was Polwhele's dreadful *The Unsex'd Females, A Poem* (1798).[63] The antifeminists had few new points; the old arguments were revived, and to clinch their position they insisted that feminism was unwomanly.

Wollstonecraft's fame and prominence as the theorist of feminism is the result of several factors. She was the first to write specifically about the political rights of women. She represented the radical cause of the 'nineties, which seemed to contemporaries far more dangerous than the Wilkesite radicalism of the 'sixties. Her own gifts and personality were, of course, remarkable, but that she lived when she did and was intimate with a remarkable group of people surely helped to build and maintain Wollstonecraft's fame. She has been the subject of many biographies, beginning with that written by her husband, Godwin's *Memoirs of the Author of a Vindication* (1798). Todd, "The Biographies of Mary Wollstonecraft" (1976) and Moers, "Vindicating Mary Wollstonecraft" (1976) discuss the large number of studies of her life and works that have appeared with the revivals of feminism in the twentieth century. For many modern writers, Wollstonecraft has become the symbol of eighteenth-century feminism, which somewhat distorts the early history of the woman's movement. The nonpolitical feminism of Hannah More was far more influential at the time and for many years thereafter.

Focusing on Wollstonecraft has also tended to obscure other women in the radical Godwin circle. Work on them has been limited, although they may have been more influential in keeping alive feminist ideas. Many of their writings were novels, which were probably more widely read than Wollstonecraft's *Mary*. Some of these women are discussed in Adams, *Studies in the Literary Backgrounds of English Radicalism* (1947). Mary Hays, whose writings not only included novels and tracts but also the invaluable *Female Biography*, has received more attention than most, but still awaits an adequate biography.[64] Amelia Opie has had two biographers.[65] But the best source for these women's ideas remains their novels: Hays, *Memoir of Emma Courtney* (1796); Opie, *Adeline Mobray* (2nd ed. 1805); Fenwick, *Secresy* (1795); Robinson, *Walsingham* (1797); Charlotte Smith, *Desmond* (1792) and *The Young Philosopher* (1798); Williams, *Julia* (1790). The radical feminism of the turn of the century must not be underestimated, though much of its initial influence was negative rather than positive. But women had learned to read, and more and more of them were writing books and pamphlets. It was difficult to stop their filling these writings with feminist ideas. The church, state, and society in general may have frowned on these ideas but could not prevent their circulation.

The eighteenth-century English woman, like her male relations, experienced vast social, political, and economic changes. Her life at the end of the century was different from that at its outset. The spread of literacy, the acceptance of writing as a respectable livelihood for women, the rising birthrate and declining death rate, and the evangelical expectations of good works for the benefit of society, were surely among the most important developments affecting women. The amount or kind of human control over the demographic changes is still unclear; that it happened is indisputable, and for women as for men—there were more of them living longer. A higher birthrate also meant more children per woman; the larger families of the later century increased women's responsibilities and their value at home. Limited though this role might be, it could lead to greater self-consciousness and self-confidence. The other changes more obviously opened opportunities for women. The importance of literacy and the creation of written works was not undervalued in the eighteenth century. One of the constant worries of writers of works on education was the influence unsuitable books might have. Literacy opened many prospects for women, not only for making a living but also for spreading ideas. In the growth of female self-consciousness, without which feminism is nothing, that women were writing books, pamphlets, and magazines meant that they were challenging men on their own ground. Having babies and raising a family was women's work; writing was not, but women could and did do it. The evangelical emphasis on good works also broadened the sphere of women's activities. Conservatives believed that women were naturally better and purer than men; could they then be denied the opportunity to extend their grace and charity to the less fortunate? This led to prison visits, antislavery meetings, and visits to orphanages, slums, and factories. All this broadened the experience of women and gave them more ideas about what they could do to improve the society in which they lived. The increasing activity of nineteenth-century women in philanthropic and social causes had its roots firmly in the eighteenth century. Political feminism too is rooted there. Just as it took the whole century for the idea of female equality to be clearly stated, so it took another for it to be achieved. Feminism is more than politics. Modern feminism, like modern society, begins in the eighteenth century.

# NOTES

1. Among the most useful works for information about women are: Buer, *Health, Wealth, and Population*; Chambers, "Enclosure and Labor Supply in the Industrial Revolution" and *Population, Economy, and Society*; Eversley, "A Survey of Population in an Area of Worcestershire"; Flinn, *British Population Growth*; Loschky and Krier, "Income and Family Size in Three Eighteenth-Century Lancashire Parishes"; Hair, "Bridal Pregnancy in Rural England Further Examined" and "Bridal Pregnancy in Rural England in Earlier Centuries"; Krause, "Changes in English Fertility and Mortality" and "Some Aspects of Population Change"; McKeown and Brown, "Medical Evidence Related to English Population Changes"; Sogner, "Aspects of the Demographic Situation in Seventeen Parishes in Shropshire."
2. These include: Chambers, "Population Change in a Provincial Town"; Tranter, "Population and Social Structure in a Bedfordshire Parish"; Wrigley, "Family Limitation in PreIndustrial England."
3. These include: Habakkuk, "English Population in the Eighteenth Century"; Razzell, "Population Change in Eighteenth Century England."
4. "Size and Structure of the Household in England"; *Household and Family in Past Time*; and, with John Harrison, "Clayworth and Cogenhoe."
5. Barley, *The English Farmhouse and Cottage*; Fussell, *The English Rural Labourer*, and *Village Life*; Fussell and Goodman, "The Housing of the Rural Population in the Eighteenth Century."
6. Beattie, "The Criminality of Women in Eighteenth-Century England"; George, *London Life*; Marshall, *The English Poor*; Thompson, "The Moral Economy of the English Crowd."
7. *An Account of Several Work-houses*; Braddon, *The Miseries of the Poor, A Proposal for Relieving*

... the Poor; Burn, *A Glimpse at the Social Condition of the Working Classes*; Colquhoun, *The State of Indigence*; Davies, *The Case of Labourers in Husbandry*; Eden, *The State of the Poor*; H. Fielding, *A Proposal for Making an Effectual Provision for the Poor*; Massie, *A Plan ... Considerations Relating to the Poor*; Ruggles, *The History of the Poor.*

8. Chambers, *Nottinghamshire in the Eighteenth Century*; George, *London Life*; Gilboy, *Wages in Eighteenth Century England*; Mann, "Clothiers and Weavers in Wiltshire"; Tickner, *Women in English Economic History.*

9. For an introduction to these women, see the relevant chapters in: Blease, *The Emancipation of English Women*; G. Hill, *Women in English Life*; Jarrett, *England in the Age of Hogarth*; Phillips and Tomkinson, *English Women in Life and Letters*; Roscoe, *The English Scene*; Rowbotham, *Hidden from History*; Stenton, *The English Woman in History.*

10. Gagen, *The New Woman*; Jaeger, *Before Victoria*; Plumb, "Reason and Unreason in the Eighteenth Century"; Quinlan, *Victorian Prelude*; Taylor, *The Angel Makers*; K. Thomas, "The Double Standard"; Benkovitz, "Some Observations on Woman's Concept of Self in the Eighteenth Century."

11. Aiken, *Epistles on Women*; Alexander, *The History of Women*; Andrews, *Remarks on the French and English Ladies*; A. L. Thomas, *Essay on the Character, Manners, and Genius of Women.*

12. Fordyce, *The Character and Conduct of the Female Sex*, and *Sermons to Young Women*; Gregory, *A Father's Legacy*; Kenrick, *The Whole Duty of Women*; E. Moore, *Fables for the Female Sex*; S. Wesley, Jr., *The Battle of the Sexes*. For the scriptural arguments on the position of women see: Ruether, *Religion and Sexism.*

13. Cressy, "Literacy in Pre-Industrial England"; Laqueur, "Literacy and Social Mobility in the Industrial Revolution in England"; Neuburg, *Popular Education in Eighteenth Century England*; Sanderson, "Literacy and Social Mobility in the Industrial Revolution in England."

14. Edwards, *Six Life Studies*; C. J. Hamilton, *Women Writers*; Jerrold, *Five Queer Women*; Manley and Belcher, *O Those Extraordinary Women*; Mayer, *Women of Letters*; Ritchie, *A Book of Sibyls*; Wallas, *Before the Bluestockings*; Wilson, *These Were Muses.*

15. Carter, *Letters from ... Carter, to ... Montagu, Memoirs of the Life*, and *A Series of Letters between ... Carter and ... Talbot.*

16. Clerke, *The Herschels and Modern Astronomy*; Lubbock, ed., *The Herschel Chronicle*; Sidgwick, *William Herschel.*

17. Ashmun, *The Singing Swan*; Lucas, *A Swan and Her Friends*; Seward, *The Swan of Lichfield.*

18. R. B. Johnson, ed., *Bluestocking Letters*; W. S. Scott, *The Bluestocking Ladies*; Wheeler, *Famous Blue-stockings.*

19. Blunt, ed., *Mrs. Montagu, "Queen of the Blues," Her Letters*; J. T. Boulton, "Mrs. Elizabeth Montagu"; Climenson, ed., *Elizabeth Montagu, the Queen of the Blue-Stockings: Her Correspondence*; Hornbeak, "New Light on Mrs. Montagu"; W. P. Jones, "The Romantic Bluestocking: Elizabeth Montagu"; E. Montagu, *Letters.*

20. Clifford, *Hester Lynch Piozzi—Mrs. Thrale*; Piozzi, *Thraliana*; Spacks, "Scrapbook of a Self."

21. Among the eighteenth-century periodicals which should prove most fruitful for the historian are: *The Family Magazine, The Female Tatler, Gallery of Fashion, The Gentleman's Magazine, The Guardian*, Eliza Haywood's *The Female Spectator* and *The Parrot, The Ladies' Diary, The Ladies' Magazine, The Ladies' Museum* (originally *The Lady's Monthly Museum*), *The Lady's Magazine, or Polite Companion for the Fair Sex, The Lady's Museum* (ed. Lennox and Kelly), *The London Magazine, The Matrimonial Magazine, The Midwife, The New Lady's Magazine, The Old Maid, The Rambler, The Royal Female Magazine, The Spectator, The Tea-Table.*

22. Blanchard, "Richard Steele and the Status of Women"; Hodges, "*The Female Spectator*, A Courtesy Periodical"; Hunter, "The Eighteenth Century Englishwoman: According to *The Gentleman's Magazine*," and "*The Lady's Magazine* and the History of the Eighteenth-Century Englishwoman"; Miller, "Eighteenth Century Periodicals for Women"; Stearns, "Early English Periodicals for Ladies," and "The First English Periodical for Women."

23. For lists of eighteenth-century novels, see: McBurney, *A Check List of English Prose Fiction; The New Cambridge Bibliography of English Literature*, vol. 2; as well as the bibliographies of works cited herein which deal with the novels.

24. Horner, *The English Women Novelists*; R. B. Johnson, *The Women Novelists*; Kavanagh, *English Women of Letters*; MacCarthy, *The Later Women Novelists*, and *Women Writers*; Masefield, *Women Novelists*; Simon, "Le Roman Féminin en Angleterre"; Whitemore, *Woman's Work in English Fiction*; Halsband, "Women and Literature in Eighteenth-Century England"; Lock, "Astrea's 'Vacant Throne': The Successors of Aphra Behn."

25. Among the most recent biographies are: Hodge, *The Double Life of Jane Austen*; Laski, *Jane Austen and Her World*; Pilgrim, *Dear Jane*.

26. Adelstein, *Fanny Burney*; Hahn, *A Degree of Prudery*; Hemlow, *The History of Fanny Burney*; Kamm, *The Story of Fanny Burney*; Montague and Martz, "Fanny Burney's Evelina."

27. Backscheider, "Defoe's Women"; Fitzgerald, *Daniel Defoe*; Rogers, "The Feminism of Daniel Defoe."

28. Anderson, "Mistress Delariviere Manley's Biography"; Needham, "Mrs. Manley: An Eighteenth-Century Wife of Bath," and "Mary de la Riviere Manley, Tory Defender"; Snyder, "New Light on Mrs. Manley?"

29. M. D. Bell, "Pamela's Wedding and the Marriage of the Lamb"; Donovan, "The Problem of Pamela"; Dussinger, "What Pamela Knew"; C. Hill, "Clarissa Harlowe and Her Times"; Moynihan, "Clarissa and the Enlightened Woman as Literary Heroine"; Watt, *The Rise of the Novel*.

30. Sherburn, "Fielding's *Amelia*"; Towers, "*Amelia* and the State of Matrimony"; Wendt, "The Naked Virtue of Amelia"; M. B. Williams, *Marriage: Fielding's Mirror of Morality*.

31. Isles, "The Lennox Collection"; Séjourné, *The Mystery of Charlotte Lennox*; Small, *Charlotte Ramsay Lennox*; Whicher, *The Life and Romances of Mrs. Eliza Haywood*.

32. Defoe, *Conjugal Lewdness, The Family Instructor, Religious Courtship, A Treatise Concerning the Use and Abuse of the Marriage Bed* (cf. *Conjugal Lewdness*).

33. *The Art of Governing a Wife*; Lovemore, *A Letter from a Father to a Son*; Truelove, *The Comforts of Matrimony*.

34. *A Dialogue concerning the Subjection of Women to their Husbands*; Foster, "Sermon XVI, On the Seventh Commandment"; Salmon, *A Critical Essay concerning Marriage*; Sprint, *The Bride-Woman's Counseller*; Wilkinson, *The Merchant Royall*.

35. E. Griffith, *Essays, Addressed to Young Married Women*; Haywood, *The Wife*; J. Hill, *The Conduct of a Married Life*.

36. Tompkins, *The Polite Marriage*, discusses this literary couple.

37. *Baron and Feme; The Laws Respecting Women; A Treatise of Feme Coverts*. Among modern sources, see: O. R. McGregor, *Divorce in England*.

38. Jourdain, *English Interiors in Smaller Houses*; Ramsey and Harvey, *Small Georgian Houses*; Richardson and Eberlein, *The Smaller English House*.

39. Bayne-Powell, *Housekeeping in the Eighteenth Century*; Rose M. Bradley, *The English Housewife*; Fussell and Fussell, *The English Countrywoman*; Hart, *The Eighteenth Century Country Parson*; Hole, *English Home-Life*; Plumb, "The Woman's Burden."

40. Richard Bradley, *The Country Housewife and Lady's Director*; Ellis, *The Country Housewife's Family Companion; The Farmer's Wife; or, The Complete Country House-Wife*; M. Johnson, *Madam Johnson's Present: or, The Best Instructions for Young Women*; Raffald, *The Experienced House-Keeper*; E. Smith, *The Compleat Housewife; Every Woman Her Own Housekeeper*.

41. Hecht, *Continental and Colonial Servants*, and *The Domestic Servant Class*; Horn, *The Rise and Fall of the Victorian Servant*; Marshall, "The Domestic Servants of the Eighteenth Century"; Stuart, *The English Abigail*.

42. Defoe, *The Behaviour of Servants in England* (cf. *The Great Law of Subordination*); *Every-Body's Business, is No-Body's Business; The Great Law of Subordination; The Maid Servant's Modest Defense*.

43. Bayne-Powell, *The English Child*; Lorence, "Parents and Children in Eighteenth-Century Europe"; Roe, *The Georgian Child*; Still, *The History of Paediatrics*.

44. Bonhote, *The Parental Monitor*; Brown, *A Letter to a Lady*; Collyer, *The Parent's and*

*Guardian's Directory*; Cutts, *Almeria: or, Parental Advice*; Hanway, *Letters on the Importance of the Rising Generation*; *The Infant's Lawyer*; Nelson, *An Essay on the Government of Children*; Tillotson, *Six Sermons*.

45. Downman, *Infancy; or, The Management of Children*; Mantell, *Short Directions for the Management of Infants*; Moss, *An Essay on the Management and Nursing of Children*, and *An Essay on the Management, Nursing, and Diseases of Children* (cf. title preceding); H. Smith, *Letters to Married Women*; Theobald, *The Young Wife's Guide*; Underwood, *A Treatise on the Disorders of Childhood*.

46. Armstrong, *An Account of the Diseases Most Incident to Children* (cf. following title), and *An Essay on the Diseases Most Fatal to Infants*; Cook, *A Plain Account of the Diseases Incident to Children*; Denison, *The Child's Physician*; Forster, *A Treatise on the Various Kinds ... of Foods.... To which is added a Discourse of the Diseases of Children*; *A Full View of All the Diseases Incident to Children*.

47. Airlie, *In Whig Society*; Aspinall-Oglander, *Admiral's Widow*, and *Admiral's Wife*; E. M. Bell, *The Hamwood Papers*; Delany, *Autobiography and Correspondence*; Dickins and Stanton, eds., *An Eighteenth-Century Correspondence*; Fremantle, *The Wynne Diaries*; Goede, *A Foreigner's Opinion of England*; Hampden, *An Eighteenth-Century Journal*; Heber, *Dear Miss Heber*; Hutton, *Reminiscences*; La Roche, *Sophie in London*; LeFanu, *Betsy Sheridan's Journal*; Lichtenberg, *Lichtenberg's Visits to England*; Napier, *The Life and Letters*; Osborn, *Letters*; Pembroke, *Pembroke Papers*; Pepys, *A Later Pepys*; Powys, *Passages from the Diaries*; Purefoy, *Purefoy Letters*; Ryder, *The Diary of Dudley Ryder*; Sherson, *The Lively Lady Townshend*; Sibbald, *The Memoirs of Susan Sibbald*; Stanley, *The Girlhood of Maria Josepha Holroyd*; Stokes, *The Devonshire House Circle*; Thomson, *The Russells in Bloomsbury*; Verney, ed., *Verney Letters*; Wyndham, *Chronicles of the Eighteenth Century*.

48. Boaden, *Memoirs of Mrs. Siddons*; Manvell, *Sarah Siddons*.

49. Based on the memoirs are: Littlewood, *Elizabeth Inchbald*; McKee, *Elizabeth Inchbald, Novelist*; Tobler, *Mrs. Elizabeth Inchbald*.

50. J. Fielding, *An Account of the Origin and Effects of a Police*; Hanway, *Letter V. To Robert Dingley*; Dingley, *Proposals for Establishing a Public Place of Reception*; Massie, *A Plan for the Establishment of Charity-Houses*.

51. See also: Smelser, *Social Change in the Industrial Revolution*.

52. See, for example: Kovačević and Kanner, "Blue Books into Novel"; and Kovačević, *Fact into Fiction*.

53. Corder, *Life of Elizabeth Fry*. See also: *Albion's Fatal Tree: Crime and Society in Eighteenth-Century England*.

54. Barbauld, *The Works of Anna Laetitia Barbauld*.

55. Trimmer, *Some Account of the Life and Writings of Mrs. Trimmer*.

56. Hopkins, *Hannah More and her Circle*; M. G. Jones, *Hannah More*; More, *The Letters of Hannah More*; Roberts, *Memoirs of the Life and Correspondence of Mrs. Hannah More*.

57. Blease, *The Emancipation of English Women*; Bouten, *Mary Wollstonecraft and the Beginnings of Female Emancipation*; O'Malley, *Women in Subjection*; Storr, *Mary Wollstonecraft et le mouvement féministe*.

58. "Mary Astell: A Seventeenth Century Advocate for Women"; F. M. Smith, *Mary Astell*.

59. Plumb, *The Growth of Political Stability*, p. xviii.

60. Donnelly, "The Celebrated Mrs. Macaulay"; Fox, "Catharine Macaulay, An Eighteenth Century Clio"; Withey, "Catharine Macaulay and the Uses of History."

61. Duncombe, *The Feminiad; or, Female Genius*; Haywood, *Epistles for the Ladies*; M. Scott, *The Female Advocate*.

62. *Appeal to the Men of Great Britain in behalf of Women*; Edgeworth, *Letters for Literary Ladies*; Hawkins, *Letters on the Female Mind*; Hays, *Letters and Essays*; Radcliffe, *The Female Advocate*; Wakefield, *Reflections on the Present Condition of the Female Sex*.

63. Other attacks included: Duff, *Letters, on the Intellectual and Moral Character of Women*; *The Female Aegis; or, The Duties of Women*; E. Hamilton, *Letter Addressed to the Daughter of a Nobleman*, and *Memoirs of Modern Philosophers*; West, *Letters to a Young Lady*.

64. Fenwick, *The Fate of the Fenwicks*; Hays, *The Love-Letters of Mary Hays*; Luria and Tayler,

"Gender and Genre: Women in the Literature of the British Romantics"; Pollin, "Mary Hays on Women's Rights in the Monthly Magazine."
65. Brightwell, *Memorials of the Life of Amelia Opie*; M. E. Macgregor, *Amelia Alderson Opie*.

# BIBLIOGRAPHY

*An Account of Several Work-Houses for Employing and Maintaining the Poor*, etc. London: 1725. (Society for Promoting Christian Knowledge.)

*An Account of the Methods Whereby the Charity-Schools Have Been Erected and Managed.* London: 1705. (Later eds. have title: *An Account of Charity Schools Lately Erected in England, Wales and Ireland.* SPCK.)

ADAMS, MARTIN RAY. *Studies in the Literary Backgrounds of English Radicalism, with Special Reference to the French Revolution.* Lancaster, Pa.: 1947.

ADBURGHAM, ALISON. *Women in Print: Writing Women and Women's Magazines from the Restoration to the Accession of Victoria.* London: 1972.

ADELSTEIN, MICHAEL EDWARD. *Fanny Burney.* New York: 1968.

AIKIN, LUCY. *Epistles on Women, Exemplifying Their Character and Condition in Various Ages and Nations.* London: 1810.

AIRLIE, MABELL FRANCES ELIZABETH (GORE) OGILVY, COUNTESS OF. *In Whig Society, 1775–1818.* London and New York: 1921.

ALEXANDER, WILLIAM. *The History of Women, From the Earliest Antiquity to the Present Time, Giving Some Account of Almost Every Interesting Particular Concerning That Sex among All Nations.* 2 vols. London: 1779.

ANDERSON, PAUL BUNYAN. "Mistress Delariviere Manley's Biography." *Modern Philology* 33 (1935–36): 261–78.

ANDREWS, JOHN. *Remarks on the French and English Ladies, in a Series of Letters; Interspersed with Various Anecdotes*, etc. London: 1783.

*Appeal to the Men of Great Britain in behalf of Women.* London: 1798.

ARBLAY, FRANCES (BURNEY) D'. *Diary and Letters of Madame d'Arblay. (1778–1840).* 7 vols. London: 1842–46.

ARMSTRONG, GEORGE. *An Account of the Diseases Most Incident to Children.* London: 1777. (Another ed. of *An Essay on the Diseases Most Fatal ....*)

——. *An Essay on the Diseases Most Fatal to Infants ... The Second edition, with Additions.* London: 1771.

*The Art of Governing a Wife; with Rules for Batchelors. To Which Is Added an Essay against Unequal Marriage.* London: 1747.

ASHDOWN, MARGARET. "Elizabeth Elstob, the Learned Saxonist." *Modern Language Review* 20 (1925): 125–46.

ASHMUN, MARGARET. *The Singing Swan. An Account of Anna Seward and Her Acquaintance with Dr. Johnson, Boswell, and Others of Their Time.* New Haven and London: 1931.

ASPINALL-OGLANDER, CECIL FABER. *Admiral's Widow; Being the Life and Letters of the Hon. Mrs. Edward Boscawen from 1761–1805.* London: 1942.

———. *Admiral's Wife; Being the Life and Letters of the Hon. Mrs. Edward Boscawen from 1719–1761.* London and New York: 1940.

ASTELL, MARY. *A Serious Proposal to the Ladies, for the Advancement of Their True and Greatest Interest. By a Lover of Her Sex.* London: 1694.

———. *Some Reflections upon Marriage, Occasion'd by the Duke & Dutchess of Mazarine's Case; Which Is Also Consider'd.* London: 1700.

AUSTEN, JANE. *Pride and Prejudice: A Novel.* 3 vols. London: 1813.

BACKSCHEIDER, PAULA. "Defoe's Women: Snares and Prey." *Studies in Eight enth Century Culture* 5 (1976): 103–20.

BALLARD, GEORGE. *Memoirs of Several Ladies of Great Britain, Who Have Been Celebrated for Their Writings or Skill in the Learned Languages, Arts and Sciences.* Oxford: 1752.

BARBAULD, ANNA LAETITIA (AIKIN). *The Works of Anna Laetitia Barbauld, with a Memoir by Lucy Aikin.* 2 vols. London: 1825.

BARKER, THEODORE CARDWELL; MCKENZIE, J. C.; and YUDKIN, JOHN, eds. *Our Changing Fare: Two Hundred Years of British Food Habits.* London: 1966.

BARLEY, MAURICE WILLMORE. *The English Farmhouse and Cottage.* London: 1961.

*Baron and Feme. A Treatise of the Common Law concerning Husbands and Wives.* London: 1700.

BAYNE-POWELL, ROSAMOND. *The English Child in the Eighteenth Century.* New York and London: 1939.

———. *Housekeeping in the Eighteenth Century.* London: 1956.

BEACHAMP, VIRGINIA WALCOTT. "Pioneer Linguist: Elizabeth Elstob." *University of Michigan Papers in Women's Studies* 1, no. 3: 9–19.

BEATTIE, J. M. "The Criminality of Women in Eighteenth-Century England." *Journal of Social History* 8 (Summer 1975): 80–116.

*Beauty's Triumph: or, The Superiority of the Fair Sex Invincibly Proved, Wherein the Arguments for the Natural Right of Man to a Sovereign Authority over the Woman are Fairly Urged and Undeniably Refuted.* London: 179-? (Contents: Part 1 Woman not inferior to man. Part 2 Man superior to woman. Part 3 Woman's superior excellence over man. Each part previously printed separately in 1739–40. Another ed., 1751, gives variant titles to parts 2 and 3. For individual eds. of 1739 and 1740, see listings under: Sophia (pseud.); *Man superior to woman . . . By a gentleman.*)

BELL, EVA MARY, ed. *The Hamwood Papers of the Ladies of Llangollen and Caroline Hamilton.* London: 1930.

BELL, MICHAEL DAVITT. "Pamela's Wedding and the Marriage of the Lamb." *Philological Quarterly* 49 (1970): 100–12.

BENKOVITZ, MIRIAM J. "Some Observations on Woman's Concept of Self in the Eighteenth Century." In *Woman in the Eighteenth Century and Other Essays,* edited by Paul Fritz and Richard Morton, pp. 37–54. McMaster Association for Eighteenth-Century Studies 4. Toronto: 1976.

BETHUNE, GEORGE WASHINGTON. *The British Female Poets: With Biographical and Critical Notices.* Philadelphia: 1848.

BEVAN, JOSEPH GURNEY. *Memoirs of the Life and Travels in the Service of the Gospel of Sarah Stephenson.* London: 1807.

*Biographium Faemineum. The Female Worthies: or, Memoirs of the Most Illustrious Ladies of All Ages and Nations.* 2 vols. London: 1776.

BLANCHARD, RAE. "Richard Steele and the Status of Women." *Studies in Philology* 26 (1929): 325–55.

BLEACKLEY, HORACE WILLIAM. *Ladies Fair and Frail. Sketches of the Demi-monde during the Eighteenth Century.* London and New York: 1909.

BLEASE, WALTER LYON. *The Emancipation of English Women.* London: 1910.

BLOCH, IVAN. *Sexual Life in England, Past and Present.* Translated by William H. Fostern. London: 1938.

BLUNT, REGINALD, ed. *Mrs. Montagu, "Queen of the Blues," Her Letters and Friendships from 1762 to 1800.* 2 vols. London: 1923.

BOADEN, JAMES. *Memoirs of Mrs. Siddons. Interspersed with Anecdotes of Authors and Actors.* London and Philadelphia: 1827.

BONHOTE, ELIZABETH. *The Parental Monitor.* 2 vols. London: 1788.

BOSWELL, JAMES. *Boswell in Search of a Wife, 1766–1769.* Edited by Frank Brady and Frederick A. Pottle. London and New York: 1957.

BOULTON, JAMES T. "Mrs. Elizabeth Montagu." *Burke Newsletter* 3 (1961–62): 96–98.

BOULTON, WILLIAM BIGGS. *The Amusements of Old London.* London: 1901.

BOUTEN, JACOB. *Mary Wollstonecraft and the Beginnings of Female Emancipation in France and England.* Amsterdam: 1922.

BRADDON, LAWRENCE. *The Miseries of the Poor Are a National Sin, Shame, and Charge.* London: 1717.

———. *A Proposal for Relieving, Reforming and Employing All the Poor of Great Britain.* London: 1721.

BRADLEY, RICHARD. *The Country Housewife and Lady's Director, in the Management of a House and the Delights and Profits of a Farm.* London and Dublin: 1727.

BRADLEY, ROSE M. *The English Housewife in the Seventeenth and Eighteenth Centuries.* London: 1912.

BRIGHTWELL, CECELIA LUCY. *Memorials of the Life of Amelia Opie.* 2d ed. Norwich: 1854.

BROWN, SARAH. *A Letter to a Lady on the Management of an Infant.* London: 1779.

BRYAN, MARGARET. *A Compendious System of Astronomy, in a Course of Familiar Lectures . . . also Trigonometrical and Celestial Problems, with a Key to the Ephemeris, and a Vocabulary of the Terms of Science. . . .* London: 1797. 2d ed., 1799. 3d ed., rev. and corr., 1805.

———. *Lectures on Natural Philosophy: The Result of Many Years' Practical Experience of the Facts Elucidated. With an Appendix: Containing a Great Number and Variety of Astronomical and Geographical Problems; also some Useful Tables, and a Comprehensive Vocabulary.* London: 1806.

BUCHAN, WILLIAM. *Domestic Medicine; or, The Family Physician.* Edinburgh: 1769.

BUER, MABEL CRAVEN. *Health, Wealth, and Population in the Early Days of the Industrial Revolution.* London and New York: 1926.

BURN, JAMES DAWSON. *A Glimpse at the Social Condition of the Working Classes during the Early Part of the Present Century.* London: 1868.

BURTON, ELIZABETH. *The Georgians at Home: 1714–1830.* London: 1967.

BUTLER, MARILYN. *Maria Edgeworth: A Literary Biography.* Oxford: 1972.

CADOGAN, WILLIAM. *An Essay upon Nursing, and the Management of Children, from Their Birth to Three Years of Age.* London: 1748.

CAPPE, CATHARINE HARRISON. *An Account of Two Charity Schools for the Education of Girls: and of a Female Friendly Society in York.* York: 1800.

———. *Memoirs of the Life of the Late Mrs. Catherine Cappe Written by Herself.* London: 1822.

CARTER, ELIZABETH. *Letters from Mrs. Elizabeth Carter, to Mrs. Montagu, between the Years 1755 and 1800, Chiefly upon Literary and Moral Subjects.* Edited by Montagu Pennington. 3 vols. London: 1817.

———. *Memoirs of the Life of Mrs. Elizabeth Carter.* Edited by Montagu Pennington. London: 1807.

———. *A Series of Letters between Mrs. Elizabeth Carter and Miss Catherine Talbot from the Year 1741 to 1770.* Edited by Montagu Pennington. 2 vols. London: 1808.

CAULFIELD, ERNEST. *The Infant Welfare Movement in the Eighteenth Century.* New York: 1931.

CHAMBERS, JONATHAN DAVID. "Enclosure and Labor Supply in the Industrial Revolution." *Economic History Review,* 2d series, 5 (1952–53): 310–343.

———. *Nottinghamshire in the Eighteenth Century: A Study of Life and Labour under the Squirearchy.* 2d ed. London and New York: 1966.

———. "Population Change in a Provincial Town: Nottingham 1700–1800." In *Studies in the Industrial Revolution Presented to T. S. Ashton,* edited by L. S. Presnell, pp. 97–124. London: 1960.

———. *Population, Economy, and Society in Pre-Industrial England.* Edited by W. A. Armstrong. London and New York: 1972.

———. "The Vale of Trent 1670–1800: A Regional Study of Economic Change." *Economic History Review.* Supplement 3.

CHARKE, CHARLOTTE. *A Narrative of the Life of Mrs. Charlotte Charke, Youngest Daughter of Colley Cibber, Esq., Written by Herself.* London: 1755.

*Cheap Repository Tracts.* etc. London: 1798. (By Hannah More and her friends.)

CLARK, ALICE. *Working Life of Women in the Seventeenth Century.* London and New York: 1919.

CLAY, CHRISTOPHER. "Marriage, Inheritance, and the Rise of Large Estates in England, 1660–1815." *Economic History Review,* 2d series, 21 (1968): 503–18.

CLERKE, AGNES MARY. *The Hershels and Modern Astronomy.* London and New York: 1895.

CLIFFORD, JAMES LOWRY. *Hester Lynch Piozzi—Mrs. Thrale.* Oxford: 1941.

CLIMENSON, EMILY J., ed. *Elizabeth Montagu, the Queen of the Blue-Stockings: Her Correspondence from 1720 to 1761.* 2 vols. London and New York: 1906.

COLLYER, JOSEPH. *The Parent's and Guardian's Directory, and the Youth's Guide, in the Choice of a Profession or Trade.* London: 1761.

COLQUHOUN, PATRICK. *The State of Indigence, and the Situation of the Casual Poor in the Metropolis, Explained.* London: 1799.

*Common Sense: or, The Englishman's Journal.* London: 1737–1743.

*The Compleat Servant Maid, or The Young Maidens Tutor, Directing Them How They May Fit Themselves for Any of These Employments, viz. Waiting-woman, House-keeper, Chamber-maid, etc.* London: 1683. 6th ed., London: 1700.

COOK, JOHN. *A Plain Account of the Diseases incident to Children; with an Easy Method of Curing Them; Designed for the Use of Families.* London: 1769.

CORDER, SUSANNA. *Life of Elizabeth Fry.* London and Philadelphia: 1853.

CRESSY, DAVID. "Literacy in Pre-industrial England." *Societas* 4 (1974): 229–40.

CUTTS, MRS. *Almeria: or, Parental Advice: A Didactic Poem. Addressed to the Daughters of Great Britain and Ireland by a Friend of the Sex.* London: 1775.

DAVIES, DAVID. *The Case of Labourers in Husbandry.* London: 1795.

DEFOE, DANIEL. *The Behaviour of Servants in England Inquired into.* London: 1726? (A reissue of *The Great Law of Subordination Consider'd....*)
——. *Conjugal Lewdness: or Matrimonial Whoredom.* London: 1727.
——. *An Essay upon Projects.* London: 1697.
——. *Every-Body's Business, Is No-Body's Business; or, Private Abuses, Publick Grievances: Exemplified in the Pride, Insolence, and Exorbitant Wages of Our Women-Servants, Footmen, &c.* London: 1725.
——. *The Family Instructor.* London: 1715.
——. *The Great Law of Subordination Consider'd; or, The Insolence and Unsufferable Behaviour of Servants in England Duly Enquir'd into.* London: 1724.
——. *The Maid Servant's Modest Defense.* London: 1725.
——. *The Fortunes and Misfortunes of the Famous Moll Flanders.* London: 1722.
——. *Religious Courtship: Being Historical Discourses, on the Necessity of Marrying Religious Husbands and Wives Only.* London: 1722.
——. *The Fortunate Mistress: or, A History of the Life ... of the Lady Roxana.* London: 1724.
——. *A Treatise concerning the Use and Abuse of the Marriage Bed.* London: 1727. (Another issue of *Conjugal Lewdness....*)
DELANY, MARY (GRANVILLE) PENDARVES. *Autobiography and Correspondence of Mary Granville, Mrs. Delany.* Edited by Lady Llanover. 1st series, 3 vols. London: 1861. 2d series, 3 vols. London: 1862.
DENISON, REV. J. *The Child's Physician, or The Mother and Nurse Instructed.* London: 1795.
*A Dialogue concerning the Subjection of Women to Their Husbands ... by a Friend to the Ladies.* London: 1765.
DICKINS, LILIAN, and STANTON, MARY, eds. *An Eighteenth-Century Correspondence.* London and New York: 1910.
DINGLEY, ROBERT. *Proposals for Establishing a Public Place of Reception for Penitent Prostitutes.* London: 1758.
DONNELLY, L. M. "The Celebrated Mrs. Macaulay." *William and Mary Quarterly,* 3rd series, 6 (1949): 173–207.
DONOVAN, ROBERT A. "The Problem of Pamela, or Virtue unrewarded." *Studies in English Literature* 3 (1963): 377–95.
DOWNMAN, HUGH. *Infancy; or, The Management of Children, a Didactic Poem in Six Books.* 4th ed. Edinburgh: 1788.
DRUMMOND, JACK CECIL, and WILBRAHAM, ANNE. *The Englishman's Food.* Rev. ed. London: 1957.
DUFF, WILLIAM. *Letters, on the Intellectual and Moral Character of Women.* Aberdeen: 1807. Reprinted in Feminist Controversy in England, 1788–1810, series. New York: 1974.
DUNBAR, JANET. *Peg Woffington and Her World.* London and Boston: 1968.
DUNCOMBE, JOHN. *The Feminiad: or, Female Genius. A Poem.* London: 1754.
DUSSINGER, JOHN A. "What Pamela Knew: An Interpretation." *Journal of English and German Philology* 60 (1970): 377–93.
DYCE, ALEXANDER. *Specimens of British Poetesses.* London: 1825.
EDEN, FREDERICK MORTON. *The State of the Poor; or, An History of the Labouring Classes in England.* 3 vols. London: 1797.
EDGEWORTH, MARIA. *Letters for Literary Ladies.* London: 1795. Reprinted in Feminist Controversy in England, 1788–1810, series. New York: 1974.

EDWARDS, MATILDA BARBARA BETHAM-. *Six Life Studies of Famous Women*. London and New York: 1880.
EHRENPREIS, IRVIN, and HALSBAND, ROBERT. *The Lady of Letters in the Eighteenth Century*. Los Angeles: 1969.
ELLIS, WILLIAM. *The Country Housewife's Family Companion*. London: 1750.
ELWOOD, ANNE KATHERINE. *Memoirs of the Literary Ladies of England, from the Commencement of the Last Century*. 2 vols. London and Philadelphia: 1843.
EPTON, NINA CONSUELO. *Love and the English*. London: 1960. Cleveland: 1961.
*An Essay in Defence of the Female Sex ... Written by a Lady*. London: 1696. (Judith Drake, fl. 1696, supposed author.)
EVERSLEY, DAVID EDWARD CHARLES. "A Survey of Population in an Area of Worcestershire from 1660–1850 on the Basis of Parish Records." *Population Studies* 10 (1956–57): 253–79.
*Every Woman Her Own House-keeper*. 4th ed. London: 1796.
*The Family Magazine; or, A Repository of Religious Instruction and Rational Amusement*. London: Jan. 1788–June 1789.
*The Farmer's Wife; or, The Complete Country House-wife*. London: c. 1780.
FAUCHERY, PIERRE. *La destinée féminine dans le roman européen du dix-huitième siècle, 1713–1807; essai de gynécomythie romanesque*. Paris: 1972.
*The Female Aegis; or, The Duties of Women*. London: 1798. Reprinted in Feminist Controversy in England, 1788–1810, series. New York: 1974.
*Female Restoration, by a Moral and Physical Vindication of Female Talents ... by a Lady*. London: 1780.
*The Female Tatler*. Nos. 1–111. London: 8 July 1709–31 March 1710. Edited by Mary Manley.
FENWICK, ELIZA. *The Fate of the Fenwicks; Letters to Mary Hays (1798–1828)*. Edited by A. F. Wedd. London: 1927.
——. *Secresy; or, The Ruin on the Rock*. London: 1795. Reprinted in Feminist Controversy in England, 1788–1810, series. 3 vols. New York: 1974.
FIELDING, HENRY. *A Proposal for Making an Effectual Provision for the Poor*. London: 1753.
FIELDING, JOHN. *An Account of the Origin and Effects of a Police ... with a Plan for Preserving Those deserted Girls Who Become Prostitutes from Necessity*. London: 1758.
FITZGERALD, BRIAN. *Daniel Defoe; A Study in Conflict*. London: 1954. Chicago: 1955.
FLEETWOOD, WILLIAM. *The Relative Duties of Parents and Children, Husbands and Wives, Masters and Servants*. London: 1705.
FLINN, MICHAEL WALTER. *British Population Growth, 1700–1850; Prepared for the Economic History Society*. London 1970.
FORDYCE, JAMES. *The Character and Conduct of the Female Sex*. Dublin: 1776. Reprint. London: 1776.
——. *Sermons to Young Women*. 2 vols. London: 1766.
FORSTER, WILLIAM. *A Treatise on the Various Kinds ... of Foods: with Aphorisms of Health; or, Rules to Preserve the Body to a Good Old Age. To Which Is Added a ... discourse of the Diseases of Children*. Newcastle-upon-Tyne: 1738.
FOSTER, JAMES. "Sermon XVI, on the Seventh Commandment." In *Sermons on the following subjects*. London: 1732.
FOX, CLAIRE GILBRIDE. "Catharine Macaulay, an Eighteenth Certury Clio." *Winterthur Portfolio* 4 (1968): 129–42.

FREMANTLE, ELIZABETH (WYNNE). *The Wynne Diaries.* Edited by Anne Fremantle. 3 vols. London: 1935–40.

*A Full View of All the Diseases Incident to Children.* London: 1742. (Edited by John Burton?)

FULLARD, JOYCE, and SCHEVELLE, RHONDA W. "A Bibliography of Eighteenth-Century Women Poets." *Mary Wollstonecraft Journal* 2 (1974): 40–46.

FUSSELL, GEORGE EDWIN. *The English Rural Labourer; His Home, Furniture, Clothing and Food, from Tudor to Victorian Times.* London: 1949.

———. *Village Life in the Eighteenth Century.* Worcester: 1947.

———, and FUSSELL, K. R. *The English Countrywoman; A Farmhouse Social History, A. D. 1500–1900.* London: 1953.

———, and GOODMAN, CONSTANCE. "The Housing of the Rural Population in the Eighteenth Century." *Economic History* 2 (1930–33): 63–90.

GAGEN, JEAN ELISABETH. *The New Woman: Her Emergence in English Drama, 1600–1730.* New York: 1954.

*Gallery of Fashion.* Vols. 1–9. London: April 1794–March 1803.

GARDINER, DOROTHY. *English Girlhood at School; A Study of Women's Education through Twelve Centuries.* London: 1929.

GAUSSEN, ALICE CECILIA CAROLINE. *A Woman of Wit and Wisdom: A Memoir of Elizabeth Carter.* London and New York: 1906.

*The Gentleman's Magazine.* Vols. 1–103, no. 3. London: Jan. 1731–Sept. 1907. (subtitle varies.)

GEORGE, MARY DOROTHY. *London Life in the XVIIIth Century.* London and New York: 1925. Reprint. New York: 1964.

GILBOY, ELIZABETH. *Wages in Eighteenth Century England.* Cambridge, Mass.: 1934.

GISBORNE, THOMAS. *An Enquiry into the Duties of the Female Sex.* London: 1797. Reprinted in Feminist Controversy in England, 1788–1810, series. New York: 1974.

GLASSE, HANNAH. *The Art of Cookery, Made Plain and Esay . . . by a Lady.* London: 1747.

———. *The Compleat Confectioner.* Dublin: 1742.

———. *The Servant's Directory, or, House-keeper's Companion.* London: 1760.

GODWIN, WILLIAM. *Memoirs of the Author of* A Vindication of the Rights of Woman. London: 1798. Reprinted in many editions, including Feminist Controversy in England, 1788–1810, series. New York: 1974.

GOEDE, CHRISTIAN AUGUSTUS GOTTLIEB. *A Foreigner's Opinion of England, Englishmen, Englishwomen.* Translated by Thomas Horne. 3 vols. London: 1821.

GRAY, ALMIRA. *Papers and Diaries of a York Family, 1764–1893.* London: 1927.

GRAY, ERNEST ALFRED. *Man Midwife; the Further Experiences of John Knyveton.* London: 1946. (Fictitious diary.)

GREENBERG, JANELLE. "The Legal Status of English Women in Early Eighteenth Century Common Law and Equity." *Studies in Eighteenth Century Culture* 4 (1975): 171–81.

GREGORY, JOHN. *A Father's Legacy to His Daughters.* London: 1774. Reprinted in Feminist Controversy in England, 1788–1810, series. New York: 1974.

GRIFFITH, ELIZABETH. *Essays, Addressed to Young Married Women.* London: 1782.

GRIFFITH, RICHARD. *A Series of Genuine Letters between Henry and Frances* [i.e., between Richard and Elizabeth Griffith]. 2 vols. London: 1757. (This work was printed in four editions with various titles, ending with a six-volume edition, London: 1786.)

GRUBB, SARAH. *Some Account of the Life and Religious Labours of Sarah Grubb*. Dublin: 1792.

*The Guardian*. Nos. 1–175. London: 12 March–1 Oct. 1713. Edited by Sir Richard Steele, Joseph Addison, et al.

HABAKKUK, H. J. "English Population in the Eighteenth Century." *Economic History Review*, 2d series 6 (1953–54): 117–33.

————. "Marriage Settlements in the Eighteenth Century." *Transactions of the Royal Historical Society*, 4th series, 32 (1950): 15–30.

HAHN, EMILY. *A Degree of Prudery; A Biography of Fanny Burney*. Garden City, N.Y. and London: 1950.

HAIR, P. E. H. "Bridal Pregnancy in Earlier Rural England Further Examined." *Population Studies* 24 (1970): 59–70.

————. "Bridal Pregnancy in Rural England in Earlier Centuries." *Population Studies* 20 (1966–67): 233–43.

HAJNAL, J. "European Marriage Patterns in Perspective." In *Population in History, Essays in Historical Demography*, edited by D. V. Glass and D. E. C. Eversley, pp. 101–43. London and Chicago: 1965.

HALIFAX, GEORGE SAVILE, 1ST MARQUIS OF. *The Lady's New-years Gift; or, Advice to a Daughter*. London: 1688.

HALSBAND, ROBERT. "'The Female Pen' Women and Literature in Eighteenth Century England." *History Today* 24 (1974): 702–709.

————. *The Life of Lady Mary Wortley Montagu*. Oxford: 1956.

————. "Women and Literature in Eighteenth-Century England." In *Woman in the Eighteenth Century and Other Essays*, edited by Paul Fritz and Richard Morton, pp. 55–72. McMaster University Association for Eighteenth-Century Studies 4. Toronto: 1976.

HAMILTON, CATHERINE JANE. *Women Writers: Their Works and Ways*. 1st series -2nd series. London and New York: 1892–93.

HAMILTON, ELIZABETH. *Letters Addressed to the Daughter of a Nobleman, on the Formation of Religious and Moral Principle*. 2d ed. 2 vols. London: 1806. Reprinted in Feminist Controversy in England, 1788–1810, series. 2 vols. New York: 1974.

————. *Memoirs of Modern Philosophers*. London: 1800. Reprinted in Feminist Controversy in England, 1788–1810, series. 3 vols. New York: 1974.

HAMPDEN, JOHN. *An Eighteenth-Century Journal, Being a Record of the Years 1774–1776*. London: 1940.

HANS, NICHOLAS A. *New Trends in Education in the Eighteenth Century*. London: 1951.

HANWAY, JONAS. *Domestic Happiness Promoted; in a Series of Discourses from a Father to His Daughter ... Abridged from Virtue in Humble Life*. London: 1786.

————. *Letter V. To Robert Dingley, Esq., Being a Proposal for the Relief and Employment of Friendless Girls and Repenting Prostitutes*. London: 1756.

————. *Letters on the Importance of the Rising Generation of the Labouring Part of Our Fellow-Subjects*. London: 1767.

————. *Virtue in Humble Life, containing Reflections on the Reciprocal Duties of the Wealthy and Indigent*. 2 vols. London: 1774.

HART, ARTHUR TINDAL. *The Eighteenth Century Country Parson (circa 1689 to 1830)*. Shrewsbury: 1955.

HAWKINS, LAETITIA MATILDA. *Letters on the Female Mind*. London: 1793.

HAYS, MARY. *Female Biography; or, Memoirs of Illustrious and Celebrated Women, of All Ages and Countries*. 6 vols. London: 1803.

————. *Letters and Essays, Moral and Miscellaneous.* London: 1793. Reprinted in Feminist Controversy in England, 1788–1810, series. New York: 1974.

————. *The Love-Letters of Mary Hays (1779–1780).* Edited by A. F. Wedd. London: 1925.

————. *Memoirs of Emma Courtney.* 2 vols. London: 1796. Reprinted in Feminist Controversy in England, 1788–1810, series. 2 vols. New York: 1974.

HAYWOOD, ELIZA. *Epistles for the Ladies.* 2 vols. London: 1749.

————, ed. *The Female Spectator.* Vols. 1–4. London: April 1744–May 1746. (Originally issued in 24 monthly parts, with two months omitted, bound in 4 vols., dated 1745.)

————, ed. *The Parrot, with a Compendium of the Times.* London: 1746. (Originally issued in 9 weekly nos., 2 Aug.–4 Oct. 1746.)

————. *A Present for a Servant-Maid.* London: 1743.

————. *The Wife.* London: 1756.

HEBER, MARY. *Dear Miss Heber, an Eighteenth Century Correspondence.* Edited by Francis Bamford. London: 1936.

HECHT, JOSEPH JEAN. *Continental and Colonial Servants in Eighteenth Century England.* Northampton, Mass.: 1954.

————. *The Domestic Servant Class in Eighteenth Century England.* London: 1956.

HEMLOW, JOYCE. *The History of Fanny Burney.* Oxford: 1958.

HERSCHEL, MARY CORNWALLIS. *Memoir and Correspondence of Caroline Herschel.* London: 1876.

HILL, CHRISTOPHER. "Clarissa Harlowe and Her Times." In *Puritanism and Revolution,* pp. 367–94. London: 1958. New York: 1964.

HILL, GEORGIANA. *Women in English Life from Medieval to Modern Times.* 2 vols. London: 1896.

HILL, JOHN (JULIANA-SUSANNAH SEYMOUR [pseud.]). *The Conduct of a Married Life.* London: 1753.

*The History of Miss Katty N————... by Herself.* London: 1757.

HODGE, JANE. *The Double Life of Jane Austen.* London: 1972 (Published in U.S. as *Only a Novel; The Double Life of Jane Austen.* New York: 1972.)

HODGES, JAMES. "*The Female Spectator,* a Courtesy Periodical." In *Studies in the Early English Periodical,* edited by Richmond Pugh Bond. Chapel Hill, N.C.: 1957.

HOLE, CHRISTINA. *English Home-Life, 1500 to 1800.* London and New York: 1947.

HOLLINGSWORTH, T. H. "A Demographic Study of the British Ducal Families." *Population Studies* 11 (1957–58): 4–26.

————. "The Demography of the British Peerage." *Population Studies* 18 (1964–65): supplement.

HOPKINS, MARY ALDEN. *Hannah More and Her Circle.* New York: 1947.

HORN, PAMELA. *The Rise and Fall of the Victorian Servant.* Dublin and New York: 1975.

HORNBEAK, KATHERINE GEE. "New Light on Mrs. Montagu." In *The Age of Johnson; Essays Presented to Chauncey Brewster Tinker,* edited by F. W. Hilles, pp. 349–61. New Haven, Conn.: 1949.

HORNER, JOYCE MARY. *The English Women Novelists and Their Connection with the Feminist Movement (1688–1797).* Smith College Studies in Modern Languages, vol. 11, nos. 1–3. Northampton, Mass.: Oct. 1929–April 1930.

HOWARD, GEORGE ELLIOTT. *A History of Matrimonial Institutions.* Chicago: 1904.

HUGHES, ANNE. *The Diary of a Farmer's Wife, 1796–1797.* Edited by Suzanne Beedell. London: 1964.

HUME, A. *Every Woman Her Own Physician; or The Lady's Medical Assistant.* London: 1776.

HUNT, MORTON N. *The Natural History of Love.* New York and London: 1959.

HUNTER, JEAN E. "The Eighteenth Century Englishwoman: According to *The Gentleman's Magazine.*" In *Woman in the Eighteenth Century and Other Essays,* edited by Paul Fritz and Richard Morton, pp. 73–88. McMaster University Association for Eighteenth-Century Studies 4. Toronto: 1976.

———. "*The Lady's Magazine* and the History of the Eighteenth-Century Englishwoman." In *Newsletters to Newspapers: Eighteenth-Century Journalism,* edited by D. H. Bond and W. R. McLeod. Morgantown, W. Va.: 1977.

HUTTON, CATHERINE. *Reminiscences of a Gentlewoman of the Last Century.* Edited by Catherine Hutton Beale. Birmingham: 1891.

INCHBALD, ELIZABETH. *Memoirs of Mrs. Inchbald: Including Her Familiar Correspondence with the Most Distinguished Persons of Her Time.* Edited by James Boaden. 2 vols. London: 1833.

*The Infant's Lawyer: or, The Law (Both Ancient and Modern) relating to Infants.* London: 1697.

ISLES, DUNCAN. "The Lennox Collection." *Harvard Library Bulletin* 18 (1970): 317–34; 19 (1971): 36–60, 165–86, 416–35.

JAEGER, MURIEL. *Before Victoria.* London: 1956.

JARRETT, DEREK. *England in the Age of Hogarth.* London and New York: 1974.

JERROLD, WALTER COPELAND, and JERROLD, CLARE. *Five Queer Women.* London and New York: 1929.

*Jesus, Altogether Lovely: or, A Letter to Some of the Single Women in the Methodist Society.* London: 1763.

JOHNSON, MARY. *Madam Johnson's Present: or, The Best Instructions for Young Women in Useful and Universal Knowledge.* London: 1754. (First published [1753] with title *The Young Woman's Companion: or, The Servant-Maid's Assistant.* The 3rd ed. [1765] has title of 1754 ed., with variant subtitle.)

JOHNSON, REGINALD BRIMLEY, ed. *Bluestocking Letters.* London and New York: 1926.

———. *The Women Novelists.* London: 1918. New York: 1919.

JONES, MARY GWLADYS. *The Charity School Movement; A Study of Eighteenth Century Puritanism in Action.* Cambridge: 1938.

———. *Hannah More.* Cambridge: 1952.

JONES, W. POWELL. "The Romantic Bluestocking: Elizabeth Montagu." *Huntington Library Quarterly* 12 (1948–49): 85–98.

JOURDAIN, MARGARET. *English Interiors in Smaller Houses, from the Restoration to the Regency, 1660–1830.* London and New York: 1923.

KAMM, JOSEPHINE. *Hope Deferred: Girls' Education in English History.* London: 1965.

———. *The Story of Fanny Burney.* London: 1966. New York: 1967.

KAVANAGH, JULIA. *English Women of Letters: Biographical Sketches.* 2 vols. London: 1863. (Copyright ed. Leipzig: 1862.)

KENRICK, WILLIAM. *The Whole Duty of Woman, by a Lady, Written at the Desire of a Noble Lord.* London: 1753.

KOVAČEVIĆ, IVANKA. *Fact into Fiction.* Leicester: 1976.

———, and KANNER, BARBARA. "Blue Books into Novel: The Forgotten Industrial Fiction of Charlotte Elizabeth Tonna." *Nineteenth Century Fiction* 25 (1970): 1952–72.

KRAUSE, J. T. "Changes in English Fertility and Mortality, 1781–1850." *Economic History Review,* 2d series, 11 (1958–59): 52–70.

———. "Some Aspects of Population Change 1690–1790." In *Land, Labour and Population in the Industrial Revolution: Essays Presented to J. D. Chambers,* edited by Eric L Jones and G. E. Mingay, pp. 187–205. London: 1967. New York: 1968.

*The Ladies' Diary for the Year of Our Lord* .... London: 1704–1840. (Annual, title varies.)

*The Ladies Library, Written by a Lady* [Mary Wray?] *and published by Mr.* [Richard] *Steele.* 3 vols. London: 1714.

*The Ladies' Magazine.* Vols. 1–4. London: 18 Nov. 1749–10 Nov. 1753.

*The Ladies Museum.* Vols. 1–5th series, vol. 3. London. 1798–1832. (Two volumes per year. Title varies: 1798–1814, *The Lady's Monthly Museum;* 1815–1828, *The Ladies' Monthly Museum*).

*The Lady's Magazine; or Entertaining Companion for the Fair Sex.* Vols. 1–3rd series, vol. 5. London: 1770–1832.

*The Lady's Magazine; or, Polite Companion for the Fair Sex.* Vols. 1–5. London: 1759–1763. Edited by Oliver Goldsmith.

*The Lady's Museum.* Vols. 1–2, nos. 1–11. London: 1 March 1760–1 Jan. 1761. Edited by Charlotte Lennox and Hugh Kelly.

LAQUEUR, THOMAS W. "Literacy and Social Mobility in the Industrial Revolution in England." *Past and Present* 64 (1974): 96–107.

LA ROCHE, SOPHIE VON. *Sophie in London, 1786; Being the Diary of Sophie v. la Roche.* Translated and introduced by Clare Williams. London: 1933.

LASKI, MARGHARITA. *Jane Austen and Her World.* London and New York: 1969.

LASLETT, PETER. "Size and Structure of the Household in England Over Three Centuries." *Population Studies* 23 (1969): 199–223.

———. *The World We Have Lost.* London and New York: 1965.

———, and HARRISON, JOHN. "Clayworth and Cogenhoe." In *Historical Essays, 1699–1750, presented to David Ogg,* edited by Henry Esmond Bell and R. L. Ollard, pp. 157–84. London and New York: 1963.

———, with WALL, RICHARD, eds. *Household and Family in Past Time.* Cambridge: 1973.

*Laws concerning Masters and Servants ... by a Gentleman of the Inner-Temple.* London: 1767.

*The Laws respecting Women, as They Regard Their Natural Rights, or Their Connections and Conduct.* London: 1777.

LeFANU, ELIZABETH (SHERIDAN). *Betsy Sheridan's Journal; Letters from Sheridan's Sister, 1784–1786, and 1788–1790.* Edited by William LeFanu. New Brunswick, N.J. and London: 1960.

LICHTENBERG, GEORG CHRISTOPH. *Lichtenberg's Visits to England as Described in His Letters and Diaries.* Translated and annotated by Margaret L. Mare and W. H. Quarrell. Oxford: 1938.

LITTLEWOOD, SAMUEL ROBINSON. *Elizabeth Inchbald and Her Circle; The Life Story of a Charming Woman (1753–1821).* London: 1921.

LOCK, F. P. "Astrea's 'Vacant Throne': The Successors of Aphra Behn." In *Woman in the Eighteenth Century and Other Essays,* edited by Paul Fritz and Richard Morton, pp. 25–36. McMaster University Association for Eighteenth-Century Studies 4. Toronto: 1976.

LOCKITT, CHARLES HENRY. *The Relations of French and English Society (1763–1793).* London and New York: 1920.

*The London Magazine; or, Gentleman's Monthly Intelligencer.* Vols. 1–2d series, vol. 4. London: April 1732–June 1785.

LORENCE, BOGNA W. "Parents and Children in Eighteenth-Century Europe." *History of Childhood Quarterly* 2 (1974): 1–30.

LOSCHKY, DAVID J., and Krier, Donald F. "Income and Family Size in Three Eighteenth-Century Lancashire Parishes: A Reconstitution Study." *Journal of Economic History* 29 (1969): 429–48.

LOVEMORE, AUGUSTUS [PSEUD.]. *A Letter from a father to a Son, on His Marriage.* London: 1778.

LUBBOCK, CONSTANCE ANN (HERSCHEL), LADY, ed. *The Herschel Chronicle; The Life-story of William Herschel and His Sister, Caroline Herschel.* Cambridge: 1933.

LUCAS, EDWARD VERRALL. *A Swan and Her Friends.* London: 1907.

LURIA, GINA M., and TAYLER, IRENE. "Gender and Genre: Women in the Literature of the British Romantics." In *What Manner of Woman: Essays in British and American Literature,* edited by Marlene Springer. New York: 1977.

MACAULAY, CATHERINE SAWBRIDGE. *Letters on Education, with Observations on Religious and Metaphysical Subjects. By Catharine Macaulay Graham.* London: 1790. Reprinted in Feminist Controversy in England, 1788–1810, series. New York: 1974.

———. *Observations on the Reflections of the Right Hon. Edmund Burke, on the Revolution in France.* London: 1790.

MCBURNEY, WILLIAM HARLIN. *A Check List of English Prose Fiction. 1700–1739.* Cambridge, Mass.: 1960.

MACCARTHY, BRIDGET G. *The Later Women Novelists. 1744–1818.* Cork, Ire.: 1947.

———. *Women Writers, Their Contribution to the English Novel, 1621–1744.* Cork, Ire.: 1944.

MACGREGOR, MARGARET ELIOT. *Amelia Alderson Opie: Worldling and Friend.* Smith College Studies in Modern Languages, vol. 14, nos. 1–2. Northampton, Mass.: Oct. 1932–Jan. 1933.

MCGREGOR, OLIVER ROSS. *Divorce in England, a Centenary Study.* London: 1957.

MCKEE, WILLIAM. *Elizabeth Inchbald, Novelist.* Washington: 1935.

MCKENDRICK, NEIL. "Home Demand and Economic Growth: A New View of the Role of Women and Children in the Industrial Revolution." In *Historical Perspectives: Studies in English Thought and Society, in Honour of J. H. Plumb,* edited by Neil McKendrick, pp. 152–210. London: 1974.

MCKEOWN, THOMAS, and BROWN, R. G. "Medical Evidence Related to English Population Changes in the Eighteenth Century." *Population Studies* 9 (1955–56): 119–41.

MADAN, MARTIN. *Thelyphthora; or, A Treatise on Female Ruin.* London: 1780–81.

*Man Superior to Woman; or, A Vindication of Man's Natural Right of Sovereign Authority over the Woman. Containing a Plain Confutation of the Fallacious Arguments of Sophia, in Her Late Treatise Intitled, Woman Not Inferior to Man ... by a Gentleman.* London: 1739.

MANDEVILLE, BERNARD. *The Fable of the Bees; or, Private Vices, Publick Benefits. The 2nd Ed., Enl. with Many Additions. As Also an Essay on Charity and Charity-Schools.* London: 1723. (First edition, 1714.)

———. *The Virgin Unmask'd; or, Female Dialogues ... on Love, Marriage....* London: 1709.

MANLEY, SEON, and BELCHER, SUSAN. *O Those Extraordinary Women! Or the Joys of Literary Lib.* Philadephia: 1972.

MANN, J. DE L. "Clothiers and Weavers in Wiltshire during the Eighteenth

Century." In *Studies in the Industrial Revolution Presented to T. S. Ashton*, edited by L. S. Presnell, pp. 66–96. London: 1960.

MANTELL, T. *Short Directions for the Management of Infants*. London: 1787.

MANVELL, ROGER. *Sarah Siddons: Portrait of an Actress*. London: 1970. New York: 1971.

MARSHALL, DOROTHY. "The Domestic Servants of the Eighteenth Century." *Economica* 9 (1929): 15–40.

————. *The English Poor in the Eighteenth Century; A Study in Social and Administrative History*. London: 1926.

"MARY ASTELL: A Seventeenth Century Advocate for Women." *Westminster Review* 149 (Jan.–June 1898): 440–49.

MASEFIELD, MURIEL AGNES. *Women Novelists from Fanny Burney to George Eliot*. London: 1934.

MASSIE, JOSEPH. *A Plan for the Establishment of Charity-Houses for Exposed or Deserted Women and Girls, and for Penitent Prostitutes. Observations concerning the Foundling-Hospital Shewing the Ill Consequences of Giving Public Support Thereto. Considerations Relating to the Poor and Poor's-Laws of England. Also, a New System of Policy . . . for Relieving the Poor*. London: 1758.

*The Matrimonial Magazine, or Monthly Anecdotes of Love and Marriage*. Vol. 1. London: Jan.–June 1775. (Merged into *The Westminster Magazine*.)

MAURICEAU, FRANÇOIS. *The Diseases of Women with Child, and in Childbed*. Translated by Hugh Chamberlen. 2d ed. London: 1683.

MAYER, GERTRUDE TOWNSHEND. *Women of Letters*. 2 vols. London: 1894.

MAYHEW, HENRY. *London Labour and the London Poor*. 2 vols. London and New York: 1851. (2d ed. in 4 vols. London: 1861–62.)

MEYER, GERALD DENNIS. *The Scientific Lady in England, 1650–1760: An Account of Her Rise, with Emphasis on the Major Roles of the Telescope and Microscope*. Berkeley, Calif.: 1955.

*The Midwife: or, Old Woman's Magazine*. Vols. 1–3. London: 1751–53.

MILLER, PETER JOHN. "Eighteenth Century Periodicals for Women." *History of Education Quarterly* 11 (1971): 279–86.

————. "Women's Education, 'Self-Improvement' and Social Mobility—A Late Eighteenth Century Debate." *British Journal of Education Studies* 20 (1972): 302–14.

MINGAY, G. E. *English Landed Society in the Eighteenth Century*. London: 1963.

MOERS, ELLEN. "Vindicating Mary Wollstonecraft." *New York Review of Books* 23 (1976): 38–42.

MOLIN, SVEN ERIC. "Dr. Johnson on Marriage, Chastity, and Fidelity." *Eighteenth Century Life* 1 (1974): 15–18.

MONTAGU, ELIZABETH. *The Letters of Mrs. Elizabeth Montagu, with Some of the Letters of Her Correspondents. Published by Matthew Montagu*. 4 vols. London: 1809–13.

MONTAGU, LADY MARY (PIERREPONT) WORTLEY. *The Complete Letters of Lady Mary Wortley Montagu*. Edited by Robert Halsband. 3 vols. Oxford: 1965–67.

————. *The Nonsense of Common-sense, 1737–1738*. Edited by Robert Halsband. 1947. Reprint. New York: 1970.

MONTAGUE, EDWINE, and MARTZ, LOUIS L. "Fanny Burney's Evelina." In *The Age of Johnson; Essays Presented to Chauncey Brewster Tinker*, edited by F. W. Hilles, pp. 171–82. New Haven, Conn.: 1949.

MOORE, EDWARD. *Fables for the Female Sex*. London: 1744.

MOORE, HENRY. *The Life of Mrs. Mary Fletcher, Consort and Relict of the Rev. John Fletcher*. London and New York: 1818.

MORE, HANNAH. *The Letters of Hannah More*. Edited by R. Brimley Johnson. London: 1925; New York: 1926.

———. *Strictures on the Modern System of Female Education. With a View of the Principles and Conduct Prevalent among Women of Rank and Fortune*. 2 vols. London: 1799. Reprinted in Feminist Controversy in England, 1788–1810, series. New York: 1974.

MOSS, WILLIAM. *An Essay on the Management and Nursing of Children in the Earlier Periods of Infancy*. London: 1781.

———. *An Essay on the Management, Nursing, and Diseases of Children*, London: 1794. (Retitled edition of *An Essay on the Mangement and Nursing of Children*.)

MOYNIHAN, ROBERT D. "Clarissa and the Enlightened Woman as Literary Heroine." *Journal of the History of Ideas* 36 (1975): 159–66.

NAPIER, LADY SARAH (LENNOX) BUNBURY. *The Life and Letters of Lady Sarah Lennox, 1745–1826*. 2 vols. London and New York: 1901.

NEEDHAM, GWENDOLYN B. "Mrs. Manley: An Eighteenth-Century Wife of Bath." *Huntington Library Quarterly* 24 (1950–51): 259–84.

———. "Mary de la Riviere Manley, Tory Defender." *Huntington Library Quarterly* 12 (1948–49): 253–88.

NELSON, JAMES. *An Essay on the Government of Children, under Three General Heads: viz. Health, Manners and Education*. London: 1753.

NEUBERG, VICTOR E. *Popular Education in Eighteenth Century England*. London: 1971.

*The New Cambridge Bibliography of English Literature*, vol. 2: *1660–1800*. Edited by George Watson. Cambridge: 1971.

*The New Lady's Magazine; or, Polite, and Entertaining Companion for the Fair Sex*. London: Feb. 1786–May 1797.

OGILVIE, MARILYN BAILEY. "Caroline Herschel's Contributions to Astronomy." *Annals of Science* 32 (1975): 149–61.

*The Old Maid ... by Mary Singleton, Spinster* [pseud.] Nos. 1–37. London: 15 Nov. 1755–24 July 1756. (Weekly, by Frances Moore Brooke.)

O'MALLEY, IDA BEATRICE. *Women in Subjection; A Study of the Lives of Englishwomen before 1832*. London: 1933.

OPIE, AMELIA ALDERSON. *Adeline Mobray; or, The Mother and Daughter*. 2d ed. London: 1805. Reprinted in Feminist Controversy in England, 1788–1810, series. 3 vols. New York: 1974.

OSBORN, SARAH (BYNG). *Letters of Sarah Byng Osborn, 1721–1773*. Edited by John McClelland. Palo Alto, Calif.: 1930.

PARREAUX, ANDRÉ. *Daily Life in England in the Reign of George III*. Translated by Carola Congreve. London: 1969.

PEARCE, CHARLES E. *"Polly Peachum"; Being the Story of Lavinia Fenton (Duchess of Bolton) and "The Beggar's Opera"*. London and New York: 1913.

PEMBROKE, HENRY HERBERT, 10TH EARL OF. *Pembroke Papers (1780–1794); Letters and Diaries of Henry, Tenth Earl of Pembroke and His Circle*. Edited by Lord Herbert. London: 1950.

PENN, JAMES. *Remarks on Thelyphthora*. London: 1781.

PEPYS, WILLIAM WELLER. *A Later Pepys: The Correspondence of Sir W[illiam]. W[eller]. Pepys, Bart., Master in Chancery, 1758–1825, with Mrs. Chapone, Mrs. Hartley, Mrs. Montagu, Hannah More, William Franks, Sir James Macdonald, Major*

*Rennell, Sir Nathaniel Wraxhall, and Others.* Edited by Alice C. C. Gaussen. 2 vols. London and New York: 1904.

PHILLIPS, MARGARET, and TOMKINSON, WILLIAM SHIRLEY. *English Women in Life and Letters.* Oxford and New York: 1926.

PHILLIPS, TERESIA CONSTANTIA. *A Letter Humbly Address'd to the Right Honourable, the Earl of Chesterfield.* London: 1750.

PILGRIM, CONSTANCE. *Dear Jane: A Biographical Study of Jane Austen.* London: 1971.

PILKINGTON, LAETITIA. *Memoirs of Mrs. Laetitia Pilkington, 1712–1750, Written by Herself.* Introduction by Iris Barry. London: 1928. (First printed 1748–54.)

PINCHBECK, IVY. *Women Workers and the Industrial Revolution, 1750–1850.* London and New York: 1930.

———, and Hewitt, Margaret. *Children in English Society.* 2 vols. London: 1969, 1973.

PIOZZI, HESTER LYNCH THRALE. *A Series of Letters on Courtship and Marriage.* Springfield: 179-?

———. *Thraliana; The Diary of Mrs. Hester Lynch Thrale (Later Mrs. Piozzi) 1776–1809.* Edited by Katharine C. Balderston. 2 vols. Oxford: 1942.

PLAISANT, MICHÈLE; DENIZOT, PAUL; MOREUX, FRANÇOISE. *Aspects du féminisme en Angleterre au 18e siècle.* Paris: 1972.

*The Pleasures of a Single Life, or, The Miseries of Matrimony.* London: 1701.

PLUMB, JOHN HAROLD. *The Growth of Political Stability in England: 1675–1725.* London: 1967. (U.S. ed. has title: *The origins of Political Stability in England, 1675–1725.* Boston: 1967.)

———. "The New World of Children in Eighteenth Century England." *Past and Present* 67 (May 1975): 64–95.

———. "Reason and Unreason in the Eighteenth Century English Experience." In *In the Light of History*, pp. 3–24. London: 1972. Boston: 1973.

———. "The Woman's Burden." In *In the Light of History*, pp. 140–46. London: 1972. Boston: 1973.

POLLIN, BURTON R. "Mary Hays on Woman's Rights in the Monthly Magazine." *Etudes Anglaises* 24 (1971): 271–82.

POLWHELE, RICHARD. *The Unsex'd Females: A Poem, Addressed to the Author of The Pursuits of Literature.* London: 1798. Reprinted in Feminist Controversy in England, 1788–1810, series, as *The Unsex'd Females* [by] *Richard Polwhele. The Female Advocate; or, An Attempt to Recover the Rights of Women from Male Usurpation* [by] *Mary Ann Radcliffe.* New York: 1974.

POPE, ALEXANDER. *Of the Characters of Women; An Epistle to a Lady.* London: 1735.

POULAIN DE LA BARRE, FRANÇOIS. *The Woman as Good as the Man: or, The Equality of Both Sexes.* Translated by A. L. London: 1677.

POWYS, CAROLINE (Girle). *Passages from the Diaries of Mrs. Philip Lybbe Powys ... 1756–1808.* Edited by Emily J. Climenson. London and New York: 1899.

PROCHASKA, F. K. "Women in English Philanthropy 1790–1830." *International Review of Social History* 19 (1974): 426–45.

PUREFOY, HENRY, and PUREFOY, ELIZABETH. *Purefoy Letters, 1735–1753.* Edited by G. Eland. 2 vols. London: 1931.

QUINLAN, MAURICE JAMES. *Victorian Prelude, a History of English Manners, 1700–1830.* 1941. Reprint. Hamden, Conn.: 1965.

RADCLIFFE, MARY ANN. *The Female Advocate; or, An Attempt to Recover the Rights of*

*Women from Male Usurpation*. London: 1799. Reprinted in Feminist Controversy in England, 1788–1810. Series. (See Polwhele.) New York: 1974.

RAFFALD, ELIZABETH WHITAKER. *The Experienced House-Keeper, for the Use and Ease of Ladies*. Manchester: 1769. (Numerous additional eds. to 1818, with slight variations in title.)

*The Rambler*. Vols. 1–8, nos. 1–208. London: 20 March 1750–17 March 1752. Edited by Samuel Johnson.

RAMSEY, STANLEY CHURCHILL, and HARVEY, J. D. M. *Small Georgian Houses and Their Details, 1750–1820*. London: 1972.

RAZZELL, P. E. "Population Change in Eighteenth Century England. A Reinterpretation." *Economic History Review*, 2d series 18 (1965): 312–32.

REYNOLDS, MYRA. *The Learned Lady in England, 1650–1760*. Boston: 1920.

RICHARDS, ERIC. "Women in the British Economy since about 1700: An Interpretation." *History* 59 (1974): 337–57.

RICHARDSON, ALBERT EDWARD, and EBERLEIN, H. DONALDSON. *The Smaller English House of the Later Renaissance, 1660–1830*. London and New York: 1925.

RITCHIE, ANNE ISABELLA. *A Book of Sibyls*. London, New York, and Leipzing. 1883.

ROBERTS, WILLIAM. *Memoirs of the Life and Correspondence of Mrs. Hannah More*. 2d ed. 4 vols. London: 1834. 2 vols. New York: 1834.

ROBINSON, MARY. *Walsingham: or, The Pupil of Nature. A Domestic Story*. London: 1797. Reprinted in Feminist Controversy in England, 1788–1810, series. 4 vols. New York: 1974.

ROE, FREDERIC GORDON. *The Georgian Child*. London: 1961.

ROGAL, SAMUEL. "John Wesley's Women." *Eighteenth Century Life* 1 (1974): 7–10.

ROGERS, KATHERINE. "The Feminism of Daniel Defoe." In *Woman in the Eighteenth Century and Other Essays*, edited by Paul Fritz and Richard Morton, pp. 3–24. McMaster University Association for Eighteenth Century Studies 4. Toronto: 1976.

ROSCOE, EDWARD STANLEY. *The English Scene in the Eighteenth Century*. London and New York: 1912.

ROWBOTHAM, SHEILA. *Hidden from History: 300 Years of Women's Oppression and the Fight aginst It*. London: 1973. (American eds. have title: *Hidden from History: Rediscovering Women in History from the 17th Century to the Present*.) New York: 1974, paperback edition, New York: 1976.

*The Royal Female Magazine: or. The Ladies General Repository of Pleasure and Improvement*. Vols. 1–2. London: 1760.

RUETHER, ROSEMARY RADFORD, ed. *Religion and Sexism; Images of Woman in the Jewish and Christian Traditions*. New York: 1974.

RUGGLES, THOMAS. *The History of the Poor*. 2 vols. London: 1793–94.

RYDER, DUDLEY. *The Diary of Dudley Ryder, 1715–1716*. Edited by William Matthews. London: 1939.

SALMON, THOMAS. *A Critical Essay concerning Marriage ... to Which Is Added, an Historical Account of the Marriage Rites and Ceremonies of the Greeks and Romans, and Our Saxon Ancestors, and of Most Nations of the World at This Day. By a Gentleman*. London: 1724.

———. *An Essay concerning Marriage* [subtitle as first ed. listed above] ... *at This Day*. 2nd ed. By Mr. Salmon. London: 1724.

SANDERSON, MICHAEL. "Literacy and Social Mobility in the Industrial Revolution in England." *Past and Present* 56 (August 1972): 75–104.

SCHNORRENBERG, BARBARA BRANDON. "Education for Women in Eighteenth Century England: An Annotated Bibliography." *Women and Literature* 4 (1976): 49–55.

SCOTT, MARY. *The Female Advocate; a Poem occasioned by Reading Mr. Duncombe's Feminead.* London: 1774.

SCOTT, WALTER SIDNEY. *The Bluestocking Ladies.* London: 1947.

SÉJOURNÉ, PHILIPPE. *Aspects généraux du roman féminin en Angleterre de 1740–1800.* Aix-en-Provence: 1966.

———. *The Mystery of Charlotte Lennox, First Novelist of Colonial America (1727?–1804).* Aix-en-Provence: 1967.

SEWARD, ANNA. *The Swan of Lichfield; Being a Selection from the Correspondence of Anna Seward.* Edited by Hesketh Pearson. London: 1936.

SHERBURN, GEORGE. "Fielding's *Amelia*: An Interpretation." *English Literary History* 3 (1936): 1–14.

SHERSON, ERROL HENRY STUART. *The Lively Lady Townshend and Her Friends, An Effort to Set Forth the Doings and Surroundings of a Typical Lady of Quality of the Eighteenth Century.* London: 1926.

SIBBALD, SUSAN. *The Memoirs of Susan Sibbald (1783–1812).* Edited by Francis Paget Hett. London: 1926.

SIDGWICK, JOHN BENSON. *William Herschel, Explorer of the Heavens.* London: 1953.

SIMON, IRÈNE. "Le Roman Féminin en Angleterre au XVIIIe Siècle." *Etudes Anglaises* 27 (1974): 205–13.

SMALL, MIRIAM ROSSITER. *Charlotte Ramsay Lennox, an Eighteenth Century Lady of Letters.* New Haven, Conn.: 1935.

SMELLIE, WILLIAM. *A Treatise on the Theory and Practice of Midwifery.* 3 vols. London: 1752–64.

SMELSER, NEIL J. *Social Change in the Industrial Revolution.* London, Toronto, Chicago: 1959.

SMITH, CHARLOTTE TURNER. *Desmond: A Novel.* 3 vols. London: 1792. Reprinted in Feminist Controversy in England, 1788–1810, series. 3 vols. New York: 1974.

———. *The Young Philosopher; A Novel.* 4 vols. London: 1798. Reprinted in Feminist Controversy in England, 1788–1810, series. 4 vols. New York: 1974.

SMITH, E. *The Compleat Housewife; or, Accomplished Gentlewoman's Companion.* 3rd ed. London: 1729.

SMITH, FLORENCE MARY. *Mary Astell.* New York: 1916.

SMITH, HUGH. *Letters to Married Women.* London: 1767.

———. *The Family Physician.* 5th ed. London: 1770?

SMITH, WILLIAM. *A Sure Guide in Sickness and Health, in the Choice of Food, and Use of Medicine.* London: 1776.

SNYDER, HENRY L. "New Light on Mrs. Manley?" *Philological Quarterly* 52 (1973): 767–70.

SOGNER, SØLVI. "Aspects of the Demographic Situation in Seventeen Parishes in Shropshire 1711–60. An Exercise Based on Parish Registers." *Population Studies* 17 (1963–64): 126–46.

SOPHIA [PSEUD.] *Woman Not Inferior to Man: or, A Short and Modest Vindication of the Natural Right of the Fair Sex to A Perfect Equality of Power, Dignity and Esteem, with the Men.* London: 1739. Reprint 174–?, 1751, in *Beauty's Triumph*, q.v.

———. *Woman's Superior Excellence over Man; or A Reply to the Author of a Late Treatise,*

*Entitled Man Superior to Woman.* London: 1740. Reprint. 174-?, 1751, in *Beauty's Triumph*, q.v.

SPACKS, PATRICIA ANN (MEYER). "Ev'ry Woman Is at Heart a Rake." *Eighteenth Century Studies* 8 (1974): 27–46.

———. *Imagining a Self: Autobiography and Novel in 18th Century England.* Cambridge, Mass.: 1976.

———. "Scrapbook of a Self: Mrs. Piozzi's Late Journals." *Harvard Library Bulletin* 18 (1970): 221–47.

*The Spectator.* Vols. 1–8. London: 1 March 1711–7 Dec. 1712. (Suspended until) 17 June 1714–20 Dec. 1714. Edited by Sir Richard Steele, Joseph Addison, et al.

SPRINT, JOHN. *The Bride-Woman's Counseller, Being a Sermon Preach'd at a Wedding.* London: 1699?

STANLEY, MARIA JOSEPHA. *The Girlhood of Maria Josepha Holroyd. Recorded in Letters of a Hundred Years Ago: from 1776 to 1796.* Edited by J. H. Adeane. London and New York: 1896.

STEARNS, BERTHA MONICA. "Early English Periodicals for Ladies (1700–1760)." *PMLA* 48 (1933): 38–60.

———. "The First English Periodical for Women." *Modern Philology* 28 (1930): 45–59.

STEBBINS, LUCY (POATE). *London Ladies; True Tales of the Eighteenth Century.* New York: 1952.

STEEVES, HARRISON ROSS. *Before Jane Austen.* New York: 1965. London: 1966.

STENTON, DORIS MARY. *The English Woman in History.* London and New York: 1957. Reprint. New York: 1977.

STILL, GEORGE FREDERIC. *The History of Paediatrics; ... to the End of the XVIIIth Century.* London: 1931.

STOKES, HUGH. *The Devonshire House Circle.* London: 1917.

STORR, MARTHE SEVEN. *Mary Wollstonecraft et le mouvement féministe dans la littérature anglaise.* Paris: 1932.

STUART, DOROTHY MARGARET. *The English Abigail.* London 1946.

SUTHERLAND, JAMES R. "The Progress of Error: Mrs. Centlivre and the Biographers." *Review of English Studies* 18 (1942): 167–82.

SWIFT, JONATHAN. "A Letter to a Very Young Lady on Her Marriage." In *The Works of Dr. Jonathan Swift ... in Twelve Volumes*, 4: 49–62. London: 1766.

TAYLOR, GORDON RATTRAY. *The Angel Makers; A Study in the Psychological Origins of Historical Changes, 1750–1850.* Rev. ed. London: 1973. New York: 1974.

———. *Sex in History.* London: 1953. New York: 1954.

*The Tea-Table.* Nos. 1–36. London: 21 Feb.–22 June 1724.

THEOBALD, JOHN. *The Young Wife's Guide, in the Management of Her Children. Containing, Every Thing Necessary to be Known Relative to the Nursing of Children, from the Time of Their Birth, to the Age of Seven.* London: 1764.

THOMAS, ANTOINE LÉONARD. *Essay on the Character, Manners, and Genius of Women in Different Ages. Enl. from the French ... by Mr. Russell.* London: 1773. (First French ed., Paris: 1772)

THOMAS, DAVID. "The Social Origins of Marriage Partners in the British Peerage in the Eighteenth and Nineteenth Centuries." *Population Studies* 26 (1972): 99–111.

THOMAS, KEITH. "The Double Standard." *Journal of the History of Ideas* 20 (1959): 195–216.

THOMPSON, E. P. "The Moral Economy of the English Crowd in the Eighteenth Century." *Past and Present* 50 (1971): 76–136.

THOMSON, GLADYS SCOTT. *The Russells in Bloomsbury, 1669–1771.* London: 1940.

TICKNER, FREDERICK WINDHAM. *Women in English Economic History.* London and New York: 1923.

TILLOTSON, JOHN. *Six Sermons ... of Stedfastness in Religion; Family Religion; Education of Children; the Advantages of an Early Piety.* London: 1694.

TILLY, LOUISE A.; SCOTT, JOAN W.; COHEN, MIRIAM. "Woman's Work and European Fertility Patterns." *Journal of Interdisciplinary History* 6 (1976): 447–76.

TINKER, CHAUNCEY BREWSTER. *The Salon and English Letters; Chapters on the Interrelations of Literature and Society in the Age of Johnson.* New York: 1915.

TOBLER, CLARA. *Mrs. Elizabeth Inchbald, eine vergessene englische bühnendichterin und romanschriftstellerin des 18. jahrhunderts.* Berlin: 1910.

TODD, JANET M. "The Biographies of Mary Wollstonecraft: Review Essay." *Signs. Journal of Women in Culture and Society.* 1 (1976): 721–34.

TOMPKINS, JOYCE MARJORIE SANXTER. *The Polite Marriage.* Cambridge: 1938.

———. *The Popular Novel in England, 1770–1800.* 1932. Reprint. Lincoln, Neb.: 1961.

TOWERS, AUGUSTUS R. "*Amelia* and the State of Martrimony." *Review of English Studies,* n.s. 5 (1954): 144–57.

TRANTER, N. L. "Population and Social Structure in a Bedfordshire Parish: The Cardington Listing of Inhabitants, 1782." *Population Studies* 21 (1967): 261–82.

*A Treatise of Feme Coverts; or, The Lady's Law.* London: 1732.

TRIMMER, SARAH. *The Oeconomy of Charity; or, An Address to Ladies, Adapted to the Present State of Charitable Institutions in England: with a Particular View to the Cultivation of Religious Principles among the Lower Orders of People.* 2 vols. London: 1801.

———. *Reflections upon the Education of Children in Charity Schools.* London: 1792.

———. *Some Account of the Life and Writings of Mrs. Trimmer with Original letters, and Meditations and Prayers, Selected from Her Journal.* 2 vols. London: 1814.

TRUELOVE, FRANCIS [PSEUD.] *The Comforts of Matrimony; Exemplified in the Memorable Case and Trial, Lately Had upon and Action Brought ... for Criminal Conversation with the Plaintiff's Wife.* 6th ed. London: 1739.

UNDERWOOD, MICHAEL. *A Treatise on the Disorders of Childhood and Management of Infants from the Birth; Adapted to Domestic Use.* 3 vols. London: 1797.

UPHAM, A. H. "English Femmes Savantes at the End of the Seventeenth Century." *Journal of English and German Philology* 12 (1913): 262–76.

UTTER, ROBERT PALFREY, and NEEDHAM, GWENDOLYN BRIDGES. *Pamela's Daughters.* New York: 1936.

VERNEY, MARGARET MARIA, lady, ed. *Verney Letters of the Eighteenth Century.* 2 vols. London: 1930.

VERRAL, WILLIAM. *A Complete System of Cookery.* London: 1759.

WAKEFIELD, PRISCILLA BELL. *Reflections on the Present Condition of the Female Sex.* London: 1798. Reprinted in Feminist Controversy in England, 1788–1810, series. New York: 1974.

WALLAS, ADA. *Before the Bluestockings.* London: 1929.

WATT, IAN. *The Rise of the Novel: Studies in Defoe, Richardson and Fielding.* Berkeley, Calif. and London: 1957.

WEARMOUTH, ROBERT FEATHERSTONE. *Methodism and the Common People of the Eighteenth Century.* London: 1945.

WENDT, ALAN. "The Naked Virtue of Amelia." *English Literary History* 27 (1960): 137–48.

WESLEY, JOHN. *The Journal of the Rev. John Wesley.* Edited by Nehemiah Curnock. London: 1909–16.

———. *Sermons on Several Occasions.* Edited by Thomas Jackson. 2 vols. London: 1825.

WESLEY, SAMUEL, JR. *The Battle of the Sexes: A Poem.* 2d ed. London: 1725.

WEST, JANE. *Letters to a Young Lady, in Which the Duties and Character of Women are Considered, Chiefly with a Reference to Prevailing Opinions.* 2d ed. 3 vols. London: 1806. Reprinted in Feminist Controversy in England, 1788–1810, series. New York: 1974.

WHATMAN, SUSANNA. *The Housekeeping Book of Susanna Whatman, 1776–1800.* Edited by Thomas Balston. London: 1956.

WHEELER, ETHEL ROLT. *Famous Blue-stockings.* London and New York: 1910.

WHICHER, GEORGE FRISBIE. *The Life and Romances of Mrs. Eliza Haywood.* New York: 1915.

WHITE, CYNTHIA LESLIE. *Women's Magazines, 1693–1968.* London: 1970.

WHITFIELD, GEORGE. *The Works of the Reverend G[eorge]. W[hitfield].* 6 vols. London: 1771–72.

WHITMORE, CLARA HELEN. *Woman's Work in English Fiction, from the Restoration to the Mid-Victorian Period.* New York and London: 1910.

WILKINSON, ROBERT. *The Merchant Royall. A Sermon.* London: 1607. (Also printed in *Conjugal Duty: Set forth in a Collection of Ingenious and Delightful Wedding-Sermons.* 2 parts. London: 1732, 1736.)

WILLIAMS, HELEN MARIA. *Julia, a Novel; Interspersed with . . . Poetical Pieces.* 2 vols. London: 1790. Reprinted in Feminist Controversy in England, 1788–1810, series. 2 vols. New York: 1974.

WILLIAMS, MURIEL BRITTAIN. *Marriage: Fielding's Mirror of Morality.* University, Ala.: 1973.

WILLIFORD, MIRIAM. "Bentham on the Rights of Women." *Journal of the History of Ideas* 36 (1976): 167–76.

WILSON, MONA. *These Were Muses.* London: 1924.

WITHEY, LYNNE E. "Catharine Macaulay and the Uses of History: Ancient Rights, Perfectionism, and Propaganda." *Journal of British Studies* 16 (1976): 59–83.

WOLLSTONECRAFT, MARY. *Mary; A Fiction.* London: 1788. Reprinted in Feminist Controversy in England, 1788–1810, series. New York: 1974.

———. *Thoughts on the Education of Daughters: with Reflections on Female Conduct, in the More Important Duties of Life.* London: 1787. Reprinted in Feminist Controversy in England, 1788–1810, Series. New York: 1974.

———. *A Vindication of the Rights of Woman, with Strictures on Political and Moral Subjects.* London: 1792. Reprinted in many editions, including Feminist Controversy in England, 1788–1810, series. New York: 1974.

WRIGLEY, E. A. "Family Limitation in Preindustrial England." *Economic History Review,* 2d series, 19 (1966): 82–109.

WYNDHAM, MAUD MARY. *Chronicles of the Eighteenth Century, Founded on the Correspondence of Sir Thomas Lyttelton and His Family.* 2 vols. London: 1924.

# The Discovery of Women
# In Eighteenth-Century
# English Political Life

KARL VON DEN STEINEN

> Women signify nothing unless they are the mistress of a first minister, which I would not be if I were young; and I think there are few if any women that have understanding or partiality enough to serve well those that they really wish to serve.
>
> —Sarah, Duchess of Marlborough[1]

The single most essential truth about women's political influence and involvement in eighteenth-century England is that their political activity must nearly always be measured through the achievements or failures of men. In an age when even universal manhood suffrage constituted an unthinkably radical objective, the politically inclined woman had no choice but to influence the conduct of men who were directly involved in politics: monarchs, ministers, members of Parliament, agents, and voters. The study of women's role in eighteenth-century political life must therefore be conducted at one remove: a woman's political influence must be measured by the actions of the men with whom she associated. The proof of influence thus becomes difficult, as few men, then or now, willingly acknowledged the responsibility of wives, mothers, mistresses, or female friends for their own political conduct. The sources of political, social, and economic history for the period reflect this very clearly. The researcher in quest of the women's role must be prepared to sift large bodies of printed and manuscript material to find the frequently circumstantial bits of evidence which reveal the nature of women's political involvement in the period.

The women in eighteenth-century English political life may be discovered at several levels of activity: at court, near Parliament and in Westminster, in local proceedings and elections, and outside the mainstream of Parliamentary political activities. The vast majority of the printed material understandably deals with those women who through birth, marriage, opportunity, inclination, and ability exercised substantial political influence. At court, the figures of Queen Anne, Sarah, duchess of Marlborough, and Queen Caroline dominate the available materials. Those involved near Parliament and in Westminster—those who became avid observers of and dabblers in politics. but who largely lacked power and influence through no fault of their own—generated a sizable, if often romanticized, literature which contributes more to social and literary history than to political history. The evidence of involvement at the local level and outside the parliamentary mainstream in an age lacking even universal manhood suffrage is rarely direct. Thus the most essential task remaining is the careful sifting of published materials and manuscripts for the evidence of women's influence and involvement in political life and elections.[2]

Only a few figures exercised significant influence at court. Of these, only Queen Anne, who ruled in her own right, participated directly in politics. The bulk of her political involvement through much of her reign came, however, under the guidance of Sarah, duchess of Marlborough, the epitome of the politically powerful woman of the eighteenth century. The duke of Marlborough's period of favor at court and power in government is the measure of Sarah's influence on Anne's politics. Sarah's involvement, however, rested upon the conduct of others, rather than direct action, and her tenure as Anne's personal confidante and political advisor proved woefully fragile in the end. While Anne may be spoken of as achieving power through birth and opportunity, Sarah's talent, marriage, and inclination sustained her only as long as the opportunity provided by her relationship with Anne remained intact.[3] Once forced away from court, Sarah retained a lively interest in politics and, after Marlborough's death, she did exercise local influence in her capacity as a major landed magnate.

Sarah's demise by no means assured her successor in Anne's favor, Abigail Hill Masham, of substantial political influence with the queen. Though contemporaries viewed Masham as an effective agent at court for

Robert Harley, recent scholarship has minimized her actual influence. Her greatest value to the queen and to Harley alike consisted of her service as an unofficial messenger between the two when Harley lacked office and the official access to the queen it provided. Neither figure saw Masham as a major force, and the queen bestowed only limited favor and position upon her. The minimal contact between Masham and Harley during his ministry from 1710 to 1713 supports the thesis that she provided a channel of communication only when a formal line did not exist. During the early part of Harley's ministry, the duchess of Somerset, who succeeded Sarah as groom of the stole and first lady of the bedchamber, exercised greater political influence on the queen than did Masham, who eventually deserted Harley for Bolingbroke in the hope of sparing her ailing queen further anguish.[4]

The literature surrounding Anne and Sarah is extensive and, in many instances, superficial. David Green's recent biographies of both figures provide a suitable starting point for the reader. His works have received mixed reviews, but contribute to our understanding of both women because of his access to the manuscripts at Blenheim. A great deal can also be gathered from Sarah's own writings, and from the standard Winston Churchill biography of the duke of Marlborough, which reveals Sarah's devotion to and furtherance of her husband's political objectives.[5]

The Hanoverian succession returned to England the issue of mistresses' influence upon monarchs, as well as upon ministers and lesser men. While a man might have a mistress with little fear of politically compromising scandal in the eighteenth century, little concrete evidence of mistresses actually exercising political influence over their men has yet appeared. In the cases of highly placed favorites, as with royal mistresses, politicians could and did seek to cultivate them for their own advantage. J. M. Beattie's work on the court of George I vividly describes the efforts of Stanhope, Sunderland, and Carteret to cultivate the duchess of Kendall, and of Walpole and Townshend to counter this. R. M. Hatton, whose biography of George I will be most welcome, has described George's relations with his women and has persuasively argued that Baroness Kielmannsegg was George's half-sister and therefore probably not his mistress. The culmination of these efforts, however, lies in Walpole's realization that influencing George II through Queen Caroline offered a far surer path.[6]

Caroline of Anspach, who served as intermediary between Sir Robert Walpole and George II, exercised extraordinary political influence for her time. Her court as princess of Wales is amply described in Lady Cowper's *Diaries*, and the proceedings at court during her political relationship with Walpole appear in Lady Sundon's *Memoirs* and Lady Suffolk's *Letters*.

Caroline's dominance of the scene is revealed by her virtual selection, approval, and keeping of Lady Suffolk as her husband's politically harmless mistress. Lady Sundon, as Caroline's mistress of the robes, influenced Caroline more than did Lady Suffolk. The works on Lord Hervey by Romney Sedgwick and Robert Halsband particularly illuminate Caroline's political role. Typically, the vast majority of the material deals with matters of court intrigue, influence, patronage, and privilege—all essential aspects of the eighteenth-century political scene. From Walpole's viewpoint, the utility of the Caroline relationship is best illustrated in Plumb's biography of the first minster.[7]

Caroline's position as princess of Wales and later as queen did not, however, assure her of political involvement and influence. She inclined in that direction and possessed sufficient determination, intelligence, and ability to follow her inclination. That the positions themselves conferred no more than opportunity is confirmed by the minimal political involvement of George III's mother, Augusta, princess of Wales, and the deliberate avoidance of political activity by George III's queen, Charlotte. Though contemporaries imagined Augusta's menacing influence on young George's character and political outlook, John Brooke, in his recent *King George III*, has convincingly described her as politically subservient to her husband, Frederick, Prince of Wales, during his lifetime, and politically dependent upon the earl of Bute's advice after the prince's death. Upon George III's accession, she retired and exercised virtually no political influence at all. In Caroline's case, she deliberately abjured political activity and deplored factional strife. Olwen Hedley's recent biography of Charlotte at once shows the court intrigue around her and Charlotte's deliberate aloofness from it.[8]

The significance of the eighteenth-century English court lay not only in personal access to high places and political influence upon the monarch per se, but in the opportunity to gain personally and politically advantageous patronage. From court to constituency, patronage was a major facet of eighteenth-century political, social, and economic life. As such, it involved women as well as men. The queen's court offered ample openings for politically motivated patronage, and the placement of key supporters in such positions of royal favor often measured the stature of a given politician. Inability to deliver such positions, by the same token, indicated political weakness. The significance of court positions became even greater in the case of so politically active a queen as Caroline, though even a figure so dedicated to avoidance of factional intrigue as Charlotte could never totally escape issues of patronage and placement. Given the frequently bitter relationships between the Hanoverian kings and Princes of Wales, women often became the pawns of political and royal familial struggles.

No less characteristic of the working of patronage in the age, however, was the plight of one Mrs. Putland, whose husband's vote was jeopardized for Newcastle's interest in Sussex in 1733 because she was

> afraid of loosing [sic.] the advantage of teaching a charity school which old Snooke had the management of during his lifetime and with which I complimented his son after his decease; and now he requites me very handsomely, by using it to compel the man to vote against his inclination.[9]

The whole area of patronage frequently touched women at all social levels; whether in terms of positions for wives, daughters, and friends of key followers, of locally administered favors to widows of deceased soldiers and sailors, or of custom for tradesmen and tradeswomen, such delivery of patronage or failure to deliver it might tell much about the relative political strengths and viabilities of such interests. Though the most politically significant patronage opportunities often lay at court, patronage as an institution must be understood to permeate all levels of English political, social, and economic life in this period.[10]

The involvement of eighteenth-century English women in and near Parliament and in the volatile constituencies surrounding that institution is more difficult to assess than women's influence at court. Many women bore close enough relationships to politically significant figures of the day to have the opportunity to exercise influence. Wives, mothers, sisters, mistresses, and friends might all affect political conduct, but few did so with any demonstrable consistency. In most instances, women active in other fields became politically involved for short periods, only later to withdraw forever from that arena. Others passively supported their men, or ignored politics entirely. None achieved very much for very long.

In the first half of the century, the figure of Lady Mary Wortley Montagu stood above the rest. Lady Mary, though known primarily for her literary activity, twice became politically active. Her vigorous support of her husband, Edward Wortley Montagu, in his quest for a seat in Commons during the 1714 election showed intense interest in and accurate awareness of the political situation, but little ability to influence either her husband or the outcome of the election. Later, she resisted her husband's opposition to Sir Robert Walpole and instead warmly supported the first minister. Her political support of Walpole culminated with the publication of the political journal, *The Nonsense of Common Sense*, which ran to nine issues in 1737. In it, she assailed Chesterfield and Lyttelton's *Common Sense*. Though initially well received, Lady Mary's journal, like so many others of the day, did not last. It marked, however, an unusual degree of direct political activism by a woman. Her correspondence also described an incident in 1738 when the House of Lords attempted to exclude a group of interested women from its gallery:

> Not withstanding which determination, a tribe of dames resolved to shew on this occasion, that neither men nor laws could resist them. These heroines were Lady Huntingdon, the Duchess of Queensbury, the Duchess of Ancaster, Lady Westmoreland, Lady Cobham, Lady Charlotte Edwin, Lady Archibald Hamilton and her daughter, Mrs. Scott, Mrs. Pendarvis, and Lady Francis Saunderland. I am thus particular in their names, since I look upon them to be the boldest assertors, and most resigned sufferers for liberty, I ever read of. They presented themselves at the door at nine o'clock in the morning, where Sir William Saunderson respectfully informed them the [Lord] Chancellor had made an order against their admittance. The Duchess of Queensbury, as head of the squadron, pished at the ill-breeding of a mere lawyer, and desired him to let them up stairs privately. After some modest refusals he swore by ——— he would not let them in. Her grace, with a noble warmth, answered, by G—— they would come in, in spite of the Chancellor and the whole House. This being reported, the Peers resolved to starve them out; an order was made that the doors should not be opened till they had raised the siege.
>
> These Amazons now shewed themselves qualified for the duty even of foot-soldiers; they stood there till five in the afternoon, without either sustenance or evacuation every now and then playing vollies of thumps, kicks, and raps, against the door, with so much violence that the speakers in the House were scarce heard. When the Lords were not to be conquered by this, the two Duchesses (very well apprized of the use of strategems in war) commanded a dead silence of half an hour; and the Chancellor, who thought this a certain proof of their absence, (the Commons also being very impatient to enter) gave order for the opening of the door; upon which they all rushed in, pushed aside their competitors, and placed themselves in the front rows of the gallery. They stayed there till after eleven, when the House rose; and during the debate gave applause, and showed marks of dislike, not only by smiles and winks (which have always been allowed in these cases), but by noisy laughs and apparent contempts; which is supposed the true reason why poor Lord Hervey spoke miserably.[11]

Mrs. Pendarvis, another of the participants, provided a tamer account of the proceedings and suggested that the group involved attended debates of the House of Lords more than once. Another member of the squadron, Selina, countess of Huntingdon, became a passionate convert to Calvinistic Methodism under the influence of her sister, Lady Margaret Hastings, in the following year. She devoted the remainder of her long life to her religious activities and never returned to the political scene. The episode described above has nevertheless remained sufficiently shocking that A. S. Turberville twice described it as "Amazonian" in his work on the House of Lords in the period.[12]

Such concerted displays of direct feminine political activity were both rare and noteworthy. Yet the political biographies of all those women named remain to be researched and written. Was this an isolated outburst, or only one manifestation of the political actitivies of a group of involved women? To what extent did such unusually active women actually influence the conduct of parliamentary politics or, more precisely, the conduct of individual politicians? Were women frequently excluded from the galleries? Upon precisely what grounds were such exclusions based when they did occur? Perhaps this debate was not their only concern—women have been noted observing the debates on the Sacheverell trial, for example—and perhaps Lord Hervey's speech was not their only victim.

A vast Lady Mary Wortley Montagu literature has emerged over the years, but far too much of it shallowly recounts the social and literary sides of her life. Robert Halsband's work, including his biography, his edited and complete editions of her correspondence, and his edition of her political journal are by far the most satisfactory sources for the study of the political side of Lady Mary's career. Much of the work on such well-known figures as Lady Mary must begin with careful rereading of the printed primary sources, and Halsband has handsomely provided the starting point for that.[13]

In the latter part of the century, Georgiana, duchess of Devonshire—Fox's duchess—emerged as the most politically active woman as she conducted salons for Fox's followers and potential supporters. Her avid support of Charles James Fox occupied many years of her life, particularly in the 1780s, and marked her for veneration by Fox's supporters and for vilification by his opponents. Occasionally, as in the hotly contested general election of 1784, the duchess became more directly involved on Fox's behalf. Her brief canvassing career began when her mother, Dowager Countess Spencer, called upon Georgiana and her sister, Harriet, Lady Duncannon, to come out to St. Albans to counter Lady Salisbury's canvassing for Viscount Fairford. The countess had inherited what had once been Sarah, duchess of Marlborough's, interest in St. Albans, and now sought to use it to support the Foxite candidate William Sloper. With the help of Georgiana and Harriet, he narrowly prevailed. Had it not already been too late, the sisters would willingly have proceeded to Northampton for more canvassing. Instead, their next opportunity occurred in Westminster itself.[14]

Georgiana's involvement in the 1784 election for the populous Westminster constituency earned her both credit and notoriety. Many accounts of her canvassing of lower-class voters exist, though the reports that she actually exchanged kisses for votes are more commonly associated with her sister, Lady Duncannon, who again accompanied her on these expeditions. She contributed significantly to the reversal of Fox's fortunes during the campaign and she must receive considerable credit for Fox's success in wresting the second seat from Sir Cecil Wray. Lady Carlisle, Lady Derby, and Lady Beauchamp, as well as Horace Walpole's three nieces, the three Ladies Waldegrave, also campaigned for Fox in that election. The other side's attempts to counter Fox's ladies by bringing in Lady Salisbury and Lady Hobart met with less success. Yet Georgiana never canvassed again.

The key to understanding her abrupt and final withdrawal from the world of electioneering she had just discovered is the vilification she suffered from Fox's opponents. Though the editors of a copious contemporary anthology of materials about the campaign repeatedly reminded their readers that the most unspeakable examples they had encountered were omitted for propriety's sake, they nevertheless printed:

> The girl condemn'd to walk the streets,
> And pick up each blackguard she meets,
>     And get him in her clutches;
> Has lost her trade—for they despise
> Her wanton arms, her leering eyes—
>     Now they can kiss a Duchess.[15]

Georgiana's anguish at such abuse became great enough to make her wish to abandon the campaign before its conclusion, but her loyalty to Fox kept her engaged to the very end. Not only she, but her contemporaries, including her mother who had induced her to canvass in the first place, considered her canvassing in Westminster to be unfeminine and socially compromising. Just how much abuse was necessary to drive an eighteenth-century duchess to that point cannot be precisely measured. On the eve of a pending Westminster election in 1788, her mother wrote to the duke of Devonshire urging him to send Georgiana out of London rather than to allow her to repeat her exertions of 1784. The duke responded sympathetically, but the issue became moot when Georgiana herself wrote to her mother and willingly agreed not to canvass actively.[16] Thus, even her influential canvassing for Fox in 1784 amounted to a single series of efforts which she never repeated. She did remain one of Fox's primary political hostesses, but her activities in that capacity usually were no more direct than the instance when, in 1805, Fox pleaded with her to get as many of their friends as possible to attend a division in Commons dealing with the abolition of the slave trade. Her efforts, however successful, were not enough, as the amendment in question lost seventy-seven to seventy.

The single most useful account of Georgiana's life and political conduct may be found in the earl of Bessborough's edition of her correspondence. Her political activities also appear in many of the biographies of Charles James Fox, most recently and effectively in those by John Derry and Loren Reid. The studies of particular episodes in Fox's political career by L. G. Mitchell and John Cannon also shed considerable light on Georgiana's work for Fox. More material exists with regard to her influence than for virtually any other politically involved woman of the late eighteenth century. Much work remains to be done not only on Georgiana's own political activities, but on those of other women named in that infamously masculine display of female canvassing in 1784. Just how influential were such expeditions on the politicians themselves and on potential voters? To what extent did such canvassing merely cause notoriety, rather than actual influence on voter conduct at the polls? Too few correlations of poll books and canvasses exist as it is. While Georgiana's political activities and those of her cohorts may tempt the researcher to wish that kisses might be correlated with these sources as well, a serious effort is in fact needed to assess the effectiveness of such female political activities. That Fox's susceptibility to female influence may have been greater than usual in the period has been suggested by D. T. Johnson, who noted the predilection of the Fox family men for marrying women without the mother-in-law-to-be's consent as a possible cause for Fox's opposition to the Royal Marriage Bill of 1772.[18]

The role of political hostess did not necessarily mean measurable political influence, though the opportunity certainly existed. The true political influence of such hostesses remains to be assessed. That the opportunity for influence might be turned to personal as well as to political ends may be gathered from the activities of Elizabeth, Viscountess Melbourne, on behalf of her dull-witted husband, Sir Peniston Lamb, who owed what little political advancement he acquired entirely to his active, intelligent, and beautiful wife. She also worked actively to develop patronage opportunities for her sons, including the eventual prime minister, Lord Melbourne. Lady Melbourne preceded Georgiana, duchess of Devonshire, as Fox's foremost political hostess, but cooperated amicably when the younger duchess arrived on the scene. Melbourne House and Devonshire House provided the two most significant meeting places for Charles James Fox's supporters in the latter years of the century. Lady Melbourne's direct political involvement, unlike Georgiana's, lay in the area of acquisition of patronage for the advancement of their men, rather than active support of major political figures. The political activities of these two women, amongst others, may be compared to gain some impression of the diverse channels political inclinations, talents, and opportunities might take for women in the eighteenth century.[19]

The extension of the assessment of women's political influence beyond those well-known women already discussed must begin with the identification of those women with the opportunity to exercise influence. An extensive list of potentially involved women may be assembled from the social commentaries and correspondence of the day, including W. S. Lewis's monumental edition of Horace Walpole's correspondence. Many relationships with political potential may be readily identified: Maria Skerett and Sir Robert Walpole; Nancy Parsons and Viscount Maynard, the duke of Grafton, and the third duke of Dorset in turn; Mrs. Armistead and Charles James Fox. In many instances, however, politically oriented women merely observed and commented upon the activities they saw, as in the cases of Lady Sarah Byng Osborn, whose only direct involvement came with her futile attempts to intercede with Lords and the Admiralty on behalf of her ill-fated brother, Admiral John Byng, or Lady Sarah Lennox, who wrote much but did little about the political activities of her nephew, Charles James Fox. Lady Hester Pitt of the Grenville family, as Lady Chatham, performed much of her ailing husband's personal business during the illness which crippled him during his ministry in 1767 and 1768. Most of the political side of the business remained in the hands of his colleagues Camden, Shelburne, and Grafton, however. Lady Hester Stanhope, the Younger Pitt's niece, acted as his political hostess and knew most of the important men of her day in 1803 and 1804, though her conduct sometimes embarrassed her uncle and scandalized his guests. Yet someone of the politically inclined lineage of Lady Mary Wortley Montagu's daughter, Lady Bute, exercised no demonstrable political influence upon her husband. Before any conclusions may be drawn, further indentification and assessment of influence must occur, with particular attention to the question of the forces which caused women to be politically active or passive in their relationships with their politically involved men.[20]

A few eighteenth-century women became politically involved through their writings. Lady Mary Wortley Montagu's publication of *The Nonsense of Common Sense* has already been discussed. She was aware, however, of the precedent of Mary Delariviere Manley's vigorous Tory writings during Anne's reign. Manley gained notoriety for the shockingly scandalous content of her writings and for her attacks against the political interests of the duke and duchess of Marlborough. Her novel, *Queen Zarah*, scarcely veiled a bitter and sometimes crude attack on Sarah, duchess of

Marlborough. That novel and a number of her Tory political tracts won her the favor of the duke and duchess of Marlborough's constant Tory critic, Dean Swift. Later in the century, Catherine Graham Macaulay won acclaim first as a "Whiggish" historian and then for her vigorous political writings, especially those attacking Edmund Burke's views. Her best known political pamphlets were her *Address to the People of England, Ireland, and Scotland*, which in 1775 attacked the government's policy toward North America, and her *Observations on the Reflections of the Right Hon. Edmund Burke on the Revolution in France*, which in 1790 assailed Burke's views on the French Revolution. Twenty years earlier she had also attacked Burke's views. She actively supported the activities of John Wilkes, and her brother, John Sawbridge, was one of Wilkes's strongest supporters. The actual political impact of such writers has not, however, yet been clearly established.[21]

The opportunity for particular women to become involved politically near Parliament or, indeed, at any level of society often related to the marriages arranged for them by their parents. From a male point of view, the choice of a wife with substantial wealth, high social station, or good political connections could enhance his estate and with it his political interest. The imaginary advice Winston Churchill has Marlborough's father giving to his promising but penniless son captures the spirit of the age accurately enough:

> You have your foot on the ladder of fortune. You have already mounted several important rungs. Every one says you have a great future before you. Every one knows that you have not got—apart from the annuity and your pay—a penny behind you. How can you on a mere whim compromise your whole future life? Catherine Sedley is known to be an agreeable woman. She holds her own in any company. The Duke listens to all she says, and the whole Court laughs at her jests. She is asked everywhere. Women have beauties of mind quite as attractive, except to enamoured youth, as those of body. Sir Charles is a really wealthy man, solid, long-established, with fine houses, broad acres, and failing health. She is his only child. With his fortune and her humour and sagacity behind you, all that poverty which has pursued us since your infancy, would be swept away. You could look any man in the face and your career would be assured.[22]

Few men of the eighteenth century would have ignored this advice as John Churchill did. And even fewer would have succeeded as handsomely as did the duke of Marlborough. Many social and economic historians, such as Gordon Mingay, have described the attitudes and conventions attending arranged marriages in the period. The institution of marriage is now undergoing the scrutiny necessary to make particular judgments about the economic, social, and political impacts of marriage as an institution and of individual marriages as well. Patricia Otto's as yet unpublished work on eighteenth-century aristocratic marriages is remarkably valuable for its thoroughness and acuity. Hopefully she and others will continue in this direction, as the conclusions she has reached are already challenging and valuable: arranged marriages not only frequently influenced the economic, social, and political potential of given families, but the aristocracy guarded the institution as a vital means of class preservation. The relative importance of economic, social, and political motives for the arrangement of marriages, however, has not yet been established.[23]

Male dominance of political involvement at the local and con-stituency levels was neither so complete nor so automatic as is commonly imagined. Although the evidence of male involvement and influence outside Parliament overwhelms the parallel evidence of female activity, this is to be expected and must be dealt with if an accurate picture of women's political involvement in the period is to be achieved. The initial task here, too, is the identification of women who had the opportunity or potential to become involved. The search must extend both to printed materials and to manuscripts—often already sifted thoroughly on other questions, including male political activity—which will yield evidence substantiating or repudiating the actual involvement and influence of given women. Much of the work yet to be done must be conducted in English archives, though a great deal of preliminary identification can be accomplished through printed primary and even secondary sources. Most of this work remains to be done.[24]

The bulk of the literature on the women's movement, including that produced in response to recent interest in the area, does little to seek the eighteenth-century origins of the women's suffrage movement or women's involvement in elections. Yet such involvement did exist and may often be discovered, though it frequently lies buried in vast bodies of material dealing primarily with male activities. The exclusion of women from the franchise rested on shaky legal grounds at best, and women theoretically held more rights in eighteenth-century England than they usually exer-cised. The absence of women from the eighteenth-century electorate rested primarily upon social constraints rather than legal prohibitions. The origins of these social constraints lay long before the eighteenth century, as may be gathered from Derek Hirst's brief but tantalizing passage on women's voting in his recent work on the Stuart electorate.[25]

Charlotte Carmichael Stopes's early work on the legal position of English women still provides a useful key to the understanding of the theoretical legal position of women in eighteenth-century England. Stopes

vigorously argued the decline of women's rights and political involvement
to an ultimate low in the seventeenth and eighteenth centuries, and
pointed to Sir Edward Coke's dictum passingly dismissing women as a
group disqualified from the franchise as one of the main sources of women's
exclusion from elections.[26] Though Sir Simon D'Ewes noted the possibility
that women might legally be allowed to vote, he nonetheless felt it
propitious to exclude them from the Suffolk election for the Long
Parliament in 1640 . The exclusion of English women from the parliamentary franchise remained almost complete from this time forward despite
the lack of actual legal constraints upon women's voting. That the
eighteenth-century exclusion of women from the parliamentary franchise
rested primarily on social attitudes rather than upon clear legal prohibitions is revealed by a careful examination of the case of Olive vs.
Ingram before King's Bench in 1739. That case found that women might
hold the office of church sexton and might vote for that office, but also
explored the question of women's voting more generally. With particular
reference to the parliamentary franchise, the justices found no absolute
legal prohibition of women's voting, but doubted the efficacy of it because
of women's supposedly limited judgment in public matters. One justice,
Page, flatly stated that he saw no legal obstacle to women's voting for
members of Parliament. The case at once demonstrated the lack of clear
legal prohibitions of women's voting and expressed the social attitudes
toward women which in practice denied them the vote. Stopes's con-
tention that the eighteenth century marked the nadir of the English
woman's rights and privileges is strongly supported by such evidence. In
practice, women in the eighteenth century did not vote in parliamentary
elections.[27]

A careful combing of published and unpublished sources of English
local history does, however, reveal women holding various local offices
during the eighteenth century. In Derbyshire, for example, women were
nominated, though disqualified, from service as overseers of the poor
during the last two decades of the seventeenth century, but one Mrs. Isabel
Eyre, a widow, was nominated and allowed to serve in that capacity in
1712. Women also served from time to time as constables, churchwardens,
and reeves of manors. Most commonly, such positions rotated amongst
residents or tenants in a given parish and the women served in their turn.
Women also commonly attended and voted in the parish vestry, though
some disputes arose over this. While males serving in local offices far outnumbered females, the available records must still be carefully reviewed to
establish the true extent of women's local office holding in the period.[28]

The eighteenth-century origins of the women's suffrage movement do
appear occasionally in some of the general treatments of that movement, as

with the first chapter of Roger Fulford's book. All too often, however, the women's movement and suffrage literature begins with the nineteenth century. Such a belated start ignores the intellectual ancestry of the suffrage movement in the increased awareness of many cultured eighteenth-century women that education for women must necessarily precede their political involvement. Whether dealing with Elizabeth Montagu and the "Blue Stockings," in which group cultural discussions prevailed over political considerations, or with the pioneering work of Mary Wollstonecraft, the theme of women's education as the key to women's advancement in all fields of endeavor occurred with increasing frequency late in the eighteenth century. Mary Wollstonecraft's vigorous *A Vindication of the Rights of Women* became at once the most outspoken and most vilified work advocating women's education as the means to improve women's station in life. Her work must stand as a cardinal document in the literature of the women's suffrage movement. That she wrote in reaction to Thomas Paine's *Rights of Man* rendered her work the more significant in the questioning literature which arose from the French Revolution and the English reaction to it.[29]

The issue of women's suffrage first arose in Parliament in the debates on Charles Grey's motion for parliamentary reform in 1797. Charles James Fox suggested that the better-educated women deserved the franchise more than the least-educated and more dependent classes of men. He suggested further that if independence were the major qualification for inclusion in the franchise, such women deserved the vote more than many groups of dependent men, including soldiers, servants, and the poor. Fox raised the issue more to show the inconsistencies in the positions of those demanding the expansion of male suffrage than as a serious proposal for the enfranchisement of women.[30]

The de facto exclusion of women from the parliamentary franchise did not, however, mean their exclusion from electoral activities at the constituency level. Despite the total subordination of married women to their husbands, women could and did inherit political interests in eighteenth-century constituencies. As widows, heiresses, and mothers of minor sons, English women often conducted political and electoral affairs as heads of interest. A careful examination of the *History of Parliament* volumes edited by Romney Sedgwick and by Sir Lewis Namier and John Brooke reveals several such instances. Sarah, duchess of Marlborough, conducted the political side of her husband's substantial interest in St. Albans, Woodstock, and Oxfordshire after his death. In Bossiney, Cornwall, Lady Bute inherited her father's fortune and political interest. Alexander Luttrell's mother managed his inherited interest in Minehead, Somerset, during his minority, as did Sir James Lowther's mother in

Appleby, Westmoreland, and the duchess of Bedford during her grandson's minority for Okehampton, Devon. Heiresses invariably lost the direction of their political interests upon marriage or remarriage, as did guardians upon the majority of their wards, however. The search for the activities of female heads of political interests is difficult insofar as male heads of interest vastly outnumbered them in the period and the sources are weighted accordingly.[31]

Women also frequently became involved in eighteenth-century electioneering outside greater London. A careful examination of Hogarth's four paintings of "The Election" reveals women in and around an election, but little suggestion of effective influence may be seen: gifts are being made available to voters' wives and daughters, women sell election ballads and attend election entertainments, but with what influence? The nature of canvassing and the carefully observed unwritten code of electioneering conduct dictated that the appropriate favors and honors be distributed to electors' wives and daughters. Omissions might well lead to the neutralization of otherwise favorable votes. Yet even the impact of aristocratic women acting as election hostesses at home has not seriously been examined.[32]

Occasionally the influence of a particular woman in particular circumstances may be established. One may search the manuscripts for evidence of direct female influence, and may indeed discover agents' canvass reports suggesting such, as in the case of one Mr. Sharps of Clift, Sussex, who in 1734 "inclined to go wrong, but his mother-in-law says he shall go right."[33] John Sharp of Clift appears in the printed poll book as voting for the "right" candidates in the duke of Newcastle's interest, Henry Pelham and James Butler, hence suggesting the success of his mother-in-law's influence.[34] The manuscripts dealing with campaigns, canvasses, and elections often reveal cases of locally influential women, including widows managing their late husbands' landed estates and political interests, and of women whose influence was presumed to exist through family ties. The latter might range from an individual expected to go wrong because his sister lived with an opposing agent to nieces married into opposing families and expected to influence their husbands' votes. So, too, might women become involved insofar as promises made about their disposition by one side or the other became political issues. In an earlier Sussex election, four votes hinged on whether a promise made to provide a widow's house to a loyal man could be fulfilled without breaking an earlier pledge that the widow might retain the house in question. Newcastle's agent, Julius Hutchinson, finally resolved the matter by persuading the widow to move to a better house to make the promised residence available to the loyal follower, thus satisfying all concerned and delivering the four votes in question.[35] Women might also become the victims of local political struggles, as with the widows of the hotly contested Sussex borough of Lewes who, in 1734, had been warned out of their houses "unless they consent to take new men into their houses who had a vote."[36] Such instances may seem trivial in and of themselves, but the record of women's involvement at the local and constituency level is so infrequent that such cases must be discovered, recorded, and evaluated if any accurate picture is to emerge from the election evidence. Male involvement dominates the manuscript material, but the evidence of female influence and activity can be sifted from it and can provide a clearer understanding of women's roles at this level of eighteenth-century political life.

Three groups of politically active women may be identified beyond the mainstream of parliamentary politics: Jacobites, rioters, and reformers. Women frequently appeared among the ranks of both Scottish and English Jacobites in the risings of 1715 and 1745 and even beyond. Whether dealing with Lady Nithsdale, who spirited her condemned husband out of the Tower of London in women's clothing on the eve of his execution after the '15, or the unnamed woman servant who suffered whipping and permanent disfigurement for her support of Prince Charles in the '45, the Jacobite movement received substantial female support. During Charles's march southward in 1745, Manchester, so the story goes, fell to "a drummer and a whore," while the Scotswoman, Flora MacDonald, was instrumental in Charles's escape after the '45. A close examination of Scottish local records will reveal the names of even more male and female Jacobites than will the English court records, as not all suspected Jacobites faced prosecution. The names of such Scotswomen as Lady Clanranald, who went mad in English custody, Lady MacKinnon, the dowager duchess of Gordon, the countess of Enroll, Mrs. Anne Leith, and Margaret Turner all appear, for example, among the ranks of Jacobites in Aberdeenshire and Banffshire during the '45. Even after the failure of the '45, Lady Primrose appeared as a prominent Jacobite hostess in London, and Clementina Walkinshaw, the prince's mistress, weakened his support when she became suspect as a spy. The motivation of Jacobite women for their support of that forlorn cause is, however, totally lacking in study. Most of the Scotswomen, at least, formed their loyalties to the Stuarts very young and very intensely, and few turned on their cause in later years. In the absence of scholarly study the temptation to assume a romanticized explanation for these loyalties must be resisted.[37]

Women's activities also sometimes extended to the civil disorders which frequently erupted in eighteenth-century England, as shown in the works of James Fitts, George Rudé, and E. P. Thompson. Such rioting often involved political motives or overtones. Rudé notes, for example, the prosecution of some twenty women among one hundred ten of the Gordon rioters who were tried and whose occupations could be identified. Similar discoveries no doubt will apear through careful examination of court records dealing with other civil disorders.[38]

Those women who became involved with the various reform movements late in the eighteenth century are more difficult to classify in an eighteenth-century political scheme. In general, the French Revolution's truncation of English reform movements for nearly a generation meant that the achievement of their objectives at the parliamentary level would belong to the nineteenth rather than the eighteenth century. A few, however, were active before the turn of the century and their achievements occurred even during the Napoleonic Wars. Hannah More, who as an Evangelical worked for basic Scriptural education of the poor and who as a reformer vigorously supported William Wilberforce's antislavery campaign, is a prime example. During the period of the French Revolution, Hannah More's political writings clearly lay within the eighteenth-century value system. Her advocacy of the support of the established government and her closeness to the views of Edmund Burke were complemented with her commitment to the "Evangelical Party" of the established church rather than to dissent. Her efforts to educate the poor aimed only at providing them with enough literacy to read the Bible and with a few basic skills, excluding writing. Her work in education was aided by her sisters and complemented by the work of Sarah Trimmer. Her involvement in education, however, placed her in the embarrassing position of employing dissenting teachers which in turn led to the infamous Blagdon Controversy and to a weakening of her educational efforts. She became committed to Wilberforce and the antislavery cause primarily from religious conviction. Neither More nor Wilberforce saw the abolition of the slave trade in 1807 as an end, and both wished to see a continuation of social and moral reforms, though More refused to countenance parliamentary reform. Though Hannah More belongs more to the eighteenth century than do many of the other reformers of both sexes, partly because of her distinguished literary career, most of the roots of the later reformers may nevertheless be found in the eighteenth century. Elizabeth Fry, for example, began to develop the religious convictions which provided the basis of her Quaker ministry and her later efforts at prison reform before the turn of the century. Her major efforts, including her well-known work at Newgate Prison, came after the Napoleonic Wars, however. The place of such reformers in the eighteenth-century political scheme is confusing, regardless of sex. Some, like Wilberforce, whose close relationship with the Younger Pitt and whose excellence as a parliamentary debater predated his career as a reformer, properly belong to the eighteenth century.

Similarly, Hannah More, in support of Wilberforce from 1790 onwards, belongs there too. But to what extent did More and other women effectively contribute to the parliamentary realization of reform? Surely her literary reputation and her Evangelical commitments gave her unusual prominence at the time, but the degree of her actual influence remains to be assessed.[39]

The researcher who is persuaded of the significance of the quest for the nature of eighteenth-century English female political involvement will unavoidably face great frustrations. The evidence will relate almost entirely to male activity. Women were not only ignored but, when politically active, vilified for seeming too masculine. Much of the evidence for women's activities and influences lies buried within the vast material dealing with male activity. If, however, the origins of the women's political movement and the place of women in eighteenth-century society are to be discovered and understood, the work must be undertaken. In terms of printed works, a vast body of light, socially oriented material must be ploughed through to identify women with political potential. Concerned researchers will find many of the attitudes expressed in the writings of the period offensive and archaic, but must not allow these feelings to divert them from their purposes.

One common factor, then, unites all female experience in eighteenth-century English political life: direct political action by women rarely occurred below the level of a queen ruling in her own right, a position occupied only by Anne in the eighteenth century. Beyond this, the entirety of women's political involvement in eighteenth-century England necessarily meant the influencing of men to act politically as the women wished them to. That women attempted such influence at all and occasionally succeeded in its exercise is more remarkable than the apolitical passivity of most eighteenth-century English women. The study of women in eighteenth-century English political life is therefore always at one remove: sources are fewer, evidence is scarcer and more circumstantial than that for male political activity. Such study requires patience, diligence, and determination. Its undertaking should provide a challenge rather than a deterrent for the committed researcher.

# NOTES

1. King, ed., *Memoirs of Sarah, Duchess of Marlborough*, pp. 331–2.

2. The researcher beginning the quest for eighteenth-century women's political involvement should become well-versed in the controversial literature about the nature and structure of eighteenth-century English politics. For many years the meticulous works of Namier, *Structure of Politics at the Accession of George III* and *England in the Age of the American Revolution*, dominated the interpretation of the period and were thought to be applicable to the entire century. The failure of Walcott's overly ambitious attempt to apply Namier's methods to the reign of Anne in his *English Politics in the Early Eighteenth Century* prompted, however, a thorough reexamination of the political structure of the early years of the century. Holmes's *Politics in the Age of Anne*; Speck's *Tory and Whig: The Struggle in the Constituencies, 1705–1715*; their cooperative documents book, *The Divided Society*; and Plumb's challenging *The Growth of Political Stability in England, 1675–1725* have contributed to the scholarly resurrection of a "party" interpretation of the politics of the period. Later in the century, such works as Ginter's *Whig Organization in the General Election of 1790*; E. A. Smith's *Whig Principles and Party Politics*; and O'Gorman's *The Rise of Party in England* have similarly reasserted the argument that a party interpretation makes the best sense of the period. In general, the resurgent party interpretation is most persuasive when applied to parliamentary politics and least convincing when it attempts to develop party identity as a voter motive in the constituencies. Namier's work retains a value for the researcher seeking women's political involvement in the period insofar as it urges a careful search for and identification of politically involved individuals as a necessary prerequisite for the interpretation of the period. For the best summary of the Namierite position, see Brooke's "Introductory Survey" to the Namier and Brooke, *The Commons, 1754–1790*, which is now printed separately as *The House of Commons, 1754–1790*. J. Owen's *The Pattern of Politics in Eighteenth Century England*, his *Rise of the Pelhams*, and his recent text, *The Eighteenth Century* are all useful. Yet all of these works deal only passingly with women. They provide a vital framework for the understanding of politics in the age at the same time that they indicate how much further the researcher in quest of women's political activities must go, often through the same materials. Much of the work on English women, including Stenton's excellent *The English Woman in History*, has the same problem in reverse: a good deal of worthwhile material on English women in the eighteenth century, amongst other periods, but no focus upon their political activities. One must now choose between politics without women or women without politics.

3. Roberts, in his recent edition of *The Diary of Sir David Hamilton, 1709–1714*, reveals much of the circumstances of and steps toward Sarah's demise in Anne's favor. Hamilton served as one of Anne's physicians and as an intermediary between Anne and Sarah as their estrangement grew, as well as a political go-between for Marlborough's supporters and the court as Harley's forces gained ministerial strength.

4. This limited view of Abigail Hill Masham's influence over Anne is presented both by Holmes in his *Politics in the Age of Anne*, pp. 210–6, where he discusses both bedchamber politics in general and Masham's influence in particular, and in Biddle's *Bolingbroke and Harley*, pp. 148–59, 257–8.

5. Sarah's own writings offer excellent insights into her political involvements. Three such items have recently been reprinted: *Letters of Sarah, Duchess of Marlborough; Memoirs of Sarah, Duchess of Marlborough*, ed. King; and *Private Correspondence of Sarah, Duchess of Marlborough*. Green's works are *Sarah, Duchess of Marlborough* and *Queen Anne*. For Sarah's political activities during her husband's life, Churchill's standard multivolume biography, *Marlborough: His Life and Times*, remains most valuable.

6. George I's relations with Kendall and Kielmannsegg are discussed in Hatton's essay, "George I as an English and European Figure," pp. 190–209. Beattie discusses the maneuverings around them in his *The English Court in the Reign of George I*. See also Robert Williams's edition of *Memoirs of Sophia Dorothea*.

7. The most revealing and useful views of Caroline's court at various times are in Cowper's edition of the *Diary of Mary Countess Cowper*; Thomson's edition of the *Memoirs of*

*Viscountess Sundon*; and in the *Letters to and from Henrietta, Countess of Suffolk*. Quennell's biography, *Caroline of England* wants a modern scholarly successor. Plumb's unfinished biography of Walpole, particularly the second volume, *Sir Robert Walpole: The King's Minister* provides a thorough view of the Walpole-Caroline relationship from the former's viewpoint. The most vivid account of Caroline's political activity appears in the material surrounding Walpole's agent at court, Lord Hervey. Halsband's *Lord Hervey: Eighteenth Century Courtier* is the most satisfactory biography, and Sedgwick's edition of *Some Materials Towards Memoirs of the Reign of George II* provides the fullest account of Caroline's political activities. Dickinson's *Sir Robert Walpole and the Whig Supremacy* and Kemp's *Sir Robert Walpole* are also useful. Much of the flavor of the period may be gathered by reading Oliver's *The Endless Adventure*, especially the second volume which deals with the Walpole-Caroline relationship. Turberville's *English Men and Manners in the Eighteenth Century* also describes the atmosphere at the Hanoverian Court.

8.  For Augusta's role, see Brooke, *King George III*, pp. 29–30, 46–49, 266; and Edwards's *Frederick Lewis, Prince of Wales*, pp. 184–5. For Charlotte's position, consult Hedley's *Queen Charlotte*.

9.  British Library, Add. MSS. 32688, ff. 228–29, William Hay to the Duke of Newcastle, 30 August 1733.

10.  Thomson's edition of *Memoirs of Viscountess Sundon* offers a vivid account of patronage and placement at Caroline's court. For a more locally oriented view of the workings of patronage, see Curtis's *Chichester Towers*, which recounts the impact of the assignment of a deanery of an English cathedral upon Sussex politics and elections. See also, Owen's "Political Patronage in Eighteenth Century England," pp. 360–87.

11.  Lady Mary Wortley Montagu to Lady Pomfret [March 1739], in Halsband, ed., *The Complete Letters of Lady Mary Wortley Montagu*, vol. 2, 1721–1751, pp. 135–37.

12.  See also Mrs. Pendarves to Anne Granville, 3 March 1738/9, in Llanover's edition of *The Autobiography and Correspondence of Mary Granville, Mrs. Delany*, vol. 2, pp. 42–46. These volumes deserve a careful combing for the identification of politically involved women of the period and their activities and interests. Stenton's *The English Woman in History* briefly describes the career of another of the women involved, Selina, countess of Huntingdon, pp. 283–84. Foster's *The Life and Times of Selina, Countess of Huntingdon* ignores her early political activities and deals exclusively with the religious side of her life, in which she found greater fulfillment. Turberville's remarks occur in his *The House of Lords in the Eighteenth Century*, pp. 15 and 238.

13.  The vast majority of the Lady Mary Wortley Montagu literature is superficial and devotes little attention to her political life. Halsband is the exception: *The Life of Lady Mary Wortley Montagu; The Complete Letters of Lady Mary Wortley Montagu; The Selected Letters of Lady Mary Wortley Montagu*; and *The Nonsense of Common Sense* are all essential. Of the many earlier biographies, Emily Morse Symonds's *Lady Mary Wortley Montagu and Her Times*, published under the pseudonym George Paston, devotes much fuller attention to her political support of her husband in 1714 than do most works.

14.  For Georgiana's St. Albans involvement, see Lansberry's "A Whig Inheritance."

15.  [Hartley et. al., eds.], *History of the Westminster Election*, p. 434.

16.  Lady Spencer to the duke of Devonshire, 27 July 1788; Georgiana to Lady Spencer, 23 July 1788, quoted in earl of Bessborough, ed., *Georgiana: Extracts from the Correspondence of Georgiana, Duchess of Devonshire*, pp. 132–33. Georgiana's wish to quit before the end of the campaign appears in George's "Fox's Martyrs: The General Election of 1784." The great need for politically oriented biographies of eighteenth-century women is illustrated by the total omission of these events in Biddulph's *The Three Ladies Waldegrave*.

17.  Georgiana's activities as Fox's primary political hostess may be gathered from such works as Iris Leveson-Gower's *The Face Without a Frown*; Foster's edition of *The Two Duchesses*; Stuart's *Dearest Bess*, a biography of Georgiana's eventual successor as duchess of Devonshire, Lady Elizabeth Foster; and in the letters and diary fragment appended to Sichel's *Sheridan*. The debate and division involved appears in Great Britain, Parliament, *Parliamentary Debates (House of Commons)*, 1st series, 3 (15 January–12 March 1805), pp. 642–74.

18. Bessborough's work, cited above, is the most satisfactory volume dealing with the duchess herself. Most of the rest of the material about her political activity is in the literature on Charles James Fox. Derry's *Charles James Fox*; Lascelles' *The Life of Charles James Fox*, and Reid's *Charles James Fox: A Man for the People* all note Georgiana's political activities for Fox. Both Cannon's *The Fox-North Coalition* and Mitchell's *Charles James Fox and the Disintegration of the Whig Party, 1782–1784* devote greater attention to Fox's political activities in general and Georgiana's support of him in particular. The most recent repetition of Georgiana's 1784 canvassing appears in McAdams' article, "Electioneering Techniques in Populous Constituencies, 1784–96." Johnson's suggestion about the origins of Fox's opposition to the Royal Marriage Bill appears in his "Charles James Fox: From Government to Opposition, 1771–1774."

19. Lady Melbourne's political involvements and her largely successful quest for patronage for her men may be seen in the countess of Airlie's *In Whig Society* and in Cecil's well-known *Young Melbourne*.

20. Important correspondences include Lewis's *The Correspondence of Horace Walpole*; Fortescue's *The Correspondence of King George III, 1760–1783*; Aspinall's *Later Correspondence of George III, 1783–1810*; Thomas W. Copeland's *The Correspondence of Edmund Burke*; and Aspinall's *The Correspondence of George, Prince of Wales*. Also important for the identification of politically involved women are the writings of individuals, such as Osborn's edition of *Political and Social Letters of a Lady of the Eighteenth Century*; the very similar edition of *Letters of Sarah Byng Osborn*, ed. McClelland; or *The Life and Letters of Lady Sarah Lennox*, ed. the countess of Ilchester and Lord Stavordale. For Lady Chatham's activities during her husband's incapacity, see B. Williams, *The Life of William Pitt, Earl of Chatham*, 2: 242–44. Lady Hester Stanhope's activities while residing with the Younger Pitt are described in Haslip's *Lady Hester Stanhope* pp. 42–48, and in her own *Memoirs* especially 2: 1–75. Lady Bute appears in the Lady Mary Wortley Montagu material cited in note 13, above, but is virtually unmentioned in biographical works dealing with Lord Bute's career. Family papers offer yet another treasure trove of material for sifting, whether in English archives, the *Reports* of the *Historical Manuscripts Commission*, or such volumes as Verney's *Verney Family Letters of the Eighteenth Century* or W. J. Smith's edition of *The Grenville Papers*. Turberville's *The House of Lords in the Eighteenth Century* lists peeresses in their own right and sometimes touches on the political activities of aristocratic women.

21. Something of Mary Delariviere Manley's political writing may be gathered from Horner's "The English Women Novelists and Their Connection with the Feminist Movement." *Queen Zarah* has recently been reprinted in Köster's edition of *The Novels of Mary Delariviere Manley*. Macaulay's eight-volume historical work is *The History of England from the Accession of James I to That of the Brunswick Line*. Her two most significant political pamphlets are *Address to the People of England, Ireland, and Scotland* and *Observations on the Reflections of the Right Hon. Edmund Burke on the Revolution in France*. Her earlier assault on Burke's views appeared as *Observations on a Pamphlet [by Edmund Burke] entitled Thoughts on the Cause of the Present Discontents*. A recent reprint of her *Address to the People . . .* appeared in P. C. Smith's edition of *English Defenders of American Freedoms, 1774–1778*, pp. 107–24. Her career and writings are discussed both in Beckwith's dissertation, "Catherine Macaulay, Eighteenth Century English Rebel" and in Donnelly's article, "The Celebrated Mrs. Macaulay." Her political support of Wilkes is discussed in Christie's *Wilkes, Wyvill, and Reform*.

22. Churchill, *Marlborough: His Life and Times*, 1: 126–27.

23. Mingay's *English Landed Society in the Eighteenth Century* provides a thorough discussion of marriage arrangements and settlements. Habakkuk's "English Landownership, 1680–1740" and "Marriage Settlements in the Eighteenth Century" both touch on this area as well. Ashley's *The Stuarts in Love* stresses the acquisition of property as a major motive for arranged marriages, a circumstance which does not change with the turn of the century. More recently, Clay's "Marriage, Inheritance, and the Rise of Large Estates in England, 1660–1815" and D. Thomas's "The Social Origins of Marriage Partners of the British Peerage" examine the area more closely. Another approach to the

subject of arranged marriages may be seen in Hill's "Clarissa Harlowe and Her Times." The foremost modern work in the area, however, may be found in Otto's "Daughters of the British Aristocracy," which stresses the Scottish peerage. Hopefully, her thorough scholarly work will be extended throughout the British aristocracy of the period. Laslett also comments on marriage as a politically significant institution in his *The World We Have Lost*, p. 183. Jane Austen's novel *Mansfield Park*, is also reflective of the utility of marriage as a means of perpetuating and strengthening local political interest. Fleishman discusses the setting of that novel in detail in his *A Reading of Mansfield Park*. The continuation of these views of marriage beyond the eighteenth century is suggested by F. M. L. Thompson in his *English Landed Society in the Nineteenth Century*, pp. 18–19, 98–99, 100–103, and 301–303. A necessary corollary to the work on marriage appears in part in McGregor's *Divorce in England*, pp. 1–34.

24.  Useful glimpses of potentially involved women occur also in Keppel's *The Sovereign Lady*, which unfortunately lacks the scholarly footnotes which would make it more useful to the serious researcher. Bass's *The Green Dragoon* depicts Mary Robinson's efforts on Tarleton's behalf and in support of Charles James Fox.

25.  Hirst, *The Representative of the People?* pp. 18–19. Hirst's work in these pages is precisely the sort of detailed work at the constituency level which must be done for the eighteenth century as well if an accurate picture of women's involvement in the constituencies is to be drawn. The nature of the social attitudes toward women in the period may readily be gathered by reading Halifax's *Advice to a Daughter*, published late in the seventeenth century. The first two chapters of Blease's *The Emancipation of English Women* also deal with attitudes toward women, as does Bouten's *Mary Wollstonecraft and the Beginnings of Female Emancipation in France and England*. Bouten discusses extensively the antifeminine attitudes of such writers as Richardson, Fielding, Pope, and Chesterfield, but he commends Addison and Steele for at least wishing to improve women's minds to overcome their supposed indolence.

26.  Sir Edward Coke, 4 Inst. 5.

27.  Stopes, *British Freewomen* deals with Coke's work and its impact upon women's political involvement, pp. 99–112. For Olive vs. Ingram, see 7 Mod. 264–74, 87 Eng. Rep. 1230–36. The case includes an enlightening discussion of the legal precedents for and against women's holding office and voting as they were viewed in the eighteenth century. The case is also mentioned in Stopes, pp. 129–30, and in John Campbell's *The Lives of the Chief Justices*, 2: 173–74, in which Lee's stand is commended. A thorough contemporary view of women's legal status in eighteenth-century England is provided in *The Laws Representing Women*, which touches nearly every area except the franchise. Thomas's "The Double Standard" adds a useful perspective to the area of women and the law by comparing the differing legalities of various acts when committed by men or women. More recently, Greenberg has provided "The Legal Status of the English Woman in Early Eighteenth Century Common Law and Equity." She passingly notes the supposed legal disability of English women to vote and to serve on juries. More work in the area is clearly needed.

28.  For the Derbyshire examples, see Cox's *Three Centuries of Derbyshire Annals* 1: 112; 2: 137–38. The Webbs also discuss women's local office holding at several points in their multivolume *English Local Government from the Revolution to the Municipal Corporations Act*.

29.  Only Fulford in his *Votes for Women* says much about the eighteenth-century origins of the movement. Wollstonecraft's *A Vindication of the Rights of Women* deserves careful study as a spiritual antecedent of the women's suffrage movement. For a useful review of recent biographies of Mary Wollstonecraft, see Tyson's "A Found Woman." Tyson discusses Edna Nixon's *Mary Wollstonecraft and Her Times*, Eleanore Flexner's *Mary Wollstonecraft*, and Claire Tomalin's *The Life and Death of Mary Wollstonecraft*, as well as the older standard, Ralph Wardle's *Mary Wollstonecraft: A Critical Biography*. It would be more accurate to say that Mary Wollstonecraft has recently been found again, given Bouten's treatment of her in the last chapter of his *Mary Wollstonecraft and the Beginnings of Female Emancipation in France and England*. Reynolds's *The Learned Lady in England, 1650–1750*

deals extensively with the education of women and the activities of educated women through the middle of the eighteenth century, and occasionally notes their political actions. Similar issues, as well as women's legal position and marriage, are discussed for the first half of the century in Wienbeck's *Die Stellung der Frau der oberen und mittleren Gesellschaftsklassen Englands in der ersten Hälfte 18. Jahrhunderts*. Turberville's *English Men and Manners in the Eoghteenth Century* also describes the activities of the "Blue Stockings," though not so well and so thoroughly as Bouten does in his sixth chapter. The actual political significance of the "Blue Stockings" and other similar groups remains to be studied. Many important political figures, including Samuel Johnson and Edmund Burke, attended such gatherings, but the influence of neither the meetings nor of the women participating in them upon the men has yet been assessed.

30. *The Parliamentary History of England from the Earliest Period to the Year 1803*, 33: 726–27.

31. Sedgwick's *The House of Commons, 1715–1754* and Namier and Brooke's *The House of Commons, 1754–1790* provide extensive details about local interests in the constituencies, including those headed by women. A combing of the "constituency" entries is a necessary step toward identification of politically involved women. The instances mentioned above are described in Sedgwick, pp. 263–64, 304, 302; Namier and Brooke, p. 224; Sedgwick, p. 316; Namier and Brooke, pp. 405, 256, respectively. See Speck, *Tory and Whig*, p. 58, for Sarah's activities in St. Albans. Lansberry's "A Whig Inheritance" discusses Sarah's interest in St. Albans, too, and indicates that the interest there originated in her own inheritance.

32. Hogarth's four paintings, "The Election," now hang in Sir John Soane's Museum in London. They are frequently reproduced in volumes dealing with Hogarth's work and the social milieu of eighteenth-century England. Reproductions and a full description of them may be found in the museum's guide book, *A New Description of Sir John Soane's Museum*.

33. British Library, Add. MSS., 32688, f. 57, Hay to Newcastle, 9 August 1733.

34. *A Poll Taken by Henry Montague, Esq., (Sheriff of the County of Sussex) at the City of Chichester, on Thursday and Friday the Ninth and Tenth Days of May 1734*, p. 20.

35. British Library, Add. MSS., 32686, ff. 245, 264, Julius Hutchinson to Newcastle, 3 March and 8 March 1722/3.

36. British Library, Add. MSS., 32689, f. 100, Thomas Pelham, Jr., to Newcastle, 27 December 1733.

37. On the Jacobites, Petrie's *The Jacobite Movement* provides a sympathetic but fair introduction. A good example of available published studies of local Jacobitism and local Jacobites, from which the cited examples are drawn, is Tayler and Tayler's *Jacobites of Aberdeenshire and Banffshire in the Forty-Five*. A combing of Scottish publications, state papers, and archives as well as English judicial records will surely yield much more on Jacobite women.

38. Several authors deal with civil disorder in this period. Rudé's *The Crowd in History* and his *Paris and London in the Eighteenth Century* touch upon women's involvement in mobs and riots. E. P. Thompson's *The Making of the English Working Class* also frequently touches on women's participation in civil disorders, though the focus is not primarily political. The work of Fitts also promises to reveal more about politically organized and motivated rioting, as in his article, "Newcastle's Mob."

39. A solid introduction to the Reformers may be found in Brown's *Fathers of the Victorians*. The best biography of Hannah More herself is Jones's *Hannah More*, though Meakin's early *Hannah More: A Biographical Study* retains some use. Her association with the "Evangelical Party" and the "Clapham Sect" are described in Hopkins's *Hannah More and Her Circle*, pp. 143–61 and 203–20 in particular. The political side of her writing is described in Courtney's *Hannah More's Interest in Education and Government*, pp. 31–51. William Roberts's edition of *Memoirs of the Life and Correspondence of Hannah More* is somewhat clouded by his personal acquaintance with her in her later years. *The Works of Hannah More* should also be consulted, especially for her political writings such as the ballad "Village Politics" in which she vigorously urged the poorer classes to support the

government. Her educational efforts may be placed in context by consulting D. Owen's *English Philanthropy, 1660–1960* and Jones's *The Charity School Movement*, pp. 158–60. The only biography of Elizabeth Fry is Kent's *Elizabeth Fry*.

# BIBLIOGRAPHY

AIRLIE, MABEL FRANCES ELIZABETH (GORE) OQILVY, COUNTESS OF. *In Whig Society, 1775–1818: Compiled from the Hitherto Unpublished Correspondence of Elizabeth, Viscountess Melbourne, and Emily, Countess Cowper, Afterwards Viscountess Palmerston.* London: 1921.

ASHLEY, MAURICE. *The Stuarts in Love with Some Reflections on Love and Marriage in the Sixteenth and Seventeenth Centuries.* London: 1963. New York: 1964.

ASPINALL, A., ed. *The Correspondence of George, Prince of Wales.* 8 vols. New York: 1963–71. London: 1963–71.

———, ed. *The Later Correspondence of George III, 1783–1810.* 5 vols. Cambridge: 1962–70.

AUSTEN, JANE. *Mansfield Park.* London: 1814, Philadelphia: 1832.

BASS, ROBERT D. *The Green Dragoon: The Lives of Banastre Tarleton and Mary Robinson.* New York: 1957. London: 1957.

BEATTIE, J. M. *The English Court in the Reign of George I.* Cambridge: 1967.

BECKWITH, MILDRED C. "Catherine Macaulay, Eighteenth-Century English Rebel." Ph.D. dissertation, Ohio State University, 1953.

BESSBOROUGH, EARL OF, ed. *Georgiana: Extracts from the Correspondence of Georgiana, Duchess of Devonshire.* London: 1955.

BIDDLE, SHEILA. *Bolingbroke and Harley.* New York: 1974. London: 1975.

BIDDULPH, VIOLET. *The Three Ladies Waldegrave (and Their Mother).* London: 1938.

BLEASE, W. LYON. *The Emancipation of English Women.* London: 1910. Reprint. New York: 1976.

BOUTEN, JACOB. *Mary Wollstonecraft and the Beginnings of Female Emancipation in France and England.* Amsterdam: 1922.

BRITISH LIBRARY [Formerly integrated with British Museum]. The Duke of Newcastle's Manuscripts, including Add. MSS., 32686, 32688, and 32689, cited in text.

BROOKE, JOHN. *The House of Commons, 1754–1790.* London: 1964. New York: 1968.

———. *King George III.* New York: 1972. London: 1972.

BROWN, FORD K. *Fathers of the Victorians: The Age of Wilberforce.* Cambridge: 1961.

CANNON, JOHN. *The Fox-North Coalition: Crisis of the Constitution, 1782–4.* Cambridge: 1969.

CECIL, DAVID. *Young Melbourne.* New York: 1939. London: 1939.

CHRISTIE, IAN R. *Wilkes, Wyvill, and Reform: The Parliamentary Reform Movement in British Politics, 1760–1785.* New York: 1962. London: 1962.

CHURCHILL, WINSTON S. *Marlborough: His Life and Times.* 4 vols. New York: 1933–38. London: 1933–38.

CLAY, CHRISTOPHER. "Marriage, Inheritance, and the Rise of Large Estates in

England, 1660–1815." *Economic History Review*, 2d series, 21 (December 1968): 503–18.

COPELAND, THOMAS, ed. *The Correspondence of Edmund Burke*. 9 vols. Chicago: 1958–70. Cambridge: 1958–70.

COURTNEY, LUTHER WEEKS. *Hannah More's Interest in Education and Government*. Waco, Texas: 1929.

COWPER, SPENCER, ed. *The Diary of Mary Countess Cowper, Lady of the Bedchamber to the Princess of Wales, 1714–1720*. London: 1814.

COX, JOHN CHARLES. *Three Centuries of Derbyshire Annals as Illustrated by the Records of the Quarter Sessions of the County of Derby from Queen Elizabeth to Queen Victoria*. London: 1890.

CURTIS, LEWIS PERRY. *Chichester Towers*. New Haven: 1966.

DERRY, JOHN W. *Charles James Fox*. New York: 1972. London: 1972.

DICKINSON, H. T. *Sir Robert Walpole and the Whig Supremacy*. Mystic, Conn.: 1973. London: 1973.

DONNELLY, LUCY MARTIN. "The Celebrated Mrs. Macaulay." *William and Mary Quarterly*, 3rd series, 6 (April 1949): 173–297.

EDWARDS, AVERYL. *Frederick Lewis, Prince of Wales, 1707–51*. New York and London: 1947.

FITTS, JAMES L. "Newcastle's Mob." *Albion* 5 (Spring 1973): 41–49.

FLEISHMAN, AVROM. *A Reading of Mansfield Park: An Essay in Critical Synthesis*. Minneapolis: 1967.

FLEXNER, ELEANORE. *Mary Wollstonecraft*. New York: 1972.

FORTESCUE, JOHN, ed. *The Correspondence of King George the Third, 1760–1783*. 6 vols. London: 1927–28. Reprint: 1967.

[FOSTER, J. K., ed.] *The Life and Times of Selina, Countess of Huntingdon*. 2 vols. London: 1844.

FOSTER, VERE, ed. *The Two Duchesses: Georgiana, Duchess of Devonshire, Elizabeth, Duchess of Devonshire: Family Correspondence relating to Georgiana, Duchess of Devonshire, Elizabeth, Duchess of Devonshire, Earl of Bristol, Bishop of Derry, the Countess of Bristol, Lord and Lady Bristol, the Earl of Aberdeen, Sir Anthony Foster, Bart., and Others, 1777–1850*. London: 1898.

FRITZ, PAUL, and WILLIAMS, DAVID, eds. *The Triumph of Culture*. Toronto: 1972.

FULFORD, ROGER. *Votes for Women: The Story of a Struggle*. London: 1958.

GEORGE, M. DOROTHY. "Fox's Martyrs: The General Election of 1784." *Transactions of the Royal Historical Society*, 4th series, 21 (1939): 133–68.

GINTER, DONALD, ed. *Whig Organization in the General Election of 1790: Selections from the Blair Adams Papers*. Berkeley, Calif.: 1967.

GOWER, IRIS LEVESON. *The Face without a Frown: Georgiana, Duchess of Devonshire*. London: 1944.

Great Britain. Historical Manuscripts Commission. *Reports*.

GREEN, DAVID. *Queen Anne*. New York: 1970. London: 1970.

———. *Sarah, Duchess of Marlborough*. New York: 1967. London: 1967.

GREENBERG, JANELLE. "The Legal Status of the English Woman in Early Eighteenth Century Common Law and Equity." In *Studies in Eighteenth Century Culture*, edited by Harold E. Pagliaro. Madison, Wis.: 1975.

HABAKKUK, H. R. "English Landownership, 1680–1740." *Economic History Review* 10 (February 1940): 1–17.

———. "Marriage Settlements in the Eighteenth Century." *Transactions of the Royal Historical Society*. (1950).

HALSBAND, ROBERT, ed. *The Complete Letters of Lady Mary Wortley Montagu*. 3 vols. Oxford: 1965–67.

———. *The Life of Lady Mary Wortley Montagu*. Oxford: 1956. New York: 1960.

———. *Lord Hervey: Eighteenth Century Courtier*. Oxford: 1973. New York: 1974.

———, ed. *The Nonsense of Common Sense*. Evanston, Ill.: 1947. Reprint. New York: 1970.

———, ed. *The Selected Letters of Lady Mary Wortley Montagu*. New York: 1970. Harlow: 1970.

[HARTLEY, J., et. al., eds.] *History of the Westminster Election, Containing Every Material Occurrence, from Its Commencement on the First of April to the Final Close of the Poll, on the 17th of May to Which Is Prefixed a Summary Account of the Proceedings of the Late Parliament, So Far as They Appear Connected with the East India Business, and the Dismissing of the Portland Adminstration with Other Select and Interesting Occurrences at the Westminster Meetings, Previous to the Dissolution on the 25th Day of March, 1784. To Which Is Now Added a Complete History of the Scrutiny, and the Proceedings of the House of Commons Therein*. London: 1785.

HASLIP, JOAN. *Lady Hester Stanhope: A Biography*. New York: 1934. London: 1934.

HATTON, R. M. "George I as an English and a European Figure." In *The Triumph of Culture*, edited by Paul Fritz and David Williams. Toronto: 1972.

HEDLEY, OLWEN. *Queen Charlotte*. London: 1975. Levittown, N.Y.: 1976.

HILL, CHRISTOPHER. "Clarissa Harlowe and Her Times." *Essays in Criticism* 5 (October 1955): 315–40.

HIRST, DEREK. *The Representative of the People? Voters and Voting in England under the Early Stuarts*. Cambridge: 1975.

HOLMES, GEOFFREY. *Politics in the Age of Anne*. New York: 1967. London: 1967.

———, and SPECK, W. A., eds. *The Divided Society*. London: 1967. New York: 1968.

HOPKINS. MARY ALDEN. *Hannah More and Her Circle*. New York and London: 1947.

HORNER, JOYCE. "The English Women Novelists and Their Connection with the Feminist Movement (1688–1797)." *Smith College Studies in Modern Languages* 11, nos. 1–3 (October 1929–April 1930): 8–18.

ILCHESTER, COUNTESS OF, and STAVORDALE, LORD, eds. *The Life and Letters of Lady Sarah Lennox, 1745–1826, Daughter of Charles, Second Duke of Richmond, and Successively the Wife of Sir Thomas Charles Bunbury, Bart.; and of the Hon. George Napier; Also a Short Political Sketch of the Years 1760 to 1763 by Henry Fox, 1st Lord Holland*. London: 1902.

JOHNSON, D. T. "Charles James Fox: From Government to Opposition, 1771–1774." *English Historical Review* 89 (October 1974): 750–84.

JONES, MARY GWLADYS. *The Charity School Movement: A Study of Eighteenth Century Puritanism in Action*. Cambridge: 1938

———. *Hannah More*. Cambridge: 1952. Reprint. New York: 1968.

KEMP, BETTY. *Sir Robert Walpole*. London: 1976.

KENT, JOHN. *Elizabeth Fry*. London: 1962. New York: 1963.

KEPPEL, SONIA. *The Sovereign Lady: A Life of Elizabeth, Third Lady Holland with Her Family*. London: 1974.

KING, WILLIAM, ed. *Memoirs of Sarah, Duchess of Marlborough, Together with Her Characters of Her Contemporaries and Her Opinions*. New York: 1930. London: 1930. Reprint. New York: 1969.

KÖSTER, PATRICIA, ed. *The Novels of Mary Delariviere Manley*. 2 vols. Gainesville, Fla.: 1971.

LANSBERRY, H. C. F. "A Whig Inheritance." *Bulletin of the Institute of Historical Research* 41 (May 1968): 47–57.

LASCELLES, EDWARD. *The Life of Charles James Fox.* New York: 1936. London: 1936. Reprint. New York: 1970.

LASLETT, PETER. *The World We Have Lost.* New York: 1965. London: 1965.

*The Laws Respecting Women, as They Regard Their Natural Rights, or Their Connections and Conduct: in Which Their Interests and Duties as Daughters, Wards, Heiresses, Spinsters, Sisters, Wives, Mothers, Widows, Mothers, Legatees, Executrixes, &c. Are Ascertained and Enumerated; Also, the Obligations of Parent and Child, and the Condition of Minors. The Whole Laid Down according to the Principles of the Common and Statute Law, Explained by the Practice of the Courts of Law and Equity, and Describing the Nature and Extent of the Ecclesiastical Jurisdiction.* London: 1777. Reprint. Dobbs Ferry, N.Y.: 1974.

*Letters of Sarah, Duchess of Marlborough.* London: 1875. Reprint. New York: 1972.

*Letters to and from Henrietta, Countess of Suffolk, and Her Second Husband, the Hon. George Berkeley, from 1712 to 1767.* 2 vols. London: 1824.

LEWIS, WILMARTH SHELDON, ed. *The Correspondence of Horace Walpole.* 39 vols. New Haven: 1937–74. London: 1937–74.

LLANOVER, LADY, ed. *The Autobiography and Correspondence of Mary Granville, Mrs. Delany.* 3 vols. London: 1861. Boston: 1879.

MCADAMS, DONALD R. "Electioneering Techniques in Populous Constituencies, 1784–96." *Studies in Burke and His Time* 14 (Fall 1972): 23–54.

MACAULAY, CATHERINE GRAHAM. *Address to the People of England, Ireland, and Scotland.* London: 1775.

———. *History of England from the Accession of James I to That of the Brunswick Line.* 8 vols. London: 1763–83.

———. *Observations on the Reflections of the Right Hon. Edmund Burke on the Revolution in France, in a Letter to the Right Hon. the Earl of Stanhope.* London: 1907.

MCCLELLAND, JOHN, ed. *Letters of Sarah Byng Osborn, 1721–1773, from the Collection of the Hon. Mrs. McDonnel.* Stanford: 1930. London: 1930.

MCGREGOR, O. R. *Divorce in England: A Centenary Study.* London: 1957.

MEAKIN, ANNETTE M. B. *Hannah More: A Biographical Study.* London: 1911.

*Memoirs of the Lady Hester Stanhope as Related by Herself in Conversations with Her Physicians; Comprising Her Opinions and Anecdotes of Some of the Most Remarkable Persons of Her Time.* 3 vols. London: 1846.

MINGAY, GORDON E. *English Landed Society in the Eighteenth Century.* London: 1963.

MITCHELL, L. G. *Charles James Fox and the Disintegration of the Whig Party, 1782–1794.* Oxford: 1971.

MORE, HANNAH. *The Works of Hannah More....* London: 1801.

NAMIER, LEWIS. *England in the Age of the American Revolution.* London: 1930. 2d ed., 1961. New York: 1961.

———. *The Structure of Politics at the Accession of George III.* London: 1929. 2d edition, 1957. New York: 1967.

———, and Brooke, John, eds. *The House of Commons, 1754–1790.* 3 vols. London: 1964.

NIXON, EDNA. *Mary Wollstonecraft and Her Times.* London: 1971.

*A New Description of Sir John Soane's Museum.* London: 1969.

O'GORMAN, FRANK. *The Rise of Party in England: The Rockingham Whigs, 1760–82.* London: 1975.

OLIVER, F. S. *The Endless Adventure*. 3 vols. London: 1930–35. Boston: 1931–35.

OSBORN, EMILY F. D., ed. *Political and Social Letters of a Lady of the Eighteenth Century, 1721–1771*. London: 1890.

OTTO, PATRICIA C. "Daughters of the British Aristocracy: Their Marriages in the Eighteenth and Nineteenth Centuries with Particular Reference to the Scottish Peerage." Ph.D. dissertation, Stanford University, 1974.

OWEN, DAVID. *English Philanthropy, 1660–1960*. Cambridge, Mass.: 1964.

OWEN, JOHN. *The Eighteenth Century*. New York: 1976. London: 1976.

————. *The Pattern of Politics in Eighteenth Century England*. London: 1962.

————. "Political Patronage in Eighteenth Century England." In *The Triumph of Culture*, edited by Paul Fritz and David Williams, pp. 369–87. Toronto: 1972.

————. *The Rise of the Pelhams*. London: 1957. New York: 1971.

PALMER, IRIS IRMA (LEVISON-GOWER). *The Face Without a Frown: Georgiana, Duchess of Devonshire*. London: 1944.

*Parliamentary History of England from the Earliest Period to the Year 1803....* 36 vols. London: 1806–20.

PASSFIELD, SIDNEY JAMES WEBB, BARON, and WEBB, BEATRICE. *English Local Government from the Revolution to the Municipal Corporations Act: The Parish and the County*. New York and London: 1924.

————. *English Local Government from the Revolution to the Municipal Corporations Act: The Manor and the Borough*. 2 vols. New York and London: 1924.

————. *English Local Government from the Revolution to the Municipal Corporations Act: Statutory Authorities for Special Purposes*. New York and London: 1922.

PASTON, GEORGE [EMILY MORSE SYMONDS]. *Lady Mary Wortley Montagu and Her Times*. New York and London: 1907.

PETRIE, SIR CHARLES. *The Jacobite Movement*. 2 vols. London: 1948–50.

PLUMB, J. H. *The Origins of Political Stability in England, 1675–1725*. Boston: 1967. London: 1967 (British edition has title: *The Growth of Political Stability in England, 1675–1725*.)

————. *Sir Robert Walpole*. 2 vols. Boston: 1956–61. London: 1956–61.

*Private Correspondence of Sarah, Duchess of Marlborough, Illustrative of the Court and Times of Queen Anne*. 2 vols. London: 1838. Reprint. New York: 1972.

QUENNELL, PETER. *Caroline of England: An Augustan Portrait*. London: 1939. New York: 1940.

REID, LOREN. *Charles James Fox: A Man for the People*. Columbia, Mo.: 1969. London: 1969.

REYNOLDS, MYRA. *The Learned Lady in England, 1650–1750*. Boston: 1920.

ROBERTS, PHILIP, ed. *The Diary of Sir David Hamilton, 1709–1714*. New York: 1975. Oxford: 1975.

ROBERTS, WILLIAM. *Memoirs of the Life and Correspondence of Mrs. Hannah More*. London: 1834. New York: 1834–35.

RUDÉ, GEORGE. *The Crowd in History: A Study of Popular Disturbances in France and England, 1730–1848*. New York: 1964.

————. "The Gordon Riots: A Study of the Rioters and Their Victims." *Transactions of the Royal Historical Society*, 5th series, 6 (1956): 93–114.

————. *Paris and London in the Eighteenth Century*. London: 1952.

SAVILE, GEORGE, FIRST MARQUESS OF HALIFAX. "Advice to a Daughter." *The Complete Works of George Savile, First Marquess of Halifax*. Edited by Walter Raleigh, pp. 1–46. Oxford: 1912.

SEDGWICK, ROMNEY, ed. *The House of Commons, 1715–1754*. 2 vols. London: 1970.
———. *Lord Hervey's Memoirs*. New York: 1963. London: 1963.
———, ed. *Some Materials toward Memoirs of the Reign of George II*. 3 vols. London: 1931. Reprint. New York: 1970.
SICHEL, WALTER. *Sheridan: From New and Original Material; Including a Manuscript Diary by Georgiana, Duchess of Devonshire*. 2 vols. London: 1909.
SMITH, E. A. *Whig Principles and Party Politics: Earl Fitzwilliam and the Whig Party, 1748–1833*. Totowa, N.J.: 1975. Manchester: 1975.
SMITH, PAUL C., ed. *English Defenders of American Freedoms, 1774–1778: Six Pamphlets Attacking British Policy*. Washington, D.C.: 1972.
SMITH, WILLIAM JAMES, ed. *The Grenville Papers: Being the Correspondence of Richard Grenville, Earl Temple, K.G., and the Right Hon. George Grenville, Their Friends and Contemporaries*. London: 1852–53. Reprint. New York: 1970.
SPECK, W. A. *Tory and Whig: The Struggle in the Constituencies, 1705–1715*. New York: 1970. London: 1970.
STENTON, DORIS MARY, *The English Woman in History*. New York: 1957. London: 1957. Reprint. New York. 1977.
STOPES, CHARLOTTE CARMICHAEL. *British Freewomen: Their Historical Privilege in Common Law and Equity*. London: 1894.
STUART, DOROTHY MARGARET. *Dearest Bess: The Life and Times of Lady Elizabeth Foster, Afterwards Duchess of Devonshire, from Her Unpublished Journals and Correspondence*. London: 1955.
TAYLER, ALISTAIR and TAYLER, HENRIETTA. *Jacobites of Aberdeenshire and Banffshire in the Forty-Five*. Aberdeen: 1928.
THOMAS, DAVID. "The Social Origins of Marriage Partners of the British Peerage in the Eighteenth and Nineteenth Centuries." *Population Studies* 26, no. 1 (March 1972): 99–111.
THOMAS, KEITH. "The Double Standard." *Journal of the History of Ideas* 20 (April 1959): 195–216.
THOMPSON, ERNEST PALMER. *The Making of the English Working Class*. London: 1963. New York: 1964.
THOMPSON, F. M. L. *English Landed Society in the Nineteenth Century*. London: 1963.
THOMSON, KATHERINE BYERLEY. *Memoirs of Viscountess Sundon, Mistress of the Robes to Queen Caroline, Consort of George II; Including Letters from the Most Celebrated Persons of Her Time*. 2 vols. London: 1847.
TOMALIN, CLAIRE. *The Life and Death of Mary Wollstonecraft*. New York: 1974. London: 1974.
TURBERVILLE, A. S. *English Men and Manners in the Eighteenth Century*. Oxford: 1926. New York: 1957.
———. *The House of Lords in the Eighteenth Century*. Oxford: 1927. Reprint. Westport, Conn.: 1970.
TYSON, G. P. "A Found Woman: Some Recent Biographies of Mary Wollstonecraft." *Eighteenth Century Studies* 9 (Winter 1975–76): 263–69.
VERNEY, LADY MARGARET MARIA, ed. *Verney Family Letters of the Eighteenth Century from the Manuscripts at Claydon House*. 2 vols. London: 1930.
WALCOTT, ROBERT. *English Politics in the Early Eighteenth Century*. Cambridge, Mass.: 1956. Oxford: 1956.
WARDLE, RALPH. *Mary Wollstonecraft: A Critical Biography*. Lawrence, Kansas: 1951.
WIENBECK, DOROTHEE. *Die Stellung der Frau der oberen und mittleren Gesellschaftsklassen Englands in der ersten Hälfte des 18, Jahrhunderts unter Ausschluss der Versund

*Prosadichtung nach Zeitgenössischen Zeugnissen dargestellt*. Halle, Germany: 1931.

WILLIAMS, ROBERT. *Memoirs of Sophia Dorothea, Consort of George I*. 2 vols. London: 1845.

WILLIAMS, BASIL. *The Life of William Pitt, Earl of Chatham*. 2 vols. New York and London: 1913.

WILLIAMS, R., ed. *Memoirs of the Life and Correspondence of Hannah More*. 4 vols. London: 1834.

WOLLSTONECRAFT, MARY. *A Vindication of the Rights of Women: with Strictures on Political and Moral Subjects*. London: 1792. Reprint. New York: 1971.

*The Works of Hannah More*. 11 vols. London: 1830. New York: 1844 (two volumes).

# Demographic Contributions
## to the History of Victorian Women

Traditional historiography has confined Victorian women to the drawing room or factory. Its fixation upon the contrasts between the supposedly privileged and the obviously exploited has often blocked creative or realistic assessment of the roles, life-styles and complex status patterns of nineteenth-century women. More importantly, hallowed stereotypes have hampered the analysis of the ways in which Victorian women shaped their own lives, and through their collective activities the amorphous process of "modernization" itself.[1] The recent resurgence of women's history, however, is creating a new appreciation for the complexity and diversity which have always characterized the experience of English women. For no century in the past is this sophistication more needed than the nineteenth, when Britain, unevenly affected by the spread of industrialization and urbanization, became regionally and socially heterogeneous to an unprecedented degree.

Demographic history provides an ideal perspective from which to approach this diversity, because it focuses on the major and measurable parameters of the ordinary woman's (and man's) existence. If everyone who was ever born must die, in between they must live in a household or institution, marry or remain single, have children or not, migrate or stay put. In the aggregate these mundane events form patterns which affect the history of a nation (or region) as much as major economic and political developments. But demographic patterns frequently differ from group to group—whether the grouping principle is derived from gender, class, race, religious, ethnic, geographical, or generational factors—so that the analysis of mortality, fertility, marriage, migration, and household structure provides us with a direct way of measuring the extent and nature of differences between and within local populations of a single nationality.

Demographic data can also be used to dramatically highlight differences between ordinary life in the past and present, as Peter Uhlenberg did in his article on nineteenth-century Massachusetts women, "A Study of Cohort Life Cycles" (1969). Uhlenberg demonstrated that until the early twentieth century only the exceptional woman managed to live out the "typical" life cycle, which included living long enough to marry, having children and surviving jointly with a husband until the last child married and grandchildren began arriving. In the nineteenth century only one out of five native-born women experienced all these phases of their life cycle; whereas one out of three females born died before the age of twenty.

Although no one has used available data to make similar calculations for the women of nineteenth-century England, the demographic profiles of the two areas were sufficiently alike to produce similar outcomes, implying that for English women as well, the "ordinary" life cycle was exceptional until the twentieth century.

In general, all nineteenth-century societies were afflicted with higher death rates (or lower life expectancies) than their twentieth-century counterparts. Inevitably the relatively greater pervasiveness of illness, death, and dying affected the quality of life itself, as well as prevailing attitudes about pain, funerals, and mourning. Social historians have recently become very interested in the interplay between demographic facts and the attitudes, values and behavior patterns dominant in any culture—in France these interconnections lie at the heart of what is now fashionably called the study of "mentalities."[2] In future research, historians of women might find it fruitful, for example, to reexamine the history of birth control, abortion, infanticide, pregnancy, childbirth, and child care from the new perspectives which stress the interrelatedness of demographic and psychological variables.

In the specific case of Victorian women, demographic research also provides a natural focus for the exploration of several key dimensions of the nineteenth-century experience—the feminine role in the translation of "progress" into improved health and greater longevity, the spread of fertility control, the role of marital status and migration in the accelerating drive for personal autonomy, and the evolution of new roles for women in and outside of family households.

Before we can explore the substantive findings of demographic history, it is necessary to review some of the available guides to the data sources and methods of analysis out of which demographic history is constructed. After some of the most general treatments are discussed, primary sources specific to the Victorian era will be examined. Subsequently, modern scholarship about or pertaining to the demographic history of Victorian women is reviewed (selectively) according to whether or not it has most relevance to fertility, mortality, marriage, migration, or household structure.

## General Guides to Sources and Methods in Demographic History

Demographic history is most interesting when it asks general questions about the role of population change in the entire complex of social change. But in order to tackle the "big questions," the demographically oriented scholar must possess a certain amount of reliable statistical data. First and foremost, demography is the *quantitative* study of population. Initially a demographer looks for data on the size of a population, and how its members are distributed by age and sex as well as geographically. Subsequently, the study of changing growth rate patterns includes the analysis of how fertility, mortality, and migration have affected the size and structure of a population over time. The analytic techniques available are diverse, and range from the elegantly simple to the extremely complex, but the specific quantitative techniques which can be used by the historical demographer are determined by the amount and nature of the data available.[3]

T. H. Hollingsworth's *Historical Demography* (1969) remains the best descriptive survey of data and source problems in demographic history, while Louis Henry's newly translated *Population Analysis and Models* (1976) is now the most comprehensive representation of the modern analytic (quantitative) techniques which can be applied to historical problems. Anyone planning to do historical research in population must be familiar with both. The best and most readable general survey of the mortality and fertility history of European populations remains E. A. Wrigley's *Population and History* (1969), but it treats preindustrial population patterns in a far more detailed fashion than industrial or postindustrial developments. Ironically, European demographic historians continue to be more interested in preindustrial demography than in the demography of industrializing Europe, despite the fact that data is often more abundant in the latter period.

The continuing preoccupation with the demographic characteristics of essentially traditional (largely European) peasant cultures is still very evident in the interesting new collection of essays edited by Ronald Demos Lee, *Population Patterns in the Past* (1977). Most valuable among them to the historian interested in women is Daniel Scott Smith's, "A Homeostatic Demographic Regime: Patterns in West European Family Reconstitution Studies." This contains a useful summary table of average values for nuptiality, mortality, and fertility in preindustrial Europe, although it involves primarily French data. All of these books contain scattered material which is relevant to our evolving understanding of how high mortality and high fertility placed effective constraints on the degree of autonomy the ordinary woman could hope to achieve in the premodern period. Unfortunately, none deal extensively with industrializing Europe, let alone Victorian English women.

Books concerned exclusively with English demography also show a similar fixation on the early modern period. The essays edited by E. A. Wrigley in *An Introduction to English Historical Demography* (1966), deal mostly with the use of Anglican parish registers as a data source. From the 1530s to the 1830s parish registers, through the recording of baptisms, burial, and marriages, are the principal (and sometimes the only) index of births, deaths, and rates of family formation available for England. These essays also contain good discussions of the respective merits and limits of aggregative analysis and family reconstitution as alternative methods of analysis (see footnote 3).

Peter Laslett's well-known *The World We Have Lost* (1965) was the first general attempt to use parish register data and other demographic material to explore the ramifications of preindustrial mortality, fertility, and family structure on the lives of ordinary men and women in a specifically English context. Despite the controversy over Laslett's approach to the analysis of class structure, the book remains a valuable introduction to ordinary life before industrialization and urbanization gradually transformed its context. In this sense it remains a useful if extremely general basis for determining continuities and discontinuities in the demographic experience of Victorian women particularly for age at marriage and fertility patterns.

In the late eighteenth century, parish registers became an increasingly inaccurate index to the actual number of births and deaths occurring in England.[4] Because of the resulting confusion, the decades between the 1780s and 1840s are a statistical wilderness which abound with conflicting estimates of national and regional mortality and fertility trends.

The best guide presently available to the source problems which generate continuing debate is M. W. Flinn's *British Population Growth 1700–1850* (1970). After reading Flinn, it becomes clear why demographic historians of the later eighteenth and early nineteenth centuries are primarily absorbed by controversies over technical problems involving the adjustment of defective data. While basic trends in national fertility and mortality remain controversial, it becomes difficult to relate them in any meaningful fashion to social and economic changes as these affect either women or men. In the meantime anyone interested in the demography of the period from 1780 to 1840 must be prepared to invest a great deal of energy in rather technical problems before dealing with substantive issues, particularly those relevant to groups of women.[5]

## SOURCES FOR THE DEMOGRAPHIC HISTORY OF VICTORIAN WOMEN

Because of data problems, the following bibliographical review concentrates on sources for demographic trends in the post-1840 era. Shortly after Victoria became queen, the principal sources for the demography of Great Britain took their modern forms. In 1837, the registration of births, deaths, and marriages became the province of civil and not religious (Anglican) authorities. This resulted in the renewed availability of more accurate vital statistics. Subsequently, the national enumeration of 1841 led to the publication of a series of census volumes which took a recognizably standard modern form, including as they did detailed data on the age and occupational structure of the male and female populations.[6]

But it is the 1851 census volumes which are the first great monument to the Victorian passion for statistics.[7] The mid-century enumeration continued the new series of tables on age and occupational structure, but it added data on marital status by age and county level migration data for the first time. More importantly, a special enumeration of religious affiliation and education was carried out as part of the census. The introductory essays to the regular and special data sets all contained particularly valuable general discussions, which ought to be read by users of the statistical volumes for background information on the data.

Between 1851 and 1900 no further special enumerations were undertaken (the religious census in particular had been much too controversial), but the standard data gathered often became more detailed. In 1891 the first tables on the employment patterns of married women were published, showing that nationally only about ten percent of all married women were employed. These and other data on the employment patterns of married women must be used with caution. Married women were engaged in a diverse range of economic activities not all of which paid a regular wage or took them out of the home. This sort of employment tended to be overlooked by or concealed from the enumerators.[8] Nevertheless, it is probably true that English women worked outside the home infrequently after marriage, and less frequently than their Continental counterparts.

The last census before the First World War included the most important special enumeration yet undertaken by the census officials—the comprehensive set of data on fertility and marriage published as part of the 1911 census.[9] Geographical and occupational differences involving children ever born and surviving to successive cohorts of women born in the nineteenth century were fully detailed in the published tables. The complex patterns of variation which emerged at the occupational level have never been entirely explained, although the fertility history of the major "status groups" was clear enough.[10]

Although the Victorian and Edwardian census volumes contain much that is essential to the study of demographic history, they are basically vast collections of numbers which can only intimidate the casual reader. Those using the published volumes should know what they are looking for, and plan to do some background reading. All census data contains some pitfalls for the unwary, but there are several general guides which discuss the kinds of data available in the Victorian censuses and the problems connected with their use (if any).[11]

Unfortunately, none of the British guides to census data discuss information specific to females in the detailed and illuminating manner of van de Walle's *The Female Population of France in the Nineteenth Century* (1974), or Coale and Zelnick's *New Estimates of Fertility and Population in the United States* (1963). Both books systematically review age misstatement and underenumeration by age group among the female population. Thus many late nineteenth-century French women who were nearing thirty continued to report their age as under twenty-five; while in late nineteenth- and early twentieth-century America, substantial fractions of women, particularly middle-aged women, appear to be missing from the census altogether. Both books are technical rather than broadly historical in orientation, and thus they provide no social explanations for the data they set out, but a social historian could easily use this kind of information to further the study of anxieties related to aging among women.

Unexpectedly, the census volumes can also be used to illuminate and even "date" changing attitudes towards women. For example, before 1891 wives not otherwise employed, and older children as well, were always classified among the "domestic" sector of the economy. This included hotel and inn keepers as well as salaried domestic servants. Although there is no evidence that the majority of British housewives subsequently abandoned their domestic duties, by 1891 they, along with older children, were shifted into the category called "Indefinite and Non-Productive," thereby joining paupers, lunatics, and gentlemen, among others. It is around this time, then, that wives became "officially" viewed as dependents, whose activities made no meaningful contribution to the economy.

Although the published census volumes can be used to illuminate many aspects of Victorian women's history, it is the unpublished enumerators' schedule books which are in many ways the most demographically revealing. The manuscript schedule books contain data on the name, sex, age, marital status, occupation, birthplace, and relationship to head of each member of a household. It is only by using these schedule books, for example, that household structure can be related to social class or occupation, or that occupation can be related to migration and marriage patterns. The schedule books from the 1841 through 1871 censuses have been microfilmed and are available for use at the Public Record Office in London.[12]

The major published source of data for the analysis of mortality, fertility, and marriage is found in the *Annual Reports of the Registrar General for Births, Deaths, and Marriages in England and Wales*.[13] (Data for Scotland and Ireland are published in separate series.) The reports for England and Wales were begun in 1837 and continued through the period under discussion. Each annual report had a valuable introductory essay which discussed the data, and occasionally related the unfolding trends to the social and economic forces acting upon women. Although these discussions are not very detailed, they do provide an indication of how demographic changes could be used to buttress or unsettle prevailing prejudices about women. For example, whenever the registrar general discussed any unfavorable aspect of female mortality patterns he tended to place the blame on the way women dressed (the corset was a particular favorite), thus shifting responsibility to women themselves.

From the standpoint of the period (cross-sectional) analysis of national and regional variations in vital rates, the most useful volumes are those which contain ten-year summaries of national, county, and "Registration District" statistics.[14] The first summary volume appeared as part of the *Fifteenth Annual Report*. Subsequently the twenty-fifth, thirty-fifth, forty-fifth reports, etc., contained similar summary tables.[15] As always when using the *Annual Reports*, background reading must be done on the completeness and accuracy of registration. Extremely useful in this respect is Teitelbaum's "Birth Underregistration in the Constituent Counties of England and Wales: 1841–1910" (1974).[16]

The aggregate statistics published in the annual reports were drawn from information provided by the unpublished, individual certificates of births, deaths, and marriages collected by local registrars. Most of these are still preserved at Somerset House in London, or in various registry or county archives around England. Although anyone is allowed to pay a fee and look up one or several specific events which, for example, may have involved an ancestor, researchers are still not allowed to do "general searches" of all the records from one particular area or time period. There is no time limit like the hundred-year rule which restricts access to census schedules. Even though local registrars have made some exceptions, the records, in order to protect privacy and prevent blackmail, are supposed to be forever sealed. The determination of the registrar general's office to perpetuate this policy is extremely unfortunate, since it is only through general access to the certificates for an area or time period that scholars can begin to relate social class and occupational factors to female mortality patterns, distinguish regional from occupational influences upon fertility in the mid-Victorian period, or do family reconstitution for the post-1840 decades which does not involve Anglicans only.

The outpouring of statistical data from the published census volumes and the *Annual Reports of the Registrar General* fascinated statistically minded Victorians. Most issues of the *Journal of the Royal Statistical Society* contained one or more demographic articles which made use of these sources, or some of the other diverse minor sources containing data on population change of one sort or another. Therefore, the journal articles can be used as a guide to other sources of demographic data for the period. The quality of the data, as well as the analytic techniques employed, varied quite considerably, but there are many interesting studies by nineteenth-century statisticians on women-related topics which deserve rereading.[17]

Another major and woefully underexplored primary source for demographic information is the vast body of literature produced by Victorian doctors, physicians, and medical practicioners. In books and journal articles they regularly addressed problems (sometimes providing data) in areas of central concern to the demographic historian interested in women. Causes of death and illnesses of particular importance to women were often discussed, as were (albeit rarely) the influence of contraception, abortion, and sexual behavior on fertility. Recently American medical literature has been used to produce several interesting studies of doctors and women in the nineteenth century, but nothing major along these lines has been done for Victorian England.[18] (The medical literature published in Victorian Britain is massive in scope, and an excellent introductory bibliography can be found in Kanner's "The Women of England in a Century of Social Change, Part II" [1973].)[19]

Continuing research on the demographic history of Victorian women must build on the scholarship which has already been done. Invaluable from this standpoint are the regularly updated entries in the bibliographical journal *Population Index*. All contemporary and historical demographic research is completely indexed by topic, area, and period. There are two journals which are exclusively devoted to historical demography: *Local Population Studies* deals almost exclusively with English material, while the

French journal, *Annales de Démographie Historique*, occasionally publishes research relevant to England. *Population Studies* publishes excellent historical articles in almost every issue, while the *Journal of Family History* often contains articles which are directly relevant to women's history.

## The Demographic History of Victorian Women

We now turn to a selective survey of how secondary works using Victorian data can be used to illuminate the demographic experience of Victorian women. Unlike other specialties in the social sciences or history, historical demography has never failed to recognize the existence and (to a lesser degree) the importance of women. But since most research was not done from the new perspectives now being explored by historians of women (indeed how could it have been?) it has certain limitations from this standpoint. Nevertheless, demographic historians have provided those focusing more intensively on women with much valuable data. Our survey begins with the most general demographic treatments, and proceeds to studies which specialize on fertility, mortality, marriage, migration, and household structure data in that order. No attempt has been made to assess the merits of the respective methodologies used by the authors cited, since this would not have been possible in the alloted space.

In the 1970s demographic history came of age, but the general works published on the Victorian period were not designed to advance our understanding of the role (passive or active) that the female half of the population had in the changing demographic picture, and thus they contain little of interest.[20]

An outstanding and welcome exception is Kennedy's *The Irish: Emigration, Marriage and Fertility* (1973). This excellent analysis of Irish demography in the nineteenth century treats the particular experiences of rural Irish peasant women and their working-class urban counterparts in rich, revealing detail. Of particular interest is the study of the mortality and migration patterns of ordinary rural women. Irish women were the last in Europe to achieve age-specific mortality rates which were consistently more favorable than those of men. Kennedy shows how this demographic lag was due to the unfavorable ways farm wives and daughters were regarded and treated in the rural economy. In the case of daughters, their unpaid labor, however important, was not counted as justifying the expenses incurred to farm families through their support and cost of dowries. Poor diets and harsh treatment were fairly general, and this led directly to higher death rates for girls than those experienced by their brothers. In an urban context it was easier to find wage-paying jobs and there was less reason for daughters to receive or endure family-inflicted oppression. Thus it was not surprising that sex-linked mortality differentials were reversed in the Irish urban context, or that Irish peasant women left the countryside in droves.

In the general treatments of English demography, it is local or special studies which tend to have the most interesting detailed data on women. Outstanding examples are Hollingsworth's demographic profiles of British ducal families and peerage families.[21] Hollingsworth's ducal study presents data on all the cohorts of these privileged women born between 1330 and 1930, describing their mortality and fertility history in great detail. The cohort or generational changes over time and unexpected contrasts between ducal sons and ducal daughters are often remarkable, but Hollingsworth is a statistical rather than a social demographer and by convention none of the observed changes are explained, except as a by-product of other statistical changes. Anyone interested in the overall experience of the well-born, however, could easily employ his data in broader social studies of women in the highest strata of British society.

Armstrong's *Stability and Change in An English County Town* (1974) is basically a broad study of demographic patterns in York around 1851. It is most useful for data on fertility and marriage patterns. One of Armstrong's most interesting findings is that place of residence in York was more important than other indicators of relative wealth in influencing fertility, suggesting the possibility that such matters were influenced by knowledge and attitudes prevailing locally among women. (The work of McLaren on abortion information also points to local communication networks among women. See footnote 38.)

Bryant's "Demographic Trends in South Devon" (1971) develops an interesting method for studying short distance migration among married rural laborers (at least those who have large families); while Haines, "Fertility, Nuptiality and Occupation" (1977) considers the social, economic, and demographic characteristics of England's coal-mining populations, the most fertile occupational group in nineteenth-century England. (An article by Friedlander on nineteenth-century coal-mining populations goes over similar evidence, but much more superficially.) The most detailed, useful and revealing study of how occupation affects fertility is David Levine's recent *Family Formation in an Age of Nascent Capitalism* (1977).

From the standpoint of the history of women all these studies are interesting, but of limited usefulness, because of their preoccupation with the family as the central unit of analysis. All the authors assume (without considering alternatives) that the interests of husbands and wives are identical with respect to family size. Undoubtedly this is often true, but it is not necessarily the case. A focus on wives as women, or even mothers, apart from wives as family members (or junior partners of their husbands) can lead to unexpected insights. This is amply demonstrated by Perdita Huston's "To Be Born a Woman is a Sin" (1977). Huston interviewed some two hundred rural peasant women in contemporary third world countries, and found that most of the women were conscious of a clear conflict of interest between their own reproductive goals and those of their husbands.[22] Historians do not usually have access to such unambiguous forms of evidence, but unless the possibility of husband/wife conflicts is kept in mind, subtle indications of it can be overlooked.

We turn now to studies which do deal more directly with women, through the selective consideration of presently available classic and recent treatments which concentrate more exclusively on fertility-related issues.

## FERTILITY

The end of intensive childbearing deserves to be regarded as the B.C./A.D. of the history of women. Despite its intrinsic importance, little as yet is known about the causes of the momentous shift from "traditional" to "modern" fertility patterns which began in Western Europe and the United States.[23] Although the European fertility transition began in earnest in the nineteenth century, its onset does not appear to be consistently correlated with a specific stage of social or economic development at the national level. In France, for example, fertility began its modern sustained decline much in advance of marked industrialization or urbanization, while in England industrialization and urbanization were "completed" at least two decades before any unbroken downturn of fertility began. Because of these and other inconsistencies analytic interest has shifted to the regional level. But in England, as noted previously, both national and regional analysis has been hampered in the existence of defective data, particularly for the late eighteenth and early nineteenth centuries. The resulting confusion about the basic chronology of fertility change at the national level has led to a plethora of conflicting theories.

Traditional scholars argued either that fertility was constant from 1750 to 1876, or that it rose from 1780 to 1820 and was constant thereafter until the 1870s. Fairly recently Hollingsworth detected a previously unsuspected decline in fertility from around 1820 to 1840 based on changing age structure data.[24] Soon afterwards Ronald Lee, using newly developed statistical techniques, challenged the validity of Hollingsworth's "discovery," and argued instead that fertility was constant from 1780 to 1836.[25] Only someone at ease with sophisticated statistical arguments can hope to judge the relative merits of either case. In the meanwhile, had

Hollingsworth gone unchallenged, it would have brought the otherwise divergent fertility history of British women more into line with their French and American counterparts, since in both countries the downward course of fertility began early in the century. Without evidence for an earlier decline, England will continue to appear economically ahead of but demographically "behind" its neighbors.

Two family reconstitution studies mentioned earlier provide local data relevant to controversies about national trends. Levine's study of Shepsted, *Family Formation in an Age of Nascent Capitalism* (1977), provides definite evidence of a rise in fertility from the middle of the eighteenth century. More importantly, it also presents good data indicating that a fall in fertility took place among couples married after 1825. This is evidence, Levine argues, that depressed economic conditions forced couples to practice birth control. Levine's explanation for changes in fertility is classically Marxist—whether rising or falling, fertility is regarded as a function of the demand for labor. However, if we return to the upper end of the social scale, and to Hollingsworth's study of ducal families it can be seen that he too uncovers similar trends in fertility—a rise in the eighteenth century and a falling off by mid-century.[26] Was there an increased demand for the labor of the leisured classes in the eighteenth century? Did the demand for ducal "hands" subsequently decrease? If so, why was it noticed first among the wives of dukes' sons and thereafter among dukes' daughters? Were these wealthy and privileged families reacting to employment pressures, or were there broader, more subtle forces at work which caused prevailing "mentalities" to shift, favoring first larger, then smaller families?

In the meantime, if fertility rose in the eighteenth century among such diverse groups as peers and rural industrial laborers, for what groups would it have been stable or declining, so as to generate stablity at the national level in the manner required by Lee's new estimates?[27] These and other questions will keep scholars fascinated by the late eighteenth and early nineteenth centuries until more painstaking research at the local level can clarify the confused situation.

It is particularly important to determine with some certainty whether or not there was a fall in fertility in the 1820s and 30s. Among other possibilities, such a fall could indicate that early birth control advocates had more success than presently imagined,[28] or alternatively that immiseration of the kind described by Levine was so widespread among certain segments of the working class that the fecundity of their women (i.e., the ability to conceive and bear live children) was impaired. The latter possibility is something on which the research of Rose Frisch on diet, puberty, and fecundity has a bearing, particularly "Population Food Intake and Fertility: Historical Evidence for a Direct Effect of Nutrition on Reproductive Ability" (1978).[29] Frisch argues that European women never had as many children as they were biologically capable of bearing (given adequate nutrition) because so many were so chronically undernourished.

When we move from the mysteries of the early nineteenth century to the Victorian era itself, data is much better and national trends more certain, but marked regional and occupational diversity makes clarity at the national level somewhat irrelevant. Carol Pearce's article, "Expanding Families" (1973) is a study of fertility contrasts in the town of Ashford, Kent, in the middle decades of the nineteenth century. For example, although retailers' wives were significantly older than laborers' wives when they married, the former were more fertile than the latter in the first five years of marriage. Over several decades, the fertility of the retailers' wives declined slightly, while that of the laborers' wives rose. Pearce does not explore the determinants of fertility in Ashford, but the contrasts are suggestive. Were the fertile retailers' wives beginning to deliberately control their fertility? Were the laborers' wives originally less fecund than their more prosperous sisters? Was their rising fertility a sign of better health? Whatever the case, Pearce does not think the observed differences are due to changes in the completeness of registration.[30]

A regional study of demographic contrasts in mid-nineteenth-century Cornwall has also demonstrated the existence of divergent fertility trends in some sections of the county. At the aggregative level, fertility was stable from 1840 to 1860, but this was the result of rising fertility in the newer mining areas and some of the agricultural districts, canceled out by declining fertility in older mining areas and some of the towns.[31] In this case declining fertility was probably heavily influenced by the magnitude of husband-only migration out of the older mining areas.

Juda Matras's "Social Strategies of Family Formation" (1965) uses data from the Fertility Census of 1911 to explore class and occupational differences at the national level in the mid-Victorian decades. Matras finds that already at least twenty percent of the Status I families (mostly upper middle-class) were making some attempts to control fertility.[32] By the First World War, seventy-two percent of this group had become "controllers," the highest percentage found among any group. Patricia Branca's study of mid-Victorian women, *Silent Sisterhood* (1975), gives the impression that the use of birth control was more widespread than this among mid-Victorian middle-class women, but her data sources appear too inadequate to sustain such a claim.

In the 1870s, national fertility rates finally began the decisive phase of their modern decline. Regional and socioeconomic differences in patterns of change were the subject of the tables published in the Fertility Census of 1911. These data were systematically analyzed by Innes in *Class Fertility Trends in England and Wales* (1938). Despite shortcomings in the way that data on various occupations were aggregated into status groups, the data clearly showed that the decline in fertility affected every region and every socioeconomic stratum. But since some were affected more than others, the process of differential decline had the effect of temporarily maximizing fertility differences among the country's social classes. Clearly the upper and middle classes led the decline, while miners and agricultural workers lagged furthest behind. Of all the working-class groups, textile workers had the lowest fertility by 1911.[33]

Women in the textile-producing areas had a long tradition of working outside the home for a wage; but when David Glass tried to systematically correlate female labor force patterns with low fertility in other regions of the country, no consistent relationship emerged over the decades 1851 to 1931. In fact, Glass could find no consistent correlation between declining fertility at the county level and any of the obvious social and economic forces at work in the country.[34] This is not entirely surprising, since the county may not be the most appropriate unit of analysis for the detection of such interactions.

It was not until the early 1950s publication of Banks' *Prosperity and Parenthood* that any general treatment appeared to make social and economic sense of declining fertility in the late nineteenth century. Banks argued that by analyzing data on the incomes, expenditures, and aspirations of the "middle classes" (the subpopulations which experienced the sharpest drops in their fertility) one could determine why the fertility decline began. The data in *Prosperity and Parenthood* clearly demonstrated that one of the few ways the "middle classes" could afford to maintain or raise their standards of living (including increasingly expensive children) in the economic context of depression and stable incomes was to deliberately reduce family size.[35] Later, in *Feminism and Family Planning* (1964), Banks and his coauthor, Olive Banks, explored the role that "feminism" may have had in independently producing fertility declines. They concluded that "feminists" were not advocates of birth control, and, moreover, the method by which family size was reduced was coitus interruptus, a male-dominated rather than female-dominated form of control. In their estimation it appeared that the decline in fertility was prompted largely by parental concerns over the cost of children and carried out primarily by a cautious paterfamilias. Any independent role for women was minimized or lost altogether.

The strictly economic approach to the social and economic analysis of late Victorian fertility trends has been attacked from several different standpoints. Banks' data on "middle-class" lifestyles are actually highly specific to the situation of the upper middle classes. It remains to be demonstrated that the strata above or below this very small minority of Victorian families were affected by a cost/income squeeze of a similar nature. Were ducal families (consistently among the wealthiest and most secure in England) also reducing their fertility for reasons related to the cost of children? Were working-class families less affected by the cost of children than middle-class families, and thus less compelled to limit family size? This seems unlikely in that opportunities for gainfully employing children were becoming less plentiful in the late nineteenth-century economy.[36]

Secondly, in exploring the impact of "feminism" on fertility the Bankses used an unjustifiably narrow definition, confining the term to organized groups working for economic or political change. But there were many kinds of "feminism" in the nineteenth century, some of which never crystallized into formal organizations. Some novelists, for example, were spreading the individualist gospel of self-realization among women who would not have thought of themselves as feminists. These and other diffuse forms of "life-style" feminism had an impact on the lives of ordinary women long before they got the vote. Daniel Scott Smith's article, "Family Limitation, Sexual Control, and Domestic Feminism in Victorian America" (1974) argues this case very persuasively. Patricia Branca stresses a similar "unofficial" drive for personal autonomy within the confines of traditional family life among Victorian English women in *Silent Sisterhood*.

Finally, with respect to the means whereby fertility control was achieved, Banks's insistence on the ultimate importance of coitus interruptus is undercut by his own multiple references to the possibility of the widespread resort to abortion among middle-class women.[37] Coitus interruptus was the major strategy that Victorian and Edwardian couples admitted to using, but doctors were convinced that many women were secretly using abortion to terminate unwanted pregnancies. The doctors testifying in *The Declining Birth Rate—Its Causes and Effects*, described towns where working-class women would go so far as to poison themselves with lead in order to induce abortions. In a recent article, Angus McLaren argues convincingly for the central importance of abortion in reducing late nineteenth-century British fertility.[38] A similar situation with respect to the prevalence of abortion existed in Victorian America and nineteenth-century France.[39]

Abortion is a woman-dominated form of family control, one which in the late nineteenth century involved a certain risk to a woman's health and safety. Were women resorting to it only because of the rising cost of children or related economic pressures? Can it be established instead that the control of fertility was part of the independently growing desire for emancipation from the confines of intensive maternity? Whatever the case, it seems unlikely that women had no role in the decline of fertility apart from their cooperation in husband-wife consumption-oriented dyads.

What of the role of women in the decline in illegitimate fertility? In England a pronounced fall in illegitimate birth rates began in the 1860s, a full decade before the decline of marital fertility.[40] No substantial explanations for this trend have yet been developed, but clearly the control of illegitimate fertility must have more to do with the restriction of pre-marital sexual behavior and/or the increasingly effective use of birth control outside marriage, than with rational calculations about the cost of raising children.

Unfortunately, we still know relatively little about changing patterns of Victorian sexual behavior. Although the phrase "Victorian women" is almost synomymous with frigidity, in reality sexual norms were quite a bit more flexible than prevailing stereotypes allow. F. Barry Smith's re-visionist essay, "Sexuality in Britain 1800–1900" (1977), reminds us of how little concrete information we actually possess on Victorian practice and how much research on sexual behavior must yet be done.

Edward Shorter's work has become rather controversial for suggesting that rising illegitimate fertility on the Continent in the early part of the nineteenth century was a result of increasing sexual activity consequent upon the early "liberation" of women by the forces of "modernization."[41] Since he implies that pleasure-seeking women casually took illegitimacy in their stride, he has been severely (and justifiably) criticized.[42] The applicability of Shorter's arguments and those of his critics to the English case, of course, depends on whether or not a genuine rise in illegitimacy is believed to have taken place.

By now it is apparent that the fertility history of nineteenth-century England is only in the early stages of exploration. Future work must start with thoroughly analyzed and adjusted data, and make use of a wide variety of techniques for measuring fertility.[43] At present the most useful contributions to the field will probably come in the form of local studies which clearly delineate differential levels and trends among well-defined groups of women in specific social and economic contexts. Ultimately, research which contributes to the history of women, as well as the history of fertility, will consciously explore how the confusing array of forces involved in rapid social change may have impinged differently on men and women, husbands and wives, thus creating an independent space within which some women might have acted on their own.

## MORTALITY

The changes which took place in nineteenth-century mortality patterns were no less dramatic than those which involved fertility, but the magnitude and direction of mortality trends in the early nineteenth century have also been obscured by similar problems with defective data. Nevertheless, mortality appears to have been drifting downward earlier and more consistently than fertility. The important question remains why the lives of both men and women became longer and less subject to catastrophic termination in the form of epidemics.[44] The historian of women will ask in addition why were there differences in the mortality differentials of males and females, and why did these differences increasingly favor females?

The first question is best answered by McKeown's new *The Modern Rise of Population* (1976). Although the author deals with the mortality history of Europe as a whole, he pays special attention to the British case. According to McKeown the modern decline in mortality was primarily a function of improvements in nutrition and sanitation, both of which made it easier for human beings to increase their life expectancy through their own strengthened natural resistance to disease. Very little credit is due to scientific breakthroughs and medical advances.

McKeown makes a good case, but in the course of its development he rarely distinguishes between the mortality history of men and women, although he could have done so in ways which would illuminate his case. Were women increasing their life expectancies at a faster rate than men because they were relatively better-fed and personally cleaner? (McKeown implies that similar differences were at the root of aristocratic mortality advantages.) More importantly women may have had a role in declining mortality by fostering personal and food hygiene at the household level.[45] Finally, the decline in infanticide, to which McKeown attributes such importance, may have been more directly influenced by the attitudes and behavior of women than men, particularly in cases involving bastardy.

Doctors rarely praised women for their efforts to improve health and sanitation, although they never hesitated to blame women for their shortcomings. It was easy enough for them to criticize working-class women who bottle-fed their babies instead of giving them the breast, but this overlooked the fact that some mothers had to work to support their families, while others were in such chronic ill health that they were incapable of producing their own milk.[46]

275

Ultimately, the detailed analysis of mortality must begin with the analysis of the enormous body of statistical data on the changing importance of specific causes of death, which were published all through the Victorian period. W. P. D. Logan in his "Mortality in England and Wales from 1848 to 1947" (1950) used the registrar general's data to distinguish between the mortality history of men and women, but he did not relate the observed changes to social and economic conditions. My own "Sex and Death in Victorian England" (1977) shows how difficult it is to do this, given the nature of the published data. All through the nineteenth century, as recognizable "modern" mortality patterns emerged [47] the changes associated with industrialization and urbanization (or modernization in general) were differentially affecting different regions and social classes, as well as the men and women of those subpopulations. Many more local studies of mortality rates by age and sex must be done before we can untangle the complex network of causes and effects as they impinged on the mortality of both men and women.

In the aggregate picture, the role of tuberculosis in giving women their first clear mortality advantages over men in most age groups is clear. Tuberculosis, the single leading cause of death in Victorian Britain, was becoming less lethal for both sexes but for women this trend proceeded more rapidly. The reasons for this are not clear. Since intensive child-bearing was thought to aggravate tubercular conditions, the reduction of fertility may have been a contributing factor. But a superficial consideration of the data, decade by decade, does not support this. Of all the leading causes of death in the nineteenth century, tuberculosis is the one most in need of further study.

The role of pregnancy and childbirth in female mortality and morbidity (the propensity to illness) also needs much more research. The official data, which gives the impression that deaths related to childbirth played a very small role in the mortality patterns of women aged twenty to forty-five, may be misleading.[48] (There were between four and five maternal deaths per thousand deliveries in the Victorian period.) At any rate one of the contributing factors to the lack of interest on the part of doctors in improving the maternal mortality picture all during the nineteenth century was the prevailing, religiously inspired mentality that it was God's will that women suffer, even to the point of dying, during childbirth.

One feature of the registrar general's data on death rates by age group is particularly striking. Throughout the nineteenth century and into the early twentieth young girls aged five to fifteen were generally at a mortality disadvantage when compared to their male counterparts. The registrar general did not try to explain this puzzling feature of his data in any serious fashion, although it clearly points to the widespread neglect and/or abuse of young vulnerable females, even among the middle classes.[49] What concrete forms this negative environment took can only be determined by future research, along lines pioneered by Kennedy for the Irish case.

Several other topics in mortality history would be extremely useful and interesting to explore. One involves the impact of marital status on mortality rates. Contemporary data from developed countries show that married women have consistently more favorable mortality patterns than never-married women.[50] In turn, never-married women have lower death rates at every age than either divorced or widowed women. Were these same patterns characteristic of the nineteenth century as well, even when the never-married state was so much more prevalent, and married women were, if not killed by intensive maternity, at least worn out by it?

In general the study of mortality patterns in Victorian England has attracted less scholarly interest and is thus less well-developed than the study of fertility. There are few local studies of mortality by age and sex. Very little analysis dealing specifically with the impact of class or occupation on feminine death rates has been done. There are no detailed studies of infant and child mortality patterns which use existing data to examine whether or not there were any pale survivals of earlier eras when discrimination against females was not simply unfair, but actually deadly.[51] Finally, there are no recent statistical studies of the volitional aspects of mortality, suicide and murder, as these affected Victorian women.[52]

## MARITAL STATUS

Like all the countries of nineteenth-century Western Europe, Britain had what is called the "European Marriage Pattern." Its characteristic features were first discovered by J. Hajnal and outlined in a deservedly famous article, "European Marriage Patterns in Perspective" (1965). Hajnal pointed out that in most third world countries, even today, the average woman is married by her middle or late teens to a man much older than herself, often by as much as ten years. Moreover, few women were allowed to remain permanently unmarried, whatever their feelings and preferences.

By contrast, in nineteenth-century Europe the average woman was married in her middle to late twenties to a man very near her own age. A more startling departure was that ten to twenty percent of all adult women remained permanently unmarried. Hajnal argued that in ancient and medieval time Europe had the same marriage patterns as the rest of the world; he thought that the gradual departure from them probably began in the late middle ages. It was not until the seventeenth century, however, that the features of the new pattern were clearly established throughout Western Europe.

Although the economic and social significance of changing marriage patterns for Western European economic development are still being explored, its importance for women's history is self-evident. Western Europe became the only cultural area which gave its women time to develop a mature sense of identity before subjecting them to the rigors of intensive maternity. If only from the standpoint of age, husbands became more like partners than father substitutes. Most importantly, some women were left permanently outside the framework of traditional social roles, both free and forced to explore new strategies of survival, gradually developing new life-styles which ultimately led to changes in the status of all women.

The forces which generated this massive departure from more traditional patterns were themselves a product of a still obscure complex of causes related to the changing exigencies of peasant life in late medieval and early modern Europe. At its height the European marriage pattern was an integral part of a system which kept land, resources, and population in an approximate balance.[53] One crucial development which probably influenced the age and extent to which women were married off, was the rise of domestic service. This made it possible for ordinary families to "store" large numbers of their young women in other households while their marriages were delayed, in some cases indefinitely.[54]

From the Victorian standpoint the interesting question then becomes what impact industrialization and urbanization had on the unique Western European marriage pattern. Very little research has been done from this standpoint,[55] the one exception being Michael Anderson's recent article, "Marriage Patterns in Victorian Britain" (1976). Anderson tried to systematically relate the available data on the age, sex, and marital status of Britain population (at the registration district level) to data on sex-ratios, employment patterns, and urban/rural (agricultural) differentials.[56]

Anderson's analysis shows that the transfer of men and women from the countryside to the towns did slightly increase their chances of marrying, but this was more true for men than for women. In towns with a large number of female domestic servants (who were supposed to remain unmarried) no departure from preindustrial patterns took place. Only where women shifted out of domestic service and into other forms of paid employment did a drop in the age of marriage and a reduction in the proportion of those remaining unmarried occur.

Levine's study of Shepsted provides a dramatic illustration of how the creation of new, non-agricultural forms of employment could affect marriage patterns. His rural industrial laborers showed a marked tendency to depart from the Western European pattern by marrying in their early twenties and reducing the amount of permanent celibacy. But *nationally* there was no well-developed departure from older patterns in the form of dramatic declines in the age of marriage or a marked reduction in the proportions remaining unmarried. For women as a whole the proportion ultimately celibate actually increased towards the late nineteenth century.[57] It was not until the twentieth century, long after England had become a "mature" industrial society, that the age of marriage for women began to fall, and fewer and fewer were left, or chose to remain, "spinsters."[58] This development was probably connected to the increasing confidence ordinary people felt over the control of fertility, but once again a shift in the prevailing mentalities about marriage may have taken place as well.

The European marriage pattern was never confined to the peasantry. Gradually it became part of upper and middle class life as well. Women of the British peerage experienced a gradual increase in their age at first marriage from 1550 to 1900.[59] The European pattern reached its fullest expression among peerage females born between 1850 and 1874. Ultimately, twenty-seven percent of them never married, while those that did had a mean age at first marriage of twenty-six. The social and economic forces which made the British peerage adopt a pattern of late marriage and extensive celibacy are not fully understood.[60] Obviously, they involve dowries and other matters of family finance. But the possibility remains that some privileged women were simply choosing not to marry in order to pursue alternative life-styles and this deserves further consideration.

Banks discusses the central importance of delayed marriage to the Victorian middle classes in *Prosperity and Parenthood*. To them it was a way of keeping living standards acceptably high and restricting family size as well. But the possibility that some middle-class women were simply choosing to "go it alone" must be considered as well, particularly in the late nineteenth century, when opportunities for respectable employment were increasing. Several authors have the impression that the extent of permanent celibacy was greatest among the middle classes, but there is no solid statistical data behind most generalizations of this nature.[61]

The study of marital dissolution, separation, and widowhood could also use further research. McGregor's *Divorce in England. A Centenary Study* (1957) provides the basic statistics on the extent of formal divorce. Rowntree and Carrier's "Resort to Divorce in England and Wales,

1858–1957" (1958) goes over the material in abbreviated form. But many couples could not be bothered with or afford official divorces. They simply lived apart. Manuscript census data could shed some light on the extent of this, although local or seasonal migration patterns must be taken into account as well. How class, occupation, and region affected the extent of widowhood would also be an interesting subject for research.[62]

## MIGRATION

We do not have enough detailed knowledge about the migration patterns of women in preindustrial England to be able to gauge how or in what ways social and economic change during the Victorian era may have introduced important departures from traditional patterns.[63] Certain general features apparently persisted. Women continued to outnumber men in rural to urban migration streams as they had done for several centuries, and for the same reason—the relative ease with which women could find employment in domestic service. As usual most of the women migrants continued to be relatively young and single.

Nevertheless the sheer volume of geographical mobility among ordinary women both before and after industrialization was quite unique in a worldwide context. Young women in non-Western cultures have never had the same amount of freedom to leave their families, and migrate to the cities while still single. Because they were (and are) married and reproductively active so much earlier than their European counterparts, many third world women (with their children) are left behind to maintain traditional village life while their husbands or brothers migrate to the towns. The women of Western Europe, through their freedom to migrate, became an integral part of urban life even if so many were only domestic servants.

The paradoxical aspects of this situation have been explored by Theresa McBride in *The Domestic Revolution* (1976). Although domestic service was such an "old-fashioned" form of employment, the Victorian women who sought positions as servants were or could be doing so in a very "modern" frame of mind. Domestic service paid relatively high wages, and it offered a young woman the opportunity to learn valuable social and household skills which might lead to better marriages and upward mobility. Unfortunately, the kind of demographic data McBride discusses pertains mostly to domestic servants in France. The demographic patterns connected with service in Victorian England, particularly those aspects which involve geographical origins or illegitimacy rates, remains untreated.

Despite the continuing importance of domestic service, occupational opportunities for women were diversifying as never before in the nineteenth century. The "classics" of migration history all contain some information on women, but, as usual, do not compare the differences between male and female migration in any systematic manner.[64] Thus the impact of industrialization on the movement of women from one area to another remains insufficiently studied.

Future research focusing on migration would do well to consider the relevance of demographic data to "push/pull" controversies. Edward Shorter has argued that migrating women felt the same "pull" of adventure and advancement as their male counterparts.[65] Paradoxically, his critics (who write from a feminist perspective) have argued that girls, although pushed out of their family households by parents who needed their wages, dutifully remained dependent on their families even at a distance.[66] The mortality rates of young girls in England and Ireland indicate that they were not well-treated at home and would have done well to have left many family situations, in which case Shorter's arguments (in modified form) ought to be considered. In any case, the range of alternative household or institutional living situations which awaited young migrants would make an interesting study.

Finally, there is the matter of overseas migration. Compared to the volume of internal movement, migration out of England was a minor form of geographical mobility for women (in Ireland this was not true). But because it was touted as the "final solution" to the "surplus woman" problem, emigration received a great deal of attention. Conservative Victorians spoke of the unmarried woman as "redundant," since her existence could only be justified through marriage. Because there were not enough husbands to go around (males left England so much more frequently than women) surplus women were told they had a duty to emigrate.[67] The societies formed to rid England of its redundant women were not very successful. Most unmarried women preferred to remain in their native land as "old maids" rather than go abroad for husbands, indicating once again that some women may have believed that there were advantages to being unmarried sufficient to outweigh the disadvantages of the single state.

## HOUSEHOLD STRUCTURE

Data on household structure is most intelligible when it is part of a comprehensive treatment of family and kinship. But the study of household structure has so many implications for the analysis of fertility, mortality, marriage, and migration, that the simple or bare presentation of data is often justified. This is one possible defense of the approach taken by Peter Laslett to the history of household structure in *Household and Family in Past Time*, (1972), an approach which is centered primarily on quantitative data and hence is often criticized for its narrow analytical framework.

Laslett is noted for arguing that because there has been no significant change in the size and structure of the average English household from the sixteenth century to the First World War, the way people arrange themselves in households has not contributed to or reflected social change.[68] Critics of Laslett have pointed out that his data for preindustrial households is insufficiently detailed, or that he ignored the evidence of change in his own data.[69]

The studies of mid-Victorian households in York and Preston done by Armstrong and Anderson, respectively, indicate that significant structural variation did indeed exist.[70] The kinds of data used by them can be gathered for other communities as well and ultimately integrated into a comparative study of how social change in the nineteenth century affected the position of women vis-a-vis society's most important micro-institution. Under what conditions were female-headed households most common? Where did females show the greatest tendency to live alone? How did aging affect the position of women in the household?

Anderson's book, *Family Structure in Nineteenth Century Lancashire* (1971), shows some sensitivity to aspects of household structure as they affect women. He demonstrates that in Preston rapid industrialization and urban growth created a housing shortage which increased the percentage of extended families. This was often the result of young married couples living with one set of parents, thus enabling the young wife to work even after the birth of a child. Levine demonstrates that pauperization forced a certain increase in household complexity.

Most needed are new studies of household structure among nineteenth-century middle- and upper-class families.[71] Neither was so directly affected by industrialization and urbanization, but because so many "privileged" women neither married nor worked outside the home, they created an unusual "dependency burden" for their male relatives. The difficulty of supporting several grown daughters or dependent sisters is thought to have caused middle-class males to take more positive attitudes toward work outside the home for respectable unmarried women, but the empirical dimensions of the dependency problem among the middle classes have never been analyzed.

Finally, what of those girls or women who found themselves, permanently or temporarily, outside of a family household either because they were lodgers, or one of the unfortunate inmates of England's workhouses, jails, or asylums? The demographic characteristics of women who lived away from home, and the institutionalized segment of Victorian womanhood have never been explored.

## Conclusion

In addition to discussing several major sources for demographic data on the women of Victorian England, this essay has selectively reviewed some classic and recent examples of demographic research which cover material relevant to the history of women. No attempt was made to evaluate the methodological techniques used by various authors to reach their conclusions.

From the standpoint of women's history the purpose of this essay was to demonstrate that a demographic perspective on the history of women is essential for the study of the most fundamental aspects of women's lives in any era. More importantly, it provides us with several measurable indices of the extent to which basic experiences are similar or different for women in various socioeconomic circumstances.

From the standpoint of demographic history this essay has tried to underscore the necessity of taking data on women more seriously in future research, not out of courtesy, but because to do so is analytically illuminating. For Western Europe the nineteenth century was *the* century of "demographic transition." As mortality and fertility gradually fell towards the "low" levels to which we are now accustomed, migration urbanized the population and industrialization totally transformed traditional patterns of work. In all these transitions, the experience of women was different than that of men, for reasons connected with biology, traditional social roles, and the autonomous striving of women themselves. Statistical descriptions of the demographic transition or the modernization process in general are incomplete unless they acknowledge sex-linked differences. Explanations of the social and demographic transformations which took place in the nineteenth century, if they are to be more successful than in the past, must not fail to take these differences into account.

# NOTES

Many thanks are due to Daniel Scott Smith for his close critical reading of the original draft, and his valuable suggestions for improving this essay, although he is not responsible for any of its shortcomings.

1.  "Modernization" is a notoriously vague term. It is used here in its usual diffuse sense, as a catch-all for the forms of social change connected with industrialization and urbanization. For a more precise analysis of "modernization," including an analysis of the ways it is distinct from and even independent of "industrialization," see E. A. Wrigley's "The Process of Modernization and the Industrial Revolution in England."

2.  "Mentalities" is also a notoriously vague term, but it can be usefully distinguished from the more mundane "attitudes" in the following manner: an individual or a culture may have an attitude toward something without any underlying implication that the attitude is connected to others in a related area or that the set of attitudes flows out of certain cultural conditions. "Mentalities" explicity refers to interlocking sets of ideas on, for example, death or pain, which are produced by or are an adjustment to certain demographic or other givens. This type of analysis is obviously related to the classical Marxist analysis of legal systems or ideas about "justice" which see both as an emanation of certain class- and property-based relationships. The analysis of mentalities, however, frequently stresses the importance of demographic parameters in shaping the attitudes, values, and behavior patterns of ordinary people in their daily lives. These are not regarded as something foisted off on the lower classes by the upper classes. Moreover, the "mentalities" themselves can independently affect underlying demographic realities. An interesting recent example (in English) of a French-style analysis of mentalities can be found in Sontag's "Images of Illness," a comparative historical analysis of attitudes towards tuberculosis and cancer. Stone's new book, *The Family, Sex, and Marriage: England 1500-1800*, also contains extended discussion of the relationship between demographic facts and cultural attitudes and behavioral patterns. For example, Stone argues that in sixteenth- and seventeenth-century England high infant and child mortality made it impossible for anyone to care much about (or for) children under two, and generally low life expectancies made it risky to invest much emotional capital in any relationship.

3.  There are two fundamental approaches to demographic measurement. The traditional school is called *aggregative, period*, or *cross-sectional* analysis. This approach to measurement begins with the absolute number of demographic events taking place in a given time period (usually a year, decade, or other familiar short-range unit of time) and converts them into rates or ratios by comparing the demographic experience of one section of the population with another, most often with the total population. Before decennial census taking began in 1801, population totals are often unavailable for regional and national analysis in England, and therefore some aggregative analysis takes the form of ratios of one vital event to another. Not presently available to this author is Schofield and Wrigley's forthcoming *English Population Change*, a study of aggregative measures applied to population data available before 1838. This undoubtedly will become the major guide to source and measurement problems for the aggregative approach to English demographic history in the preindustrial period. *Cohort* or *longitudinal* analysis, by contrast, measures the experience of distinct generations as they move through time. A cohort is a group of people who experienced a demographic event like birth or marriage in the same year, decade, or half-century, etc. In longitudinal analysis one asks what the average completed family size of a given cohort of women was, once all had moved through their fertile years. In aggregative analysis one would be more likely to measure the age specific fertility rates of all women or all married women in a given time period, irrespective of the extent to which relevant characteristics like age distribution or marital duration were different between generations. The historical demographic techniques grouped under the name "family reconstitution" are basically the application of longitudinal methods of measurement to

parish register data on baptisms, burials, and marriages through the piecing together of the vital histories of individual families and the subsequent grouping of family level data into cohorts. The best guide to modern approaches to family reconstitution using English records is by E. A. Wrigley and Schofield, "Nominal Record Linkage by Computer and the Logic of Family Reconstitution." For doubts about the representativeness of data resulting from reconstitution see, R. S. Schofield, "Representativeness and Family Reconstitution."

4. See Krause, "The Changing Adequacy of English Registration, 1690–1837"; and E. A. Wrigley, "Baptism Coverage in Early Ninteenth Century England: The Colyton Area." See also Levine, "The Reliability of Parochial Registration and the Representativeness of Family Reconstitution"; Berry and Schofield, "Age at Baptism in Pre-industrial England"; Razzell, "The Evaluation of Baptism as a Form of Birth Registration"; and James, "Infant Mortality in Rural North Shophire, 1561–1810."

5. There are, however, some local censuses dating from the late eighteenth and early nineteenth centuries which have not been explored from the women's history stand-point. See Law, "Local Censuses in the 18th Century." Articles based on the use of other local sources for the late eighteenth and early nineteenth centuries are: Edwards, "Norwich Bills of Mortality, 1707–1830"; and Forbes, "Mortality Books for 1774–1793 and 1833–1835 from the Parish of St. Giles, Criplegate, London." One article does carry a reconstitution analysis into the early nineteenth century and explores the social and economic implications of the data. See Levine, "The Demographic Implications of Rural Industrialization."

6. All the 1841 census volumes were originally published as part of *House of Commons' Sessional Papers*. As such they are indexed in the *General Alphabetical Index to the Bills, Reports, Estimates, Account, and Papers, Printed by Order of the House of Commons*, for various time periods. These general indexes are available in most college and university libraries. The volumes do not generally appear in the year of enumeration but were published several years later. Each census volume therefore has two different volume numbers, a *Sessional Papers* volume number for a given year of publication, and a volume number within the series of census volume published as a result of one enumeration (see below).

7. The *Census of Great Britain* volumes for 1851 were published as part of the *Sessional Papers* for 1852 to 1853. *Part I* (two volumes) included the Introductory Report and *Population Tables* (1801–51) for all the major civil and ecclesiastical divisions of Great Britain (vols. 85, 1 and 86, 1 of the *Sessional Papers*). *Population Tables, Part II*, included the data on ages, civil condition occupations, and birth places as well as the number of blind, deaf and dumb, and the inmates of workhouses, prisons, lunatic asylyms, and hospitals (*Sessional Papers*, 1852–53, vol. 88). The special study of *Religious Worship (England and Wales)* appears as part of volume 89 of the *Sessional Papers* 1852–53; while the *Education Report* was published in Volume 90. *Religious Worship and Education* for Scotland was published as part of the *Sessional Papers* for 1854, Vol. 59: 301.

8. Alexander, "Women's Work in Nineteenth Century London: 1820–1850."

9. *Census of England and Wales*, 1911, vol. 13, "Fertility and Marriage," Part I (part of the *Sessional Papers* for 1917). London, HMSO 1917.

10. Innes, *Class Fertility Trends in England and Wales 1876–1934*. Innes also discusses the shortcomings of the chief occupationally derived "status" groups in the fertility census. No single "status" group, for example, includes all "middle class" families. Michael Teitlebaum is working on the analysis of the decline of fertility in England and Wales in the modern period as part of the Princeton group's study of this aspect of European history in general. When published, this work will update and expand Innes's treatment.

11. There are two main books which provide excellent background reading on the nineteenth-century censuses. E. A. Wrigley, ed., *Nineteenth Century Society* contains articles which discuss the various kinds of data found in the middle and later nineteenth-century censuses, and the shortcomings connected with each kind of data. (Of particular value is Michael Drake's essay "The Census, 1801–1891," which contains a complete index to

all the published census volumes, by title and volume, as they appeared in the *Sessional Papers.*)The essays also provide models for how various statistical series can be applied to the study of social structure. However, little information deals specifically with women. Another book which also provides general background reading on the censuses is Lawton, ed., *"The Censuses and Social Structure."*

12   There is a hundred-year limit on public access to the enumerators' manuscript schedule books. Thus, in 1981, the 1881 set of schedule books will be microfilmed and made available to qualified users through the Public Record Office. Microfilm reels of data from selected areas may also be ordered for use elsewhere. The Mormons have complete sets of the British 1841, 1851, 1861, and 1871 microfilmed schedule books in the Geneological Library in Salt Lake City. In addition, they have microfilmed all other available sources of British geneological data. Under a grant fron England's Social Science Research Council, Michael Anderson is currently preparing a "public use" sample of the data from an ecologically stratified set of communities in 1851. All the data for these communities found in the enumerators' schedule books for 1851 is being coded and put on tape for later use by interested researchers. The set of sample data should be ready soon.

13.   The "Reports of the Registrar General" also appeared as part of the *Sessional Papers.* The specific volume number of an annual report can be found by consulting any complete index of the *Parliamentary Papers.*

14.   The registration district contained a set of parishes all of which were supposed to report their vital events in one specified location. Registration districts were geographical equivalents to local poor law unions, and so data for one can be used along side data for the other in certain sorts of analyses.

15.   The "15th Report of the Registrar-General" (hereafter RRG) appears as part of the *Sessional Papers* for 1854, 19, 50. The "Supplement to the 25th RRG" was part of the *Sessional Papers* for 1865, 13, 1. For the "Supplement to the 35th RRG" see the *Sessional Papers* for 1875, 18, Part II, 1. The "Supplement to the 45th Report" was published in 1884, 20, 50, and the "Supplement to the 55th RRG" appeared as part of the *Sessional Papers* for two different years; 1895, 23 Part I., and 1897, 21, Part II, 1.

16.   Birth registration was not complete until the 1870s.

17.   *The Journal of the Royal Statistical Society* was known by this name only after 1887. Previously it had been the *Journal of the Statistical Society* (1873–86) and earlier, the *Journal of the Statistical Society of London* from 1838 (when the journal started) to 1872. Alternative sources of demographic data which various journal articles made use of include insurance statistics, the vital registers of non-Anglican groups like the Quakers, and miscellaneous parliamentary reports which are published as parts of the *Sessional Papers.* In addition all Anglican churches still kept their registers of baptisms and burials as well as marriages. These registers could still be used for purposes of family reconstitution even after civil registration became mandatory, but the families recon-stituted would probably be unrepresentative.

18.   See the discussion of this in Kanner's "The Women of England in a Century of Social Change, Part II," p. 232. Branca's *Silent Sisterhood* makes a start along these lines.

19.   Medical journals were abundant during this period and various articles often contain some demographic material. A few titles are: *British Medical Journal, London Journal of Medicine, British and Foreign Medical Review*, etc.

20.   *Population Problems in the Victorian Age*, intro. J. J. Spengler, contains some Victorian reprints. Tranter, *Population Since the Industrial Revolution* has a short section on the "status" of women and the decline of fertility, but the generalizations are shallow and out of date. Tranter asserts that the late nineteenth-century fertility decline was connected to a rise in the employment of married women outside the home, although no such trend is statistically demonstrable. *Population in Industrialization*, ed. Drake, contains reprints of some classic articles on the population controversy, but none contain material relevant to women.

21.   Hollingsworth, "The Demography of the British Peerage," and "A Demographic Study of British Ducal Families."

22. In *Populi*. A substantial majority of her interviewed subjects wanted to limit their families, but their husbands were against it. The fear of divorce or polygyny prevented many women from using contraception. Neither fear was relevant to women in Victorian England.

23. In Europe, "traditional" fertility generally meant that the average woman gave birth to between five and six children in her lifetime, although women married at twenty and surviving to fifty would have had around eight live births. "Modern" levels of fertility were first achieved in Britain by women born at the turn of the twentieth century and marrying in the 1920s. These women completed fertility with an average of 2.4 children. See Kelsall, *Population*, p. 24. The volume of essays edited by Charles Tilly, *Historical Studies of Changing Fertility*, contains the most comprehensive and useful treatment of the subject available, including an analysis of the importance of regional variations in understanding the fertility transition.

24. Hollingsworth, *Historical Demography*, pp. 339–52.

25. Lee, "Estimating Series of Vital Rates and Age Structure from Baptisms and Burials," pp. 495–511.

26. Hollingsworth, "British Ducal Families," p. 370. Hollingsworth's cohorts are too broad to permit the pinpointing of the ducal fertility decline to a specific decade. It appears as if the decline in fertility began among ducal daughters in the 1850s, and earlier for the wives of dukes' sons.

27. Loschky and Krier, "Income and Family Size in Three Eighteenth Century Lancashire Parishes," find evidence among eighteenth-century gentry and tradesmen's wives for even earlier attempts to control fertility.

28. See Fryer, *The Birth Controllers*, pp. 43–106, and Peel, "Birth Control and the British Working Class Movement."

29. See also Laslett, "Age at Menarche in Europe Since the 18th Century." The average age at first menstruation has been declining slowly since the late eighteenth or early nineteenth century. This is generally thought to indicate that girls were getting healthier, most probably because they were better-fed. For a general treatment of the relation between diet, weight gain, and menstruation see Frisch, "Critical Weights: A Critical Body Composition, Menarche, and the Maintenance of Menstrual Cycles."

30. Pearce, "Expanding Families," p. 34.

31. Johansson, "The Demographic Transition in England."

32. Matras, "Social Strategies of Family Formation," table 2.

33. Innes, *Class Fertility*, p. 44. For Scotland, see Dunlop, "The Fertility of Marriage in Scotland."

34. Glass, "Changes in Fertility in England and Wales, 1851–1931." It seems doubtful at this point that the late Victorian decline in marital fertility was tied to the employment patterns of married women. Throughout the nineteenth century married women had been *withdrawing* from the work force, and their participation in it was probably at its historical low point as fertility began to decline. See McDougall, "Working Class Women During the Industrial Revolution, 1780–1914" and McBride, "The Long Road Home: Woman's Work and Industrialization."

35. Banks, *Prosperity and Parenthood*, p. 200.

36. The cost of children cannot be dismissed as a relevant explanatory factor but it needs to be evaluated more systematically as in Henderson, "The Cost of Children, Part I" and "Parts II & III." For some general Victorian background see William H. Bronson, "Social Legislation and the Birth Rate in Nineteenth Century Britain."

37. *Prosperity and Parenthood*, pp. 143–44, 157–59.

38. "Abortion in England 1890–1914." McLaren presents interesting information which suggests that information about fertility control was spread locally, woman to woman.

39. For America, see the references in Barker-Benfield, *Horrors of the Half-Known Life*. For France, see McLaren's "Abortion in France."

40. Laslett and Oosterveen, "Long Term Trends in Bastardy in England."

41. Shorter summarizes his theories in *The Making of the Modern Family*. See also: "The Decline in Non-Marital Fertility in Europe 1880–1940."

42. For criticisms of Shorter on this point see Scott's review in *Signs*. For a more general criticism of Shorter's theories about women and their relationship to the family unit see Scott and L. A. Tilly, "Women's Work and the Family in Nineteenth Century Europe."

43. The precise dating of a change in fertility generally depends on the methods used to measure it. Fluctuations in the crude birth rate, for example can take place independently of marital fertility rates, because crude birth rates are sensitive to changes in migration which lead to changes in the age distribution and marriage rates. In the short run marital fertility can rise or fall independently of crude birth rates.

44. By preindustrial standards, epidemics in Victorian England were mild affairs. Only Ireland experienced a disaster of traditional proportions during the famine and dislocation resulting from the potato blight. More work could be done on male/female differentials during the famine. See Cousens, "Regional Death Rates in Ireland during the Great Famine."

45. Kanner, *Women of England, Part II*, p. 235. McKeown, *The Modern Rise of Population*, pp. 138–41.

46. Howe, *Man, Environment and Disease in Britain*, p. 198.

47. A "modern" mortality pattern is one in which women have markedly lower death rates than men in all five-year age groups. In the "traditional" pattern death rates for women often exceed those for men—particularly during the childbearing years. An indispensable research aid to the careful delineation of changing mortality patterns at the national level by specific causes is Preston, Keyfitz, and Schoen's *Causes of Death*, which contains all the main life tables for nineteenth- and twentieth- century Britain.

48. Oakley, "Wisewomen and Medicine Men: Changes in the Management of Childbirth." Oakley points out that all through the nineteenth century delivery at home under the care of a midwife was far safer than giving birth in a hospital, not only because so many doctors refused to follow proper sanitary precautions, but also because they mismanaged so many births, (pp. 45–47). Oakley discusses how prevailing medical mentalities about childbearing influenced the management of hospital births.

49. Johansson, "Sex and Death in Victorian England," p. 173.

50. The best review of the contemporary data is Gove's "Sex, Marital Status and Mortality." Gove argues that the mortality advantage of the married population reflects the emotional benefits of marriage rather than the physical deficiencies of the never married population. Daniel Scott Smith thinks that in the nineteenth century, by contrast, it is probable that the mortality of the never married was relatively higher than at present, because so many spinster/bachelors were in ill health, this being one of the factors influencing their marital state. (In correspondence, letter dated 19 February 1978.) However, the point stressed here is the total lack of research in this area.

51. Ursula Cowgill finds evidence for female infanticide in "Life and Death in the 16th Century in the City of York." Keith Wright's "Infanticide in Earlier 17th Century England" does not. See also Langer, "Infanticide: A Historical Survey."

52. The General data is reviewed by Hair in "Deaths from Violence in Britain."

53. The essays in *Population Patterns in the Past*, ed. Lee, contain detailed material on the relationship between mortality, inheritance and age of marriage in the preindustrial peasant economy.

54. The upper and middle classes of Catholic Europe were able to store some of their surplus daughters in convents, but there was never enough room to dispose of all of them in that fashion. Protestant parents could not use convents for any of their daughters, which is perhaps one reason they became more and more amenable to sending girls away to school. Late-marrying girls learned skills which enabled them to organize their leisure time, while permanently unmarried women pioneered careers in teaching.

55. Ogle, "On Marriage Rate and Marriage Ages," pp. 253–380. Ogle's work was done in the 1880s.

56. Anderson's analysis comprises a critique of Ogle.

57. Hollingsworth, "Demography of the British Peerage," p. 20.

58. See also Outhwaite's "Age at Marriage in England from the Late Seventeenth to the Nineteenth Century," and Crafts and Ireland's study, "A Simulation of the Impact of

Changes in the Age of Marriage." The latter contains an excellent summary of the literature and the problems involved in historical study of changing marriage patterns.

59. Hollingsworth, "British Peerage," p. 27.
60. A thesis not read by this author may contain some relevant information on this point. See Otto, "Daughters of the British Aristocracy: Their Marriages in the Eighteenth and Nineteenth Centuries." See also Davit, "The Social Origins of Marriage Partners of the British Peerage in the Eighteenth and Nineteenth Centuries"; and Davidoff, *The Best Circles.*
61. Anderson cites several sources relating to middle-class marriage patterns which supposedly have data on the extent of celibacy among middle class daughters, ("Marriage Patterns," p. 72) but none of the sources present detailed statistics. Branca (*Silent Sisterhood*) thinks that middle-class women were more likely to marry than the average women, but once again has no supporting evidence for her claim. See also Harrison et al., "Social Class and Marriage patterns in Some Oxfordshire Populations," for a local study.
62. Widowhood, and the older female in general, is also an important but neglected area of the history of Victorian women. Laslett has begun the exploration of ageing in "Societal Development and Ageing."
63. One of the most detailed studies of male and female migration patterns in a preindustrial context is Schofield's "Age-Specific Mobility in an Eighteenth-Century Rural English Parish." Forthcoming is Vivien Brodsky's important dissertation "Marriage and Mobility in Pre-industrial England." Brodsky's data comprises the first comprehensive analysis of marriage and migration among women before industrialization. She shows that girls who remained at home tended to marry in their early twenties to men seven or more years older than themselves. Girls who migrated and entered domestic service, by contrast, tended to marry in their middle or late twenties. Their husbands were their own age or slightly older. Brodsky's groundbreaking research demonstrates crucial links between the use of domestic service and the spread of the European marriage pattern. (In correspondence between Vivien Brodsky and Barbara Kanner, 26 May 1977.)
64. Redford, *Labor Migration in England 1800–1850,* and Saville, *Rural Depopulation in England and Wales, 1851–1951.*
65. *The Making of the Modern Family.* See also: "Female Emancipation, Birth Control and Fertility in European History."
66. L. Tilly, Scott, and Cohen, "Women's Work and European Fertility Patterns."
67. Hammerton, "Femininism and Female Emigration, 1861–1886," and for more general background on emigration, Glass and Taylor, *Population and Emigration.*
68. "Preface," *Household and Family in past Time,* p. ix.
69. On the latter point, see Nixon, "Size and Structure of the Household in England Over Three Centuries."
70. W. A. Armstrong, "A Note on the Household Structure of Mid-Nineteenth Century York in Comparative Perspective," and Anderson, "Household Structure and the Industrial Revolution."
71. Some data can be found in Crozier's "Kinship and Occupational Succession," but Crozier never published the full set of data she gathered on middle-class households in London's Highgate.

# BIBLIOGRAPHY

ALEXANDER, SALLY. "Women's Work in Nineteenth Century London: 1820–1850." In *The Rights and Wrongs of Women,* edited by Juliet Mitchell and Ann Oakley. Harmondsworth, England: 1976.

ANDERSON, MICHAEL. *Family Structure in Nineteenth Century Lancashire.* Cambridge Studies in Sociology, 5. London: 1971.

———. "Household Structure and the Industrial Revolution: Mid-ninteenth Century Preston in Comparative Perspective." In *Household and Family in Past Time,* edited by Peter Laslett with Richard Wall. Cambridge: 1972.

———. "Marriage Patterns in Victorian Britain: An Analysis Based on Registration District Data for England and Wales, 1861." *Journal of Family History* 1 (1976): 55–79.

ARMSTRONG, ALAN. *Stability and Change in an English Country Town: A Social Study of York 1801–51.* London: 1974.

———. "A Note on the Household Structure of Mid-Nineteenth Century York in Comparative Perspective." In *Household and Family in Past Time,* edited by Peter Laslett with Richard Wall. Cambridge: 1972.

BANKS, J. A. *Prosperity and Parenthood: A Study in Family Planning among the Victorian Middle Classes.* London: 1954.

———, and BANKS, OLIVE. *Feminism and Family Planning in Victorian England.* Studies in Sociology. Liverpool: 1964. Reprint. New York: 1972.

BARKER-BENFIELD, G. J. BEN. *Horrors of the Half-Known Life: Male Attitudes towards Women and Sexuality in Nineteenth Century America.* New York: 1976.

BERRY, B. MIDI, and SCHOFIELD, R. S. "Age at Baptism in Pre-industrial England." *Population Studies* 25 (1971): 453–63.

BRANCA, PATRICIA. *Silent Sisterhood: Middle Class Women in the Victorian Home.* London and Pittsburgh: 1975.

BRASON, WILLIAM H. "Social Legislation and the Birth Rate in Nineteenth Century Britain." *Western Economic Journal* 6 (1968): 134–44.

BRYANT, DAVID. "Demographic Trends in South Devon in the Mid-Nineteenth Century." *Exeter Essays in Geography,* edited by K. J. Gregory and W. L. D. Ravenhill. Exeter: 1971.

COALE, ANSLEY J., and ZELNICK, MELVIN. *New Estimates of Fertility and Population in the United States.* Princeton: 1963.

COUSENS, S. H. "Regional Death Rates in Ireland during the Great Famine from 1846–1851." *Population Studies* 14 (1960): 55–74.

CRAFTS, N. F. R., and IRELAND, J. J. "A Simulation of the Impact of Changes in Age at Marriage before and during the Advent of Industrialization in England." *Population Studies* 30 (1976): 495–510.

CROZIER, DOROTHY. "Kinship and Occupational Succession." *Sociological Review,* n.s. 13 (1965): 15–43.

DAVIDOFF, LENORE. *The Best Circles. Women and Society in Victorian England.* London and Totowa, N.J.: 1973.

DAVIT, THOMAS. "The Social Origins of Marriage Partners of the British Peerage in the Eighteenth and Nineteenth Centuries." *Population Studies* 26 (1972): 99–111.

DRAKE, MICHAEL. "The Census, 1801–1891." In *Nineteenth Century Society: Essays in the Use of Quantitative Methods for the Study of Social Data.* Cambridge: 1972.

————, ed. *Population in Industrialization*. In Debates in Economic History, series. London and New York: 1969.

DUNLOP, J. C. "The Fertility of Marriage in Scotland: A Census Study." *Journal of the Royal Statistical Society* 77 (1914): 259–88.

EDWARDS, J. K. "Norwich Bills of Mortality, 1707–1830." *Yorkshire Bulletin of Economic and Social Research* 21 (1969): 94–113.

FLINN, M. W. *British Population Growth: 1700–1850*. New York and London: 1970. 2d ed. London: 1972.

FORBES, T. R. "Mortality Books for 1774–1793 and 1833–1835 from the Parish of St. Giles, Criplegate, London." *Bulletin of the New York Academy of Medicine* 47 (1971): 1,524–36.

FRIEDLANDER, DOV. "Demographic Patterns and Socio-economic Characteristics of the Coal-Mining Population in England and Wales in the Nineteenth Century." *Economic Development and Cultural Change* 22 (1973): 39–51.

FRISCH, ROSE. "Critical Weights: A Critical Body Composition, Menarche and the Maintenance of Menstrual Cycles." In *Biosocial Interrelations in Population Adaptation*, edited by E. S. Watts, F. E. Johnson, G. W. Lasker. The Hague: 1975.

————. "Population Food Intake and Fertility: Historical Evidence for a Direct Effect of Nutrition on Reproductive Ability." *Science* 199 (1978): 22–30.

FRYER, PETER. *The Birth Controllers*. London: 1965. New York: 1966.

GLASS, D. V. "Changes in Fertility in England and Wales, 1851–1931." In *Political Arithmetic*, edited by L. Hogben. New York: 1938.

————, and TAYLOR, P. A. M. *Population and Emigration*. In Government and Society in Nineteenth Century Britain: Commentaries on British Parliamentary Papers, series. Dublin: 1976.

————. "Population and Population Movements in England and Wales, 1700 to 1850." In *Population in History*, edited by D. V. Glass and D. E. C. Eversley. Chicago: 1965.

GOVE, WALTER R. "Sex, Marital Status and Mortality." *American Journal of Sociology* 79 (1973): 45–65.

Great Britain, *Parliamentary Papers*: 1. *Decennial Censuses*. For a complete index to the censuses taken between 1851 and 1891 see: *General Alphabetical Index to the Bills, Reports, Estimates, Accounts, and Papers, Printed by Order of the House of Commons, 1852–1899*. London: 1909.

————. *Parliamentary Papers*: 2. *Annual Reports of the Registrar General, Births, Deaths, and Marriages, England and Wales*. For a complete index of the annual reports see: *General Alphabetical Index to the Bills, Reports, Estimates, Accounts, and Papers, Printed by Order of the House of Commons, 1852–1899*. London: 1909.

————. *Census of England and Wales, 1911*. "Fertility and Marriage. XIII; Part I." London: 1917.

HABAKKUK, H. J. *Population Growth and Economic Development Since 1750*. Leicester: 1971.

HAINES, MICHAEL. "Fertility, Nuptiality and Occupation: A Study of British Mid-Nineteenth Century Coal Mining Populations." *Journal of Interdisciplinary History* 7 (1977): 245–81.

HAIR, P. E. H. "Deaths from Violence in Britain: A Tentative Secular Survey." *Population Studies* 25 (1971): 5–24.

HAJNAL, J. "European Marriage Patterns in Perspective." In *Population in History*, edited by D. V. GLASS and D. E. C. EVERSLEY. Chicago: 1965.

HAMMERTON, A. JAMES. "Feminism and Female Emigration, 1861–1886." In *A Widening Sphere: Changing Roles of Victorian Women*, edited by Martha Vicinus. Bloomington: 1977.

HARRISON, G. A., et. al. "Social Class and Marriage Patterns in Some Oxfordshire Populations." *Journal of Biosocial Science* 3 (1971): 1–12.

HENDERSON, A. "The Cost of Children, Parts II and III." *Population Studies* 3 (1949): 267–98.

HENRY, LOUIS. *Population Analysis and Models*. Translated by Etienne van de Walle. New York: 1976.

HOLLINGSWORTH, T. H. "The Demography of the British Peerage." *Supplement to Population Studies* 18, no. 2 (1964): 1–108.

———. "Demographic Study of British Ducal Families." In *Population in History*, edited by D. V. Glass and D. E. C. Eversley. Chicago: 1965.

———. *Historical Demography*. In The Sources of History: The Uses of Historical Evidence, series. Ithaca, N.Y.: 1969.

HOWE, G. MELVYN. *Man, Environment and Disease in Britain—A Medical Geography Through the Ages*. Newton Abbot, England, and New York: 1972.

HUSTON, PERDITA. "To Be Born a Woman is a Sin." *Populi* 4 (1977): 27–36.

INNES, JOHN W. *Class Fertility Trends in England and Wales, 1876–1934*. Princeton: 1938.

JAMES, R. E. "Infant Mortality in Rural North Shopshire, 1561–1810." *Population Studies* 30 (1976): 305–308.

JOHANSSON, SHEILA RYAN. "The Demographic Transition in England: A Study of the Economic, Social and Demographic Background to Mortality and Fertility Change in Cornwall, 1800–1900." Ph.D. dissertation, University of California, Berkeley, 1974.

———. "Sex and Death in Victorian England. An Examination of Age and Sex-Specific Death Rates, 1840–1910." In *A Widening Sphere: Changing Roles of Victorian Women*, edited by Martha Vicinus, pp. 163–81. Bloomington: 1977.

KANNER, S. BARBARA. "The Women of England in a Century of Social Change: 1815–1914. A Select Bibliography." In *Suffer and Be Still: Women in the Victorian Age*, edited by Martha Vicinus. Bloomington: 1973.

———. "The Women of England in a Century of Social Change, 1815–1914: A Select Bibliography, Part II." In *A Widening Sphere: Changing Roles of Victorian Women*, edited by Martha Vicinus. Bloomington: 1977.

KELSALL, R. K. *Population*. In The Social Structure of Modern Britain, series, John Barron Mays and Maurice Croft, general editors. London: 1967. Rev. ed.: 1970.

KENNEDY, ROBERT E., Jr. *The Irish: Emigration, Marriage and Fertility*. Berkeley: 1973.

KRAUSE, J. T. "The Changing Adequacy of English Registration, 1690–1837." In *Population in History*, edited by D. V. Glass and D. E. C. Eversley. Chicago: 1965.

LANGER, W. L. "Infanticide: A Historical Survey." *History of Childhood Quarterly* 1 (1974): 351–65.

LASLETT, PETER. "Age at Menarche in Europe Since the 18th Century." *Journal of Interdisciplinary History* 2 (1971): 221–36.

———, and Oosterveen, Karla. "Long Term Trends in Bastardy in England and

Wales: A Study of the Illegitimacy Figures in the Parish Registers and in the Reports of the Registrar General, 1561–1960." *Population Studies* 27 (1973): 255–86.

———. "Mean Household Size in England Since the Sixteenth Century." In *Household and Family in Past Time*, edited by Peter Laslett with Richard Wall. Cambridge: 1972.

———. "Societal Development and Ageing." In *Ageing and the Social Sciences*, edited by Robert H. Binstock and Ethel Shanas. New York: 1976.

———. *The World We Have Lost*. London: 1965. New York: 1965, 1966. 2d ed. New York: 1971.

LAW, C. M. "Local Censuses in the 18th Century." *Population Studies* 23 (1969): 87–100.

LAWTON, R., ed. *The Censuses and Social Structure: An Interpretive Guide to Nineteenth Century Population Censuses of England and Wales*. London: 1972.

LEE, RONALD. "Estimating Series of Vital Rates and Age Structure from Baptism and Burials: A New Technique with Application to Pre-Industrial England." *Population Studies* 28 (1974): 495–512.

———, ed. *Population Patterns in the Past*. In collaboration with Richard A. Easterlin, Peter H. Lindert, and Etienne van de Walle. London and New York: 1977.

LEVINE, DAVID. "The Demographic Implication of Rural Industrialization: A Family Reconstitution Study of Shepsted Leicestershire, 1660–1851." *Social History* 2 (1976): 177–98.

———. "The Reliability of Parochial Registration and the Representativeness of Family Reconstitution." *Population Studies* 30 (1976): 107–22.

———. *Family Formation in an Age of Nascent Capitalism*. New York: 1977.

LOGAN, W. P. D. "Mortality in England and Wales from 1848 to 1947: A Survey of Changing Causes of Death during the Past Hundred Years." *Population Studies* 4 (1950): 132–78.

LOSCHKY, DAVID J., and KRIER, DONALD F. "Income and Family Size in Three Eighteenth Century Lancashire Parishes: A Reconstitution Study." *Journal of Economic History* 29 (1969): 429–48.

MCBRIDE, THERESA M. *The Domestic Revolution: The Modernization of Household Service in England and France, 1820–1920*. New York: 1976.

———. "The Long Road Home: Women's Work and Industrialization." In *Becoming Visible: Women in European History*, edited by Renate Bridenthal and Claudia Koonz. Boston: 1977.

MCDOUGALL, MARY LYNN. "Working Class Women during the Industrial Revolution, 1780–1914." In *Becoming Visible: Women in European History*, edited by Renate Bridenthal and Claudia Koonz. Boston: 1977.

MCGREGOR, O. R. *Divorce in England: A Centenary Study*. London: 1957.

MCKEOWN, THOMAS. *The Modern Rise of Population*. New York: 1976.

MCLAREN, ANGUS. "Abortion in England, 1890–1914." *Victorian Studies* 20 (1977): 379–400.

———. "Abortion in France: Women and the Regulation of Family Size, 1800–1914." Paper read at the conference on Women and Power, 16–18 November 1977, at the University of Maryland, College Park, Maryland.

MATRAS, JUDAH. "Social Strategies of Family Formation: Data for Britain Female Cohorts born 1831–1910." *Population Studies* 19 (1965): 167–81.

National Birth Rate Commission (Reports and Evidence of). *The Declining Birth Rate: Its Causes and Effects.* London: 1916.

NIXON, J. W. "Size and Structure of the Household in England over Three Centuries: A Comment." *Population Studies* 24 (1970): 445–47.

OAKLEY, ANN. "Wisewomen and Medicine Men: Changes in the Management of Childbirth." In *The Rights and Wrongs of Women*, edited by Juliet Mitchell and Ann Oakley. Harmondsworth, England: 1976.

OGLE, W. "On Marriage Rate and Marriage Ages with Special Reference to the Growth of Population." *Journal of the Royal Statistical Society* 53 (1890): 253–80.

OTTO, PATRICIA C. "Daughters of the British Aristocracy: Their Marriages in the Eighteenth and Nineteenth Centuries with Particular Reference to the Scottish Peerage." Ph.D. dissertation, Stanford University, 1974.

OUTHWAITE, R. B. "Age at Marriage in England from the Late Seventeenth to the Nineteenth Century." *Transactions of the Royal Historical Society* 23 (1973): 55–70.

PEARCE, CAROL, G. "Expanding Families: Some Aspects of Fertility in a Mid-Victorian Community." *Local Population Studies* 10 (1973): 22–35.

PEEL, JOHN. "Birth Control and the British Working Class Movement." *Bulletin for the Study of Labour History* 7 (1963): 16–22.

PRESTON, SAMUEL H.; KEYFITZ, N.; and SCHOEN, R. *Causes of Death: Life Tables for National Populations.* New York: 1972.

RAZZELL, P. E. "The Evaluation of Baptism as a Form of Birth Registration through Cross-Matching Census and Parish Register Data: A Study in Methodology." *Population Studies* 26 (1972): 121–46.

REDFORD, ARTHUR. *Labor Migration in England, 1800–1850.* 2d ed. Manchester: 1964.

ROWNTREE, GRISELDA and CARRIER, NORMAN. "The Resort to Divorce in England and Wales, 1858–1957." *Population Studies* 11 (1958): 188–233.

SALAFF, JANET W. "The Status of Unmarried Hong Kong Women and the Social Factors Contributing to their Delayed Marriage." *Population Studies* 30 (1976): 391–412.

SAVILLE, JOHN. *Rural Depopulation in England and Wales, 1851–1951.* London: 1957.

SCHOFIELD, R. S. "Age-Specific Mobility in an Eighteenth-Century Rural English Parish." *Annales de Demographie Historique* (1970): 261–74.

———, and Wrigley, E. A. *English Population Change.* Forthcoming.

———. "Representativeness and Family Reconstitution," *Annales de Demographie Historique* (1972): 119–30.

SCOTT, JOAN W., and TILLY, LOUISE A. "Women's Work and the Family in Nineteenth Century Europe." *Comparative Studies in Society and History* 17 (1975): 36–64.

———. "Review of the 'Making of the Modern Family' by Edward Shorter." *Signs. Journal of Women in Culture and Society* 2 (1977): 692–97.

SHORTER, EDWARD. "Female Emancipation, Birth Control and Fertility in European History." *American Historical Review* 78 (1973): 604–40.

———. "The Decline in Non-Marital Fertility in Europe, 1880–1940." *Population Studies* 25 (1971): 375–93.

———. *The Making of the Modern Family.* New York: 1975. Reprint. New York. 1977.

SMITH, DANIEL SCOTT. "Family Limitation, Sexual Control, and Domestic

Feminism in Victorian America." In *Clio's Consciousness Raised*, edited by Mary Hartman and Lois Banner. New York: 1974.

———. "A Homeostatic Demographic Regime: Patterns in Western European Family Reconstitution Studies." In *Population Patterns in the Past*, edited by Ronald Lee. New York: 1977.

SMITH, F. BARRY. "Sexuality in Britain 1800–1900: Some Suggested Revisions." In *A Widening Sphere*, edited by Martha Vicinus. Bloomington: 1977.

SONTAG, SUSAN. "Images of Illness." (Part 2 of 3 Parts). *New York Review of Books*, 9 February 1978, p. 27.

STONE, LAWRENCE. *The Family, Sex and Marriage: England 1500–1800*. New York: 1977.

TILLY, CHARLES, ed. *Historical Studies of Changing Fertility*. Princton: 1978.

TILLY, LOUISE A.; SCOTT, JOAN A.; and COHEN, MIRIAM. "Women's Work and European Fertility Patterns." *Journal of Interdisciplinary History* 6 (1976): 447–76.

TEITELBAUM, MICHAEL S. "Birth Underregistration in the Constituent Counties of England and Wales: 1841–1910." *Population Studies* 28 (1974): 329–43.

TRANTER, N. L. *Population since the Industrial Revolution: The Case of England and Wales*. New York and London: 1975.

UHLENBERG, PETER. "A Study of Cohort Life Cycles: Cohorts of Native Born Women, 1830–1920." *Population Studies* 23 (1969): 407–20.

VAN DE WALLE, ETIENNE. *The Female Population of France in the Nineteenth Century*. Princeton: 1974.

WRIGLEY, E. A. "Baptism Coverage in Early Nineteenth Century England: the Colyton Area." *Population Studies* 29 (1975): 299–316.

———, ed. *An Introduction to English Historical Demography*. London and New York: 1966.

———, ed. *Nineteenth Century Society: Essays in the Use of Quantitative Methods for the Study of Social Data*. Cambridge: 1972.

———, and SCHOFIELD, R. S. "Nominal Record Linkage by Computer and the Logic of Family Reconstitution." In *Identifying People in the Past*, edited by E. A. Wrigley. London: 1973.

———. *Population and History*, New York: 1969.

———. "The Process of Modernization in the Industrial Revolution in England." *Journal of Interdisciplinary History* 4 (1974): 228–34.

# Women in the Mirror:

# Using Novels to Study Victorian Women

## PATRICIA OTTO KLAUS

When you asked me to speak about women and fiction I
sat down on the banks of a river and began to wonder
what the words meant. They might mean simply a few
remarks about Fanny Burney; a few more about Jane
Austen; a tribute to the Brontës.... But at second sight
the words seemed not so simple. The title women and
fiction might mean, and you might have it mean, women
and what they are like; or it might mean women and the
fiction that is written about them; or it might mean that
somehow all three are inextricably mixed together.

VIRGINIA WOOLF, *A Room of One's Own*

At first sight, the Victorian novel with its detail and emphasis on
women, love, marriage, and the family seems an obvious and rich
storehouse of information about women in nineteenth-century England.
But upon closer inspection, as Virginia Woolf noted, it is a complex, even
confusing, source. How does one employ novels as a historical source? The
purpose of this essay is to encourage careful, critical use of novels for
research on Englishwomen, and to provide a guide for the mass of writings
novelists, historians, and literary scholars have published on women and

the novel. The essay is in two parts: first, a brief discussion of women and the novel; second, an introduction to the use of novels in historical study. Its intention, differing from most bibliographic essays, is not to assess the existing critical literature, but to stimulate the use of novels in the historical study of women and Victorian society. There is no specific body of literature on this subject. Historians sporadically sift through novels in search of lively quotations or illustrations and literary scholars sometimes include history to provide background for their primarily literary arguments. Only relatively recently have researchers interested in women begun to focus on the relationship among the writer, society, and the novel.[1] The newness of the field is evidenced by the fact that, with the exception of the works of Patricia Thomson, Wanda Neff, and Aina Rubenius, most of the studies which combine the sources and methods of history and literature to study women in the past either have been just published, like Morroe Berger's *Real and Imagined Worlds* (1977), or are doctoral dissertations.[2]

The resurgence of the feminist movement and the growth of women's studies at universities has stimulated an interest in women's lives and roles in the past and has increased the number of dissertations on women and literature. As Martha Vicinus noted recently, "Fortunately the interdisciplinary nature of women's studies encourages us to place literature in a broader context; the next decade should see the expansion of the study of cultural and social forces that brought women writers and a female literary sensibility to the fore during the Victorian period."[3] Almost all of these dissertations are in English literature or modern literature, reflecting the historian's reluctance to use novels. Barbara S. Frankle's discussion of Anthony Trollope in "The Genteel Family: High Victorian Conceptions of Domesticity and Good Behavior" (1969) is a welcome exception.[4] If historians have been wary of novels, students of literature have been hesitant to go beyond the well-established authors, even when comparing Victorian ideals and reality. The reason for this lies in part in the approaches of the two disciplines. Whereas literary scholars turn to "real life" to augment their interpretation and understanding of "great" literature, historians use novels to supplement their analysis of Victorian reality. Although the number of dissertations on women and literature has increased, only about half of them deal directly with the interaction of women, society, and their characterization in novels.[5] The others concentrate primarily on literary questions or are descriptive and of little use to the historian.[6] In recent dissertations, scholars have described Victorian women as exploited and restricted, examined how male and female authors regarded women, and shown how the writer's sex and Victorian values affected the portrayal of heroines.[7]

The main source for anyone who wishes to use novels to learn about women in Victorian England is, of course, the novels themselves. The Victorian novelists were tremendously productive. Robert A. Colby has estimated that over forty thousand novels were published between 1800 and 1900; Mackenzie Bell mentioned over 1,030 authors in his anthology, *Representative Authors of the Nineteenth Century* (1927); Frances Trollope published over one hundred novels in her lifetime; Catherine Gore wrote twenty-four in a single decade.[8] Such numbers make it impossible to list their works individually. The researcher looking for novels on particular themes written during certain parts of the century or by a particular author can consult bibliographies. Bibliographies on the period can be divided into three sorts: the "comprehensive" bibliography which surveys the major (and, in some cases, minor) literature and usually includes references to the novels, their authors, and critical assessments; the annual bibliographies; and guides and surveys of authors.

Richard Altick in *The Art of Literary Research* (1963) and Lionel Stevenson in *Victorian Fiction: A Guide to Research* (1964) provide useful introductions to methodological and bibliographical resources. The major bibliographies are F. W. Bateson, ed., *The Cambridge Bibliography of English Literature*, III, 1800–1900 (1941), and George Watson, ed., *The New Cambridge Bibliography of English Literature*, III, 1800–1900 (1969). The *CBEL* contains references on the education of women, publishing, book distribution, literary memoirs, archival holdings, literary relations with the continent, and major and minor novelists. The sections on the major novelists include lists of their works, bibliographies, a brief biography, and critical evaluations. The sections on over two hundred minor novelists list works and some critical assessments. The *New CBEL* is an updated revision which emphasizes literary references over social and political background.[9] These bibliographies can be supplemented with Lucien Leclaire, ed., *A General Analytical Bibliography of the Regional Novelists of the British Isles, 1800–1950* (1954), which is organized chronologically with an author index; and *XIX Century Fiction* (1951), based on Michael Sadleir's extensive holdings of first editions, is a good source for obscure novels and includes brief insightful comments on the authors. In his four-volume bibliography, *Victorian England in Its Novels*, (1968), Myron Brightfield arranged hundreds of novels by topic, for example, "The Pure English Girl."[10]

In this essay I have included references to critical works on novels written by male and female authors which I think would be valuable to someone using literature to study women. While some pertain directly to the subject of women and literature, others add background or methodological information. Because of the vast amount of published material I do not attempt to be inclusive and concentrate, with a few exceptions, on critical studies published in English.[11] Additional references can be located by consulting the annual bibliography published by the Modern Language Association (the most comprehensive) and the Humanities Research Association's *Annual Bibliography of English Language and Literature*. Both the MLA bibliography and the *ABELL* contain sections on nineteenth-century literature and include critical works published the previous year. The English Association of London's annual bibliography, *This Year's Work in English Studies*, a critical essay on the more important books and articles published each year, is less comprehensive but useful in identifying trends. The *Victorian Periodicals Newsletter* publishes a bibliography of books, articles, and reviews on Victorian literature, art, history, economics, and biography.[12]

## NOVELS AND THE STUDY OF WOMEN

The nineteenth-century novel, often characterized as the literature by and for women, is a particularly rich source for the study of women in the past. It is no wonder that a society which extolled the family and regarded marriage as the "one great profession" for women produced novels which, as Thomas Carlyle complained, "made love and marriage seem the main business of life."[13] Male as well as female authors wrote primarily for and about women. Even such "political" novels as Anthony Trollope's *The Prime Minister* or Joseph Conrad's *The Secret Agent* have important subplots about love and marriage. Anthony Trollope, believing that the lessons of fiction should "appertain chiefly to the intercourse between young men and young women," described the "love plot" as one of the five essential elements of the Victorian novel.[14]

Women may well have formed a majority of the reading audience. One of the best sources of information about the tastes of the Victorian reading public and the preponderance of female readers are the comments made by contemporary reviewers, such as Florence Layard in "What Women Write and Read" (1887–88); [M-M] in "Novels of the Day: Their Writers and Readers" (1860); Edward Salmon in "What Girls Read" (1886); and articles in contemporary periodicals, for example, "What American Girls Read" in *The Pall Mall Gazette* (they favored "the romantic or sensational old-time favorites like *Jane Eyre, East Lynne* and *Lady Audley's Secret*"). "The man," asserted *The Pall Mall Gazette* in 1888, "... once he has entered a business or profession has no longer time for reading novels ... the maiden, however, reads on.... The national outcome of this is that novels are mostly written for women, and not only for but also by women."[15] Authors and critics believed that the characters and morals portrayed in novels had an effect upon their readers. As Henry Trail commented at a Toynbee Hall lecture in 1888, "Anthony Trollope used constantly to say that boys and girls—men and women, too—drew their current notions of the duties, the courtesies and the ideals of life more from novels they read than from anything else, and the statement is just as true today." Young women, as W. R. Greg pointed out, were regarded as especially susceptible: "Novels constitute a principal part of the reading of women who are always impressionable, in whom at all times the emotional element is more awake and more powerful than the critical, whose feelings are more easily aroused and whose estimates are more easily influenced than ours [men's]." The novelist had a duty to encourage morality and proper behavior. As Florence Layard approvingly quoted Thomas Carlyle, "'The writer of a book, is he not a preacher, preaching not to this parish or that, but to all men in all times and places? Not the wretchedest circulating library novel, but will help regulate the actual practical weddings and households of those foolish girls.'" In *The Pall Mall Gazette* the American W. D. Howells expanded on the theme of Victorian novelist as moralist: "He assumes a higher function, something like that of a physician or a priest...."[16] Women in autobiographies or memoirs substantiated this association when they recalled, as did Emmeline Pethick-Lawrence, that the novels they read as young girls affected their lifelong interests.[17]

Victorians, convinced of the influence of novel reading on behavior, worried about moral standards in books. When Charles Pelham, a younger son of the Duke of Newcastle, wished to make what his father deemed a "ripped and wholly objectionable marriage" (to a woman who was, however, a daughter of Lady Orde and the niece of the Duchess of Hamilton), the Duke wrote in anger, "An idle mind has induced you to amuse yourself with novel reading, the poison of every young mind, and this has led you to act as you have." This concern about the deleterious effects of novel reading, originally directed toward romances and gothic tales, intensified with the publication of the sensational novels in the 1860s and the translation of French novels, particularly those of Zola, into English. Articles about the sensational novels appeared frequently in periodicals.[18] Speakers in the House of Commons addressed themselves to this "problem." The National Vigilance Association, founded in 1886, devoted part of its energies to preventing the sale of "disgraceful" literature. In 1887, *The Pall Mall Gazette* seriously noted:

> A priest in Limerick lately commenced an agitation against "English light literature" and the other evening there was a public demonstration in connection with the movement. Thousands of people walked in a procession after an effigy of Satan, and a banner with the inscription, "Burn immoral literature," ... It is to be hoped that the movement will spread; but it should be remembered that the "penny dreadful" is not the worst form of noxious literature. In many instances the expensive three-volume novel is quite as impure, and quite as dangerous.[19]

Much of the criticism of novel reading stemmed from the fear that girls and women would be debased by the stories they read. Henry Mayhew, in *London Labour and the London Poor*, drew a direct and simple connection between behavior and novels:

> The ruin of many poor girls is commenced by reading the low wishy-washy cheap publications that the news-shops are now gorged with, and by devouring the hastily written, immoral, stereotyped tales about the sensualities of the upper classes, the lust of the aristocracy, and the affection that men about town—nobles, lords, illustrious dukes, and even princes of the blood—are in the habit of imbibing for maidens of low degree "whose face is their fortune."[20]

Considered equally damaging was the possibility that women, aspiring to unattainable fantasies, would become unhappy or undutiful daughters or wives. With this in mind, conduct manuals and books of advice, such as Henry Roger's admonitions on novel reading in "The Greyson Letters," continually warned parents about the dangers of the novel. Mrs. Hester Chapone in *Letters on the Improvement of the Mind, Addressed to a Young Lady*; James Fordyce in *Sermons to Young Women*; and Dr. John Gregory in *A Father's Legacy to His Daughters*, written in the eighteenth century but still popular in the nineteenth century, all cautioned against those novels "that so enchant the mind—most of which tend to inflame the passions of youth" (Chapone, 2: 146) and recommended specific "safe" authors.[21] The numerous guides written in the nineteenth century, such as Mrs. Sarah Ellis's *Daughters of England* (1836); and Harriet Martineau's *How to Observe Morals and Manners* (1838), *Home Duties. A Book for Girls* (1869); and *The Young Lady's Book of Advice and Instruction* (1869) all advised young women to read history and serious books which would neither inflame their sensibilities nor make them overly learned.[22]

Although novel reading, particularly of the wrong sort of novels, could be dangerous to the morals of young girls, some authors and critics believed that reading proper novels could improve values and standards, and teach them, through example, the proper way to live. Novel reading was one way for middle-class girls and women to learn about the world. As the *Westminister Review* argued in an article on novels about prostitution:

> The best justification for such novels ... assuredly is that women may perhaps be redeemed from the possibility of remaining in that imbecile and ignorant condition which the romanticist commonly regards as innocence and which woman is so generally encouraged to regard as her special virtue, even by those who are so earnest in describing it as the principal cause of her ruin.[23]

Despite the fears that parents of daughters may have had concerning novel reading, novel writing was one of the few acceptable means of earning a living for middle-class women. The fact that novels could be written at home and that some female authors were notable commercial successes encouraged women to become writers.

Even though novel writing was "acceptable" and did not involve a loss of social status for the middle-class woman, the "lady novelist" aroused a great deal of comment, such as G. H. Lewes's famous article, "The Lady Novelists" (1852), and the anonymous "The Lady Novelists of Great Britain" (1853) in the Victorian periodical press. Reviewers concerned themselves with questions about the proper interests and occupations for women. Although most female authors came from middle-class homes and were daughters of clergymen, barristers, and commercial men, a minority were of aristocratic origin, such as Lady Emmeline Stuart-Wortley, a daughter of the duke of Rutland, and Lady Georgina Fullerton, a daughter of Lord Grenville.[24] Their works enable us to read what women had to say, though couched in fictional settings and with imagined characters, about Victorian society, the position of women, and the relations between women and men. The woman novelist, though perhaps "invisible" in the legal and political sense,[25] is very visible through her writing. "Novels," noted Dorothy Hale in her introduction to the exhibition on nineteenth-century novelists at the University of California, Los Angeles, "were not only a major vocational outlet for Victorian women, they were also one of their few imaginative outlets in a society which suppressed its women even more than its men. For the social scientist, therefore, the novels can be used as an index both to feminine feelings and ideals and the facts of their everyday existence." Even though few women novelists were publically involved with the "Woman Question," their novels expressed doubts and conflicts about the limited life they were allowed to lead, revealed and protested the problems and restrictions women faced, and, if only by the fact of their authorship, subtly suggested the possibility of more opportunities for women.[26]

Recent historical scholarship has not only provided more information about women's lives in Victorian England, but has also underscored the usefulness of novels for historical studies. Patricia Branca uses domestic advice manuals, some women's periodicals, and census data in her speculative *Silent Sisterhood. Middle Class Women in the Victorian Home* (1975) to describe the middle-class housewife's responses to "modernization." Unlike the leisured lady pictured by Walter Houghton, J. A. Banks, Duncan Crow, and others, Branca's women are busily preoccupied with running a household on a limited budget, filled with anxiety about their changed socioeconomic situation, and concerned with their ability to discharge their new duties as managers of urban middle-class households.[27] In *Victorian Ladies at Work: Middle Class Working Women in England and Wales, 1850–1914* (1973), a useful descriptive study, Lee Holcombe discussed the gentlewomen who had to seek work outside the home because of economic circumstances or because they did not marry. Turning to the helping occupations of nursing and teaching, and later to clerical work, civil service, and the distributive trades, they attempted to earn a living in a world that offered limited career opportunities to women. Leonore Davidoff, in her excellent study of manners and social conventions, *The Best Circles: Women and Society in Victorian England* (1973), examines the functional (rather than decorative) role of upper-class women who, as the guardians of "Society," supervised the assimilation of new wealth and talent into England's elite. Barbara S. Frankle has effectively used etiquette books and novels to analyze middle-class women who employed manners and etiquette as a means of defining their own gentle status and of protecting their households from encroachment from nongentle, newly prosperous outsiders. Pamela Horn and Theresa McBride's recent studies on the Victorian servant supplement the more substantial earlier works by Ivy Pinchbeck and Margaret Hewitt on working women and provide information about the recruitment, treatment, and working conditions of women employed in domestic service, the largest occupational category for women in the nineteenth century. Ray Strachey, Roger Fulford, Constance Rover, and Andrew Rosen have written the best of many studies of women's attempts to gain the parliamentary vote and eventually be recognized as men's political equal. These and other studies show the Victorian woman actively managing a home, consulting doctors, working, and being active in politics and philanthropies.[28]

Barbara Kanner's bibliographical chapter in *Suffer and Be Still*, edited by Martha Vicinus, the essential starting place for anyone interested in the position of women in Victorian society, provides references to contemporary and recent articles and books on women and employment, work, prostitution, women's roles in sciety, emigration, philanthropy, and education. An excellent second bibliographical essay, Barbara Kanner's "The Women of England in a Century of Social Change, 1815–1914: A Select Bibliography, Part II" in *A Widening Sphere*, edited by Martha Vicinus, contains over six hundred references to recent and contemporary studies of women's relationships to their families, their health, marriage, child care and childbirth, views about women's intellectual capacities, sex, and voluntary organizations. In addition, both *Suffer and Be Still* and *A Widening Sphere* include articles of interest and varying usefulness on women and Victorian society.

Intriguing questions remain, however, which cannot be answered by census data, etiquette books, or parliamentary commissions on working conditions, divorce, and property laws. How did women feel about their lives, about being women in Victorian society? One can turn to letters, autobiographies, and memoirs but, as Lawrence Stone has noted, "many of the most important questions about family relations, love and marriage deal with values, states of mind, and intimate habits of thought which do not usually find their way on to paper." Although such sources are important and must be used, the reader cannot necessarily rely on their candor. Even diary and letter writers are aware of style and literary convention.[29]

Novels offer another source for this intimate world of emotions and relationships because love, marriage, and family relations were themes in most nineteenth-century works. This is particularly true for the nineteenth century, when propriety and self-restraint, especially for women, were very highly valued. Victorian women, those who wrote as well as those who did not, can be seen as sharing an "increasingly secretive and ritualized physical experience" and training in "repression, concealment and self-censorship."[30] As Vicinus has suggested:

> So often concerned with love, courtship, and marriage, fiction rarely dealt directly with the growing complexity of women's sphere. Despite these seeming limitations, Victorian literature functioned as both an expression of and a shaper of the culture and its conflicts. For many men and women, reading the works of the best known and loved writers was a means of managing the emotional ambivalences they felt in regard to their changing roles. Art gave order to an understanding of the conflicting demands placed on individuals by personal needs, families, and society .... The classic works of Victorian literature cannot tell us much specifically about female suffrage, the rising number of single women, or job opportunities, but they can illuminate the emotional conflicts and resolutions of men and women concerned with woman's proper place.[31]

By writing novels, women were able to express what they thought or felt, under the guise of writing fiction, just as male authors were able to discuss relations between men and women and their feelings about women at the time. Of course, the researcher, in order to use these novels, must be aware of the conventions of plot, language, and style employed by Victorian authors.

Literary scholars interested in the questions of how and why women wrote and how authors have portrayed women have produced critical studies on women and literature that are essential for the historian using novels to study women.[32] Three fundamental questions have been posed that are of interest to historians: why do women write? do women write differently from men, and if so, why? and how have women been represented in fiction by male and female authors? Victorian women had practical and psychological reasons for writing. As I mentioned earlier, writing was a socially acceptable occupation for a middle-class woman, in part because it could appear as an avocation and could be done at home. Virginia Woolf, thinking of the complicated lives of George Eliot and Charlotte Brontë, commented that women wrote fiction because it required less concentration than other art forms and could be pursued by women who had other things to do.[33] Novel writing promised substantial financial rewards for the successful. Catherine Gore earned over 20,000 pounds from her novels; Elizabeth Gaskell and Frances Trollope supported their families on their earnings; Mrs. Hodgson Burnett, *The Pall Mall Gazette* noted, received 3,750 pounds for a single story.[34] Women may also have turned to novel writing because other opportunities for achievement, such as politics, law, business, or medicine, were closed to them.[35] Writing may have given women a way to share experiences and express their solidarity with other women and, in a covert way, to vent their anger and protest the place of women in Victorian society. Many English women would have agreed with the advice given by Fanny Fern, an American novelist: "Look around and see innumerable women to whose barren and loveless lives this would be an improvement and solace and I say to them write! write! write! it will be a safe outlet for thoughts and feelings."[36]

In such matters as style, point of view, and choice of themes, many literary scholars have agreed that there are basic differences in the writing of men and women. They have pointed to something distinctly "female": narrowness of focus, "smaller feminine outlook," sentimentality, greater sensitivity, more trivial detail, controlled resentment, self-consciousness, and reiteration of certain themes.[37] Is this a biological imperative or a product of social conditions and restrictions placed on women? Do women write in this "feminine" style, as Cynthia Ozick has suggested, because they have learned a set of standards, language, and control for their own self-preservation, or in order to be accepted seriously as writers?[38] Such critics as Bald, Courtney, and Johnson, despite their antifeminist attitudes and often patronizing comments, implicity (if not explicitly) have agreed with feminist critics, Margaret Lawrence and Virginia Woolf among others, that women wrote as they did because of their narrow range of experience. According to this interpretation, socialization practices and restricted opportunities encouraged a fiction full of details, emotional, and small in scope. Taught to be submissive, manipulative, and concerned for others, women wrote in a pleading tone; though at the same time, resentful of their place, they protested their situation.[39] It did not help that critics responded to women writers first as women and second as novelists.[40]

While more recent scholars have concurred that restricted lives and narrow experience influenced women's literature, they have placed new emphasis on the effects of the ambivalence of the female role. Patricia Spacks in *The Female Imagination* (1975) argues that the restrictiveness of society and the ambivalence of the accepted female role forced women to turn inward and develop a richer fantasy life and a creative, though narcissistic and masochistic, preoccupation with the self. Showalter, after studying over two hundred minor and major female novelists of the nineteenth and twentieth centuries, has concluded that there is a distinct and developing tradition in women's writing.[41]

The factors which influenced women's style and encouraged them to write also affected their portrayal of women and their situation in fiction, just as male authors' experiences influenced their representation of women and the relations between the sexes.[42] Reflecting the perceived difficulties of women and the conventional attitudes toward them in Victorian society, the theme of woman as victim recurs in both the novels and the critical literature. As artists and even as people, women were restricted, demeaned, exploited, idealized, made to doubt themselves, taught to sacrifice themselves for others and to bow before the greater wisdom of men.[43] In *Middlemarch*, *The Mill on the Floss*, and *Daniel Deronda*, the innate abilities of Dorothea, Maggie, and Gwendolyn go unrealized because of the inhibitions circumscribing Victorian women.[44] According to Leonore Hoffman, the conflicts Charlotte Brontë, George Eliot, George Egerton, and Olive Schreiner felt between the need to assert themselves as people and the impulse to submerge their selves in the service of others resulted in their creation of heroines characterized by fragmented personalities and contradictory behavior.[45] Ellen Moers, Spacks, and Showalter have noted the recurrence of the heroine who renounces, compromises, or dies.[46] Portrayals of the "strong-minded" heroine provide a case in point; whereas male authors depicted her as destructive and made her reform in the end, female authors were more sympathetic. Although Roni Natov has seen this sympathy as paving the way for a more complex characterization of women and the "new woman" heroine, it should be noted that all her strong-minded heroines (Catherine Earnshaw, Maggie Tulliver, Jane Eyre, and Dorothea Brooke) meet one of the conventional fates of a Victorian heroine.[47] Elizabeth Hardwick has observed that in novels by both men and women, the heroine inevitably is betrayed and suffers. Even though suffering may be considered an ennobling experience, she comments, somehow it is always the women, such as Hester Prynne and

Tess, who were distressed and not the men who victimized them.[48] The prevalence of the Victorian heroine who is ennobled by suffering has led literary scholars and historians to question the effect that this idealization of womanhood had on women.

Françoise Basch, in a comparison of the fictional representation of women by major Victorian novelists with the actual position of women, has suggested that idealization was merely another means of restricting women and also that this myth of the ideal woman inhibited novelists.[49] Her study, although it does not go far enough into the reasons for the disparity between the position and the portrayal of women, reflects the sensitivity of the "new feminist" criticism to questions of power, oppression, and the relationship between fictional heroines and the actual situation of women.[50] Historians should also heed feminist critics' admonitions to literary scholars to pay attention to the material details of women's lives, their reminders that stereotypes need to be analyzed in relation to society, and their interest in relating the representation of women in fiction to the position of women in society. The ways in which male and female authors have portrayed women in fiction provide important information to the historian about women's experiences and attitudes toward them.

Annis Pratt, a "new feminist" critic, has suggested that feminist literature deals not only with women's moral superiority over men or their struggle to gain rights, but also with an existential struggle as a female character strives to be someone. There are numerous studies discussing women as they are portrayed in novels, however, most of them lack a theoretical framework and are weak on analysis. These descriptive accounts, though of limited usefulness for the historian, do provide information about women characters and writers and are sources of anecdotes about them. R. P. Utter and G. B. Needham's *Pamela's Daughters* (1937) is a history of literary taste and fashions; Katherine West's *Chapter of Governesses* (1949) and Katherine Moore's *Cordial Relations: The Maiden Aunt in Fact and Fiction* (1967) and *Victorian Wives* (1974) are simply descriptive. Others, such as John D. Kennedy's "Trollope's Widows: Beyond the Stereotypes of Maiden and Wife" (1975), a study of the problems of the mature woman in Trollope's novels, do not analyze the relationship between women in society and their representation in literature.[51] Although most literary scholars have seen the relationship between Victorian society and the portrayal of women as basically static and stressed how the narrow experience of women writers, the expectations of women's conduct, and male attitudes toward women resulted in characters who are submissive or defeated, some scholars have described a dynamic relationship. Showalter has employed a developmental model derived from studies of literary subcultures to describe how women's writing, in response to changes in women's position and attitudes toward them, progressed from the imitation of male authors and internalization of their standards to a protest against those standards and a search for a distinct female identity and literary voice.[52]

In one of the first studies of this sort, *The Victorian Heroine: A Changing Ideal, 1837–73* (1956), Patricia Thomson explores the effect of the growth of the ideas of the feminist movement (in education, employment, rights of women, and attitudes toward prostitution, among others) on the portrayal of female characters. Believing that novelists are influenced, even against their will, by new ideas, Thomson proposed that although the ideal of woman may have remained static between 1837 and 1873, the heroines, reflecting the impact of feminist ideas, changed. Marcia Fox, Sara Davis, Lloyd Fernando, Leone Scanlon, and A. R. Cunningham have suggested that interest in the "woman question," changes in opportunities for women in such areas as education, employment, property owning, voting, control over family size, and a new questioning of conventional attitudes toward women and marriage were reflected in the appearence of the New Woman.[53] The New Woman was a more independent woman who pursued a career, perhaps like George Gissing's Rhoda Nunn, bore a child out of wedlock like Grant Allen's Herminia, or questioned traditional assumptions about marriage and male-female relationships like Olive Schreiner's Lyndall.[54] The change in the heroine suggests some interesting lines of inquiry to the historian studying women, especially since even New Women are usually made to suffer for their independence.

Influenced by the feminist movement, the growth of women's studies, and new feminist literary criticism, scholars are now investigating the representation of women in literature as one means of discovering attitudes and tensions in the past and examining the lives of women authors for information about women's experiences. Increasingly, literary critics are analyzing the connections between fictional and real women. Historians can further explore this relationship and its implications for Victorian society. From the representation of women in fiction by male and female authors, we can discover attitudes about women, tensions which existed between men and women, and the conflicts that Victorian women felt. Women who wrote, especially the minor novelists whose work did not bring critical acclaim or great recognition, were not so different from other women of their time. Many of their necessary personal adjustments were not due to their creativity, but because they had been born women in a society which inculcated ambivalent expectations and restricted activities. The lives of women writers, and the literature they produced, provide a source of information about the experience and emotions of Victorian women. As Margaret Lawrence has observed, "in the century and a half women have been writing they have set down enough of what drives them emotionally, and of what passes in their minds to bring the race much closer to an understanding of itself and perhaps a little nearer to easing the pain there is between men and women."[55]

## Using Novels As Historical Evidence

"All very interesting," might reply the historian trained to regard novels as the creation of the author's imagination and therefore unreliable, "but can we use novels as serious evidence?" Walter Laquer, in "Literature and the Historian" (1967), suggested that in the nineteenth century a clear distinction between literature and history was not drawn. Thomas Babington Macaulay's famous dictum, "history begins in literature and ends in essay," more a comment on the standards of literary excellence expected from historians than on method, nevertheless reflects the contemporary feeling that the novel, the essay, and history were all forms of literature. Later in the century, as history became increasingly accepted as a scientific discipline with a distinct methodology, the use of literary sources fell into disrepute. They were considered subjective, impressionistic, and inaccurate. But all historical sources are subjective to some extent. E. H. Carr has offered us a useful reminder, recently noted by Lawrence Stone, that "no document can tell us more than what the author of the document thought—what he thought happened, what he thought ought to happen or would happen, or perhaps only what he wanted others to think he thought, or even only what he himself thought he thought."[56]

Discussion of the use of literature in studying history has become more frequent with the growing interest in interdisciplinary studies. John V. Fleming, in "Historians and the Evidence of Literature" (1973), encouraged historians to overcome their reticence about using literary materials. A. J. Lehmann, in "Writer as Canary" (1967), and R. Gordon Kelly, in "Literature and the Historian" (1974), discussed the insights that can be gained from using literature. The usefulness of the novel to the historian depends in part on what questions are asked. Novels have little to add to the history of diplomacy, politics, or the actions of the powerful. But to the history of attitudes, responses, and values, the Victorian novel has a great deal to offer since one of its main functions, according to serious Victorian authors and critics, was to provide insights into the nature of man and society. Marc Bloch believed that "We can speak of earlier ages only through the accounts of eye-witnesses...." Novelists, though they present their accounts in fictional terms, are one set of eyewitnesses of life in Victorian England.[57]

Novels can be a rich source for the historian, providing insights into values, emotions, and conflicts, when they are examined with the same scrutiny as other historical evidence.[58] As Carr, among others, has suggested, the historian needs "imaginative understanding of the minds of the people with whom he is dealing." Novels offer us a unique opportunity to understand the minds of Victorian women and the Victorian period. Richard Hoggart has claimed that "properly read—read in and for themselves, with an openness to the author's imagination and art—works of literature give an insight into the life of an age, a kind and intensity of insight, which no other source can give."[59]

Novels operate on two basic levels: what the authors conciously set out to say through plot, theme, characters, and details; and what they unconsciously say through their work about their values and their relationship with society. Both levels are influenced by the authors' relations with their society. The first level is the story itself and the development of the characters—how they behave, what they want or fear, the meaningful details of their lives. Recurring themes and characters, such as the passive heroine, suggest what the public's reading preferences were. Such information raises questions about the readers; for example, why did the middle- and working-class women, who apparently formed the majority of the nineteenth-century reading audience, choose to read about passive dependent heroines? Why is the desirability of womanliness stressed in minor and major novels while in reality many women struggled to acquire more rights and opportunities? How much is the recurrence of themes and character types the result of Victorian literary conventions, and what functions did those conventions serve?

Novels can also give us an invaluable sense of the Victorian milieu. The details of the characters and their setting supply us with a mental picture of the time—a sort of backdrop against which we can bring the people and events of Victorian England into clearer focus. Frank Kermode, in his discussion of the bombing scene in Joseph Conrad's *The Secret Agent*, suggested that "It makes us *see*. It explains. It takes us into a region of historical explanation from which historians feel themselves disbarred by their primary adherence to the documents. Yet it is recognizably historical...."[60] There is a clear distinction between the use of conventional historical sources and novels. Fiction, though it may be based on real people and feelings, is the creation of the writer's imagination. Historians cannot go to novels and expect to find a document that purports to describe what a certain time or place in Victorian

England looked like or what actual people said or did. But they can find a dramatic interpretation which can augment the facts. *The author, not the fictional character, is the historial figure.* Though we may learn about George Eliot from studying Maggie Tulliver, we should never treat Maggie as if she had been a real person. While never taking the world of the novel as fact or assuming its representativeness, and always using it in conjunction with conventional evidence to ensure that its interpretation is not misleading, we can develop, as does Humphrey House in *Dickens World*, an invaluable feeling for the period which enhances our sense of what was important to the people and how it might have felt to have lived in particular situation in nineteenth-century England.

Let us look at three examples: how novelists illustrate particular problems of their time, how they give a sense of the Victorian milieu, and how they provide insights into emotions and conflicts experienced by Victorian women. These examples are taken from the works of male and female authors. Though for different reasons, the writings of both are valuable to the historian. The sex of the authors had a great effect on the literature they wrote: men and women had different experiences, different opportunities, and saw the Victorian world through different eyes. Even though a man might create believable women characters, he still revealed how he thought women felt and what he himself felt about women. It is here that the two views are valuable: from male authors we see Victorian society as men saw it; from female authors, as women saw it.

In *The Prime Minister*, Anthony Trollope describes how Mr. Wharton, a wealthy barrister of high principles, threatens to disinherit his beloved daughter Emily so that her fortune will not enrich the unscrupulous bounder she insists on marrying. He goes through considerable mental and emotional turmoil trying to decide if he should forbid the marriage which he knows, because of Lopez's character and the disparity between his background and Emily's, would be a disaster. Emily tells him, "You claim a right to my obedience, and I acknowledge it. I am sure you believe me when I promise not to see him without your permission." But in spite of Wharton's disapproval and misgivings,

> a feeling began to grow upon him already that his daughter had a mode of pleading with him which he would not ultimately be able to resist. He had the power, he knew, of putting an end to the thing altogether. He had only to say resolutely and inchangeably that the thing shouldn't be, and it wouldn't be. If he could steel his heart against his daughter's sorrow for, say a twelvemonth, the victory would be won. But he already began to fear that he lacked the power to steel his heart against his daughter.[61]

This passage is an excellent illustration of the conflict between parental authority and freedom of choice which created problems for many nineteenth-century families. The scenes in *The Prime Minister* also give a feeling for the affection between fathers and daughters, and popular attitudes about the importance of marriage for a woman, as shown by Wharton's admission to Authur, Emily's unsuccesful suitor and close family friend:

> I am thinking very much about it. I do not know that I have really been able to think of anything else for the last two months. It is all the world to me,—what she and Everett [his son] do with them-selves; and what she may do in this matter of marriage is of infinitely greater importance than anything that can befall him. If he makes a mistake, it may be put right. But with a woman's marrying—, *vestigula nulla retrorsum.*[62]

Marriage customs of propertied families, changing since the late seventeenth century, were still in transition. Parents, believing their authority to be, theoretically, inalienable, had to face the fact that their daughters were increasingly able to meet, at social gatherings or through their school friends or their brothers, young men who had not passed parental scrutiny. What was a parent to do when a daughter wished to marry someone who was on the periphery of the gentle class and not quite acceptable? The decision was made even more difficult in the nineteenth century because parents, even though they wished to retain their right of veto, increasingly believed that women should make a choice and that love was important in marriage. In addition, young men were more frequently able to earn their own living in a profession, thus making parental economic sanctions less effective. A parent could forbid the marriage, or could, as in the case of Wharton, sadly acquiesce and take legal steps to protect the family fortune. If one looks at Chancery Court cases, one will find real life Mr. Whartons who tried to exert some control over their daughters' marriage choices by specifying in their wills that their daugh-ters had to have the permission (often in writing) of their guardians or trustees before marrying, and that if they married without permission, they would forfeit most or all of their fortune.[63]

In our second example, from Charlotte Brontë's *Villette* and Anne Brontë's *Agnes Grey*, we get a sense for the helplessness and frustration that a governess could experience. Elizabeth Hardwick has pointed perceptively to the incident in *Agnes Grey* where the sensitive heroine has to watch her charges mutilate baby birds. Horrified and repulsed, she was nevertheless powerless to stop them. In George Gissing's *The Odd Women* we find another vivid picture of the redundant governess's bleak existence, written from a man's point of view. Virginia and Alice Madden (one an ex-companion, the other a poorly paid ex-nursery governess) shared a bed-sitting room in London. Unable to find remunerative employment and living off tiny legacies from their families, they spent their days counting their meager resources and rationing their food.

> They were preparing their midday meal, the substantial repast of the day. In a little saucepan on an oil cooking stove was some plain rice, bubbling as Alice stirred. Virginia fetched from downstairs [Mrs. Conisbee had assigned them to a shelf in her larder] bread, butter, cheese, a pot of preserve, and arranged the table (three feet by one and a half) at which they were accustomed to eat.... At their meal they calculated that they must cut back their expenses. "Seven shillings rent; that leaves only seven and two-pence a week for everything—everything!" "We *could* do it, dear!" persisted the other. "If it came to the very worst, our food need not cost more than a sixpence a day ... I do really believe, Virgie, we would support life on less—say, on fourpence—Yes, we could, dear!" "Is such a life worthy of the name?"[64]

For details of despair we could turn to the brief histories in the 1851 Report of the Governesses Benevolent Association and other available contemporary documents. From M. Jeanne Peterson's excellent article, "The Victorian Governess: Status Incongruence in Family and Society" (1970), we know that governesses, usually middle-class women forced to earn their living, often faced nothing better than unemployment or old age on a meager pension from the Governesses Benevolent Association. A. James Hammerton has added that by the 1860s finding a situation had become more difficult and that alternative opportunities for these women in genteel occupations were very limited.[65]

Gissing's account, though it should be supplemented with historical studies, increases our understanding of the redundant woman's plight. He dramatized the situation and offered a general comment about the lives of single women as well as providing specific examples. *The Odd Women* illuminates Victorian life and values and reveals the author's feelings about himself, women, and the society around him. It is also a document of a man's anger at a socioeconomic system which, because of notions of gentility inculcated into middle-class children, made it impossible for them to hold nongentle jobs. The value placed on gentility and the lack of genteel opportunities for women caused the spiritual and physical decline of redundant gentlewomen. Frustration with a society which pushed women into loveless marriages for economic security lay behind this criticism. Women married in order to avoid poverty, ignominy, and uselessness. Women were not the only casualities in this system: men married fools because "They must marry someone, and in the case of most men choice is seriously restricted." Gissing's critique of marriage in late Victorian England reflects both his personal circumstances (two unhappy marriages), his hostility toward women, and the mounting criticism of the institution of marriage voiced at the end of the century by journalists, novelists, and social writers.[66] Since people did not often express their intimate feelings about marriage, novels were, as Showalter has brilliantly shown in her discussion of the female sensationalist writers, a way for both men and women to show their real feelings.[67]

Reading novels was also, as Martha Vicinus has noted, "a means of managing the emotional ambivalences [men and women] felt in regard to their changing roles." One reason for this was that Victorian writers, in their novels, expressed their own ambivalences about the position of women. One of the important questions to Victorians was how was one to live and lead a worthy life. The code of respectability and the concept of duty were only partial answers. Dinah Mulock Craik provided a typical response in her "A Woman's Thoughts about Women:"

> A definite answer to this question is simply impossible. So diverse are characters, tastes, capabilities, and circumstances, that to lay down a distinct line of occupation for any six women of one's own acquaintance would be the merest absurdity. To few is the choice so easy, the field of duty so wide, that she need puzzle very long over what she ought to do. Generally—and this is the best and safest guide—she will find her work lying very near at hand: some desultory tastes to condense into regular studies, some faulty household quietly to remodel, some child to teach, or parent to watch over. All these being needless or unattainable, she may extend her service out of the home into the world, which perhaps never at any time so much needed the help of us women. And how many of its charities and duties can be best done only by a wise and tender woman's hand.[68]

These were, however, not satisfactory answers. Dorothea Brooke may have sought a cause to make her life meaningful, but she also tried to develop herself as a person. This question came to the fore when Victorian novelists depicted young girls. Although the sensationalist female novelists showed that it was possible for women to flee their familial duties, most women's options narrowed once they married and had families because they then had direct responsibilities. But girlhood and adolescence was a time of potential when one could aspire, like Maggie Tulliver, to learning and knowledge, and of adjustment to the restrictions circumscribing women in Victorian society. Novels on the development of girls' characters provide the historian with an opportunity to learn about attitudes toward women's lives and how these changed during the nineteenth century. One can follow the development of young girls, such as Caroline Norton's heroine in her romance *Stuart of Dunleath*, George Eliot's Maggie Tulliver, Mollie in Elizabeth Gaskell's *Wives and Daughters*, and Olive Schreiners' Lyndall in *Story of an African Farm*; examine how the authors portrayed them; ask whether their experiences were meant to be representative of the conflicts felt by Victorian girls; and study the comments the authors made through their representations. Norton, Eliot, and Schreiner each directly protested the limitations placed on women. Norton, through a romance, shows the injustice of forced marriages and the dilemma of the woman trapped in marriage to a man she loathes. By her sympathetic presentation of Maggie, Eliot causes one to question a system which educates Tom but will not allow Maggie to fulfill her potential. Schreiner protests the institution of marriage much more directly, reflecting the change in women's position by 1883 and the much more outspoken criticism of marriage.[69] Gaskell, through her portrayal of Mrs. Kirkpatrick and Cynthia, gently chides the social institutions that create women who have no purpose but to marry. Tracing the ways in which female authors depict the development of their girl characters is of particular interest to the historian since it reveals changing attitudes.

Literature is one way of transmitting and inculcating the values that society (or interest groups which control the writing and publication of books) regards as necessary to its perpetuation.[70] Literature as historical evidence can be employed to discover values and tensions existing in Victorian society.[71] The lovely, gentle, submissive, restrained, and virtuous heroine recurs in popular literature at a time when women began to make more choices for themselves in marriage and had increasing access to employment. We think of Gaskell's Mary Barton who, though the daughter of a factory worker, behaved as much like a lady as she could in her circumstances. Dalziel, Neff, and, to a lesser degree, Thomson have all noted the "lag" between the actual advancement of women and how they were portrayed in novels. Significantly, female characters who did not conform to the ideal frequently died or were forced to compromise their desires in order to survive. Even George Eliot, a woman who defied one of society's strongest conventions by living with G. H. Lewes, created heroines who learned they could not do or be what they wished, but had instead to limit their hopes and ambitions. This effort to encourage the submissive and male-dominated female character was perhaps an attempt, conscious or unconscious, to balance the standards of behavior thought essential to the preservation of the Victorian family and women's new choices and opportunities.

In "Literature and the Historian" (1974), Kelly discusses several ways in which novels could be used to reveal social tensions and values and also criticizes the manner in which novels generally have been used. He argues that the analysis of the text of a book does not provide any evidence of its reader's response and that "great" literature is often an inferior historical source.[72] Victorian novelists can be divided, roughly, into three groups: those we continue to study as the creators of great literature (Jane Austen, Emily and Charlotte Brontë, Charles Dickens, George Meredith, George Eliot, Thomas Hardy, William Thackeray, and Anthony Trollope); the serious novelists, or as Carolyn Heilbrun has referred to them, "middle-range novelists,"[73] who are rarely studied today as important writers in literature courses (for example, Elizabeth Gaskell, Charles Kingsley, and Mrs. Humphrey Ward); and the more numerous "popular" novelists (Catherine Gore, Margaret Oliphant, Frances Trollope, G. P. R. James, to name but a few). The popular novels, written with the specific intention of satisfying a mass audience, tended to say what the public wanted to read and therefore suggest something about their readers' tastes, fears, and aspirations. As Lady Mary Wortley Montagu explained in the eighteenth century, "Perhaps you will say I should not take my ideas of the manner of the times from such trifling authors; but it is more truly to be found among them, than from any historian—as they write merely to get money, they always fall into the notions that are most acceptable to the present taste."[74] In her analysis of the popular literature heroines of the 1850s Dalziel discovered that in the vast majority of these stories the heroine conformed to a type: she blushed easily, had long, beautiful hair, was very young, pretty, and frail. Submissive and virtuous, she was dependent upon her parents, brother, or husband. Marriage to a healthy, rational gentleman of good birth and large estates who rode and was a member of parliament was her destiny. Characters in popular novels adhered to the ideal of Victorian womanhood and manhood recommended by etiquette books and advice manuals: the woman demure, attractive, submissive; the man guiding, strong, in control. The minor novels frequently featured stock middle-class or aristocratic characters who provided entertainment for their middle- and working-class readers, especially those who either hoped to better themselves by marriage—the theme of most of these novels—or to escape from the marriage they had made.[75]

While the popular novelists' reliance on stock characters and situations reflected their perception of the audience's preferences, the major or serious novelists were more innovative.[76] Great literature, according to Leo Lowenthal, provides "one of the essential sources for studying the relation between man and society" and contains "the most telling truths about society and the individual." Like Lehmann who compared writers with their intuitive powers to canaries discovering gas pockets in mines, Lowenthal has suggested that the creative artist has special powers. He argued that the "writer's desire to create the unique and important work forces him to discover those new and telling expressions that often successfully bring hitherto nameless anxieties and hopes into focus."[77] The major Victorian novelists were concerned with self-awareness and the search for individual values and purpose in a world which had its own standards.[78] From them we can learn about the values of Victorian society and the woman's quest for her own identity and sense of worth within that society.

Studies of specific genres also provide background information for the researcher working in a particular period. The "silver-fork" novels, replete with details about society and catering to the desire for escape and entertainment, have been examined by M. W. Rosa, *The Silver-Fork School: Novels of Fashion Preceding Vanity Fair* (1936) and, briefly, by Michael Sadleir, *Bulwer and His Wife* (1933). Historical novels, another form of Victorian wish fulfillment, have been studied by Nicholas Rance, *Historical Novel and Popular Politics in Nineteenth-Century England* (1975); Avrom Fleishman, *The English Historical Novel* (1971); James C. Simmons, *The Novelist as Historian* (1973); and, in great detail, by E. A. Baker, *History in Fiction* (1907) (a guide to historical romances) and *A Guide to Historical Fiction* (1941). The social reform novel, which made novels "respectable" in the eyes of many Victorians, contains vivid details about Victorian life and class attitudes. These novels have been analyzed by Tillotson, and Louis Cazamian, *The Social Novel in England 1830–1850* (1973; translated from original 1904 French edition). Barbara Kanner and Ivanka Kovačević's study of one of the minor women novelists in "Blue Book into Novel: The Forgotten Industrial Fiction of Charlotte Elizabeth Tonna" (1970) is an example of the method and sources used by the social reform novelists. Domestic realism, the subject of Vineta Colby's *Yesterday's Woman* (1974), should interest the researcher on women in nineteenth-century England because these novels, written principally by women, provide detailed accounts of middle-class people's lives and work.

Since the novel reflects the attitudes and experiences of its author, it needs to be handled critically when used as historical evidence—precisely because it is the creation of a single person's perceptions and conditioned by that person's environment. As Lehmann has pointed out, historians often fail to cross-examine literature with the same rigor they use for other sources and often credit writers with undeserved special powers. Researchers, he advised, should remember that authors wrote for specific social groups and that they represented the values of their own class.[79]

When historians use the novel, they should consider the constraints which affected its author's observations of women in Victorian society: the author's purpose, sex, education, talent, social position, personal experience, and general outlook. Biographies, autobiographies, letters and memoirs are the most obvious sources for this sort of background information.[80] The historian must not regard Victorian novels as isolated documents, but take into account specific literary and trade conventions in order to assess accurately the novel and its author. To this end, scholars should be familiar with Albert Baugh, *A Literary History of England* (2d ed., 1967); E. A. Baker, *A History of the English Novel* (1924), volume seven on "Dickens and Thackeray," and eight on "From the Brontës to Meredith: Romanticism and the English Novel"; E. C. Batho and Bonamy Dobrée, *The Victorian and After*, volume four of *The Oxford History of English Literature*, which describes and analyzes the contributions of major and some minor nineteenth-century novelists. John R. Reed has a chapter on women in his study, *Victorian Conventions* (1974). The chapters on Victorian novels in David Daiches, *A Critical History of English Literature* (1968) and Walter Allen, *The English Novel, A Short Critical History* (1954) provide quick introductions to the novelists. John Chapman, in *The Victorian Debate: English Literature and Society 1832–1901* (1968), surveyed some of the main social and intellectual themes in Victorian society and how these themes influenced and were expressed in literature.

Together with Victorian literary conventions, the historian must examine the audience's environment and expectations.[81] R. K. Webb's *Modern England* (1970) is an excellent survey, especially for the first half of the nineteenth century. Harold Perkin's *The Origins of Modern British Society 1780–1880* (1969) and J. F. C. Harrison's *The Early Victorians 1832–1851* (1971) offer stimulating analyses of the relations between classes and— Perkin in particular—the conflicts experienced by the middle classes as they refined the "entrepreneurial ideal." G. Kitson Clark's discussion of religion and the gentry, in *The Making of Victorian England* (1962), is useful, as is the wealth of detail about living conditions, recreation, and other aspects of Victorian life included in Geoffrey Best's *Mid-Victorian Britain 1851–1875* (1971). G. M. Young's classic *Victorian England: Portrait of an Age* (1936) is an excellent brief account which gives a sense of what it was like to live in Victorian England. Historical studies of the later Victorians are not as rich. Peter Stansky's *England Since 1867: Continuity and Change* (1973) is insightful but too brief; R. K. Ensor's *England 1870–1914* (1936) is very detailed but in need of revision. More specialized histories are very useful in integrating the novel into the study of Victorian women in society: Houghton's study of Victorian anxieties in *The Victorian Frame of Mind, 1830–1870* (1957), especially his chapter on love and the Victorian ideal of womanhood; Michael Anderson's *Family Structure in Nineteenth-Century Lancashire* (1973), an excellent study in family and kin relations in the industrial north; Roy Lewis and Angus Maude's *The English Middle Classes* (1949), a compact introduction; J. A. Banks, *Prosperity and Parenthood* (1954), on the rising expectations of the Victorian upper middle classes about standards of living; and F. M. L. Thompson's thorough examination of the upper classes in *English Landed Society in the Nineteenth Century* (1963). In addition, the chapter on "The Victorian Family: Illusion and Reality" in O. R. McGregor, *Divorce in England* (1957), provides useful statistical data on marriage, separation, reasons for divorce, and divorce.

Lionel Stevenson has suggested that the Victorian novelist had to be entertaining, moralistic, and realistic to please his readers. In a society without television, radio, and films, novel reading supplied a principal form of entertainment. As even Mrs. Austin, a friend of John Stuart Mill, remarked:

> about Charlotte Yonge's novel; *The Heir of Redcliffe* I have not read. It sounded too good for me. I am not worthy of superhuman flights of virtue—in a novel. I want to see how people act and suffer who are as good-for-nothing as I am myself. Then I have the sinful pretension to be amused, whereas all our novelists want to reform us. . . .[82]

Historians, interested in the effects of literacy upon political and social behavior, have studied the working-class reading public.[83] People read more as their leisure time, money, and opportunities to travel increased—and they read popular novels. The reading public became divided into serious and light readers, and authors and publishers became increasingly responsive to mass preferences. Readers had access to novels through circulating libraries which could be found all over the country and, by mid-century, novels became the most requested item at these libraries. The publication of novels in installments as magazine serials, monthly serials, and, after 1848, in cheap railway editions which catered to the traveler, also affected their style, veracity and form. Installment publication also accentuated the need for excitement and suspense to encourage readers to buy forthcoming editions. Since the last chapters of most serials were being written as the first chapters were being read, authors knew how their readers were responding. The result, fortunately for the historian, was a literature which closely reflected its audience's tastes, aspirations and interests.[84] The need to entertain and instruct affected the novelists' portrayal of their society. The desire to cater to the public thirst for romance and adventure resulted in a preponderance of stories about the aristocracy, especially in the 1830s and 1840s when the high fashion or "silver-fork" novels about the affluent classes were in vogue. These stories, with their set plots and characters, tell us more about the audience's hopes and interests than about actual conditions or behavior. The future historians and social scientists who look at the tremendous commercial success of passionate "women's historical romances" in the 1970s, such as *Sweet Savage Love* and *Moonstruck Madness*, will not learn anything about how women dressed, spoke, or behaved.[85] But they will discover something about popular tastes, fantasies, and more, if they ask why women, at a time when they were entering the job market, divorcing their husbands, and even attending graduate school in unprecedented numbers, found such books appealing.

The novelists' efforts to improve their world could also distort their representation of people and events. Domestic realists such as Harriet Martineau and Charlotte Yonge, social reformers like Elizabeth Gaskell and Charlotte Elizabeth Tonna, and even such "great" novelists as Anthony Trollope and George Eliot were all concerned with elucidating problems of morality, conduct, and ethics. The attempt to reform morals and behavior meant that accuracy occasionally had to be sacrificed for didactic effect or moral purpose. For example, the prostitute in most Victorian novels had to die, perhaps like Mary Barton's Aunt Esther, a wasted, cough-wracked wraith slipping through dark, rainy streets until she expired in sorrow on the doorstep of her chaste niece's dwelling. She was not allowed to ply her trade for a few years and then marry a customer and live to old age in modest circumstances.[86] Young women who married for money or status instead of love were also made to repent their choice.[87] There were lessons to be learned from these novels.

Although we must recognize the distortions caused by the novelists' efforts to be entertaining and instructive, most authors tried to portray life convincingly so that their stories and lessons would be credible. As Margaret Oliphant maintained in her review of Bulwer Lytton in *Blackwood's Magazine*, "It is not the vocation of the novelist ... to startle us with exaggerated events ... but to order his world on the general principles of nature as the outer world is regulated ... in a word, indeed, to be true to nature...." In the same vein, George Eliot pronounced in her famous paragraph in *Adam Bede*:

> Certainly I could, if I held it the highest vocation of the novelist to represent things as they never have been and never will be. Then of course, I might refashion life and character entirely after my own liking....But it happens on the contrary, that my strongest effort is to avoid any such arbitrary picture, and to give a faithful account of men and things as they have mirrored themselves in my mind. The mirror is doubtless defective; the outlines will sometimes be disturbed, the reflection faint or confused; but I feel as much bound to tell you as precisely as I can what that reflection is, as if I were in the witness-box narrating my experience on oath.[88]

The use of the mirror image recurs in recent as well as nineteenth-century literary scholarship.[89] But though, as Leslie Stephen declared, the "whole interest of the novel may be in the representation of the truth," the vision in the mirror is inevitably curved, magnified, or even distorted by the author's perceptions, fears, anxieties, moral judgments, and limitations of talent.[90] The ability of authors to recreate reality is limited by the nature of art, the fact that their writing is influenced by personal perceptions, the publishing format of Victorian novels, and the demands of Victorian readers. As *The Pall Mall Gazette* pointed out, "In all works of fiction it is impossible to discern where the real and the ideal begin and end: everywhere they are blended." What the reader finds in the novel is a composite of reality filtered through the artist's perceptions and abilities, and our own reading. Although Thomas Hardy argued that "a work of fiction should be a precise transcript of life," we do not see a real picture in his novels, "but rather a heightening, an exaggeration of those features which afforded his particular insight ... at the end he will have reproduced what is not just a counterpart or replacement of the actual but a heightening of it."[91] As Lowenthal has suggested, novelists' selective reproduction of reality does not, however, make it impossible for the historian to use novels as a source; in fact it can be used to learn more about man's relation to his society:

> But whether it is the literary artist or the sociologist who constructs the image for us, that image will rest upon a human—and therefore biased—interpretation. But when we turn our attention to the problem of *how* a literary character dissents from a social order or how he seeks to justify it, then we have descriptive materials of prime importance. A study of the modes of rejection or acceptance of existing social orders found in literature enables us to fill in the blanks left by political and economic history.... They [attitudes] may look forward, or backward, to a different age but they tend to do so from within the confines of an existing reality. Thus, the "bias" of a writer is not the kind of drawback that it would appear at first sight. The writer is ... concerned ... with a *human* reality that involves attitudes and feelings which are never neutral.[92]

The Victorian novel, with its wealth of detail and many female characters, offers the historian a very special source for understanding the Victorian woman. Historians must subject these novels to the same critical reading as that with which they examine other sources by recognizing the constraints on the novel as historical evidence. Once considered, the effect of the writers' perceptions, the demands of their audiences, the personal and social factors which affected them, can afford the sensitive scholar the novel's insights into society. The novel does not provide us with a photograph of Victorian women, but it is, to paraphrase Richard Altick, "an eloquent artistic document" of women's journey, the autobiography of their soul and struggle.[93]

# NOTES

1. Perhaps I ought to say "refocus" since literary scholars, before the rise of the New Criticism often examined the environment of literary works. Some literary scholars, such as Colie, "Literature and History," and Altick, *The Art of Literary Research*, reacting to New Criticism, have urged students to be aware of the contributions of history to literary study.

2. W. F. Neff attempted, unsuccessfully she felt, to use fiction as the basis for a history of women in *Victorian Working Women*; Rubenius compared conventional expectations with Elizabeth Gaskell's portrayal of women in *The Woman Question in Mrs. Gaskell's Life and Work*; and Thomson explored the effect of feminist ideas on the characterization of women in *The Victorian Heroine: A Changing Ideal 1837–1873*. Although W. F. Neff was pessimistic, Rubenius downplayed the importance of the woman question, and Thomson's historical analysis has been questioned, all three are interesting in terms of methodology. See also Berger, *Real and Imagined Worlds*, pp. 32–39, 146–49; and Baym, *Women's Fiction*.

3. Between 1953 and 1958, fewer than five abstracts for dissertations on women and literature in the Victorian period were published in *Dissertation Abstracts*; between 1963 and 1967, fewer than ten; and between 1973 and 1977, over thirty. These numbers do not include dissertations on the work of female authors which examined themes, style, or the like with little or no reference to the effect of the authors' sex upon their novels. The publication of a new journal, *Women and Literature* (1975–ㅤ), a continuation of *The Mary Wollstonecraft Journal*, also reflects this increased interest; Vicinus, *A Widening Sphere*, p. xii.

4. Frankle, "The Genteel Family: High Victorian Conceptions of Domesticity and Good Behavior."

5. For examples, see Lawson, "Class Structure and the Female Character in Anthony Trollope's *The Way We Live Now*"; W. T. Williams, "Women's Roles as Delineated by Victorian Society"; Ewbank, "The Role of Women in Victorian Society"; and Sporn, "The Transgressed Woman." While the growth in women's studies and feminist approaches to literature may have encouraged dissertations examining women's position in society, earlier dissertations also discussed women's roles and compared the portrayal of female protagonists to women in Victorian society: for example, Meers, "Victorian Schoolteachers in Fiction"; Adams, "The Victorian Woman in Fact and Fiction 1870–1901"; Davies, "The Social Status of the Middle Class Victorian Woman"; Rorabacher, "Victorian Women in Life and Fiction"; and Zinn, "Love and Marriage in the Novels of English Women: 1740–1840." For additional titles, see the bibliography.

6. For example, see Portner's thematic study, "A Study of Marriage in the English Novel"; or the descriptive studies of Essex, "A Study of the Role of Woman in Thomas Hardy's Novels"; and Gandesbery, "Versions of the Mother in the Novels of Jane Austen and George Eliot."

7. Altick and Matthews, eds., have compiled a list of over two thousand doctoral dissertations in their *Guide to Doctoral Dissertations in Victorian Literature 1886–1958*. The *Guide* also provides a sense of trends in scholarly interests: for example, during that seventy-two year period, there was only one female author (George Eliot) among the eleven most frequently studied writers. For dissertations completed in the United States, *Dissertation Abstracts*, arranged by subject, is useful for locating these in literature and history. For history, see the American Historical Association, *List of Doctoral Dissertations in History; Retrospective Index to Theses in Great Britain and Ireland, 1716–1950*. ed. Roger Bilboul, which is arranged by topic; and the Institute of Historical Research's bulletin, *Historical Research for University Degrees in the United Kingdom, 1931/32–*.

8. R. A. Colby, *Fiction with a Purpose: Minor and Major Novelists*, p. 4; and Bell, *Representative Novelists of the Nineteenth Century*. These numbers are even more impressive when one realizes that for most of the nineteenth century, novels were "triple-deckers," three volumes per novel.

9. Altick, *Research*; and Stevenson, ed., *Victorian Fiction: A Guide to Research*. Watson also edited a supplement to the *CBEL* in 1959, in which he expanded the section on political and social background and included critical work published since 1941.

10. Leclaire, ed., *A General Analytical Bibliography of the Regional Novelists of the British Isles 1800–1900*; Sadleir, *XIX Fiction*; Brightfield, *Victorian England in Its Novels 1840–1870*; see also Ray, *Bibliographical Resources for the Study of Nineteenth Century Fiction*. Other bibliographies should be noted: Dick, ed., *A Student's Guide to British Literature*, and Altick and Wright, eds., *Selective Bibliography for the Study of English and American Literature*, are briefer surveys; Fidell and Flory, eds., *Fiction Catalog*, with supplements, lists over four thousand works published in English; Cotton and McGill, eds., *Fiction Guides General: British and American* includes references to bibliographies and critical studies; Sadleir, *Excursions in Victorian Bibliography* contains critical essays and a bibliography of first editions; Block, ed., *The English Novel 1740–1850*, briefly lists novels, is marred by omissions, and is rather difficult to use; Jefferson, ed., *Victorian Social Fiction* is an exhibition catalog which contains lists of novels written by workers and other Victorians.

11. This means that I omit the important theoretical work on literature, history and society done in French, and most of the interesting recent work on women and literature in the United States, some of which would provide fruitful comparisons with English women and their literature.

12. The MLA bibliographies (published under several names) date from 1919, as does *TYWES*. *ABELL* began in 1920. See also the bibliographies on Victorian literature edited by William D. Templeman, Austin Wright, and Robert C. Slack.

13. As quoted by Tillotson, *Novels of the Eighteen-Forties*, p. 150.

14. Showalter, *A Literature of Their Own*, noted that only about twenty percent of Victorian novelists were women. Anthony Trollope, *An Autobiography*, ed. Book, p. 186, as quoted in Stang, *The Theory of the Novel*; Trollope, *Four Lectures*, p. 108; L. James, "The Rational Amusement: 'Minor Fiction' and Victorian Studies"; and Berger, pp. 32–39.

15. For comments on the novel as the genre for women, see D. Stone, *Novelists in a Changing World*, and Wagner, *Five for Freedom*. For discussion of the female reading public, based on qualitative rather than quantitative evidence for the most part, see Tillotson; Dalziel, *Popular Fiction 100 Years Ago*; Cruse, *The Victorians and Their Reading*; and "Fashion and Fiction," *The Pall Mall Gazette*, 10 January 1888, p. 14. For these and other *PMG* quotations I would like to thank Tim Clifford. Additional contemporary articles on women and novels can be located by consulting *Poole's Index to Periodical Literature* (covering the period 1802–1906 and organized by subject, e.g. "novels," "women," and "fiction") and Houghton's *Wellesley Index to Victorian Periodicals, 1824–1900*, 2 vols., (organized by author and periodical). Both are invaluable resources.

16. *PMG*, 21 February 1887, p. 3; Greg, "False Morality of Lady Novelists," p. 86; Layard, p. 376; Howells, "In Praise of Pure Fiction: 'English Novels versue French,'" p. 7. See also Howells, *Heroines of Fiction*; L. Stephen, "The Duty of Authors"; Trollope, "Novel Reading"; and Stang, *Theory of the Novel*, chapters 1 and 2.

17. Pethick-Lawrence, *My Part in a Changing World*, pp. 66–67.
18. For examples, see Oliphant, "Sensational Novels"; Mansell, "Sensation Novels"; [Hannigan], "Sex in Fiction"; "The New Dangers of Sensational Fiction"; and "Our Female Sensation Novelists"; Surtees, *Beckford Inheritance*, p. 35.
19. *PMG*, 2 June 1887, p. 13. In the 1880s *PMG* carried extensive articles about the debate over realism versus moral concern in literature. See also Frierson, "The English Controversy over Realism in Fiction, 1885–1895."
20. As quoted by Dalziel, p. 51. For the concern about the specific effects of novel reading on girls' morals, see the discussion in Dalziel; Mayhew, p. 221; and the bibliography in Engelman, "The Ideal English Gentlewoman in the Nineteenth Century."
21. Watt in *The Rise of the Novel* discussed some of the doubts people felt about novels in the eighteenth century.
22. Articles in contemporary periodicals and women's magazines also discussed the effects of poor reading literature and recommended certain authors and subjects. For a guide to the latter see White, *Women's Magazine 1693–1968*.
23. As quoted in Thomson, p. 137. See also Stang, chapters 1 and 2.
24. For the brief synopsis of the social and religious backgrounds of a number of Victorian women authors, see the biographical appendix in Showalter, *Literature*.
25. For discussion of the economic, social, political, and legal restrictions which limited women's opportunities to participate actively in Victorian society see Strachey, "*The Cause*"; McGregor, *Divorce in England*; J. S. Mill, *The Subjection of Women*, and Harriet Taylor Mill, *The Enfranchisement of Women*, in *Essays in Sex Equality*, ed. Rossi; Milne, *Industrial and Social Position of Women in the Lower and Middle Ranks*; and Reiss, *Rights and Duties of English Women*. For the psychological and social constraints under which the Victorian woman lived, see Houghton, *Victorian Frame of Mind*; Cunnington, *Feminine Attitudes in the Nineteenth Century*; Klein, *The Feminine Character*; and contemporary writing on women by Coventry Patmore, John Ruskin, and the numerous conduct guides for women. For additional references, see Kanner, "The Women of England in a Century of Social Change, 1815–1914," and the essays in both *Suffer* and *Widening Sphere*.
26. Hale, "'A d____d mob of scribbling women,' Nineteenth-Century British Novelists"; Gorsky, "The Gentle Doubters: Images of Women in Englishwomen's Novels, 1840–1920"; Showalter, "Dinah Mulock Craik and the Tactics of Sentiment," and "Desperate Remedies: Sensation Novels of the 1860's"; K. Ellis, "Paradise Lost: The Limits of Domesticity in the Nineteenth Century Novel"; and McDaniel, "Charlotte Brontë and the Feminist Novel."
27. Branca, *Silent Sisterhood*, and "Image and Reality: The Myth of the Idle Victorian Woman." Houghton in his chapter on love in *The Victorian Frame of Mind* discussed the Victorian ideal of the woman as angel in the home as it appeared in the works of Coventry Patmore, Alfred Lord Tennyson, and John Ruskin, which has dominated much of the thinking about Victorian women. Banks, *Prosperity and Parenthood*, described the "paraphernalia" surrounding the upper-middle-class woman. In *Feminism and Family Planning among the Victorian Middle Classes*, Banks and Banks analyzed the shift from the "perfect wife" to the "perfect lady." See also Crow, *The Victorian Woman*; Vicinus, *Widening Sphere*, p. xii.
28. Holcombe, *Victorian Ladies at Work*; Davidoff, *The Best Circles*; Horn, *The Rise and Fall of the Victorian Servant*. McBride, *The Domestic Revolution*; Pinchbeck, *Women Workers in the Industrial Revolution 1750–1850*; M. Hewitt, *Wives and Mothers in Victorian Industry*; Rover, *Women's Suffrage and Party Politics 1866–1914*; Fulford, *Votes for Women*; and Rosen, *Rise Up Women!* See also Marshall, *The English Domestic Servant in History*; Stearns, "Working Class Women in Britain, 1890–1914"; Oren, "The Welfare of Women in Laboring Families"; and Roe's review article, "Modernisation and Sexism."
29. L. Stone, *The Family, Sex and Marriage in England 1500–1800*, p. 13; Fothergill, *Private Chronicles: A Study of English Diaries*, p. 33. Fothergill noted that by the early nineteenth century personal diaries were being published.
30. Showalter, *Literature*, pp. 16–25. She makes this point in reference to its effect on women

writers. I would argue that this training in repression and concealment also affected letter writing, memoirs, and conventional historical sources.

31. Vicinus, *Widening Sphere*, p. xii.

32. There are numerous studies of women and literature which concentrate on questions of interest to the literary scholar. These studies, which emphasize style, form, or other aspects of literary creation without reference to the author as a woman or to the historical background of the work, are of minimal value to the historian and have not been included in this essay.

33. Woolf, "Women and Fiction", p. 143. See also Showalter, *Literature*, pp. 53–71.

34. Hale; *PMG*, 3 November 1888, p. 3; see also the discussion in Showalter, *Literature*, pp. 47–52; and Moers, pp. 119–20.

35. V. Colby, *Yesterday's Women* and *The Singular Anomaly*.

36. Moers; see Wood, "The 'Scribbling Women' and Fanny Fern," p. 24.

37. Baker, *History of the English Novel*, 10: 194; George Eliot, "Silly Novels by Lady Novelists," pp. 442–61; Johnson, *The Women Novelists*; Colby, *Yesterday's Women*; Lewes, "The Lady Novelists"; Courtney, *The Feminine Note in Fiction*; Bald, *Women-Writers of the Nineteenth Century*; Lawrence, *The School of Femininity*.

38. Ozick, "Women and Creativity." See also Kaplan, *Feminine Consciousness in the Modern British Novel*; Heilbrun, *Towards a Recognition of Androgyny*; Denne and Rogers, "Women Novelists: A Distinct Group?" and the discussion in the first chapter of Showalter, *Literature*.

39. Woolf, "Women and Fiction," pp. 143–45.

40. D. Stone, "Victorian Feminism and the Nineteenth Century Novel"; Showalter, *Literature*, chapter 2, and "Women Writers and the Double Standard"; Ozick; and Ohlmann, "Emily Brontë in the Hands of Male Critics."

41. Spacks, *The Female Imagination*; Showalter, *Literature*.

42. There are several studies which examine how attitudes toward women result in misogynistic literature: Rogers, *The Troublesome Helpmate* traced misogynous stereotypes from the middle ages to the present; M. Ellmann in *Thinking About Women* has shown that such attitudes persist despite improvements in women's position in society.

43. In particular see R. West, "And They All Lived Unhappily Ever After," who questions why it is that even now women write about their humiliations by men and their insecurity; Sage, "The Case of the Active Victim"; Hardwick, *Seduction and Betrayal*; and Woolf, *A Room of One's Own* and *Three Guineas*. Several scholars have noted the differential treatment accorded women writers by critics: Showalter, "Women Writers and the Double Standard"; Ohlmann, "Emily Brontë in the Hands of Male Critics"; Harworth, "Romantic Female Writers and the Critics"; and Greer, "Flying Pigs and Double Standards."

44. Levenson, "The Artist and the Woman in George Eliot's Novels."

45. Hoffman, "A Delicate Balance."

46. Moers; Spacks; and Showalter, *Literature*. See also Elliott, "A Lady to the End."

47. Natov, "The Strong-Minded Heroine in Mid-Victorian Fiction."

48. Hardwick.

49. Basch, *Relative Creatures*.

50. For discussion of the "new feminist" literary criticism see Pratt, "The New Feminist Criticism"; Robinson, "DWelling in Decencies: Radical Criticism and the Feminist Perspective"; Margaret Anderson, "Feminism and the Literary Critic"; Blecki, Gelpi, Juhasz, and Burkon, eds., *Feminist Literary Criticism*; Donovan, ed. *Feminist Literary Criticism*; Kolodny, "Some Notes on Defining a 'Feminist Literary Criticism'"; Showalter, "Literary Criticism"; and Diamond and Edwards, eds., *The Authority of Experience*.

51. Pratt, "New Feminist Criticism"; Showalter, *Literature*. Other scholars have examined the way being a woman affected women's works: Beer's *Reader I Married Him* (an unsuccessful study); Wagner, *Five for Freedom*; and Mews, *Frail Vessels*. For additional "descriptive" studies, see Hinkley, *Ladies of Literature*; Weismann, "'Old Maids Have

Friends': The Unmarried Heroine of Trollope's Barsetshire Novels"; Skinner, "Mr. Trollope's Young Ladies"; and Delafield, *Ladies and Gentlemen in Victorian Fiction.*

52. Showalter, *Literature.*
53. Thomson, *Victorian Heroine*; Fox, "The Woman Question in Selected Victorian Fiction 1883–1900"; S. deS. Davis, "The Female Protagonist in Henry James' Fiction, 1870–1890"; Fernando, "The Radical Ideology of the 'New Woman'" and *"New Women" in the Late Victorian Novel*; Scanlon, "The New Woman in the Literature of 1883–1909"; A. R. Cunningham, "The 'New Woman Fiction' of the 1880's"; Harris, "The New Woman in the Literature of the 1890's"; and Schwalbe, "H. G. Wells and the Superfluous Woman."
54. Gissing, *Odd Women*; G. Allen, *The Woman Who Did*; Schreiner, *The Story of an African Farm.*
55. Lawrence, *The School of Femininity*, p. 11.
56. Laqueur, "Literature and the Historian"; Macaulay, "History and Literature." See also Collingwood, *The Idea of History*; Hutchinson, "The Role of Clio"; Carr, *What is History?*, p. 16, as quoted by L. Stone in *The Family*, pp. 11–12.
57. Fleming, "Historians and the Evidence of Literature"; Lehmann, "Writer as Canary"; Kelly, "Literature and the Historian"; Bloch, *The Historian's Craft*, p. 48; see also Berger.
58. For two excellent examples of using literature to elucidate tensions and attitudes, see J. E. C. Hill, "Clarissa Harlowe and Her Times," and D. B. Davis, *Homicide in American Fiction.* See also Banks, "The Way They Lived Then: Anthony Trollope and the 1870's," and House, *The Dickens World.*
59. Carr, pp. 26–27; Hoggart, "Literature and Society." See also D. Hewitt, *The Approach to Fiction.*
60. Kermode, "Novel, History and Type." See also Gottschalk, "The Historian and the Historical Document."
61. Trollope, *The Prime Minister*, 1: 44.
62. Ibid., 1: 139.
63. For an example of this, see LeJeune v. Budd (1834) in *Reports of Cases Decided in the High Court of Chancery*, ed. Simon.
64. Hardwick, pp. 13–14; Gissing, *Odd Women*, pp. 12, 14.
65. Peterson, "The Victorian Governess: Status Incongruence in Family and Society," pp. 3–19; and Hammerton, "Feminism and Female Emigration, 1861–1886," pp. 52–71.
66. Sporn, "Gissing's *Demos*: Late Victorian Values and the Displacement of Conjugal Love"; Haydock, "The Woman Question in the Novels of George Gissing"; and Fernando, *"New Women."*
67. Showalter, *Literature*, pp. 153–82.
68. Craig, "A Woman's Thoughts about Women," pp. 88–9. Several recent doctoral dissertations have examined the theme of development, though mostly from a literary perspective: Susan E. Siefert, "The Dilemma of the Talented Woman: A Study of Nineteenth Century Fiction"; Sawdrey, "Between Two Worlds: A Study of the Heroine in the Novels of Mrs. Elizabeth Gaskell"; Francone, "Women in Rebellion: A Study of the Conflict Between Self-Fulfillment and Self-Sacrifice in *Emma, Jane Eyre*, and *The Mill on the Floss*"; and McDaniel, "Fettered Wings Half-Loose: Female Development in the Victorian Novel." See also Cadogan and Craig, *You're a Brick, Angela! A New Look at Girls Fiction from 1839–1975.*
69. See E. Chapman, *Marriage Questions in Modern Fiction and Other Essays.*
70. Kelly, "Literature and the Historian" discussed the question of the transmission of cultural values through literature. He used character development in nineteenth-century children's books to discover what sorts of values and behaviors were highly regarded at the time and, by implication, behaviors which parents and authors found threatening. R. Williams in *Culture and Society* and *The Long Revolution* examined the relationship between social, economic, and political change and literary response. Hoggart, working at the Centre for Contemporary Cultural Studies at Birmingham University, has explored the relationship between culture, values, and society in modern England, "The Literary Imagination and the Study of Society"; "An Approach to the

Study of Literature and Society"; and *The Uses of Literacy*. Although Bradbury in *The Social Context of Modern British Literature* virtually ignored women, his survey of literature as an aspect of society from 1870 to the present is a very competent introduction.

71. Kelly, p. 14.

72. Ibid.

73. Heilbrun, *Androgyny*.

74. As quoted in Leavis, *Fiction*, p. 82.

75. Tillotson has suggested that lesser novelists, being imitative rather than innovative, revealed more about Victorian society because they filled their novels with detail and reflected popular notions. Lowenthal in his very useful study, *Literature, Popular Culture, and Society* contrasted "art" and mass or popular literature from "which we learn about the typical forms of behavior, attitudes, commonly held beliefs, prejudices and aspirations of large numbers of people" (p. vii). For additional discussions of the usefulness of popular novels, see R. Colby, Dalziel, and Frankle.

76. Although recent critical studies of the major novelists, such as those by Barbara Hardy, Ian Watt, David Daiches, Albert Guerard, F. D. Leavis, Lionel Trilling, Northrup Frye, U. C. Knoepflmacher, and Donald Stone concentrate on questions of particular interest to the literary scholar, they may be of some use for the historian using the "great" novels.

77. Lowenthal, *Literature*, p. vii; Lehmann, p. 19. See also Lowenthal, *Literature and the Image of Man*.

78. One of the bodies of criticism, along with sociology of literature and American Studies, which has dealt specifically with literature as a means for studying life and social relations in the past is Marxist literary criticism. Lukács, *The Theory of the Novel*, and Goldmann, *Towards a Sociology of the Novel*, have regarded the novel as the story of the problematic hero searching for real values in an unauthentic world. The hero is problematic because as an artist the writer is himself searching for authentic values yet must exist in a world controlled by the degrading market economy. Many of the nineteenth-century novels can be seen as fitting into Lukács' third category of novel, the *Bildungsroman*, characterized by the hero who gives up his search for authentic value and settles for a self-imposed limitation or compromise. For an introduction to sociological studies of literature, consult Watson, *The Study of Literature. A New Rationale of Literary History*, chapter 10; Lowenthal, "Literature and Sociology"; and Laurenson and Swingewood, *The Sociology of Literature*.

79. Lehmann, p. 19; Lowenthal, p. xiii.

80. R. Williams in *The Long Revolution* analyzed the social origins, education, and occupation of 350 writers born between 1470 and 1920. Altick attempted a more detailed survey in "The Sociology of Authorship: The Social Origins, Education, and Occupation of 1,100 British writers 1800–1935," though his conclusions about the relative homogeneity of the "author class" until the twentieth century are similar to Williams. Both discuss the ratio of male to female authors. Most minor and major novelists have been the subject of reputable biographies. For these and other references, consult the *CBEL*; the *New CBEL*; the annual bibliographies; Bell, *Representative Novelists*; Black, *Notable Women Authors of the Day*; and the *Dictionary of National Biography*. Two contemporary sources, Allibone, *A Critical Dictionary of English Literature* and Kirk, *A Supplement to Allibone's Critical Dictionary*, should be used with caution. Matthews has compiled a list of autobiographies, *British Autobiographies*, and diaries, *British Diaries: An Annotated Bibliography*. For diaries in manuscript, see Batts, *British Manuscript Diaries of the Nineteenth Century*. For archival material in the United States, consult Philip A. Hamer, ed., *A Guide to Archives and Manuscripts*; the *National Union Catalog of Manuscript Collections*; and the holdings of major university libraries and the New York Public Library. For Great Britain, consult *Catalogues of the Manuscript Collections* of the British Library, and the catalogues for the Bodleian Library at Oxford and the Cambridge University Library. The *CBEL* and the *New CBEL* often list manuscript sources, as well as collections of letters and reputable biographies.

81. Urban and local historians provide detailed information about the environment. They

enable the researcher to have a more distinct picture of the locale with which to compare the novelist's portrayal. See Dyos and Wolff, eds., *The Victorian City: Images and Realities*; Ashby, *The Changing English Village*; F. Hill, *Victorian Lincoln*; as well as studies based on photographs, such as Chandler, *Edwardian Manchester and East Lancashire from Old Photographs*; and on memoirs, such as that of Avery, *The Echoing Green*. The annual bibliography in the June issue of *Victorian Studies* and Altholz, *Victorian England 1837-1901* are the first bibliographies to consult when seeking additional references to historical background. The *Journal of British Studies*, *Victorian Studies*, and *The Victorian Periodicals Newsletter* regularly contain articles of interest to the Victorian scholar; *Journal of Interdisciplinary History*, *American Historical Review*, *Journal of Modern History*, *Past and Present*, *Journal of Social History*, and *Social History* should also be consulted.

82. As quoted in Cruse, p. 53.

83. Vicinus, *The Industrial Muse*, has described working-class literary culture, especially ballads and poetry. L. James, *Fiction for the Working Man*; Daiches, *An Enquiry into the Reading of the Lower Classes*; Webb, *The British Working Class Reader*; and Altick, *The English Common Reader* have described working-class reading habits and preferences and have analyzed the expansion of the reading public. Keating, *The Working Classes in Victorian Fiction*, shows how fictional portrayal and responses lagged behind social and political reforms. See also Dalziel and R. Williams, *Long Revolution*. Cruse, in her attempt to give an idea of what people read, successfully provides a sense of the range of Victorian reading material, as does Tomlinson in *The English Middle Class Novel*.

84. As Leavis has pointed out, the shift from patronage by a cultivated elite to a mass book market directly affected the novelist's craft. Sutherland in *Victorian Novelists and Publishers* describes the Victorian publishing industry and the demands and constraints it placed upon authors. Tillotson's excellent study on the novels of the 1840s contains information on publishing, the reading public, and themes of the novels in the 1840s. Dalziel is especially informative on popular novels and the Penny Press. Sadleir in *XIX Century* has written the best study to date on the railway editions. See also Keech, "Three-Deckers and Installment Novels"; Ewing, "The Three Volume Novel"; Tanzy, "Publishing the Victorian Novel"; Carwell, "Serialization and the Fiction of Mrs. Gaskell"; Polsgrove, "They Made it Pay." Contemporary reviewers in periodicals such as *Cornhill Magazine*, *Westminster Review*, and others discussed the reading public. For some late nineteenth-century examples see R. C., "What People Read"; Humphrey, "The Reading of the Working Class"; Gattie, "What English People Read"; and the references to the reading audience in the *CBEL*.

85. For information about the commercial success of these novels, read Ray Walters's column, "Paperback Talk," in *The New York Times Book Review*, especially 8 and 14 January 1978.

86. For example, compare the representation of the prostitute in novels by Trollope, Gaskell, George Moore, and others with contemporary studies by Henry Mayhew and William Acton, and with the results of recent research by Walkowitz, "'We Are Not Beasts of the Field': Prostitution and the Poor in Plymouth"; and "The Making of an Outcast Group: Prostitutes and Working Women in Nineteenth Century Plymouth and Southampton."

87. Trollope was criticizing young women who married men for whom they did not care when he portrayed Lady Laura's unhappy marriage in the Palliser series. See Sadleir, *Anthony Trollope*, p. 274.

88. Margaret Oliphant, "Bulwer," p. 472; George Eliot, *Adam Bede*, p. 171.

89. For examples of the use of mirror metaphors, see Praz, who regarded Dickens as a "curved mirror" and Anthony Trollope as the "supremely faithful mirror" in *The Hero in Eclipse in Victorian Fiction*; Hopkins's reference to Mary Barton as "the faithful mirror of the wretchedness of the industrial masses" in "Mary Barton: A Victorian Bestseller"; and Collins's opinion that in *Emma* "mirrors changing social attitudes," in "Jane Austen and the Victorian Novel."

90. Stephen, "The Past and Future of 'English Novels,'" *PMG*, 4 May 1887, p. 3. For

studies of realism and the novel, see Auerbach's classic study, *Mimesis*; R. Williams, "Realism and the Contemporary Novel," and Watt's chapters, "Realism and the Novel Form" and "Realism and the Later Tradition, A Note," in *The Rise of the Novel*. Becker's collection of excerpts and brief comments, *Documents of Modern Literary Realism*, provides a useful introduction to this difficult question. I. Williams, *The Realist Novel in England: A Study of Development* contains an analysis of the relationship between the desire to present accurate detail and romanticism. Levine's, "Realism Reconsidered," is a brief essay on the impossibility of portraying "real" life. All fiction, Levine maintained, even realistic fiction, is a creation. Scholes, ed., *Approaches to the Novel* is a useful introduction to conventions of the novel. Stevenson, "The Relativity of Truth in Victorian Fiction"; H. James, *The Art of the Novel*; J. F. Stephen, "The Relation of Novels to Life"; Levine, "Can You Forgive Him? Trollope's *Can You Forgive Her* and the Myth of Realism"; Rust, "The Art of Fiction in George Eliot's Reviews"; Eile, "The Novel as an Expression of the Writer's Vision of the World"; Arthur, "The Victorian Ideal of Realism"; and Dunbar, "The Faithful Recorder: Mrs. Humphry Ward."

91. *PMG*, 13 October 1887, p. 14; Hyde, "Hardy's View of Realism," pp. 54–59.
92. Lowenthal, *Literature*, p. xvi.
93. Altick, *Literary Research*, p. 12.

# BIBLIOGRAPHY

ADAMS, RUTH. "The Victorian Woman in Fact and Fiction 1870–1901." Ph.D. dissertation, (Radcliffe College) Harvard University, 1951.

ADKINS, LORNA F. B. "The English Novel in the Eighteen-Fifties." Ph.D. dissertation, University of Texas, Austin, 1975.

AITKEN, DAVID HARED. "The Victorian Idea of Realism: A Study of the Aims and Methods of the English Novel between 1860 and 1875." Ph.D. dissertation, Princeton University, 1962.

AGRESS, LYNNE. "The Feminine Irony: Treatments of Women by Women in Early Nineteenth-Century Literature." Ph.D. dissertation, University of Massachusetts, 1975.

ALLEN, GRANT. *The Woman Who Did*. London and Boston: 1895.

ALLEN, WALTER. *The English Novel: A Short Critical History*. New York: 1954.

ALLIBONE, S. AUSTIN. *A Critical Dictionary of English Literature, and British and American Authors....* 3 vols. Philadelphia: 1859–71.

ALTHOLZ, JOSEPH, ed. *Victorian England 1837–1970*. Cambridge: 1901.

ALTICK, RICHARD D. *The Art of Literary Research*. New York and Toronto: 1963.

———. *The English Common Reader*. Chicago: 1957.

———. "Nineteenth Century English Best Sellers: A Further List." *Papers of the Bibliographical Society* 22 (1969): 197–206.

———. "The Sociology of Authorship: The Social Origins, Education and Occupation of 1,100 British Writers 1800–1935." *New York Public Library Bulletin* 66, no. 6 (1962): 389–404.

———, and MATTHEWS, WILLIAM, eds. *Guide to Doctoral Dissertations in Victorian Literature 1886–1958*. Urbana, Ill.: 1960.

————, and WRIGHT, ANDREW, eds. *Selective Bibliography for the Study of English and American Literature*. 3d ed. 1967.

*American Historical Review*.

ANDERSON, MARGARET. "Feminism and the Literary Critic." *Atlantis* 1 (1975): 3–13.

ANDERSON, MICHAEL. *Family Structure in Nineteenth Century Lancashire*. Cambridge: 1971.

ANDERSON, RACHEL. *The Purple Heart Throbs: The Sub-Literature of Love*. London: 1974.

ASHBY, M. K. *The Changing English Village*. Kineton, England: 1974.

AUERBACH, ERICH. *Mimesis: The Representation of Reality in Western Literature*. Translated by W. R. Trask. Princeton, N.J.: 1953.

AUERBACH, NINA. *Communities of Women: An Idea in Fiction*. Cambridge, Mass. and London: 1977.

AVERY, GILLIAN. *The Echoing Green: Memoirs of Regency and Victorian Youth*. New York: 1974.

BAKER, ERNEST A. *A Guide to the Best Fiction, British and American*. . . . New York and London: 1932.

————. *A Guide to Historical Fiction*. New York: 1914. Reprint: 1969.

————. *History in Fiction: a Guide to the Best Historical Romances*. 2 vols. New York and London: 1907.

————. *History of the English Novel*. Vols. 7, 8, 10. London: 1924–39. Reprint. New York: 1964–67.

BALD, MARJORY A. *Women-Writers of the Nineteenth Century*. Cambridge: 1923. Reprint. New York: 1963.

BANKS, J. A. *Prosperity and Parenthood: A Study of Family Planning among the Victorian Middle Classes*. Liverpool and New York: 1954.

————. "The Way They Lived Then: Anthony Trollope and the 1870's." *Victorian Studies* 12, no. 2 (1968): 177–200.

————, and BANKS, OLIVE. *Feminism and Family Planning in Victorian England*. Liverpool and New York: 1964.

BASCH, FRANÇOISE. *Relative Creatures. Victorian Women in Society and the Novel*. Translated by Anthony Rudolf. New York: 1974.

BATESON, F. W., ed. *The Cambridge Bibliography of English Literature*. Vol. 3: *1800–1900*. Cambridge: 1941.

BATHO, E. C., and DOBRÉE, BONAMY. *The Victorians and After*. 3d ed. rev. *The Oxford History of English Literature*, vol. 4, edited by F. P. Wilson and Bonamy Dobrée. London: 1950.

BATTS, JOHN STUART. *British Manuscript Diaries of the Nineteenth Century*. Totowa, N.J.: 1976.

BAUGH, ALBERT C., ed. *A Literary History of England*. 2d ed. New York: 1967.

BAYM, NINA. *Woman's Fiction: A Guide to Novels by and about Women in America, 1820–1870*. Ithaca, New York: 1978.

BECKER, GEORGE, ed. *Documents of Modern Literary Realism*. Princeton: 1963.

BEER, PATRICIA. *Reader I Married Him*. London and New York: 1974.

BELL, MACKENZIE. *Representative Novelists of the Nineteenth Century*. New York: 1927.

BERGER, MORROE. *Real and Imagined Worlds: The Novel and Social Science*. Cambridge, Mass. and London: 1977.

BEST, GEOFFREY. *Mid-Victorian Britain 1851–1875*. London and New York: 1971.

BLACK, HELEN. G. *Notable Women Authors of the Day*. Glasgow: 1893. Reprint. Freeport, N.Y.: 1972.

BLECKI, CATHERINE; GELPI, BARBARA; JUHASZ, SUZANNE; and BURKON, SELMA. *Feminist Literary Criticism: A Symposium.* San Jose, Calif.: 1974.

BLOCH, MARC. *The Historian's Craft.* Translated by Peter Putnam. New York: 1953.

BLOCK, ANDREW, ed. *The English Novel 1740–1850.* New rev. ed. London: 1961.

BOLSTAD, ROBERT M. "The Passionate Self in George Eliot's *Adam Bede, The Mill on the Floss, and Daniel Deronda.*" Ph.D. dissertation, University of Washington, 1976.

BOOS, FLORENCE, ed. "Bibliography of Literature in English by and about Women 1600–1900." *Women and Literature* 4, no. 2 (1976): supplement.

BRADBURY, MALCOLM. *The Social Context of Modern English Literature.* New York: 1971.

BRANCA, PATRICIA. "Image and Reality: The Myth of the Idle Victorian Woman." In *Clio's Consciousness Raised,* edited by Mary Hartman and Lois Banner. New York: 1974.

———. *Silent Sisterhood: Middle-Class Women in the Victorian Home.* London: 1975.

BRIGHTFIELD, MYRON F. *Victorian England in Its Novels 1840–1870.* 4 vols. Los Angeles: 1968.

British Museum, Department of Manuscripts. *The Catalogues of the Manuscript Collections.* London: 1962.

C., R. "What People Read." *Academy* 52–54 (1897–98).

CADOGAN, MARY, and CRAIG, PATRICIA. *You're a Brick, Angela! A New Look at Girls' Fiction from 1839–1975.* London: 1976.

CALDER, JENNI. *Women and Marriage in Victorian Fiction.* London: 1976.

CARR, E. H. *What Is History?* New York: 1962.

CARRIER, ESTHER J. *Fiction in Public Libraries 1876–1900.* New York: 1965.

CARWELL, VIRGINIA A. "Serialization and the Fiction of Mrs. Gaskell." Ph.D. dissertation, Northwestern University, 1965.

CAZAMIAN, LOUIS. *The Social Novel in England 1830–1850: Dickens, Disraeli, Mrs. Gaskell, Kingsley.* Translated by Martin Fido (from original French ed., 1904). London and Boston: 1973.

CHANDLER, GEORGE. *Victorian and Edwardian Manchester and East Lancashire from Old Photographs.* London: 1974.

CHAPMAN, ELIZABETH. *Marriage Questions in Modern Fiction and Other Essays.* London and New York: 1897.

CHAPMAN, JOHN. *The Victorian Debate: English Literature and Society 1832–1901.* New York: 1968.

CHAPONE, MRS. HESTER. *Letters on the Improvement of the Mind, Addressed to a Young Lady.* 2 vols. London and Boston: 1822.

CLARK, GEORGE KITSON. *The Making of Victorian England.* Cambridge, Mass.: 1962.

COLBY, ROBERT A. *Fiction with a Purpose: Minor and Major Nineteenth-Century Novels.* Bloomington, Ind.: 1967.

COLBY, VINETA. *The Singular Anomaly: Women Novelists of the Nineteenth Century.* New York: 1970.

———. *Yesterday's Women: Domestic Realism in the English Novel.* Princeton, N.J.: 1974.

COLIE, ROSALIE. "Literature and History." *Relations of Literary Study: Essays on Interdisciplinary Contributions,* edited by James Thorpe. New York: 1967.

*College English.*

COLLINGWOOD, R. G. *The Idea of History.* Oxford: 1946.

COLLINS, BARBARA BASIL. "Jane Austen and the Victorian Novel." *Nineteenth Century Fiction* 4 (1949): 175–86.

CORNILLON, SUSAN KOPPELMAN, ed. *Images of Women in Fiction*. Rev. ed. Bowling Green, Ohio: 1972.

COTTON, GERALD, and McGILL, HILDA, eds. *Fiction Guides General: British and American*. London and Hamden, Conn.: 1967.

COUCH, RUTH L. "Women and Thomas Hardy: A Study of Sex-Linked Qualities in the Characters." Ph.D. dissertation, Oklahoma State University, 1975.

COURTNEY, W. L. *The Feminine Note in Fiction*. London: 1904.

CROW, DUNCAN. *The Victorian Woman*. New York: 1971.

CRUSE, AMY. *The Victorians and Their Reading*. Boston: 1935. (Published in Great Britain as *The Victorians and Their Books*. London: 1935.)

CUNNINGHAM, A. R. "The 'New Woman Fiction' of the 1880's." *Victorian Studies* 17 (1973): 1,177–86.

CUNNINGTON, C. W. *Feminine Attitudes in the Nineteenth Century*. London: 1938. Reprint. New York: 1973.

DAICHES, DAVID. *A Critical History of English Literature*. 2d ed. 2 vols. New York and London: 1968.

———. *Some Late Victorian Attitudes*. New York: 1969.

DALZIEL, MARGARET. *Popular Fiction 100 Years Ago*. Philadelphia: 1958.

DAVIDOFF, LEONORE. *The Best Circles: Women and Society in Victorian England*. London and Totowa, N.J.: 1973.

DAVIES, BERNICE F. "The Social Status of the Middle Class Victorian Woman as It Is Interpreted in Representative Mid-Nineteenth Century Novels and Periodicals." Ph.D. dissertation, Stanford University, 1943.

DAVIS, DAVID B. *Homicide in American Fiction*. Ithaca, N.Y.: 1957.

DAVIS, SARA DE S. "The Female Protagonist in Henry James' Fiction, 1870–1890." Ph.D. dissertation, Tulane University, 1974.

DEGLER, CARL N. "What Ought to Be and What Was: Women's Sexuality in the Nineteenth Century." *American Historical Review* 79, no. 5 (1974): 1467–89.

DELAFIELD, ELIZABETH MONICA. *Ladies and Gentlemen in Victorian Fiction*. London: 1937.

DENNE, CONSTANCE AYERS, and ROGERS, KATHARINE M. "Women Novelists: A Distinct Group?" *Women's Studies* 3, no. 1 (1975): 5–28.

DETTER, HOWARD M. "The Female Sexual Outlaw in the Victorian Novel: A Study in the Conventions of Fiction." Ph.D. dissertation, Indiana University, 1971.

DIAMOND, ARLYN, and EDWARDS, LEE R., eds. *The Authority of Experience: Essays in Feminist Criticism*. Amherst, Mass.: 1977.

DICK, ALIKI L., ed. *A Student's Guide to British Literature: A Selective Bibliography of 1,128 Titles and Reference Sources from the Anglo-Saxon Period to the Present*. Littleton, Colo.: 1972.

*Dictionary of National Biography*. Edited by Sir Leslie Stephen and Sir Sidney Lee. 22 vols. London: 1921–22.

*Dissertation Abstracts International*. Ann Arbor, Mich.: 1969–. (1939–51, *Microfilm Abstracts*; 1952–69, *Dissertation Abstracts*.)

DONOVAN, JOSEPHINE, ed. *Feminist Literary Criticism: Explorations in Theory*. Lexington, Ky.: 1975.

DUNBAR, GEORGIA D. S. "The Faithful Recorder: Mrs. Humphry Ward and the Foundation of Her Novels." Ph.D. dissertation, Columbia University, 1953.

DUNBAR, JANET. *The Early Victorian Woman: Some Aspects of Her Life, 1837–1857.* London: 1953.

DYLLA, SANDRA M. "Jane Austen and George Eliot: The Influence of Their Social Worlds on Their Women Characters." Ph.D. dissertation, University of Wisconsin, 1974.

DYOS, H. J., and WOLFF, MICHAEL, eds. *The Victorian City: Images and Realities.* 2 vols. London and Boston: 1973.

EILE, STANISLAW. "The Novel as an Expression of the Writer's World." *New Literary History* 9, no. 1 (1977): 113–28.

ELIASBERG, ANN P. "The Victorian Anti-Heroine: Her Role in Selected Novels of the 1860's and 1870's." Ph.D. dissertation, City University of New York, 1975.

ELIOT, GEORGE. "Silly Novels by Lady Novelists." *Westminster Review* 66 (1856): 442–61.

ELLIOTT, JEANNE. "A Lady to the End: The Case of Isabel Vane." *Victorian Studies* 19, no. 3 (1976): 329–44.

ELLIS, KATHERINE. "Paradise Lost: The Limits of Domesticity in the Nineteenth Century Novel." *Feminist Studies* 2, no. 2/3 (1975): 55–63.

ELLIS, MRS. SARAH STICKNEY. *Daughters of England: Their Society, Character, and Responsibilities.* London: 1836. New York: 1842.

———. *The Wives of England.* London: 1843.

———. *The Women of England.* London: 1839.

ELLMANN, MARY. *Thinking About Women.* New York: 1968.

ELLMANN, RICHARD, and FEIDELSON, CHARLES, JR., eds. *The Modern Tradition: Backgrounds of Modern Literature.* New York: 1965. London and New York: 1968.

ENGELMAN, HERTA. "The Ideal English Gentlewoman in the Nineteenth Century: Her Education, Conduct, and Sphere." Ph.D. dissertation, Northwestern University, 1956.

English Association. *This Year's Work in English Studies.* London, 1919/20–.

*English Literary History.*

ENSOR, R. K. *England 1870–1914.* Oxford: 1936.

ESSEX, RUTH. "A Study of the Role of Woman in Thomas Hardy's Novels." Ph.D. dissertation, New York University, 1976.

EWBANK, DAVID R. "The Role of Woman in Victorian Society: A Controversy Explored in Six Utopias 1871–1895." Ph.D. dissertation, University of Illinois, 1968.

EWING, DOUGLAS C. "The Three Volume Novel." *Papers of the Bibliographical Society of America* 61 (1966): 201–07.

FAIREY, WENDY W. "The Relationship of Heroine, Confessor, and Community in the Novels of George Eliot." Ph.D. dissertation, Columbia University, 1975.

FERNANDO, LLOYD. *"New Women" in the Late Victorian Novel.* University Park, Penn. and London: 1977.

———. "The Radical Ideology of the 'New Woman.' " *Southern Review* 2 (1967): 206–22.

FIDELL, ESTELLE A., and FLORY, ESTHER V., eds. *Fiction Catalog.* New York: 1961.

FLEISHMAN, AVROM. *The English Historical Novel.* Baltimore: 1971.

FLEMING, JOHN V. "Historians and the Evidence of Literature." *Journal of Interdisciplinary History* 4, no. 1 (1973): 95–105.

FORDYCE, JAMES. *Sermons to Young Women.* 4th ed. 2 vols. London: 1767.

FOTHERGILL, ROBERT A. *Private Chronicles: A Study of English Diaries.* London and New York: 1974.

Fox, Marcia R. "The Woman Question in Selected Victorian Fiction 1883–1900." Ph.D. dissertation, City University of New York, 1975.

Francone, Carol B. "Women in Rebellion: A Study of the Conflict between Self-Fulfillment and Self-Sacrifice in *Emma, Jane Eyre,* and *The Mill on the Floss.*" Ph.D. dissertation, Case Western Reserve University, 1975.

Frankle, Barbara S. "The Genteel Family: High Victorian Conceptions of Domesticity and Good Behavior." Ph.D. dissertation, University of Wisconsin, 1969.

Frerichs, Sarah C. "Elizabeth Missing Sewell: A Minor Novelist's Search for the *Via Media* in the Education of Women in the Victorian Era." Ph.D. dissertation, Brown University, 1974.

Frierson, W. C. "The English Controversy over Realism in Fiction, 1885–1895." *PMLA* 43 (1928): 533–50.

Fryer, Peter. *Mrs. Grundy: Essays in English Prudery.* London and New York: 1964.

Fulford, Roger. *Votes for Women.* London: 1957.

Gandesbery, Jean J. "Versions of the Mother in the Novels of Jane Austen and George Eliot." Ph.D. dissertation, University of California, Davis, 1976.

Gattie, Walter Montagu. "What English People Read." *Fortnightly Review* 52 (1889): 307–21.

George, H. B. *Historical Evidence.* Oxford: 1909.

Gissing, George. *The Odd Women.* London: 1891. London and New York: 1971.

Goldmann, Lucien. *Towards a Sociology of the Novel.* Translated by Alan Sheridan. Paris: 1964. London: 1975.

Goode, John. "Woman and the Literary Text." In *The Rights and Wrongs of Women,* edited by Juliet Mitchell and Ann Oakley. London: 1976.

Gorsky, Susan. "The Gentle Doubters: Images of Women in English women's Novels, 1840–1920." In *Images of Women in Fiction: Feminist Perspectives,* edited by Susan Cornillon. Bowling Green, Ohio: 1972.

———. "Old Maids and New Women: Alternatives to Marriage in English Women's Novels: 1847–1915." *Journal of Popular Culture* 7 (1973): 68–85.

Gottschalk, Louis. "The Historian and the Historical Document." In *The Use of Personal Documents in History, Anthropology and Sociology,* edited by Louis Gottschalk, Clyde Kluckhorn, and Robert Angell. New York: 1945.

Greenwald, Fay T. "The Young Girls in the Novels of W. D. Howells and Henry James." Ph.D. dissertation, New York University, 1974.

Greer, Germaine. "Flying Pigs and Double Standards." *Times Literary Supplement,* 26 July 1974, pp. 784–85.

Greg, W. R. "False Morality of Lady Novelists." [anonymously] *National Review* 8 (1859): 144–67. Reprint. In *Literary and Social Judgments.* London and Boston: 1873.

Gregory, Dr. John. *A Father's Legacy to His Daughters.* London: 1774.

Gross, George C. "Mary Cowden Clarke, 'The Girlhood of Shakespeare's Heroines,' and the Sex Education of Victorian Women." *Victorian Studies* 16, no. 1 (1972): 37–58.

Hale, Dorothy. "'A d____d mob of scribbling women.' Nineteenth Century British Novelists." Exhibition of the University Research Library, U.C.L.A. May-June 1977.

Hammerton, A. James. "Feminism and Female Emigration, 1861–1886." In *A Widening Sphere,* edited by Martha Vicinus, q.v.

[Hannigan, D. F.] "Sex in Fiction." *Westminster Review* 143 (1895): 616–25.

HARDWICK, ELIZABETH. *Seduction and Betrayal: Women and Literature*. New York and London: 1974.

HARRIS, KATHERINE S. "The New Woman in the Literature of the 1890's: Four Critical Approaches." Ph.D. dissertation, Columbia University, 1963.

HARRISON, J. F. C. *The Early Victorians 1832–1851*. London and New York: 1971.

HARTLEY, SUSAN. "The Later Novels of George Meredith: Women's Struggle for Emancipation." Ph.D. dissertation, Florida State University, 1973.

HARVEY, SIR PAUL. *The Oxford Companion to English Literature*. 4th ed., revised by Dorothy Eagle. Oxford: 1967.

HARWORTH, H. E. "Romantic Female Writers and the Critics." *Texas Studies in Literature and Language* 16, no. 4 (1975): 725–36.

HAYDOCK, JAMES J. "The Woman Question in the Novels of George Gissing." Ph.D. dissertation, University of North Carolina, 1965.

HEILBRUN, CAROLYN. *Towards a Recognition of Androgyny*. New York: 1973.

HENKIN, LEO, J. "Problems and Digressions in the Victorian Novel 1860–1900." Serialized in the *Bulletin of Bibliography* 18 (1944) to 20 (1950).

HEWITT, DOUGLAS. *The Approach to Fiction: Good and Bad Readings of Novels*. London: 1972.

HEWITT, MARGARET. *Wives and Mothers in Victorian Industry*. London: 1958.

HILL, FRANCES. *Victorian Lincoln*. Cambridge: 1975.

HILL, JOHN EDWARD CHRISTOPHER. "Clarissa Harlowe and Her Times." In *Puritanism and Revolution*. London: 1958.

HINKLEY, LAURA. *Ladies of Literature*. New York: 1946.

HOFFELD, LAURA. "The Servant Heroine in Eighteenth and Nineteenth Century British Fiction: The Social Reality and Its Image in the Novel." Ph.D. dissertation, New York University, 1975.

HOFFMAN, LEONORE N. "A Delicate Balance: The Resolutions to Conflict of Women in the Fiction of Four Women of the Victorian Period," Ph.D. dissertation, Indiana University, 1975.

HOGGART, RICHARD. "An Approach to the Study of Literature and Society." In *Contemporary Cultural Studies*, Occasional Paper no. 6. Birmingham, England: 1969.

———. "The Literary Imagination and the Study of Society." In *Speaking to Each Other*, vol. 2. London: 1970.

———. "Literature and Society." In *A Guide to the Social Sciences*, edited by Andrew McKenzie. London: 1966.

———. *The Uses of Literacy*. London: 1957. New York: 1970.

HOLCOMBE, LEE. *Victorian Ladies at Work: Middle-Class Working Women in England and Wales, 1850–1914*. Newton Abbot, England, and Hamden, Conn.: 1973.

HOPKINS, ANNETTE. "Mary Barton: A Victorian Bestseller." *Nineteenth Century Fiction* 3 (1948): 1–18.

HORN, PAMELA. *The Rise and Fall of the Victorian Servant*. Dublin and New York: 1975.

HOUGHTON, WALTER E. *The Victorian Frame of Mind*. New Haven and London: 1957.

———, ed. *The Wellesley Index to Victorian Periodicals, 1824–1900....* 2 vols. Toronto: 1966–1972.

HOUSE, HUMPHREY. *The Dickens World*. London and New York: 1942.

HOWELLS, W. D. *Heroines of Fiction*. New York and London: 1901.

———. "In Praise of Pure Fiction: 'English Novels versus French.'" *Pall Mall Gazette*, 10 June 1887.

HUMPHREY, GEORGE. "The Reading of the Working Class." *Nineteenth Century* 33 (1893): 690–701.

HUTCHINSON, JOANNE T. "The Role of Clio in Victorian Literature: Changing Ideas of Historiography as Reflected in Nineteenth-Century Historical Literature." Ph.D. dissertation, Temple University, 1974.

HYDE, WILLIAM J. "Hardy's View of Realism: A Key to the Rustic Character." *Victorian Studies* 2, no. 1, (1958): 45–59.

Institute of Historical Research. *Historical Research for University Degrees in the United Kingdom.* London: 1931/32–.

JACK, IAN. *English Literature, 1815–1832.* Oxford: 1963.

JAMES, HENRY. *The Art of the Novel: Critical Prefaces.* Edited by R. P. Blackmur. New York and London: 1934.

JAMES, LOUIS. *Fiction for the Working Man, 1830–1850. A Study of the Literature produced for the Working Class in Early Victorian Urban England.* London and New York: 1963.

———. "The Rational Amusement: 'Minor' Fiction and Victorian Studies." *Victorian Studies* 14, no. 2 (1970): 193–99.

JAMESON, ANNA. *Memoirs and Essays Illustrative of Art, Literature and Social Morals.* New York and London: 1846.

JARMUTH, SYLVIA. "Dickens' Use of Women in His Novels." Ph.D. dissertation, New York University, 1966.

JEFFERSON, MICHAEL, ed. *Victorian Social Fiction.* New Haven, Conn.: 1965. London: 1975.

JOHNSON, R. BRIMLEY. *The Women Novelists.* London: 1919. Reprint. New York: 1967.

JOSEPHS, LOIS S. "A Historical and Critical Study of Diana, Heroine of *Diana of the Crossways* by George Meredith." Ph.D. dissertation, University of Pittsburgh, 1966.

*Journal of British Studies.*

*Journal of Interdisciplinary History.*

*Journal of Modern History.*

*Journal of Social History.*

KANNER, BARBARA S. "The Women of England in a Century of Social Change, 1815–1914." In *Suffer and Be Still,* edited by Martha Vicinus. Bloomington, Ind. and London: 1973.

———. "The Women of England in a Century of Social Change: Part II." In *A Widening Sphere,* edited by Martha Vicinus. Bloomington, Ind.: 1977.

———, and KOVAČEVIĆ, IVANKA. "Blue Book into Novel: The Forgotten Industrial Fiction of Charlotte Elizabeth Tonna." *Nineteenth Century Fiction* 25, no. 2, (1970): 152–73.

KAPLAN, SYDNEY JANET. *Feminine Consciousness in the Modern British Novel.* Urbana, Ill.: 1975.

KATZ, SEYMOUR. "Culture and Literature in American Studies." *American Quarterly* 20, no. 2, pt. 2 (1968): 318–29.

KEATING, PETER. *The Working Classes in Victorian Fiction.* London: 1971.

KEECH, JAMES M., JR. "Three-Deckers and Installment Novels: The Effect of Publishing Format upon the Nineteenth Century Novel." Ph.D. dissertation, Louisiana State University, 1966.

KELLY, R. GORDON. "Literature and the Historian." *American Quarterly* 26, no. 2 (1974): 141–59.

KENNEDY, JOHN D. "Trollope's Widows: Beyond the Stereotypes of Maiden and Wife." Ph.D. dissertation, University of Florida, 1975.

KERMODE, FRANK. "Novel, History and Type." *Novel* 1, no. 3 (1968): 231–58.

KIELY, ROBERT. *The Romantic Novel in England.* Cambridge, Mass.: 1972.

KIRK, JOHN FOSTER. *A Supplement to Allibone's Critical Dictionary....* 2 vols., Philadelphia: 1891. Reprint. Detroit: 1965.

KLEIN, VIOLA. *The Feminine Character: History of an Ideology.* New York: 1949. London: 1971.

KOLODNY, ANNETTE. "Some Notes on Defining a 'Feminist Literary Tradition.'" *Critical Inquiry* 9, no. 1 (1975): 75–92.

KOVAČEVIĆ, IVANKA. *Fact into Fiction.* Leicester, England, and Belgrade, Yugoslavia: 1975.

KROEBER, KARL. "Fictional Theory and Social History: The Need for a Synthetic Criticism." *Victorian Studies* 19 (1975): 99–106.

KUNITZ, STANLEY J., and HAYCRAFT, HOWARD, eds. *British Authors of the Nineteenth Century.* New York: 1936.

"The Lady Novelists of Great Britain." *Gentleman's Magazine,* n.s. 40, pt. 2 (1853): 18–55

LAQUER, WALTER. "Literature and the Historian." *Journal of Contemporary History* 2, no. 2 (1967): 5–14.

LAURENSON, DIANA, and SWINGEWOOD, ALAN. *The Sociology of Literature.* New York and London: 1972.

LAWRENCE, MARGARET. *The School of Feminity: A Book for and about Women as They Are Interpreted through Feminine Writers of Yesterday and Today.* New York: 1936. Reprint. Folcroft, Penn.: 1976.

LAWSON, MARY S. "Class Structure and the Female Character in Anthony Trollope's *The Way We Live Now.*" Ph.D. dissertation, Bowling Green University, 1975.

LAYARD, FLORENCE. "What Women Write and Read." *National and English Review* 10 (1887–88): 376–81.

LEAVIS, Q. D. *Fiction and the Reading Public.* London: 1965. Folcraft, Pa.: 1974.

LECLAIRE, LUCIEN, ed. *A General Analytical Bibliography of the Regional Novelists of the British Isles, 1800–1950.* Trans. 2d ed. Paris: 1954.

LEHMANN, A. J. "Writer as Canary." *Journal of Contemporary History* 2, no. 2 (1967): 15–24.

LEVENSON, SHIRLEY F. "The Artist and the Woman in George Eliot's Novels." Ph.D. dissertation, Brandeis University, 1975.

LEVINE, GEORGE. "Can You Forgive Him? Trollope's *Can You Forgive Her* and the Myth of Realism." *Victorian Studies* 18, no. 1 (1974): 5–30.

———. "Realism Reconsidered." In *The Theory of the Novel: New Essays,* edited by John Halperin. New York and London: 1974.

LEWES, G. H. "The Lady Novelists." *Westminster Review* 58 (1852): 129–41.

LEWIS, ROY, and MAUDE, ANGUS. *The English Middle Classes.* London: 1949. Reprint. Bath: 1973.

*Literature and History.*

LOCKHEAD, MARION, "Century of Matriarchs." *Blackwoods Magazine* 305 (1969): 527–37.

LONGERBEAM, LARRY. "Seduction as Symbolic Action: A Study of the Seduction Motif in Six Victorian Writers." Ph.D. dissertation, George Peabody College for Teachers, 1975.

LOWENTHAL, LEO. *Literature, Popular Culture, and Society.* Englewood Cliffs, N. J.: 1961.

———. "Literature and Sociology." In *Relations of Literary Study*, edited by James Thorpe, q.v.

LUKÁCS, GEORGE. *The Theory of the Novel.* Translated by Anna Bostock. London and Cambridge, Mass.: 1971.

[M-M]. "Novels of the Day: Their Writers and Readers." *Fraser's Magazine* 57 (1860): 205–18.

MACANDREW, ELIZABETH, and GORSKY, SUSAN. "Why Do They Faint and Die?— The Birth of the Delicate Heroine." *Journal of Popular Culture* 8 (1974): 735–45.

MCBRIDE, THERESA. *The Domestic Revolution: The Modernization of Household Service in England and France 1820–1920.* New York and London: 1976.

MCDANIEL, JUDITH. "Charlotte Brontë and the Feminist Novel." *University of Michigan Papers on Women's Studies* 2, no. 3 (1976): 90.

———. "Fettered Wings Half Loose: Female Development in the Victorian Novel." Ph.D. dissertation, Tufts University, 1973.

MCGREGOR, O. R. *Divorce in England: A Centenary Study.* London: 1957.

MACAULAY, THOMAS BABINGTON. "History and Literature." In *The Varieties of History*, edited by Fritz Stern. Cleveland, Ohio: 1956.

MAISON, MARGARET. "Adulteresses in Agony." *Listener*, 19 January 1961, pp. 133–34.

MADDEN, LIONEL, and DIXON, DIANA, comps. *The Nineteenth Century Periodical Press in Britain: A Bibliography of Modern Studies. 1901–1971. Victorian Periodicals Newsletter* 8, no. 3 (1975): supplement.

MANSELL, HENRY. "Sensation Novels." *Quarterly Review* 108 (1863): 481–514.

MARDER, HERBERT. *Feminism and Art: A Study of Virginia Woolf.* Chicago: 1968.

MARSHALL, DOROTHY. *The English Domestic Servant in History.* London: 1949.

MARSHALL, WILLIAM H. *The World of the Victorian Novel.* South Brunswick, N. J., and New York: 1967.

MARTINEAU, HARRIET. *How to Observe Morals and Manners.* New York: 1838.

———. *Home Duties: A Book for Girls.* London: 1869.

MATTHEWS, WILLIAM. *British Autobiographies: An Annotated Bibliography of British Autobiographies Published or Written Before 1951.* Berkeley, Calif.: 1955. Reprint. Hamden, Conn.: 1968.

———. *British Diaries: An Annotated Bibliography of British Diaries Written between 1442 and 1942.* Berkeley, Calif.: 1950.

MAYHEW, HENRY. *London Labour and the London Poor.* 1851; Reprint (2 vols. in 4). New York: 1969.

MEERS, GENEVA M. "Victorian Schoolteachers in Fiction." Ph.D. dissertation, Northwestern University, 1953.

MELANI, LILLIAN. "Hidden Motives: A Study of Power and Women in British Periodical Fiction, 1864." Ph.D. dissertation, Indiana University, 1973.

MEWS, HAZEL. *Frail Vessels.* London: 1969.

MILES, ROSALIND. *The Fiction of Sex: Themes and Functions of Sex Differences in the Modern Novel.* London: 1974.

MILNE, J. D. *Industrial and Social Position of Women in the Lower Ranks.* London: 1867.

MITCHELL, SALLY. "Lost Women: Implications of the Fallen in Works by Forgotten Women Writers of the 1840's." *University of Michigan Papers in Women's Studies* (1974): 110–24.

338

Modern Humanities Research Association. *Annual Bibliography of English Language and Literature*. London: 1920–.

Modern Language Association. *MLA International Bibliography of Books and Articles on the Modern Languages and Literature*. New York: 1963–. (Title varies: 1921–55, *American Bibliography*; 1956–62, *Annual Bibliography*.)

MOERS, ELLEN. *Literary Women*. Garden City, N.Y.: 1976.

MOORE, KATHERINE. *Victorian Wives*. London and New York: 1974.

———. *Cordial Relations: The Maiden Aunt in Fact and Fiction*. London: 1967.

MOSCINSKI, JOSEPH. "The Victorian Woman." *Victorian Newsletter* 28 (1964): 26–27.

MOWAT, C. L. *Great Britain Since 1914*. London and Ithaca, N. Y.: 1971.

MURPHY, MARY J. "Dickens' 'Other Women'; The Mature Women in His Novels." Ph.D. dissertation, University of Louisville, 1975.

*National Union Catalog of Manuscript Collections, 1959–1961*.

NEFF, EMERY E. *The Poetry of History: The Contribution of Literature and Literary Scholarship to the Writing of History....* New York: 1947.

NEFF, WANDA F. *Victorian Working Women*. New York: 1929. Reprint. London: 1966. New York: 1967.

"The New Dangers of Sensational Fiction." *The Critic* 13 (1888): 281–82.

*Nineteenth Century Fiction*.

*Nineteenth Century Reader's Guide to Periodical Literature, 1890–1899....* 2 vols. New York: 1944.

*Novel*.

NUNNALLY, JOSEPH C. "The Victorian Femme Fatale: Mirror of the Decadent Temperament." Ph.D. dissertation, Texas Tech University, 1968.

NATOV, RONI L. "The Strong-Minded Heroine in Mid-Victorian Fiction." Ph.D. dissertation, New York University, 1975.

OHLMANN, CAROL. "Emily Brontë in the Hands of Male Critics." *College English* 32, no. 8 (1971): 906–13.

OLIPHANT, MARGARET. "Sensational Novels." *Blackwood's Magazine* 16 (1862): 564–84.

OREN, LAURA. "The Welfare of Women in Laboring Families: England, 1860–1950." *Feminist Studies* 1, no. 3/4 (1973): 107–25.

"Our Female Sensation Novelists." In *The Christian Remembrancer*. Reprinted in *Living Age* 78 (1863): 352–69.

*Oxford History of English Literature*. Edited by F. P. Wilson and Bonamy Dobrée. Oxford: 1945–. Vol. 10: Ian Jack, *English Literature*, p. 963.

OZICK, CYNTHIA. "Women and Creativity." In *Woman in Sexist Society*, edited by Vivian Gornick and Barbara K. Moran. New York: 1971.

PALMEGIANA, E. M. *Women and British Periodicals 1832–1867: A Bibliography*. New York and London: 1976.

*Past and Present*.

PERKIN, HAROLD. *The Origins of Modern British Society 1780–1880*. Toronto and London: 1969.

PETERSON, M. JEANNE. "The Victorian Governess: Status Incongruence in Family and Society." In *Suffer and Be Still*, edited by Martha Vicinus, q.v.

PETHICK-LAWRENCE, EMMELINE. *My Part in a Changing World*. London: 1938. Reprint. Westport, Conn.: 1976.

PINCHBECK, IVY. *Women Workers in the Industrial Revolution 1750–1850*. London: 1930. Reprint. London: 1969.

POLHEMUS, ROBERT. *The Changing World of Anthony Trollope*. Berkeley and Los Angeles: 1968.

POLSGROVE, CAROL. "They Made It Pay: British Short-Fiction Writing 1820–1840." *Studies in Short-Fiction* 11 (1974): 417–21.

*Poole's Index to Periodical Literature*. Compiled by William F. Poole. 5 vols. Rev. ed. Boston: 1882–1908. Reprint. New York: 1938.

PORTNER, RUTH LEE. "A Study of Marriage in the English Novel." Ph.D. dissertation, City University of New York, 1977.

PRATT, ANNIS. "The New Feminist Criticism." *College English* 32, no. 8 (1971): 872–78.

PRAZ, MARIO. *The Hero in Eclipse in Victorian Fiction*. Translated by Angus Davidson. London and New York: 1956.

*Publications of the Modern Language Association.*

RANCE, NICHOLAS. *The Historical Novel and Popular Politics in Nineteenth Century England*. London and New York: 1975.

RAY, GORDON N. *Bibliographical Resources for the Study of Nineteenth Century Fiction*. Los Angeles: 1964.

REED, JOHN R. *Victorian Conventions*. Athens, Ohio: 1975.

REISS, ERNA. *Rights and Duties of English Women: A Study in Law and Public Opinion*. New York and Manchester, England: 1934.

*Retrospective Index to Theses of Great Britain and Ireland, 1716–1950*. Edited by Roger Bilboul. Santa Barbara, Calif.: 1975.

RINEHART, NANA M. "Anthony Trollope's Treatment of Women, Marriage, and Sexual Morality Seen in the Context of Contemporary Debate." Ph.D. dissertation, University of Maryland, 1975.

ROBINSON, LILLIAN. "Dwelling in Decencies: Radical Criticism and the Feminist Perspective." *College English* 32, no. 8 (1971): 879–89.

ROE, JILL. "Modernisation and Sexism: Recent Writings on Victorian Women." *Victorian Studies* 20, no. 2 (1977): 179–92.

ROGERS, HENRY. "The Gryson Letters." In *The Young Ladies' Guide*. American Tract Society: 1872.

ROGERS, KATHARINE M. *The Troublesome Helpmate: A History of Misogyny in Literature*. Seattle, Wash.: 1966.

RORABACHER, LOUISE. "Victorian Women in Life and Fiction." Ph.D. dissertation, University of Illinois, 1942.

ROSA, M. W. *The Silver-Fork School: Novels of Fashion Preceding Vanity Fair*. New York: 1936.

ROSEN, ANDREW. *Rise Up Women! The Militant Campaign of the Women's Social and Political Union 1903–1914*. London and Boston: 1974.

ROSENBERG, ROSALIND. "In Search of Woman's Nature, 1850–1920." *Feminist Studies* 3, no. 1/2 (1975): 141–45.

ROSSI, ALICE, ed. *Essays on Sex Equality*. Chicago: 1970.

ROTH, MARY BETH. "*Tiresias Their Muse:* Studies in Sexual Stereotypes in the English Novel." Ph.D. dissertation, Syracuse University, 1973.

ROVER, CONSTANCE. *Women's Suffrage and Party Politics in Britain 1866–1914*. London: 1967.

RUBENIUS, AINA. *The Woman Question in Mrs. Gaskell's Life and Works*. Cambridge, Mass.: 1950.

RUST, JAMES D. "The Art of Fiction in George Eliot's Reviews." *Review of English Studies* 7 (1956): 164–72.

SABISTON, ELIZABETH J. "The Provincial Heroine in Prose Fiction: A Study in Isolation and Creativity." Ph.D. dissertation, Cornell University, 1969.

SADLEIR, MICHAEL. *Anthony Trollope: A Commentary.* Boston and New York: 1927.

———. *Bulwer and His Wife, a Panorama, 1803–1836.* London: 1933.

———. *Excursions in Victorian Bibliography.* London: 1922. Reprint. Folkestone: 1974

———. *XIX Century Fiction: A Bibliographical Record based on His Own Collection.* 2 vols. Berkeley, Calif., Cambridge and London: 1951.

SAGE, LORNA. "The Case of the Active Victim." *Times Literary Supplement,* 26 July 1977, pp. 803–1804.

SALMON, EDWARD. "What Girls Read." *Nineteenth Century* 20 (1886): 515–29.

SANDERSON, MRS. WARREN. *Female Improvement.* London: 1836.

SAWDREY, BARBARA. "Between Two Worlds: A Study of the Heroine in the Novels of Elizabeth Gaskell." Ph.D. dissertation, University of Illinois, Urbana, 1975.

SCANLÒN, LEONE. "Essays on the Effect of Feminism and Socialism upon the Literature of 1880–1914." Ph.D. dissertation, Brandeis University, 1973.

———. "The New Woman in the Literature of 1883–1909." *University of Michigan Papers in Women's Studies.* 2 vols, no. 2 (1976): 133–58.

SCHOLES, ROBERT, ed. *Approaches to the Novel.* Rev. ed. San Francisco: 1966.

SCHREINER, OLIVE. *The Story of an African Farm.* London: 1883.

SCHUPF, HARRIET WARM. "Single Women and Social Reform in Mid-Nineteenth Century England: The Case of Mary Carpenter." *Victorian Studies* 17, no. 3 (1974): 301–17.

SCHWALBE, DORIS J. "H. G. Wells and the Superfluous Woman." Ph.D. dissertation, University of Colorado, 1962.

SHOWALTER, ELAINE. "Desperate Remedies: Sensation Novels of the 1860's." *Victorian Newsletter* 49 (1976): 1–5.

———. "Dinah Muloch Craik and the Tactics of Sentiment: A Case Study in Victorian Female Authorship." *Feminist Studies* 2, no. 2/3 (1975): 5–23.

———. *A Literature of Their Own: Women Novelists from the Brontës to Doris Lessing.* Princeton: 1977.

———. "Literary Criticism." *Signs. Journal of Women in Culture and Society* 1, no. 2 (1975): 435–60.

———."Women Writers and the Double Standard." In *Woman in Sexist Society,* edited by Vivian Gornick and Barbara K. Moran. New York: 1971.

———, and L'ESPERANCE, JEAN. "Notes from London." *Women's Studies* 1, no. 2 (1973): 223–33.

SIEFERT, SUSAN E. "The Dilemma of the Talented Woman: A Study of Nineteenth Century Fiction." Ph.D. dissertation, Marquette University, 1975.

SIMMONS, JAMES C. *The Novelist as Historian. Essays on the Victorian Historical Novel.* Studies in English Literature, vol. 88. The Hague: 1973.

SIMON, NICHOLAS, ed. *Reports of Cases Decided in the High Court of Chancery....* vol. 6. New York: 1851.

SINFELT, FREDERICK. "The Unconventional Realism of George Moore: His Unique Concepts of Men and Women." Ph.D. dissertation, Pennsylvania State University, 1967.

SKINNER, E. L. "Mr. Trollope's Young Ladies." *Nineteenth Century Fiction* 4, no. 3 (1949): 197–208.

SLACK, ROBERT C., ed. *Bibliographies in Victorian Literature for the Ten Years 1955–1964.* Urbana, Ill.: 1967.
SMITH, SYDNEY. "Female Education." *Edinburgh Review* 15 (1810): 299–315.
*Social History*
SPACKS, PATRICIA. *The Female Imagination.* New York: 1975.
SPORN, PAUL. "Gissing's *Demos*: Late Victorian Values and the Displacement of Conjugal Love." *Studies in the Novel* 1, no. 3 (1969): 334–46.
———. "The Transgressed Woman: A Critical Description of the Heroine in the Works of George Gissing, Thomas Hardy, and George Moore." Ph.D. dissertation, State University of New York at Buffalo, 1967.
STANG, RICHARD. *The Theory of the Novel in England 1850–1870.* New York and London: 1959.
STANSKY, PETER. *England Since 1867: Continuity and Change.* New York: 1973.
STEARNS, PETER. "Working Class Women in Britain, 1890–1914." In *Suffer and Be Still*, edited by Martha Vicinus, q.v.
STEIN, SONDRA G. "Woman and Her Master: The Feminine Ideal as Social Myth in the Novels of Charles Dickens, William Thackeray and Charlotte Brontë." Ph.D. dissertation, University of Washington, 1976.
STEPHEN, SIR JAMES FITZJAMES. "The Relation of Novels to Life." *Cambridge Essays.* . . . 1855–58.
STEPHEN, LESLIE. "The Duty of Authors." *National Review* 25 (1894): 319–39.
———. "The Past and Future of 'English Novels.'" *Pall Mall Gazette*, 4 May 1887.
STEVENSON, LIONEL. "The Rationale of Victorian Fiction." *Nineteenth Century Fiction* 27, no. 4 (1973): 391–404.
———. "The Relativity of Truth in Victorian Fiction." In *Victorian Essays: A Symposium*, edited by Warren Anderson and Thomas D. Clareson. Kent, Ohio: 1967.
———, ed. *Victorian Fiction: A Guide to Research.* Cambridge, Mass., and London: 1964.
STOEHR, TAYLOR. "Realism and Versimilitude." *Texas Studies in Literature and Language* 11 (1969): 1,269–88.
STONE, DONALD. "Victorian Feminism and the Nineteenth Century Novel." *Women's Studies* 1 (1972): 65–91.
———. *Novelists in a Changing World: Meredith, James, and the Transformation of English Fiction in the 1880's.* Cambridge, Mass.: 1972.
STONE, LAWRENCE. "Literacy and Education in England, 1640–1900." *Past and Present* 42 (1969): 69–139.
———. *The Family, Sex, and Marriage in England 1500–1800.* New York and London: 1977.
STRACHEY, MRS. RACHEL. *"The Cause"*: *A Short History of the Women's Movement in Great Britain.* London: 1928.
SUKENICK, LYNN. "Sense and Sensibility in Women's Fiction: Studies in the Novels of George Eliot, Virginia Woolf, Anaïs Nin, and Doris Lessing." Ph.D. dissertation, City University of New York, 1974.
SURTEES, VIRGINIA. *The Beckford Inheritance: The Lady Lincoln Scandal.* London: 1977.
SUTHERLAND, JOHN. *Victorian Novelists and Publishers.* Chicago and London: 1976.
SYKES, RICHARD. "American Studies and the Concept of Culture: A Theory and Method." *American Quarterly* 15, no. 2, pt. 2 (1963): 253–70.

TANZY, CONRAD. "Publishing the Victorian Novel: A Study of the Economic Relationships of Novelists and Publishers in England, 1830–1880." Ph.D. dissertation, 1961–62.

TAWNEY, R. H. *Social History and Literature.* London: 1950.

TEICHGRAIBER, STEPHEN E. "The Treatment of Marriage in the Early Novels of Henry James." Ph.D. dissertation, Rice University, 1967.

TEMPLEMAN, WILLIAM D., ed. *Bibliographies of Studies in Victorian Literature for the Thirteen Years 1932–1944.* Urbana, Ill.: 1945.

THOMPSON, F. M. L. *English Landed Society in the Nineteenth Century.* London: 1963.

THOMSON, PATRICIA. *The Victorian Heroine: A Changing Ideal, 1837–73.* London and New York: 1956.

THORPE, JAMES, ed. *Relations of Literary Study.* New York: 1967.

TILLOTSON, KATHLEEN. *Novels of the Eighteen-Forties.* Oxford: 1954.

TINDALL, WILLIAM YORK. *Forces in Modern British Literature, 1885–1946.* New York: 1947. Reprint: 1956.

TOMLINSON, T. B. *The English Middle Class Novel.* London: 1976.

TOTH, EMILY. "The Independent Woman and Free Love." *Massachusetts Review* 16, no. 4 (1975): 64–76.

TROLLOPE, ANTHONY. *Four Lectures.* Edited by Morris L. Parrish. London: 1938.

———. "Novel Reading." *Nineteenth Century* 5 (1879): 24–43.

TRUDGILL, ERIC. *Madonnas and Magdalens.* London: 1976.

TYE, J. R. ed. *Periodicals of the Nineties.* Oxford: 1974.

U.S. NATIONAL HISTORICAL PUBLICATIONS COMMISSION. *A Guide to Archives and Manuscripts in the United States.* Edited by Philip M. Hamer. New Haven, Conn.: 1961.

UTTER, R. P., and NEEDHAM, G. B. *Pamela's Daughters.* London: 1937.

VICINUS, MARTHA. *The Industrial Muse: A Study of Nineteenth-Century Working-Class Literature.* London: 1974.

———, ed. *Suffer and Be Still.* Bloomington, Ind., and London: 1972.

———, ed. *A Widening Sphere: Changing Roles of Victorian Women.* Bloomington, Ind., and London: 1977.

*Victorian Newsletter.*

*Victorian Periodicals Newsletter.*

*Victorian Studies.*

WAGNER, GEOFFREY. *Five for Freedom: A Study of Feminism in Fiction.* London: 1972.

WALKOWITZ, JUDITH. "The Making of an Outcast Group: Prostitutes and Working Women in Nineteenth Century Plymouth and Southampton." In *A Widening Sphere*, edited by Martha Vicinus, q.v.

———, and WALKOWITZ, DANIEL. "'We Are Not Beasts of the Field': Prostitution and the Poor in Plymouth and Southampton under the Contagious Diseases Acts." *Feminist Studies* 1, no. 3/4 (1973): 73–107.

WATSON, GEORGE, ed. *The New Cambridge Bibliography of English Literature.* Vol. 3: *1800–1900.* Cambridge: 1969.

———. *The Study of Literature: A New Rationale of Literary History.* New York: 1960.

———. *Supplement to the CBEL: A.D. 600–1900.* Cambridge: 1957.

WATT, IAN. *The Rise of the Novel.* Berkeley, Calif., and London: 1957.

WEBB, R. K. *The British Working Class Reader 1790–1848.* Kelley: 1955.

———. *Modern England.* New York and Toronto: 1970.

———. "The Victorian Reading Public." *The Pelican Guide to English Literature*, edited by Boris Ford. Vol. 6. London: 1969.

WEISER, IRWIN H. "Alternative to the Myth of the Family: A Study of Parent-Child Relationships in Selected Nineteenth-Century English Novels." Ph.D. dissertation, Indiana University, 1976.

WEISMANN, JUDITH. "'Old Maids Have Friends': The Unmarried Heroine of Trollope's Barsetshire Novels." *Women and Literature* 5, no. 1 (1977): 15–25.

WEST, KATHERINE. *Chapter of Governesses: A Study of the Governess in English Fiction 1800–1949.* London: 1949.

WEST, REBECCA. "And They All Lived Unhappily Ever After." *Times Literary Supplement,* 26 July 1974, p. 779.

"What American Girls Read." *Pall Mall Gazette,* 7 October 1889.

WHITE, CYNTHIA. *Women's Magazines 1693–1968.* London: 1970.

WILCOX, JAMES M. "East End Novelists: Working Class in English Fiction, 1800–1900." Ph.D. dissertation, Wayne State University, 1968.

WILDEBLOOD, JOAN, and BRINSON, PETER. *The Polite World: A Guide to English Manners and Deportment from the Thirteenth to the Nineteenth Century.* Oxford: 1965.

WILLIAMS, A. M. *Early Female Novelists.* Glasgow: 1904.

WILLIAMS, IAN. *The Realist Novel in England: A Study of Development.* Pittsburgh, Pa.: 1975.

WILLIAMS, RAYMOND. *Culture and Society* 1780–1950. London and New York: 1958.

———. *The Long Revolution.* New York and London: 1961.

———. "Realism and the Contemporary Novel." *Partisan Review* 26 (1955): 200–13. Reprinted in *The Long Revolution.*

WILLIAMS, WILLIE T. "Women's Roles as Delineated by Victorian Society: A Study of Heroines in the Major Novels of Mrs. Elizabeth Gaskell." Ph.D. dissertation, Florida State University, 1975.

*Women and Literature.*

*Women's Studies.*

WOOD, ANN D. "The 'Scribbling Women' and Fanny Fern: Why Women Wrote." *American Quarterly* 23 (1971): 3–24.

WOOLF, VIRGINIA. *A Room of One's Own.* London: 1929. Reprint. Harmondsworth, England, and New York: 1945. New York: 1957, 1963, 1965. London: 1959.

———. *Three Guineas.* London: 1938. Reprint. New York: 1963. London: 1968.

———. "Women and Fiction." *Collected Essays II.* New York: 1967.

WRIGHT, AUSTIN, ed. *Bibliographies of Studies in Victorian Literature for the Ten Years 1945–1954.* Urbana, Ill.: 1956.

YEAZEL, RUTH. "Fictional Heroines and Feminist Critics." *Novel* 8 (1974): 29–38.

YOUNG, G. M. *Victorian England: Portrait of an Age.* London and New York: 1936. Reprint: 1953.

*The Young Ladies' Guide.* American Tract Society: 1872.

*The Young Lady's Book of Advice and Instruction.* Glascow: 1869.

ZINN, ZEA. "Love and Marriage in the Novels of English Women: 1740–1840." Ph.D. dissertation, University of Wisconsin, 1935.

# Women

## in Twentieth-Century England

### NEAL A. FERGUSON

The "total" history of English women since 1900 has yet to be written from an approach that traces the interactions among economic, social, political, and cultural currents.[1] Although there has been an ever-increasing output of popular and scholarly writings from various orientations that describe women's individual and collective experiences, little historical analysis exists for the period after 1914.[2] Scarce also are studies that inquire about women's changing status within a framework that recognizes an enduring conflict between the traditional English prescription of the female role as dependent, and the traditional English claim to upholding a society of equals. The bibliographical discussion that follows is an attempt to encourage more inquiry into this attitudinal paradox, and into the changes in women's status during the first half of the twentieth century. Limitations of space prevent a full application of the advocated "total" approach, but this essay suggests a constructive start by exploring three categories of consideration after a brief introduction: family and society, education, and employment.

On the assumption that socialization and role differentiation in the private sphere of the family are related directly to attitudes, participation, and status of family members in the public sphere of society, it is clear that the subjects selected for discussion here are interrelated. The connection between domestic origins and social position, gained largely through education and employment, of course applies equally to women and men. Therefore, the deliberate concentration on women in this paper is not intended to endorse the concept of distinctions between woman's world and man's world. Rather, the thrust is in precisely the opposite direction. Using the sources that follow, one might write a history that speculates to what degree English women, by mid-century, had obliterated traditional distinctions between the realms of Hermes and Hestia.[3]

Conventional social history has detailed how, increasingly, as the twentieth century progressed, women were expected to have two vocations: family and career, Hestia and Hermes. The stresses that were involved in attempting to cope concurrently with both vocations produced sharp conflicts in society, so that "managing two roles" was for a long time an *idée fixe* in historical questioning about twentieth-century English women.[4] Until recently, feminist writers concerned themselves mainly with women's efforts to gain equal entry with men into Hermes' world, and invested little attention in studying that of Hestia. At the turn of the century, the "woman question" from the feminists' point of view was a matter of the perception that Hermes and Hestia had served long enough as an operative social myth in Western culture.[5] But equality between the sexes was sought still in what was conventionally regarded as Hermes' realm. Access to careers, equality before the law, and equal educational opportunities were pleaded as women's rights. Juliet Mitchell, in "Women and Equality" (1976) describes the link between John Stuart Mill's concept (1869) of equality of opportunity and that of the later feminists. Representing the polemical writings of late nineteenth- and early twentieth-century feminists, Emily Davies and Dorothea Beale advanced arguments for equal education of women (1869–1910). Olive Schreiner made claims for women in employment in *Women and Labour* (1911). Annie and Marie Chapman called for changes in the law in *Status of Women* (1909). More equitable attitudes toward sexual behavior were also among feminist demands, with Christabel Pankhurst campaigning: "Votes for women and chastity for men."[6]

It is clear that access to careers was by 1900 a driving goal of women who, in growing numbers, had to support themselves. Yet, gaining the franchise has been described by historians as the largest single goal in the minds of most feminists. A negative opinion about placing so much emphasis on suffrage is Wilma Meikle's *Towards a Sane Feminism* (1917): "The vote is one of the least important of feminists' demands and needs." But this is generally considered to have been a minority viewpoint in the era of World War I and just after.[7] Ray Strachey's *The Cause* (1928) and her edited volume, *Our Freedom* (1935), are more typical of statements of women's belief that the vote had yielded a new status in public life, law, employment, sexual expression, and social life.

In 1945 sociologist Viola Klein enunciated the growing realization that political and legal reform would not remove from social gospel the notion that women were inferior to men by nature. In *Feminine Character*, Klein examined the work of eight well-known early twentieth-century psychologists, anthropologists, and sociologists for their theories of female nature and feminine character, and revealed the bias in the "scientific" assertion that sex characteristics (especially sex role stereotypes) were innate rather than learned, and that women's characters were designed by nature to be complementary to the male. Sharing Klein's perspective (and expanding on the number and kinds of questions), sociologist Ann Oakley in *Sex, Gender and Society* (1974) uses recent scholarship to sort out biological from environmental determinants in women's roles. She is historically oriented, and her excellent bibliography explores the full range of the issues.

Traditional role expectations and inferior status of women in English marriage and family patterns have been seen as impediments to women's free choice of domestic and social activity irrespective of culture or class.[8] August Bebel's *Woman in the Past* (n.d.) served turn-of-the-century socialist feminists as a point of departure for this argument. For example, Ethel Snowden, in *Feminist Movement* (1913), presents the argument that women's achievement of equality is dependent upon the overthrow of capitalism.[9] More recently, Simone de Beauvoir, in *Second Sex* (1949), follows this conjecture, but extends the range of feminist questions, moving well beyond political and economic structures as determinants behind making woman "the Other." And by the 1970s, feminists of various ideological persuasions seem ready to agree that full equality is hampered as much by intransigently maintained sexual divisions in society as by capitalistic social class designation. They claim that both sex and class biases operate against women in all modern societies regardless of sociopolitical structure.[10] Juliet Mitchell, in *Woman's Estate* (1971), exemplifies this modern feminist viewpoint, and in *Psychoanalysis and Feminism* (1974) she asserts the necessity of understanding Freudian and neo-Freudian psychology in order to appreciate the power of male-dominance ideology. By contrast, Ann Oakley argues that sociological aspects such as sex role stereotyping are more important: as long as woman's major role is housewife, male dominance will remain unchallenged. Oakley lays out both her theoretical and empirical testimony in *Sociology* (1974) and in *Woman's Work* (1976). Mitchell and Oakley's differences are explored in the introduction to their own anthology, *Rights and Wrongs of Women* (1976).

Ruth Adam's *A Woman's Place* (1975) is the only single volume that surveys the status of women over the entire twentieth century. While it has the advantage of being comprehensive and clearly written, it lacks sustained analysis and unifying theoretical perspective. Sheila Rowbotham in *Women, Resistance and Revolution* (1972), *Hidden from History* (1973), and *Woman's Consciousness, Man's World* (1973), makes important contributions from the vantage point of working-class and socialist perspectives, showing the relationship between the living and working conditions of women and the socioeconomic structure of capitalism. She theorizes the development of "woman's consciousness" growing out of social changes since the seventeenth century.

Paul Thompson, *The Edwardians* (1975), provides a fascinating reconstruction of Edwardian society by using present-day social science survey techniques—notably oral history. His book includes chapters ranging from conditions of childhood to problems of old age. He also presents case studies of individual women from different classes and regional backgrounds. In *The Deluge* (1965), Arthur Marwick analyzes women's changing roles during World War I, but fails to emphasize that the changes were temporary in some respects. Jane Lewis in "Beyond Suffrage" (1975) presents a valuable discussion of the difficulties of maintaining feminist organizations and goals in the 1920s. Noreen Branson discusses women in *Britain in the Nineteen Twenties* (1976), covering politics, employment and sexual behavior. Her chapter on education ignores women's special problems. The 1930s and 1940s have scarcely been touched, except fr Marwick's recent *Home Front* (1977), and Longmate's *How We Lived* (1972), both studies about British society during World War II, the latter containing important data on women's experiences and daily activities.[11]

FAMILY AND SOCIETY

Historically, in England a woman's social status and roles have derived from her relationships within the family. Before marriage her status derived from her father, and afterwards she assumed that of her husband. Familial and social expectations of her performance of domestic and occupational roles vared somewhat according to her class, regional locaton, and ethnic background. This equation between women's roles and status and her family background has undergone changes during the present century along with demographic change, urbanization, expanded industrialism, modernization, and wars. But family experience remains a crucial variable in the history of women.

Although accounts and analyses of particular aspects of family structure, communal relationships, and kinship ties are now appearing on a regular basis, they are largely the work of sociologists, only some of whom are historically minded. Historians have still to devise an approach to family studies that is capable of reconstructing and interpreting with flexibility the diverse historical experiences of the wide variety of English family types. Certainly, for the early twentieth century, a suitable model would take geographical variants into account, would be capable of explaining relationships between socioeconomic circumstances and family structures (thus accounting for continuity and change), and would put to rest the notion that there is a single prototype of "the English family."[12] Working in this direction are the practitioners of oral history whose research is reported in *Oral History*, journal of the Oral History Society. Particularly important issues of this journal are that of fall 1975, which is devoted to family history and contains Thea Vigne's article "Parents and Children: Distance and Dependence," and that of autumn 1977, devoted to women's history and containing Joanna Bornat's "Women's History and Oral History: An Outline Bibliography"; both are recommended as introductions to new approaches. The publications of the History Workshop Group, under the leadership of Raphael Samuel, also illustrate new directions in methodology and historical questioning about the family and women's roles.

A line of inquiry that has been fruitful lately is the questioning of changes in the relationship between the family as a basic social unit and alterations in social structure, economic conditions, and social attitudes.[13] A number of authors have taken a catastrophic view of family history. Modernization and industrialization of society marks a point of decline, they say. As the family passes on its functions to agencies of the state, a forecast of imminent decline is described as plausible.[14]

Scholarly approaches to the study of the family are indebted to the pioneering work of anthropologists such as Bronislaw Malinowski and Alfred Reginald Radcliffe-Brown.[15] Their suppositions and attitudes were later influential in sociological studies of English families per se. In particular, structural-functionalist sociologists not only borrowed some of their assumptions but also their conventional middle-class sentiments about the sanctity and universality of the nuclear family.[16] From the historian's point of view, two of their assumptions were extremely important. First, that industrialization is the decisive event in the development of the family; second, that the nuclear or conjugal family is the form of the family most compatible with the needs of modern industrial society. Methodologically, they were ahistorical and sometimes antihistorical. They were concerned with describing and analyzing what existed at that time, without expanding their contexts and variables to traditional cultural patterns and values or to social developments. Fortunately, a number of British sociologists such as Anderson, Oakley, Willmott, and Young, despite the dominance of structural-functionalist orientations, have continued to assert history's importance.[17]

The work of Peter Willmott and Michael Young is an example of scholarship that integrates sociology and history. In *Symmetrical Family* (1973) they posit a four-stage model to explain what has happened to the family since about 1750. Stage 1 refers to the preindustrial family. Stage 2 designates the disrupted, transitional, industrializing family. Stage 3 in the development of the family began about 1900 and is still with us. Stage 4 families exist only as a set of tendencies, and are of less concern to historians since they deal more with the future than with the past or present. Young and Willmott propose that not all segments of English society have undergone change at the same rate. Stage 1 and 2 families continue to exist, although the proportion of them is small in comparison to that of Stage 3 families. The Stage 3 family, the family of the twentieth century, is described by characteristics of home centeredness (privatization), by deemphasis of kinship ties, and by the increasing equality of husband-wife sex roles (the companionate marriage). The authors refer to the family which exhibits these attributes as the "symmetrical family." The strength of their approach is vitiated, however, by its failure to link changes in family to changes in the wider social matrix.[18]

Edward Shorter is more aware of the interdisciplinary demands of family studies, and writes from the vantage point of sociological history. In *The Making of the Modern Family* (1975) he argues that the essential historical change in the family has been "the first sexual revolution" which occurred around 1800 and led to the privatized, domestically oriented, child-centered, twentieth-century nuclear family. Another change has occurred, says Shorter, in the post-World War II era by a "second sexual revolution"—one that places individual fulfillment above family solidarity. No doubt Shorter's assumptions not less than his methodology and conclusions will be challenged, and already, existing critiques of his work deserve scrutiny.[19]

The various approaches to the family have generated a series of problems which the historian of the family has to sort out. One of the most vexing has to do with the importance of kinship ties in modern industrial society. Two well-known English kinship studies are Willmott and Young's *Family and Kinship* (1957) and *Family and Class* (1960). The two books, which have explicit historical dimensions, investigate the relative strength of kinship in two areas of London: Bethnal Green and Woodford. They find that kinship is more important in working-class Bethnal Green than in middle-class Woodford. Extensive discussions of the literature on kinship may be found in William J. Goode's *World Revolution* (1963) and in Colin Rosser and Christopher Harris's *Family and Social Change* (1965).

Between the wars, books from a variety of viewpoints about marriage were published. Norman Haire, in *Hymen* (1927) and *Marriage and Morals* (1929) contends that twentieth-century marriage patterns underwent change at an increasingly rapid rate. Bertrand Russell's *Marriage and Morals* (1929) questions monogamy. Ralph De Pomerai, in *Marriage* (1930), analyzes the ethics of matrimony. Winifred Cullis's "Impact of the War" (1942) takes a brief look at wartime's influence on marital institutions. Margaret Cole's perspective in *Marriage* (1938) is the most historical.[20] Perhaps the most thorough investigation of marriage as a social institution remains that of Edward A. Westermarck, *History of Human Marriage* (5th ed., 1921).[21] The best recent analytic study of modern sociology of the family is D. H. J. Morgan's *Social Theory and the Family* (1975).

During the past century and a half, married middle-class women have fulfilled two major functions: housewife and mother. Early in this century both functions were thought to be "natural" ones for women. In *The Best Circles* (1973), Leonore Davidoff brilliantly analyzes the cult of "true domesticity" among English elites during the late nineteenth and early twentieth centuries. Focusing attention on lower middle-class housewives is Patricia Branca in *Silent Sisterhood* (1975).[22]

Women at the turn of the century found themselves in roles that were generally subordinate to their husbands. A major premise of modern sociology, however, is that the strict division of labor wherein the man is provider and the woman domestic worker has broken down. Marriages in all classes during the century have tended to become "companionate." Elizabeth Bott, in *Family and Social Network* (1957), uses an approach that has gained a measure of acceptance. She conceptualizes roles as tending towards sexually segregated ones at one end of the spectrum and towards joint ones at the other end. She finds that marriages have become more joint-role oriented.

Modern feminist perceptions of wife-husband roles tend to focus on the issue of housework and are less optimistic than Bott as to the degree to which traditional stereotypic roles have disintegrated.[23] Ann Oakley has contributed two books about housework: *Sociology of Housework* (1974) and *Woman's Work* (1976). The latter is the more historical. She argues that the concept of housework has developed during the past century and a half. Housework is a consequence of industrial society which brought about the division of the family's activities into work and home. She sees the dichotomy as somewhat false since work is done in both places. Housework is work, but it is unpaid work. With the decline of domestic service in the twentieth century, middle-class women do housework. Thus, both middle-class and working-class women are exploited because the role of housewife is one that all married women are expected to assume. Two recent articles focus on aspects of housework and both have excellent bibliographies: Leonore Davidoff, "Rationalization of Housework" (1976), and Jean Gardiner, "Political Economy of Domestic Labour" (1976).

Mothering has been the other dominant role for married women of all social classes. Throughout the century, until quite recently, both pro-fessional and lay observers have attempted to convince women that serving as the bearers and socializers of the future's young is the natural and noble end towards which all women ought to incline.[24] Much of the defense of motherhood has come about because it has been thought to be under attack. Charlotte Haldane's *Motherhood and its Enemies* (1928) is an example of the genre. She noted the conjunction of a number of disconcerting trends. The birth rate among "the better sort" of families was declining. She observed that illegitimacy had risen precipitously since World War I. Middle-class women had not only lost their servants, but many left home every day in order to pursue a career. Who was taking care of the children? Who was doing the housework? All in all Haldane was dismayed that women were abandoning motherhood (except for the unwed) for the "unfeminine" satisfactions of the working world.[25]

Motherhood embraces a number of sensitive topics: birth control practices, sexual practices within and outside of marriage, proper social and family roles for women, and the class nature of English society. Until the Great Depression, birth control was an emotional public issue. Much of the concern, it must be emphasized, was expressed relative to the decline of the number of children in middle-class families. There was an acknowled-ged fear that the rising tide of lower-class children would dilute the influence of the "more successful part of the nation." In reality, the birthrate among working-class families had begun to drop by 1910. In the long run, the perception that lower-class families had finally begun to restrict their procreation may have done as much to defuse the birth control issue as the fact that the Great Depression made small families more desirable. Charles Vickering Drysdale, writing in *The Small Family System* just before World War I, thought birth control to be "the most important question of our time."[26] But the English legal system tended to consider it immoral. Rose Witcop was convicted of obscenity for publish-ing Margaret Sanger's *Family Limitation* in 1922. Discussions of voluntary family limitation were gaining public acceptance nonetheless. Marie Stopes described birth control methods in *Married Love* (1920) and in *Wise Parenthood* (1919). In 1921 she established the first birth control clinic in England. In *The First Five Thousand* (1925), she described her experiences and related that coitus interruptus was the most prevalent form of contraception.[27]

The franker public discussion of birth control spilled over into a general reassessment of women's sexuality. Theodore van de Velde, in *Ideal Marriage* (1928), wrote that married couples ought to enjoy one another sexually and described various techniques to enhance such pleasures. Even though his views were considered avant-garde, he still accepted the Victorian assumption that women were more sexually passive than men. Whether discussions of sexual practices led to or followed actual changes in sexual behavior is a murky issue. Irene Clephane, in *Towards Sex Freedom* (1935), advocated freer sexual expression for all.[28]

Enhanced work opportunities for women and expanded economic circumstances were among the stimuli that encouraged prospective parents to make conscious decisions about having children and how to rear them. Actual child-rearing practices among the various classes, except for very recent history, are difficult to discern. Interesting insights were presented in *Maternity* (1915). The candid comments by working-class women showed that they were not entirely enchanted with their children's behavior but did not really know what to do about it.[29] Recent studies of child-rearing practices have often turned on the issue of which parent's influence is more necessary to insure that the child is brought up to be healthy, normal, and well-adjusted.[30] The bulk of such research supports the notion that the mother's influence is more crucial than the father's. Josephine Klein, *Child Rearing Practices* (1965), synthesizes literature on the subject.[31]

The employment of women and children has been a subject of continuing concern for more than a century and a half. The genesis of this concern, both in terms of establishing social policy and framing public opinion, was the working conditions in the nineteenth-century factories and mines. Buttressing the expressed concerns about the very real hazards posed by such employment has been the underlying assumption that women belong in the home tending the children and doing housework. The belief has been that children of working mothers are neglected and that women endanger their physical and emotional well-being by working. A classic treatment of the topic is Margery Spring-Rice, *Working-Class Wives* (1939), which also shows that working-class wives who remained at home exhibited pathologies as well. A more recent discussion by two well-known sociologists, Alva Myrdal and Viola Klein, is *Women's Two Roles* (2d rev. ed. 1968). It includes a substantial bibliography and useful statistical tables.

The literature on female children, adolescents, and young women is sparse. Most of the writing on people in these age groups is male oriented.

Typical of the few works about women is Lily H. Montague, "The Girl in the Background," *Studies of Boy Life* (1904), which regards them strictly in terms of the emotional and social support systems that they provide for males. Agnes Pearl Jephcott's *Girls Growing Up* (1942) and *Rising Twenty* (1948) are noteworthy because they specifically discuss women.[33]

## EDUCATION

Formal education has become identified in the present century as an avenue of social mobility along which meritorious youngsters may travel. According to prevailing belief, it is the method by which social, economic, and political distinctions may be earned—as opposed to those which one receives by virtue of birth or wealth. It is no exaggeration, however, to suggest that conventional wisdom about the relationship of education to social mobility has tended to ignore the special place of women. It is not clear whether English women achieve social mobility through educational achievement. Traditionally, women had their father's status while unmarried and took on their husband's after the nuptials. Has this situation changed during the present century? Do women now achieve some independent rank and status through education? These and similar questions have neither been asked nor answered in existing histories of education.[34]

Historians of English education have generally restricted their approaches to the topic to three overlapping perspectives. First, they have intensively studied the manner in which the state has established increasingly tighter control over the plethora of educational institutions that have historically existed in Great Britain.[35] Second, they have traced the state's attempt to forge a democratic educational system that allows children to receive as much formal education as they can assimilate.[36] Typically these studies have concentrated on the degree of class bias that has existed at any given moment in time, but have tended to ignore sex or ethnic biases.[37] Finally, historians of education have written social histories of education which attempt to place it in its wider social context.[38]

Lamentably, this corpus has ignored the experience of girls and women.[39] It is not clear why histories of education about the twentieth century have been so sex blind. A defense might be that the battles for women's access to education were fought and won in the nineteenth century and that there have been no distinctive issues in the present century specifically related to women. This seems to be the implicit point of view of John Lawson and Harold Silver, *Social History of Education* (1973). Rita McWilliams-Tullberg, "Women and Degrees at Cambridge" (1977), suggests that turn-of-the-century reformers may be somewhat responsible for this view. On the other hand, most of the legislation guaranteeing females equal educational opportunities has been adopted in the present century. The question cannot be answered, however, by eliciting the views of turn-of-the-century reformers or by citing laws that assure women access to educational facilities. The point is hammered home in *Discrimination against Women* (1972), a report by the Labour Party, and in Barry Turner, *Equality for Some* (1974). There is historical work still to be done on the topic of women's equality of educational opportunities in the twentieth century.

There are a few works that treat the topic of women's twentieth-century education in a general way but they are inadequate and have serious flaws. John Newsome, *Education of Girls* (1948), is not strictly a history. It is, rather, a position paper in which he reviews some history in order to make the point that the place of women is in the home. An educational administrator and reformer, Newsome contends that the education provided to girls during the present century has been too academic. They ought to receive training which would make them better mothers and homemakers. Even though published in 1948, his book is reminiscent of turn-of-the-century concerns about the future of the "race." Kathleen Ollerenshaw, *Education for Girls* (1961), summarizes the educational opportunities as they existed in the 1950s but provides some historical perspective. Josephine Kamm's *Hope Deferred* (1956), a rather brief volume, traces the history of women's education since the middle ages. Her discussion of the twentieth century is slight. She expresses a critical attitude about the achievement of parity of educational opportunities between girls and boys. As her title denotes, it has been a case of hope deferred.

These three books, as well as much history of education in general, has been written from a perspective that Herbert Butterfield might well have included under the rubric "the Whig interpretation of history."[40] That is, the implicit—and often explicit—approach has been one that measures the amount of progress made during a particular historical era towards some goal that the historian values. The goals towards which educational reformers have been striving, extrapolating from the subject matter of recent histories, are state control, equality among the social classes, and the expansion of opportunities for higher education. While useful work can be done from the Whig viewpoint, in the long run other approaches will have to be formulated that try to place the history of female education within the socioeconomic and intellectual context of a particular historical epoch and within a perspective that covers the spectrum of women's domestic and public life-styles.

Three recent studies demonstrate the potential for writing non-Whig history. Pauline Marks's "Femininity in the Classroom" (1976) is a chronologically wide-ranging essay that traces social attitudes about femininity and their repercussions on the kind of education that girls should receive. Carol Dyhouse, in two separate articles for the period from 1880 to 1920, traces the impact of social Darwinism on social policy. In "Good Wives and Little Mothers" (1977) and "Social Darwinistic Ideas" (1976), Dyhouse analyzes the impact of social Darwinism on school curricula for girls. After 1900 curriculum reforms tended to deemphasize intellectual studies and to increase the amount of domestic science taught in the expressed hope that English girls would be "better mothers" than their mothers had been—the idea prevailing that the future of the English nationality and race depended largely upon the quality of English motherhood.[41]

An introduction to the history of female education may be found in Ray Strachey. *The Cause* (1928); in the first three chapters of Elsie M. Lang, *British Women* (1929); and in Christine Sinclair Bremner, *Education of Girls and Women* (1897).

Educational reformers often justified their position on the basis of equal human rights, and more pragmatically, by noting that the potential of the English populace was being wasted by half. Two recent treatments of these views are Michael Young, *Rise of the Meritocracy* (1958), and Maureen Woodhall, "Investment in Women" (1973). From the beginning, however, reformers who wished to see girls' educational opportunities expanded met with resistance from many angles. In recent articles, "Education and Sex" (1973) and "Religious Arguments Against Higher Education for Women" (1972), Joan N. Burstyn (1972; 1973) analyzes religious and medical opposition to women's higher education in the closing decades of the nineteenth century. William and Catherine Whetham were eugenicists who, in *Heredity and Society* (1912), opposed expanding women's education. Alice Ravenhill, a popular lecturer, also wrote from this viewpoint at the turn of the century, in *Eugenic Education* (1908). Eugenicists were still concerned about education after the First World War, as evidenced by Arabella Kenealy's *Feminism and Sex Extinction*(1920), a shrill indictment of contemporary girls' and women's education. Meyrick Booth, a eugenicist and evolutionist, wrote a series of books and articles in which he attacked the idea of equal educational opportunity. Representative of his views is the following statement:

> It is my charge against the existing system that it tends to obliterate the life-giving difference of sex, that it trains girls to imitate and compete with men, rather than to fulfil their own natural gifts and to rejoice in all their feminine potentialities, welcoming even such limitations as they may impose. ["Present Day Education," p. 169][42]

Discussions of girls' secondary education fall into three areas: general overviews, biographies and autobiographies, and histories of particular schools. Aside from practical descriptions of the schools, these books reveal—perhaps for future comparative analysis—environmental and social characteristics as well as academic expectations. Headmistresses and teachers, not to mention individual students, come alive in these accounts, which comprise a good set of references for studying change and continuity in girls' education. Dorothy Gardiner, *English Girlhood at School* (1929), and Alicia C. Percival, *The English Miss* (1939), both written between the wars, are popular general accounts. More useful, though sparse on the twentieth century, are Sara Annie Burstall and M. A. Douglas, *Public Schools for Girls* (1911), and Burstall, *English High Schools for Girls* (1907). Two recent studies are helpful for those who wish to measure "progress": Kathleen Ollerenshaw, *The Girls' Schools* (1967); Felicia Lamb and Helen Pickthorn, *Locked-Up Daughters* (1968). Examples of biographies and autobiographies are Josephine Kamm, *How different from Us* (1958), about two early educational reformers; Florence Cecily Steadman, *In the Days of Miss Beale* (1931); Elizabeth Raikes, *Dorothea Beale* (1908); Burstall, "Frances Mary Buss" (1924), and *Retrospect and Prospect* (1933), in which she describes her own and others' educational activities in Manchester; and Catherine Beatrice Firth, *Constance Louise Maynard* (1949). Histories of particular schools are typically official or semiofficial in character and suffer to some extent as a result. A representative selection includes Hazel Bates and A. A. M. Wells, eds., *History of Shrewsbury High School* (1962); Ruth Florence Butler, *History of St. Anne's Society* (1949); Amy Key Clarke, *History of Cheltenham Ladies' College* (1953); Julia Mary Grant, *St. Leonard's School* (1927); F. M. Greeves, *Leyton County High School for Girls* (1962); G. M. Hine, *Lancastrian School for Girls* (1962); W. G. Hughes and M. Sweeney, *Walford Grammar School* (1954); Josephine Kamm, *Indicative Past* (1971); and Laurie Magnus, *Jubilee Book* (1923).

In higher education, Queen's College was the first women's college and was specifically established to train teachers. Historically, a high proportion of degrees granted to women have been teaching degrees, a situation lamented by Margaret Tuke, "Women Students in the Universities" (1928). Perhaps the situation has changed slightly since World War II. Kitty Anderson, *Women and the Universities* (1965), discusses this and other issues. Discussions of women's higher education have tended to focus on Oxford and Cambridge. Gemma Bailey, ed., *Lady Margaret Hall* (1923), furnishes perspectives on the first of the Oxford women's colleges. Sommerville's history is traced by Muriel St. Clare Byrne and Catherine Hope Mansfield, *Sommerville College* (1923); Ruth Florence Butler, ed., *Society of Oxford Home-Students* (1930), is a collection of student recollections;

Winifred H. Moberly, "The Oxford Women's College" (1921) outlines some of the pecuniary reasons for women's second-class status; Annie M. A. H. Rogers, *Degrees by Degrees* (1938), traces the fight by women for degrees and membership in the university. Also enlightening are *Women of Oxford* (1960) and *Testament of Youth* (1933) by Vera Brittain, an Oxford graduate. For Cambridge, Rita McWilliams-Tullberg's *A Men's University* (1974) is definitive. In addition she discusses the interrelationships of educational and suffrage reform in "Women and Degrees at Cambridge" (1977). The essay has wider relevance than the title suggests. Emily Davies, a pioneer of women's education at Cambridge, discusses her ideas in *Thoughts on Some Questions* (1910). Another trail blazer was Mrs. Henry Sidgwick; see the biography of her by Ethel Sidgwick and the history by Hamilton of the college that Sidgwick founded.[43] The history of technical education and vocational education for careers has not yet received adequate attention.[44]

EMPLOYMENT

In a society that places so much emphasis on work and economic worth, a consideration of economic opportunities for women is fundamental to a consideration of their changing status. In gross terms, changes have been slow. For instance, in 1911 women comprised roughly 29.6 percent of the work force. In 1951, the percentage was 30.8. Of all women aged fourteen or over in 1911, 35.3 percent were employed. In 1951 the percentage had dropped to 34.7. Only during the past two decades has either of these situations changed significantly. Now, for instance, nearly half of all women are employed.

But these statistical details fail in tracing historical developments, especially for the years between the two world wars, for the unprecedented employment of women during World War I and the expansion of feminist activity since the prewar period had seemed to point in the direction of increased opportunities for women's full participation in the mainstream of socioeconomic life. Certainly the flood of new legislation following 1918 appeared to reflect growing social and legal status that should have assisted the expansion of employment and careers for women. Reality, however, did not coincide with the new expectations. Although women had improved their position as skilled and unskilled workers in war-oriented industries and activities, these gains tended to evaporate within a few years after 1918. Even professional women, whose hopes had been perhaps the highest, did not reach the level of their expectations for successful careers. In part, the economic dislocations of the twenties and thirties were responsible for stemming the tide of change. But it is probably most accurate to suggest that expanded employment during the wartime emergency was not accompanied by a necessary alteration of Britain's attitudes and beliefs about women's economic roles.

This is not to deny that women's contributions to wartime society and industry were without ramifications for improved social and political position. A partial franchise was granted in 1918. New laws expanded women's rights and responsibilities. The Matrimonial Causes Act of 1923 was considered by some as the most important of the new statutes because it made the grounds for divorce the same for women as for men. Looking at a skyrocketing divorce rate, a more articulate feminism, the declining birthrate, and the legal modifications of the 1920s, some social commentators described a social revolution in the making. In any event, women's traditional roles appeared on the way to being recast, with the consequences that alterations were due in the social structure. Irene Clephane observes a social revolution in *Towards Sex Freedom* (1935). Among others who appear to have concurred were G. Evelyn Gates, et al., *The Woman's Year Book*; Charlotte Haldane, *Motherhood and Its Enemies* (1928); Ida Hirschmann, "The Surplus of Women and the Declining Birthrate" (1935); and Geoffrey May, *The Social Control of Sex Expression* (1931). In historical perspective, however, whatever gains women made in the course of rapid post-war social change, it cannot be said to have extended to the means of earning a living.

For more specific details of female employment from 1900 to 1950, and for historical understanding of shifts and limitations, it is important to perceive the employment market generally. During the twentieth century, the structure of employment shifted away from manufacturing and extractive industries and towards service-oriented ones. In 1911, 74.6 percent of all employment was in occupational groups classified as manual; by 1951 it had dropped to 64.2 percent. Women's employment has reflected this shift, with two important exceptions. The fastest growing of all women's employment groups between 1911 and 1951 was in the category of clerks, which includes secretaries and stenographers, but excludes sales personnel. By 1951 women comprised 60 percent of this white-collar, service-oriented, but low-paid occupational group. The other important exception has been in the unskilled part of the manual workers category. There, women's experiences have not paralleled those of the work force as a whole. In this work—the lowest status and most poorly paid of all—women have continued to be employed in ever greater numbers.[45]

Studies which treat the general topic of women's employment and labor outside of the home include Ruth Adam's *A Woman's Place* (1975), an overview of the twentieth century.[46] For the period before the war, a book with which to begin is Olive Schreiner's *Woman and Labour* (1911). A highly factual and comprehensive recent treatment is Lee Holcombe, *Victorian Ladies at Work* (1973). The notes contain excellent bibliography. For World War I, Irene Osgood Andrews, *Economic Effects of the War*, has the advantage of immediacy, being published in 1918; her concern is less with economic effects of the war upon women and children than with physical, emotional, and moral effects. During the war, with high female employment, the enforcement of protective legislation for women and children was allowed to weaken. Over a million women flooded into various types of employment, some having deplorable conditions. Arthur Marwick, *The Deluge* (1965), and David Mitchell, *Monstrous Regiment* (1965), both discuss the process of women's integration into the work force in this period. Most women were drawn into war-related industries, particularly munitions manufacturing. Barbara Drake, *Women in the Engineering Trades* (1917) is the most detailed account, though it does not include notes or bibliography. The government was intimately connected with almost every detail of this extremely complex and interesting story. In this connection, the role of David Lloyd George is discussed in *Arms and the Wizard* (1978), by R. J. Q. Adams.[47]

Between the wars, women's overall employment returned to prewar levels. Women went home. Oswald Mosley, the British fascist, in "Women's Work," thought this was as it should be. He was not alone. There seemed to be widespread agreement that during tough economic times, men should have the jobs rather than women.[48] With the return of the war in 1939, however, women were pulled back into employment. This time, the shift was permanent. The best book on women's employment during World War II is Vera Douie, *The Lesser Half* (1943). It is an evaluative discussion of women's drive for economic opportunity and equality before and during the war. She is concerned mainly with how women can change long-standing discriminatory practices.[49] W. K. Hancock and M. M. Gowing, *British War Economy* (1949), discuss without analysis the recruitment of women into industry during the war under the rubric "Mobilization of Manpower." Arthur Marwick, in *The Home Front* (1977), briefly discusses women's employment during the war. For the Second World War, however, there is nothing comparable to Drake's volume on World War I.

During the twentieth century, the single largest category of women's employment has been in manual labor jobs, particularly the unskilled classification. Clara E. Collet, *Women in Industry* (1911), was interested in working conditions and unemployment. She does not have the perspective necessary to see the long-term shift in women's employment from the textile to other industries.[50] Women's employment in the skilled trades has undergone a long-term decline during this century. This and other topics of relevance to women are discussed in Gertrude Williams, *Recruitment to Skilled Trades* (1957), a sociological study.[51] Until World War II, the largest single kind of employment for women was as domestic servants. It is the subject of numerous governmental reports, and, more recently, scholarly works.[52] Perhaps the reason that the "servant problem" has elicited so much concern is that it affected dramatically the life-styles of the middle and upper classes—especially the middle-class housewives who were obliged to take on themselves the roles and functions of domestic workers. After 1900, the employment of servants began to slacken due to numerous interlocking trends, among them decline in family size, modernization in domestic living with availability of prepared foods and household appliances, the increasing privatization of the middle-class household, and a shortage of domestic workers, who turned to other occupations. What had been a slow trend away from domestic employment up to 1914, became a flood during the war as young women flocked into higher-paid employments which had the added benefit of allowing them more freedom. After the war, however, tens of thousands of women were willing to return to domestic employment, when servant-employing households turned increasingly from live-in servants and towards daily or hourly employment of charwomen. Two recent books consider the history of the domestic servant in the twentieth century: Pamela Horn, *Rise and Fall of the Victorian Servant* (1975), and Theresa McBride, *Domestic Revolution* (1976). Although the two differ in style and approach, both are worthwhile. Horn's study is a more traditional history, while McBride's tends towards sociological and comparative perspectives. Leonore Davidoff, in *The Best Circles* (1973) and in "Mastered for Life" (1974), analyzes how domestic servants fitted into upper-class life in Victorian and Edwardian England. "Mastered for Life" draws some interesting parallels between the status of wives and the status of servants in English homes.

The retail and distributive trades have provided extensive employment opportunities for women.[53] James B. Jefferys' *Retail Trading* (1954) is an analysis of the revolution in the distributive trades. While working in a shop may have been cleaner than factory work and may have provided slightly more status than working as a domestic, it was not an easy way to earn a living, as Joseph Hallsworth, *Protective Legislation for Shops and Office Employees* (1932), and Hallsworth and Rhys J. Davies, *Working Life of Shop Assistants* (1910), show. Perhaps a step up from the retail trades, in terms of status, was employment as a clerical worker. There is no adequate discussion of the topic for the twentieth century. Lee Holcombe, in *Victorian Ladies at Work*, studies middle-class female employment for the period up to 1914. F. D. Klingender, *Condition of Clerical Labour* (1935);

Fred Hughes, *By Hand and Brain* (1953); and David Lockwood, *The Blackcoated Worker* (1958), discuss aspects of the subject.

Until this century, middle-class women's opportunities for professional employment were almost entirely limited to teaching and nursing.[54] In teaching, however, the higher the educational level, the fewer women teachers there were. There have been almost no women university instructors until quite recently. On the other hand, women came to dominate primary education early in the 1900s. Geoffrey Partington, *Women Teachers* (1976), covers most aspects of their twentieth-century experience. Written from a "progress" point of view, he reviews developments relative to salary, promotion, and status. Also useful are Asher Troop, *The School Teachers* (1957), and Lance G. E. Jones, *Training of Teachers* (1924).[55] As for nursing, the situation at the turn of the century is discussed by Sarah A. Tooley in *History of Nursing* (1906). A more recent survey is Lucy Ridgley Seymer's *General History of Nursing* (1954). Jean Donnison, *Medical Men and Midwives* (1977), shows how male physicians attempted to force midwives out of birth-supervising functions.[56]

In 1919 Parliament passed the Sex Disqualification (Removal) Act, which opened all the professions to women. Many professions had already removed the barriers against women. Even with the antidiscrimination law, the numbers of women actually entering such professions as law, medicine, accounting, and architecture remained quite small. Still, the rate of entry for women into the professions was higher during the decade following the act's adoption than for any other decade in this century thus far. Women were more likely to become physicians than members of any other profession, excluding teaching and nursing. Even so, they were often isolated in low-status medical fields, such as obstetrics, and had difficulty getting clinical appointments in regular hospitals. E. Moberly Bell, *Storming the Citadel* (1953), details this and other hurdles that women physicians confronted.[57]

One profession left untouched by the Sex Disqualification Act was the civil service. Although women had long been employed in the clerical grades of the civil service, only the crisis of the war prompted the doyens of His Majesty's Civil Service to recruit women actively into the service's higher grades. Hilda Martindale, *Women Servants of the State* (1938), written entirely from governmental reports, surveys employment of women in all levels of the service, while R. K. Kelsall, *Higher Civil Servants* (1955), concentrates on the administrative grades. Although Kelsall does not treat women exclusively, he has included valuable chapters on their situation.[58]

A vital but insufficiently explored subject is women's trade unionism. Lucy Middleton's anthology, *Women in the Labour Movement* (1976), partly fills the lacuna. A series of articles from different contributors, it has the disadvantage of not having a unified perspective and of being too brief. Sheila Lewenhak, *Women and Trade Unions* (1977), is an "outline history" that surveys from the middle ages to the present. For the twentieth century, she covers the campaigns for women's entry into mixed unions, abolition of sweating, right to strike, and equal pay. Lewenhak also describes government policy toward these issues. Norbert C. Soldon's *Women in Labour*, due for publication soon, will be helpful. Elizabeth B. L. Hutchins, *Women in Modern Industry* (1915), includes a discussion of women's trade unionism prior to 1914. Lee Holcombe discusses the subject in several of her chapters and included a bibliography. G. D. H. Cole, *Trade Unionism and Munitions* (1923) concentrates on the reaction of male-dominated unions to the employment of scab labor (women and adolescents) in the munitions industries during the war, but also includes relevant information on the activities of women's unions. Mary Agnes Hamilton, *Mary Macarthur* (1925), provides a romanticized biography of the preeminent union organizer of women. Also, her *Women at Work* (1941) is a general history of women's trade union activity from 1876 to 1939. An appendix has a census of women in the principal trade unions as of 1939.[59]

In addition to the difficulty that women have faced in gaining and maintaining employments in various manual, white-collar, and professional occupations, they have also been subjected to more stringent work conditions than men and have generally been paid less.[60] Rules for hours, wages, and conditions at locations of employment have come in the form of factory legislation, but also in the form of social attitudes. In certain occupations women could work only so long as they remained unmarried. Gradually the practice of marriage barriers broke down, but it was still an issue in World War II.[61] The equal pay question had emerged by 1900.[62] At the turn of the century, women's wages averaged about half of men's. As a result of governmental intervention during the war, they reached two-thirds. During the next two decades, they backslid to the one-half level, where they remained until the 1960s. The principle of equality was established by a royal commission in 1945, but reality has been otherwise. Teachers' salaries, which are established on a nationwide basis, were to be equal for the sexes by 1961, but parity was not achieved. The most recent expression of the principle of equal pay for equal work was the passage of the Equal Pay Act in 1970. On this topic, see Guy Routh, *Occupation and Pay* (1965), a highly technical statistical study of the entire British pay structure. For the early twentieth century, Edward Cadbury, *Women's Work and Wages* (1907) and C. Black, *Sweated Industry and the Minimum Wage* (1907) are valuable. J. W. F. Rowe, *Wages in Practice and Theory* (1928) studies and compares wages in five basic industries from 1886 to 1926. Agatha L. Chapman, *Wages and Salaries* (1953) is definitive for the period between the wars. Hilda R. Kahn's *Salaries in the Public Services* (1962) is an extensive treatment of the equal pay issue in governmental employment.

The employment of women in traditionally male-dominated jobs and professions has proceeded at an excruciatingly slow pace. Even when admitted to a previously closed position, women have been confronted at every step with a host of hurdles to advancement. With expansion of vocational and higher education, women have been able to give proof of equal ability to men in an increasing number of occupations, so that by mid-century it was already conventional to accept the idea that women who worked should be limited only by their capabilities. In practice, however, British society at mid-twentieth century had only just begun to redefine women's traditional roles and occupational status.

# NOTES

1.  The notion of "total" history is associated with the Annales School. A recent discussion of this historical approach is Stoianovich, *French Historical Method*. Many approaches to women's history are being formulated; for a selection of them see the essays in Carroll, ed., *Liberating Women's History*; Davis, "'Women's History'"; and Kelly-Gadol, "Social Relations of the Sexes."
2.  Kanner has published two lengthy bibliographical chapters on nineteenth-century women: "Women of England" and "Women of England, Part II." Also helpful are McGregor, "Social Position of Women"; Hanham, *Bibliography*; and Rowbotham, *Women's Liberation and Revolution*.
3.  These two Greek gods who resided on Mt. Olympus are convenient symbols for the duality of roles in which men and women historically have been cast. Hermes, the messenger god, was a god of the world and one who exemplified the "instrumental" values of the world, that is, how to get along and get ahead in the world outside of the home. Hestia, the hearth goddess, on the other hand, had control over the domestic scene and exemplified social and emotional values.
4.  Pleck, "Two Worlds," argues that it is time to abandon the strict dichotomy between work and home life. Instead research ought to be pursued that shows how the two affect one another.
5.  The term "woman question," used from the late nineteenth century onwards, refers to the broad range of women's concerns for greater self-determination, equity, and employment. Feminists applied the phrase to circumstances in private life as well as to public issues. The phrase could also reflect the befuddlement and anger of some men when they thought about or reacted to the activities of the feminists. For examples, see Hynes's discussion in *The Edwardian Turn of Mind*. Contemporary treatments generally supportive of feminism include Blease, *Emancipation of English Women*; I. Ford, *Women and Socialism*; Reiss, *Rights and Duties*; Snowden, *Feminist Movement*; Sharp, *Rebel Women*; and Swiney, *The Awakening of Women*. Critical of the feminist movement are Bax, *The Fraud of Feminism* and "Monstrous Regiment"; Colquhoun, *The Vocation of Women*; Fairfield,

*Woman's Movement*; and Hartley, *the Truth about Women*. Hutchins, *Conflicting Ideals*, attempts to be balanced.

6.  Rover, *Love, Morals, and the Feminists*.
7.  Other works on feminism that appeared near the end of the war or immediately after are T. R. Smith, ed., *The Woman Question*, a series of essays by feminist leaders; Key, *Woman Movement*; Arnold Bennett, *Our Women*; M. Booth, *Woman and Society*; and Lane and MacNamara, *Nails*.
8.  The middle-class perspective of most feminist thought has often been pointed out. One author who attempted to consider the viewpoint of working-class women is Eyles, *Women's Problems* and *The Woman in the Little House*, although she is somewhat patronizing. For a decidedly middle-class view, read Woolf's *A Room of One's Own* and *Three Guineas*. Marder discusses Woolf's ideas in *Feminism and Art*. Jerome, in *The Secret of Woman*, challenges H. L. Mencken. Holtby, *Women in a Changing Civilization*, asks women to stand united against fascism. Sayers's views, as expressed through her heroine, Harriet Vane, in *Gaudy Night* are entertaining. Sayers summarizes her thoughts on the subject in "The Woman Question." Munro, *The True Woman*, and Curle, *Women* are guides to those who wish to cling to the traditional male ethic. Luetkens in *Women and a New Society* surveys the post-World War II scene.
9.  See the discussion in J. Mitchell, *Woman's Estate*.
10. Bridges and Hartmann, "The Unhappy Marriage of Marxism and Feminism," provide a detailed discussion of the theoretical issues involved.
11. R. Strachey, "*The Cause*," provides a history of emancipation up to 1928; Brittain, *Lady into Woman*, extends Strachey's discussion to 1953. Other general treatments are Branson and Heinemann, *Britain in the 1930's*; R. Graves and Hodge, *Long Weekend*; Mowat, *Britain between the Wars*; Newitt, *Women Must Choose*; Normanton and Fawcett, "Women"; Phillips, ed., *Women and the Labour Party*; P. Strachey, *Position of English Women*; Taylor, *English History, 1914–1945*; and Zweig, *Women's Life and Labour*.
12. Class-oriented studies of women, arranged by publication date, are C. Booth, *Life and Labour*; Knowles, *The Upholstered Cage*; Gallichan, *The Great Unmarried*; Reynolds, *The Learned Lady*; H. L. Smith, *New Survey of London Life*; Percival, *The English Miss*; Schneider, "Class Origin and Fame"; Nottingham, "Toward an Analysis of the Effects of Two World Wars"; and R. Lewis and Maude, *The English Middle Classes*. Regional and local studies similarly arranged are F. Bell, *At the Works*; M. Davies, *Life in an English Village*; D. C. Jones, *Social Survey of Merseyside*; Mogey, *Rural Life in Northern Ireland*; Rees, *Life in a Welsh Countryside*; Stacey, *Tradition and Change*; Baker, *English Village*; Brennan, Cooney, and Pollins, *Social Change in South-west Wales*; Dennis, Henriques, and Slaughter, *Coal is Our Life*; W. M. Williams, *Sociology of an English Village*.
13. Fletcher, *Family and Marriage in Britain*, discusses some of these views, as does Ogburn, *Social Change*. Examples are Beveridge, *Changes in Family Life*; Urwin, *Can the Family Survive?* and H. G. Wells, *Socialism and the Family*. See also Ryder and Silver, *Modern English Society*, which contains revealing documented chapters on family and economics and on women in particular.
14. E. Paul, *Chronos*; see the modern treatment by Cooper, *Death of the Family*.
15. See Malinowski, *Argonauts* and *Father*; Radcliffe-Brown, *Andaman Islanders* and *Structure and Function*; a statement and a critique is in Gouldner, *The Coming Crisis*; also important are Rivers, *Social Organisation*; and Skolnick, "Family Revisited."
16. P. Thompson, *The Edwardians*, p. 144, gives the following definition of functionalist sociology: "The analysis of a society or institution on the assumption that all its elements are interdependent and each plays a function in maintaining social organisation. The theory is based on the analogy of a complex living creature like a mammal. It is assumed that normal societies have a consensus on central social values and purposes"; see Parsons and Bales, *Family, Socialization and Interaction Process*, and the extensive critique in Morgan, *Social Theory*.
17. M. Anderson, *Sociology of the Family* and *Family Structure*; Willmott and Young, *Symmetrical Family*; Oakley, *Woman's Work*. Discussions of historical studies of families are Berkner, "Recent Research," and Lasch, "Family and History."

18. Additional sociologies of the family with historical perspectives are Farmer, *Family*; Fletcher, *Family and Marriage*; Goode, *World Revolution and Family Patterns*; Harris, *Family*; Rosser and Harris, *Family and Social Change*.

19. Tilly, Scott, and Cohen, "Women's Work," contains a rigorous critique; R. V. Wells's review in *Journal of Social History* is kinder. For Shorter's reply to his critics, see his introductory essay to the paperback edition of his *Making of the Modern Family* (1977).

20. Since World War II, some scholarly studies of note have emerged. Hajnal, "Aspects of Recent Trends"; Pierce, "Marriage in the Fifties"; and Slater and Woodside, *Patterns of Marriage*. In addition to these, see the interesting discussions by Bernard, *Future of Marriage* and "Paradox."

21. Not to be overlooked are Bosanquet's *Family* and *Rich and Poor*. For the study of twentieth-century divorce, the Royal Commission on Divorce, 1912 to 1913, is a source with which to begin. Historical and sociological accounts are McGregor, *Divorce in England*; Glass, "Divorce in England and Wales"; and G. Rowntree and Carrier, "Resort to Divorce." Two literary offerings are Arnold Bennett, *Whom God Hath Joined*, and G. B. Shaw, *Getting Married*. Opposed to easier divorce are Hartley, *Divorce*, and C. G. Beale, *Wise Wedlock*. Reformers include Haynes, *Divorce as It Might Be*; Herbert, *Holy Deadlock* and *The Ayes Have It*; and Gribble, *The Fight for Divorce*.

22. See also J. Fisher, *World of the Forsytes*; and Davidoff et. al, "Landscape with Figures."

23. Examples are Comer, *Wedlocked Women*; Davidoff, "Rationalization of Housework"; and J. Gardiner, "Political Economy of Domestic Labour." See Glazer-Malbin, "Housework," who discusses the literature on the question. An early critic of housework was C. Hamilton, *Marriage as a Trade*.

24. See Ayling, *Retreat from parenthood*; Chesser, *Woman, Marriage and Motherhood*; Drysdale, *Small Family System*; Hirschmann, "Surplus of Women." Hoggart's *Uses of Literacy* makes a valuable interpretation of working-class women as mothers. See also Marsden, *Mothers Alone*, a very useful study.

25. Banks, *Prosperity and Parenthood*, is the classic study on the dramatic increase of voluntary family limitation in nineteenth-century England; a follow-up study is *Feminism and Family Planning*, coauthored by O. Banks. Interpretations of the declining birthrate and other vital statistics, arranged by publication date, are Yule, "Changes in the Marriage and Birth-rate"; Webb, *Declining Birth-Rate*; Elderton, *Report on the English Birth-Rate*; Innes, *Class Fertility Trends*; Titmuss and Titmuss, *Parents Revolt*; Glass and Grebnick, *Trend and Pattern of Fertility in Great Britain*; Johansson, "Sex and Death in Victorian England."

26. Drysdale was expressing a view which found support from many eugenicists. They argued that the marked decrease in the number of middle-class children threatened the continued existence of the present civilization. They assumed that British glory depended to a marked degree on the biologically inherited racial and class characteristics of the "brightest and the best." Eugenics continued to be a popular topic until the 1930s. Of interest are Chesterton, *Eugenics and Other Evils*; Ellis, *The Problem of Race-Regeneration*; Pearson and Elderton, *On the Correlation of Fertility with Social Value*; Saleeby, *The Eugenic Prospect*; Scharlieb, *Womanhood and Race Regeneration*; Whetham, *The Family and the Nation*. Kanner, "Women of England, part II" has a more complete bibliography.

27. Briant, *Marie Stopes*; Box, *Trial of Marie Stopes*; and Hall, *Passionate Crusader*, give excellent accounts of her life and battles; see also, *Birth Control News*. Two physicians—Merchant, ed., *Medical Views on Birth Control*, and Haire, *Some More Medical Views on Birth Control*— provide opposing sides to the birth control issue. Other relevant studies are Sutherland, *Birth-Control*, and Pierpoint, *Report*. Browne et al., *Abortion*, and Chance, *The Cost of English Morals* are discussions of abortion. Three recent studies are McLaren, "Abortion in England," and *Birth Control*; and Rowbotham, *Stella Browne*.

28. Popular studies about female sexuality were published in increasing numbers in the freer air of the 1920s. A selection of them includes Hartley, *Sex Education and National Health*; Royden, *Sex and Common Sense*; May, *Social Control of Sex Expression*; A. Craig, *Sex and Revolution*; Clephane, *Ourselves*; and Caudwell, *Studies in a Dying Culture*. Some literary

treatments are H. G. Wells, *Modern Utopia* and *Ann Veronica*; G. B. Shaw, *Misalliance*; and Forster, *Howard's End*. The most important study on sexology was Ellis, *Studies in the Psychology of Sex*. Recent scholarly treatments are Bullough, *The Subordinate Sex*; Cominos, "Late-Victorian Sexual Respectability"; Conway, "Stereotypes of Femininity"; and Henriques, *Love in Action*.

29. Other studies that describe working-class experiences are Reeves, *Round about a Pound a Week*; Spring-Rice, *Working-Class Wives*; Young, "Distribution of Income"; Rathbone, *The Disinherited Family*; K. D. Courtney et al., *Equal Pay*; Dearle, *Cost of Living*; Hoffner, "Recent Developments"; Dingle, "Drink and Working-Class Living Standards"; Oren, "Welfare of Women"; and Stearns, "Working-Class Women."

30. See Graveson and Crane, *A Century of Family Law*, for a discussion of guardianship.

31. Also Blagg, *Analysis of Infant Mortality*; Hartley, *Motherhood and the Relationships of the Sexes* and *Mother and Son*; C. Haldane, *Motherhood and Its Enemies*. A recent work is Rutter, *Maternal Deprivation Reassessed*.

32. In order by publication date: Martin, "The Married Working Woman"; Hogg, "Dependents on Women Wage-Earners"; Rowntree and Stuart, *Responsibility of Women Workers for Dependents*; "Employment of Married Women and Mothers of Families"; Jephcott, *Married Women Working*; Hubback, *Wives Who Went to College*; Wootton, "Twelve Criminological Hypotheses"; Winnicott, *Child*; Rapoport and Rapoport, *Dual-Career Families*.

33. Historical studies of some value are Aries, *Centuries of Childhood*; Gillis, "Evolution of Juvenile Delinquency" and *Youth and History*; Marwick, "Youth in Britain"; Pinchbeck and Hewitt, *Children in English Society*. Published early in the century are Bray, *The Town Child*, and C. Russell, *Problem of Juvenile Crime*.

34. On social mobility, see Glass, *Social Mobility*; Halsey, *Trends in British Society*; and Marsh, *Changing Social Structure*. McMillan, *The Child and the State* offers the view that education is the key to social mobility.

35. Standard accounts are Curtis, *History of Education* and *Education in Britain*; Dent, *Educational System of England* and *1870–1970*. All have useful bibliographies. Also, Akenson, "Patterns of English Educational Change"; and Middleton and Weitzman, *A Place for Everyone*. Eaglesham, *Foundations*, summarizes early twentieth-century efforts by the state to extend its control; Rubinstein, *School Attendance in London*; and "Education, 1909–1950," in *Parliamentary Papers*, are also helpful.

36. Helpful are Armfelt, *Our Changing Schools*; Doherty, "Hadow Report, 1926"; Drake, *Some Problems of Education*; H. A. L. Fisher, *Unfinished Autobiography*; J. Graves, *Policy and Progress*; C. G. Paul, *The Headmistress Speaks*; and Wakefield, *On Leaving School*. On testing, see Gray and Moshinsky, "Ability and Educational Opportunity"; Ikin, "Educable Capacity"; and a government report, *Psychological Tests*.

37. Lindsay, *Social Progress and Educational Waste*, argues that the scholarship system was biased against working-class children. In the 1920s, the Labour Party made an issue of class bias; see Tawney, *Secondary Education for All*, and Simon, *Education and the Labour Movement*. Lowndes, *The Silent Social Revolution* (1935), a classic study, contended that education was everyone's passport to social mobility, women included. Recent treatments include O. Banks, *Parity and Prestige*, and F. Cambell, *Eleven-Plus*. Ethnic bias is discussed in Burgin and Edson, *Spring Grove*.

38. An early work was Dobbs, *Education and Social Movements*. Lawson and Silver, *Social History of Education*, may be too general to be of much help for the present century; Bernbaum, *Social Change and the Schools*, is well-written and has an extensive bibliography. Other helpful studies include Allaway, "Social and Educational Change"; O. Banks, *The Sociology of Education*; Collier, *The Social Purposes of Education*; Halsey, ed., *Trends in British Society*; Jackson and Marsden, *Education and the Working Class*; Selleck, *The New Education*; Stewart, *Progressives and Radicals*.

39. Government reports have not been systematically mined. Useful sources are "General Reports of the Board of Education," published annually from 1901 to 1938, discontinued until 1947, and then divided into two annual reports retitled as "Report of the Ministry of Education" and "Statistics of Public Education." Full citations for each of

the "General Reports" are given in P. Ford and G. Ford, *A Breviate of Parliamentary Papers, 1900–1916*, pp. 457–58. Each of the reports of the Ministry of Education and the annual educational statistics are listed in P. Ford and G. Ford, *A Breviate of Parliamentary Papers*, 1940–1954, p. 505. The "Special Reports" edited by Sadler from 1897 to 1914 are excellent sources; a complete list of them is contained in P. Ford and G. Ford, *Breviate 1900–1916*, pp. 451–52. Additional parliamentary reports and studies include: "Industrial Training of Girls"; "Partial Exemption from School Attendance"; "Attendance, Compulsory or Otherwise at Continuation Schools"; "Practical Work in Secondary Schools"; "Scholarships, Free Places, and Maintenance Allowances"; and "The Number of Boys and Girls in Public Elementary Schools," all of which are in *Parliamentary Papers. Abolition of Tuition Fees in Grant-Aided Secondary Schools* and *Differentiation of Curricula between the Sexes in Secondary Schools*, both published by H.M.S.O., are also helpful sources.

40. See the pertinent comments by Dyhouse in "Social Darwinistic Ideas," p. 41.

41. Two other recent studies are Blackstone, "The Education of Girls Today," and J. Shaw, "Finishing School."

42. Other articles by M. Booth that make similar points are "Feminism and Marriage" and "The Vicious Circle." Grove responded to Booth in "Feminism and Marriage: A Reply." Also, see P. Magnus, *Educational Aims and Efforts*, and Sellers, "Boy and Girl War Products."

43. Other discussions of higher education are Fawcett, "Cambridge and Women's Education"; "General Reports on Higher Education," in *Parliamentary Papers* (1903); "University Education in London," in *Parliamentary Papers* (1913); and *Higher Education Report* (H.M.S.O., 1963). Halsey, ed., "Higher Education," in *Trends in British Society*, includes relevant statistics.

44. For teaching see the government studies *Supply of Women Teachers* and *Training and Supply of Teachers*. Scholarly studies include L. G. E. Jones, *Training of Teachers*; Kelsall, *Women in Teaching*; and Partington, *Women Teachers*. The standard work on nursing is Abel-Smith, *A History of the Nursing Profession*. Two older works remain useful: Nutting and Dock, *A History of Nursing*; and Tooley, *The History of Nursing*. For an extensive listing of sources, see A. M. C. Thompson, ed., *A Bibliography of Nursing Literature, 1859–1960*. Medical instruction for women is discussed in Little, "Undergraduate Medical Education"; Scharlieb, "Medical Education of Women." The standard account is Bell, *Storming the Citadel*. Women's adult education has been equally neglected by researchers. See E. S. Haldane, "Adult Education in Rural Districts." Harrison's *Learning and Living* is the standard work on adult education.

45. These statistics, based mostly on official figures, are discussed in Halsey, ed. *Trends in British Society*; D. C. Jones, "Notes on the Census of Occupations"; Routh, *Occupation and Pay*; Saunders and Jones, *A Survey of the Social Structure*; and Saunders et al., *A Survey of the Social Conditions*.

46. See also Papworth and Zimmern, *The Occupations of Women*. A complete list of parliamentary papers on the subject is in P. Ford and G. Ford, *Breviate 1900–1916*. Additional studies are Brittain, *Women's Work*, which has footnotes and a bibliography; MacArthur, *Women in Industry*; and Tickner, *Women in English Economic History*.

47. In addition, the following are useful: Hobman, *Olive Schreiner*; Payne, *Women without Men*; Bulkey, *Bibliographical Survey*. Government reports printed in 1920 or before include "Health of Munition Workers," "Clerical and Commercial Employment," and "Women's War Employment" all of which are in *Parliamentary Papers*; and *Employment of Women in Agriculture*, published by H.M.S.O. Also see the journal *The Labour Woman*.

48. Bowley, *Some Economic Consequences*; Ferguson, "Women's Work"; and R. Strachey, "*The Cause.*"

49. Additional studies are Beauchamp, "Women and the War Effort"; Beveridge, *Full Employment*; Douie, *Daughters of Britain*; Goldsmith, *Women at War*; Priestly, *British Women Go to War*; G. Williams, *Women and Work*; Williams-Ellis, *Women in War Factories*.

50. Also, James, "Women at Work."

51. MacDonald, *Women in the Printing Trades*; Hutchins, "Woman's Industrial Career";

Adler, "Women's Industry after the War"; Bondfield, "The Future of Women in Industry"; G. D. H. Cole et al., *Some Problems of Urban and Rural Industry.*

52. On domestic labor, see Elliott, "The Status of Domestic Workers"; Powell, *Below Stairs*, is autobiographical; Burton, *Domestic Work*; and Franklin, "Troops of Servants"; as well as the following government reports: "Domestic Service," "Domestic Help," "Post-War Organisation of Private Domestic Employment," all of which are in *Parliamentary Papers*; and *Supply of Domestic Servants* and *Staffing the Hospitals*, both published by H.M.S.O.

53. Halmos, "The Personal Service Society."

54. For the situation in professional employment at the turn of the century, see Collet, *Educated Working Women*; Castle, *A Statistical Study of Eminent Women*; and Morley, ed., *Women Workers.*

55. Government studies include *Supply of Women Teachers* and *Training and Supply of Teachers*, both published by H.M.S.O. Scholarly works are by Kelsall, *Women in Teaching*; Collins, *Women Graduates*; and Sommerkorn, "Position of Women."

56. Also, Oakley, "Wisewoman and Medicine Man."

57. Studies of women in a variety of professions include Aberdeen, *Women in professions*; Dodd, "Women as Justices of the Peace"; Frankenstein, "Women in Industrial Welfare Work"; Franz, *English Women Enter the Professions*; V. Klein, "The Demand for Professional Womanpower"; Lipinska and Mackenzie, "Women Doctors"; A. H. Bennett, *English Medical Women*; Murray, *Women as Army Surgeons*; and Peto, "Police Work for Women."

58. For historical perspective, Abramowitz and Eliasberg, *Growth of Public Employment*, is excellent. See also, Evans, *Women in the Civil Service*; M. Jefferys, "Married Women in the Higher Grades of the Civil Service"; Morley, *Women Workers*; Cohen, *The Growth of the British Civil Service*; J. Craig, *A History of Red Tape.* An evaluation of women's service during the war is "Women in the Government Departments," in *Parliamentary Papers.*

59. General studies and sources are Drake, *Women in the Trade Unions*; Heinemann and Thompson, *Professional Solidarity among Teachers*; Humphreys, *Clerical Unions in the Civil Service*; F. Hughes, *By Hand and Brain*; *Labour Year Book*; Phillips, *Women and the Labour Party*; Roberts, *Trade Union Government*; Sturmthal, *White-Collar Trade Unions*; Webb, *History of Trade Unionism*; *Women's Trade Union Review*; *Women's Industrial News*; and Boone, *The Women's Trade Union Leagues in Great Britain and the United States.*

60. In order by publication date: MacArthur, *Woman in Industry*; Benson, *Legislation for the Protection of Women*; "Health of Munition Workers" and "Employment of Women" in *Parliamentary Papers*; Mess, *Factory Legislation*; Hallsworth, *Protective Legislation*; *Physique of Women in Industry*, a government study; Blelloch, "A Historical Survey of Factory Inspection."

61. A short but perceptive essay that points out the class aspects of the marriage bar is O. Strachey, "Married Women and Work"; see also "The Marriage Bar in the Civil Service," in *Parliamentary Papers.*

62. In order by publication date: Cadbury, et al., *Women's Work and Wages*; Black, *Sweated Industry*; "Expenditures of Wage-Earning Women and Girls," in *Parliamentary Papers*; Fawcett, "Equal Pay for Equal Value"; "Salaries for Teachers," in *Parliamentary Papers*; "Women in Industry," in *Parliamentary Papers*; Edgeworth, "Equal Pay to Men and Women"; Shepherd, *The Fixing of Wages*; Rowe, *Wages in Practice and Theory*, studies and compares wages in five basic industries from 1886 to 1926; Royal Commission on Equal Pay, in *Parliamentary Papers*; and Harrod, "Equal Pay for Men and Women."

# BIBLIOGRAPHY

ABEL-SMITH, BRIAN. *A History of the Nursing Profession*. London: 1960. (American ed. New York: 1960.)

ABRAMOWITZ, MOSES, and ELIASBERG, VERA F. *The Growth of Public Employment in Great Britain*. Princeton, N.J.: 1957.

ADAM, RUTH. *A Woman's Place, 1910–75*. London: 1975. (American ed. New York: 1977.)

ADAMS, R. J. Q. *Arms and the Wizard*. London and Austin, Tex.: 1978.

ADLER, N. "Women's Industry after the War." *Contemporary Review* 108 (1915): 780–88.

AKENSON, D. H. "Patterns of English Educational Change: The Fisher and Butler Acts." *History of Education Quarterly* 11 (1971): 143–56.

ALLAWAY, A. J. "Social and Educational Change since 1900." *Sociological Review* 43 (1951): 143–57.

ALLEN, SHEILA, and BARKER, DIANA, eds. *Sexual Divisions and Society: Process and Change* London: 1976.

———. *Dependence and Exploitation in Work and Marriage*. London: 1976.

ANDERSON, KITTY. *Women and the Universities: A Changing Pattern*. Fawcett Lectures. Bedford College, London: 1965.

ANDERSON, MICHAEL. *Family Structure in Nineteenth Century Lancashire*. Cambridge: 1971.

———, ed. *Sociology of the Family*. London: 1971.

ANDREWS, IRENE OSGOOD. *Economic Effects of the War upon Women and Children in Great Britain*. London: 1918.

ARIES, PHILIP. *Centuries of Childhood: A Social History of Family Life*. Translated by Robert Baldick. New York and London: 1962.

ARMFELT, ROGER. *Our Changing Schools*. London: 1950.

AYLING, JEAN. *The Retreat from Parenthood*. London: 1930.

BAILEY, GEMMA, ed. *Lady Margaret Hall*. London: 1923.

BAKER, N. P. *The English Village*. London: 1953.

BANKS, JOSEPH A. *Prosperity and Parenthood*. Liverpool and New York: 1954.

———, and BANKS, OLIVE. *Feminism and Family Planning in Victorian England*. London and New York: 1964.

BANKS, OLIVE. *Parity and Prestige in English Secondary Education: A Study in Educational Sociology*. London: 1955.

———. *The Sociology of Education*. London and New York: 1968.

BANNER, LOIS, and HARTMANN, MARY, eds. *Clio's Consciousness Raised*. New York: 1974.

BARKER, DIANA, and ALLEN, SHEILA, eds. See Allen, Sheila, and Barker, Diana, eds.

BATES, HAZEL, and WELLS, A. A. M., eds. *A History of Shrewsbury High School (Girls' Public Day School Trust), 1885–1960*. Shrewsbury: 1962.

BAX, ERNEST BELFORT. *The Fraud of Feminism*. London: 1913.

———. "The Monstrous Regiment of Womanhood." In *Essays in Socialism*. London: 1907.

BEALE, C. G. *Wise Wedlock*. London: 1922.

BEALE, DOROTHEA. "Girls' Schools, Past and Present." *The Nineteenth Century* 23 (April, 1888): 541–54.

———; SOULSBY, LUCY H. M.; and DOVE, JANE FRANCES. *Work and Play in Girls' Schools by Three Head Mistresses*. London: 1898.

BEAUCHAMP, JOAN. "Women and the War Effort." *Labour Monthly* 24 (1942): 53–56.

BEAUVOIR, SIMONE DE. *Le Deuxième Sexe.* 2 vols. Paris: 1949.(*The Second Sex.* New York: 1953. London: 1968.)

BEBEL, AUGUST. *Woman in the Past, Present and Future.* Translated by H. B. Adams Walther. London and New York: [c. 1884].

BELL, E. MOBERLY. *Storming the Citadel: The Rise of the Woman Doctor.* London: 1953.

BELL, FLORENCE. *At the Works: A Study of a Manufacturing Town.* London: 1907.

BENNETT, A. H. *English Medical Women.* London: 1915.

BENNETT, ARNOLD. *Our Women: Chapters on the Sex-Discord.* London and New York: 1920.

———. *Whom God Hath Joined.* London: 1906.

BENSON, GODFREY R. *Legislation for the Protection of Women.* London: 1912.

BERKNER, LUTZ K. "Recent Research on the History of the Family in Western Europe." *Journal of Marriage and the Family* 35 (1973): 395–405.

BERNARD, JESSIE. *The Future of Marriage.* New York: 1972.

———. "The Paradox of the Happy Marriage." In *Woman in Sexist Society*, edited by Vivian Gornick and Barbara K. Moran. London and New York: 1971.

BERNBAUM, GERALD. *Social Change and the Schools, 1918–1944.* London and New York: 1967.

BEVERIDGE, WILLIAM HENRY. *Changes in Family Life.* London: 1932.

———. *Full Employment in a Free Society.* London and New York: 1944.

*Birth Control News.* London, 1921–.

BLACK, CLEMENTINA. *Sweated Industry and the Minimum Wage.* London: 1907.

BLACKSTONE, TESSA. "The Education of Girls Today." In *The Rights and Wrongs of Women*, edited by Juliet Mitchell and Ann Oakley. London: 1976.

BLAGG, HELEN M. *Analysis of Infant Mortality and Its Causes in the United Kingdom.* London: 1910.

BLEASE, W. LYON. *The Emancipation of English Women.* London: 1913.

BLELLOCH, DAVID HABERSHON. "A Historical Survey of Factory Inspection in Great Britain." *International Labour Review* 38 (1938): 614–59.

BONDFIELD, MARGARET. "The Future of Women in Industry." In *Labour Year Book, 1916.* London: 1917.

BOONE, GLADYS. *The Women's Trade Union Leagues in Great Britain and the United States.* London and New York: 1942.

BOOTH, CHARLES. *Life and Labour of the People in London.* 9 vols. London: 1892–97.

BOOTH, MEYRICK. "Feminism and Marriage." *Nineteenth Century and After* 100 (1926): 83–93.

———. "The Present-Day Education of Girls: An Indictment." *Nineteenth Century and After* 102 (1927): 259–69.

———. "The Vicious Circle." *Nineteenth Century and After* 104 (1928): 100–107.

———. *Woman and Society.* London: 1929.

BORNAT, JOANNA. "Women's History and Oral History: An Outline Bibliography." *Oral History Review* 5, no. 2 (Autumn 1977).

BOSANQUET, HELEN. *The Family.* London: 1916.

———. *Rich and Poor.* London and New York: 1899.

BOTT, ELIZABETH. *Family and Social Network.* London: 1957.

BOWLEY, ARTHUR L. *Some Economic Consequences of the First World War.* London: 1927.

BOX, MURIEL. *The Trial of Marie Stopes.* London: 1967.

BRADBROOK, MURIEL CLARA. *"That Infidel Place:" A Short History of Girton College, 1869–1969.* London: 1969.

BRANCA, PATRICIA. *Silent Sisterhood: Middle Class Women in the Victorian Home.* London: 1975. Pittsburgh, Pa., 1976.

BRANSON, NOREEN. *Britain in the Nineteen Twenties.* London and Minneapolis: 1976.

———, and HEINEMANN, MARGOT. *Britain in the 1930's.* London and New York: 1971.

BRAY, REGINALD. *The Town Child.* London: 1907.

BREMNER, CHRISTINE SINCLAIR. *The Education of Girls and Women in Great Britain.* London: 1897.

BRENNAN, T.; COONEY, E.; and POLLINS, H. *Social Change in South-west Wales.* London: 1954.

BRIANT, KEITH. *Marie Stopes.* London: 1962.

BRIDGES, AMY B., and HARTMANN, HEIDI I. "The Unhappy Marriage of Marxism and Feminism: Towards a More Progressive Union." Draft of an essay submitted to *Marxist Perspectives.*

BRITTAIN, VERA MARY. *Lady into Woman: A History of Women from Victoria to Elizabeth II.* London and New York: 1953.

———. *Testament of Youth.* London: 1933.

———. *The Women of Oxford: A Fragment of History.* London: 1960.

———. *Women's Work in Modern England.* London: 1928.

BROWNE, FRANCES WORSLEY STELLA, et al. *Abortion.* London: 1935.

BULKLEY, B. A. *Bibliographical Survey of Contemporary Sources for the Economic and Social History of the War.* Oxford: 1922.

BULLOUGH, VERN. *The Subordinate Sex: A History of Attitudes toward Women.* Urbana and London: 1973.

BURGIN, TREVOR, and EDSON, PATRICIA. *Spring Grove: The Education of Immigrant Children.* London: 1967.

BURSTALL, SARA ANNIE. *English High Schools for Girls, Their Aims, Organisation and Management.* London: 1907.

———. "Frances Mary Buss and the Association of Head Mistresses, 1874–1924." *Fortnightly Review* 116 (1924): 242–50.

———. *Retrospect and Prospect: Sixty Years of Women's Education.* London: 1933.

BURSTALL, SARA ANNIE, and DOUGLAS, M. A., eds. *Public Schools for Girls.* London: 1911.

BURSTYN, JOAN N. "Education and Sex: The Medical Case against Higher Education for Women in England, 1870–1900." *Proceedings of the American Philosophical Society* 117 (1973): 79–89.

———. "Religious Arguments against Higher Education for Women in England, 1840–1890." *Women's Studies* 1 (1972): 11–31.

BURTON, ELAINE. *Domestic Work: Britain's Largest Industry.* London: 1944.

BUTLER, RUTH FLORENCE. *A History of St. Anne's Society.* London: 1949.

———, ed. *The Society of Oxford Home-Students: Retrospects and Recollections (1879–1921).* Oxford: 1930.

BYRNE, MURIEL ST. CLARE, and MANFIELD, CATHERINE HOPE. *Sommerville College, 1879–1921.* Oxford: 1923.

CADBURY, EDWARD, et al. *Women's Work and Wages.* London: 1907.

CAMPBELL, FLANN. *Eleven-Plus and All That.* London: 1956.

CAMPBELL, G. A. *The Civil Service in Great Britain.* London: 1954.

CARROLL, BERNICE A., ed. *Liberating Women's History: Theoretical and Critical Essays.* Urbana, Ill., and London: 1976.

CASTLE, CORA SUTTON. *A Statistical Study of Eminent Women.* New York: 1906.

CAUDWELL, CHRISTOPHER. *Studies in a Dying Culture.* London: 1938.

CHANCE, JANET. *The Cost of English Morals.* London: 1935.

CHAPMAN, AGATHA L. *Wages and Salaries in the United Kingdom, 1920–1938.* Cambridge: 1953.

CHAPMAN, ANNIE, and CHAPMAN, MARIE. *Status of Women under the English Law.* London: 1909.

CHESSER, E. S. *Woman, Marriage and Motherhood.* London: 1913.

CHESTERTON, G. K. *Eugenics and Other Evils.* London: 1922.

CLARKE, AMY KEY. *History of Cheltenham Ladies' College, 1853–1953.* London: 1953.

CLEPHANE, IRENE. *Ourselves, 1900–1930.* London: 1933.

———. *Towards Sex Freedom.* London: 1935.

COHEN, EMMELINE W. *The Growth of the British Civil Service, 1780–1939.* London: 1941.

COLE, G. D. H., et al. *Some Problems of Urban and Rural Industry.* London: 1917.

COLE, G. D. H. *Trade Unionism and Munitions.* Oxford: 1923.

COLE, MARGARET. *Marriage: Past and Present.* London: 1938.

COLLET, CLARA E. *Educated Working Women.* London: 1902.

———. *Women in Industry.* London: 1911.

COLLIER, K. G. *The Social Purposes of Education.* London: 1959.

COLLINS, M. *Women Graduates and the Teaching Profession.* Manchester: 1964.

COLQUHOUN, ETHEL. *The Vocation of Woman.* London: 1913.

COMER, LEE. *Wedlocked Women.* London: 1974.

COMINOS, PETER J. "Late-Victorian Sexual Respectability and the Social System." *International Review of Social History* 8 (1963): 18–48, 216–50.

CONWAY, JILL. "Stereotypes of Femininity in a Theory of Sexual Evolution." *Victorian Studies* 14 (1970): 47–62.

COOPER, DAVID. *Death of the Family.* New York: 1970. London: 1972.

CORIN, JAMES. *Mating, Marriage, and the Status of Women.* London: 1910.

COURTNEY, JANET ELIZABETH. *Countrywoman in Council.* London: 1933.

COURTNEY, K. D., et al. *Equal Pay and the Family.* London: 1918.

CRAIG, ALEC. *Sex and Revolution.* London: 1934.

CRAIG, SIR JOHN. *A History of Red Tape: An Account of the Origin and Development of the Civil Service.* London: 1955.

CULLIS, WINIFRED C. "The Impact of the War upon British Family Life." *Journal of Marriage and the Family* 4 (1942): 10–11.

CURLE, RICHARD. *Women: An Analytical Study.* London: 1947.

CURTIS, STANLEY JAMES. *Education in Britain since 1900.* London: 1952.

———. *History of Education in Great Britain.* 7th rev. ed. London: 1967.

DAVIDOFF, LEONORE. *The Best Circles: Society, Etiquette and the Season.* London: 1973. (*The Best Circles: Women and Society in Victorian England.* Totawa, N.J.: 1973.)

———. "Mastered for Life: Servant and Wife in Victorian and Edwardian England." *Journal of Social History* 7 (1974): 406–28.

———. "The Rationalization of Housework." In *Dependence and Exploitation in Work and Marriage,* edited by Sheila Allen and Diana Barker. London: 1976.

————; L'Esperance, Jean; and Newby, Howard. "Landscape with Figures: Home and Community in English Society." In *The Rights and Wrongs of Women*, edited by Juliet Mitchell and Ann Oakley. London: 1976.

Davies, Emily. *Home and the Higher Education of Women*. London: 1898.

————. *Thoughts on Some Questions Relating to Women*. Cambridge: 1910.

————. *Women in the Universities of England and Scotland*. Cambridge: 1896.

Davies, Maude. *Life in an English Village*. London: 1909.

Davis, Natalie Zemon. "'Women's History' in Transition: The European Case." *Feminist Studies* 3 (1976): 83–103.

Dearle, Norman. *The Cost of Living*. London: 1926.

Dennis, Norman; Henriques, Fernando; and Slaughter, Clifford. *Coal is Our Life: An Analysis of a Yorkshire Mining Community*. London: 1956.

Dent, Harold Collett. *The Educational System of England and Wales*. 3d rev. ed. London: 1966.

————. *1870–1970: Century of Growth in English Education*. London: 1970.

Dingle, E. E. "Drink and Working-Class Living Standards in Britain, 1870–1914." *Economic History Review*, 2d series, 25 (1972): 608–22.

Dobbs, A. E. *Education and Social Movements*. London: 1919.

Dodd, J. Theodore. "Women as Justices of the Peace." *Contemporary Review* 112 (1917): 320–27.

Doherty, B. "Hadow Report, 1926." *Durham Research Review* 4 (1964): 117–27.

Donnison, Jean. *Medical Men and Midwives*. London and New York: 1977.

Douie, Vera. *Daughters of Britain*. London: 1949.

————. *The Lesser Half*. London: 1943.

Drake, Barbara. *Some Problems of Education*. Fabian Tract no. 198. London: 1922.

————. *Women in the Engineering Trades*. London: 1917.

————. *Women in the Trade Unions*. London: 1920.

Drysdale, Charles Vickering. *The Small Family System: Is It Injurious or Immoral?* London: 1913.

Dyhouse, Carol. "Good Wives and Little Mothers: Social Anxieties and the Schoolgirl's Curriculum. 1890–1920." *Oxford Review of Education* 3 (1977): 21–35.

————. "Social Darwinistic Ideas and the Development of Women's Education in England, 1880–1920." *History of Education* 5 (1976): 41–58.

Eaglesham, E. J. R. *The Foundations of Twentieth Century Education in England*. London and New York: 1967.

Edgeworth. J. "Equal Pay to Men and Women for Equal Work." *Economic Journal* 32 (1922): 431–57.

*The Education of Women and Girls: A List of Books and Articles in the Institute Library*. Leeds: 1966.

Elderton, E. M. *Report on the English Birth-Rate*. London: 1914.

Elliott, Dorothy M. "The Status of Domestic Workers in the United Kingdom." *International Labour Review* 63 (1951): 125–48.

Ellis, Havelock. *The Problem of Race-Regeneration*. London: 1911.

————. *Studies in the Psychology of Sex*. 6 vols. London: 1894–1910.

————. "Employment of Married Women and Mothers of Families." *International Labour Review* 63 (1951): 677–97.

Evans, Dorothy. *Women in the Civil Service*. London: 1934.

Eyles, Leonora. *The Woman in the Little House*. London: 1922.

————. *Women's Problems of Today*. London: 1926.

FAIRFIELD, ZOE. *The Woman's Movement*. London: 1911.

FARMER, MARY. *The Family*. London and New York: 1970.

FAWCETT, G. M. "Cambridge and Women's Education," *Contemporary Review* 116 (1919): 518–22.

———. "Equal Pay for Equal Value." *Contemporary Review* 114 (1918): 387–90.

FERGUSON, NEAL A. "Women's Work: Employment Opportunities and Economic Roles, 1918–1939." *Albion* 7 (1975): 55–68.

FIRTH, CATHERINE BEATRICE. *Constance Louisa Maynard, Mistress of Westfield College: A Family Portrait*. London: 1949.

FISHER, HERBERT A. L. *Unfinished Autobiography*. London: 1940.

FISHER, JOHN. *The World of the Forsytes*. New York: 1976.

FLETCHER, RONALD. *The Family and Marriage in Britain: An Analysis and Moral Assessment*. London and Baltimore: 1966.

FORD, ISABELLA. *Women and Socialism*. London: 1904.

FORD, PERCY, and FORD, GRACE. *A Breviate of Parliamentary Papers, 1900–1916*. Oxford: 1957. Reprint rev. ed. Shannon: 1969. (Rev. ed. has subtitle: *The Foundation of the Welfare State.*)

———. *A Breviate of Parliamentary Papers, 1917–1939*. Oxford: 1951. Reprint rev. ed. Shannon: 1969.

———. *A Breviate of Parliamentary Papers, 1940–1954: War and Reconstruction*. Oxford: 1961.

FORSTER, E. M. *Howard's End*. London: 1910.

FRANKENSTEIN, LUISE. "Women in Industrial Welfare Work." *International Labour Review* 40 (1939): 297–319.

FRANKLIN, JILL. "Troops of Servants: Labour and Planning in the Country House, 1840–1914." *Victorian Studies* 19 (1975): 211–40.

FRANZ, NELLIE ALDEN. *English Women Enter the Professions*. Cincinnati, Ohio: 1965.

GALLICHAN, W. M. *The Great Unmarried*. London: 1916.

GARDINER, DOROTHY. *English Girlhood at School*. Oxford: 1929.

GARDINER, JEAN. "Political Economy of Domestic Labour in Capitalist Society." In *Dependence and Exploitation in Work and Marriage*, edited by Sheila Allen and Diana Barker. London: 1976.

GATES, G. EVELYN, ed. *The Woman's Year Book, 1923/24–*. London: 1924–.

GAVRON, HANNAH. *The Captive Wife: Conflicts of Housebound Mothers*. London and New York: 1966.

GILLIS, JOHN R. "Evolution of Juvenile Delinquency in England, 1890–1914." *Past and Present*, no. 69 (1975): 96–126.

———. *Youth and History*. London and New York: 1974.

GLASS, DAVID V. "Divorce in England and Wales." *Sociological Review* 26 (1934): 288–308.

———, ed. *Social Mobility in Britain*. London: 1954.

———, and GREBNIK, ERNEST. *The Trend and Pattern of Fertility in Great Britain: A Report on the Family Census of 1946*. London: 1954.

GLAZER-MALBIN, NONA. "Housework." *Signs. Journal of Women in Culture and Society*. 1 (1976): 905–22.

GOLDSMITH, MARGARET. *Women at War*. London: 1943.

GOODE, WILLIAM J. *World Revolution and Family Patterns*. New York: 1963.

GORER, GEOFFREY. *Exploring English Character*. London and New York: 1955.

GOULDNER, ALVIN W. *The Coming Crisis of Western Sociology*. New York: 1970.

GRANT, JULIA MARY. *St. Leonard's School, 1877–1927*. Oxford: 1927.

GRAVES, J. *Policy and Progress in Secondary Education, 1902–1942.* London: 1943.

GRAVES, ROBERT, and HODGE, ALAN. *The Long Weekend: A Social History of Great Britain, 1918–1939.* London: 1940.

GRAVESON, RONALD HARRY, and CRANE, FRANCIS ROGER, eds. *A Century of Family Law.* London: 1957.

GRAY, J. L., and MOSHINSKY, PEARL. "Ability and Educational Opportunity in English Education." *Sociological Review* 27 (1935): 113–61.

GREAT BRITAIN. *Abolition of Tuition Fees in Grant-Aided Secondary Schools.* London: 1943.

————. *Adult Education in England and Wales.* London: 1954.

————. *Differentiation of Curricula between the Sexes in Secondary Schools.* London: 1923.

————. *Education and Industry.* London: 1926, 1928.

————. *Education and the Adolescent.* London: 1926.

————. *Employment of Women in Agriculture in England and Wales.* London: 1920.

————. *Higher Education Report.* London: 1963.

————. *Parliamentary Papers*, vol. 17, "Attendance, Compulsory or Otherwise at Continuation Schools." Cd. 4757, 1909, p. 1.

————. *Parliamentary Papers*, vol. 13, "Clerical and Commercial Employment." Cd. 8110, 1914–16. p. 1.

————. *Parliamentary Papers*, vol. 4, "Domestic Help." Cmd. 6481, 1942–43, p. 271.

————. *Parliamentary Papers*, vol. 29, "Domestic Service." Cmd. 67, 1919, p. 1.

————. *Parliamentary Papers*, vol. 11, "Education, 1900–1950." Cmd. 8244, 1950–51, p. 261.

————. *Parliamentary Papers*, vol. 11, "Employment of Older Men and Women." Cmd. 8963, 1952–53, p. 1

————. *Parliamentary Papers*, vol. 25, "Employment of School Children." Cd. 849, Cd. 895, 1902, p. 261.

————. *Parliamentary Papers*, vol. 19, "Employment of Women and Young Persons on the Two Shift System." Cmd. 1037, 1920, p. 519.

————. *Parliamentary Papers*, vol. 89, "Expenditures of Wage Earning Women and Girls." Cd. 5963, 1911, p. 531.

————. *Parliamentary Papers*, vol. 21, "General Reports on Higher Education." Cd. 1738, 1903, p. 243.

————. *Parliamentary Papers*, vol. 23, "Health of Munition Workers." Cd. 8185, 1916, p. 417.

————. *Parliamentary Papers*, vol. 16, "Health of Munition Workers." Cd. 8511, 1917–18, p. 1019.

————. *Parliamentary Papers*, vol. 73, "Industrial Training of Girls." Cd. 237, 1900, p. 335.

————. *Parliamentary Papers*, vol. 10, "The Marriage Bar in the Civil Service." Cmd. 6886, 1945–46, p. 871.

————. *Parliamentary Papers*, vol. 65, "The Number of Boys and Girls in Public Elementary Schools." (28), 1912–13, p. 475.

————. *Parliamentary Papers*, vol. 17, "Partial Exemption from School Attendance." Cd. 4791, 1909, p. 731.

————. *Parliamentary Papers*, vol. 5, "Post-War Organisation of Private Domestic Employment." Cmd. 6650, 1944–45, p. 1.

————. *Parliamentary Papers*, vol. 20, "Practical Work in Secondary Schools." Cd. 6849, 1913, p. 291.

———. *Parliamentary Papers*, vol. 11, Royal Commission on Equal Pay. Cmd. 6937, 1945–46, p. 651.

———. *Parliamentary Papers*, vol. 19, Royal Commission on Population. Cmd. 7695, 1948–49, p. 635.

———. *Parliamentary Papers*, vol. 21, "Salaries for Teachers in Public Elementary Schools." Cmd. 443, 1919, p. 413.

———. *Parliamentary Papers*, vol. 8, "Scholarships for Higher Education." Cd. 8291, 1916, p. 327.

———. *Parliamentary Papers*, vol. 15, "Scholarships, Free Places, and Maintenance Allowances." Cmd. 968, 1920, p. 385.

———. *Parliamentary Papers*, vol. 19, "School Training and Early Employment of Lancashire Children." Cd. 1867, 1904, p. 681.

———. *Parliamentary Papers*, vol. 40, "University Education in London." Cd. 6717, 1913, p. 297.

———. *Parliamentary Papers*, vol. 30, "Women in Industry." Cmd. 135, 1919, p. 219.

———. *Parliamentary Papers*, vol. 29, "Women in the Government Departments." Cmd. 199, 1919, p. 153.

———. *Parliamentary Papers*, vols. 37, "Women's War Employment." Cd. 7848, 1914–16, p. 669.

———. *Physique of Women in Industry*. London: 1927.

———. *Practical Education for Women in Rural Life*. London: 1928.

———. *The Primary School*. London: 1931.

———. *Psychological Tests of Educable Capacity*. London: 1924.

———. *Secondary Education*. London: 1938.

———. *Staffing the Hospitals—An Urgent National Need*. London: 1945.

———. *Supply of Domestic Servants*. London: 1923.

———. *Supply of Women Teachers*. London: 1949.

———. *Teachers' Salaries*. London: 1947, 1948, 1951.

———. *Training and Supply of Teachers*. London: 1951.

GREEVES, F. M. *Leyton County High School for Girls: A Golden Jubilee History*. Leyton: 1962.

GRIBBLE, FRANCIS. *The Fight for Divorce*. London: 1932.

GROVE, LADY AGNES. "Feminism and Marriage: A Reply." *Nineteenth Century and After* 100 (1926): 467–70.

GRYLLS, ROSALIE GLYNN. *Queen's College, 1848–1948*. London: 1948.

HAIRE, NORMAN. *Hymen, or the Future of Marriage*. London: 1927.

———. *Marriage and Morals*. London: 1929.

———. *Some More Medical Views on Birth Control*. London: 1928.

HAJNAL, J. "Aspects of Recent Trends in Marriage in England and Wales." *Population Studies* 1 (1947): 72–98.

HALDANE, CHARLOTTE. *Motherhood and Its Enemies*. London and New York: 1928.

HALDANE, ELIZABETH SANDERSON. "Adult Education in Rural Districts." *Nineteenth Century and After* 95 (1924): 609–17.

HALL, RUTH. *Passionate Crusader: The Life of Marie Stopes*. New York and London: 1977. (British edition has title: *Marie Stopes*.)

HALLSWORTH, JOSEPH. *Protective Legislation for Shops and Office Employees*. London: 1932.

———, and DAVIES, RHYS J. *The Working Life of Shop Assistants: Conditions of Labour in the Distributive Trades*. Manchester: 1910.

HALMOS, P. "The Personal Service Society." *British Journal of Sociology* 8 (1967): 13–27.

HALSEY, ALBERT H., ed. *Education, Economy, and Society*. London: 1961.

———, ed. *Trends in British Society since 1900*. London and New York: 1972.

HAMILTON, CICELY. *Marriage as a Trade*. London: 1910.

HAMILTON, MARY AGNES. *Newnham, an Informal Biography*. London: 1936.

———. *Mary Macarthur*. London: 1925.

———. *Women at Work*. London: 1941.

HANCOCK, W. K., and GOWING, M. M. *British War Economy*. London: 1949.

HANHAM, HAROLD J. *Bibliography of British History, 1851–1914*. London: 1976.

HARRIS, CHRISTOPHER C. *The Family: An Introduction*. London: 1969.

HARRISON, JOHN F. C. *Learning and Living, 1790–1960: A Study in the History of the English Adult Education Movement*. London: 1961.

HARROD, ROY. "Equal Pay for Men and Women." In *Economic Essays*. London: 1952.

HARTLEY, CATHERINE GASQUOINE. *Divorce*. London: 1921.

———. *Mother and Son: A Psychological Study of Character Formation in Children*. London: 1923.

———. *Motherhood and the Relationships of the Sexes*. London and New York: 1917.

———. *Sex Education and National Health*. London: 1920.

———. *The Truth about Women*. London: 1913.

HAYNES, E. S. P. *Divorce as It Might Be*. Cambridge: 1915.

HEINEMANN, WILLIAM, and THOMPSON, DONNA F. *Professional Solidarity among Teachers of England*. London and New York: 1927.

HENRIQUES, FERNANDO. *Love in Action: The Sociology of Sex*. London: 1960 (c. 1959). (American ed. New York: 1960 [c. 1959].)

HERBERT, ALAN PATRICK. *The Ayes Have It*. London: 1937.

———. *Holy Deadlock*. London: 1934.

HINE, G. M. *The Lancastrian School for Girls, Chichester, 1812–1962*. Chichester: 1962.

HIRSCHMANN, IDA. "The Surplus of Women and the Declining Birth-Rate." *Sociological Review* 27 (1935): 344–58.

*History Workshop Journal: A Journal of Socialist Historians*. Edited by Raphael Samuel, et al. London: 1976–.

HOBMAN, D. L. *Olive Schreiner: Her Friends and Times*. London: 1955.

HOFFNER, CLAIRE. "Recent Developments in Compulsory Systems of Family Allowances." *International Labour Review* 41 (1940): 337–61.

HOGG, M. H. "Dependents on Women Wage-earners." *Economica* 1 (1921): 69–86.

HOGGART, RICHARD. *The Uses of Literacy: Aspects of Working-Class Life, with Special References to Publications and Entertainments*. London: 1957. Reprint. Oxford: 1970. (U.S. ed. has title: *The Uses of Literacy: Changing Patterns in English Mass Culture*. Boston: 1961.)

HOLCOMBE, LEE. *Victorian Ladies at Work: Middle-Class Working Women in England and Wales, 1850–1914*. Camden, N.J.: 1973. London: 1974.

HOLTBY, WINIFRED. *Women in a Changing Civilization*. London: 1957.

HORN, PAMELA. *The Rise and Fall of the Victorian Servant*. Dublin and New York: 1975.

HUBBACK, JUDITH. *Wives Who Went to College*. London: 1957.

HUGHES, FRED. *By Hand and Brain: The Story of the Clerical Administrative Workers' Union*. London: 1953.

HUGHES, W. G., and SWEENEY, M. *Walford Grammar School for Boys and Girls, 1704–1954: A History of Their Foundations and Development*. Walford: 1954.

HUMPHREYS, B. V. *Clerical Unions in the Civil Service*. London: 1958.
HUTCHINS, (ELIZABETH) B. L. *Conflicting Ideals: Two Sides of the Woman's Question*. London: 1913.
————. "Woman's Industrial Career." *Sociological Review* 2 (1909): 338–48.
————. *Women in Modern Industry*. London: 1915.
HYNES, SAMUEL J. *The Edwardian Turn of Mind*. Princeton, N.J.: 1968.
IKIN, A. E. "Educable Capacity—Statistical Results of an Enquiry." *Times Educational Supplement*, 26 September 1918.
INNES, J. W. *Class Fertility Trends in England and Wales, 1876–1934*. Princeton, N.J.: 1938.
JACKSON, BRIAN, and MARSDEN, DENNIS. *Education and the Working Class*. London: 1959.
JAMES, EDWARD. "Women at Work in Twentieth Century Britain: The Changing Structure of Female Employment." *Manchester School of Economic and Social Studies* 30 (1962): 283–99.
JEFFERYS, JAMES B. *Retail Trading in Britain, 1850–1950*. Cambridge: 1954.
JEFFERYS, MARGOT. "Married Women in the Higher Grades of the Civil Service and Government Sponsored Research Organisations." *British Journal of Sociology* 3 (1952): 361–64.
JEPHCOTT, AGNES PEARL. *Girls Growing Up*. London: 1942.
————. *Married Women Working*. London: 1962.
————. *Rising Twenty*. London: 1948.
————. *Some Young People*. London: 1954.
JEROME, HELEN (BRUTON). *The Secret of Woman*. London and New York: 1923.
JOHANSSON, SHEILA RYAN. "Sex and Death in Victorian England: An Examination of Age- and Sex-Specific Death Rates, 1840–1910." In *A Widening Sphere: Women in the Victorian Age*, edited by Martha Vicinus. Bloomington, Ind.: 1977.
JONES, D. CARADOG. "Notes on the Census of Occupations for England and Wales." *Royal Statistical Journal* 78 (1915): 55–78.
————, ed. *The Social Survey of Merseyside*. Liverpool: 1934.
JONES, LANCE G. E. *The Training of Teachers in England and Wales*. London: 1924.
KAHN, HILDA R. *Salaries in the Public Services in England and Wales*. London: 1962.
KAMM, JOSEPHINE. *Hope Deferred*. London: 1956.
————. *How Different from Us: A Biography of Miss Buss and Miss Beale*. London: 1958.
————. *Indicative Past: One Hundred Years of the Girls' Public Day School Trust*. London: 1971.
KANNER, BARBARA. "The Women of England in a Century of Social Change, 1815–1914: A Select Annotated Bibliography, Part II." In *A Widening Sphere: Women in the Victorian Age*, edited by Martha Vicinus. Bloomington, Ind.: 1977.
————. "The Women of England in a Century of Social Change, 1815–1914: A Select Bibliography." In *Suffer and Be Still: Women in the Victorian Age*, edited by Martha Vicinus. Bloomington, Ind.: 1972.
KELLY-GADOL, JOAN. "The Social Relations of the Sexes: Methodological Implications of Women's History." *Signs. Journal of Women in Culture and Society* 1 (1976): 809–28.
KELSALL, R. K. *Higher Civil Servants in Britain*. London: 1955.
————. *Women in Teaching*. London: 1963.

KENEALY, ARABELLA. *Feminism and Sex Extinction.* London: 1920.

KEY, ELLEN. *Woman Movement.* New York: 1919.

KLEIN, JOSEPHINE. *Child Rearing Practices.* Vol. 2 of *Samples from English Cultures.* London: 1965.

KLEIN, VIOLA. "The Demand for Professional Womanpower." *British Journal of Sociology* 17 (1966): 183–97.

———. *Feminine Character: History of an Ideology.* London: 1945. Reprint. Urbana, Ill.: 1971.

KLINGENDER, F. D. *The Condition of Clerical Labour in Britain.* London: 1935.

KNOWLES, JOSEPHINE PITCAIRN. *The Upholstered Cage.* London: 1913.

Labour Party, Great Britain, Study Group on Discrimination Against Women. *Discrimination against Women: Report of a Labour Party Study Group.* London: 1972.

*The Labour Woman: A Political Monthly Journal for Working Women.* London: 1922–27.

*Labour Year Book.* London: 1916–32.

LAMB, FELICIA, and PICKTHORN, HELEN. *Locked-up Daughters: A Parents' Look at Girls' Education and Schools.* London: 1968.

LANE, EDITH, and MacNAMARA, FANNY. *Nails.* London: 1920.

LANG, ELSIE M. *British Women in the Twentieth Century.* London: 1929.

LASCH, CHRISTOPHER. "The Family and History." *New York Review of Books* 22 (13, 27 Nov.; 11 Dec. 1975): 33–38, 37–42, 50–55.

LAWSON, JOHN, and SILVER, HAROLD. *A Social History of Education in England.* London and New York: 1973.

LEWENHAK, SHEILA. *Women and Trade Unions: An Outline History of Women in the British Trade Union Movement.* London and Tonbridge: 1977.

LEWIS, JANE. "Beyond Suffrage: English Feminism in the 1920's." *Maryland Historian* 6 (1975): 1–17.

LEWIS, ROY, and MAUDE, ANGUS. *The English Middle Classes.* London: 1953.

LINDSAY, KENNETH. *Social Progress and Educational Waste.* London: 1926.

LIPINSKA, MELANIE, and MACKENZIE, MUIR. "Women Doctors: An Historic Retrospect." *Contemporary Review* 108 (1915): 504–10.

LITTLE, E. GRAHAM. "Undergraduate Medical Education of Women in London." *Nineteenth Century and After* 103 (1928): 665–77.

LOCKWOOD, DAVID. *The Blackcoated Worker: A Study in Class Consciousness.* London: 1958.

LONGMATE, NORMAN. *How We Lived Then: A History of Everyday Life during the Second World War.* London: 1971.

LOW, FLORENCE B. "The Educational Ladder and the Girl." *Nineteenth Century and After* 42 (1907): 395–405.

LOWNDES, G. A. N. *The Silent Social Revolution: An Account of the Expansion of Public Education in England and Wales, 1895–1965.* 2d rev. ed. Oxford and New York: 1969.

LUETKENS, CHARLOTTE. *Women and a New Society.* London: 1946.

MACARTHUR, MARY R., et al. *Woman in Industry from Seven Points of View.* London: 1908.

McBRIDE, THERESA. *The Domestic Revolution: The Modernization of Household Service in England and France, 1820–1920.* London and New York: 1976.

MacDONALD, J. RAMSAY. *Women in the Printing Trades.* London: 1904.

McGREGOR, OLIVER ROSS. *Divorce in England.* London: 1957.

———. "The Social Position of Women in England, 1850–1914: A Bibliography." *British Journal of Sociology* 6 (1955): 48–60.

McLaren, Angus. "Abortion in England, 1890–1914." *Victorian Studies* 20 (1977): 379–400.

———. *Birth Control in Nineteenth Century England*. London and New York: 1978.

McMillan, Margaret. *The Child and the State*. Manchester: 1911.

McWilliams-Tullberg, Rita. *A Men's University; but of a Mixed Type*. Cambridge: 1974.

———. "Women and Degrees at Cambridge University." In *A Widening Sphere: Women in the Victorian Age*, edited by Martha Vicinus. Bloomington, Ind.: 1977.

Magnus, Laurie. *The Jubilee Book of the Girl's Public Day School Trust, 1873–1923*. Cambridge: 1923.

Magnus, Sir Philip. *Educational Aims and Efforts, 1880–1910*. London: 1910.

Malinowski, Bronislaw. *Argonauts of the Western Pacific*. London and New York: 1922.

———. *The Father in Primitive Psychology*. London: 1927.

Marchant, James, ed. *Medical Views on Birth Control*. London: 1926.

Marder, Herbert. *Feminism and Art: A Study of Virginia Woolf*. Chicago: 1968.

Marks, Pauline. "Femininity in the Classroom: An Account of Changing Attitudes." In *The Rights and Wrongs of Women*, edited by Juliet Mitchell and Ann Oakley. London: 1976.

Marsden, Dennis. *Mothers Alone: Poverty and the Fatherless Family*. London: 1969. Paperback edition. Harmondsworth, England: 1973.

Marsh, David C. *The Changing Social Structure of England and Wales, 1871–1951*. London: 1958.

Martin, Anna. "The Married Working Woman." *Nineteenth Century and After* 68 (1910): 1,102–18.

Martindale, Hilda. *Women Servants of the State, 1820–1938*. London: 1938.

Marwick, Arthur. *The Deluge: British Society and the First World War*. London: 1965.

———. *The Home Front: The British and the Second World War*. London: 1977.

———. "Youth in Britain, 1920–1970." *Journal of Contemporary History* 5 (1970): 37–51.

*Maternity: Letters from Working-Women Collected by the Women's Cooperative Guild*. London: 1915.

May, Geoffrey. *Social Control of Sex Expression*. New York: 1931.

Meikle, Wilma. *Towards a Sane Feminism*. New York and London: 1917.

Mess, Henry Adolphus. *Factory Legislation and Its Administration, 1891–1924*. London: 1926.

Middleton, Lucy, ed. *Women in the Labour Movement*. London: 1976.

Middleton, Nigel, and Weitzmann, Sophie. *A Place for Everyone: A History of State Education from the End of the 18th Century to the 1970's*. London: 1976.

Mitchell, David. *Monstrous Regiment: The Story of the Women of the First World War*. London and New York: 1965.

Mitchell, Juliet. "Four Structures in a Complex Unity." In *Liberating Women's History: Theoretical and Critical Essays*, edated by Bernice Carroll. Urbana, Ill., and London: 1976.

———. *Psychoanalysis and Feminism*. London and New York: 1974.

————. "Women and Equality." In *The Rights and Wrongs of Women*, edited by Juliet Mitchell and Ann Oakley. London: 1976.

————. *Woman's Estate*. London and New York: 1971.

MOBERLY, WINIFRED H. "The Oxford Women's College." *Contemporary Review* 11 (1921): 384–88.

MOGEY, JOHN MACFARLANE. *Rural Life in Northern Ireland*. London: 1947.

MONTAGUE, LILY H. "The Girl in the Background." In *Studies of Boy Life in Our Cities*, edited by E. J. Urwick. London: 1904.

MORLEY, E. J., ed. *Women Workers in Seven Professions*. London: 1914.

MORGAN, DAVID H. J. *Social Theory and the Family*. London and New York: 1975.

MOSLEY, OSWALD. *The Greater Britain*. London: 1932.

MOWAT, CHARLES LOCH. *Britain between the Wars, 1918–1940*. Chicago: 1940.

MUNRO, C. K. *The True Woman: A Handbook for Husbands and Others*. London: 1932.

MURRAY, FLORA. *Women as Army Surgeons*. London: 1920.

MYRDAL, ALVA, and KLEIN, VIOLA. *Women's Two Roles: Home and Work*. 2d rev. ed. London: 1968. Atlantic Highlands, N.J.: 1970.

NEWITT, HILLARY. *Women Must Choose: The Position of Women in Europe Today*. London: 1937.

NEWSOME, JOHN. *The Education of Girls*. London: 1948.

NORMANTON, H., and FAWCETT, M. G. "Women." *Encyclopedia Britannica*. 13th ed. London and Chicago: 1926.

NOTTINGHAM, ELIZABETH K. "Toward an Analysis of the Effects of Two World Wars on the Role and Status of Middle-Class Women in the English Speaking World." *American Sociological Review* 12 (1947): 666–75.

NUTTING, MARY ADELAIDE, and DOCK, LAVINIA L. *A History of Nursing: The Evolution of Nursing Systems from the Earliest Times to the Foundation of the First English and American Training Schools for Nurses*. 4 vols. New York: 1907–12. Reprint. Buffalo, New York: 1974–.

OAKLEY, ANN. *Housewife!* London: 1974. (American ed. has title: *Woman's Work: The Housewife, Past and Present*. New York: 1976.)

————. *Sex, Gender, and Society*. London: 1972.

————. *The Sociology of Housework*. London: 1974. New York: 1975(c. 1974).

————. "Wisewoman and Medicine Man: Changes in the Management of Childbirth." In *The Rights and Wrongs of Women*, edited by Juliet Mitchell and Ann Oakley. London and New York: 1976.

OGBURN, W. F. *Social Change*. New York: 1922.

OLLERENSHAW, KATHLEEN. *Education for Girls*. London: 1961.

————. *The Girls' Schools: The Future of the Public and Other Independent Schools for Girls in the Context of State Education*. London: 1967.

*Oral History*. Vol. 1–(1973–). Journal of the Oral History Society, Essex University.

OREN, LAURA. "The Welfare of Women in Laboring Families: England, 1860–1950." In *Clio's Consciousness Raised*, edited by Mary Hartmann and Lois Banner. New York: 1974.

PAPWORTH, LUCY WYATT. *Women in Industry: A Bibliography*. London: 1915.

————, and ZIMMERN, D. M. *The Occupations of Women*. London: 1914.

PARSONS, TALCOTT, and BALES, ROBERT B., eds. *Family, Socialization and Interaction Process*. Glencoe, Ill.: 1955.

PARTINGTON, GEOFFREY. *Women Teachers in the Twentieth Century*. London and New York: 1976.

PATON, GRACE M. *The Child and the Nation*. London: 1915.

PAUL, CHARLES KEGAN. *The Headmistress Speaks.* London: 1935.

PAUL, EDEN. *Chronos or the Future of the Family.* London: 1930.

PAYNE, DOROTHY. *Women without Men: Creative Living for Singles, Divorcees and Widows.* Philadelphia: 1969.

PEARSON, KARL, and ELDERTON, E. M. *On the Correlation of Fertility with Social Value.* London: 1913.

PERCIVAL, ALICIA C. *The English Miss Today and Yesterday.* London: 1939.

PETO, D. O. G. "Police Work for Women." *Contemporary Review* 113 (1918): 531–37.

PHILLIPS, MARION, ed. *Women and the Labour Party.* London: 1918.

PIERCE, RACHEL M. "Marriage in the Fifties." *Sociological Review* 11 (1963): 215–40.

PIERPOINT, RAYMOND. *Report of the Fifth International Neo-Malthusian and Birth Control Conference.* London: 1922.

PINCHBECK, IVY, and HEWITT, MARGARET. *Children in English Society,* Volume II: *From the Eighteenth Century to the Children Act of 1848.* London and Toronto: 1973.

PLECK, ELIZABETH H. "Two Worlds in One." *Journal of Social History* 10 (1976): 178–95.

POMERAI, RALPH DE. *Marriage: Past, Present, and Future.* London: 1930.

POWELL, MARGARET. *Below Stairs.* London: 1968. New York: 1970.

PRIESTLY, J. B. *British Women Go to War.* London: n.d.

RADCLIFFE-BROWN, ALFRED REGINALD. *The Andaman Islanders.* Cambridge: 1922.

———. *Structure and Function in Primitive Society.* London: 1952.

RAIKES, ELIZABETH. *Dorothea Beale of Cheltenham.* London: 1908.

RAPOPORT, RHONA, and RAPOPORT, ROBERT. *Dual-Career Families.* London: 1971.

RATHBONE, ELEANOR FLORENCE. *The Disinherited Family: A Plea for the Endowment of the Family.* London: 1924.

RAVENHILL, ALICE. *Eugenic Education for Women and Girls.* London: 1908.

REES, ALWYN D. *Life in a Welsh Countryside.* Cardiff: 1950.

REEVES, MRS. PEMBER. *Round about a Pound a Week.* London: 1913.

REISS, ERNA. *Rights and Duties of Englishwomen: A Study in Law and Public Opinion.* Manchester: 1934.

REYNOLDS, MYRA. *The Learned Lady in England.* New York: 1920.

RIVERS, W. H. R. *Social Organisation.* London: 1924.

ROBERTS, BENJAMIN C. *Trade Union Government in Great Britain.* London: 1956.

ROGERS, ANNIE M. A. H. *Degrees by Degrees: The Story of the Admission of Oxford Women Students to Membership of the University.* London: 1938.

ROSSER, COLIN, and HARRIS, CHRISTOPHER. *The Family and Social Change.* London: 1965.

ROUTH, GUY. *Occupation and Pay in Britain, 1906–60.* Cambridge: 1965.

ROVER, CONSTANCE. *Love, Morals, and the Feminists.* London: 1970.

ROWBOTHAM, SHEILA. *Hidden from History: 300 Years of Women's Oppression and the Fight against It.* London: 1973. (American eds. have title: *Hidden from History: Rediscovering Women in History from the 17th Century to the Present.* New York: 1974. Paperback ed. New York: 1976.)

———. *Stella Browne, Feminism and Birth Control.* London: 1977.

———. *Woman's Consciousness, Man's World.* Harmondsworth, England: 1974.

———. *Women, Resistance and Revolution.* London: 1972. (American eds. have title: *Women, Resistance, and Revolution; A History of Women and Revolution in the Modern World.* New York: 1972. Paperback ed. New York: 1973.)

———. *Women's Liberation and Revolution: A Bibliography.* 2d rev. ed. Bristol: 1973.

ROWE, J. W. F. *Wages in Practice and Theory.* London: 1928.

ROWNTREE, B. SEEBOHM, and STUART, FRANK D. *The Responsibility of Women Workers for Dependents*. London: 1922.
ROWNTREE, G., and CARRIER, N. H. "The Resort to Divorce in England and Wales, 1858–1957." *Population Studies* 11 (1958): 188–223.
———, and PIERCE, R. M. "Birth Control in Britain." *Population Studies* 15 (1961): 3–31, 121–60.
Royal Commission on Divorce and Matrimonial Causes. *Report*. London: 1912.
ROYDEN, AGNES MAUDE. *Sex and Common Sense*. London: 1924.
RUBINSTEIN, DAVID. *School Attendance in London, 1870–1904: A Social History*. London: 1969.
RUSSELL, BERTRAND. *Marriage and Morals*. London: 1929.
RUSSELL, CHARLES. *The Problem of Juvenile Crime*. London: 1917.
RUSSELL, DORA WINIFRED. *Hypatia or Woman and Knowledge*. New York: 1925.
RUTTER, MICHAEL. *Maternal Deprivation Reassessed*. Harmondsworth, England, and Baltimore: 1972.
RYDER, JUDITH, and SILVER, HAROLD. *Modern English Society: History and Structure, 1850–1970*. London: 1970.
SALEEBY, CALEB W. *The Eugenic Prospect: National and Racial*. London: 1921.
SAMPSON, ANTHONY. *Anatomy of Britain Today*. Rev. ed. London: 1965.
SAMUEL, RAPHAEL, ed. *Miners, Quarrymen and Saltworkers*. London: 1977.
———. *Village Life and Labour*. London: 1975.
———. See also *History Workshop Journal*.
SANGER, MARGARET. *Family Limitation*. London: 1922.
SAUNDERS, ALEXANDER M. CARR, and JONES, D. CARADOG. *A Survey of the Social Structure of England and Wales*. London: 1937.
———, et al. *A Survey of Social Conditions in England and Wales*. Oxford: 1958.
SAYERS, DOROTHY L. *Gaudy Night*. London: 1935.
———. "The Woman Question." *Vogue* 109 (1947): 86, 128, 133.
SCHARLIEB, MARY ANN. "The Medical Education of Women." *Nineteenth Century and After* 92 (1922): 317–29.
———. *Womanhood and Race Regeneration*. London: 1911.
SCHNEIDER, JOSEPH. "Class Origin and Fame: Eminent English Women." *American Sociological Review* 5 (1940): 700–12.
SCHREINER, OLIVE. *Woman and Labour*. London and New York: 1911.
SELLECK, RICHARD J. W. *The New Education*. London: 1968.
SELLERS, EDITH. "Boy and Girl War Products." *Nineteenth Century and After* 84 (1918): 702–16.
SEYMER, LUCY RIDGLEY. *General History of Nursing*. 3rd ed. London: 1954.
SHARP, EVELYN. *Rebel Women*. London: 1915.
SHAW, GEORGE BERNARD. *Getting Married*. London: 1908.
———. *Misalliance*. London: 1910.
SHAW, JENNY. "Finishing School: Some Implications of Sex-Segregated Education." In *Sexual Divisions and Society: Process and Change*, edited by Sheila Allen and Diana Barker. London: 1976.
SHEPHERD, E. Colston. *The Fixing of Wages in Government Employment*. London: 1923.
SHORTER, EDWARD. *The Making of the Modern Family*. New York: 1975. Paperback ed. New York: 1977.
SHREWSBURY, JOHN FINDLAY DREW. *A History of Bubonic Plague in the British Isles*. London: 1970.
SIDGWICK, ETHEL. *Mrs. Henry Sidgwick*. London: 1938.

SIMON, BRIAN. *Education and the Labour Movement.* London and New York: 1965.

SKOLNICK, ARLENE. "The Family Revisited: Themes in Recent Social Science Research." *Journal of Interdisciplinary History* 5 (1975): 703–19.

SLATER, ELIOT, and WOODSIDE, MOYA. *Patterns of Marriage.* London: 1951.

SMITH, HUBERT LLEWELLYN. *The New Survey of London Life and Labour.* 9 vols. London: 1932–35.

SMITH, THOMAS ROBERT, ed. *The Woman Question.* New York: 1919.

SNOWDEN, ETHEL. *The Feminist Movement.* London: 1913.

SOLDON, NORBERT C. *Women in Labour.* New York, forthcoming.

SOMMERKORN, I. "The Position of Women in the University Teaching Profession in England." Ph.D. thesis, London University, 1966.

SPRING-RICE, MARGERY. *Working-Class Wives: Their Health and Conditions.* London: 1939.

STACEY, MARGARET. *Tradition and Change: A Study of Banbury.* London: 1953.

STEADMAN, FLORENCE CECILY. *In the Days of Miss Beale: A Study of Her Work and Influence.* Cheltenham: 1931.

STEARNS, PETER N. "Working-Class Women in Britain, 1890–1914." In *Suffer and Be Still: Women in the Victorian Age,* edited by Martha Vicinus. Bloomington, Ind.: 1972.

STEWART, W. A. C. *Progressives and Radicals in English Education, 1750–1970.* London: 1972.

STOIANOVICH, TRAIAN. *French Historical Method: The Annales Paradigm.* Ithaca, N.Y., and London: 1976.

STOPES, MARIE C. *The First Five Thousand.* London: 1925.

———. *Married Love.* London: 1920.

———. *Wise Parenthood.* London: 1919.

STRACHEY, OLIVER. "Married Women and Work." *Contemporary Review* 145 (1934): 332–36.

STRACHEY, PHILIPPA. *The Position of English Women in Relation to That of Men.* London: 1935.

STRACHEY, RAY (RACHEL CONN [COSTELLOE]). *"The Cause": A Short History of the Women's Movement in Great Britain.* London: 1928. (American ed. has title: *Struggle, The Stirring Story of Woman's Advance in England.* New York: 1930.) Reprint. Port Washington, N.Y.: 1969.

———. *Millicent Garrett Fawcett.* London: 1931.

———, ed. *Our Freedom and Its Results.* London: 1936.

STURMTHAL, ADOLF, ed. *White-Collar Trade Unions: Contemporary Developments in Industrialized Societies.* Urbana, Ill.: 1966.

SUTHERLAND, HALLIDAY. *Birth Control: A Statement of Christian Doctrine against the Neo-Malthusians.* London: 1922.

SWANWICK, HELENA MARIA. *The Future of the Women's Movement.* London: 1913.

SWINEY, FRANCES. *The Awakening of Women.* London: 1899.

TAWNEY, R. H., ed. *Secondary Education for All.* London: 1922.

TAYLOR, A. J. P. *English History, 1914–1945.* London: 1965.

THOMPSON, ALICE MARY CHARLOTTE, ed. *A Bibliography of Nursing Literature, 1859–1960.* London: 1968.

THOMPSON, BARBARA, and FINLAYSON, ANGELA. "Married Women Who Work in Early Motherhood." *British Journal of Sociology* 14 (1963): 150–68.

THOMPSON, PAUL. *The Edwardians: The Remaking of British Society.* London and Bloomington, Ind.: 1975.

TICKNER, FREDERICK WINDHAM. *Women in English Economic History.* London: 1923.

TILLY, LOUISE A.; SCOTT, JOAN W.; and Cohen, Miriam. "Women's Work and European Fertility Patterns." *Journal of Interdisciplinary History* 6 (1976): 447–76.

*Times Educational Supplement.* London: 1910–.

TITMUSS, RICHARD M. "The Position of Women in Relation to the Changing Family." In *British National Conference on Social Welfare.* London: 1953.

———, and TITMUSS, KATHLEEN. *Parents Revolt: A Study of the Declining Birth-Rate in Acquisitive Societies.* London: 1947.

TOOLEY, SARAH A. *The History of Nursing in the British Empire.* London: 1906.

TROOP, ASHER. *The School Teachers.* London: 1957.

TUKE, MARGARET. "Women Students in the Universities." *Contemporary Review* 133 (1928): 71–77.

TURNER, BARRY. *Equality for Some: The Story of Girls' Education.* London: 1974.

URWIN, EVELYN CLIFFORD. *Can the Family Survive?* London: 1944.

VELDE, THEODORE VAN DE. *Ideal Marriage.* Translated by Stella Browne. London: 1928.

VIGNE, THEA. "Family and Youth." *Oral History* 3, no. 2 ("Family History Issue," autumn 1975): 5.

———. "Parents and Children, 1890–1918: Distance and Dependence." *Oral History* 3, no. 2 ("Family History Issue," autumn 1975): 6–13.

WAKEFIELD, CHARLES C. *On Leaving School.* London: 1927.

WEBB, SIDNEY. *The Declining Birth-Rate.* Fablan Tract no. 131. London: 1911.

———, and WEBB, BEATRICE. *The History of Trade Unionism.* Rev. ed. London: 1920.

WELLS, H. G. *Ann Veronica.* London: 1909.

———. *A Modern Utopia.* London: 1905.

———. *Socialism and the Family.* London: 1906.

WELLS, ROBERT V. Review of Edward Shorter, *The Making of the Modern Family. Journal of Social History* 10 (1977): 361–64.

WESTERMARCK, EDWARD A. *The Future of Marriage in Western Civilisation.* London: 1937.

———. *The History of Human Marriage.* 5th rev. ed. London: 1921.

WHETHAM, W. C. D., and WHETHAM, CATHERINE. *The Family and the Nation: A Study in National Inheritance and Social Responsibility.* London: 1909.

———. *Heredity and Society.* London: 1912.

WILLIAMS, GERTRUDE. *Recruitment to Skilled Trades.* London: 1957.

———. *Women and Work.* London: 1945.

WILLIAMS, WILLIAM MORGAN. *The Sociology of an English Village: Gosforth.* London: 1956.

WILLIAMS-ELLIS, ANNABEL. *Women in War Factories.* London: 1943.

WILLMOTT, PETER, and YOUNG, MICHAEL. *Family and Class in a London Suburb.* London: 1960.

———. *Family and Kinship in East London.* London: 1957.

———. *The Symmetrical Family.* London: 1937. New York: 1974.

WINNICOTT, MORRIS. *The Child, the Family and the Outside World.* Harmondsworth, England: 1964.

WINSTANLEY, D. A. *Unreformed Cambridge.* London: 1935.

*Women's Industrial News.* London: 1895–1919.

*Women's Trade Union Review.* London. 1891–1919.

WOODHALL, MAUREEN. "Investment in Women: A Reappraisal of the Concept of Human Capital." *International Review of Education* 19 (1973): 9–29.

WOOLF, VIRGINIA. *A Room of One's Own*. London: 1929.

———. *Three Guineas*. London: 1938.

WOOTTON, BARBARA. "Twelve Criminological Hypotheses." In *Social Science and Social Pathology*. London: 1960.

*Year Book of Education*. London: 1932–40, 1948–.

YOUNG, MICHAEL. "Distribution of Income within the Family." *British Journal of Sociology* 3 (1952): 305–21.

———. *The Rise of the Meritocracy, 1870–2033: An Essay on Education and Equality*. London: 1958. New York: 1959.

YULE, G. UDNY. "On the Changes in the Marriage and Birth-rate in England and Wales during the Past Half-Century." *Journal of the Royal Statistical Society* 69 (1906): 88–132.

ZWEIG, FREDERICK. *Women's Life and Labour*. London: 1952.

# A Survey

## of Primary Sources and Archives

## for the History

## of Early Twentieth-Century English Women

JEFFREY WEEKS

The past decade has seen a major academic and political revival of interest in the history of women. Developments in social history, particularly the growth of subdisciplines such as demographic history, family history, and the history of sexuality, have helped to broaden the concept of what a "history of women" involves. Meanwhile, the revival on a mass scale of a feminist movement, with an active engagement with its prehistory and an on-going analysis of current attitudes towards women, has produced a new surge of research activity. One common theme amongst modern researchers is the interest in locating and using primary sources: correspondence, diaries, journal and informal records of organizations, occasional leaflets and pamphlets, and ephemera. It goes without saying that this trend has not gone forward without problems, particularly relating to the accessibility and preservation of such material.

In Britain, recent years have seen the development of a sustained interest in the preservation of twentieth-century archives, a significant element of which has been the growth of specialist archive centers. Though no single center has emerged for documenting the history of women, the Fawcett Library, which has grown from what was essentially a private collection, has become the best-known locus for the history on nineteenth- and early twentieth-century feminism. Manuscripts in the Fawcett collection include a great deal of material relating to the suffrage struggle, and there are also records of individuals and organizations involved in a wide range of other activities. In addition to a large collection of autograph letters and papers of organizations discussed in detail below, the collection also houses the records of a variety of groups such as the various women's emigration societies from 1862 (the Society for the Overseas Settlement of British Women and its predecessors), the Nationality of Women Committee, the Equal Pay Committee, the Association of Post Office Women Clerks, the Council of Women Civil Servants, the National Association of Women Civil Servants, the Consultative Committee of Women's Organizations, and the British Federation of Business and Professional Women. The nature and quality of these records vary from a small cache of unsorted material to a complete run of minutes and reports. *In toto* the records constitute a major collection of material, illustrating the wide range of women's social and professional activities. Some of the material, such as that relating to the emigration societies, is of unique significance. Many of the major collections of papers have been catalogued with the aid of financial assistance from the Social Science Research Council. In its new home at the City of London Polytechnic, the Fawcett Library is being carefully rearranged, both to uncover some of the hidden riches and to make its individual collections more easily available to researchers.

But, apart from this unique collection, the archives potentially valuable to the history of twentieth-century women are widely scattered. Consequently, the starting point for information on material in Britain must be the Historical Manuscripts Commission.[1] A statutory body, it acts as a coordinating center for a vast range of information on historical documents, from manorial records to recent papers. The local record offices in England and Wales send annual lists of accessions to the commission, as do many of the major public and university libraries. The commission's National Register of Archives has over twenty thousand reports on collections of papers, and a regularly updated personal index provides a name guide to personal collections and other relevant material. There is also a subject index to the reports, though this is by no means comprehensive. In particular, the references to women are sparse. A mine of information exists here, however, if the researcher pursues coherent lines of inquiry. For example, a vitally important source which is only now being tapped is the material in the local record offices on education, the division of labor between men and women, attitudes toward marriage, prostitution, and many other fields of investigation. The commission's information can provide an important entree into this field. The chief defect of the system is that it is almost entirely dependent on information offered to the commission, so there are major gaps which must be filled in by individual work. Over the past ten years there has been some effort to collate the available information.

Between 1968 and 1970 a pilot project at Nuffield College, Oxford, conducted a survey of the papers of British Cabinet Ministers from 1900 to 1951, including, of course, the few women ministers.[2] The success of this project led to the establishment of a major investigation at the British Library of Political and Economic Science (BLPES, in the library of the London School of Economics) in 1970. During the six and a half years of its existence (September 1970 to March 1977) the Historical Records Project produced five volumes of guides, *Sources in British Political History, 1900–1951*, which are indispensable for researching the history of women.[3] The various volumes include descriptions of the records of women's organizations and the private papers of individual women—feminists, politicians, administrators, and writers. The project not only actively researched the whereabouts of papers still in private hands and documented their present location, but was concerned also with preserving the material for posterity. An essential by-product of its work was providing advice (with the support of the Historical Manuscripts Commission) on depositing papers in relevant libraries.

Another vital source is the vast collection of the National Archives, for the twentieth century has seen a massive intervention of the state in the regulation of social life, and this has inevitably affected the lives of women. The Public Record Office in London, which holds the records of the central government departments, gives general access to its records on a thirty-year rule (though some classes are reserved for longer). Its various *Handlists* provide an entree into the records. Of obvious relevance are such department files as those of the Home Office (with, for example, details of the planning of protective legislation), the Ministry of Labour files (ref LAB; with information on female employment), and the Cabinet papers.[4] The Scottish Record Office in Edinburgh and the Public Record Office of Northern Ireland in Belfast house similar records for their respective areas.

Most of the major public and university libraries have valuable material. The Manchester Central Library, for instance, has a large suffrage collection as well as the papers of Dame Millicent Fawcett. The John Rylands University Library of Manchester has a variety of material, including press cuttings relating to the women's movement. Other major archives, such as the British Library, the national libraries of Scotland and Wales, the major university libraries (especially the Bodleian Library, Oxford, and Cambridge University Library), the libraries of the major urban areas, private libraries (such as the Marx Memorial Library), the Museum of London, and the important record offices (particularly the

Greater London Record Office), all contain a variety of collections relating to feminism and women in politics.[5] Additionally, numerous documents relating to the history of women in the first half of the twentieth century survive in private hands, in the libraries or storerooms of political pressure groups, in public and national libraries, in local record offices, and in the memories of the participants themselves.

The discussion which follows, using information gathered from the various sources, attempts to suggest broad areas for which documents survive, but given the nature of research, it cannot be fully comprehensive. The organization is thematic, the topics or themes having been selected from among those presently considered important to the study of early twentieth-century British women: social morality, suffrage, postwar feminism, access to public office, the labor movement, maternity and child welfare, birth control, and reform of attitudes toward sexuality. Broadly speaking, an attempt has been made to cover two major, if closely interlinked, areas of interest. First, the history of women's own activities both in the various feminist organizations and in wider social activity, and second, the social and political definition and control of women. No attempt has been made to explore the sources relating to women in other areas, such as art and culture. These demand a special study. Three appendices are provided for the convenience of the researcher. The first appendix lists libraries and archives mentioned in the text, and gives their addresses. The second and third appendices list, respectively, individuals and organizations mentioned in the text, along with the abbreviated names of libraries or archives containing their records and papers.

## SOCIAL MORALITY

Early feminism had many complex roots, but one strong and persistent theme was expressed in the campaign against the "double standard" of morality which merged into a long-lasting drive for "social purity." The key figure in the late nineteenth century was Josephine Butler, substantial collections of whose papers and correspondence have survived. Liverpool University Library has a group of letters, many of which were used in A. S. G. Butler's *Portrait of Josephine Butler* (1954). The collection includes letters from Josephine Butler to her family and colleagues from 1853 to 1903, of which 157 letters are addressed to Fannie Forsaith, a colleague in the campaign against the Contagious Diseases Acts. Other letters, pamphlets, and cuttings have been deposited in the library by the Josephine Butler Memorial House in Liverpool. St. Andrews University Library holds a further small collection of Butler correspondence. Most of the letters are addressed to Josephine or Canon George

Butler, and most concern the campaign against the state regulation of prostitution, in Britain and abroad. The Fawcett Library has on deposit the letters and documents owned by the Josephine Butler Society, still extant as the successor to the Association for Moral and Social Hygiene which grew out of the organizations formed to fight the Contagious Diseases Acts. Amongst these papers is a substantial collection of Butler letters. The Josephine Butler Society records include minutes of the executive committee and subcommittee of the Ladies' National Association for the Abolition of the State Regulation of Vice (founded to fight the Contagious Diseases Acts in 1869) and certain records of the National Association for the Repeal of the Contagious Diseases Acts from 1869 to 1886. Complimentary papers relating to the campaign against the acts are in the H. J. Wilson collection held by Sheffield City Library. Henry Joseph Wilson was Liberal M. P. for Holmfirth from 1885 to 1912, and very active in "social purity" matters.

The Josephine Butler Society has always been primarily concerned with prostitution. The records of the British Vigilance Association, also in the Fawcett Library, reflect a wider campaign for public morality. The association grew out of the National Vigilance Society founded amidst the agitation over the Criminal Law Amendment Act of 1885. It became the British Vigilance Association in 1953 on its amalgamation with the National Committee for the Suppression of Traffic in Women. This collection consists of a fascinating group of minutes, correspondence, and reports, and reflects a variety of campaigns: over the age of consent (with the aim of raising it), against "obscene" displays in shops, and for the detection of various forms of prostitution. A collection of papers relating to the complementary Public Morality Council is in the Greater London Record Office.

Also relevant here are the records of various temperance organizations. Lambeth Palace Library has, for instance, the minutes and papers of the Church of England Temperance Society, founded in 1872, and some records of the Police Court Mission, founded in 1876. The present heir to these bodies, the Church of England Council for Social Aid, still campaigns to promote the "moral life" of the individual and the family. A similar ambition lies behind the work of the National British Women's Total Abstinence Union, formed in 1876, which has retained in its London offices a complete run of minute books and other papers. Other relevant records on this theme can be found in the London headquarters of the United Kingdom Alliance. A number of records of local women's temperance groups have been deposited in various archives—for example, the papers of the Aberystwyth Women's Temperance Association in the National Library of Wales, and the papers of the Ulster Women's

Christian Temperance Union in the Public Record Office of Northern Ireland.

## SUFFRAGE

### CONSTITUTIONALISTS

The Suffrage campaigns are undoubtedly the best-known and best-documented aspects of the women's movement. The National Union of Women's Suffrage Societies, founded in 1897 as a federation of all the existing suffrage groups (some dating back to 1867), was the chief "constitutionalist" suffrage organization. Its history and work can be traced in collections at the Fawcett Library, which include correspondence and papers of Millicent Fawcett. Apart from papers relating directly to the suffrage campaign there is material relating to her work on the Ladies Commission of Inquiry into the Boer War Concentration Camps. The library has records of the Fawcett Society and its predecessors (the London suffrage groupings), and correspondence and papers both of the NUWSS and of smaller suffrage groups, such as the Artists Franchise League and the St. Joan's Social and Political Alliance (formerly the Catholic Women's Suffrage Society). The literary executrix of Dame Kathleen D'Olier Courtney, secretary of the NUWSS from 1911 to 1914 and a founder of the Women's International League, recently deposited a collection of her papers with the Fawcett Library. Letters and diaries of Dame Kathleen, especially relating to her work with the Friends' Relief Service during World War I, are at the Imperial War Museum.

Records at the Manchester Central Library include papers of the Manchester District Federation of the NUWSS and further material of Mrs. Fawcett's, including her in-correspondence, notes, her analyses of parliamentary divisions, notes for speeches, press cuttings, and papers on other topics, such as women's education and employment, the drink problem, the Boer War, and the World War I British Women's Patriotic League.

The papers of Catherine E. Marshall (1880–1961) at the Cumbria Record Office are also important. She was parliamentary secretary of the NUWSS before World War I, helped found the Women's International League in 1915, and from 1916 worked full-time for the No-Conscription Fellowship. Later she was active in the international peace movement and the Labour Party. Her papers reflect all these activities.

Other record offices have small collections of papers illustrating local suffrage campaigns. These include some records of the Cambridge Women's Suffrage Association from 1884 to 1939, in the Cambridgeshire and Isle of Ely Record Office, and items relating to the Great Yarmouth Women's Suffrage Societies in the Great Yarmouth Borough Archives. The Historical Manuscripts Commission has further information on these local records. The British Library has seven volumes of letters and papers exchanged between Mrs. Elizabeth C. Wolstenholme Elmy and Harriet McIlquham between 1889 and 1914 (Add MSS 47449–55), which concern the organization of the suffrage movement, and in particular the Women's Franchise League and the Women's Emancipation Union. Finally, many records remain in private hands. Dame Margery Corbett Ashby, for instance, who has been an active feminist since the beginning of the century, retains various unsorted papers.

MILITANTS

The chief collection of suffragette papers are those deposited by the Suffragette Fellowship in the Museum of London. Important amongst these are papers relating to the Women's Social and Political Union, including diaries, correspondence, autobiographical notes by various suffragettes, letters from Emmeline and Christabel Pankhurst and Mrs. Pethick Lawrence, material relating to demonstrations, and papers concerning the organization of the WSPU. The Museum of London also has material of the Women's Freedom League (founded in 1907 as a breakaway from the WSPU) concerning its formation, constitution, and policy. The Fawcett Library has formal records of the league and papers of one of its leaders, Teresa Billington Greig. The Greig papers include material on the Independent Labour Party (ILP) and WSPU, biographical items, and notes for her uncompleted biography of Charlotte Despard. The records of the Women's Tax Resistance League, which developed from the Women's Freedom League in 1909, are similarly split between the Fawcett Library and the Museum of London.

Papers relating to the best known suffragette leaders, Christabel, Emmeline, and Sylvia Pankhurst, can be found in a variety of libraries. The material collected by David Mitchell for his various works on the suffragette movement and the Pankhursts now forms part of the Museum of London collection.[6] Manchester Central Library has material concerning the relations of the WSPU and the Independent Labour Party. The Sylvia Pankhurst papers at the International Institute of Social History, Amsterdam, contain family papers dating back to the 1860s, including correspondence of Dr. R. M. Pankhurst and Mrs. Pankhurst, as well as a great deal of material relating to Sylvia's own political activities in the East London Federation of the Suffragettes, in the Communist movement and in antifascist activity between the wars. The British Library has correspondence between Christabel Pankhurst and H. D. Harben (Add MS 58226), and there is also aboundant relevant correspondence in other collections there, including the Balfour papers.

The political and personal involvement of the Pankhursts with the Labour movement can be traced in the papers relating to Keir Hardie in the National Library of Scotland and in the archives of the Independent Labour Party, not currently open to researchers but to be placed in the care of the British Library of Political and Economic Science (BLPES). The papers of other men close to the campaign for women's suffrage are also useful sources. The George Lansbury collection at BLPES contains relevant items. There is a file on women's suffrage in the papers of W. H. Dickinson, first baron Dickinson, in the Greater London Record Office. The papers of H. W. Nevinson and his wife Margaret at the Bodleian Library, Oxford, also have useful material. The Bertrand Russell collection at McMaster University, Hamilton, Ontario, has papers on his involvement in the women's movement. Particularly important on this theme is the Maud Arncliffe Sennett collection in the British Library (Department of Printed Books), a useful source for the Men's League for Women's Suffrage, particularly in the north of England. The collection consists of thirty-seven volumes of press cuttings, pamphlets, and letters, many annotated by Maud Arncliffe Sennett.

Antisuffrage records are scattered. Papers of Lord Curzon, a leader of the antisuffrage campaign, are in the India Office Library and contain relevant material, including copies of speeches, three bundles of letters from the period from 1910 to 1913, papers appealing for subscriptions to the antisuffrage cause (1910), and files of correspondence, including letters from Lord Cromer, another antisuffrage leader. A note by Curzon (October 1918) in the collection indicates that he destroyed a vast amount of correspondence relating to the National League for Opposing Women's Suffrage as he felt the cause was now lost. The papers of Mrs. Humphry Ward, one of the founders of the earlier Women's National Anti-Suffrage League (set up in 1908) are available in the Library of University College, London, and in Pusey House, Oxford. The family papers of the countess of Jersey, president of the league, are in the Greater London Record Office, while the Cromer papers are in the Public Record Office.

## POSTWAR FEMINISM

Before World War I, the suffrage campaign represented the most public and dramatic manifestation of feminism. After the achievement of a limited female suffrage in 1918, this single focus was lost and feminist involvement dispersed into a number of disparate organizations. The constitutionalist line of the NUWSS and its associates was continued after 1918 by various successor organizations. The NUWSS itself eventually became the National Council for Equal Citizenship which survived until 1946. In that year it amalgamated with the National Women Citizen's Association, founded in 1918 to develop "educative work on women citizenship, and on the methods of using the new voting power given to women." The records of these organizations are now in the Fawcett Library. The Six Point Group, founded in 1921 by Lady Rhondda as a nonparty pressure group working for the equality of women, has retained minutes and newsletters from its foundation and these were preserved by a long-serving member, Mrs. Hunkins Hallinan. The collection also includes records of the now defunct Women for Westminster group, which pressured for more female M.P.' s. Further records of this group are in the Greig papers in the Fawcett Library.

An older pressure group, the National Council of Women of Great Britain, which from the 1890s has acted as a coordinating body for various aspects of women's work, has retained many of its records in its London offices, including an early minute book, though most of the remaining records consist of printed rather than manuscript material. Many feminists put their energies in the inter-war years into campaigns for disarmament and international cooperation. Their prime vehicle was the Women's International League for Peace and Freedom, founded in 1915.[7] Its records, in BLPES, contain papers relevant to the work of Helena Swanwick (first editor of *The Common Cause* and president of the British section of the league); files concerning and emanating from Catherine Marshall, onetime secretary of the league, complementing those in Cumbria Record Office; formal records such as minutes and reports; and other documents such as press cuttings and pamphlets. Other feminists engaged in work with the National Federation of Women's Institutes, founded in 1917, which has retained not only its own formal records, but files on all its constituent Women Institutes. Other inter-war activities relating to the family and motherhood will be discussed below.

## WOMEN IN PUBLIC OFFICE

Fed by the stream of feminism, but not always coterminus with it, is the history of women's participation in philanthropy, politics, education, and social affairs. An excellent example is provided by the career of Dame Henrietta Octavia Barnett (1851–1936), a dedicated social reformer in her own way, involved in various social causes (housing, poor law, the feeble-minded) and a prominent supporter of the garden city ideal. Her career is reflected in collections of Barnett family papers at the Greater London Record Office and at Lambeth Palace Library. The papers at the Greater London Record Office (correspondence, sermons, lecture notes, etc.) were collected by Dame Henrietta in preparation for her biography of her husband, Canon Samuel Augustus Barnett, founder of the Charity Organisation Society in 1868.[8] The COS played a major role in the emergence of "social work" and family casework, which in turn has had important consequences for the social definition of women's role. The records of the COS in the Greater London Record Office include minute books complete from 1869, case cards and papers, and local area papers.[9] Another collection which reflects a range of interest and involvement similar to that of Dame Henrietta Barnett is that of Helen Bosanquet (1860–1925), district secretary of the Charity Organisation Society and member of the Royal Commission on the Poor Laws. The papers, which are in the University of Newcastle-upon-Tyne Library, include much correspondence.

The evolution of British social policy from the early philanthropists and social reformers to the welfare state can be clearly traced in the papers of one of its prime architects, Sir William, first baron Beveridge, at BLPES. This large collection covers his early work in planning labour exchanges and insurance schemes, his academic work, his involvement in the debate over population policies, and the planning of the Beveridge Report itself. No other single collection so clearly illustrates the ways in which traditional assumptions about the family and women's role were embedded in the fabric of the new welfare state.

The direct involvement of women in national politics both before and after the attainment of the vote can be documented in a number of collections. Beatrice Webb's strenuous efforts for Fabian socialism are amply recorded in the Passfield papers at BLPES. The papers include her famous diaries, extensive correspondence between her and Sidney Webb (Baron Passfield), and letters to both of them from a vast range of correspondents. BLPES also has the papers of Violet Rosa Markham (d. 1960), politician and administrator, onetime chairman of the advisory council, National Institute of Houseworkers. The material covers the wide range of her work, including her involvement in the Women's Volunteer Reserve, the National Assistance Board, factory inspection, domestic service, and the postwar organization of women's employment. After 1918, women such as Beatrice Webb and Violet Markham often exercised more influence on public events than the average female M.P., but lacked the symbolic significance.

The National Library of Ireland has a number of letters of the

Countess Markievicz (Constance Gore-Booth), the first woman to be elected to the Westminster Parliament, though as a Sinn Feiner she did not take her seat. The Public Record Office in London has other papers concerning the countess in class CO 904.[10] The papers of Lady Astor, the first woman actually to sit in the House of Commons, form part of the substantial and wide-ranging collection in Reading University Library. There is extensive correspondence, including papers on her parliamentary work, material on Christian Science, and documents relating to her interest in nursery schools (1931–64). Not all women M.P.' s kept so important a collection, though there are exceptions such as Eleanor Rathbone.[11] The records of the major political parties are thus often more revealing of the attitudes of and towards female politicians.

The records of the Labour Party will be discussed below. The records of the Conservative Party detail its attitudes to women politicians. The party has, for example, papers of the Women's Conferences of the National Union of Conservative and Unionist Associations dating from 1921, and seven minute books of the Central Women's Advisory Committee dating from 1935. The Liberal Party has a less coherent collection of papers, but the National Liberal Club[12] collection includes a group of records of the Women's National Liberal Federation, while records of the Scottish Women's Liberal Federation are held in Edinburgh University Library. The papers of Baroness Asquith of Yarnbury (Lady Violet Bonham-Carter), for many years a dominant force in Liberal politics, are retained by her son, Hon. Mark Bonham-Carter. The papers of Lady Megan Lloyd-George, a onetime Liberal member of Parliament, and later a Labour politician and M.P., are in the National Library of Wales.

If progress at the peak of national politics was difficult, education and academia has offered some women a more accessible career during this century. Girton College, Cambridge, has a considerable collection of material relating to Emily Davies, pioneer and promoter of higher education for women and secretary of Girton College, but it is not made generally available pending cataloging. The papers of a number of heads of women's colleges do in fact survive. St. Hilda's College, Oxford, has records of C. M. E. Burrows, its principal from 1910 to 1918. Lady Margaret Hall, Oxford, has college and personal papers of Lynda Dorothea Grier, principal from 1921 to 1945. Girton College, Cambridge, has items concerning Dame Bertha Surtees Newall (Phillpotts), principal of Westfield College from 1919 to 1921, and mistress of Girton from 1922 to 1925. At a lower level of education, records of the Parents' National Educational Union (founded 1887) and its founder Charlotte Mason are available in London University Library.

## WOMEN AND THE LABOR MOVEMENT

The relationship between the various strands of feminism and the labor movement has always been complex and in many ways problematical. The history of the Women's Social and Political Union, from its birth within the Independent Labour Party, to its later antisocialist position, is evidence of this, though the radical fissure was more evident at a national level than in the local activity of numerous women who were both feminist and socialist.

The best known example of a counter-tendency is the work of Estelle Sylvia Pankhurst and the East London Federation of Suffragettes. The Sylvia Pankhurst collection in Amsterdam includes minute books, leaflets and correspondence concerning the federation. Its trajectory, from a suffragette organization to becoming the Workers' Suffrage Federation in 1916 and later still the Workers' Socialist Federation reveals another strand in the growth of a type of socialist feminism, from which the new Communist Party of Great Britain benefited yet found difficult to accommodate.

There has been, nevertheless, a long line of women whose dedication to socialism and the labor movement has been of major importance in the growth of both. The best known of the pioneer socialists of the 1880s is Annie Besant. Most of her own surviving papers are with the Theosophical Society, International Headquarters, Adyar, Madras, India, but these do not appear to predate her involvement with the Theosophical movement. There is little for the 1880s or 90s, but there are, however, scattered letters in other British collections, such as her letters to George Bernard Shaw in the British Library (Add MSS 50529; Shaw seems to have destroyed many others). The sources relating to Eleanor Marx have been abundantly documented in Yvonne Kapp's two-volume biography.[13] A number of papers relating to Enid Stacy, another pioneer socialist of the 1890s, are currently in the care of her niece, Angela Tuckett, who is preparing a biography. Papers of Katherine Bruce Glasier remain with her son, Malcolm, but it is expected that they will eventually be placed in a major library.

With regard to women's trade union involvement, various records survive for the early part of the century, though the records of the National Federation of Women Workers have not been discovered. The Tuckwell collection in the Library of the Trades Union Congress includes records of the Women's Trades Union League (founded in 1874 as the Women's Protective and Provident League to Promote Female Trades Unionism), such as minute books and annual reports. The collection has the Trade

Union notebooks of Lady Dilke, onetime president of the league, as well as other records of her niece, Gertrude Tuckwell, secretary of the league from 1892 to 1904 (and later president of the Women Public Health Officers Association). Some correspondence of Lady Dilke with her first husband is in the British Library (Add MSS 44886) and the Bodleian Library, while the papers of her second husband, Sir Charles Dilke, also relevant to this theme, are in the British Library, Birmingham University Library, and Churchill College, Cambridge.

The Modern Records Centre, University of Warwick Library, has two interesting collections directly concerning female employment. The first consists of some papers of Clara E. Collet (1860–1948), assistant commissioner to the Royal Commission on Labour, 1892, and labor correspondent, Board of Trade from 1893 to 1903; there are selections from her diaries and documents on women's employment, especially in the textile or sewing machine trades and domestic employment. The second collection consists of copies of papers of Lucy Anne Evelyn Streatfield, the first woman senior inspector of factories. There are business diaries concerning her inspectorate from 1893 to 1897, and material on the disease known as "phossy-jaw" in match factories, sweating, etc. Papers given by Lady Clark (née Barbara Keen) to the Bodleian Library are chiefly concerned with female trade union affairs, dating from around 1912. Wider questions concerning the unionization of women, and the attitude of male trade unionists towards women workers, can be traced in the records of the Trades Union Congress (retained at Congress House, London) and in the records of individual trade unions.[14]

A very important source for the lives of working-class women, especially up to the 1920s, is the archive of the Women's Cooperative Guild.[15] The guild had been founded in 1883 to organize women on consumer issues, but under the general secretaryship of Margaret Llewelyn Davies (from 1889 to 1921) it concerned itself with all the wider questions of women's emancipation including the problems of housing, health insurance, employment of young people, maternity, divorce law reforms, antisweating campaigns, as well as the suffrage question and the organization of women in trade unions. The guild's own records, dating from the first decade of the century and covering most of these topics, are housed in Hull University Library. These are complemented by the eleven volumes of guild material presented to BLPES by Lillian Harris, life-long friend and companion of Margaret Llewelyn Davies. This collection is particularly useful in illustrating the personal influence of these two women in encouraging the spread of cooperation amongst working-class women.

The records held by the Labour Party are the other major source for documenting the political activities of working-class and socialist women. There are subject files on many topics relating to women, but also several discrete groupings which are of major importance. The Labour Party holds, for instance, the surviving records of the Women's Labour League, founded in 1906, including minutes and notes, together with the correspondence of Mary Middleton, secretary from 1907 to 1911. (Papers of Margaret MacDonald, one of the founders of the League, can be found in BLPES, while the Public Record Office has a large collection of J. R. MacDonald's papers.) There are also minutes of the Standing Joint Committee of Industrial Women's Organizations. This committee was a constituent of the Consumers' Council, founded in 1918, and while the council's own formal records do not appear to have survived amongst the public records, there are eight boxes of relevant papers with the Labour Party, including correspondence and material on national kitchens and mass catering. These were the papers of Dr. Marion Phillips, a member of the council, Labour women's organizer, and later M.P. for Sunderland. The Labour Party also holds her constituency files, her papers as a member of the Rent Restrictions Act Committee from 1930 to 1931, papers relating to domestic service, and correspondence. Few papers are yet readily available for the Communist Party of Great Britain. An autobiography of Helen Crawfurd, first woman organizer of the CPBG is in private hands, but may be accessible via the Marx Memorial Library. This library has, of course, many other items, including press cuttings, on women.

Another stream of socialist and feminist propaganda during the interwar years can be discerned in three other collections—the papers of the novelist Winifred Holtby and those of Vera Brittain and Winifred Horrabin. Winifred Holtby's papers, including letters, notebooks, diaries, and manuscripts, are housed in the Hull Library of Humberside Public Libraries. The papers of her close friend and literary executrix, Vera Brittain, are even more comprehensive. McMaster University Library, Hamilton, Ontario, has manuscripts, some twenty-five thousand letters belonging to her and her husband, Sir George Catlin, and press cuttings, while her interest in Anglo-Indian relations, and her involvement in the World Pacifist Conference in India, is represented in notebooks in the Bodleian Library. A book of *Selected Letters of Winifred Holtby and Vera Brittain* was published in a limited edition in 1960. The papers of Winifred Horrabin (1887–1971), another feminist and socialist writer, are in Hull University Library. The collection includes extensive correspondence, a series of diaries, journals and notebooks dating from 1922, and several folders of notes, press cuttings, manuscripts, and typescripts relating to

"Citizen of the World, Olive Schreiner" (1937). (The papers of Olive Schreiner herself are in the South African Library, Cape Town.) Also in Hull University Library is an interesting collection of the papers of Julia Varley (1888–1953), suffragette and trade unionist.

## MATERNITY AND CHILD WELFARE

Another recurrent theme in twentieth-century social theory and practice is a concern with the conditions and responsibilities of motherhood and the corollary, an emphasis on the development of healthy children. This was partly, no doubt, a necessary humanization of attitudes, part of the preconditions for the establishment of a welfare state. But its history, like that of the welfare state, is more complex than this would suggest. One of the roots of the new concern with "motherhood" in the early part of the century was undoubtedly related to the wave of imperialist sentiment, and the fear of national decline and "racial suicide" that the problems of fighting the Boer War accentuated and underlined. The revelation in the war that working-class children were often ill-fed and unhealthy—boding ill for the future of the race—was one of the major factors behind the formation of the National League for Physical Education and Improvement founded in 1905 (and known from 1918 to its dissolution in 1928 as the National League for Health, Maternity and Child Welfare). This acted as a link between many voluntary national organizations concerned with safeguarding motherhood and the health of the young. No direct records of the league are known, but the records of several organizations closely associated with it have survived. The National Association for Maternal and Child Welfare, for instance, is a direct descendant of the infant welfare movement of the late nineteenth century. Between 1899, when the first was established, and 1910, over a hundred child welfare centers sprang up in the United Kingdom, and in 1911 the Association of Infant Welfare and Maternity Centres was formed to assist these institutions. This was followed in 1912 by the establishment of the National Association for the Prevention of Infant Mortality. These amalgamated in 1935 to found the existing national association. This has retained a useful collection of records, including minutes of the National Conference on Infant Mortality from 1906 to 1912, and formal records of the associations. Similarly, the National Society of Day Nurseries, founded in 1906, which had an active existence until 1973 (latterly known as the National Society of Children's Nurseries) retained a valuable collection of papers, which have been given to BLPES. In 1973 the society amalgamated with the Nursery School Association to form the British Association for Early Childhood Education. The new association has retained for the moment the records of the NSA. Complementing these are the papers of Lady Allen of Hurtwood, who died in 1976. She was chairman of the Nursery School Association from 1942 to 1948, president from 1948 to 1951, and founder president of the World Organisation for Early Childhood Education. Her papers, very revealing on these themes, are housed in the Modern Records Centre, University of Warwick Library. It appears that the records of the National Baby Week Council, later known as the National Baby Welfare Council, were destroyed during the Second World War, but records of the National Birthday Trust, founded in the 1930s by Juliette Rhys-Williams, which amongst other work investigated nutrition and feeding schemes, survive with her daughter, Elspeth Rhys-Williams, in London.

Records of the Health Visitors' Association and the Royal College of Midwives are also relevant in this context. The Health Visitors' Association was founded in 1896 as the Women Sanitary Inspectors' Association, and was registered as a trade union in 1918. Its formal records (minutes, etc.) survive, and date from the early part of this century. The Royal College of Midwives has records dating back to the foundation of the Midwives' Institute in 1881, and they include minutes, accounts, papers and correspondence.[16] These have been usefully listed.

During the inter-war years a highly significant strand of feminism launched a movement that became the campaign for state support of the family (which, in a post-Beveridge form, became known as Family Allowances). Eleanor Rathbone, a feminist and later Independent M.P., was the founder of two related organizations, the Family Endowment Society and the Children's Nutrition (formerly Minimum) Society. Their secretary, Mrs. Marjorie Soper, knew of no formal records, but Eleanor Rathbone's own papers, including extensive correspondence, survive in Liverpool University Library. They are, however, disappointing on this theme. Her papers relating to the franchise for Indian women are in the Fawcett Library.[17]

With regard to attitudes towards children, abundant records survive and there has been in particular a growing interest recently in youth movements and the social role of childhood. Records of organizations such as the National Society for the Prevention of Cruelty to Children, founded in 1884, are of obvious importance, and a full set survive in the society's offices. Brian Harrison has ably documented the significance of the history of the Girls' Friendly Society (in *Past and Present*, no. 61, 1973). Its records are held by the society in London. Other records that might be mentioned are those of the Young Women's Christian Association of Great Britain, and the Girl Guides Association. Both associations retain ample records in their respective offices. The records of the Young Women's Christian

Association include material on women emigrants, industrial legislation, and women in wartime. The Girl Guides Association, founded as a counterpart to the Scouts, has papers (formal records, correspondence, press cuttings) from its foundation in 1910. In addition, the papers of Dame Katherine Furse, Director of the Women's Royal Naval Service from 1917 to 1919, and of the World Bureau of Girl Guides and Girl Scouts from 1928 to 1938, are preserved in Bristol University Library. These papers provide a further useful insight into the work of a woman active in public affairs.

## BIRTH CONTROL

With the new social emphasis on motherhood came a prolonged debate on what Margaret Sanger was the first to term "birth control," but which in a significant ideological switch in the 1930s became known as "family planning." Various organizations sprang up after the 1870s, but they all manifested contrasting, and sometimes conflicting ambitions and aims. The Malthusian League (known from the 1920s as the New Generation League) was the oldest, founded in 1877 to advocate the restriction of births as a stage in the elimination of poverty and social unrest, and it survived in an exiguous form until the 1950s. Certain papers of C. V. Drysdale (1873–1961), secretary to the league, editor of its journal, and later its president, are in BLPES. They consist largely of notes, drafts, and other materials used in his published works on the Malthusian doctrine. Other papers relating to the league survive in private hands.[18] BLPES has also a major collection of birth control pamphlets and ephemera.

The Eugenics Education League, founded in 1907 and known since 1926 simply as the Eugenics Society, had a different emphasis: the scientific study and control of heredity as the major avenue to a racially more secure future. The society has retained in its London headquarters a substantial and valuable collection of records dating from its foundation, including a very useful assemblage of press cuttings and albums, organized chronologically and by subject (e.g., population, genetics, genes, heredity, birth control). Eugenics proved a most influential doctrine amongst a certain strata of intellectuals. University College, London, has large collections of the papers of Sir Francis Galton, founder of the society, Karl Pearson, its high priest, and Lionel Penrose, a later defender. Other collections where the influence of eugenics can be traced are those of Beveridge, Havelock Ellis, Leonard Darwin (care of the History and Social Studies of Science Division, University of Sussex) and Reginald Ruggles Gates, first husband of Marie Stopes (in the library of King's College, London).

The Bodleian Library has the letters received by Sir James Marchant (d. 1950), who was secretary of the National Birth Rate Commission which examined the population crisis during World War I.

The best known advocate of birth control after the First World War is undoubtedly Dr. Marie Stopes, and the collection of her correspondence and papers in the British Library (Add MSS 58447–770) is probably the most important single source. It contains a vast grouping of correspondence—personal, scientific, and political—as well as records of the Society for Constructive Birth Control and Racial Progress, material concerning the clinics, and papers concerning her relationship (often uneasy) with other birth control organizations. The collection is indispensable both for understanding Marie Stopes's own dynamic and controversial role and for grasping the immensely complex crosscurrents in the study and advocacy of sex reform. There is a fascinating correspondence with such reformers as Havelock Ellis, Aylmer Maude, and representatives of a wide range of medical and scientific opinion. There is also a large correspondence from the many women (often working-class) and men whom she helped. This section is, however, closed to researchers at the moment. Certain other papers, emanating from the Marie Stopes Memorial Foundation are in Hull University Library. Another collection relevant here is that of Norman Haire, medical officer in charge of the Walworth Welfare Centre in 1921, and a leading advocate of birth control and sex reform during the 1930s and 1940s. His surviving papers are in the rare book library of the University of Sydney, Australia, but there is also extensive correspondence in the Marie Stopes collection at the British Library. The more controversial parts of his papers, such as his diaries, were destroyed after his death.

The activities of the Malthusian League and Marie Stopes during the 1920s in sponsoring clinics led in 1930 to the establishment of the National Birth Control Council. This was the forerunner of the Family Planning Association, which has retained an extremely valuable and comprehensive collection of records, now deposited, together with records of the international family planning organization, in the David Owen Centre for Population Growth Studies. The collection includes minutes and papers relating to the administration of the association, as well as full records of the North Kensington Centre and the Walworth Welfare Centre and Clinic dating from the 1920s. An appeal by the association for records of local clinics brought a wide response so that, for example, records of the Liverpool Clinic from 1931, and of the Birkenhead Clinic from 1934, are now with the main collection.

The Abortion Law Reform Association, formed in 1936, also retained many of its records, the earlier material being preserved in the Medical

Sociology Research Unit of Aberdeen University. Of course, many of the pioneers of abortion law reform are still alive, but the private papers of the more controversial pioneers such as F. W. Stella Browne have not been traced.[19]

## REFORM OF ATTITUDES TOWARD SEXUALITY

Questions of birth control or family planning can quickly merge into wider questions about the control of one's sexuality, but in the first half of the century few made the vital connections. The British Society for the Study of Sex Psychology, founded in 1914 by, amongst others, Edward Carpenter, George Ives and Laurence Housman, with F. W. Stella Browne as an active member, was the main reform organization, becoming in the 1920s closely linked with the World Leaque for Sexual Reform, and remaining active until the mid-1930s. Edward Carpenter's papers, in Sheffield City Library, are an excellent source for piecing together the work of the early sex reformers, and include his often intimate correspondence with feminists (such as Olive Schreiner) and reformers not only in Britain but throughout the world. The other major influence on the early reformers was the sex psychologist Havelock Ellis.[20] Some of his papers remain in private hands, but many are now in the United States: at the University of Texas at Austin, in Yale University Library, with the Menninger Foundation, Topeka, Kansas, and at the University of California at Los Angeles. These contain manuscripts and drafts of his work and extensive correspondence. Of particular importance is the correspondence with Olive Schreiner in the University of Texas.

Also with the University of Texas at Austin are the minutes and correspondence of the British Society for the Study of Sex Psychology itself. This collection is complemented by a revealing correspondence in the same Library between George Ives, an English criminologist, and the writer Laurence Housman. This concerns not only their efforts for the British Society for the Study of Sex Psychology during the decades of the 1910s to the 1930s, but also for a highly secretive homosexual reform organization active from the 1890s. This had international links, and featured many prominent people who were urged by the ardent leaders to use their positions to promote law reform. Not until the late 1950s do we find another, and this time more public, homosexual reform organization appearing in Britain. The university of Texas also has papers relating to the lesbian writer, Radclyffe Hall. The furor surrounding the publication in 1928 of her book *The Well of Loneliness* marked a significant stage in the emergence of a widespread consciousness of lesbianism.[21]

Norman Haire's papers in the University of Sydney Library contain items relating to the World League for Sexual Reform. This organization, founded in the 1920s by the German sexologist Dr. Magnus Hirschfeld, attempted to bring together on an international basis most of the progressive sex reformers from the various countries of the world. Its peak of influence was probably reached in 1929 when its London World Congress discussed topics such as abortion, birth control, censorship and homosexuality. Though not formally dissolved until 1935, its effective demise came in 1933 with the Nazi rise to power in Germany. Its international records, together with Hirschfeld's major library and case records were burnt by the Nazis. Haire's correspondence is thus an important source and is also useful for his own sex reform work in the 1940s.

The development of the Freudian movement in Britain can be traced in records held by the British Institute of Psychoanalysis. Of particular importance are the private papers of Ernest Jones (d. 1958), president of the International Psycho-Analytical Association, and the leading British interpreter of Freud. The collection includes much correspondence from and with leading psychoanalysts, papers relating to his biography of Freud, lectures, addresses, and so forth. This collection, however, is only available for research purposes in exceptional circumstances.

Another discipline which exercised some influence in the discussion of sexuality and the role of women was anthropology, and several collections reveal this. The Robert Briffault papers at the British Library (Add MSS 58440–43) contain items relating to his classic anthropological work, *The Mothers* (1927), which continued the long debate traceable through the work of Lewis Henry Morgan and Friedrich Engels. His opponent in the debate that ensued was the anthropologist Bronislaw Malinowski, whose papers should prove to be a major source. They are in the BLPES and in Yale University Library, and contain relevant correspondence with fellow anthropologists, sex psychologists such as Havelock Ellis, reformers such as Bertrand Russell, and many others.

The mention of Bertrand Russell (whose papers are at McMaster University) reminds us of the importance of sex education—always a highly controversial subject—to this discussion. Some evidence of the pitfalls involved can be found in the Russell papers themselves, which have details of the progressive school sponsored by Bertrand and Dora Russell in the late 1920s and early 1930s. Another progressive educationalist, much influenced by the sexual theories of Wilhelm Reich, was A. S. Neill. His surviving papers are retained by his widow at Summerhill School, Leiston, Suffolk.

## CONCLUSION

It should by now be apparent that the sources for the history of women in Britain are many and various, and by no means confined to familiar types of collections. The major sources will continue to be private, personal collections and the records of organizations, particularly pressure groups of or for women. But the various struggles of or relating to women during the century—for the vote, for education, for social morality, for birth control or (very occasionally) for "sexual freedom"—became at various times central elements in political and social debate. The abundance of records now becoming available makes it possible for the first time to fully document this process.

## NOTES

1. The computer printout of the personal index is available in the commission's search room and in major libraries such as the Bodleian Library, Oxford, and Cambridge University Library. The commission publishes an annual list of *Accessions to Repositories and Reports Added to the National Register of Archives* (London: H.M.S.O., 1972–), which is the successor to the *List of Accessions to Repositories*. This summarizes information on major collections accessioned by local record offices and many public libraries. There is also a National Register of Archives (Scotland), General Register House, Edinburgh EH1 3YY. The most comprehensive guide to the major record centers is *Record Repositories in Great Britain*, 5th ed., (London: H.M.S.O., 1976).

2. Cameron Hazlehurst and Christine Woodland, *A Guide to the Papers of British Cabinet Minister, 1900–1951* (London: 1974) prints the findings of the project, which was directed by Dr. Hazlehurst.

3. Chris Cook, with Philip Jones, Josephine Sinclair, and Jeffrey Weeks, *Sources in British Political History*, 5 vols. (London and New York: 1975–78) prints the findings of the research team. The subjects considered by each of the individual volumes are divided as follows: *Vol. 1, A Guide to the Archives of Selected Organisations and Societies* (1975); *Vol. 2, A Guide to the Private papers of Selected Public Servants* (1975); *Vols. 3 and 4, A Guide to the Private Papers of Members of Parliament, A–K, L–Z* (1977); and *Vol. 5, A Guide to the Private Papers of Selected Writers, Intellectuals and Publicists* (1978). In many cases the information in this article can be amplified by reference to the relevant volume of this work.

4. Brenda Swann, "The Public Record Office as a Source for Labour History," *History Workshop* 2 (Autumn 1976) provides a useful introduction to the PRO with reference to the needs of specialist historians.

5. Another important source, not discussed in the text, is that produced by oral history techniques. The significance of these methods is already being recognized by some historians. The "Family History Issue" of *Oral History: The Journal of the Oral History Society* 3, no. 2 (published by the Department of Sociology, University of Essex, Colchester), has several articles which underline the real insights which can be provided by oral techniques. Amongst other collections, the Oral History Project, Department of

Sociology, University of Essex, and also the South Wales Miners' Library, University College, Swansea, West Glamorgan, are very important sources.

6. Much material, of course, remains at the moment in private hands. For instance, David Mitchell has used additional material in his biography of Christabel Pankhurst, while Jill Craigie has apparently amassed a large collection of unpublished suffragette material in preparation for a study.

7. The British Library of Political and Economic Science (BLPES) has several other major collections of pacifist records, in which many women are of course prominent. Reference should also be made here to the records of the Society of Friends (The Quakers) which also contain various collections of and relating to women; the records are held at Friends' House, Euston Road, London WC1.

8. Now known as the Family Welfare Association.

9. It should be mentioned that the library of the Charity Organisation Society is on deposit at the Goldsmith Library, London University Library, which also has a manuscript diary of Sir C. S. Loch, longtime secretary of the society.

10. The Public Record Office has similar files on other women active in the Irish struggle, as, for example, Maud Gonne, also in class CO 904.

11. *Sources in British Political History*, vols. 3 and 4 (above, n. 3), detail the surviving papers of women M.P.'s from 1918 to 1951.

12. At the time of writing the future of the National Liberal Club Library was in doubt. It is expected that it will eventually become part of a university library.

13. Yvonne Kapp, *Eleanor Marx*, 2 vols. (London: 1972, 1976).

14. *Sources in British Political History*, vol. 1, pp. 261–63, describes the Trades Union Congress archive. Probably the largest single collection of trade union records is that at the Modern Records Centre, University of Warwick Library. A guide to its holdings, edited by Richard Storey and Janet Druker, has been published by the Library: *Guide to the Modern Records Centre: University of Warwick Library* (Occasional Publications, no. 2, 1977).

15. Now known as the Cooperative Women's Guild.

16. These records form the basis of a recent study by Jean Donnison, *Midwives and Medical Men* (London: 1977).

17. Relevant here (though perhaps suggesting a different direction) are the records of the organizations which campaigned to change the divorce laws. In fact, only post-1939 records of the Divorce Law Reform Union (founded 1906) appear to survive, and only a few papers survive of the Marriage Law Reform Society (founded 1946, amalgamated with the union in the 1960s). Papers of individual campaigners, such as Sir A. P. Herbert, do survive: his family has a substantial collection, while other papers are with the University of Texas at Austin.

18. See Rosanna Ledbetter, *History of the Malthusian League, 1877–1927* (Columbus, Ohio: 1976).

19. No substantial collection of records of the Workers' Birth Control League, active in the 1920s, appear to survive, though one of its members, Dora Russell, still has a lively memory. No papers of another leading member, F. W. Stella Browne, have been discovered; see Sheila Rowbotham, *A New World for Women: Stella Browne, Socialist Feminist* (London: 1977).

20. Phyllis Grosskurth is preparing the authorized biography and will have access to available papers.

21. Mr. Lovat Dickson has some additional papers. He owns the world copyright of Hall material.

# BIBLIOGRAPHY

Appendix A

Addresses of libraries, organizations, and archives mentioned in the text. Conditions of access to papers vary, and researchers are advised to inquire in advance about the availability of specific collections. In the case of private organizations and societies listed here, a preliminary letter of inquiry is absolutely essential. Such private bodies are noted with an asterisk. It should not be assumed that the holdings of these libraries and archives will be open to researchers.

For a fuller list of libraries and archives, the researcher should refer to the guide published by the Historical Manuscripts Commission, *Record Repositories in Great Britain*, 5th ed., 2d impression (London: HMSO, 1976).

Abbreviations for each archive are provided for quick reference to appendixes B and C.

\* Abortion Law Reform Association (ALRA), 88b Islington High Street, London N1.

Birmingham University Library (Birmingham UL), The Main Library, P. O. Box 363, The University, Edgbaston, Birmingham B15 2TT.

Bodleian Library (Bodl.), Oxford OX1 3BG.

Bristol University Library (Bristol UL), Wills Memorial Library, Queens Road, Bristol BS8 1RJ.

\* British Association for Early Childhood Education (Brit. Assoc. ECE), Montgomery Hall, Kennington Oval, London SE11.

\* British Institute of Psycho-Analysis (Brit. Inst. Psycho-Analysis), 36 New Cavendish Street, London W1.

British Library (BL), Department of Manuscripts, Great Russell Street, London WC1B 3DG.

British Library of Political and Economic Science (BLPES), London School of Economics, Houghton Street, Aldwych, London WC2A 2AE.

Cambridge University Library (Cambridge UL), West Road, Cambridge CB3 9DR.

Cambridgeshire and Isle of Ely Record Office (Camb. and Ely RO), County Record Office, Shire Hall, Castle Hill, Cambridge CB3 OAP.

Churchill College, Cambridge (Churchill Coll., Camb.), Cambridge CB3 ODS.

\* Church of England Council for Social Aid (C of E Council for Social Aid), Church House, Dean's Yard, London SW1.

\* Conservative Party (Conservative P), 32 Smith Square, London SW1P 3HH.

Cumbria Record Office (Cumbria RO), The Castle, Carlisle CA3 8UR.

David Owen Centre for Population Growth Studies (David Owen Centre), University College, P. O. Box 78, Cardiff, CF1 1XL.

\* Divorce Law Reform Union (Divorce Law RU), 117 Easton Road, Milton, Portsmouth, Hants.

Edinburgh University Library (Edinburgh UL), Department of Manuscripts, George Square, Edinburgh EH8 9LJ.

\* Eugenics Society (Eugenics Soc.), 69 Eccleston Square, London SW1V 1PJ.

\* Family Planning Association (Fam. Plan. Assoc.), 27 Mortimer Street, London W1N 8BQ.

Fawcett Library (Fawcett), City of London Polytechnic, Calcutta House Precinct, Old Castle Street, London E1 7NT.

* Girl Guides Association (GGA), 17 Buckingham Palace Road, London SW1W 0PT.

* Girls' Friendly Association (GFS), Central Office, 126 Queen's Gate London SW7.

Girton College, Cambridge (Girton Coll., Camb.), Cambridge CB3 0JG.

Great Yarmouth Borough Archives (Great Yarmouth), Town Hall, Great Yarmouth (see also Norfolk RO).

Greater London Record Office (GLRO), The County Hall, London SE1 7PB.

* Health Visitors' Association (HVA), 36 Eccleston Square, London SW1.

Historical Manuscripts Commission (Hist. MSS Comm.), Quality House, Quality Court, Chancery Lane, London WC2A 1HP.

History and Social Studies of Science Division, University of Sussex (HSSSD, U Sussex), Sussex House, Falmer, Brighton BN1 9RH.

Hull University Library (Hull UL), The Brynmor Jones Library, The University, Hull HU6 7RX.

Humberside Public Libraries (Humberside PL), Central Library, Albion Street, Hull, Humberside.

Huntington Library (HL), San Marino, California, 91108, U.S.A.

Imperial War Museum (Imp. War Mus.), Department of Libraries and Archives, Lambeth Road, London SE1 6HZ.

India Office Library (India Office), Foreign and Commonwealth Office, 197 Blackfriars Road, London SE1 8NG.

International Institute of Social History (IISH), Herengracht 262, Amsterdam, Netherlands.

King's College, London (King's Coll., London), Strand, London WC2R 2LS.

* Labour Party (Labour P), Transport House, Smith Square, London SW1.

Lady Margaret Hall, Oxford (Lady Margaret Hall), Oxford OX2 6QA.

Lambeth Palace Library (Lamb. Pal.), London SE1 7JU.

Liverpool University Library (Liverpool UL), The University, P. O. Box 123, Liverpool L69 3DA.

McMaster University Library (McMaster UL), Hamilton, Ontario, Canada.

Manchester Central Library (Manchester Central), St. Peter's Square, Manchester M2 5PD.

Manchester: John Rylands University Library of Manchester (Rylands), Deansgate, Manchester M3 3EH.

Marx Memorial Library (Marx Mem.), Marx House, 37A Clerkenwell Green, London EC1.

Medical Sociology Research Unit of Aberdeen University (Med. Soc. RU, Aberdeen U), Aberdeen University Library, Manuscripts and Archives Section, University Library, King's College, Aberdeen AB9 2UB.

Menninger Foundation (Menninger), 3616 W. Seventh Ave., Topeka, Kansas, U.S.A.

Modern Records Centre (MRC), University of Warwick Library, Coventry CV4 7AL.

Museum of London (Mus. of London), Barbican, London EC2.

* National Association for Maternity and Child Welfare (Nat. Assoc. Mat. Child Welf.), Tavistock House North, Tavistock Square, London WC1.

* National British Women's Total Abstinence Union (Nat. Brit. Women's TAU), 23 Dawson Place, London W2.

* National Council of Women of Great Britain (Nat. Coun. Women GB), 36 Lower Sloane Street, London SW1.
* National Federation of Women's Institutes (Nat. Fed. Women's Inst.), 39 Eccleston Street, London SW1.

National Liberal Club (Nat. Lib. Club), 1 Whitehall Place, London SW1.

National Library of Ireland (NL Ireland), Department of Manuscripts, Kildare Street, Dublin 2, Republic of Ireland.

National Library of Scotland (NL Scotland), George IV Bridge, Edinburgh EH1 1EW.

National Library of Wales (NL Wales), Aberystwyth, Dyfed SY23 3BU.

* National Society for the Prevention of Cruelty to Children (Nat. Soc. Prev. Cruelty to Children), National Headquarters, 1 Riding House Street, London W1.

Newcastle-upon-Tyne University Library (Newcastle-upon-Tyne UL), Queen Victoria Road, Newcastle-upon-Tyne NE1 7RU.

Norfolk and Norwich Record Office (Norfolk and Norwich RO), Central Library, Norwich NOR 57E (contains material from Great Yarmouth, exclusive of borough charters and assembly books).

Public Record Office (PRO), Kew, Richmond, Surrey.

Public Record Office of Northern Ireland (PRO Northern Ireland), 66 Balmoral Avenue, Belfast BT9 6NY.

Pusey House (Pusey), St. Giles, Oxford.

Reading University Library (Reading UL), Whiteknights, Reading, Berkshire, RG6 2AE.

* Royal College of Midwives (Midwives), 15 Mansfield Street, London W1.

St. Andrews University Library (St. Andrews UL). The University, St. Andrews, Fife, KY16 9TR.

St. Hilda's College, Oxford (St. Hilda's Coll.), Oxford OX4 1DY.

Scottish Record Office (Scottish RO), P. O. Box 36, H. M. General Register House, Edinburgh EH1 3YY.

Sheffield City Libraries (Sheffield City), Central Library, Surrey Street, Sheffield, Yorkshire, S1 1XZ.

* Society of Friends (Quakers), Friends House, Euston Road, London NW1.

South African Library (SA Lib.), Queen Victoria Street, Cape Town, South Africa.

* Summerhill School (Summerhill), Leiston, Suffolk.

Texas University Library (Texas UL), Austin, Texas, 78712, U.S.A.

Theosophical Society (Theos. Soc.), International Headquarters, Adyar, Madras, India.

Trades Union Congress Library (TUC Lib.), Congress House, Great Russell Street, London WC1.

* United Kingdom Alliance (UK Alliance), 12 Caxton Street, London SW1.

University College London Library (University Coll., London), Gower Street, London WC1E 6BT.

University of California at Los Angeles, Research Library (UCLA), Special Collections Department, 405 Hilgard Avenue, Los Angeles, California, 90024, U.S.A.

University of London Library (U London L), Senate House, Malet Street, London WC1E 7HU.

University of Sydney, Australia (U Sydney L), Fisher Library, Parramatta Road, Sydney, Australia.

Yale University Library (Yale UL), New Haven, Connecticut, 06520, U.S.A.

* Young Women's Christian Association of Great Britain (YWCA of GB), Administrative Headquarters, 2 Weymouth Street, London W1.

## Appendix B

Individuals mentioned in the text, and the location of sources relevant to them, abbreviated according to appendix A. Arranged alphabetically.

ASHBY, MARGERY CORBETT [Dame]: retains her own papers.

ASTOR, NANCY WITCHER (Langhorne) [Viscountess]: Reading UL.

ASQUITH, BARONESS: see BONHAM-CARTER.

AVELING, ELEANOR (Marx): see n. 13.

BALFOUR, ARTHUR JAMES [Earl]: BL

BARNETT, HENRIETTA OCTAVIA (Rowland) [Dame]: Barnett Family Papers, GLRO; Lamb. Pal.

BARNETT, SAMUEL AUGUSTUS [Canon]: GLRO; see also Charity Organisation Society.

BESANT, ANNIE (Wood): Theos. Soc.; BL (letters).

BEVERIDGE, WILLIAM HENRY BEVERIDGE [Baron]: BLPES.

BONHAM-CARTER, LADY VIOLET ([Baroness] Asquith): retained by Hon. Mark Bonham-Carter.

BOSANQUET, HELEN (Dendy): Newcastle-upon-Tyne UL.

BRIFFAULT, ROBERT: BL.

BRITTAIN, VERA MARY: McMaster; Bodl.

BROWNE, FRANCES WORSLEY STELLA: no known surviving papers.

BURROWS, CHRISTINE MARY ELIZABETH: St. Hilda's Coll.

BUTLER, ARTHUR STANLEY GEORGE: St. Andrews UL; Liverpool UL (letters).

BUTLER, GEORGE [Canon]: St. Andrews UL (letters).

BUTLER, JOSEPHINE ELIZABETH (Grey): Fawcett; Liverpool UL (letters); St. Andrews UL (letters); see also Josephine Butler Society.

CARPENTER, EDWARD: Sheffield City.

CATLIN, SIR GEORGE EDWARD GORDON: McMaster.

COLLET, CLARA ELIZABETH: MRC.

COURTNEY, KATHLEEN D'OLIER [Dame]: Fawcett; Imp. War Mus.

CRAWFURD, HELEN: retained in private hands; see also Communist Party of Great Britain (CPGB).

CROMER, EVELYN BARING [Earl]: India Office (letters).

CURZON, GEORGE NATHANIEL CURZON [Marquis]: India Office (letters).

DARWIN, LEONARD: HSSSD, U Sussex.

DAVIES, EMILY: Girton Coll., Camb.

DAVIES, MARGARET LLEWELYN: BLPES; see also Women's Cooperative Guild.

DESPARD, CHARLOTTE: Fawcett (material for biography, prepared by T. B. Greig, q.v.)

DICKINSON, SIR WILLOUGHBY HYETT [Baron]: GLRO.

DILKE, SIR CHARLES WENTWORTH: BL; Birmingham UL; Churchill Coll., Camb.

DILKE, EMILIA FRANCIS (Strong) [Lady]: BL; Bodl.; Tuckwell Collection, TUC Lib. (letters).

DRYSDALE, CHARLES VICKERY: BLPES.

ELLIS, HAVELOCK: Yale UL; Menninger; UCLA; Texas UL; some papers retained in private hands; see also M. Stopes, B. Malinowski.

ELMY, ELIZABETH C. WOLSTENHOLME: BL.

FAWCETT, MILLICENT (Garrett) [Dame]: Fawcett; Manchester Central; see also Fawcett Society.

FORSAITH, FANNIE: Liverpool UL (letters).

FURSE, KATHERINE (Symonds) [Dame]: Bristol UL.

GALTON, SIR FRANCIS: University Coll., London.

GATES, REGINALD RUGGLES: King's Coll., London.

GLASIER, KATHARINE ST. JOHN (Conway) BRUCE: retained by her son, Malcolm Glasier.

GONNE, MAUD: see MacBride.

GREIG, TERESA BILLINGTON: Fawcett.

GRIER, MARY LYNDA DOROTHEA: Lady Margaret Hall.

HAIRE, NORMAN: U Sydney L; M. Stopes Collection, BL (letters).

HALL, RADCLYFFE: Texas UL; some papers retained by Mr. Lovat Dickson.

HALLINAN, HAZEL HUNKINS: see Six Point Group; also Women for Westminster.

HARBEN, HENRY DEVENISH: BL (letters).

HARDIE, JAMES KEIR: NL Scotland; some papers held by the Independent Labour Party (ILP), soon to be turned over to the BLPES.

HARRIS, LILLIAN: BLPES; see also Women's Cooperative Guild.

HERBERT, SIR ALAN PATRICK: papers survive with family; Texas UL.

HIRSCHFELD, MAGNUS: see N. Haire; also World League for Sexual Reform.

HOLTBY, WINIFRED: Hull UL; Humberside PL.

HORRABIN, WINIFRED (Batho): Hull UL.

HOUSMAN, LAURENCE: Texas UL (letters).

HURTWOOD, LADY ALLEN of: MRC.

IVES, GEORGE: Texas UL.

JERSEY, MARGARET ELIZABETH LEIGH (Villiers) [Countess]: GLRO.

KEEN, BARBARA, LADY CLARK: Bodl.

LANSBURY, GEORGE: BLPES.

LAWRENCE, EMMELINE PETHICK: Mus. of London.

LLOYD-GEORGE, LADY MEGAN: NL Wales.

LOCH, SIR CHARLES STEWART: Goldsmith Library, London UL.

MACBRIDE, MAUD (Gonne): PRO (Class CO 904).

MACDONALD, JAMES RAMSAY: PRO.

MACDONALD, MARGARET ETHEL (Gladstone): BLPES.

MCILQUHAM, HARRIET: BL.

MALINOWSKI, BRONISLAW: BLPES; Yale (correspondence with H. Ellis).

MARCHANT, SIR JAMES: Bodl.

MARKHAM, VIOLET ROSA: BLPES.

MARKIEVICZ, CONSTANCE GEORGINA (Gore-Booth) de: NL Ireland; PRO (Class CO 904).

MARSHALL, CATHERINE E.: Cumbria RO; see also Women's International League for Peace and Freedom.

MASON, CHARLOTTE MARIA SHAW: U London L.

MAUDE, AYLMER: BL (correspondence with M. Stopes).

MIDDLETON, MARY: Labour P; see also Women's Labour League.
NEILL, ALEXANDER SUTHERLAND: retained by his widow at Summerhill School.
NEVINSON, HENRY WOODD: Bodl.; see also Sharp, Evelyn, who was Nevinson's second wife.
PANKHURST, CHRISTABEL: Mus. of London; BL (correspondence with H. D. Harben).
PANKHURST, EMMELINE (Goulden): Mus. of London.
PANKHURST, ESTELLE SYLVIA: Mus. of London; IISH.
PANKHURST, RICHARD MARSDEN: IISH.
PASSFIELD, SIDNEY JAMES WEBB [Baron]: Passfield Papers, BLPES.
PEARSON, KARL: University Coll., London.
PENROSE, LIONEL SHARPLES: University Coll., London.
PHILLIPS, MARION: Labour P.
PHILLPOTTS, BERTHA SURTEES [Dame]: Girton Coll., Camb.
RATHBONE, ELEANOR FLORENCE: Liverpool UL; Fawcett.
RHONDDA, MARGARET HAIG (Thomas) MACKWORN [Viscountess]: see Six Point Group.
RHYS-WILLIAMS, JULIETTE EVANGELINE (Glyn) [Lady]: retained by her daughter Elspeth Rhys-Williams.
RUSSELL, BERTRAND [Earl]: McMaster.
RUSSELL, DORA WINIFRED (Black) [Countess]: see B. Russell.
SCHREINER, OLIVE: SA Lib.; Texas UL.
SENNETT, MAUD ARNCLIFFE: BL.
SHARP, EVELYN: Bodl.
SHAW, GEORGE BERNARD: BL.
STACY, ENID: retained by her niece, Angela Tuckett.
STOPES, MARIE CHARLOTTE CARMICHAEL: Marie Stopes Mem. Foundation, Hull UL; BL (includes correspondence with H. Ellis, A. Maude, N. Haire).
STREATFEILD, LUCY ANNE EVELYN: MRC.
SWANWICK, HELENA MARIA (Sickert): see Women's International League for Peace and Freedom.
TUCKWELL, GERTRUDE M.: Tuckwell Collection, TUC Lib.
VARLEY, JULIA: Hull UL.
WARD, MARY AUGUSTA (Arnold) ["Mrs. Humphry Ward"]: University Coll., London; Pusey.
WEBB, BEATRICE (POTTER): Passfield Papers, BLPES.
WILSON, HENRY JOSEPH: Sheffield City.


Appendix C

Organizations mentioned in the text, and the location of sources relevant to them. Arranged alphabetically.

Aberystwyth Women's Temperance Association: NL Wales.
Abortion Law Reform Association: earlier papers in Med. Soc. RU, Aberdeen U.
Artists Franchise League: Fawcett.
Association for Moral and Social Hygiene: (predecessor to Josephine Butler Society, q.v.)

Association of Infant Welfare and Maternity Centres: (predecessor to National Association for Maternity and Child Welfare, q.v.)
Association of Post Office Women Clerks: Fawcett.
British Association for Early Childhood Education: (successor to National Society of Day Nurseries and Nursery School Association, q.v.)
British Federation of Business and Professional Women: Fawcett.
British Institute of Psycho-Analysis: retains papers.
British Society for the Study of Sex Psychology: Texas UL.
British Vigilance Association: Fawcett.
British Women's Patriotic League: Manchester Central.
Cambridge Women's Suffrage Association: Camb. and Ely RO.
Catholic Women's Suffrage Society: (predecessor to St. Joan's Social and Political Alliance, q.v.) Fawcett.
Central Women's Advisory Committee (Conservative Party): Conservative P.
Charity Organisation Society (COS): GLRO; Goldsmith Lib., U London L.
Children's Nutrition (formerly Minimum) Society: see Rathbone, E. F.
Church of England Council for Social Aid: retains papers.
Church of England Temperance Society: Lamb. Pal.
Communist Party of Great Britain (CPGB): Marx Mem.
Consumers' Council: see Standing Joint Committee of Industrial Women's Organisations (Labour Party).
Cooperative Women's Guild: Hull UL; BLPES.
Council of Women Civil Servants: Fawcett.
Divorce Law Reform Union: retains some papers.
East London Federation of Suffragettes: IISH.
Equal Pay Committee: Fawcett.
Eugenics Education League: (predecessor to Eugenics Society, q.v.)
Eugenics Society: retains papers.
Family Endowment Society: see Rathbone, E. F.
Family Planning Association: David Owen Centre.
Family Welfare Association: (descendant of Charity Organisation Society, q.v.)
Fawcett Society: Fawcett.
Friends' Relief Service: Imp. War Mus.
Girl Guides Association: retains papers.
Girls' Friendly Society: retains papers.
Great Yarmouth Women's Suffrage Societies: Great Yarmouth.
Health Visitors' Association: retains papers.
Independent Labour Party (ILP): Fawcett; Manchester Central; retains papers to be given to BLPES; see also Greig, T. B.
International Psycho-Analytical Association: see Jones, E.
Josephine Butler Society: Fawcett.
Ladies Commission of Inquiry into the Boer War Concentration Camps: Fawcett.
Ladies' National Association for the Abolition of the State Regulation of Vice: see Josephine Butler Society.
Malthusian League: (predecessor to New Generation League, q.v.)
Marriage Law Reform Society: see Divorce Law Reform Union.
Men's League for Women's Suffrage: M. A. Sennett Collection, BL (Department of Printed Books).
Midwives Institute: (predecessor to Royal College of Midwives, q.v.)
National Assistance Board: V. R. Markham Papers, BLPES.

National Association for Maternal and Child Welfare: (predecessor to National Association for Maternity and Child Welfare, q.v.)

National Association for Maternity and Child Welfare: retains papers.

National Association for the Prevention of Infant Mortality: (predecessor to National Association for Maternity and Child Welfare, q.v.)

National Association for the Repeal of the Contagious Diseases Acts: see Josephine Butler Society.

National Association of Women Civil Servants: Fawcett.

National Baby Week Council: (predecessor to National Baby Welfare Council, q.v.)

National Baby Welfare Council: papers destroyed in WW II.

National Birth Control Council: (predecessor to Family Planning Association, q.v.)

National Birthday Trust: see Rhys-Williams, J.

National British Women's Total Abstinence Union: retains papers.

National Committee for the Suppression of Traffic in Women: (predecessor to British Vigilance Association, q.v.)

National Conference on Infant Mortality (1906–12): (predecessor to National Association for Maternity and Child Welfare, q.v.)

National Council for Equal Citizenship: (descendant of National Union of Women's Suffrage Societies [NUWSS], q.v.)

National Council of Women of Great Britain: retains papers.

National Federation of Women Workers: no known surviving papers.

National Federation of Women's Institutes: retains papers.

National Institute of Houseworkers: V. R. Markham Papers, BLPES.

National League for Health, Maternity and Child Welfare: no known surviving papers.

National League for Opposing Women's Suffrage: most papers destroyed by G. N. Curzon.

National League for Physical Education and Improvement: (predecessor to National League for Health, Maternity and Child Welfare, q.v.)

National Liberal Club: retains papers.

National Society for the Prevention of Cruelty to Children: retains papers.

National Society of Children's Nurseries: (predecessor to National Society of Day Nurseries, q.v.)

National Society of Day Nurseries: BLPES.

National Union of Conservative and Unionist Associations (Women's Conferences): Conservative P.

National Union of Women's Suffrage Societies (NUWSS): Fawcett.

National Vigilance Society: (predecessor to British Vigilance Association, q.v.)

National Women Citizens' Association: Fawcett.

Nationality of Women Committee: Fawcett.

New Generation League: BLPES; see also Drysdale, C. V.

No-Conscription Fellowship: Catherine E. Marshall Papers, Cumbria RO.

Nursery School Association: temporarily retained by its successor, British Association for Early childhood Education; see also National Society of Day Nurseries (merged with NSA, 1973), and Hurtwood, Lady Allen of.

Parents' National Educational Union: U London L.

Police Court Mission: Lamb. Pal.

Public Morality Council: GLRO.

Royal College of Midwives: retains papers.
St. Joan's Social and Political Alliance: Fawcett.
Scottish Women's Liberal Federation: Edinburgh UL.
Six Point Group: retained in care of H. H. Hallinan, q.v.
Society for Constructive Birth Control and Racial Progress: M. Stopes Collection,
    BL; M. Stopes Mem. Foundation, Hull UL.
Society for the Overseas Settlement of British Women: Fawcett.
Society of Friends (Quakers): retains papers.
Standing Joint Committee of Industrial Women's Organisations (Labour Party):
    Labour P.
Suffragette Fellowship: Mus. of London.
Theosophical Society: retains papers.
Ulster Women's Christian Temperance Union: PRO Northern Ireland.
United Kingdom Alliance: retains papers.
Women for Westminster: some records retained amongst papers of Six Point
    Group, q.v.; see also Greig, T. B.
Women Public Health Officers Association: Tuckwell Collection, TUC Lib.
Women Sanitary Inspectors' Association: (predecessor to Health Visitors'
    Association, q.v.)
Women's Cooperative Guild: (predecessor to Cooperative Women's Guild, q.v.)
Women's Emancipation Union: BL; see also Elmy, E. C. W., and McIlquham, H.
Women's Franchise League: BL; see also Elmy, E. C. W., and McIlquham, H.
Women's Freedom League: Mus. of London; Fawcett.
Women's International League: Fawcett; Catherine E. Marshall Papers, Cumbria
    RO.
Women's International League for Peace and Freedom: BLPES.
Women's Labour League: Labour P.
Women's National Anti-Suffrage League: Ward Papers, University Coll., London;
    Pusey.
Women's National Liberal Federation: Nat. Lib. Club.
Women's Protective and Provident League to Promote Female Trades Unionism:
    (predecessor to Women's Trades Union League, q.v.)
Women's Social and Political Union (WSPU): Mus. of London; Manchester
    Central.
Women's Tax Resistance League: Mus. of London; Fawcett.
Women's Trades Union League: Tuckwell Collection, TUC Lib.
Women's Volunteer Reserve: V. R. Markham Papers, BLPES.
Workers' Birth Control League: no known surviving papers.
Workers' Socialist Federation: IISH.
Workers' Suffrage Federation: IISH.
World League for Sexual Reform: no known surviving papers; see Haire, N.
World Organisation for Early Childhood Education: MRC.
Young Women's Christian Association of Great Britain: retains papers.

# Contributors

KATHLEEN CASEY teaches in the history department of the University of California, Los Angeles. She received the Bsc. Econ from London School of Economics and the Ph.D. in history from the University of California, Berkeley. She is the author of "The Cheshire Cat: Reconstructing the Experience of Medieval Woman," and coauthor of "Women in the Middle Ages: A Working Bibliography."

SHEILA C. DIETRICH teaches at the University of Washington, Seattle, where she is a member of the Medieval Colloquium. She received the Ph.D. in history at Cornell University. Among her recent papers are "Women in Power from the First through the Sixteenth Century," and "Matilda Empress: Critics and Chroniclers."

NEAL A. FERGUSON teaches modern English and European history at the University of Nevada, Reno. He received the Ph.D. in history at the University of Oregon at Eugene. His publications include, "Women's Work: Employment Opportunities and Economic Roles, 1918–1939." He is president of the Rocky Mountain Conference on British Studies.

JEAN E. HUNTER teaches modern English history and women's studies at Duquesne University. She received the Ph.D. in history from Yale University. Her publications include "The Eighteenth Century Englishwoman according to Gentleman's Magazine," and "The Images of Woman." She is the editor of *Eighteenth Century Life*, a quarterly newsletter.

SHEILA RYAN JOHANSSON is research associate, Center for Studies in Demography and Ecology at the University of Washington, Seattle and teaches English history and women's history. She received the Ph.D. in history at the University of California at Berkeley. She is the author of "Sex and Death in Victorian England: An Examination of Age- and Sex-Specific Death Rates, 1840–1910" and "'Herstory' as History: A New Field or Another Fad?"

BARBARA KANNER teaches historiography, English history, and women's history at Occidental College in Los Angeles. She received the Ph.D. at UCLA. Her publications include "The Women of England in a Century of Social Change, 1815–1914," "Blue Book into Novel: The Forgotten Industrial Fiction of Charlotte Elizabeth Tonna," and *The Victorian Woman in English Social History: An Essay and a Critical Bibliography*.

RUTH KITTEL taught most recently English Medieval and legal history at Mills College. She received the Ph.D. in history at the University of California at Berkeley. Her recent papers include "The Position of Women in Thirteenth Century English Criminal Law," and "Common Law Limitations on the Canon Law of Marriage."

ROSEMARY MASEK teaches Tudor-Stuart English history and women's studies at the University of Nevada, Las Vegas. She received the Ph.D. in history at the University of Illinois. She is a contributor to the *Biographical Dictionary of British Radicals in the Seventeenth Century*. Her recent papers include "The Emergence of Self-Concept in Women of Seventeenth Century England," and "Misogyny in the Medieval Romance: Rhetoric or Reality?"

MARC ANTHONY MEYER is a regents fellow at the University of California, Santa Barbara, where he teaches Medieval history and women's history. He is completing his doctoral dissertation, "The Legal Position of Women in Anglo-Saxon England." His publications include" The Greater Royal

Nunneries of Wessex" and "Women and the Tenth Century English Monastic Reform."

PATRICIA OTTO KLAUS teaches modern English and women's history at Yale University. She received the Ph.D. in history at Stanford University. Her recent papers include "Control of Courtship: The Marriage Act of 1753," "Seduction or Marriage: Reform of the Scottish Marriage Law," and "The Redundant Woman in late-Nineteenth Century England."

BARBARA B. SCHNORRENBERG has been research associate and has taught at University of North Carolina, Chapel Hill. She received the Ph.D. in history from Duke University. Her recent papers include "Catherine Macaulay Graham" and "The Blue Stockings and English Education." She is the author of "Education for Women in Eighteenth Century England: An Annotated Bibliography." She is president of the Southeastern American Society for Eighteenth Century Studies.

KARL VON DEN STEINEN teaches British and Empire history at California State University, Sacramento. He received the Ph.D. in history from UCLA. He has presented numerous papers on eighteenth-century politics and published "The Harmless Papers: Gladstone, Granville, and the Censorship of the Madagascar Blue Books of 1884" and "The Fabric of Interest in the County: The Buckinghamshire Election of 1784."

JEFFREY WEEKS, formerly research officer, Historical Records Project, London School of Economics, is research fellow in the Department of Sociology, University of Essex. He is the author of "Notes on Sources: The Women's Movement," coauthor of *Socialism and the New Life,* and a major contributor to *Sources for British Political History.* His study on homosexuality is forthcoming.

# Index

*See* ends of chapters for alphabetical lists of authors discussed.